LIBRARY

Tel: 01244 375444   Ext: 3301

This book is to be returned on or before the last date stamped below. Overdue charges will be incurred by the late return of books.

UNIVERSITY COLLEGE
CHESTER

CONTEMPORARY SOCIAL THEORY

General Editor: ANTHONY GIDDENS

Theoretical Traditions in the Social Sciences

Introductory Sociology

Tony Bilton, Kevin Bonnett, Philip Jones,
Ken Sheard, Michelle Stanworth and
Andrew Webster

MACMILLAN

First edition 1981
Reprinted 1982 (twice — with corrections), 1983 (twice), 1984

Published by
Higher and Further Education Division
MACMILLAN PUBLISHERS LTD
London and Basingstoke
Companies and representatives throughout the world

ISBN 0 333 28204 3 (hard cover)
ISBN 0 333 28205 1 (paper cover)

Typeset in 11/12 Baskerville by
ILLUSTRATED ARTS

Printed in Hong Kong

Distributed in USA by Sheridan House Inc., 145 Palisade St, Dobbs Ferry, NY 10522, USA

For Helen
Aileen
Cicely and Richard
Janet, Jennifer, Norma and Anna
David
Helen

ACKNOWLEDGEMENTS

The authors and publishers wish to thank the following who have kindly given permission for the use of copyright material:

Cambridge University Press for a chart from *Poverty, Inequality and Class Structure*, edited by Dorothy Wedderburn, and for a table and diagram from *The Wealth of the Nation* by J. Revell; The Controller of Her Majesty's Stationery Office for tables and data from official publications; Fontana Paperbacks for a table from *Trade Unions Under Capitalism* by Clarke and Clements, derived from *Department of Employment Gazette*, HMSO, Nov 1975, Nov 1976 and Dec 1976, and R. Price and G. S. Bain, 'Union Growth Revisited: 1948–1974 in Perspective', *British Journal of Industrial Relations*, vol. XIV, Nov 1976; Heinemann Educational Books for tables from *Class in a Capitalist Society*, edited by Westergaard and Resler, F. H. McClintock for a table from *Crime in England and Wales,* edited by McClintock and Avison and published by Heinemann Educational Books; Routledge & Kegan Paul Ltd for a table from *Schooling in Capitalist America* by S. Bowles and H. Gintis; University of California Press for a table from *Social Mobility in Industrial Society* by S. M. Lipset and R. Bendix.

Contents

viii   *Contents*

Foreword

Sociology is a subject that has undergone some major transformations over the past decade or so. Both on the level of
social theory and in terms of the expansion of empirical
research, sociology has developed along many fronts. The
task of incorporating the main elements of these developments within an introductory textbook is a formidable one.
But it is a task that the authors of *Introductory Sociology*
have accomplished in a very impressive fashion. This book, in
my opinion, is simply the best and most comprehensive
introductory text currently available. Its virtues are several.
All of the chapters are written in a clear and cogent style, but
manage to initiate the reader into debates of a complex
character. The authors are particularly concerned to emphasise that sociology is an inherently controversial subject, and
try to summarise several different competing views on the
major topics that are analysed. The book includes reference
to the latest empirical studies, and at the same time has
lengthy sections dealing with problems which have rarely
figured in introductory texts previously (e.g. sexual divisions
in society). Not least important, the authors show themselves
to be sensitised to contemporary trends in social theory: the
'sociological theories' chapter presents an exemplary discussion, accessible to the beginning reader, of basic theoretical issues that anyone studying sociology today must confront. Like several of the other chapters in the book, it is an
independent contribution in its own right. This book will
deservedly become the standard introduction to sociology in
schools and colleges.

King's College   Anthony Giddens
Cambridge

Preface

In many ways this has been a difficult book to write. We have tried to meet the varying requirements of students approaching sociology for the first time at different levels of study. Moreover, we have been especially concerned to produce a book which is not only comprehensive in its coverage of substantive areas in sociology but which locates them firmly within theoretical perspectives and debates.

We hope we have been able to do justice to these objectives. Our experience of teaching at both GCE Advanced level and degree level allows us to appreciate the varying needs and expectations which students bring to a sociology textbook. Furthermore, while each of us teaches all the topics covered in the book at A level, the fact that we specialise in different areas at degree level has enabled us to draw upon specific expertise for the separate chapters.

Our objectives — of comprehensiveness, theoretical rigour and substantive depth — ruled out the possibility of a small introductory monograph. But students need not feel compelled to read the book at one sitting from cover to cover. The book is structured in such a way that each of the chapters can be read as a self-contained entity. The discrete nature of each chapter has required the occasional repetition of material, but such repetition has been kept to a minimum and, particularly through the use of cross-referencing, helps to ensure continuity of discussion.

At the same time, some chapters can be usefully combined and treated as a unit. Chapters 2, 3, 4 and 6, on 'Patterns of Inequality', 'Forms of Subordination', 'Power and Politics' and 'Sexual Divisions in Society', can be approached in this way, as can Chapters 5 and 6, on 'The Family' and 'Sexual

Divisions'. In particular, Chapters 11 and 12 — 'The Production of Sociological Knowledge' and 'Sociological Theories' — were written as a pair and designed to be read together. Our general objective has been to achieve a balance in the level at which the chapters are pitched; however, Chapters 11 and 12 tackle very complex methodological and theoretical sociological issues, and students are more likely to understand them fully after they have immersed themselves fairly extensively in the rest of the book.

References included in abbreviated form in the body of the text are reproduced fully at the end of each chapter. These are not meant to be a comprehensive list of the major contributions in a particular area of sociology, nor should students feel it necessary to read them all. The relative importance of particular books or articles should be clear from their prominence within the chapter in which they appear.

Writing this book has certainly helped us clarify and order our ideas about sociological issues and has reinforced our conviction that studying sociology can be an exciting and stimulating experience. We hope that after reading the result of our efforts you will share this belief.

ACKNOWLEDGEMENTS

While the writing of this book has involved the collective efforts of six authors, its successful completion would not have been possible without the assistance and advice of a large number of other people.

We are particularly grateful to John Winckler at Macmillan. He has proved a most reasonable and encouraging publisher, bearing our enthusiasm and occasional frustration equally calmly and consistently sharing our commitment to this book. We are very grateful to Tony Giddens, who (besides offering many useful suggestions and criticisms on individual chapters) did much to help us view the book as a whole at the crucial stage of final editing. We would also like to thank Louella Hodgson for her part in the book's early stages, and Graham Day, Eric Dunning and David Held for constructive comments and criticisms on particular sections of the manuscript. Needless to say, only we are responsible for any weaknesses the book may have.

Keith Povey performed the monumental task of copy-editing with exceptional thoroughness and efficiency. His work would have been even more difficult had it not been for the considerable typing and decyphering skills of Sue Barnard, Jenny Connor, Rosemary Leach, Rosemary Jolley, Deborah Allsop, Lynn Dopson, Ola Holasz, Barbara Sporne and Verna Cole. Our thanks go, too, to Ron Stellitano for the cover photograph.

Finally, we would like to thank all our sociology students at the Cambridgeshire College of Arts and Technology, past and present, whose stimulation and friendship have not only made teaching sociology here so enjoyable but have also contributed in no small measure to the writing of this book.

Cambridgeshire College of
Arts and Technology

Tony Bilton
Kevin Bonnett
Philip Jones
Ken Sheard
Michelle Stanworth
Andrew Webster

1

Sociology: Themes and Issues

1.1 INTRODUCTION: DEFINING SOCIOLOGY

All academic disciplines or areas of study are faced with the initial problem of providing the layperson or newcomer to the discipline with some idea as to what their subject 'is all about'. Most people feel that they have some understanding of the focus of disciplines like History or Physics, but are less familiar with Sociology. For sociologists the question 'What *is* Sociology?' frequently poses an awkward and embarrassing problem; indeed they may feel tempted to reply 'History', 'English' or 'Economics' when asked what they teach or study in order to simplify conversations with strangers! Offering a single-sentence, short-hand definition such as 'Sociology is the study of human society and human social behaviour' may seem rather vague and uninformative (though being essentially accurate), or not sufficiently precise as to distinguish sociology from other disciplines such as psychology.

Sociologists may attempt to improve on this by detailing specific *areas* of behaviour in which they are interested: how people behave in families, why some people are involved in crime, why some children perform better at school, and so on. Such brief 'thumb-nail' sketches do give some indication of the essence of sociology, but ultimately it is both necessary and perhaps more fruitful to emphasise that the most important and distinctive feature of sociology is not so much *what* is studied but *how* it is studied, i.e. it is important to indicate what is the particular *perspective* of sociology, its distinct *way of looking* at the individual and society.

Collectively, the population of Britain perform millions of acts every day during their waking hours, yet the net result of all this is *not chaos* and confusion, but a reasonable approximation of *order*: motorists drive on the left-hand side of the road, not on the right; shoppers offer coins and banknotes, cheques and cheque cards in exchange for goods and services, not goats and chickens or nothing at all; love-making takes place indoors in bedrooms, and not outside on the pavement. In short, behaviour occurs in more or less co-ordinated, regular sequences and patterns: social life involves patterned regularities. The sociologist would also suggest that these *patterned regularities* in social life mean that social behaviour is predictable, i.e. that one can safely say that individuals in similar social situations will behave similarly. Furthermore, the sociological perspective maintains that these patterns in behaviour are the products of specific social 'forces' or factors, and more specifically are the consequence of the *social relationships and experiences* which go to make up human social living.

There has occurred a rapid growth of interest in this kind of perspective on human behaviour in post-war Britain, especially from the 1960s onwards. Sociology degree courses at universities, polytechnics and colleges have increased considerably, sociology has found its way into some schools, sociologists have been increasingly recognised and consulted by various organisations, from national government downwards, in research programmes, policy planning, etc., and some sociologists have also found fame in the national media.

But despite this, there remains a widespread ignorance and rejection of a sociological perspective when people think about human behaviour. Other, more familiar, 'common-sense' perspectives predominate in people's minds. They may, for instance, employ a *biological* perspective in attempting to explain family and marital arrangements: 'women rear children because they have a maternal instinct (biologically determined) for this task'. Similarly, they may use a pseudo-*psychological* perspective in explaining suicide ('People commit suicide when they are mentally unbalanced'), or a *moralistic* perspective in explaining crime ('Criminals are people who have not developed a conscience regulating their actions'). Because ordinary people are more familiar with these kinds of common-sense perspectives in their everyday lives a sociological approach does not come easily to them.

This is further compounded by a deeply held commitment to the idea that we are all individuals, unique beings with our own special qualities and idiosyncrasies, which sociologists deny, preferring to 'put people in boxes' without regard for their individuality.

Sociology, however, insists on a willingness to reject what is 'obvious', 'common sense', 'natural', and to go beneath the surface of such understanding of the world. As Berger (1966, pp. 32–4) puts it:

The fascination of sociology lies in the fact that its perspective makes us see in a new light the very world in which we have lived all our lives . . . It can be said that the first wisdom of sociology is this — things are not what they seem.

Sociologists emphasise that what is 'common sense' or 'natural' may be by no means universal or eternal, but is frequently relative to particular societies or to particular periods in time. We can illustrate this by reference to a basic and familiar area of human social experience, courtship and marriage.

The common-sense view of differences in behaviour between men and women in the family in our society tends to assume that because there are biological and physiological differences between men and women, certain aspects of their behaviour are therefore 'natural'. For example, it is often argued that it is common sense and natural that because of their respective biological make-ups women will engage in child-rearing and domestic tasks and that men will make sexual advances and will work outside the home. Mead's study of New Guinea, *Sex and Temperament in Three Primitive Societies* (1935), revealed the partiality of such common-sense interpretations of behaviour patterns. Among the Arapesh, she found very few 'natural differences' in men's and women's behaviour, with neither sex exhibiting aggression: women did the heavy carrying (because of their supposedly strong foreheads), and the men lay with their wives during and after childbirth, 'sharing' the pain and strain. Among the Mundugamor, both sexes were aggressive, children were treated brusquely by both parents, and love-making was rather like a pitched battle. Among the Tchambuli, yet further variation occurred: men adorned themselves, gossiped, made things for trade, while women selected their partners, made the sexual advances, did all the trade, and were the more aggressive sex. Obviously, we cannot explain these very striking variations in behaviour via biology, since the people in the various societies were all the same biologically.

In the realm of courtship and falling in love, sociology further questions common-sense notions. In Western societies, men and women are popularly said to choose marriage partners by the uniquely personal act of falling in love — love strikes willy-nilly, 'across a crowded room', in a 'magical chemistry', etc. Sociologically speaking, nothing could be further from reality. As Berger (1966, p. 48) says:

> As soon as one investigates which people actually marry each other one finds that the lightning shaft of Cupid seems to be guided rather strongly within very definite channels of class, income, education, racial and religious background.

That is, falling in love is regulated and constrained by very powerful social factors: the odds against HRH Prince Charles falling in love with Elsie from the Tesco supermarket are very high indeed. Numerous other examples abound. For instance, to the Hopi Indians of North America it is 'common sense' that rain-clouds are gods and must therefore be enticed to rain by rain-dances, a view not entirely consistent with that of the Meteorological Office. Similarly, in medieval Europe, it was 'common sense' that one could determine the guilt or innocence of an accused person through 'trial by ordeal', e.g. accused people carried a red-hot iron bar for ten paces, and if their wounds were healed after x days they would be declared innocent — again, this method is noticably absent in modern trials!

The essential point, then, is that one person's 'common sense' is somebody else's nonsense, and there are numerous examples of sociological and anthropological investigation questioning and exploding many common-sense notions about behaviour.

Although the use of everyday common-sense beliefs is

usually not only unsystematic and inadequate but also often contradictory, if we look more closely at common sense it is likely such explanations of the world are based on what we shall call here 'individualistic' and/or 'naturalistic' assumptions. What do we mean by these labels?

An individualistic explanation of some event or phenomenon assumes that the event can be readily understood and explained solely through reference to the behaviour of the individual(s) involved in it. There is no attempt to understand or explain the phenomenon in terms of wider *social* forces. A naturalistic explanation of behaviour rests on the assumption that one can readily identify 'natural' (or sometimes 'God-given') reasons for behaviour, such that, for example, it is 'only natural' that two people should fall in love, get married, live together, and raise a family.

Both types of explanation are rejected by the sociologist: the individualistic because it does not recognise the importance of wider social forces acting on the individual which he or she cannot control; the naturalistic because it fails to recognise that behaviour patterns are not primarily biologically determined but rather reflect social conventions that have been learned by individuals as members of social groups or, more generally, society.

In Tables 1.1 and 1.2 are presented an outline of the major differences between the everyday and sociological explanations of phenomena. Table 1.1 contrasts the accounts of poverty, industrial conflict, and suicide as provided by the individualistic and sociological approaches.

The reader may be familiar with aspects of the individualistic account sketched in Table 1.1: in particular, he or she may have noticed similar explanations of poverty or industrial conflict in the press or on television. Inasmuch as the media does reproduce such accounts it sustains the status quo, since 'the problem' is said to lie within the individual and not wider social processes, implying that a solution comes through changes in the individual rather than in society. The predominance of the individualistic perspective in our everyday life is not difficult to understand: the birth of modern capitalist society was accompanied by a philosophy of individualism, the belief that individuals were free to choose their rulers,their

TABLE 1.1

Explanation of:	Individualistic	Sociological
Poverty	People who are poor are so because they are afraid of work, come from 'problem families', are unable to budget properly, suffer from low intelligence and shiftlessness.	Contemporary poverty is caused by the structure of inequality in class society and is experienced by those who suffer from a chronic irregularity of work and low wages.
Industrial conflict	Industrial conflict is caused by the interference of influential individuals or 'agitators' in the work-place.	Industrial conflict only occurs and is only sustained because of the existence of widespread grievances among the work-force.
Suicide	The most individual of all acts committed by a person of unsound mind.	The frequency, location, and type of suicide is governed primarily by social factors such as religion, family and marriage patterns and not individual factors.

employers, and their religion. At a time when structural unemployment means that many — particularly the young — will be out of work for long periods of time, the old individualistic idea that 'all we need is a bit of enterprise and motivation' seems to get stronger the more inappropriate it becomes.

We can repeat our exercise and briefly characterise the divergence between the naturalistic and sociological explanations, this time through reference to marriage and the position or role of women in the family (Table 1.2).

That there is nothing 'natural' about our marriage pattern or the role of women in society is clear from the sociological account. However, the naturalistic account should not be rejected on the grounds that it is inadequate, as though it could be polished up a bit and made more acceptable: rather,

TABLE 1.2

Explanation of:	Naturalistic	Sociological
Marriage	It is only natural that a man and woman should live together for life because they fall in love and want to raise children.	Monogamy is only one form of marriage, predominant in Western society. For example, polygyny (a man with more than one wife) and polyandry (a woman with more than one husband) also exist in other societies. Marital patterns depend on a variety of economic and social factors. The eligibility of marriage partners depends on the class and status position of the individuals.
Woman's role	It is important that the woman should be at home to raise her children because this satisfies her maternal instinct and the children's need for a mother.	Women stay at home because it is a widespread social expectation that the home is the correct place for them to be and because of limitations on the opportunity to do otherwise. Socialisation of children is just one function of the institution of the family which could be performed in non-familial contexts.

it should be dismissed because it presents an entirely *distorted* picture of social reality. That marriage forms and the role of women in society are not 'God-given' is clearly demonstrated in Chapter 5 on the family and Chapter 6 on sexual divisions in society. These show how what is taken for granted in one society would be looked upon as being not only strange but perhaps also immoral in another society. We are not then just talking about the French eating frogs' legs and the English black pudding: we could eat frogs' legs in England without affecting our social structure. Eating habits are simply a matter of fashion and individual taste. But if marriage patterns were to be drastically altered, significant changes in the social structure would occur. In short, it is sociology's comparative perspective, its cross-cultural vision, that provides its strongest refutation of the naturalistic explanations or accounts outlined above.

Sociology reveals the rich variety of human societies, the vast differences between cultures, both in the past and in the present. What would be considered to be 'human nature' in one society might appear to be positively extraterrestrial in another: quite simply sociology tells us that there is no such thing as *the* 'Human Nature', We *learn* to become members of a particular society and the most important forces involved in this process are *social*, not biological or instinctual. Let us look at what this means in more detail.

1.2   THE INDIVIDUAL IN SOCIETY

Society as constraint

It is a fundamental assumption for sociology that when we are born we are confronted by a *social* world which is just as real — at least in its consequences for our behaviour — as other realities which we also confront. What we are as individuals is decided by the particular society in which we live, and by the particular social groups to which we belong. This is so because the world around us — including the social world — channels our actions, *constraining* us to act in particular ways. As a result, regularities and patterns can be observed in the behaviour of different individuals. Let us look at a simple example.

If I want to leave a room, I must do so by the limited number of means available to me, which will be by the door or the windows; if they are locked, I cannot leave. I have a strictly limited choice of action, and the extent of the choice is determined for me by the constraints of my physical environment. Other sorts of things can constrain my actions too, of course; I may not be able on my income to afford a Ferrari. So I am constrained by my material world — the practicalities of my material circumstances — just as much as by my physical world. (We will return to look at the importance of such practical constraints on human action shortly.)

Yet there are other aspects of my world which exercise similar constraints over my behaviour. Having bought my car, if I want to travel from A to B in Britain I have to do so by travelling on the left-hand side of the road. What sorts of factors constrain me to do so?

First of all my physical world constrains me in so far as every other car will be travelling on the left-hand side and my progress might be somewhat impeded if I chose otherwise; secondly, it is a *rule* that is being followed by every car. Like every rule, it has means by which it is enforced; in this case, if I break the rule of driving on the left-hand side of the road I can be prosecuted under a law of the land. Now although such a rule is not part of my physical or material world, its existence constrains my action just as effectively as they do; we can call it a *social* constraint — a constraint of the *social* world.

However, not every social constraint has a law to back it up. In fact most of the rules we follow in our social lives are not legally enforced, but they are rules nevertheless. For example, if I had all the money in the world I could quite easily buy a hundred Ferraris if I wished. But I might *not* wish to do so because I might believe it to be wrong to buy an Italian car for one reason or another. Now what is constraining my action here? Of course, it is my belief about what is right or what is wrong; if I believe something to be right, I am prepared to do it, whilst if I believe it to be wrong I am not. So my beliefs constitute an extremely important constraint on my behaviour and, bearing in mind that what we believe to be right or wrong is, to a large extent, *learnt* behaviour, that we do not *inherit* such beliefs, it is obvious that the *source* of these beliefs has to be seen as a major constraint on, and determinant of, our behaviour. Clearly, this source is society and the particular social groups within it. Thus in our society we believe it to be right and normal for one man and woman to marry. In others it is considered normal for one man to marry many women. Both are rules which are believed to be right by those following them; however one is not 'right' and the other 'wrong' — they are simply different rules, found in different societies.

Culture

This sort of learned behaviour in any particular society includes those ideas, techniques and habits which are passed on
by one generation to another — in a sense, a *social* heritage —
and which are virtually a set of solutions to problems that, in
the course of time, others have met and solved before. This
learned behaviour, or social inheritance, of any society is
called its *culture*.

It is the possession of a common culture and the ability to
communicate and pass it on to others that distinguishes the
human being from other animals. Humans are human *because*
they share with others a common culture, a culture which
includes not only the artefacts of its living members but also
those of members of past generations. This is the heritage
awaiting those as yet unborn. Human beings are able to develop and pass on their culture by means of language, which is,
of course, itself a product of culture. Language has to be
learned in the same way as other elements of a culture and,
once this has been accomplished, the individual can acquire
the rest of his or her culture. How is this done?

Socialisation

The process by which we acquire the culture of the society
into which we are born — the process by which we acquire
our *social* characteristics and learn the ways of thought and
behaviour considered appropriate in our society — is called
socialisation. When individuals, through socialisation, accept
the rules and expectations of their society that make up its
culture and use them to determine how they should act, we
say they have *internalised* society's cultural rules.

Now, in a very real sense socialisation can only be properly
understood as an aspect of *all* activity within human societies.
In the course of our social lives we are constantly learning
about ways of thinking and behaving considered appropriate
by those other members of society with whom we come into
contact (as well as those considered inappropriate by them)
and this learning process only ceases when social life itself
ceases — on death. However, despite recognising this fundamental general and continuing character which it possesses,

we can nevertheless identify specific vehicles, or *agencies* of socialisation. In particular, since the socialisation undergone by a human being in the early years of its life will obviously be of crucial influence in affecting the attitudes and behaviour of the social adult, then the *family*, as the first human group an individual in any society usually belongs to, is clearly a socialising agency of major importance.

Most of the influence of the family in this initial stage during the socialisation process is unintended, and takes place informally, as a product of social interaction between people in extremely close physical and emotional proximity to one another. In such a setting we learn as much through observation and experience as we do through deliberate instruction or training. Thus, though our parents tell us not to stare at strangers, not to speak with our mouths full, etc., they unintentionally teach us much more besides. For example, it is in the family that we first encounter the way in which people who have authority behave, and the differences in the way men and women behave.

Despite the primacy of its influence, socialisation in the early years of life is not confined to the family, however. As the child gets older, other agencies get in on the act. For example, other children with whom a child comes into contact — friends, playmates, and so on — can have a significant socialising influence. This agency, called the *peer group*, is probably the first means by which children encounter ideas and ways of behaving different from those at home.

Then, of course, the whole process of formal *education* is a crucial socialising agency. In complex and highly differentiated societies like ours there is such an abundance of different sorts of skills and knowledge which one might learn that a reliance on informal means for their successful acquisition would be useless. The more complex a society and the more varied the skills possessed by its members, the greater the need for institutions deliberately designed to effect the formal dissemination of specialised skills and knowledge — educational establishments like schools, colleges and universities.

From a sociological point of view, however, such places are 'learning' establishments in a much broader sense than most people would ordinarily recognise and, as such, have to be seen as major agencies of socialisation.

When a child goes to school he or she is not only confronted with the traditional school subjects, but also with codes and practices governing behaviour. The pupil has to learn not only history and geography, but also how to relate to teachers and fellow students: for example, when it is acceptable to claim the attention of the teacher and to ask questions, or when conversation with friends is allowed. He or she also has to learn which strategies are acceptable in which classroom, since teachers' demands will vary.

Research seems to indicate that pupils are evaluated on their mastery of this 'hidden curriculum' just as they are evaluated on their mastery of the formal syllabus. In some cases mastery of the 'hidden curriculum' can almost compensate for lack of ability. Jackson (1968, p. 34) draws attention to this in his study *Life in Classrooms*:

> What do teachers mean when they say a student tries to do his work? They mean in essence that he complies with the procedural expectations of the institution. He does his homework (though incorrectly), he raises his hand during discussions (though he usually comes up with the wrong answer), he keeps his nose in his book during free study periods. He is in other words a model student though not necessarily a good one.

The socialisation process pupils encounter in schools therefore involves not only the acquisition of formally defined skills, but also the gaining of many other social skills, such as learning how to live in a group and how to respond to those in authority.

So, in the classroom, as in the family and the peer group, socialisation largely takes place as an unintended consequence of the interaction of its members. Much of *adult* socialisation is equally informal and unintentional, deriving from informal norms developed within groups.

Social groups are often deliberately set up for a purpose. Their goals cover an infinite range, from the manufacturing of nappies to campaigning for free abortion. Of equal sociological interest, however, is that any group, whatever its purpose, will always unintentionally develop distinctive *patterns* of behaviour. Members of the group will come to expect one another to conform to these patterns if they wish to remain members of it. This group pressure for conformity may often override values imposed from outside: for example, the child may refuse to 'tell tales on his or her friends' despite demands from the teacher, or soldiers may infringe Queen's Regulations rather than be disloyal to their comrades in the platoon. Groups evolve expected ways to behave which their members must normally obey.

This is not to say that *all* socialisation is unintended behaviour, or that the actors involved are necessarily unaware of the process they are undergoing. At a basic level, we are all aware of the responses of others to us in our dealings with them, and most of us, with a greater or lesser degree of skill and more or less self-consciously, tend to modify our behaviour in order to elicit the response we desire, both from particular individuals with whom we come into contact and from groups in which we are members. Thus we may vary our behaviour to suit our membership of different groups. For example, in the golf club the young member may play down the fact that he is also a member of the left-wing Socialist Workers Party, while at Party meetings he may play down the fact that he is in the golf club. In this example what is being sought is an approval of behaviour. In other cases modification or manipulation of behaviour can sometimes be deliberately designed to elicit an *un*favourable response from others. For example, Hell's Angels and punk rockers tend to structure their behaviour in order to gain the active disapproval of others.

Another level at which the self-manipulation of attitude and behaviour can take place occurs when someone self-consciously takes on the attitudes and standards of a group he or she wishes to join in order that entry and acceptance may be made less difficult. This is called *anticipatory socialisation*. An example might be of the young man from a working-class background who deliberately rejects or modifies much of the behaviour he learnt while growing up — so far as patterns of speech and dress and leisure-time activities are concerned, for example — so that he might more easily pursue his chosen career in, say, the Higher Administrative Section of the Civil Service.

So far we have identified specific group agencies of social-isation, but it is obviously a mistake to restrict our definition of the concept to a process taking place only in these settings. In effect, since socialisation is present as part of all social relationships, whether the parties to the relationship are aware of it or not, it is clear that it is a much more subtle, complex and pervasive process than it might at first appear and that we can only properly understand it as an aspect of *all* human activity. Moreover, since our involvement in social relationships and membership of social groups only ends when our social existence ends (at death), socialisation must be seen as an inevitable and a lifelong process. Even at the point of death we are nevertheless still members of a social group — be it a family, a hospital ward, a platoon of soldiers, or whatever. As a consequence we are still constrained to conform to standards of behaviour expected of us by the group. Where death is a normal occurrence — in a hospital ward, for instance — this constraint on us to behave in ways determined by our interaction with others will extend even to the actual process of dying itself. This has been well documented in Sudnow's book *Passing On* (1967).

From all this, it is apparent that socialisation cannot be seen as an entirely rigid process as some have assumed. In fact, as an informal process, socialisation rarely involves the internal-isation of a fixed set of universally approved standards. We should not expect the result of socialisation to be some sort of across-the-board agreement throughout society — a societal consensus — about the way to think and act, even though some renowned sociologists have assumed this to be the case. Rather, we should expect socialisation to operate at different levels of generality. Where a group's standards and values are peculiar to that group itself, e.g. hippies, Satan-worshippers, the socialisation experienced by its members will be corres-pondingly unique. However, where a group exhibits more general characteristics — that is, where they duplicate those in other similarly structured groups — then the socialisation experienced by its members will be correspondingly more general.

Some socialisation takes place on an extremely particular level: for example, individual families will in many respects differ from each other and as a result the content of much of the socialisation characteristic of each will be correspondingly variable. In contrast, socialisation can be much more general. This is so where the structure and organisation of social groups and collectivities is fairly precisely defined by some overall set of rules, as, for example, in the armed services, or in other bureaucratic organisations like local government departments, the Civil Service, ICI, or in similarly organised work-groups (for instance in the coal or motor industries).

Less deliberately structured groupings can exhibit similar patterns of socialisation, too. In British public schools, for instance, not only are the majority of pupils deliberately drawn from that small section of British society committed to the standards which the public school promotes, but teaching staff are similarly rigorously selected, not merely on the basis of academic competence, but also on the basis of the extent to which they have successfully internalised the standards they are expected to foster among their pupils. (In fact, this is really an example of intentional and deliberate socialisation in education, since one of the self-conscious functions of the British public school is the perpetuation of that distinctive life-style by which the elite marks itself off from the rest of society.)

The *most* general level at which socialisation takes place will obviously be where it is common to the society as a whole. The principal agency at this level is the *mass media* in all its forms: books, magazines, newspapers, cinema, theatre and television are all influential mechanisms for the dissemination of ideas and of particular sets of values and beliefs. (This book is itself an instrument of socialisation.) As we will examine in more detail in Chapter 9, the mass media can in a very important sense direct the way we look at the world and the questions we ask about it. In effect, it can, along with other phenomena, structure reality for us. Furthermore, it is too easy to assume that this structuring of reality takes place in some sort of 'neutral' fashion. We should at least be prepared to ask questions about this; in particular, we should consider whether the way we are persuaded to look at the world by such media benefits certain interests or groups in society rather than others. Furthermore, although the censorship and control of such vehicles of mass communication by the state in some societies provides clear evidence of this, we should not assume that manipulation of the media can only take a deliberate form. Media presentation of the world can often work less intentionally to the advantage of particular groups, even in societies like ours where much is made of 'the freedom of the press'. We will return to this point.

The effects of non-socialisation

From what we have said so far, it should be clear that socialisation is a crucial concept for sociology, since it directs attention to a key element in the process by which the individual becomes social and acquires those qualities usually referred to as 'human'. In fact, proof of this can be seen by examining some of the available evidence concerning human beings who have failed to be 'made social' via socialisation in the way we have been describing. Such people manifestly lack those human characteristics a society both produces in its members and relies on for its continued existence.

There have been a number of recorded cases of children living in the wild and presumed to have been nurtured and reared by animals; such children are often referred to as feral (wild) children. Some of the better-known cases include the 'wild boy of Aveyron', found in a French forest in 1799, Amala and Kamala, two sisters found in a wolf-den in 1920, or the recent case of the Indian boy, Shamdev, found playing with wolf cubs near the Musafirkhana forest.

It has still to be proved conclusively that these children were reared exclusively by animals, but it is clear that they all had minimal human contact. Descriptions of their behaviour show how many of the characteristics which are considered natural or essentially human are not instinctive but learnt, indicating the necessity of human contact and care for the development of social behaviour and for the development of fundamental human faculties.

Consider how Shamdev first behaved when rescued from the forest at the age of about 5:

At first Shamdev cowered from people and would only play with dogs. He hated the sun and used to curl up in shadowy places. After dark he grew restless and they had to tie him up to stop him following the jackals which howled around the village at night. If anyone cut themselves, he could smell the scent of blood and would scamper towards it. He caught chickens and ate them alive, including the entrails. Later, when he had evolved a sign language of his own, he would cross his thumbs and flap his hands: this meant 'chicken' or 'food' (*The Observer*, 30 August 1978).

Although such behaviour corresponds closely to the descriptions of other feral children, it is impossible to know whether these children might have developed similar patterns of behaviour even if brought up in greater contact with people, and it has been suggested that feral children might have been abandoned by their parents *because of* their behaviour problems. However, another case of a child brought up in semi-isolation illustrates how unusual behaviour patterns would seem to be the product of minimal socialisation rather than the result of any inherent deficiency or abnormality. Isabelle is a case referred to by Kingsley Davis. She was an illegitimate child who spent most of her first six years of life in a darkened room with a deaf mute mother. When found, her behaviour was such that she was thought to be mentally deficient:

Her behaviour towards strangers, especially men, was almost that of a wild animal, manifesting much fear and hostility. In lieu of speech she made only a strange croaking sound. In many ways she acted like an infant ... At first it was even hard to tell whether or not she could hear, so unused were her senses. Many of her actions resembled those of deaf children (Davis, 1970, p. 206).

In addition she was unable to speak or walk properly. What is interesting about Isabelle's case, though, is that after two years of rehabilitation and skilled training she covered the stages of learning that would normally require six years. It would seem in this case that her unusual behaviour patterns and impaired development were not a product of personal inadequacy, but were due to her restricted early experiences and minimal human contact.

From these examples it is clear that the acquisition of fundamental human characteristics does not occur instinctively; indeed, such behaviour is predominantly shaped by an individual's immediate social environment. Socialisation is essential for a person to develop into a social being.

Status, role, norm, sanction

Because of socialisation it is only rarely that we have to puzzle out a meaning for an action which we come across in our normal social encounters — most actions seem perfectly intelligible to us the moment they occur — because we have learnt the *rules* by which others are playing the 'game'. To put this another way, we can predict what is going to happen in most of the situations in which we find ourselves because we have expectations that certain rules will be followed. For example, we would be surprised if the police did not wear a particular uniform or if a traffic warden did not book us for parking on a yellow line. Furthermore, we utilise such expectations about the way an individual in a particular position should behave, *irrespective* of whether we know that individual personally. All of us know how the police and traffic wardens behave, whether or not we actually *know* police or traffic wardens. The social position that a person occupies we call a *status* and the behaviour that we expect from a person occupying that position we call a *role*.

A social role is rather similar to a role played by an actor: people occupying certain positions or statuses in society are expected to behave in certain predictable ways, as if 'scripts' had been prepared for them. For example, if we go to the doctor, we expect him or her to behave in a particular way, to ask questions about our illness and symptoms, possibly to examine us, to make a diagnosis and perhaps write a prescription. Any other behaviour, such as suggesting a game of cards, would surprise and confuse us, as it would not conform to our notion of the appropriate role that someone occupying the status of doctor should perform.

Furthermore, we would expect *any* doctor, not just our

own, to behave in the 'proper' manner, in the same way that we expect the same sort of behaviour from all shop assistants, or all priests, or all fathers. But the expectations involved in roles are not simply one-directional; it is not merely the case that a person is expected to play a role in certain typical ways. Rather, that person is also entitled to expect others to behave towards *him or her* in certain ways. Doctors can ask us all sorts of intimate questions and expect honest answers; in return, we expect them to treat this knowledge confidentially and not to gossip about the state of our health. A social role thus involves *mutual* expectations.

Social roles, therefore, are not just a matter of the way people can be *observed* to behave (in the usual run of things) but concern the way it is thought that people *ought* to behave. Ideas about what people *should* do, about what behaviour is 'proper' or 'fitting', we call *norms*. The most important expectations surrounding social roles are not just statements about what *actually* happens — about what a person *will* do, out of habit and so on — but are norms outlining things which a person occupying his or her status is *obliged* to do. That is, roles are *normatively defined*: the expectations are about an *ideal* pattern of behaviour to which actual behaviour only approximates.

The relationship between norms and socialisation is plain. While norms define society's rules, it is through socialisation that individuals come to embrace as their own the norms of others concerning the performance of their roles, and learn to regard the rules and traditions of their society as rightful.

However, there is something else to consider. Knowledge of the rules, the standards required of us, does not *necessarily* ensure that they will always be kept, for we still have the *choice* of breaking them if we wish. So, even though internalisation does in large measure explain the remarkable degree of conformity exhibited in social life, we have to recognise that there is another reason for this. Suppose you sometimes feel tempted to drive faster than the allowed speed limit, perhaps because you are in a hurry or because you decide that it is quite safe to do so and that the speed limit is unnecessary. Do you therefore automatically break this legal rule? Only with great care, of course, because you know that if you are caught breaking the limit by the police, the consequences will be unpleasant — a summons, a court case, a fine, perhaps an endorsement. That is, the rule — in this case, a legal one — is backed up or underwritten by *sanctions* — in this case, legal ones — designed to ensure compliance with it. All of society's rules have sanctions of one sort or another backing them up, although most are non-legal since most of society's rules are not legal ones. However, sanctions do not always work to ensure conformity by constituting a *threat* of some sort or another, for some encourage conformity instead by offering *inducement*.

There are two broad types of sanctions: *positive*, or rewarding, sanctions; and *negative*, or punitive, sanctions. The constraint of positive sanctions really refers to the general way in which the desire to seek the approval of others (though, sometimes, their disapproval) can influence our behaviour.

In contrast negative sanctions operate by encouraging behaviour designed to avoid the *disapproval* of others. These can be more or less *organised*. The most obvious example of such a sanction, of course, is the action taken by a state against those who break its laws. Less organised, but equally important, are those sanctions which involve the mobilisation of public disapproval in a more *diffuse* way against those who break society's non-legal rules. Thus, by the use of gossip, ostracism, satire, and, probably most important of all, ridicule, offenders against society's standards are punished for their transgressions. In small-scale and closely knit communities, where self-respect is very closely tied up with the esteem in which one is held by one's fellows, any sanction of this sort designed to erode it is likely to be particularly effective. Thomas Hardy shows this very clearly in his description of a 'skimmity ride' in his novel *The Mayor of Casterbridge*. He describes how Michael Henchard, the disgraced and bankrupt former mayor of the town, and his one-time mistress are publicly disgraced by an informal gathering of some of the townsfolk (complete with hideous effigies of the couple swaying drunkenly in a horse-drawn cart) outside the mayor's house. The shame of having her 'dirty linen' ritually washed in public in this way by representatives of the community is too great for the woman and she suffers a stroke from which she dies shortly afterwards.

Similar customs to this, all designed to hold up social mis-creants to public ridicule, can be found in many different sorts of small-scale societies. Often such societies lack legal machinery, as they lack state institutions generally, and so this sort of diffuse sanction can be the most important means of punishing offenders against society's norms.

With all these formal and informal constraints, we can see that pure freedom for the individual actor is very unlikely; considering all these expectations and controls that surround us, Berger's portrayal of society as a prison begins to seem plausible: 'Our considerations of the sociological perspective have led us to a point where society looks more like a gigantic Alcatraz than anything else' (Berger, 1966, p. 107). But un-like ordinary prisons, members of most societies conform freely and willingly — they actually *want* to do what they are expected to do. As Berger (1966, pp. 140–1) graphically des-cribes it:

> Society penetrates us as much as it envelops us. Our bondage to society is not so much established by conquest as by collusion . . . we are entrapped by our own social nature. The walls of our imprisonment were there before we appeared on the scene, but they are ever rebuilt by ourselves. We are betrayed into captivity with our own co-operation.

Functionalism

So far we have been describing the ways in which the processes of socialisation and internalisation come to bind societies together and reproduce practices and institutions. In the traditional sociological view, these processes were vital, for they were the means by which to achieve *social integration* and *moral regulation* in society. Let us imagine a society where social integration and moral regulation are perfect, and exist throughout society. There would then be complete agreement — consensus — on the rules of behaviour governing people as they occupy different social positions. Social expectations would cover all circumstances and problems perfectly. All members of society would be efficiently socialised into a complete acceptance of the social rules, perhaps leading to complete internalisation of the rules. Social harmony and peace would prevail as everyone would have their range of roles to play and would know how to play them. All would be committed to common goals and values, but they would 'know their place' and accept the ration of power and advantage deemed suitable for their social position.

Unlike some politicians who cling to mythical notions of a past golden age, no sociologist actually believes that society is, or could be, really like this. However, many, beginning with Emile Durkheim, believe that society approximates to this model. Durkheim and his followers (many of whom are known as 'functionalists') have been concerned with one basic and overriding question — how society can continue as an integrated whole and not collapse into a mass of warring individuals. Their answer to this 'problem of social order' is in terms of socialisation into a consensus of norms and values. For them the key to societal continuity is conformity due to learnt rules of conduct. Individual people may come and go, but society carries on continuously — because it can shape the incoming individuals to fit the existing state of affairs.

From this point of view, societal characteristics cannot be explained as the product of actors' choices, since these choices are themselves the product of socialisation. If this is so, how do societies come to be organised in the way they are? For the functionalist, the answer is that societies have *built-in* tendencies towards harmony and self-regulation, analogous to biological organisms or machines. In the same way that the human body, for instance, is an integrated whole whose individual parts serve particular 'needs' of the system (for example, the heart performs the function of pumping blood around the body, the bowel functions to collect and evacuate solid-waste products, and so on), so society comprises a system of interdependent institutions each with a contribution to make to the overall stability and continuity of the whole. According to the functionalist, then, to explain the existence of a social institution we must not look for purposive intention on the part of individuals but, rather, we should investigate the fact that the social system as a whole requires its needs to be satisfied.

Of course, such sociologists do not agree with this model entirely. As it stands, it gives a picture of a society that is totally static, without change, and totally without conflicts between opposed social groups. Any sociologist has to accept that there are some differences in values between separate groups in society and that people must adapt and innovate to cope with changing social circumstances. But the function-alist starting-point is still the idea that people are socialised strongly into conformity and that social phenomena can be explained in terms of the functions they perform. This view remained dominant for a long time in sociology, but more recently sociologists have become reluctant to view people as happy robots, acting out predetermined roles.

For one thing, they feel the functionalist approach does not only neglect change and conflict but tends to 'reify' society — to treat it as a thing — by attributing to social structures capacities for thought and purposive action which only humans can possess. To explain the existence of institutions in society not in terms of individual intention but in terms of societal need ultimately implies that societies are capable of *deciding* what they need. But, of course, societies do not think, only people do. Furthermore, critics feel the function-alist approach overemphasises the determining nature of the socialisation process, which leads to a false and oversimplified view of human personality and human action.

1.3 THE INDIVIDUAL AS A CREATIVE SOCIAL ACTOR

The perspectives we have discussed so far emphasise the important truth that societies exist and persist as solid, real entities. For any individual, society is a massive external reality, and it is necessary to emphasise this simply because we tend to take for granted these social arrangements as natural, immovable and inevitable. This is less so today in rapidly changing societies where great efforts are made to adapt and modify social institutions; indeed, it is plausible to suppose that the roots of sociology lie in the experience of rapid and far-reaching social change. However, even in modern Western societies, most people live within their culture as a given 'natural' world. In contrast, the sociologist is forced to recognise the *precariousness* of social existence. This is not just because of the threat from disease, famine or a self-inflicted nuclear holocaust; all social worlds are precarious in a deeper sense. This is because social arrangements are fundamentally *arbitrary* ways of organising human life — there is an apparently endless range of variations in social rules, ideas and conventions. In this sense, there is a shared 'common-sense' view of 'reality' which is taken for granted by individuals who share a culture.

Social action theory

One important perspective in sociology, social action theory, emphasises these features of social life. Building especially upon the work of Alfred Schutz, recent action theorists pay close attention to the ways in which these 'definitions of reality' are used and sustained by actors. They show how these definitions may be disputed by individuals or groups, and how actors *negotiate* shared rules and ideas.

What this implies is neatly summed up by a famous phrase of W. I. Thomas (1966): 'If men define situations as real, they are real in their consequences.' Thomas is emphasising that the social behaviour of human beings is a product of what *they decide* is going on around them, of what they take the behaviour of others to *mean*. Whether or not these definitions are correct, *every* social encounter involves a process of interpretation on the basis of available evidence, whether this is self-conscious or not.

At the simplest level this means deciding that someone wearing, say, a skirt in our society is female and acting on the basis of this decision, or deciding that someone shouting at the top of his or her voice is excited or angry and acting accordingly. The 'female' *could* be a female impersonator, or someone in disguise, or an actor on the way to a theatre; the 'angry' or 'excited' person could be deaf, or someone calling out to a friend some distance away. But the 'truth' is not the point at issue; what matters is that as human beings we necessarily engage in an interpretative process when we encounter others, as they do with us. From this point of view society is an aggregate of such activities; social order is negotiated order.

The emphasis here is on the individual's capacity to understand and interpret what other individuals *mean* by their social actions. The most distinctively human aspect in this respect is the capacity to communicate verbally: language is the principal medium by which humans exchange meaning. Although other vehicles are available — gesture, touch, dress, etc., all sometimes speak as loudly as words — for the action theorists the capacity to give meaning to the world through a shared language enables people to interact socially and to create a social order.

In contrast to the functionalist, then, who sees the capacity of the human being to communicate as simply a vehicle for the 'activation' of imposed cultural rules, for the action theorist this capacity is the essential creative ingredient in social life. From this viewpoint cultural rules are not given determinants of individual action but are continually built up and broken down as the result of individual choices and decisions.

Although the negotiation of rules is a constant process, this does not completely undermine the power of socialisation. Societies are still largely reproduced through this process. However, from a social action perspective socialisation can never be simply a matter of internalisation of fixed social rules. Socialisation is, by its nature, a means to create *change* as well, because human behaviour is learned rather than imprinted. Human cultures can change rapidly because cultural innovation is infinitely faster than biological evolution. Patterns of social life can change radically and still be passed to the next generation, and so adaptation and innovation can be rapidly institutionalised. This is the key to the human being's evolutionary break with other species. Culture and symbolic language, once developed through evolution, allow humans to race ahead.

These elements distinctive to humans were emphasised in the work of G. H. Mead and W. I. Thomas, two of the early American sociologists who contributed to social action theory. They demonstrated the importance of early socialisation for the development of social and mental skills in the individual. Symbolic language, and the concepts and shared meanings embodied within the use of language, can only be learnt through socialisation. However, Mead, Cooley and Thomas also recognised that socialisation is not a simple one-way process, and that potential for change is also generated *within the individual*. There is a close connection between the learning process and the development of a thinking, reasoning *self*. This self has an individual identity and an individual capacity for reflexive thought: that is, actors can reflect on their own actions and *the way others respond to them*. For Mead, the actor was shaped by these responses from others, so that the self was a social product. But at the same time, the self was complex enough to initiate actions and innovate new ideas. The mature actor is self-conscious, and so begins to learn rules and expectations in a less passive way. As we take on new roles — plumber, husband, father, shop steward, etc. — we are partly aware of the demands and constraints involved and we can exercise choice. It may be that some of our roles conflict (e.g. fatherly responsibilities might conflict with commitments at work) or different groups might impose conflicting expectations in relation to one particular role (e.g. in a man's role as shop steward the managers might expect him to calm disputes while his work-mates might demand that he never compromise with the bosses). In either case, the individual must make choices, innovate, and if necessary abandon a role altogether.

Equally important, the whole notion of set role behaviour may come to seem problematic. In many situations, actors are faced with no clear rules for action, or the action may be hard to sustain. First of all, a 'frame' or definition of the situation must be established — 'is this an intellectual conversation between colleagues or an attempt at flirtation?' — and the situation might waver between definitions or be both at once. This means that social interaction requires mutual effort by the actors as they attempt to establish the definition of the situation for each other and negotiate appropriate behaviour for themselves and for the other. Much of the time the problem is eased by set rules for encounters and by rituals (e.g. the polite formality between bank manager and client) but there is *always* some scope for challenging and redefining these and hence helping to redefine rules of appropriate behaviour.

The general social action approach thus emphasises fluidity

and change in social interaction; it has a conception of the individual that emphasises people's creativity and capacity for innovation. For social action theory socialisation is a complex process running throughout life and roles arise from practical interaction; they do not derive from some static central value-system.

As a general approach, this presents a very attractive picture of human beings, but we must not, on the other hand, allow this to distract us from the pressing reality of society as an institutionalised, patterned, constraining system. We *are* creative, innovatory individuals but only by virtue of socially created selves, and our actions all take place in the context of patterned social relationships with others. Social action can never be separated from *practical constraints* or from *social control*.

Practical constraints

We must never forget that people do not act and make choices in a vacuum. The factors influencing their choices can be understood, and these influences lie at two levels. The first level is that of the values and beliefs they have learnt through socialisation. For example, a couple might choose either to limit family size and have more money, or instead to maximise the number of children. The choice they make will depend in large part on their learnt values, but there is a second level of explanation, concerned with influences we mentioned earlier (pp. 8–9) – *practical constraints* on action. In choosing family size, the couple's decision will be affected by factors such as the unemployment of the father, or government banning of contraceptives. In addition, the desire to keep up a respectable level of income or the desire of the woman to have a job or career, may lead to the woman going to work. At the same time there may be little provision of help in child care, and so the couple will have to organise their lives accordingly. Possibly this will mean changes in behaviour (such as the role of the man in housework) which violate the norms and values into which they were socialised. On the other hand, if they were sufficiently wealthy they might be able to afford a nanny or a private nursery school. This illustrates the crucial point that practical constraints affect people in differing degrees, depending on their level of material advantage. Power and reward are distributed unequally in most societies, and so the privileged will be much freer. They are relieved of many practical constraints on action. Thus even individual choice cannot be understood in isolation from the wider social structure.

This example demonstrates what we mean when we say that choices are never totally 'free' but are influenced in complex ways by the socialisation process and by practical constraints. In addition, we should consider whether there might be a link between the *dominant ideas* transmitted through socialisation and those people who benefit from the existing distribution of power and reward. In other words, we should always look for the *origin* of social norms and consider whether the values and expectations reproduced through socialisation serve the interests of any particular group or class. If they do, then we may wish to explore this issue of *ideology* to see whether socially dominant groups use their power to *impose* ideas and patterns of behaviour on their subordinates.

1.4   SOCIAL CONTROL, POWER AND CONSTRAINT

Dominant values

In exploring the origins of norms, it is important at this stage to distinguish two sources of change. One is the innovative adaptation by people to changed circumstances; the other consists of conscious, concerted attempts by groups to influence behaviour. For an example of innovative action in relation to norms we can return to the couple we met earlier. In the end, they make the same decision as most others and decide to go ahead and have children, and to try to reconcile this with their material aspirations. Therefore, they produce two or three children and the mother goes out to work. To cope with this, the father has to take a very active part in housekeeping and child-rearing, violating traditional conceptions of gender roles. However, these traditional role expectations prove weaker than the pressure of the other goals and practical constraints, and so the gender role is modified. As more people find themselves in the same position, men stop mocking each other for doing housework and mothers-in-law cease criticising their sons' wives about going out to work. Their expectations have had to change.

At the same time, there are other groups operating at the second level of influence on norms. Traditionalist 'defenders of the family' may actively attempt to influence behaviour. After the Second World War, fears of a decline in family size led to a fashion for theories of 'maternal deprivation' which, together with more direct exhortation, encouraged women to refrain from paid employment (see Chapter 5).

It might be argued, in addition, that there is a further level of influence, where the unanticipated effects of communication become important. This may be seen as very significant today when we consider the way that advertising and women's magazines continue to portray women as finding all their fulfilment in the home. The role of woman as employee is systematically ignored, and this may unintentionally help to maintain a situation where women form a docile and cheap work-force.

We can see, then, that there are many elements and factors in this change in gender roles. One aspect is the spontaneous adaptation by members of society to new circumstances; another is the level of open attempts by groups to influence behaviour; a third is the whole range of unintended consequences which benefit different groups unequally.

This idea of unequal benefit links crucially to the point that competition for influence over behaviour is itself very far from free and equal. Many sociologists would argue that privileged groups are able to sustain a system of dominant values which helps to maintain the social structure. This social structure is itself unequal, and works to the benefit of this dominant group. We can see this system of dominant values as operating in two main ways. First, these values may limit conflict in crisis situations. For example, some historians have argued that Methodism and other non-conformist sects were deliberately encouraged by employers in the nineteenth century in order to placate the workers and persuade them to look for salvation in the next world rather than in this. This was perhaps successful in moderating opposition to the new industrial social order. In more normal times, however, we may see a second effect of dominant values. This strategy is simply to defend existing institutions and social relations as naturally right and inevitable. As long as things remain the same, the privileged will automatically retain their privilege. This concept of dominant values will be discussed more fully in Chapter 9; here we can simply note the role of such values in securing the acquiescence of the subordinate and less privileged members of society.

The behaviour of members of society is also directly affected, as we saw earlier, by *sanctions* designed to ensure compliance to its standards, that is, by *social control*. There are plenty of examples of such a control being effected by the use of *coercive* sanctions in the world today — from the killing of real or imagined enemies by despots like Idi Amin in Uganda, to the widespread use of torture and incarceration in prisons and camps in many different countries. (In fact, it might be said that the use of torture in the 'civilised' world today is more widespread and certainly much more sophisticated than was the case in the 'barbaric' Middle Ages.) However, direct coercive sanctions require continuous effort, and may in fact be a rather brittle form of social control, so we should not expect dominant groups in different societies to rely wholly and simply on such crude means of retaining their power and privilege, especially where their position has long been entrenched. Since the downfall of military regimes in South America and elsewhere provide clear evidence that no political structure relying solely on coercion can hope to survive for long, we should not be surprised to find that the most effective form of social control involves attempts not to crush opposition but to stop it arising in the first place: that is, by the control of people's ideas, rather than of their actions.

We can see, then, that dominant values can make life easier for rulers. If the subordinate members of society can be persuaded to believe that those who dominate have a *right* to do so, and that those who have great material advantage have a *right* to it, then they are very unlikely to challenge or threaten the privileged. Thus ruling groups are likely to attempt to 'engineer the consent of the ruled' so that they accept their own subordination and disadvantage. It must be said that this has apparently been achieved with a good deal of success in many societies in many different periods.

Powerlessness and constraint

It may be, however, that the acceptance of dominant values is not as great as it might seem — we should not assume that actors conform because they wish to (even if these wishes were manipulated). Much more pressing considerations may produce a sullen acceptance of the existing social order which entails no strong commitment to the status quo. As we shall see in Chapter 4, much conformity may be explained by *powerlessness* in the face of social circumstances, where the actors recognise their inability to change things, and so resign themselves to making the best of it. This resigned attitude is an understandable response if individuals suffer subordinate positions in many of their social relationships. People may have little chance to argue with their foreman at work, with the council housing department, with the teacher of their child, or with the police officer who forces obedience to the law. All these figures of authority act in some degree as agents of social control, making decisions and issuing instructions which will bind those dependent on, or subordinate to them. Most areas of our lives involve us in institutionalised power relationships, and most of us are subordinate most of the time. We know that if we really step out of line, then the police or the armed forces may step in with their right to use legitimate violence to force our conformity. As we show in Chapter 4, all patterned social relations involve relations of power and dependence, domination and subordination. Very often we conform because we know we dare not risk the consequences of non-conformity.

If power is distributed unequally in patterned ways, it is even more obvious that material resources are spread unequally. Sartre is reported to have said that he did not feel free without a thousand francs in his pocket; this is clearly a freedom which can only be enjoyed by a few. Chapter 2 will document the gross material inequalities which exist in wealth and income — and also in basic benefits such as health and job security. It is perfectly obvious that the choices made by creative social actors are limited by the practical resources available to them. What needs to be explained is the *origin* of concentrations of wealth and security or of poverty and deprivation. As we shall see in Chapter 2, we can distinguish different types of social structure which systematically generate unequal distributions of power and reward. Poverty and dependence are the result of particular systems of social relationships, which means that we can never understand the actions, choices and motives of actors unless we relate them to the position of the actor in the social structure. Knowledge, power and economic resources are the raw materials of social action, and they are all unequally available.

All of this seems to have painted a rather gloomy picture. Our ideas are shaped by the pressures of socialising agencies, our actions are regulated by forces of social control, and society limits the resources available to us. Everything seems to indicate that we should accept the inevitable and just lie back and be happy robots. Needless to say, most sociologists are reluctant to relax into this supine position — and with good reason. Societies *do* change, and their social institutions are *not* immune to innovation, reform or rebellion. Although social arrangements constrain and control us, they are still constructed and reproduced by human action. People, especially when acting collectively, can come to break these barriers, overcome these constraints and reconstruct their social world. Many sociologists feel that their body of knowledge has a central contribution to make towards such reconstruction.

1.5   THE PRACTICE OF SOCIOLOGY

Developments within sociology

In order to appreciate fully the emphasis of a sociological perspective, it is important to realise that sociology as a discipline arose within distinct historical, intellectual and social contexts, and that it is the product of a particular era in particular societies. Major questions about the individual and society have preoccupied thinkers in all periods of history: the philosophers of Ancient Greece and Rome reflected upon the way society operated and/or should operate, and for centuries afterwards social and political theorists and philosophers applied themselves to similar questions. But these 'philosophical' analyses of society were essentially based on speculation, on dubious and untested assumptions about the motives of human beings in their behaviour, and on undisciplined theorising, and they lacked *systematic* analysis of the structure and workings of societies. Philosophers and thinkers frequently constructed grand models and schemes about humans and their societies without looking at how societies *actually worked*.

However, from the eighteenth century onwards in Western Europe, important changes took place in perspectives on and understanding of society and the individual's place in it. Many considerable advances were taking place in scientific discovery with regard to the structure and composition of the physical world surrounding human beings, and with regard to the physical nature and make-up of human beings themselves. The natural sciences, though essentially in their infancy, were beginning to develop systematic methods for studying the physical world and the individual's part in (and relation to) it, and they were being increasingly recognised and valued for providing this more 'certain' knowledge. Could such a scientific, 'rational' approach also be applied to the analysis of humans' social worlds, their relationships, experiences and behaviour within it?

Alongside these developments there were also extensive social, economic and political changes which had and were to have profound effects on societies in Western Europe and elsewhere. Scientific and technological advances laid the foundations for the transformation from a predominantly rural, agricultural, 'manual' way of life to an urban, industrial, 'mechanised' pattern of living. New inventions and developments in methods of production, transport, etc., changed the scale and location of production at work from the land and small enterprises to the town and city and larger-scale enterprises like factories. A greater variety of occupations emerged.

These extensive changes integral to the process of industrialisation involved, moreover, a major paradox, in that they brought a 'new' society with great productive potential and more sophisticated and complex ways of living, while at the same time generating extensive disruptions in traditional patterns of life and relationships, as well as creating new material problems of overcrowded and unpleasant urban conditions, poverty and unemployment.

Sociology as a distinct discipline emerged against the background of these intellectual and material changes in the second half of the nineteenth century. The early sociologists were greatly influenced by the changes in patterns of life which they saw going on around them as industrialisation proceeded, and they were often deeply disturbed by what they saw. It is important to stress at this point that these early sociologists were *not* intensely 'radical' individuals, but rather could frequently be more accurately labelled as 'conservatives' made uneasy by the changes they were observing in society. Nevertheless, they were greatly concerned with the idea of obtaining exact knowledge of the workings of society, and, living in a period when the natural sciences were making real strides in knowledge, felt that the application of natural science methods to the study of society might produce similar advances in understanding. Thus, from the very beginning, there was a great emphasis on the need to analyse social life scientifically. Auguste Comte, the so-called 'founder' of sociology, who stressed the adoption of a scientific method of analysing society so that we might improve society through a thorough understanding of it, summed up in his famous phrase, 'To know, to predict, to control.' This early emphasis on the 'scientific' analysis of social life was to have (and still has) considerable implications for the subsequent development of the discipline, as we shall see in Chapters 11 and 12.

Although we have located the beginnings of sociology in Western Europe in the second half of the nineteenth century, its development and acceptance as an academic discipline was not a uniform and uncomplicated process. Sociology became firmly established in universities in France and Germany earlier than in Britain. British universities for a long time were relatively much more interested in the anthropological investigation of so-called 'primitive' societies in the more remote areas of the world, and British sociology constituted a relatively minor discipline, centred mainly on the London School of Economics. The focal points of British academic life were, of course, the universities of Oxford and Cambridge, traditionally the cornerstones of the established social elite, and the critical examination of British society (in such areas as inequality, the distribution of power, the basis of industrial conflict, and so on) was perhaps a less acceptable enterprise than the socially and politically 'safer' study of unfamiliar cultures.

The early classical works in sociology of the late nineteenth and early twentieth centuries were produced in France and Germany, with Emile Durkheim in France and Max Weber in Germany as the outstanding figures. Sociology developed markedly in the USA, too, and received more widespread acceptance there than in Britain: in many ways the USA early this century was ideal sociological material — a rapidly expanding and industrialising, cosmopolitan, immigrant-based society which was experiencing a wide range of social changes. Sociology in the USA during the inter-war period was characterised by detailed empirical studies of a variety of areas (particularly the more 'seamy' side) of American social life — of delinquent gangs and neighbourhoods, of particular ethnic minorities, etc.

As an established discipline, however, sociology is a relatively new arrival on the academic scene, and the real expansion in its popularity has occurred in the post-war period, particularly in the 1960s. We can point to some factors which have influenced this expansion:

(i) In the post-war period there has developed a rather more critical awareness of how societies operate: fewer people simply sit back and accept their societies unthinkingly — they see that alongside the many technological and social advances that have been made there still exist problem areas like overpopulation, poverty and crime.

(ii) Alongside this, there has developed an increasing concern with social reform and the reordering of society, accompanied by the belief that in order to make such reforms effective and soundly based, knowledge about society and its members is needed.

(iii) There has also developed an increasing awareness of other societies and ways of life as a result of better systems of communication in travel and the mass media.

(iv) Increasingly, it has been claimed that people who work in government, industry, the social services, etc., ought to have some sort of specialist knowledge of society on the grounds that they will be better equipped to meet the demands of their work.

So far, then, we have stressed how sociology's development as an academic discipline has not been uniform all over the world. One important implication of this must be stressed: in the same way that there is no single pattern of development of sociology, so also is there *no single* sociological perspective. Rather there are a *variety* of perspectives which do share the common emphasis of viewing social behaviour as the product of social arrangements, social forces and conditions, etc., but which may differ in the relative emphasis which they assign to certain specific factors or variables for explaining that behaviour. Put more simply, sociologists themselves often disagree in explaining society and social behaviour because they may start with different 'background assumptions'. You will see later, for example, that Marxist sociologists often disagree with functionalist sociologists, in that the former stress the unequal distribution of economic and material resources as a crucial element in the way societies operate, while the latter emphasise the importance of extensive commitment to shared norms and values by the members of society. Though the existence of a variety of competing perspectives in sociology can sometimes be confusing and a little frustrating to the new student, he or she must recognise that there simply is no nice, neat package of 'sociology' which is universally accepted and which provides all the answers.

Sociology and social policy

At the beginning of this chapter we discussed the difficulties faced by the sociologist in answering the layperson's question 'What is sociology all about?' The second question (if his interest has been maintained) is frequently 'OK, what *good* is sociology?' Such an enquiry raises a whole range of issues concerning the application of sociological knowledge and its role in policy and reform.

As we have suggested, a concern with social problems and

social reform was an integral part of sociology from its beginnings. Many of the early sociologists were anxious about the social changes occurring around them and wanted to establish sociology as a comprehensive scientific discipline, charged with discovering sociological laws of behaviour and constructing social policy based on these laws. In other words, a scientific sociology was to be used for the reorganisation of society.

A similar conception of the role of sociology (though with a more 'radical' political orientation) is held by certain contemporary sociologists who want sociology to be not simply a discipline which analyses and explains social life but rather a vehicle for changing society, a discipline committed to the extensive alteration of existing social structural arrangements. At the opposite end of the pole there is the view of sociology as a completely objective, non-evaluative discipline, a way of looking at societies and developing knowledge about social behaviour, in which opinions or perspectives on policy-making, the solution of problems, and so on have no place.

Though these different perspectives on the role of sociology have been and still are the source of much debate among sociologists themselves, for the layperson no such complications exist: that is, many people understand sociology as being only concerned with social problems, social policies and social reform. While it is undoubtedly the case that sociology does attract people with a strong concern over social issues and problems, such preoccupations do not exhaust the subject-matter of the discipline.

Sociologists are interested in *sociological* problems. Any social phenomenon, be it 'nice' or 'nasty', that requires explanation is a sociological problem. *Social* problems (i.e. something identified as harmful to society and needing something doing about it) are merely one type of sociological problem.

However, the fact remains that demands are made on sociology to 'pay its way', to produce practical returns which can be utilised for policy purposes. There has been a considerable growth in the demand for applied social science from industry and, particularly, government, reflecting the increased willingness of governments to intervene in society (whether their own or someone else's), so that sociologists are being increasingly consulted in respect of certain problems ranging from population control to terrorist control. Even if sociologists do not actually provide a solution themselves, their data are often used in the formulation of policy by others.

Such a task for sociology may appear reasonable and innocuous, particularly in societies which embrace a commitment to the principle of using knowledge for practical purposes and not to any principle of 'knowledge for knowledge's sake'. Some would say that there is nothing remarkable or wrong in working for some group and being paid to answer some question that the group regards as important. But a whole host of questions are raised by the demand that sociology be geared towards assisting in the solution of social problems, policy formulation and social reform. In particular it is vital to remember that the recommendation, provision and implementation of social policies and reforms involve *political* questions and decisions — after all, who is to decide what is an 'appropriate' social policy, a 'desirable' social reform, an 'effective' solution to a social problem? As Bottomore (1962, p. 319) says:

> Every solution of a problem and act of policy is a political decision. It expresses the resolve of a social group to maintain or change a particular way of life, and to act in accordance with certain ideals. The sociologist may supply information, elucidate the context of problems, point to causes or conditions, indicate the advantages and costs of alternative courses of action . . . But in the last resort, political decisions rest upon judgement, or political wisdom, and upon interests.

It cannot be assumed, either by the sociologist or by anyone else, that particular policy measures are in any way neutral instruments which are somehow divinely 'right' for the particular society concerned. Policies inevitably reflect ideologies, frameworks of values, either hidden or overt, and the sociologist employed on work in particular policy areas is inevitably bound up with these frameworks of values. Sociologists who lend their names or their work to a particular social policy are engaging in a political act; they cannot escape by saying that the use of their work to *justify* a particular social policy (even if they did not advocate that policy) is not their concern. The sociologist as a 'citizen' has to ask about the uses to which his or her work is to be put (see, for example, the discussion of Project Camelot in Chapter 12).

What *has* been the contribution of sociologists to social policy and reform, and what can they realistically expect to do in these areas? Probably the major contribution has been and will continue to be to encourage a more realistic and informed approach to social problems and matters of social policy. Sociology has an important role to play in exploding myths and misconceptions about social phenomena and institutions, and in providing a context in which controversial issues can be examined critically and analytically. Hence, sociological analyses of race relations, crime and the treatment of offenders, poverty and the like have helped to bring 'hot' issues out into the open and to clarify understanding of these areas. A good example of this can be seen in the area of educational research: before 1944 in England and Wales, education at a grammar school was predominantly the preserve of middle-class children whose parents had the ability to pay, with only a minority of 'free-place' pupils attending. The 1944 Education Act claimed to eliminate such inequality of opportunity by making entry to grammar schools the result of an examination open to all via the competition of the '11-plus'. The inadequacies of such a claim were starkly illustrated by subsequent sociological investigations in educational achievement (see Chapter 7 on education) during the 1950s and 1960s, which revealed sharply unequal chances in grammar school entry between middle-class and working-class children. Not only did these investigations reveal the fallacy of the claim about equal opportunity in the selective system, but they were also highly influential elements in the ammunition of the campaigners for the abolition of this system and the introduction of comprehensive education.

In a real sense, then, sociology can be seen as having an important 'critical' role to play in monitoring and assessing the impact of social policy, and in questioning accepted assumptions in these areas. A major contribution here has been to demonstrate that such social problems are the product of *social structural arrangements* and not the consequences of individual or personal qualities (see above on individualistic versus sociological explanations). Sociological studies have emphasised the need to investigate fully the complexities behind social problems, the need to reject the inadequate, simplistic, monocausal explanations of these phenomena often suggested by laypeople, politicians and the media. Sociologists have also strongly questioned the fallacy that social problems are necessarily the product of 'bad' things. Such problems may well be the product of social arrangements which are regarded as 'good', 'right' and 'desirable'; for example, high divorce rates may be the product of the high expectations and demands centred on monogamous marriage.

We must also underline a further dimension of sociology's 'critical' role in examining social problems. A major contribution of the discipline has been to emphasise how the identification and designation of a particular phenomenon or pattern of behaviour as a 'social problem' is not an unambiguous matter, but a process of *social definition*. Hence, for many sociologists, what is frequently most interesting is *why* a society defines a pattern of behaviour as a 'problem' and the process by which it *becomes* a 'problem'. As we shall see in Chapter 10 on deviance, the activities of groups with fewer power resources are much more likely to be labelled as 'social problems' and be given greater publicity than are those of the more dominant social groups in society. For instance, the use of cannabis by the young is far more likely to be branded as 'drug-taking'/'drug addiction' and hence a 'social problem' than is the consumption of thirty cigarettes a day by adults or half a bottle of brandy by middle-class businessmen. Thus 'social problems' are problems defined as such by the powerful; sociological problems concern the understanding of social life.

Sociology and social change

If it is necessary to draw a clear distinction between social problems and sociological questions then it follows that sociology must maintain a critical distance from the ideas — whether dominant or otherwise — of any particular society at any particular time. Any form of scientific endeavour must attempt to transcend its time and place to sustain an independent, doubting stance. This is obviously a pressing necessity — and source of difficulty — for sociology. Sociologists are only too well aware that ideas arise in particular social climates and contexts, and yet they have to seek a way of standing apart from society and analysing it objectively. The very project of sociology assumes the possibility of such knowledge, and implies that this knowledge should be made available to guide human action. If sociology produces more exact information, more rigorous analysis and new concepts to illuminate social life, then this knowledge can be used by people in society. All social action has to take place on the basis of ideas, assumptions and information, however false and mistaken these may be. Thus, whether individual sociologists like it or not, the fact that they produce knowledge is a significant contribution to the changing flux of social life. Some degree of influence cannot be avoided, and in fact many sociologists would now argue that the sociologist has a definite *responsibility* to disseminate this knowledge in order to criticise delusions and misconceptions. In this sense, sociological findings can be a resource available to all, to be used for whatever purpose the user decides. In this view, the social scientist produces neutral science and takes no responsibility for the ways in which it is used.

The simplicity of such a view disguises its danger. Is it really acceptable for knowledge to be used for any goal? Has science got no connection with the pursuit of human fulfilment and liberation? Certainly, many powerful groups with an interest in preserving the existing order do see sociology as threatening. They resent the disclosure of inconvenient truths, but above all they fear the disclosure that things need not be the way they are. The diversity and changeability of social structures is a central theme in this knowledge, together with the revelation that human action can recast social relations and institutions. If sociology reveals the extent of constraint and deprivation in societies, it also reveals the human potential for liberation and creative social reconstruction. If this know-

42 *Introductory Sociology*

ledge is disseminated widely, and not restricted to already powerful groups, sociology can and must aid members of society to act more knowledgeably, more rationally, with more self-understanding; it will be a tool aiding people to build themselves a better society.

REFERENCES TO CHAPTER 1

Berger, P. (1966) *Invitation to Sociology*, Harmondsworth, Penguin.
Bottomore, T. (1962) *Sociology*, London, Allen & Unwin.
Davis, K. (1970) *Human Society*, London, Macmillan.
Jackson, P. (1968) *Life in Classrooms*, New York, Holt, Rinehart & Winston.
Mead, M. (1935) *Sex and Temperament in Three Primitive Societies*, London, Routledge & Kegan Paul.
Sudnow, D. (1967) *Passing On*, Englewood Cliffs, N. J., Prentice-Hall.
Thomas, W. I. (1966) in M. Janowitz (ed.), *Organization and Social Personality: Selected Papers*, University of Chicago Press.

2
Patterns of Inequality

2.1 INTRODUCTION

Inequality of power and advantage has been an extremely common, if not universal, feature of human societies, even if the degree of inequality has varied very greatly. It has almost always been the case that some group or groups have controlled and exploited other groups. At some points in the history of a given society people have rebelled and challenged this inequality; at other points they have meekly accepted their subordination.

In this chapter we are not concerned with these responses of the oppressed — they will be discussed in Chapter 4 on power. Instead, the main task here is to understand the systems of stable inequality which have existed in different types of society. Inequality is not something which is randomly distributed between individuals in society. The sociologist is concerned with the way different *groups* are in an unequal relationship with other groups. Members of a given group will have features in common and will usually see their unequal position passed on to their children. The concept of *stratification* refers, then, to the idea that society is divided into a patterned structure of unequal groups, and usually implies that this structure tends to persist across generations. Now the actual nature of these groups, and the relationships between them, varies enormously. In this chapter we shall examine only some of the more important types of stratification structure.

The issue of inequality is absolutely central for sociology, not only because of the moral and political implications, but

also because of the crucial place of stratification in the organisation of society. Every aspect of the life of every individual
and household is affected by stratification, whether they
realise it or not. As we shall see in the discussion of evidence
from Britain, opportunities for health, long life, security,
educational success, fulfilment in work and political influence
are all unequally distributed in systematic ways. Values and
patterns of behaviour are equally affected: for example, not
only can social position strongly predict voting behaviour but
also, some would claim, whether the person prefers to make
love in the dark or with the light on!

Since stratification is so important, it is vital that concepts
and explanations are employed in a clear and unambiguous
way. Unfortunately, the very fact that the study of inequality
is the central issue means that there have been a great variety
of competing theories and concepts attempting to describe
and explain it. This diversity is closely linked to the political
importance of inequality. Different theories have been linked
to different ideas on the value or otherwise of inequality, and
also, as we shall see later, to different views on society and its
future.

We described stratification earlier as a stable structure of
inequality between groups which persists across generations.
However, it is clear that we still need to distinguish between
different advantages which can be distributed unequally.
There are three basic forms of advantage which privileged
groups may enjoy:

(a) *Life-chances*: that is, all those material advantages
which improve the quality of life of the recipient — this may
include not only economic advantages of wealth and income,
but also benefits such as health or job security.

(b) *Social status*: that is, prestige or high standing in the
eyes of other members of the society.

(c) *Political influence*: that is, the ability of one group to
dominate others, or to have preponderant influence over
decision-making, or to benefit advantageously from decisions.

Now it may well be that privileged social groups tend to be
advantaged in all three areas, while subordinate groups norm-

ally enjoy poor life-chances, low status *and* little political influence. But we cannot assume that this is always the case. It is important to keep the three elements conceptually distinct, especially when trying to explain the basic nature of a given type of stratification structure. Inequality in one of these areas may be the root cause of inequality in the other spheres — caste society, as we shall see, appears to be based on *status* differences. Other inequalities follow as a result from this.

Furthermore, we must be clear on the differing nature of these types of advantage. Life-chances are *facts*. They describe the actual material benefits and opportunities of a group, whether or not the members of the group recognise these facts. Thus we can call these *objective inequalities*, which can be measured objectively by the sociologist. In contrast, inequalities of social status only exist by virtue of the fact that status differences are *constructed* and *recognised* by members of social groups. The basis for status may vary: it may be anything a social group claims as giving superiority and which is recognised by other groups — examples might include wealth, religious purity, political position or sexual prowess. Whatever the basis, status can only be sustained by conscious social action — groups claim status, and others actively defer to their 'superiority'. We can term this *subjectively based inequality*. Finally, inequality in political influence can normally be seen as deriving from either material advantage or high status, but it may be that political office may independently form the basis for gaining status and/or privileged life-chances. This can be termed *politically based inequality*.

Thus, structures of inequality may be based on any one of these three types of advantage; the root of inequality may lie in economic relationships, in status relationships, or in relationships of political domination.

However, most societies today, including Britain, have stratification systems based almost entirely on economic relationships. Inequalities in material life-chances are fundamental; status differences and differences in political influence follow on from this. Structures where economic relationships are primary we call *class societies*, and in these we refer to the different unequal groups as *classes*. There is considerable dispute over the precise definition of this term, but we shall use *class* to refer to *a group sharing a similar position in a structure of objective material inequalities, produced by a particular system of economic relationships characteristic of a particular mode of production.*

This means that the class position of a given group is determined by its relationship to other groups in the way production is organised. Different societies have different ways of organising production, and this creates different kinds of classes. For example, agricultural production might be organised on the basis of the *master-slave* relationship, as in Ancient Rome or in the southern states of the USA, or based on the *lord-serf* relationship, as in feudal Europe, or on the *capitalist-proletarian* relationship, as in modern Western societies. Each of these economic relationships, which will be explained in detail later in this chapter, forms the basis for a totally different *class structure*. In each case, these economic relationships create inequality as one class dominates and exploits the other. This is not to say that economic relationships always constitute the main bases of inequality in a society.

2.2 CASTE AND AGE-SET STRATIFICATION

In a *caste* stratification system — traditional India provides the most complete version — an individual's position totally depends on those *status* attributes ascribed by birth rather than on any which are achieved during the course of one's life. This is not to say, as we shall see later on in this chapter and elsewhere in the book, that there is not a strict and systematic constraint on achievement imposed by ascribed status attributes in class societies too: those of race and gender are particularly significant ones in our society, for example. However, status attributes ascribed by birth in a *caste* society define an individual's position in the stratification system much more completely and securely than they do in a class society. The difference is clearly seen by comparing the ideologies of mobility held by the members of the two sorts of system. Thus, in a class society members typically believe that mobility is easily available and secured on merit. Though this chapter will demonstrate that this is largely nonsense in practice, this belief still contrasts with that underlying caste inequality. The social position into which an individual is born here is the one in which, theoretically, he is bound to remain for the rest of his life. In reality, individuals, families and even groups can change position, although it is far from usual.

In traditional India, each position in the caste structure is defined in terms of its *purity* relative to others. The under-lying ethos of the allocation of such status is that those who are most pure — the Brahmin or priest caste — are superior to all others, whilst those who are least pure — sometimes called the untouchables — are inferior to all other castes. (The tradi-tional castes, or Varna, also included the Kshatriyas, or war-riors, the Vaishyas, traders, and the Shudras, servants and labourers.) According to the ideology, such relative purity can only be retained by the ritual avoidance of contact between members of the different castes and as such determining the extent to which one can enter into any sort of activity or relationship. Here, then, we have a stratification system whose strata are defined in terms of ascribed status attributes and which is legitimated by religious values.

Another stratification system based just as exclusively on ascribed status attributes is characteristic of what are known as *age-set* societies. All societies differentiate and, to a greater or lesser extent, allocate unequal rewards on the basis of age. This age-based inequality in our society is most marked in the years of youth and early adulthood: thus, in British law, 16 is the age of consent, 18 is the age at which one can vote and drink in a pub, and so on.

In primitive societies the fact that as people get older they pass through socially recognised statuses is usually of much greater *structural* significance than in our society, and as a result is usually symbolically recognised by what van Gennep called *rites de passage*. In our society, such ritual celebrations of changes of status through ageing are now restricted to religious occasions like baptism, confirmation and burial, though 'coming-of-age' parties amount to the same thing. The process is much more serious for primitive society, how-ever, for getting older in this sort of world is not just a question of securing certain basic legal rights as it is for us, but is fundamentally concerned with acquiring prestige. And this remains throughout life, for the old occupy a much higher status in primitive society than they do in societies like ours. A particularly crucial stage of status acquisition occurs when an individual enters social adulthood and is allowed to do things only an adult can, like marry and fight and so on. The *rite de passage* celebrating this change of status typically involves, for boys, circumcision.

In *age-set* societies, the changes in status involved in getting older are institutionalised to such a degree that they often constitute the very basis of political organisation. In such societies, those males who are initiated together — between the ages of, say, 13–18 — constitute an *age-set* and the members of each set together pass through a series of *age-grades*. Different sets perform different political tasks. Typically there will be a warrior set, composed of those of the suitable age for fighting, while beneath them, in both age and status, will be a set of initiates. Above them will be the set of newly retired warriors, while above this set will be sets of elders, their relative status depending on their social ages, who will be responsible for internal political and legal matters and perhaps for communicating with the gods.

A person's social development is thus determined purely and simply by the physical fact of ageing: no one can be fixed in a low position, but must eventually succeed to the highest status, simply by staying alive.

2.3 SLAVERY

Of all patterns of social stratification, it is the system of slavery which draws the most rigid legal boundaries between members of one class and those of another. In this system, some human beings are regarded as chattel, or items of property, belonging to another individual or social group.

Slavery has taken different forms, depending in part on the particular economic use to which slaves have been put. In the fifth and fourth centuries B.C. in Greece, for example, slaves, acquired through conquest and trade, were a recognised form of investment for well-to-do citizens. Rich Athenians set up small factories in which the chief, but not the sole, source of labour was slaves. These factories, which produced a range of goods from shoes to armour, brought in a regular profit for their owners, but the reliance on slave labour had disadvantages from the owners' point of view; the market for industrial goods was uncertain, and in slack times, when it was difficult to sell the products from the workshop, slaves still had to be fed and housed, even though their labour brought no immediate return for the owner. Consequently, most such factories employed free labourers, as well as slaves, who could be laid off in slack periods.

As well as working in factory production, slaves were often responsible members of wealthy households, entrusted with keeping accounts, tutoring children and protecting the family while the master was away on military excursions; slaves were frequently trained as craftsmen, and occasionally acted for wealthy owners as captains of ships, managers of banks, or directors of small workshops. Since the value of these slaves to their masters lay so often in the slaves' intelligence, initiative and skill, incentives (such as the possibility of purchasing freedom) were used more consistently than physical coercion as a means of persuading slaves to accept their inferior status.

But many workers found their enslavement to be a virtual death sentence. In the silver mines of Laurium, where about 10,000 Greek slaves were employed, slave labour completely replaced wage labour. The profit from mining was so immense that owners could afford to treat slaves — their only major capital investment — as expendable; the treatment of slaves in these mines was brutal in the extreme, and many were literally worked to death.

Slavery is, then, under certain conditions, a highly profitable system of exploitation. In North America, where the enslavement of Africans and their descendants continued until the last quarter of the nineteenth century, this exploitation was 'justified' by beliefs about racial inferiority, and reinforced by a form of Christian preaching which emphasised to slaves the virtues of humility and submission. Furthermore, the harsh treatment of slaves was fully supported by the legal system. Slaves in North America had few civil or property rights. They were forbidden to enter into contracts, and consequently the marriage of two slaves was not considered legally binding; the slave owner could, if he wished, separate husbands from wives, and parents from children. Strict laws regulated every aspect of slave behaviour, restricting the slave's right to travel, to defend himself against attacks by whites, and to use as he might wish what little leisure time was available. The penalties for breaking the regulations were severe, including beatings and death. An important aspect of the slave's position was the perpetual nature of slavery – slaves were destined to occupy this status throughout their lives, and their children in turn because they were the property of the owner. Slaves, as property, were under the absolute power of their owners; they could be bought, sold or traded at the whim of the master, and were occasionally awarded as prizes in lotteries, or wagered at gaming tables.

The economic significance of slavery, both for the North American colonies and for European capitalism, is too important to be overlooked. Exploitation of the rich natural resources of the new world required far more labour power than European colonists themselves could provide. Approximately 20 million healthy young Africans were forcibly transported as slaves to the 'new world' between the sixteenth and mid-nineteenth centuries, and this had a critical effect on Africa's own development.

2.4   FEUDALISM

Feudal societies emerged in Europe at the point at which the state was unable to exercise direct control over the population. Political power was decentralised in the sense that warriors were able to claim rights over a local territory and enforce their own brand of justice by means of military might. Unarmed peasants were unable to challenge the power of a warrior (or noble) who had personal supporters with horses and weapons. Military power was linked to wealth, which meant, in this case, agricultural land. The greater a noble's military power, the more land he could control; and the larger his estates, the more warriors he could support in order to secure his domain.

Wider patterns of trade were common before the emergence of feudalism, but when these were disrupted by wars and invasions, local communities became virtually self-sufficient. Productive activity was carried out by peasants, who lived on and cultivated the land which was controlled by the feudal lords. The lords compelled the peasants to hand over a considerable portion of the agricultural goods that they produced as tenant farmers on small strips of land, and also to perform customary services directly for the benefit of the lord.

In early periods of feudalism, the link between a noble and his peasants was maintained in the form of a personal agreement which ended upon the death of either party. (The same was true initially of the oath of allegiance linking lords to other, more powerful nobles through rights to the use of land and military alliance.) But eventually the servile condition of the peasants (and the privileged status of nobles) became hereditary, passed down from one generation to the next. Serfs were tied to the land which they cultivated, with little opportunity of changing or improving their position. They became, in a sense, a captive labour force; those who tried to escape from the land to neighbouring towns could be forcibly returned or punished. Most serfs lived in miserable poverty, although the communal traditions of medieval villages went some way towards alleviating the worst forms of hardship.

The nobility and the serfs emerged, then, as two of the distinct strata in feudal society. However, the clergy formed a third stratum in feudal society. The Catholic Church had enormous secular (as well as spiritual) power, since it possessed the right to income from vast expanses of land. Like nobles, powerful clergymen had access to estates, which were cultivated by serfs and guarded by armed retainers. To some extent, the Church was an independent force in feudal society, in competition with the nobility and the king. However, as 'men of learning', clergymen were able to promulgate a view of the world which was taken for granted by most of the population, a world view which included the notion that the supremacy of the king, the privileges of the nobility and the lowly position of serfs were all ordained by God. Thus the power of the Church was used to legitimate the system of social inequality.

In Europe from the twelfth century onward, feudal society was affected by the gradual transformation of local markets into permanent towns, with important implications for the emergence of a fourth stratum. Eventually the townsmen (or burgesses), using wealth acquired from trade, purchased considerable freedoms from feudal obligations. Their newly acquired rights (to come and go as they pleased, to own and dispose of property, to buy and sell goods) contributed to the growth of trade and also strengthened the economic power of the burgesses in relation to that of the nobility.

Thus feudal society came to comprise four distinct social strata: the nobility and the clergy, who controlled most of the land and enjoyed the agricultural surplus; the serfs, who cultivated the land and were bound to it; and the burgesses. These classes were, by and large, closed; access to the nobility or the peasantry was determined by birth, though occasionally peasants could escape from feudal bondage to the towns, and rich merchants were sometimes able to purchase titles and estates. The clergy was, of course, an exception to the rule of hereditary classes; since clergymen were (in theory at least) celibate, they had no legal heirs, and so the lower ranks of the clergy were open to the younger sons of noblemen or, more rarely, to commoners.

The burgesses constituted a growing challenge to the social relations of feudalism. Expansion of their wealth depended upon drawing serfs away from the land to labour in the towns (thus serfs who could remain hidden within town walls for a year and a day gained freedom from the land) and on undermining those aristocratic privileges, such as control over roads, which inhibited commercial activity. The challenge of the burgesses paved the way for the eventual emergence of a large class of landless labourers with no means of livelihood other than the sale of their labour for a wage; this was, therefore, one of the conditions for the development of capitalism.

2.5 THEORIES OF STRATIFICATION

Marx (1818–83)

Marx's general approach

Karl Marx has provided modern sociology and politics with

one of its most wide-ranging and powerful theoretical approaches. At the same time, his account of society has been one of the most bitterly contested of all social theories, for it is not only a sociological theory, but also a philosophy of man and a programme for revolutionary change in society. A large portion of the world's population sees Marx's as the most illuminating of all man's intellectual products; our own area of the globe in the West sees Marxism as a false and dangerous dogma.

Different sociologists have adopted these different views, and others fall in between, but it is certain that any theory of stratification owes a great debt to Marx's account of classes, even if the sociologist ends up rejecting Marx as mistaken or overtaken by history. The reason for debt is that Marx's theory of society is entirely based on the study of economic relationships, and these economic relationships form the basis of *classes*. Class relations are the key to all aspects of society.

For Marx, all non-Communist societies are *class societies*. Economic reward, political power and social prestige all flow from the structure of classes. These classes are more than 'income groups', they are created by the way in which production is socially organised. In the Marxist view,

> mankind must first of all eat, drink, have shelter and clothing, before it can pursue politics, science, art, religion, etc.; and therefore the production of the immediate material means of subsistence . . . forms the foundation upon which the State institutions, the legal conceptions, art, and even the ideas on religion, of the people concerned have been evolved (F. Engels, speech at the graveside of Karl Marx).

The production of material goods is the primary activity of humans, and it must come before all other activities. As soon as a society is able to produce more than the bare minimum needed for survival, it is possible for classes to emerge. One class (the majority) does the productive work, while a minority class dominates them and seizes all the surplus produced. Any class society is founded on this relationship between the exploiters — those who take the surplus and rule the society — and the exploited — those who actually produce through their labour.

The history of 'civilised' society, for Marx, has been the history of different forms of class exploitation and domination. It is the form of class domination present which determines the general character of the whole social structure. It is crucial to understand that this class relationship is a *social* relationship which is not automatically and directly produced by specific techniques of production. For example, the growing of wheat using traditional, non-mechanical techniques is compatible with a wide range of social relations of production. A Roman citizen often owned slaves who worked his land growing wheat; a feudal lord would seize the surplus wheat grown by the serf on the lands of medieval Europe; the early capitalist farmers began to employ landless labourers to do their manual work for a wage which was less than the total value of the product which they created. In each case, wheat is grown on land by the labour of men and women, but the social arrangements are *totally* different. There are *totally* different class relationships, leading to *totally* different forms of society: ancient, feudal and capitalist. The only thing that unites these three arrangements is that in each case a minority class rules and takes the surplus away from the producers. Each society, says Marx, embodies class exploitation based on relationships of production. It is this that Marx calls the *mode of production*. The key to understanding a given society is to discover which is the dominant mode of production within it. We then know the basic pattern of social and political relationships, and can appreciate what conflicts and potentials for change are built into the society.

The capitalist mode of production, for example, developed in Britain prior to industrialisation. Capitalistic economic relations were established in the countryside through the 'enclosures', where land became the private property of landowners and the rural work-force was stripped of the land-use rights that gave them an independent source of subsistence. The workers, replaced by sheep and by mechanised farming techniques, were forced to become landless proletarians, dependent on employment in a labour market. The machine-breaking resistance of the Luddites against these changes was only one sign of the growing class conflicts to come. In later stages, cottage and craft industries were moved into factories, which then led on to the development of 'machinofacture' (mechanised production) through technological innovation. This quickened the growth of an urban proletariat in the mid-nineteenth century, which gradually came to develop the collective organisations (unions and political parties) necessary to struggle against exploitation. Quite apart from the class conflict endemic in capitalism, the economic system itself is beset with instabilities. Periodic slumps occur when trade and investment collapse and unemployment rises. Capital then emerges again more efficient, but concentrated in larger firms — the successful absorbing the weak. This eventually results in 'monopoly capitalism', where economic power is concentrated in the hands of a few very large enterprises. In Marx's view there are also longer-term threats to the survival of capitalism, especially through the tendency for the rate of profit to fall. When Marx tells us in the *Communist Manifesto* that 'all history is the history of class struggles', he is claiming that all conflict and change in societies can ultimately be traced back to the underlying class conflict, based on the opposing class interests arising from exploitation. These fundamental economic relations shape, in addition, all other aspects of the social structure. The state, laws, and even religion come to reflect and justify the basic class relations. The 'superstructure' of ideas and social institutions comes to reproduce the economic base: 'the ideas of the ruling class are the ruling ideas in every epoch', Marx claimed, and 'the state is but the executive committee of the whole bourgeoisie'.

However, this 'integration' of different institutions can never be perfect. There is always some potential for opposition and change; this comes to a climax in periods of revolutionary social transformation.

According to Marx, revolutions can only occur on the basis of appropriate material conditions, where economic development is being *held back* by the existing social relations. For example, the 'enclosures' concentrated land and allowed new techniques, but only through completely disrupting the social relations existing in the countryside. Thus, relations of production are transformed in a revolution. Secondly, people must become conscious of the opposed interests and fight them out through political struggle. Many historians regard the English Civil War of the seventeenth century as a crucial transition period where an emerging bourgeoisie removed old political barriers to its development — it was a 'bourgeois revolution'. The triumph of a new ruling class goes together with the eventual emergence of a whole new social structure based on the new mode of production.

For Marx, the final revolution will be made by the proletarian class. Unlike earlier revolutions, there will not be a new exploiting class, for rule by the proletariat means self-government by the working-class majority. Thus, class society is abolished, with all its evils, and a new realm of human freedom begins in Communist society. Here at last, people have an abundant society where all benefit and all are free to live and work in a flexible, creative way. Man comes to control his own destiny and 'make his own history'. Equality brings emancipation: according to Marx it will be 'possible for me to do one thing today and another tomorrow, to hunt in the morning, fish in the afternoon, rear cattle in the evening, criticise after dinner, *just as I have a mind* without ever becoming hunter, fisherman, shepherd or critic'. Thus, only here in Communist society can people fulfil their potential for creativity and goodness.

Marx's account of the capitalist mode of production

Some sociologists have tried to describe the general features of 'industrial society' or even 'modern society', arguing that 'industry' imposes a special pattern on society and social institutions. Marx could never have accepted such a view. It was not only industry that gave advanced European nations their character, but the way in which industrialisation took place, developing the growth of capitalist social relations. For Marx, the growth of industry promised wealth and abundance for all, but because industry had so far developed in a capitalistic way, the new-found wealth was monopolised by one class, while the mass of the working people were made poorer, not richer, by the advances in production.

Let us examine the class relations of capitalism, as Marx describes them. The key classes in the capitalist mode of production are the bourgeoisie and the proletariat, or capitalists and landless wage labourers. While Marx recognises that (as we shall see later) there are other classes, the fundamental class division is between this pairing of exploiter and exploited. The bourgeoisie derive their class position from the fact that they own productive wealth. It is not their high income that makes them capitalists, but the fact that they own the means of production (i.e. inputs necessary for production — factories, machines, etc.)

Indeed, the ability of workers to work (labour-power) itself is a marketable commodity, bought for the least cost to be used at will by the capitalist. There is a general tendency, Marx claimed, for wages to stick at a general exploitative level, except when some skills are temporarily scarce. In addition, the capitalist owns the product and will always pocket the difference between the value of the labour and the value of the product — 'surplus value' as Marx called it — purely and simply by virtue of his ownership. His property rights also allow the capitalist the control of the process of production and the labour he buys. The proletariat, in contrast, own no means of production whatever.

Before capitalism, the worker had rights of use over some land, and had enough tools to grow some food and have some produce left to barter for other goods. Additionally, some of the worker's surplus was seized by the feudal lord. In the capitalist mode of production, however, the workers are landless and have no independent means of subsistence. They have to sell their labour-power in order to live and so labour-power becomes a marketable commodity, apparently no different from any other exchangeable object. Thus, the crucial division between classes is based on *property* ownership or non-ownership of the means of production.

Nevertheless, it might seem that the workers must get their just reward under capitalism, for they are free to work for whom they like, and to bargain for their wage. However, this can never be a free and equal contract, because the individual worker must have work at any price simply in order to survive, while the capitalist (though needing workers) can employ or sack any individual he chooses. The employer could even suspend production and live off his wealth for some considerable time.

This process of exploitation is not so obvious as the direct payment of tithes or forced labour under feudalism, but it is still, according to Marx, economic exploitation. Thus the capitalists have economic power, controlling and exploiting the worker, and this also gives them political power as well. The only ultimately effective way the worker can resist is through collective class action to overthrow the capitalist mode of production. More limited forms of resistance such as normal trade union activity do not alter the fundamental relationships of class inequality in capitalist society. The revolution, however, will not turn the clock back and abolish industry. Instead, it will reorganise industry on the basis of equal power and reward, spreading wealth throughout society and abolishing the ownership of productive property by a minority.

In his massive work *Capital*, Marx analyses the strains and disruptive tendencies built into capitalism. He argues that class conflicts and economic crises are built into the way the economic system works, and they cannot be avoided. The capitalists are themselves forced continually to maximise profits and maximise exploitation of the workers, because they are under pressure of competition and hit by economic crises. These and other pressures keep the worker in poverty (at least relative to the capitalists), but other forces will also create, Marx claimed, the conditions for revolt.

The urbanisation of workers and their employment in ever-larger factories break down old barriers of skill and status among the workers, and bring about a realisation of collective class identity and shared interests. In addition, the economies of the most advanced capitalist nations would advance to a point where any further development of production would be held back by the crises of capitalism and by the desire to produce for profit rather than the general good. The material conditions for revolution would evolve and the working class would develop into a revolutionary class ready to seize their opportunity. With this successful revolution, there would be the construction of the Communist Utopia, 'where society inscribes on its banners: "From each according to his ability, to each according to his needs!" '

Can Marx's analysis be applicable today?

It is obvious that there are some serious problems in Marx's account. Revolution has occurred in nations on the verge of entry into capitalism, not in societies which are mature and 'ripe' for change. The working class in capitalist societies has enjoyed, in the long term, a rise in the standard of living, and labour movements have won enough welfare concessions to ease the lot of many of the poor. By no means all Western societies have strong Communist parties. In addition, the growth of the new middle class of managerial, professional and clerical workers appears to contradict Marx's view that divisions among those without wealth would disappear. Western economies are certainly prone to crises, but the state seems able to keep them in check.

Generally, then, Marx's ideas seem to many people to have been 'disproved' by twentieth-century developments. In fact, however, this is a rather limited view. The real issues are firstly whether Marx's general perspective on stratification was sound, and secondly, whether contemporary Western societies are still capitalist in the general basic character of their social relations. The first issue is important because Marx provides an account of stratification which is significantly different from that of many other social theorists. Very often today, sociologists see classes as merely groupings of people with similar attributes such as income, type of occupation, and so on. Marx, in contrast, saw classes as systematically linked in a particular structure of social relationships. An *explanation* of inequality is given through the analysis of the mode of production. Marx points out the deeper class relations and potential conflicts below the surface of society. This strength, however, is linked to a crucial failing in the eyes of many sociologists. They argue that Marx's class analysis is too simplistic to account adequately for the complexity of social inequality. For them, Marx's overwhelming emphasis on the ownership of productive wealth leaves us unable to explain adequately all the differences in rewards and in consciousness within the mass of the population who are not capitalists.

Every middle-class employee is certainly not a member of the bourgeoisie, but most sociologists would also feel that the middle class are not true proletarians either, even though they own no wealth. In order to cope with these problems, the ideas of Max Weber have often been employed in addition to, or instead of, those of Marx, and we will examine Weber's approach shortly. Before that, however, we must address the question of whether contemporary Western societies are still capitalist.

Quite clearly, the Western economies are vastly changed today in comparison with Marx's time. There is far more economic intervention by the state in most societies of the West, and state employees of one kind or another form a large part of the work-force (a quarter of all workers in Britain). Nationalisation and the frequent replacement of individual owner-managers by shareholders and managerial bureaucracies have both changed the structure of industry. However, as is indicated elsewhere in this chapter and in Chapter 4, it can still be argued that private ownership of the means of production is the basis of economic power and wealth, and that the labour market is still the prime determinant of wage-levels. The worker is still in a subordinate position in the work-place, and the incomes of workers are still very low *in comparison with* those who control them. Other interpretations are possible: it is commonly argued, for example, that the West has 'mixed economies' which work in everyone's interest, but in our view this is mistaken — Western economies are still best described as capitalist.

Our next theorist of stratification, Max Weber, agreed with this view, but took a very different perspective on the class structures of capitalist societies.

Weber (1864–1920)

Weber's general approach

Weber's ideas differed from those of Marx in a variety of ways. His political goals were quite contrasting — Weber had no objection to seeing his native Germany ruled by the capitalists through a parliament. He rejected the goals and policies of the

German socialists and regarded communism as an unattainable Utopia. More generally, Weber rejected the idea that sociologists could generalise about social structures by using the analysis of modes of production. For Weber, every society was historically unique and complex. Above all, he rejected the Marxist view that economic relations were always the explanation of social structure and the prime mover of social change. He believed that religious ideas had an independent historical influence, and that the realm of politics was usually the crucial controlling force in social change. This led him to reject Marxism as a one-sided sociology, unable to deal adequately with the full complexity of society and social change.

Weber's approach to inequality was to present a range of descriptive categories that could be used to describe it in any given society. He gave no priority to any particular relationship of inequality: for example, he believed that the relation between money-lender and debtor might be as significant as a basis for class as that between workman and employer. A wide range of economic bases for class could therefore be found. Additionally, Weber emphasised in his essay 'Class, Status and Party' (see Gerth and Mills, 1948) that inequality in society might not be based on economic relations at all, but on prestige or on political power, mobilised through a party. Thus, unlike Marx, Weber did not see every unequal social structure as a class society — caste, for example, was based on status differences, grounded in religious ritual.

Indeed, Weber emphasised that 'economic power may result from the possession of power which rests on other foundations'. Social status, or prestige, may derive from economic power, but this is not necessarily the case; Weber cites the case of the newly rich businessman who does not possess the education or 'culture' to command high status. Also, status may form the basis of political power — Weber saw this as especially relevant in the case of the German Junker aristocracy, who were economically weak but still held the reins of political power. For Weber it was a matter for social and historical analysis to discover the real basis of inequality in a particular society.

In spite of these considerations, Weber certainly did regard capitalism as a class society — economic relations form the basis of inequality. We might suppose from this that Weber is merely echoing Marx's theories, but in fact Weber emphasises the importance of the *market* as the economic basis for class much more than *property*. For him, the primary cause of inequality in capitalism is *market capacity* — this is the skills brought to the labour market by the employee. Differences in reward between occupations result from the scarce skill held by the occupational group. If the skill is in demand, the reward will be high.

A good contemporary example can be seen in the typographers on Fleet Street newspapers. These skilled workers control entry to their craft of type-setting, and hence 'keep themselves scarce'. As a result they have traditionally commanded higher wages than most other manual workers. Unfortunately for them, however, new computer technology is rapidly replacing the antiquated machines now in use, resulting in a great cut in demand for the old craft skills. The strong market capacity of the typographers is now undermined, and they are likely to suffer a fall in *life-chances*. This concept is Weber's term for all those rewards and advantages afforded by market capacity. Life-chances include income, perks and pensions, together with less tangible benefits such as security or good working conditions. We can therefore distinguish groups with similar market capacity, and these can be termed 'classes'. We can see, then, that Weber agrees with Marx that the crucial economic features of capitalism are private ownership of the means of production, and markets for goods and labour. The crucial difference is that Marx emphasised the first element, while Weber emphasised the second.

Sociologists are often attracted by Weber's account because it gives an explanation for the distinct differences in life-chances between different strata in contemporary capitalism. We can see that there is a broad division in life-chances between manual and non-manual workers; the skills of the non-manual employees, especially professionals, give this class significant advantages in market capacity and hence in life-chances. At the same time, we may distinguish unequal strata within a class. The working-class occupations may be divided into skilled, semi-skilled and unskilled strata, and life-chances broadly differ according to the skill level. Normally, though, sociologists have argued that these three strata have enough in common to make them components of one class, because they are all divided by a considerable gulf from the non-manual middle class, which contains its own strata.

Weber's consideration of the capitalist market therefore appears to give an explanation of the hierarchy of occupational reward found in capitalist societies, and gives us the means to describe sociologically the complexity of inequality in reward and advantage.

Evaluation of Weber's theory

There are, however, a number of problems in Weber's account. One problem is that we may have no clear criterion for dividing up the work-force into classes and strata. In other words, taken to its logical conclusion, Weber's analysis of market capacity would put each person into a separate class because each individual would have a minutely different skill from everyone else. (In fact, Weber himself tended to use much broader class categories in his own empirical research.) More importantly, Weberian approaches tend to concentrate on occupation and neglect *wealth* as a crucial element in the class structure. If we are concerned with concentrations of economic advantage and power, we cannot neglect that small minority — Marx's bourgeoisie — who monopolise the ownership of the means of production. As this chapter will go on to show, a small, economically dominant class undoubtedly does still exist in Western societies.

Marx and Weber: conclusions

We have seen that both Marx and Weber see contemporary Western societies as capitalist, and both agree that the crucial distinctive features of this are private ownership of the means of production, and a market for labour. If we wish to understand the structure of objective economic inequality in capitalist society, we must understand both of these economic relations and see both elements of capitalist social relations as producing distinct social classes. Consequently, we can distinguish three main classes in contemporary capitalist society. The small 'upper class' consists of those with substantial holdings of productive wealth. This class — only a small percentage of the adult population — has succeeded in preserving and expanding its wealth, and has developed effective means to ensure that both this wealth and the accompanying social attributes are transmitted across generations. The ownership of productive property defines this class and separates it from the rest of society. This class coincides with Marx's bourgeoisie. The non-owners of the means of production, however, cannot all be described as proletarians. Many managerial positions involve the employee being both a representative of the capitalist *and* a worker who is in some degree exploited. These positions have been labelled by Wright (1978) as 'contradictory class locations'. They contain elements of both

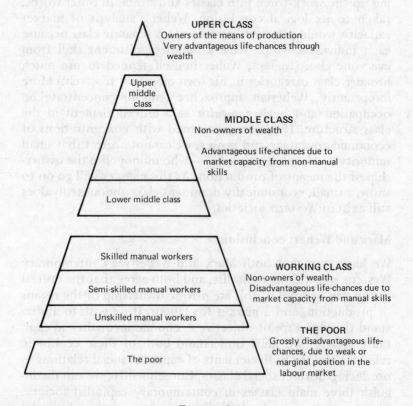

UPPER CLASS
Owners of the means of production
Very advantageous life-chances through wealth

Upper middle class

MIDDLE CLASS
Non-owners of wealth

Advantageous life-chances due to market capacity from non-manual skills

Lower middle class

Skilled manual workers

WORKING CLASS
Non-owners of wealth
Disadvantageous life-chances due to market capacity from manual skills

Semi-skilled manual workers

Unskilled manual workers

THE POOR
Grossly disadvantageous life-chances, due to weak or marginal position in the labour market

The poor

FIGURE 2.1

worker and bourgeois class positions. Generally, however, we can divide up those below the upper class on the grounds of life-chances, based on market capacity. Broadly speaking, the working-class/middle-class division still reflects crucial differences in life-chances between manual and non-manual workers, and so we are justified in seeing non-manual workers as members of a distinct class. A wide range of differences in attitude and life-style are associated with these objective economic differences between middle and working class.

However, it is not these differences in behaviour which form the *basis* of the class structure; rather these differences are an indirect reflection of objective economic inequalities.

We can therefore conclude that the ideas of Marx and Weber can, for our purposes, be partly combined to produce a three-class model of contemporary capitalist societies (see Figure 2.1).

2.6 THE OWNERSHIP OF WEALTH

Just as every citizen has the right to enjoy a meal at the Savoy Grill, so every individual has the right to be a millionaire. As we shall see, however, the enormous and persistent inequality in the distribution of personal wealth is one of the most important features of capitalist class structure. The question of changes in patterns of inequality in the distribution of wealth must therefore be considered in detail; our empirical evidence will relate to contemporary Britain.

What is wealth?

The distinction between income and wealth is not entirely rigid. We can say, though, that income is a flow of disposable (spendable) money, while wealth refers to fixed assets such as land, shares, buildings or durable possessions. Wealth thus seems to mean the same as 'property', but 'property' is a term commonly used to refer to anything from Henry Ford II's car company to the clothes you are wearing. Both of these count, in legal terms, as private property, and the individual owner has the right to buy, sell, control and even destroy personal wealth. (These rights, we might note, are specific to capitalist society. Ownership of land in many pre-industrial societies meant 'rights of use' and not complete personal control.) These rights of control over one's own possessions are valued rights — we would not want our shirt to be stolen, torn, or dyed by someone else — but this all-embracing idea of 'property rights' conceals a crucial difference between different forms of property. We must distinguish between *consumption property* and *production property*. Property for personal consumption includes consumer durables (e.g. washing-machines, motor-cars) and family homes which are owner-occupied. Productive property is significantly different, for this includes factories, farming or building land, and stocks and shares. This kind of property is *capital* and yields income through profit on the productive use of property. It is a defining feature of capitalist society that the productive wealth of the society (on which the whole population depends for employment and products) is privately owned and controlled. Private productive property provides massive unearned income, and also frequently forms the basis of economic power. Unearned income derives from:

(i)   rent on buildings or land;
(ii) dividends paid from profit of firms to shareholders; and
(iii) interest on monetary investments such as deposit accounts or government securities.

In addition, the right to buy and sell property provides *capital gains*: where the market value of an item of property has risen, this provides a profit on its sale. This is the basis for property speculation and investment in antiques or works of art. In the latter cases, capital gains are being made from what might be termed special kinds of consumption property, only available to the rich.

It is crucial to note that 'wealth begets wealth': that is, productive property provides a return which may itself be reinvested to provide further return. Indeed, the more you possess, the faster this wealth begets more. Those whose income wealth exceeds their consumption must always get richer, and hence the gap between the property-owner and the propertyless must always widen (unless there are counter-vailing measures such as wealth tax). The dynamics of capital accumulation thus ensure that property is distributed un-equally, and that it remains so. We shall see that this concen-tration of productive wealth creates a propertied upper class, which can also be regarded as an economically dominant class.

The distribution of wealth in Britain

The statistical description of the distribution of wealth is by no means straightforward. One reason is that the distinction we have made between productive and consumption property is not always maintained, or it is applied in differing ways. Sometimes income gets included as well — for example, should the contents of current accounts in banks or building societies be included as wealth? In addition, most information comes from official statistics, especially from the Inland Revenue, deriving from tax returns and death duties. These sources are neither totally reliable, nor do they always provide the information required. The records typically understate the concentration of wealth, for they rely on individual declara-tions which are manipulated and presented so as to minimise apparent wealth holdings. There is, therefore, a great need for interpretation and adaptation of the figures which in turn gives rise to conflicting views among different researchers.

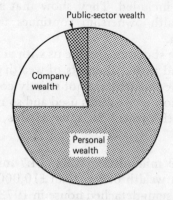

Source: Atkinson (1974).

FIGURE 2.2

This account draws upon the important recent contributions of Atkinson (1974), Westergaard and Resler (1975), Revell (1967), and the Diamond Commission (1979).

In asking the question 'who owns Britain's wealth?' it is not immediately obvious that we should deal with individuals. After all, the state owns many buildings and assets, and much emphasis has been put on the institutional shareholdings of insurance companies, for example. It is important to note, however, that the majority of Britain's wealth is still owned by identifiable individuals (see Figure 2.2).

Let us examine, then, the 1974 distribution of this personally held wealth, as described in the government publication *Social Trends 1975*. According to this official source:

(i)   92.8 per cent of personal wealth is owned by 25 per cent of the adult population. Thus 75 per cent of Britain's adults share a mere 7.2 per cent of personal wealth.

(ii) 67.5 per cent of personal wealth is owned by 10 per cent of all adults.

(iii) 51.1 per cent is owned by 5 per cent of all adults.

(iv) 26.0 per cent of personal wealth is owned by 1 per cent of the adult population.

These figures exclude minor forms of consumption property, and hence give a more accurate picture than if all durable possessions were included. They show that a vast degree of inequality in wealth ownership continues to exist in contemporary Britain.

Inland Revenue statistics provide us with actual numbers of wealth-owners and actual amounts of wealth (see Table 2.1). Unfortunately, the statistics are not strictly comparable, since a broader definition of wealth is used and so more people are classified as wealth-owners. In spite of this, the figures are still startling:

(i)   Out of 19 million taxpayers, 14.7 million (77.1 per cent) own wealth of *less* than £10,000. (Roughly the value of a semi-detached house in 1973.)

(ii) On the other hand, 4.4 million taxpayers (22.9 per cent) own wealth of over £10,000. This group owns

TABLE 2.1
Estimated wealth of individuals in Great Britain, 1973

Range of net capital value* (lower limit)	Number of cases (thousands)	Per cent	Amount (£ million)	Per cent
Nil	3,599	18.8	1,649	1.0
1,000	4,804	25.1	8,529	5.2
3,000	2,279	11.9	8,979	5.5
5,000	4,082	21.3	29,847	18.2
Under 10,000	14,764	77.1	49,006	29.9
10,000	2,229	11.6	27,738	16.9
15,000	782	4.1	13,854	8.5
20,000	1,044	5.5	30,723	18.8
50,000	211	1.1	13,109	8.0
100,000	79	0.4	10,025	6.1
200,000	31	0.2	19,414	11.8
Over 10,000	4,376	22.9	114,866	70.1
Total	19,140	100.0	163,872	100.0

* = 'net assets' or wealth.

Source: Inland Revenue, *Estimated Wealth of Individuals in Great Britain 1973*, London, HMSO, 1975, table 1.

70.1 per cent of all personal wealth in Britain, a total of £114, 866 million.

(iii) The other 77.1 per cent of taxpayers share between them £49,006 million.

These figures understate the degree of inequality because they include such a wide range of small assets, but the table goes on to show the further concentration of wealth at the highest levels. There is a definite hierarchy of wealth within the top few per cent of the population:

(i) Those owning wealth worth between £10,000 and £20,000 account for a further 15.7 per cent of taxpayers.

(ii) Thus 92.8 per cent of taxpayers owned wealth of less than £20,000 in 1973. This accounts for the great bulk of those owning houses and having relatively small investments or savings.

(iii) A further 5.5 per cent of taxpayers have wealth between £20,000 and £50,000, accounting for 18.8 per cent of national wealth.

(iv) An elite 1.1 per cent own wealth worth between £50,000 and £100,000, 8 per cent of Britain's total.

(v) An even more select group of 0.4 per cent own assets valued between £100,000 and £200,000, accounting for 6.1 per cent of total wealth.

(vi) Finally the super-rich (numbering 31,000), with wealth worth over £200,000, formed 0.2 per cent of taxpayers and owned £19,414 million, which is 11.8 per cent of Britain's personal wealth. This does not include, of course, their extensive overseas investments.

(vii) 'Taxpayers' here refers to married couples or single earners. Thus the wealthy form a smaller proportion of the *total* adult population than these figures indicate.

We can see from this evidence that objective differences in material advantage have hardly disappeared from the British social structure. Furthermore, it makes no sense at all to refer to the wealthy as 'the middle class'. Certainly, the white-collar occupations enjoy higher levels of consumption property, especially home-ownership, but the bulk of non-manual workers fall well below the top 7.2 per cent who own 44.7 per cent of total personal assets.

No doubt some higher professionals fall into this group, as do many smaller businessmen and senior managers. However, as we have seen, a smaller band of the really rich form 1.7 per cent of all taxpayers and account for 25.9 per cent of total personal assets. Whether businessmen, financiers, landowners or simply heirs to wealth, there exists here an upper class whose economic and social position is crucially and primarily defined by their ownership of productive property. We can thus define the *upper class* as *that group in the population who own substantial amounts of productive property, and for whom this provides their predominant source of income.*

For most people, income comes through earned wages: the vast majority of employees, whether manual working-class or non-manual middle-class, *simply do not possess* productive property.

The propertied upper class can partly be identified through studies of share-ownership. Wilsher (1973) presents a list of some of Britain's richest capitalists. Many products with household names are still made by firms where descendants of the founder retain huge personal shareholdings: the Cadbury family, for example, own a total of £15 million worth of shares at 1969 prices. The Earl of Iveagh had a personal holding in Guinness worth £1.4 million in 1969, while his family had shares in trust to the tune of £9.4 million. Nearly all major wealth-owners have such large shareholdings distributed in trusts in the name of family members — thus *apparently* spreading the wealth for the purpose of avoiding taxation and death duties. The owner of Scottish & Newcastle Breweries, Sir William McEwan Younger, had in 1969 a personal holding of 80,000 shares worth £320,000, while his family trusts accounted for £1.3 million. As we shall see, such generous bequests are one explanation for changes in the distribution of wealth.

Income from wealth

Before gaining income from wealth, one first has to join the ranks of the propertied. Today, no less than earlier in this century, the surest way of entering this class is to choose one's parents carefully, for inheritance is by far the most important single factor in the gaining of wealth. In 1939, Josiah Wedgewood published his study of inheritance and concluded that of the wealthy

> about one third owe their fortunes almost entirely to inheritance (including gifts before death), another third to a combination of ability and luck with a considerable inheritance of wealth and business opportunity, and the remaining third largely to their own activities.

Atkinson, commenting on this conclusion, states that 'there is no apparent tendency for the importance of inheritance to decline over the course of this century' (1974, p. 76). Atkinson cites Harbury's finding that two-thirds of rich sons (1956–7) had fathers who were in the top 0.25 per cent of wealth-owners. Only a quarter of these sons had fathers who left only small estates on death. Thrift alone will not produce wealth. Atkinson calculates that a man saving 5 per cent of his £2,000 net pay would only amass £16,000 by the age of 65 (assuming a net return of 6 per cent).

Having gained wealth, a member of the upper class can expect unearned income to be produced, as we have seen, in the form of rent, interest, share dividends, or capital gains.

Personal holdings of shares are a clear illustration. The more wealth owned by an individual, the more likely it is that these will be in the form of shares. Thus personal share-holding is highly concentrated: 'Some 93% of all adults in 1970 held not even a single share . . . or government bond. Most of the 7% or so who did had only small or modest hold-ings. A minority of 1% owned about four-fifths of all capital of this kind in personal hands' (Westergaard and Resler, 1975, p. 117). Even within that 1 per cent, there is considerable concentration in a smaller minority of the super-rich, as we have seen above.

The return on shares through dividends clearly depends upon the profitability of industry, and so the rate varies with economic conditions. In general, however, a shareholder has been able to expect a real return (after inflation is taken into account) of about 10.5 per cent per year since the war. This is not as productive as during the years of the British Empire, 1919–29, when the real return was 19.5 per cent, but still better than the depression of 1939–49, when returns were on average only 2 per cent. A personal shareholding of £500,000 thus brings a real return (before taxes) of about £55,000 per year. Westergaard and Resler present data (p. 108) on un-earned income that show how much of the income of the wealthy is derived from investments: in 1971, 25 per cent of the income of those getting £5,000–6,000 a year came from investment; and this formed 40 per cent of the income of those getting over £10,000. Westergaard and Resler also esti-mate that six out of seven taxpayers have no investment income whatever, while 10 per cent of taxpayers shared two-thirds of all such income. Within that, 1 per cent of taxpayers gained one-third of all unearned income. The great majority of the population, in contrast, have to work to earn their living.

Changes in the distribution of wealth

While statistical evidence seems to suggest some reduction in the degree of inequality in the distribution of wealth, we must regard this as merely a quantitative change, rather than any qualitative change in the class structure. That is to say, the system of inequality remains the same, and remains massively unequal, despite those changes observed in the last fifty years. As can be seen from Table 2.2 and Figure 2.3:

(i)   The share of the richest 1 per cent has fallen from 69 per cent of total personal wealth in 1911–13 to 42 per cent in 1960.

(ii) The share of the next 2–5 per cent below that 1 per cent actually *increased* from 18 per cent of all wealth to 33 per cent of all wealth.

TABLE 2.2
Groups within adult population owning wealth

Groups within adult population owning proportions of wealth	Estimated proportion of total personal wealth				
	1911–3 (%)	1924–30 (%)	1936–8 (%)	1954 (%)	1960 (%)
Richest 1% owned	69	62	56	43	42
Richest 5% owned	87	84	79	71	75
Richest 10% owned	92	91	88	79	83
Richest 1% owned	69	62	56	43	42
Next 2–5% owned	18	22	23	28	33
Next 6–10% owned	5	7	9	8	8
95% owned	13	16	21	29	25
90% owned	8	9	12	21	17

Sources: Westergaard and Resler (1975, p. 112); Revell (1967).

74   *Introductory Sociology*

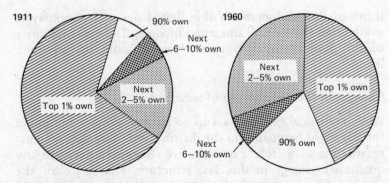

Source: Revell (1967).

FIGURE 2.3 *Changes in proportion of wealth owned by different groups*

   (iii) Some increase in the share of the next 6–10 per cent also occurred — from 5 per cent of wealth in 1911–13 to 8 per cent in 1960.

   (iv) An important shift took place between 1936–8 and 1954.

One primary explanation of these changes is the tendency for personal wealth-holders to share out their wealth amongst kin, especially through trusts which are beneficial in avoiding tax. As death duties and other taxes increased in severity during and after the Second World War (especially through the post-war Labour Government), the incentive to spread wealth-holding became very great. Thus much of the apparent redistribution of wealth is simply a formality — it remains within the same family who merely come to own it in legal name sooner rather than later when the holder dies. Clearly, we must include all such wealth-holders within the ranks of the upper class, rather than claiming that much wealth has diffused down into the middle class. One illustration of this phenomenon is the great rise in the number of women who are owners of wealth; the share of wealth held by women rose from 33 per cent to 42 per cent between 1927 and 1960. Wives merely gain legal title to family wealth which was previously in the name of the husband.

Death duties can be avoided if wealth is transferred through gifts at least seven years before the death of the donor. Thus sons and daughters become richer earlier, and this produces the apparent reduction in the proportion of wealth held by the top 1 per cent. As Atkinson (1974, p. 23) points out:

> among male wealth-holders the share of younger age-groups has increased. Whereas the average man of 65 plus used to own more than six times as much as the average man under 45, he now owns only three times as much ... the distribution of wealth over this century has not been between the rich and the poor, but between successive generations of the same family.

This hardly constitutes a qualitative change in the class structure.

Conclusion: the propertied upper class

The importance of inheritance, and the barriers to gaining substantial wealth through saving or employment mean that the upper class has maintained a considerable degree of social closure. That style of life and demeanour characteristic of Britain's dominant class is a result of its peculiar history. Unlike many other European countries, the ancient British aristocracy has managed to preserve and transmit its wealth through judicious marriage and inheritance. Marriage to foreign heiresses — German in the last century, American in this — helps to maintain the financial standing of noble families. Far more important, however, has been the merging of the new bourgeoisie with the traditional aristocracy.

The landed rich became economically active, especially in the eighteenth century, through the rise of commercialised farming, banking, and trade with the colonies. When the new class of bourgeois manufacturers and traders arose in the nineteenth century, it was able to merge with the commercialised aristocracy through marriage, and through the newly reformed public schools and universities. Old values and class patterns of behaviour became grafted on to a new economic class. The rise of the Empire and British trading dominance allowed a gentlemanly upper class of senior colonial administrators and City financiers to sustain and nurture distinctively upper-class characteristics. The continued dominance of City and Civil Service elites has often been seen as a barrier to dynamism in

British industry; in fact, it has merely been one aspect of a secure and integrated dominant class, linked by kinship, ownership of wealth and distinctive patterns of education.

2.7   THE DISTRIBUTION OF LIFE-CHANCES

In the previous section we described and accounted for the unequal distribution of wealth in Great Britain in terms of the ownership and control of forms of private productive property. We argued that the ownership of this form of property and its effect — wealth — is the defining feature of the dominant or upper class. In this section, we shall shift our attention to the two remaining strata of our model, the middle and working classes. Rather than the result of differential access to productive property *per se*, the inequality between these two broad *occupational* strata can be explained in terms of Weber's emphasis on their different *market capacities*. Market capacity generates its own effects which are expressed in terms of different material rewards, conditions of work, health, housing, and education. In general, one can distinguish between the fundamental conditions of any capitalist system which *explain* its continuation — private property and market capacity — and the *resulting* inequalities of wealth-ownership and life-chances.

The market capacity of the individual depends on the sort of skills that he or she can bring to the labour market as an employee. Clearly, given inequality of skills — primarily caused by an unequal *opportunity* between classes to obtain such skills — inequality of reward is inevitable. The crucial point is that rewards are important in determining an individual's life-chances; in other words, inequalities of reward are accompanied by and produce inequalities in all areas of life: conditions at work, health, housing, education, mortality, and justice.

Material rewards

Income distribution

Social commentators of the 1950s and early 1960s claimed that with the burgeoning of the 'affluent society' the major economic inequalities of class society were a thing of the past. We have seen that any such claim about the distribution of wealth could not have been and cannot today be legitimately sustained. What then of income? What evidence is there of a more equal distribution of income over the past thirty years? Table 2.3 provides some general information about the distribution of personal income after tax from the late 1930s to the mid-1970s.

TABLE 2.3
Distribution of personal income after direct taxes

Groups of income units[1]	Estimated % share of total value of all personal income						
	1938	1949	1954	1957	1963	1967	1974
Richest 1% received	11.5	6.5	5.5	5	5	5	4
Richest 5% received	24	17	15.5	14.5	15.5	15	13.7
Richest 10% received	33.5	27	25	24	25	24.5	23.2
Richest 20% received	46.5	42	42	38	*	*	39
Richest 40% received	*	64	65.5	63	64.5	64	63.6
Poorest 50% received	*	26.5	25.5	27.5	*	*	27
Poorest 30% received	*	14.5	11	13	12	11.5	12.8

[1] The 'income unit' is the tax unit, i.e. a married couple or single person (never married, divorced, widowed), aged 16 and over.
*No data given in sources.
Sources: *Social Trends 1977*; Westergaard and Resler (1975).

What conclusion can be drawn from these figures? First, within the top range of earners, the richest 5 per cent and 10 per cent have experienced some reduction in their share of total earned income. However, this move towards greater equality occurred primarily during the first part of the period: after 1954 this trend had practically ended. Any redistribution was primarily an effect of both the Second World War and the reformist government of Atlee. Second, gross inequalities across income units are evident. Thus, in 1974:

(i)   the richest 1 per cent earned 4 times their 'parity share', i.e. the amount they would have earned if income had been equally distributed among the total working population;

    (ii)   the richest 5 per cent earned nearly 3 times their parity share;

    (iii) the richest 10 per cent earned nearly 2½ times their parity share;

    (iv) the poorest 30 per cent only a third of their parity share.

But even then, such estimates do not take into account certain types of income which must be included for an accurate picture. These are employers' national insurance contributions, employees' superannuation contributions, benefits in kind as provided to all by the state (e.g. hospitals, schools, etc.), and finally, benefits received in the form of expense-account living. The latter benefits have become increasingly important for top wage earners as a means of 'topping up' salaries. In 1978 67 per cent of typical managers had a company car and 44 per cent were entitled to free private medical insurance, 37 per cent receiving a 'bonus' worth £1,200 on average. Finally, Table 2.3 shows only the effect of direct taxation on earnings: as we shall see, if *indirect* tax, such as VAT and that on beer and tobacco, is taken into account, taxation falls more heavily in real terms on the poorer sectors of the working population. A tax on a given commodity takes a higher proportion of a smaller income. Thus, by neglecting these other forms of income and the effect of indirect taxation, the figures presented so far *underestimate* the full extent of inequality in income distribution.

If we now move away from regarding income distribution in terms of the relative amount received by different groups of 'income units' to that received by different occupational strata, we gain a much more concrete indication of inequality. Dividing the strata into two broad bands — the male non-manual and the male manual workers — Table 2.4 demonstrates the degree to which the distribution of earnings between them has remained relatively constant over the past fifty years.

Furthermore, as Table 2.5 shows, within the broad non-manual/manual categories inequalities of reward between the sexes are very much in evidence. Table 2.5 describes the broad occupational and sexual hierarchy of reward in Britain in des-

TABLE 2.4

Indices of earnings — occupational group average expressed as a percentage of average for all men in the same period

	1913–14	1922–4	1935–6	1955–6	1960
Non-manual workers	142	158	152	144	145
Manual workers	88	83	85	83	82

Source: Westergaard and Resler (1975, p. 74).

TABLE 2.5

Average gross weekly earnings of full-time workers by sex and occupational strata (GB) (including overtime, shift premium payments and excluding fringe benefits)

	1970 (£)	1973 (£)	1975 (£)	1976 (£)	1978 (£)
Male non-manual (21+)	35.8	48.1	68.4	81.6	100.7
Male manual (21+)	26.8	38.1	55.7	65.1	80.7
Female non-manual (18+)	17.8	24.7	39.6	48.8	59.1
Female manual (18+)	13.4	19.7	32.1	39.4	49.4

Sources: Adapted from *Department of Employment Gazette*, October 1973; and *Social Trends*, 1977, table 6.12.

cending order. For both occupational strata female employees earn approximately 50 per cent of their male counterparts, and this discrimination against and exploitation of women's labour has only marginally decreased through recent legislation such as the Equal Pay Act of 1970. As Westergaard and Resler (1975, p. 101) say, 'sex inequality in pay reinforces class inequality: it strikes hardest at the lowest levels of the occupational hierarchy'.

The marked inequalities between manual and non-manual earnings is even more significant when one considers the importance that overtime and similar variable payments play in the gross figures of Table 2.5. That is, if we exclude such payments, the manual sector — in particular the male manual worker — suffers a major reduction in average weekly earnings while the non-manual workers do not, since their gross wages depend on very little overtime. This fact is illustrated in Table 2.6.

TABLE 2.6
*Average gross weekly earnings of male (21+) full-time manual and
non-manual employees (all industries and services, April 1978)*

	Manual (£)	% of earnings	Non-manual (£)	as % of earnings
Average gross earnings	80.70		100.70	
of which overtime				
payments	11.60	14	3.0	3
Payment by results				
and bonus or				
commission	7.20	9	2.9	2.9
Shift-work	2.40	3	0.6	0.6
Remaining earnings	59.50	74	94.20	93.5 (approx.)

Source: *Department of Employment Gazette* (*New Earnings Survey* 1978),
October 1978. (Note the figures in bold type.)

The figures in Table 2.6 demonstrate the importance of
overtime and other payments for the male manual workers'
earnings (over 25 per cent) and their minimal significance for
non-manual workers. For some male manual employees in
certain industries overtime and other payments are even more
important in determining average earnings: for example, on
average, 30 per cent of the wages of manual employees in
the metal manufacture and mining industries is made up in
overtime payments, etc. In other words, in general, manual
workers have to *work more hours* per week to achieve a gross
average wage which is *still about 25 per cent less* than that of
the non-manual worker. Moreover, as mentioned earlier, the
figures presented so far do not include a range of fringe benefits usually the privilege of non-manual employees which
have a real income value: among these are luncheon vouchers,
company cars, credit facilities (cheap company loans), and so
on. There appears to be, then, no justification for the claim
that manual and non-manual earnings are starting to overlap
and becoming more comparable.

What of the distribution of earnings *within* the broad occupational and sex categories? Obviously, in April 1978 not every male manual worker earned the average of £80.70, nor every male non-manual worker £100.70. Table 2.7 provides some initial figures on distribution. It is worth while consulting the table to recall the average gross earnings for comparison. Table 2.7 shows, first, that within the male occupational strata there is a much wider range of earnings among the non-manual employees, with the better-paid earning amounts near to or considerably above the average compared with earnings within the manual strata. In each industrial and service area of employment there are a considerable number of manual occupational groups, the majority of whose members earn considerably less than the average gross weekly earnings. In other words, in the manual sector, lower than average wages are not confined to those traditional low-paid occupational groups — farmworkers, gardeners and general labourers. Among male non-manual employees, however, the picture is very different. Apart from the low-level clerical, sales and nursing occupational groups, the overriding majority of members in other occupational groups enjoy wages near to or much above the average.

TABLE 2.7

Distribution of gross weekly earnings (April 78) (including overtime), etc.	Male Manual (£)	Male Non-manual (£)	Female Manual (£)	Female Non-manual (£)
10% earned less than	53.4	57.7	33.7	37.1
25% earned less than	63.3	72.0	39.6	44.2
50% earned less than	76.8	91.8	47.6	53.9
25% earned more than	93.1	117.4	57.0	68.7
10% earned more than	112.2	150.4	67.1	88.8

Source: *Department of Employment Gazette,* October 1978.

In general, then, there appears to be no overlap of earnings: there is no general level of earnings which 'most people' enjoy. Later on, we consider the impact of taxation on real income levels and its distribution. We shall show that taxation does

very little to relieve the inequalities of reward and general
life-chances between different occupational strata, and that,
in fact, in many ways it encourages further inequality.

The life-cycle of earnings

People also experience radically unequal patterns of earnings
over the span of their working lives as employees. For the
majority in all occupational groups, earnings are roughly similar in the early years of employment, that is, between the ages
of 20 and 25. But from age 25 onwards the earnings gap between the groups widens in favour of those in the non-manual
sector. For the latter, those in the higher occupational categories, such as managers, professional employees, academics,
engineers, scientists and technologists, earnings increase
rapidly because of an incremental system of reward — a regular and progressive increase in earnings in addition to any pay
awards negotiated — whereby earnings rise steeply up till their
late forties. At this stage in their careers employees enjoy
salaries which are about twice that received in their early
twenties (i.e. referring to their 'real' earnings when allowance
has been made for inflation, etc.). After this peak has been
reached, their real earnings fall, but only very moderately.
For manual workers, however, including skilled, semi-skilled
and unskilled, wages increase only slightly over their working
lives; wages increase on average by only 15 per cent, reaching
their peak in the employee's mid-thirties. They then tail off
to a level which, for the majority of the manual working population, is less than that enjoyed in their early twenties. This
is due to many factors, one of the more obvious of which is
that the cumulative physical demands of manual work may
well affect the worker's health. Moreover, as a worker gets
older, overtime, shift work and so on become less and less a
physical possibility. Similarly, job-related sickness may mean
that the ageing worker is more frequently unable to turn up
for work. The effect of these factors on earnings is suggested
by Table 2.8. Differences in life cycle of earnings clearly have
a number of consequences: for example, they will be expressed in the consumption patterns of the two classes. Non-
manual workers, given their greater security and better

financial prospects, could, for example, make some provision for replacing their car once every two years, or afford to obtain and pay off a mortgage. Only those non-manual workers who engage in low-level clerical and sales work experience a life cycle of earnings akin to that of the manual workers. But even these may envisage some possibility of promotion to a sub-managerial or supervisory position, a prospect which

TABLE 2.8

Variations in median gross earnings by age, for full-time men in selected occupations, 1970

Age group	Median earnings at each age expressed as per cent of median earnings in the same occupational group at age 21–24											
	M	E	A	P	T	O	S	SM	SSM	UM	All non-manual*	All manual*
18–20	–	56	–	52	60	70	66	63	72	85	63	70
21–24	100	100	100	100	100	100	100	100	100	100	100	100
25–29	128	132	130	145	122	123	124	110	110	108	130	110
30–39	166	157	179	175	140	138	139	114	114	113	157	116
40–49	180	171	199	188	144	137	135	113	112	110	163	114
50–59	180	165	193	194	136	125	127	105	105	101	155	105
60–64	162	155	192	171	130	114	114	98	97	92	132	95
All ages	166	146	176	155	123	119	119	104	104	101	133	105

Source: *Department of Employment Gazette*, January 1971, pp. 51–5 (data from *New Earnings Survey* of April 1970).

– = insufficient cases for separate presentation.
*For lack of space, data are shown only for selected main occupational groups. The totals for non-manual employees include groups M to S and other non-manual workers not listed here; those for manual employees, groups SM, SSM and UM and other manual employees not listed here.

Occupational groups

M	= managers	O	= office and communications work
E	= professional engineers, scientists and technologists	S	= sales workers
A	= academic staff and teachers (especially schoolteachers)	SM	= skilled
P	= other professional and technical	SSM	= semi-skilled
T	= technicians	UM	= unskilled

manual workers in a wide range of selected industries and trades is probably as far from the mind of the manual worker as it is from the reality of his or her employment situation. As Westergaard and Resler (1975, p. 83) say, the difference between the classes in terms of their life cycle of earnings 'plays a large part in differences of approach to the management of everyday life, and of responses to the social order, between the classes'. Table 2.8 illustrates that once again there is no evidence of a strong overlap between the manual and non-manual sectors.

Differences in terms and conditions of work

In this section we are not so much concerned with how many pounds are 'in the pay packet', i.e. *what* is earned, but rather with the general conditions of employment experienced by the manual and non-manual sectors. Thus, we shall consider such factors as hours, sick pay, pension schemes and holiday entitlements.

Hours worked per week vary considerably between the two broad occupational sectors. As was seen earlier, overtime plays a much greater role in pushing up the average gross weekly earnings of the male manual than of the male non-manual worker. For the former, the average working week in 1978 was forty-six hours, for the latter about thirty-eight hours. Besides being paid less per hour the majority of women employees in both sectors work fewer hours than their male counterparts. This is a result of a number of factors such as the much larger proportion of part-time work, the artificial restriction of female overtime by male-dominated trade unions, and social measures against women at work in general. (These factors are examined in more detail in our chapters on the family and sexual divisions.) In terms of historical change, manual workers of both sexes work today almost as many hours each week as they did in the late 1930s and early 1940s; this demonstrates the fact that, where available, overtime is a crucial necessity for the manual worker if he or she is to receive a wage at or above the 'average' for all manual occupations. In short, although the 'standard working week' has been reduced since the war, in reality the working week for the manual worker is much the same. Table 2.9 gives some of the relevant figures.

TABLE 2.9
*Average weekly hours and distribution of hours worked by sex and
occupational strata (1978)*

| | Full-time males (21+) | | Full-time females (18+) | |
	Manual	Non-manual	Manual	Non-manual
Average weekly hours	46.0	38.7	39.6	36.7
of which overtime	6.1	1.4	1.1	0.4
Distribution of hours				
(% employed)	(%)	(%)	(%)	(%)
36 hours or less	1.5	23.3	18.1	34.8
36–40 hours	37.1	57.5	64.1	59.9
40–48 hours	32.2	13.4	13.9	4.6
48+ hours	29.2	5.8	3.9	0.7

Source: *Department of Employment Gazette*, October 1978.

Hours of work are only one aspect of the conditions of
employment that must be considered: holidays, sick pay,
the provision of pension schemes, penalties for lateness at
work and so on are additional conditions that must come
into any assessment of overall occupational inequality. A
survey conducted by Wedderburn (1970) provides some useful information about inequality between and within the
manual/non-manual division regarding these conditions of
employment. Her findings are reproduced in Table 2.10 (p. 86).

As Wedderburn's figures indicate, manual workers are much
worse off than non-manual employees. This is true not only
of the relative provision of benefits but also of the extent to
which disciplinary measures are used. Note, for example, that
most manual workers — the 'operatives' — are penalised for
late arrival at work, whereas very few non-manual workers
suffer pay loss for lateness. This derives from a work ideology
that assumes that manual workers will be less 'responsible',
and so will need more discipline, than non-manual workers.
As Wedderburn says, employers assume 'that the non-manual
worker will "behave responsibly", will "have the interests of
the firm at heart" and "not abuse privileges"'. Such ideological assumptions help to maintain the material and symbolic inequalities between manual and non-manual workers,

TABLE 2.10

Selected differences in terms and conditions of employment

	Per cent of establishments in which the condition applies					
	Operatives	Foremen	Clerical workers	Technicians	Middle managers	Senior managers
Holiday: 15 days+	38	72	74	77	84	88
Choice of holiday time	35	54	76	76	84	88
Normal working 40+ hours per week	97	94	9	23	27	22
Sick pay — employers' scheme	57	94	98	97	98	98
Pension — employers' scheme	67	94	90	94	96	96
Time off with pay for personal reasons	29	84	83	86	91	93
Pay deductions for any lateness	90	20	8	11	1	0
Warning followed by dismissal for persistent lateness	84	66	78	71	48	41
No clocking on or booking in	2	46	48	45	81	94

Source: Wedderburn (1970).

while working against the possibility of manual workers ever getting such privileges. Of course, the assumption that manual workers would abuse certain 'privileges' and non-manual workers not is simply *that — an assumption*, historically unwarranted and ideologically divisive.

Pension coverage

Whether or not an employer provides sick pay and a private pension scheme has a direct and obvious influence over an employee's material life-chances. Even though there has been some increase in the distribution of pension schemes over the past ten years, employee coverage is still very unequal. Wedderburn's figure of 67 per cent for her sample of male manual workers, based on data collected in 1968, is still a good indicator today, since on average only 60 per cent of all male employees in the manual sector are currently covered by an employer's pension scheme. As with any average figure, this hides significant differences within the different areas of manual employment: for example, only 30 per cent of those workers employed in unskilled occupations are covered. Moreover, as is typical, private pension coverage was markedly less for female manual labour.

Furthermore, the *terms* of the pension schemes favour non-manual employees. For example, in 1970, employers paid about three times as much into their non-manual pension funds than they paid into those of their manual employees. Additionally, the eventual pension of most non-manual workers is linked to their level of earnings enjoyed at or near to retirement; manual worker schemes, on the other hand, are typically on a flat-rate basis. Thus, the differences in the life cycle of earnings are compounded by differences in post-employment income between the manual and non-manual sectors.

Sick pay

The provision of sick pay tells a similar story. For example, in 1977:

  (i)   between the ages of 15 and 65, on average, 68 per cent of male and 56 per cent of female manual workers were entitled to sick pay;

  (ii)   between the ages of 15 and 65 virtually 100 per cent of both male and female non-manual workers were entitled to sick pay benefits.

Such differences in the provision of sick pay, marked though they are, do not take into account the fact that certain employees, because of the sort of work they do, are more likely than others actually to be absent from work with temporary or chronic illnesses, as we shall now see.

Illness and death

The sons and daughters of those manual workers — particularly the unskilled — with large families, low incomes and poor housing are more likely to be subject to poor physical development, ill-health and infant mortality than those born of middle-class parents. For the former, then, 'life-chances' can often be taken literally, i.e. the chance of actually living. The 1969 National Child Development Study (in Wedge and Prosser, 1973) compared, through a longitudinal survey, the health prospects of a sample (10,000+) of children from what were defined as 'ordinary' and socially 'disadvantaged' backgrounds. The latter were considered to be children of large or single-parent families who lived in poor housing conditions on low wages. The main findings were:

(i)   Children from disadvantaged backgrounds were less likely to be protected from disease, partly due to the fact that their parents failed to use the immunisation and screening services of the NHS. For example, 1 in 8 children had not received a polio vaccination compared with only 1 in 40 from 'ordinary' backgrounds. This does not reflect a lack of *concern* on the part of the disadvantaged parents but rather a lack of *knowledge* about the facilities that are available and how to make effective use of them. The ability to use the health service effectively is more characteristic of middle- than of working-class individuals because they share a material and status position with medical professionals. Thus they can also talk to doctors and hospital staff in a common language; they may know a patient's rights as well as the responsibilities and duties of medical staff; in general, they know how to work the system.

(ii)   The disadvantaged children were more likely to have accidents in the home — especially burns, scalds and wounds. This was seen to be a result of overcrowding in the home, whereby, for example, the boiling kettle was more likely to be knocked over, the chance of this happening being greater when the kettle was used as the *only* source of hot water in the house.

(iii) By the age of 11, disadvantaged children were reported to have been absent from school due to ill-health and emotional disorder more frequently than was the case for those from ordinary backgrounds. Again, overcrowding, both during the waking and sleeping hours, encouraged contagion and by definition denied the children an important vehicle of emotional development — privacy.

(iv) Children born into disadvantaged homes were more likely to die in early infancy than children born into 'ordinary' family environments. Although there is evidence to show that over the past 100 years the *overall* infant mortality rate, i.e. the number of deaths in the first year of life, has fallen from over 150 to about 15 per 1,000 live births, the *relative* gap between the higher and lower social classes has hardly changed and some even argue that it has widened since the beginning of this century. Approximately 30 per 1,000 live births of children of unskilled backgrounds die compared with approximately 15 per 1,000 of children born to upper middle-class families. (See also Spicer and Lipworth, 1966.) One of the main reasons why there is a greater chance of infant mortality among children of unskilled workers is the higher incidence of *premature* births in the lower classes. The National Child Development Study discovered that 1 in 12 disadvantaged children weighed less than 5.5lb (2.4 kilos) compared with 1 in 20 of 'ordinary' background offspring. Prematurity can be caused by many factors, but those which seem particularly relevant in the case of unskilled families include: (a) minimal or no use of NHS antenatal facilities, with greater reliance on kin-advice as the major source of information; (b) earlier and more numerous pregnancies; (c) greater incidence of smoking by the prospective mother; and (d) a greater likelihood of parturition and birth within the home rather than in the more controlled environment of the hospital.

The inequalities of health and mortality are not restricted to the young. Working-class adults — particularly the unskilled

— experience the physically damaging and mentally stultify-
ing effects of a disadvantaged home and work environment.
Specific occupational hazards, along with diet, poor housing
and home environment, personal habits such as smoking,
mental stress and relatively lower use of the health service
result in a higher rate of illness and injury for manual compared with non-manual workers. Social class differences are
most apparent at the extremes, i.e. between professional
and unskilled occupational groups. The annual report of the
General Household Survey provides information on the distribution of chronic illness by socio-economic group. The
incidence of chronic, or 'long-standing', illness in the population was derived from respondents' answers to the following
two questions: 'Do you suffer from any long-standing illness,
disability, or infirmity? IF YES: Does it limit your activities
compared with most people of your age?'

Table 2.11 summarises the findings of the 1975 *Survey*.
Clearly, age is an important factor in increasing the reporting
of illness, but even allowing for this, members of lower socio-
economic groups have much higher rates of illness. Overall, it
is evident that illness rates increase as one moves down the
occupational hierarchy (from 1 to 6) and that in the lower
levels of the manual sector the rate increases considerably. So,
for example, within the 15–44 age group, unskilled manual
workers (group 6) were nearly three times as likely to suffer
from chronic illness as the upper middle class (group 1).

TABLE 2.11

*Rates per 1,000 reporting (1) long-standing illness, (2) limiting
long-standing illness, by social class*

	Social class (Registrar General definition)						
	1	2	3	4	5	6	All
Long-standing illness	130	168	192	192	265	317	206
Limiting long-standing illness	65	90	104	113	162	208	121

Source: *General Household Survey*, 1975.

Mortality rates among the adult working population parallel the progressive incidence of illness that occurs as one moves down the social hierarchy. In 1972, the death rate for adult professional and managerial employees was 23 per cent below the overall average, while for unskilled workers the death rate was almost 40 per cent above the average. The gap between mortality rates for the two groups has in fact widened since the 1930s, when the rates were 10 per cent below the average for professional and managerial workers, and 11 per cent above for unskilled workers.

The redistributive effect of taxation

Most people believe that the British tax system is highly progressive, that is, the more you earn the more you pay, and the routine chant of those who earn most is that they are over-taxed, that 'if taxes were reduced we'd have more incentive to work harder'. But just how progressive is the tax structure? What is the effect of the combination of direct *and* indirect taxes? What opportunities are there for people to avoid paying tax? Answers to these and other questions should allow us to develop a more accurate picture of the impact of tax on people's earnings and hence the extent to which it redistributes income within Britain.

All employees in 1980 earning more than £1,375 p.a. (the individual's so-called 'personal allowance') are subject to an income tax at the *basic rate* of 30 per cent to a maximum of £11,250. Only that portion of income above this figure is taxed at a higher rate with, for example, earnings in excess of £16,750 taxed at 50 per cent and a maximum of 60 per cent being levied on taxable income over £27,750. However, the majority of employees receive earnings which are below the £11,250 threshold. This means that the 30 per cent rate is imposed on a wide range of incomes, from the lowest to the relatively highly paid employee. Within this large sector of the population, therefore, income tax is virtually non-progressive, with the lower paid paying a disproportionately large amount of their earnings in tax compared with those in the higher income bracket. Indeed in terms of *marginal* rates of taxation, i.e. the proportion of any additional earnings that are taxed, those on below-average incomes may in fact suffer a rate higher than those on incomes in excess of £11,250. This is the so-called 'poverty-trap' of the lower paid: a small increase in earnings takes them over a threshold, whereby they may lose certain welfare benefits and at the same time have to pay a disproportionately large increase in tax on their original income. Within the broad range of incomes taxed at the standard rate, the relative proportions of tax to original incomes illustrate the minimal progressiveness of direct tax: for example,

(i)   in 1970, those earning £60 per week or more paid on average no more than about 20-25 per cent of their original incomes in direct tax;

(ii)   in 1970, those manual workers earning the average weekly wage of £30 paid over 15 per cent of their original income in direct tax;

(iii) thus, those in the higher income bracket earning *twice* as much as those on average male manual wages paid only 5 to 10 per cent more taxation on their original incomes.

When indirect taxes — taxes such as VAT which are levied mainly on commodities purchased — are taken into account the tax burden on income is even less progressive. Indirect tax, sometimes known as 'expenditure tax', is generally *regressive*, i.e. it hits those with lower purchasing power the hardest.

Thus, in general, when all taxes, both direct and indirect, are combined the tax burden is for the most part far from progressive.

At the higher income levels the higher marginal tax rate encourages employers and their wealthier employees respectively to provide and seek forms of income that are untaxable or only slightly taxed. This has led to the development of top executives receiving not a salary but a 'total remuneration package' which includes a whole range of fringe benefits. For example, in 1975 94 per cent of top managers were given a company car for personal use (Diamond Commission Report, No. 3, 1976). Cheap mortgages supplied by employers are another important income through which higher income earners maintain real higher standards of living.

Investment income that is gained over £5,500 p.a. is subject to an investment income tax rate of 15 per cent. However, as a recent text on the British tax system says, there are 'major methods of getting round the taxation of investment income in this country, and together they enable those potentially liable to this tax to drive a coach and horses, or perhaps a large Rolls Royce, through the structure of the tax' (Kay and King, 1978, p. 51). There are three main ways in which this tax is avoided:

(i)   By investing one's income in capital gains (e.g. buying Treasury Stock over a fixed period generating both interest and resale capital gains) — no tax is levied on any capital gains up to £3,000 made in any one year;

(ii) By investing one's money in institutions — particularly life insurance companies, corporations and trusts, which are *not* subject to the surcharge and so many on the richest earnings will deposit income here where it can be increased by the institution itself rather than by their own dealings;

(iii) By investing one's money in durable goods — large houses, pictures, cars, farms, yachts, etc. None of these generate a taxable income and their increasing value over the years is only subject to the low rate of capital gains if sold.

Thus, even at these higher levels of income the tax system is *effectively* minimally progressive, reinforcing yet again the inequalities of British society. Kay and King (1978, p. 56) summarise the position by saying that:

It is possible that although the politicians and administrators most closely involved know that the appearance of immense progressivity is a sham, they believe that this appearance will deceive others into thinking that such objectives are being achieved. It is hard to imagine that the deception is successful, and the explanation is not one which flatters either group. The hypocritical nature of the

present situation reflects little credit on the British tax
system or on the British political system.

Summary

We have seen in our discussion that major inequalities still exist
between the non-manual and manual occupational strata.
Wide differences in earnings, conditions and terms of employment, health, housing and the general quality of life have all
been illustrated and documented. Primarily, these differences
derive from the different market capacities of the middle and
working classes. Inequality generated by the labour market is
a defining characteristic of an industrial society that is essentially capitalist. The extent to which redistribution through
taxation occurs is in real terms negligible.

Inequality, then, is the dominant characteristic of British
capitalism today, and is hardly affected by so-called 'redistribution measures'. The inequality we have documented in this
part of the chapter is often that which is said to have long
gone — that 'most people' earn the same, that 'most' are
middle class, and so on. Such opinions are blatantly false:
class inequality still exists.

The simple notion of a stratified society as being one based
on structured social inequality places no limitations on the
range or extremes of inequality and deprivation which might
occur within any one society. In our everyday existence in a
stratified society we recognise that there are groups for whom
these inequalities are experienced more extremely. We recognise that the 'comfortable', the 'affluent', the 'well-to-do'
and the 'rich' are distinguishable from the 'poor'.

2.8   POVERTY: ITS EXTENT AND INCIDENCE

The first problem in the analysis of poverty is one of definition: how does one decide what constitutes a condition of
'poverty' and hence who is 'poor'? The simple but crucial
answer is that no *absolute* definition of poverty *is* possible;
that is, there are no universal standards which can be used
as a basis for comparisons between cultures and over time.
Poverty is, then, essentially a relative concept, a condition

measurable only in terms of the living standards and resources of any one society at a particular time. For instance, a person seen as poor in Britain in 1981 will have better absolute living standards than a medieval peasant or someone living in the slums of Rio de Janeiro. Individuals are poor when they are significantly deprived relative to the circumstances of their fellow nationals. As Galbraith (1958, p. 252) says:

> People are poverty-stricken when their incomes, even if adequate for survival, fall markedly below those of the community. Then they cannot have what the larger community regards as the necessary minimum for decency . . . They are degraded for, in the literal sense, they live outside the grades or categories which the community regards as acceptable.

What is 'necessary' for a decent standard of living is a matter of social definition which may change over time. For example, as expectations have changed during this century, first indoor running water, then hot water, and finally an indoor fixed bathroom have come to be regarded as necessities.

The fact remains, however, that the poor are not simply at the bottom of the stratification hierarchy, but are almost, in a sense, *outside* the margins of that hierarchy. They form what some have called an 'underclass' in the stratification system. It is important to recognise that such a circumstance may have significant psychological implications for the *self-images* of the individuals concerned: not only do they have less than everyone else, but they may *feel* and *see* themselves as different — less significant, less integrated, almost outside the mainstream of society.

It is tempting to view the existence of extensive poverty in industrial societies as a thing of the past, for example being associated with the economic depression of the inter-war years of the twentieth century. Indeed, by the 1950s and 1960s many politicians and social commentators were confidently predicting that the age of extensive poverty was virtually gone in industrial societies of the West, including Britain.

However, such optimism about the alleged disappearance

of poverty has been largely shattered by sociological investigations since then. A number of studies in the 1960s and 1970s, both in Britain and elsewhere, have indicated the very real persistence of large numbers of poor people:

(i) Wedderburn's study (1962) found 12 per cent of the population existing at or below the official poverty line as defined by the National Assistance Board.

(ii) Abel-Smith and Townsend (1965) found some 7½ million people (14.2 per cent of the population) living at or below a poverty line.

(iii) Coates and Silburn (1970) examined St Ann's in the fairly prosperous city of Nottingham and found that nearly 40 per cent of this working-class district were living in poverty.

(iv) Townsend's latest survey (1979) shows that *over half* the people in Britain are likely to experience poverty at some stage in their lives by being significantly deprived of enjoying the conventional 'style of living' normal to the society.

Similar studies by Atkinson and Kincaid in Britain, Harrington in the USA, and official government studies in both countries, reveal a persistent and significant section of the population living in poverty-stricken circumstances at any one time, to say nothing of the many others, who, at certain crucial periods of their life (e.g. the old, families with young children), may temporarily lapse into poverty. Such investigations indicate clearly and forcefully that poverty is still very much with us, and that any complacency about rising standards of living in the post-war period inevitably banishing poverty must be quickly dismissed.

Who are the poor?

It is apparent that certain social categories appear at greater risk of being poor than others. Those most vulnerable to poverty at present are the old; the sick and disabled; the unemployed and the insecurely employed low-wage-earner; the large family and the single-parent (usually fatherless) family.

(i)   The *elderly* are particularly vulnerable to poverty. As life expectancy has increased and earlier retirement has become more widespread in the twentieth century, so the elderly have come to comprise an ever larger section of the poor. Thus, one-third of Abel-Smith and Townsend's poor were the aged, and almost half the old-age pensioners in their study were living below the poverty line.

(ii)   The period of so-called full employment of the 1950s and early 1960s prompted many to dismiss *unemployment* as a factor in poverty, yet all the British studies indicate the seriousness of even temporary unemployment for large numbers of families. The high unemployment of the 1970s and 1980s seems unlikely to be a temporary phenomenon: in fact many experts predict a persistent and probably increasing level of unemployment in Western economies for the rest of the century. So, prolonged unemployment for the principal breadwinners and their offspring is thrusting more and more families into poverty and threatens to do so for many years to come.

(iii)   Despite reports of 'fabulous' wages earned by manual workers, the receipt of *low pay* remains the fate of many workers in Western industrial economies. In Coates and Silburn's study, low-paid families were the second highest group of the poor, and in 1971 100,000 working fathers (with about 400,000 dependants) received wages below the official poverty line. The problems of the low paid are further compounded by the fact that their jobs are also frequently *less secure*. Moreover, they frequently work in declining industries lacking effective union organisation and political representation, so that their prospects of escaping the low pay treadmill are slim indeed.

(iv)   Though large families are less widespread in the twentieth century, the *large family* still remains vulnerable to poverty, if relatively less so than in the nineteenth century. The addition of subsequent mouths to feed merely compounds the problem, and this remains true despite the accompanying welfare state provisions of family allowance and so on. But even the *first* child can throw a low-income family into poverty.

(v)   *Single-parent families*, whether the result of choice, death, desertion, or divorce, constitute a significant portion of the poor. Coates and Silburn's third largest category of poor were those without a male breadwinner, and Abel-Smith and Townsend's study found 10 per cent of the poor belonging to fatherless families.

(vi) The *sickness* or *disablement* of one parent, whether temporary or permanent, can have major implications for families near the poverty margin. In the St Ann's study, the sick and disabled constituted the fourth largest category of the poor.

While recognising the relative vulnerability of certain groups to poverty, it must be emphasised that they do share one crucial common feature, their *social class position*. The poor are an integral part of the working class, poverty is the *direct product* of the general pattern of class inequality. As Miliband (1974) says, 'Old age, disablement, low pay, unemployment, etc. become synonymous with poverty insofar as those involved are members of the working class.'

2.9   CHANGES IN THE CLASS STRUCTURE

As we have already seen, in industrial societies the economic or material reward for most individuals is largely determined by their occupation; in Parkin's (1971) phrase, the occupational structure is the 'backbone of the class structure'. It follows, then, that any changes in the structure of economic inequality in our society will largely be related to changes in its occupational structure. These changes can be of two main kinds: either the *proportion* of the population doing a particular job can change or the *sorts* of job done can change. The class structure will be correspondingly affected:

(i)   If the sorts of occupation pursued in a society change then the reward structure must change too; either new occupations can simply displace old ones in the hierarchy, or the *whole* hierarchy may be modified. Thus, for example, if an occupation emerges claiming greater rewards than existing ones, the whole hierarchy is *de*moted, so to speak, relative to this one.

(ii) Changes in the proportion of a particular occupation in the labour force may also affect the rewards that occupation can demand. Thus, for example, if the number of people doing a particular job increases, thereby increasing the practice of a particular skill among the working population, other things being equal, the advantages that that occupation can claim may well be diminished, too.

During this century, largely as a result of economic changes, Britain's occupational structure has undergone two major changes, one each of the types to which we have just referred. On the one hand, a massive growth in large-scale organisations relying heavily on an equally large administrative work-force has resulted in an enormous expansion in *clerical* or *white-collar* work, while, on the other hand, a shift in emphasis in the industrial sector of the economy, from heavy to light and manufacturing industry, has had equally significant repercussions on the nature of *manual* work, giving rise to new sorts of manual worker.

The consequences of these two changes for Britain's class structure have been the source of much popular debate, frequently characterised by rather ill-informed and naive analysis. (Media clichés that 'class is dead' or that 'cloth-cap politics is old hat' are clear examples.) Fortunately, however, two major pieces of sociological scholarship have exposed the weaknesses of much of this 'common-sense' thinking and have provided real insights into the nature of work and stratification in a changing industrial society. These are Lockwood's study of the clerk, *The Blackcoated Worker* (1958), and the research into *The Affluent Worker in the Class Structure* in Britain carried out in Luton in the early 1960s by Lockwood and Goldthorpe (Goldthorpe *et al.*, 1971).

We will examine both these works in close detail shortly, but first we must properly understand those changes that have taken place in Britain this century, the consequences of which have made the contemporary position of clerical and manual work of such sociological interest.

The expansion of clerical, or white-collar occupations

A large proportion of Britain today is engaged in clerical

or white-collar work of one sort or another. Think of the number of people who work in local government departments, in central government departments like Health and Social Security or the Inland Revenue, in an administrative capacity in colleges and universities and hospitals, and in business or industrial organisations generally. Because of this it is sometimes rather difficult to appreciate how relatively recently such developments in this sort of work have taken place. Clerks *do* work in smaller scale contexts, too, of course – in banks, solicitors' offices, accountants' offices, and so on. But at the turn of the century, before the growth of larger-scale organisations demanding an associated growth in clerical staff to administer them, the clerk was *only* to be found in these latter sorts of small social settings. Then clerical work was exclusively a matter of close personal contact with one's employer, a job that could demand initiative and responsibility, and given the lack of state-provided educational facilities, one demanding the possession of relatively scarce skills.

The growth of large-scale organisations, combined with the twin developments of educational expansion and a large influx of women into clerical work, changed all this. Clerical work no longer took place solely in small-scale settings, but increasingly in large impersonal offices. Clerks now worked with many other clerks and often under the impersonal authority of an unseen employer. Crucially, because of the proliferation of at least rudimentary reading and writing skills amongst a majority of the population, they no longer possessed those relatively scarce attributes formerly enabling them to lay claim to special advantages.

One popular interpretation of these changes holds that as a result of the expansion in white-collar work, the clerk's status has depreciated to such an extent that the position of white-collar work in the class structure today is indistinguishable from that of manual work. This in turn is used to support a claim that Britain, and societies like it, are largely 'classless' and that occupations are today by and large similarly rewarded.

Since this argument frequently uses as supporting evidence the changes in the nature of manual work that have taken place in Britain since the Second World War, before we examine its validity more closely, we must also analyse these changes in manual work.

The rise of the affluent worker

An industrial society typically experiences a number of changes in its economic base over time. Early industrialisation normally amounts to little more than the exploitation of raw materials – in Britain's case, these included coal, iron ore, wool, water, etc. – together with the refining of some imported goods, for example cotton in Britain. Now this directly affects not only a society's occupational and, hence, class structures, but also the geographical distribution of its population. Thus, in Britain, since manual work was confined almost exclusively to these traditional industries, the industrialisation and urbanisation of the country occurred largely where the raw materials themselves were located and could be worked, in areas such as Lancashire, the North East, South Wales, Humberside and Clydeside. It was in these areas that the majority of manual workers and their families had to live.

All industrial societies must develop and diversify, however, especially as raw materials and markets have only a finite life. The 1930s depression and the Second World War, coupled with general technological progress, precipitated such developments in Britain, and brought changes in the nature of manual work. Thus, after 1945, Britain's economy came to rely less on its traditional heavy industries and more on new light and manufacturing industries largely concerned with the factory production of consumer goods like cars, televisions, washing machines, cookers, themselves the product of relatively recent invention. The location of production in these new industries was not primarily determined by the whereabouts of raw materials, but also partly by central government concern to alleviate unemployment. Broadly speaking, this can be done in one of two ways: either work can be provided where people are unemployed or the unemployed can be moved to the work. Both strategies were used.

Where work was brought to the workers, this usually meant building factories on the outskirts of old urban areas (in contrast to the traditional picture of urbanisation taking place around the location of production). Yet the changes these peripheral areas underwent were not confined merely to this new industrialisation. On the one hand many of Britain's urban centres had been bombed into ruins during the war. On the other, there were powerful demands for slum clearance and urban renewal programmes. As a result, much of the manual population formerly exclusively based in the centre of these traditional industrial areas were being relocated on new estates, often near new factories. Similarly, in the purpose-built new and expanded towns, the manual worker lived and worked on housing and industrial estates, while the centre of these urban areas tended to be given over to office blocks and administrative institutions.

All of this fundamentally altered traditional urban and industrial life; in particular, it meant the growth of the *mobile* manual worker. Because traditional manual work had always taken place where the raw materials were located, working-class communities grew up around these sources, and work opportunities and skills tended to be handed down through the generations from father to son. We discuss in Chapter 5 the consequences of this immobility for certain aspects of the social structures of these older communities.

The shift from traditional heavy industry to light manu-facturing industry also meant a change in the technique of production, particularly with the introduction of mechanised mass production, often using the assembly line. We examine the consequences of this change for the nature of work in more detail in Chapter 8. Here we must note that relatively high wages were paid for such work, with consequences for occupational stratification.

The new manual worker emerging in post-war Britain in fact differed from his traditional counterpart not only in his family and community life but also in terms of his relative affluence. By this time real increases in material prosperity as a result of the economic boom of the 1950s and the develop-ment of welfare provisions produced a section of the manual work-force in this country for whom the truth of the boast of the then Prime Minister, Harold Macmillan, that the British people 'had never had it so good' seemed self-evident — or at least so far as their purchasing power was concerned. It also seemed self-evident to many media commentators that the principal consequence of these changes in white-collar and manual work was the destruction of class differences in Britain. We were, it was loudly and generally asserted, 'all middle class now'.

Both *The Blackcoated Worker* and *The Affluent Worker in the Class Structure* seek to examine the truth of such claims. *The Blackcoated Worker* examines changes that have taken place in the class position of the clerk during the course of the century, and also compares this position with that of the manual worker. *The Affluent Worker* research assesses the true extent of any improvement in the class position of the manual worker and also compares this position with that of those engaged in middle-class occupations. It is to these attempts that we now turn.

'The Blackcoated Worker': Lockwood

Lockwood seeks to analyse changes in the stratification position of the clerk by using a framework based essentially on Weber's distinction between class and status as bases of stratification. Following Weber, he argues that the stratification position of *any* occupation can be most successfully located by distinguishing between those *material* (or factual) rewards which accrue to it in what he calls its *market* and *work situations* — which together amount to its class situation — and those *symbolic* rewards which accrue to it in what he calls its *status situation*.

Work situation refers to the hours worked, the degree of segregation from other sorts of employees, the holidays allowed, the degree of responsibility and authority involved, the physical conditions of the work, and so on: that is, the conditions of work enjoyed or endured by an individual while doing the job.

Market situation refers to an occupation's income, sick pay, job security, pension arrangements, superannuation schemes, incremental scale structure, hidden incomes or 'perks', career structure, and so on: that is, those rewards an individual receives for selling skills in society's market-places.

In contrast *status situation* refers to the prestige attached to an occupation — the position it occupies in a society's hierarchy of symbolic reward. Using this framework, Lockwood seeks:

(i)   to identify the extent of any changes in the market, work and status situations of the clerk over time;

(ii) to examine the extent to which any changes represent a blurring of class differences between clerical and manual work.

Lockwood's conclusions can be summarised as follows.

The work situation

This has changed substantially over the last century or so. Formerly, clerks typically worked on their own and often in a close physical and often paternalistic relationship with their employers. However, increased mechanisation has made much clerical work more routine in character and, in this respect, similar to much manual work. Furthermore, the bureaucratisation of clerical work in large organisations tends to produce a common identity among clerks through an increased awareness of their shared economic position.

Clerks experience bureaucratisation when their work is organised and directed in terms of rigidly defined impersonal rules, standardised working conditions, appointments made on universalistic criteria, and a clear separation of management and staff. This constitutes a work situation likely to produce, amongst clerical workers, the sort of collective awareness of their common circumstances traditionally only associated with manual workers in large industrial organisations. Thus, Lockwood argues that the rapid post-war growth in the *unionisation* of clerks must be understood primarily as an expression of the emergence of this sort of collectivist orientation out of a bureaucratic work situation. It does not arise as a result of the influence of market situation factors (since the least well paid and least secure clerks are not the most organised) or status situation factors, as 'there is no general correlation between social status and unionism in the clerical field'. The bureaucratic work situation is the decisive influence, then: for example, Lockwood found that 80 per

cent of (bureaucratised) local government clerks were unionised, while among (unbureaucratised) commercial and industrial clerks the number was only 5 per cent.

However, Lockwood insists that this growth in collective
awareness is the only area in which there has been any convergence of clerical and manual workers in this century, for
real differences *still* remain in their respective work situations.
First, of course, many clerks today still work in relatively
small-scale surroundings — in accountants' offices, solicitors'
offices, banks, etc. — where face-to-face contact with management remains a feature of their work situation lacking in that
of most manual work. Such clerks still identify with their
firm or employer in ways uncharacteristic of manual workers:
for example, seeing themselves 'on the same side' as management. While the growth of large-scale organisations has in
many cases weakened this identification of white-collar employees with management, they still share advantages with
clerks working in small firms and offices and their situation
vis-à-vis manual workers is still differentiated. Thus, clerks
still experience much less supervision than manual workers:
for example, rarely having to clock in and out, or take tea
breaks between hooters, and so on. Again, their overall working hours tend to be fewer and their use of overtime far less
routine than in the case of manual workers. Crucially, their
use of office facilities is often the same as management's, yet
different from that of manual workers in the same organisation: according to Lockwood, the segregation of clerks and
manual workers is 'perhaps the most outstanding feature of
industrial organisation'.

Lockwood argues not only that these real differences remain in the respective work situations of the clerk and the
manual worker, but also that a comparison of their market
and status situations does not support the conclusion that
such occupations occupy largely indistinguishable positions
in the stratification system.

Market situation

Although things have changed — for example, the clerical/
manual gap in earnings has narrowed, and in some cases been

reversed (though manual workers generally have to work longer hours for equivalent pay) — real differences remain. Clerks enjoy a greater stability and security of employment than manual workers, are much more likely to be members of pension and superannuation schemes (which are major instruments of inequality in retirement), and are often in a well-defined career structure, which itself produces additional benefits (such as steadily rising earnings, the opportunity for getting house mortgages, etc.).

Status situation

Although the traditional higher status of the clerk has been reduced somewhat, Lockwood argues that the symbolic rewards to white-collar work remain significantly higher than those attached to manual work: 'brain-work' is still more highly regarded than manual work. Overall, then, Lockwood argues that despite changes in the position of clerks in the stratification system, important differences between them and manual workers remain, and that it is illegitimate to talk of the 'erosion of class differences' between these two sorts of occupation.

'The Affluent Worker in the Class Structure': Goldthorpe et al.

As we mentioned earlier, this research evaluated the so-called 'embourgeoisement thesis'. This somewhat mystifying phrase refers to the notion that the 'lower' classes, specifically wage-earning manual workers, are becoming, through increasing affluence, 'bourgeois': they are gradually losing their working-class identity, life-style, values, and so on, and adopting middle-class values and behaviour patterns.

Zweig (1961) and others identified a number of significant changes which had undoubtedly occurred and which they interpreted as proof of embourgeoisement: the expansion of white-collar jobs; the expansion of education at all levels; a narrowing of income differentials; and an increase in residential mobility among the working class with the consequent erosion of the family and kinship ties found in the traditional community. The working classes were allegedly losing their traditional political attitudes and social values as they became more individualistic, keen to 'get on', to buy high-cost consumer durables such as fridges and radios, and less concerned with maintaining traditional working-class culture.

According to the thesis, then, the old pyramid-shaped class structure was now being recast into something like a diamond pattern, most people sharing a similar economic and status position in the middle stratum, with only a minority at the highest and lowest levels: the good fairy of capitalist affluence had apparently granted our wish — we had all become middle class.

Goldthorpe and his colleagues argued that *if* the process of embourgeoisement was in fact occurring, if manual wage workers were actually becoming assimilated into the middle class, we would expect to find three crucial alterations to the class structure:

(1) *The economic aspect of class*: that working-class members and their families would be more prosperous in terms of levels of income and material possessions, and would be enjoying the occupational security and prospects historically the privilege of the non-manual middle class.

(2) *The relational aspect of class*: that these improvements in their economic position would promote attitudinal changes in working-class members such that they would enjoy a social status equal to that of the middle class, who would treat affluent working-class individuals as social equals in both formal and informal social interaction.

(3) *The normative aspect of class*: that these workers would gradually acquire new norms, expectations and forms of behaviour more typical of the middle class than of the old traditional working class.

To test whether these three major changes had in fact occurred, Goldthorpe *et al.* undertook a lengthy empirical study, of Luton. They chose Luton because:

(i)   it was a rapidly growing and prosperous town where a large proportion of the workers were geographically mobile;

(ii)   a high proportion of this population lived in recently constructed housing estates;

(iii) as the industrial expansion was relatively new, Luton was not subject to the traditional 'them *vs* us' industrial relations typical of the long-established industrial regions of Britain.

The sample comprised 229 manual and 54 lower-level white-collar workers, drawn from three major high-wage manufacturing concerns, each with progressive welfare policies and good industrial relations — Vauxhall Motors, Skefko Ball Bearing Company, and Laporte Chemicals.

The manual sample was restricted to married men: between the ages of 21 and 46; who were regularly earning at least £17 per week (October 1962); and who were living in Luton or on nearby housing developments. These workers earned roughly the same as the white-collar workers, had a similar range of high-cost consumer goods, and compared favourably in terms of house ownership. Moreover, 71 per cent were not native to Luton, only 13 per cent had ever been unemployed for longer than one month, and 55 per cent lived outside traditional working-class areas such as council estates or the centre of town. Both the location and the sample would provide a critical case: if, under conditions such as these, the process of embourgeoisement was *not* in evidence, then there would be little reason for assuming that the process was occurring generally within British society.

Economic aspect

Though most of the manual workers in the sample earned wages comparable with those received by the non-manual staff, *how* each group experienced their work and earned their money was radically different.

Most of the *manual* workers saw their work as mere labour, as work which brought little intrinsic satisfaction or interest. Their jobs were monotonous, routine, lacking in responsibility and challenge, often performed under unpleasant physical conditions. Though the more skilled workers experienced some satisfaction from their work, a majority (60 per cent) of the machinists and assembly workers found their work boring: 84 per cent said that it did not command their full attention, while 47 per cent found it physically tiring. When asked, 'What is it that keeps you here?', the most important reason appeared to be the high level of pay which could be earned compared with other jobs. 'The money' was the *only* reason why 24 per cent remained at the work. Only 29 per cent of the skilled and 14 per cent of the semi-skilled said that they stayed in the job because they liked the work. However, among the white-collar sample, only 2 (out of 54) said they stayed because of the level of pay: most thought that their jobs were intrinsically satisfying.

Thus, the manual workers' increasing affluence has only been won through jobs which offer little or no immediate reward except money: the enjoyment of a middle-class income and consumption level is achieved through a work situation not typically experienced by non-manual workers.

Furthermore, the *way* the manual workers earned their wages must be considered. On average, most workers with overtime worked 50 hours per week, while 75 per cent of the sample were on shift-work permanently. Having to work overtime and on shifts to earn their money meant that their physical fitness, family life, leisure activities and so on were affected. White-collar work, however, was much more on a 'nine to five' basis, such that they were not as constrained in their non-work activities by the demands of work as were the manual workers.

Moreover, the manual workers differed from the non-manual sample in terms of job security and prospects of advancement or promotion. The white-collar workers both hoped for and sought promotion more keenly than the manual workers, but also they had a much greater chance of actually enjoying such advancement. They believed that they could 'get ahead', that individual hard work would be rewarded by increased income and upward mobility. The manual workers, however, acknowledged that, given their economic position in the factory, they could only improve their rewards and their security through the strength of the trade union: union strength rather than *individual* effort was (and still is) the way to protect and improve the workers' life-chances. For the manual worker, then, increased affluence may, in fact, depend on increased unionisation of the work-force.

Relational aspect

As we suggested, the sample differed markedly from the older, traditional, working-class areas where community and kinship ties, both economic and social, dominate the individual's life. For the majority of the Luton sample, relatives no longer lived close by. Consequently, if embourgeoisement is occurring, we would expect to find the Luton workers, now for the most part freed from the obligations and ties associated with a traditional working-class community, adopting middle-class life-styles and mixing with the middle-class workers in and out of work. The evidence does *not*, however, support this view.

Despite the fact that most of their relatives lived some way off, kinship ties were still strong for most of the manual workers. The majority who actually had relatives living in the Luton area maintained frequent contact with them, and this was also true of those who, despite the distances involved, had relatives living elsewhere. For both, contact with kin was much more frequent than with neighbours, work-mates or other friends. When wives were asked about the people they had visited, or had been visited by, during the week, relatives accounted for 52 per cent and 20 per cent respectively.

More important, the majority of the members of the sample made up for any relative decline in kin contact, not through selecting friends from among the Luton community, but rather by falling back on *neighbours*, whom the researchers roughly defined as persons living within ten minutes walk. The white-collar group, on the other hand, had a much wider range of social interaction, both kin and non-kin based, particularly with friends who were neither neighbours nor work-mates. Furthermore, compared with the white-collar workers, the manual workers rarely entertained 'friends' at home, such entertainment being reserved for family members. According to Goldthorpe *et al.*, this reflects the traditional working-class attitude that the private world of 'the home' is a place open only to the family and a very few 'special' friends.

Finally, the evidence indicates that the overriding majority of the manual workers did not develop social relationships with middle-class individuals. Most associated either with kin or with individuals of a similar socio-economic status, i.e. fellow manual workers. Only 7 per cent of the sample associated primarily with members of a middle-class status group. This lack of involvement in 'middle-class society' was also exemplified by the type of associations or organisations that the manual workers joined: working men's clubs, allotment associations, angling societies, etc., all noticeably lacking in middle-class membership. Most, in fact, had little desire to join associations likely to have a strong middle-class membership.

In general, then, there is no real evidence to support the claim that increased affluence breaks down class and status barriers between manual and non-manual workers. Changes in the worker's objective economic position — job and residential mobility, overtime and shift working, for example — certainly influence the development of non-traditional attitudes and behaviour characteristic of the 'new' affluent worker. The important point, however, is that these changes tend to promote a more *home-centred* way of life among the manual workers. As Goldthorpe *et al.* say: 'the *direction* of these changes, we would suggest, is not toward middle-classness, but rather towards what might be termed a more "privatised" mode of living'.

The normative aspect

Individuals who encounter similar experiences in their work and community lives tend to share a general image of society, their place in it, and their relationship to each other. Different images foster a range of social values, expectations and norms specific to the different classes. The character of such values has been generally described as 'individualistic' for the middle class and 'collectivistic' for the working class. If embourgeoisement is occurring, we would expect members of the working class gradually to dissociate themselves from the collectivistic orientations and behaviour patterns of their class, and aspire to and identify with the more individualistic middle-class value system. This transformation would be subject to two conditions: first, such aspirants must be able to resist pressures to conform to the norms of their working-class membership groups, perhaps by withdrawing from them or by a weakening of the integration within the group itself; secondly, aspirants must have the opportunity to associate with middle-class individuals, who in turn must accept such association. The Luton study demonstrates that increased affluence has not been a sufficient condition for embourgeoisement, particularly with regard to this third factor, the normative aspect of class.

For the affluent manual workers at Luton, collectivist orientations were still a significant feature of their view of the world. This was particularly apparent in their continued support for the Labour Party. By far the most frequent reason given for voting Labour was that it represented the material interests of the working class: it was the party which 'looks after ordinary working-class people like us'. Affluence, then, has not weakened the working-class support for the Labour Party, with little sign of the socially aspiring Conservative worker — the manual worker who feels he is moving up the 'social ladder' by voting Tory.

As we have suggested, there was little or no identification with the middle-class life-style through either aspiration or association, and the manual workers did not believe that they could be socially mobile through individual effort.

From this evidence Goldthorpe and his colleagues conclude that the process of embourgeoisement is not occurring in the more affluent Britain of the post-war era. Major differences in both economic and social advantages and in general images of society still exist for members of different occupational groups.

What changes, then, have occurred in the life of the relatively affluent manual worker? The most important development has been the 'privatisation' of the worker and his family, with home-centredness consequently amplified: the manual worker's family and its fortunes become his 'central life interest'. Secondly, although unionism is still strong, it expresses an instrumentalist rather than solidaristic orientation: that is, the newly affluent worker is likely to regard the union as the means to a particular end: e.g. he no longer sees union membership as the expression of a strong, ideological, working-class solidarity. Attracted to the Luton firms through higher pay he joined the unions even though this was not compulsory. These two factors, privatisation and instrumentalism, encourage 'a more individualistic outlook' among the manual workers, with a simultaneous weakening of communal and kin orientations. But this has *not* led to any strong desire to attain and identify with the middle-class life-style and values of the white-collar workers.

The latter, for their part (as we have seen) have experienced a process of bureaucratisation and a reduction in their career mobility: these factors have promoted a greater sense of solidarity among white-collar workers, and they have become 'more prone to collective, trade-union action of a deliberately apolitical and instrumental type'.

Thus, there appears to be a convergence between the two groups, in that the relatively affluent workers are becoming more home- and 'family-centred' and more instrumental in their unionism, while the non-manual, lower level workers are more likely to entertain ideas of 'instrumental' collectivism. But Goldthorpe *et al.* stress that such convergence, if it is occurring, does not imply that the two groups are merging or coming to share a common identity with comparable positions in the class structure.

The crucial point is that rising affluence does not bring about any *fundamental* alterations to the class structure; it may have some effect on workers' incomes, possessions and the type of houses and areas in which they live. But these changes do not necessarily transform the stratification system. As Goldthorpe *et al.* (1971, p. 162) say:

A factory worker can double his living standards and still remain a man who sells his labour to an employer in return for wages; he can work at a control panel rather than on an assembly line without changing his subordinate position in the organisation of production; he can live in his own house in a 'middle-class' estate or suburb and still remain little involved in white-collar social worlds.

2.10 SOCIAL MOBILITY

Introduction

Social stratification is, as we have seen, structured inequality in society, such that some strata have more power and reward than others. In many societies this has been an avowed and recognised feature of social organisation — acknowledged and (usually) justified both by those who benefit and those who are disadvantaged. Normally in such societies — for example, in the form of castes or feudal estates — social positions are defined and fixed by birth. Unequal power or benefit is inherited — 'ascribed' — and in theory this position cannot be changed by the efforts of the occupant of such a stratum. However good, however servile, the untouchables in India can never make themselves anything other than untouchable (and equally important, they accept this fact). Thus social hierarchy is fixed, rigid, and transmitted across generations in these societies.

For industrial societies, the position has often been portrayed in very different terms. Many sociologists have assumed that social position is gained by individual *achievement* rather than by birth — at least for the majority of the population. Inequality, they argue, is attached to *positions*; the crucial concern is, therefore, with how one gets into these positions and how much movement there is across generations. Social mobility thus becomes the focus of attention. It is accepted that individual positions are unequally rewarded, but the questions of access and opportunity now become central, and although Western capitalist societies do not claim to be equal, they *do* claim to offer equal opportunity to all in the competition for unequal positions. That is, they claim to be meritocratic.

As we have seen, the inheritance of wealth and educational advantage make this ideology of 'free competition for unequal reward' a very dubious claim, but in studying social mobility we are still comparing the actual amount of social mobility with the ideal of totally free movement through totally equal opportunity. In such a perfectly mobile society, the social position of the individual need bear no relation to the social position of his or her family of origin. The individual would move up or down according to merit.

In comparing societies with this ideal, *open* condition, we can distinguish two aspects of mobility:

(i) Intergenerational mobility: that is, the son or daughter has a different social position (higher or lower) than that of the parents (for example, a miner's daughter might train to become a teacher). This is usually seen as the most important form of mobility today.

(ii) Intragenerational mobility: that is, where an individual changes social position during a career (for example, a clerk might be promoted to a managerial position during his or her working life).

Mobility can refer to any movement, long-range or short-range. Social mobility occurs if the son of an unskilled dustman becomes a skilled electrician, just as if he becomes a solicitor. Usually, however, sociologists have concentrated on mobility across the manual/non-manual division, or 'cross-class' mobility.

Comparisons between Western industrial societies

A classic study of social mobility was made by Lipset and Bendix (1959) using data from the late 1940s. They were attempting to discover whether the USA was in fact a more 'open' society than the industrialised nations of Western Europe. The widespread assumption was that the USA, being a 'new' society, free from the feudal and aristocratic hierarchies typical of Europe, was a land of opportunity, where chances were open to all. European societies, with their long-established history of such hierarchies, were seen as more rigid and closed to movement.

Lipset and Bendix's findings are summarised in Table 2.12. Their primary discovery was that cross-class mobility (upward and downward) was around 30 per cent for nearly all Western industrial societies. That is to say, three out of ten occupied males had fathers of a different occupational class. Despite problems in comparing cross-national data, this shows a re-

TABLE 2.12
National social mobility rates

Country	Upward mobility (percentage of sons of manual fathers who are in non-manual employment)	Downward mobility (percentage of sons of non-manual fathers who are in manual employment)	Total vertical mobility (percentage of sons who have crossed classes)
USA	33	26	30
West Germany	29	32	31
Sweden	31	24	29
Japan	36	22	27
France	39	20	27
Switzerland	45	13	23
Denmark	22	44	31
Britain	20	49	29
Italy	8	34	16

Source: Lipset and Bendix (1959).

markably similar pattern. Lipset and Bendix's idea that this was somehow a 'natural' rate for industrial society is backed by Rogoff (1953), who argues that this overall rate of mobility changed very little between 1910 and 1940, thus questioning the idea that mobility opportunities have increased significantly during this century. There are, however, some significant differences between the countries despite this overall similarity of rates. If we compare Britain with the USA, for example, in Table 2.12 we find that:

(i)   in Britain, half of the sons of 'high prestige' fathers found themselves in 'low prestige' occupations, whereas

(ii) in the USA, only 26 per cent of sons from high backgrounds moved down into the working class;

(iii) by contrast, only 20 per cent of sons of working-class fathers could move into the middle class in Britain, as opposed to 33 per cent in the USA.

Miller (1960) points out that this denotes a major difference in 'openness': he argues further that the real test of open mobility is if privileged sons still move down, in which case Britain is markedly more open than the USA. This is debatable, however.

Social mobility in England and Wales

Changes in the occupational structure and the education system have produced important developments in the patterns of social mobility since 1945. We shall examine the changes through a series of important studies.

Lipset and Bendix (1959) discovered, as mentioned above that 50 per cent of the sons of the middle class experienced downward mobility, while 20 per cent of the working class moved up. This may seem something of a paradox, since people can only move up to fill vacant positions above them. The answer is of course that the working class formed a majority of the population at this time, and so 20 per cent of their sons provided sufficient people to fill the gaps left by 50 per cent of the middle class moving down.

Glass (1954) found that social mobility was by no means uncommon. Like Lipset and Bendix, he found that one-third of employees had moved across classes through intergenerational mobility. A further third had experienced mobility within the same class, and a final third had exactly the same position as their fathers. Glass emphasised, however, that nearly all this mobility was across a *short range*, that most of the cross-class mobility discovered was merely movement between lower white-collar and skilled manual positions (in either direction). This area of the class structure was seen as a 'buffer zone' — most people did *not* move out of their class, and if they did, they did not pass beyond this zone. The actual rate of social mobility in the 'buffer zone' was 50 per cent. This contrasted markedly with the picture at the extreme ends of the hierarchy. Among the higher professionals, 47 per cent of sons retained this upper middle-class position, while only 20 per cent of sons descended to routine non-manual jobs; but the lowest rates of all are shown by unskilled manual workers. Here the family gives very little impetus for upward mobility, thanks to its relative poverty and educational disadvantages. By contrast, the highest groups can protect their sons from downward mobility through devices such as public schools, as we shall see in Chapter 4.

Glass emphasised that despite apparent openness, social mobility was neither long-range nor disruptive of the class structure. If manual and routine non-manual workers are grouped together, one can see that only 20 per cent achieved upward mobility into 'solid' middle-class positions; four out of five remained within this broad grouping.

However, Glass was studying adults who were educated before the Second World War; perhaps the picture is quite different for the generation affected by the changes in the education system since 1944, which have greatly widened opportunities.

This has recently been examined by the Oxford social mobility study: a major study conducted by J. H. Goldthorpe and others (1980) of men aged between 20 and 64 years, and producing evidence for significant changes in mobility trends.

Their primary finding is that the number of highly rewarded positions has expanded, given the expansion of professional and managerial occupations and the relative decline in the proportion of manual positions. This means that the middle class can have a higher chance of staying middle class, *and* that the working class can still have a higher chance of moving up. They also suggest that there is more long-range mobility, and Glass's notion of the 'buffer zone' no longer holds true.

Thus, the researchers discovered that:

(i) the proportion of middle-class employees with working-class origins had remained the same at 50 per cent; however,

(ii) the proportion of manual workers with non-manual parents had fallen from 20 per cent to 14 per cent;

(iii) amongst the higher professionals, only 25 per cent now came from higher professional backgrounds; and

(iv) 25 per cent of higher professionals had risen from working-class backgrounds.

However, this may not mean that these professionals are less able to secure similar positions for their sons, for higher and lower professionals now form 25 per cent of the work-force, as opposed to 12½ per cent in the previous generation. There is room for professionals' sons *and* many newcomers. It was also found that those persons who went down into the working class were not especially likely to go into skilled positions, thus providing evidence against the 'buffer zone'. On the other hand, they were more likely to experience intragenerational (or 'work-life') mobility which eventually would bring them into the middle class. It is also interesting to note that of those sons of manual workers who remained working-class, 30 per cent achieved work-life mobility into the lower middle-class. This suggests that the role of intragenerational mobility may not be as unimportant today as some have suggested.

Overall, however, the Oxford group emphasises that there is still much less than 'perfect' mobility. It is still the case that:

(i)   three out of four manual workers come from manual backgrounds; and that

(ii) sons of manual workers have only half the chance of entering the professions which they would have, given equality of opportunity.

On the other hand:

(iii) the sons of higher professionals are three times more likely to follow their fathers than they would have, given equality of opportunity.

Let us examine these statistics. If we assume that merit or talent is spread randomly through the population (a not unrealistic assumption), and if we take a certain position (e.g. solicitor), then the social origins of the occupants of this position should exactly mirror the proportions of people in different strata in the society as a whole. Thus, about two-thirds of solicitors would be from working-class origins, and only about 10 per cent should come from higher professional backgrounds.

The reality of social mobility is still far removed from such an ideal model. There have been changes since the war, especially in the opportunities for long-range mobility, but the middle class have usually been the first to seize new opportunities (such as free education) to *avoid* downward mobility.

Routes for social mobility

It is generally assumed that the rise of more widespread educational opportunities has given children of working-class parents the chance to study for the qualifications necessary to enter middle-class occupations. At the same time, it is argued, the increasing demand for competitively gained qualifications means that children from middle-class families cannot assume that they will avoid downward mobility. Hence, those who enter an occupation holding few qualifications are, it is argued, less likely to achieve work-life mobility (i.e. intragenerational mobility), because qualified trainees will be recruited directly to these higher positions. Thus, these trends towards a greater stress on educational qualifications imply that intragenerational mobility within work caused through promotion becomes much less important as a route for advancement.

The primary form of mobility is intergenerational, through the *education* system. This means that inequalities in educational *opportunities* are crucial. These trends also mean that, given the occupants' lack of educational qualifications, as Goldthorpe *et al.* put it, 'a manual job is now, more than ever, a life sentence'. Similarly, the opportunities for advancement out of routine clerical work are also significantly diminished because managerial positions are often filled directly by external candidates with graduate or professional qualifications. The Oxford study, however, suggests that these changes have been misinterpreted; the researchers argue that we must not assume that work-life mobility is entirely replaced by direct entry to occupations through education. To examine the relative importance of these two routes, the researchers compared a sample of respondents born between 1908 and 1927 with a sample born between 1928 and 1948.

Respondents with manual working-class parents

(i)　In the older sample, a total of 16 per cent had obtained solid middle-class occupations. Less than one-fifth of these (3 per cent of the total) entered these positions as their first job. The other four-fifths achieved work-life mobility.

(ii) In the younger sample, a total of 19 per cent gained professional or managerial positions — hardly a startling increase. One-third of these entered these occupations directly — a small increase.

Respondents with professional or managerial parents

(i)   A total of 59 per cent of the older sample stayed within this category of occupations. Two-fifths of these entered such jobs directly, the other three-fifths went down in status and then succeeded in regaining their position through work-life mobility.

(ii)   Among the younger sample, 65 per cent retained their parents' occupational status. Of the total, 38 per cent never experienced downward mobility, and only 27 per cent had to achieve work-life mobility to regain their initial status.

Thus, not only are more of the sons of the solid middle class able to avoid downward mobility, but a higher proportion are able to retain their status from the start of their careers. While educational opportunities and the demand for qualifications have allowed a small increase in long-range mobility from the working class, they have at the same time very substantially strengthened the ability of the middle class to guarantee that their children do not suffer a loss of privilege through downward mobility.

The researchers conclude from all this that work-life mobility has not declined in absolute terms, and that inter-generational mobility through education has become much more common, increasing the overall level of social mobility. Despite this evidence of an increase, however, it is still true that long-range mobility in Britain is experienced by only a small minority.

While the routes discussed so far are the primary ones, marriage as a means of changing one's social position by acquiring a partner of a different class is also important. However, while cross-class marriages are by no means unknown, there is seldom a wide gulf between the social origins of husband and wife. A host of social factors serve to encourage 'homogamy', or marriage between social equals, ranging from barriers of wealth, status and value, to the simple fact that those from different backgrounds are unlikely to meet at work or at leisure. There is little evidence to suggest that long-range social mobility is at all common through marriage.

Causes of the level of social mobility

When assessing the overall level of social mobility in a stratification system, three crucial causal factors must be considered:

(1) the number of high positions available to be filled.
(2) the number of high-origin offspring available to fill these places.
(3) the methods used to fill them.

Even if all offspring from high origins entered similarly high positions, there could still be scope for upward mobility from below if those in higher occupations did not produce enough children to fill all the vacancies. This shortfall could happen either through a sudden expansion in the number of high positions, or through a single failure by the higher group to reproduce its own numbers. Additionally, not all the offspring from high backgrounds will avoid downward mobility if there is some degree of competition for access to the better positions — for example, through educational qualifications. As we shall see, the expansion of the number of high positions is the crucial causal factor of the degree of mobility in Britain, together with the inequalities in educational opportunity which give a better chance to the middle and upper classes in the competition for highly rewarded occupations.

The number of high positions available to be filled

The enormous expansion in non-manual occupations at professional, managerial and routine levels has been by far the most important factor in expanding opportunities for upward mobility and lessening the threat of downward mobility for the middle class. The proportion of women in manual employment has fallen steadily since 1911, while the change in male employment has occurred rapidly since 1950 (see Table 2.13).

TABLE 2.13
Changes in the British occupational structure

	Occupation (%)	1921	1951	1961	1966	1971
Males	Manual	75.5	73.6	68.1	67.1	62.6
	Non-manual	24.5	26.4	31.9	32.9	37.4
Females	Manual	68.3	—	48.1	47.6	45.7
	Non-manual	31.7	—	51.9	52.4	54.3

Source: *Census* data.

Number of offspring from high origins available

If those in middle-class positions do not reproduce sufficiently
to replace their own numbers, there will be a shortage of new
people to fill these positions. There have been long-term
differences in fertility rates between social classes, and at
times the middle class have produced fewer children than

TABLE 2.14
Family size by occupation

Husband's occupation	Average number of children of all families in 1961
Employers and managers	1.69
Professionals — self-employed	1.91
Professionals — employees	1.52
Routine non-manual	1.53
Skilled manual	1.86
Semi-skilled manual	2.04
Unskilled manual	2.36

Source: *Census 1961.*

replacement would require, that is, just over two children per couple — to allow for early mortality among some (see Table 2.14). Thus even if all the children of the middle class entered non-manual occupations, some recruits would still be needed from below. While there are significant differences in fertility, it must be emphasised that far more important processes are at work in determining overall mobility levels.

Methods of selection for high positions

If selection were purely on merit, then a fairly high level of social mobility would be expected. Those from higher backgrounds would only secure their continued position by showing talent — for example, through educational qualifications. However, this would not lead to purely open mobility as long as those from higher backgrounds gained significant advantages in the education system, whether through private schooling, or through their more successful use of the state sector. These limitations are crucially important in the supposedly open societies of the West, and to some extent in socialist societies. Achievement-based systems are not necessarily open.

Additionally, however, there are definite biases in recruitment which systematically favour those from higher-class backgrounds. The qualities demanded in competitors for a position may effectively produce *social closure*, so that only those with a certain class background, or a certain degree of wealth, are considered suitable. Data in Chapter 4 show how a public school education, followed by Cambridge or Oxford University, is the primary route into many positions of power in Britain. Thus it would seem that *ascription* rather than achievement is more important for those in the upper class. The inheritance of wealth, and the gaining of accent and demeanour through a distinct and expensive education, are 'qualifications' for power-holding in many British institutions. The broad studies of social mobility we have examined tend to neglect this propertied upper class. Here, the generalisations about mobility and achievement become inapplicable. The 'self-made millionaire' is a rare and peripheral member of this propertied class: overall it makes more sense to refer to the social closure of the upper class to mobility — whether upward into it, or downward out of it.

For the middle and working classes, however, changes in the occupational structure are the key factors affecting the overall level of social mobility.

Social mobility and class structure

It is important to realise that changes in the level of social mobility have no direct connection with patterns of inequality in society: movement between classes does not abolish objective class structures. *The structure of class positions is a separate matter from the recruitment of individuals to fill these positions.*

While these positions constitute the structure of objective inequalities, sociologists have often regarded stratification as including a broader range of features, including subjective aspects of inequality. We have seen that in capitalist societies, different classes exhibit differences in social characteristics, such as values and patterns of behaviour. If class membership is transmitted across generations (that is, if there is little social mobility) then it is more likely that these classes will become distinct social entities, differing in many ways in their social characteristics. Giddens (1973, p. 107) emphasises this idea with his concept of 'structuration': 'The greater the degree of "closure" of mobility chances the more this facilitates the formation of identifiable classes. For the effect of closure in terms of intergenerational movement is to provide for the reproduction of common life experiences over the generations.'

If, on the other hand, there is a constant flux, with high levels of social mobility, such sharp differences are less easily sustained. The upper class in Western societies have normally succeeded in maintaining a high degree of social closure, and show very distinct values and patterns of behaviour. These partly result from their objective position — their concern with wealth and its management — but also from a sustained upper-class culture. Even when considering the middle and working classes, though, we must not forget that mobility levels are still low enough to sustain different class cultures, especially at the extreme 'ends' of these classes in the upper middle class and the unskilled working class. In any society, as long as objective classes remain, there will be different opportunities and experiences available to different classes, and these will be sufficient to produce differing ideas and behaviour. This is still most emphatically true of contemporary societies, where the class structures are far from fully 'open' and hence where the degrees of structuration remain substantial.

2.11 THE FUNCTIONALIST THEORY OF STRATIFICATION

As we have seen, the Marxist perspective on stratification and inequality envisages a time when class inequality can and will eventually disappear, after the destruction of capitalism and its replacement by a new socio-economic order. Such a view contrasts starkly with that of functionalist theorists which see stratification and inequality as permanent, necessary and inevitable features of human societies.

The functionalist approach in sociology rests on two major assumptions:

(i) social phenomena exist because they have some positive function to perform in society;
(ii) if societies are to be viable, a number of basic conditions have to be achieved — a number of 'functional prerequisites' must be effectively satisfied (e.g. reproduction of the species, socialisation of the young, etc.).

Functionalists emphasise that inequality has been a prominent feature of past human societies and continues to be so in contemporary societies of West and East. It would appear, then, they argue, that stratification and inequality perform some necessary and positive function for society. Such assumptions are an integral part of the theory formulated by Davis and Moore (1945). Two extracts from this article confirm the essence of their arguments:

Social inequality is [the] device by which societies insure

that the most important positions are conscientiously filled by the most qualified persons. Hence, every society, no matter how simple or complex, must differentiate persons in terms of both prestige and esteem, and must therefore possess a certain amount of institutionalised inequality (Davis and Moore, 1945, p. 243).

As a functioning mechanism a society must somehow distribute its members in social positions and induce them to perform the duties of these positions. Inevitably, then, a society must have some way of distributing these rewards differentially according to positions. The rewards and their distribution become a part of the social order and thus give rise to stratification (Davis and Moore, 1945, pp. 242–3).

Their argument can be summarised briefly:

(i)   some positions in society are functionally more important than others (i.e. vital to the continued existence of society) and require particular skills;

(ii) not everyone in society has the talent to fill these positions;

(iii) the exclusive few have to have 'raw' talent converted into specialist skills by a training period which involves their making sacrifices;

(iv) the talented will only be induced to train for these socially vital positions if sufficient rewards are attached to their future positions;

(v)   there must exist, therefore, a system of unequal rewards built into a hierarchy of positions in society.

So, according to Davis and Moore, stratification and inequality are both positively functional and inevitable in human societies, because societies have to fill a number of 'key' positions with the 'right' people, and this can only be achieved by allocating unequal rewards to these positions.

This theory has been heavily criticised from various theoretical standpoints, and notably by Tumin (1953). His points have been taken up and expanded by others.

Much controversy has centred on the concept of 'functional

importance'. Critics argue that it is a highly value-laden term: deciding which positions are functionally more important than others cannot be done objectively, but will inevitably involve arbitrary value-judgements. How does one decide whether company directors are functionally more important than their workers, and if they receive five times as much as workers, does this mean they are five times more important? The problems involved in assessing 'functional importance' render the concept highly dubious sociologically.

Many critics have questioned the functionalists' emphasis on the limited availability of talented people in societies. Are sufficiently talented people as few and far between as functionalists suggest? There is much evidence to suggest (as we have indicated in Chapter 7 on education) that considerable potential talent is wasted, and that it is the *stratification system itself* which restricts the development of potentially talented members of society from the lower orders. The unequal distribution of resources in stratified societies enables the better-off to obtain privileged access to educational facilities to have their talent developed, while at the same time disadvantaging those at the bottom.

The theory wrongly assumes the existence of a 'meritocracy' — that there is equal opportunity for all to develop their talent: public schoolboys in Britain and white South African children, for example, do *not* start alongside their age-peers in an equal contest. As Tumin (1953, p. 389) points out, the very reverse is so: 'Smoothly working and stable systems of stratification tend to *build in* obstacles to the further exploitation of the range of available talent.'

It is by no means certain that material rewards are the *only* means by which societies can induce their members to fill social positions, as the theory seems to suggest. People may be, and frequently are, motivated to take up certain occupations by the prospect of intrinsic satisfaction from the job, by altruistic motives such as giving service to others, or by feelings of social duty or sense of mission — motives frequently unconnected with material wealth, status or power.

The functionalist theory also justifies high rewards for the occupants of certain positions partly as a compensation for the 'sacrifices' of loss of earning power and cost of training during the period of preparation for functionally important positions. Many critics regard this line of argument as dubious or, at best, misleading. The loss of earning power experienced by such as doctors, lawyers, etc., can be recouped fairly quickly after training (Tumin and others have estimated that no more than ten years is generally required), and is more than compensated by higher rewards after this time. The cost of training is generally the responsibility of parents or the state and not that of the trainees themselves.

Furthermore, the training period may be an attractive rather than depriving experience, offering gratification and stimulation to elite trainees which are not available to their age-peers working in less interesting jobs. The elite trainees may frequently enjoy higher prestige ('Our son Justin is training to be a doctor' sounds far more impressive than 'Our lad Jim's a barrow-boy'). Further, they have greater opportunities to develop their minds and personalities (the atmosphere of a university campus is more stimulating than that of an assembly line), and greater autonomy in deciding how they will organise their work and leisure time.

Functionalist theorists have also been attacked for their emphasis on the functional nature of stratification. Even in terms of their own theoretical approach, it is surely obvious that in many respects stratification is *dysfunctional*, producing many negative and damaging social consequences. We have already pointed to the way in which stratification may well inhibit the full development of talent in a society as a result of inequality of opportunity, which inevitably means that a stratified society is not utilising its talent resources fully. Furthermore, a stratified, hierarchically divided society may well generate conflict and antagonism among the various strata, rather than provide social integration (which Marxist explanations recognise and rightly emphasise). Functionalists fail to acknowledge that social institutions do not operate 'magically' in the interests of all but frequently work to the benefit of some at the expense of others.

The functionalist explanation of stratification appears especially naive in its emphasis on 'functional' importance as the determining factor in inequality of reward, at the expense of other crucial influences. Certain groups are better rewarded, *not* because they are functionally more important than others, but because they are well organised in trade unions or professional associations, having developed and used strategies and ideologies which further their claims for differential rewards effectively. Similarly, some people have access to unequal reward, not because of any talent or functional importance, but by accident of birth. Family inheritance is a crucial factor in sustaining inequality, quite simply because families are able to hand on both material and social advantages.

This is at the crux of one of the two major criticisms which Parkin (1971) makes of the functionalist theory.

First, Parkin argues, whilst a hierarchy of material reward does indeed usually represent the unequal distribution of 'marketable skills' (as he calls it) in a society, it is illegitimate to extrapolate from this, as the functionalists do, and assume it *also* represents the distribution of these skills, as an innate quality amongst society's members. We must also consider the opportunity that some occupations have for deliberately restricting access to the acquisition of the skills needed to do the job, thereby keeping down their distribution amongst the population, and enabling them to claim higher rewards in the market place. Such a strategy, says Parkin, is adopted by professions like law and medicine, where long periods of training, very often only marginally relevant or even unnecessary to the actual performance of the job, restrict the numbers of those prepared, or able to afford, to forgo the rewards of an occupation for a long period. (This willingness to delay seeking rewards is sometimes called 'deferred gratification'.)

Parkin secondly criticises the use which functionalists make of evidence which seems to indicate a consensus about the prestige ranking of occupations. A whole series of studies, he admits, appear to demonstrate that there is a broad agreement concerning the relative worth of different occupations, which apparently supports the functionalists' contention that it is possible to identify those positions which are most important in society. However, although people *seem* to agree on a hierarchy of symbolic rewards, this apparent consensus is not the sum of people's *personal* evaluations regarding the relative importance of different jobs, but a reproduction of what they have been socialised into accepting and which, when asked, they reproduce as though this sort of thing is a matter of fact. Thus, for example, although a miner might not *personally* believe that a university professor teaching three hours a week for 25 weeks of the year is doing a more worthy or important job than himself, he will nevertheless rank this occupation above his own in the construction of a prestige hierarchy because he has learnt that 'professors are more important than miners'. So, argues Parkin, this apparent consensus is, in fact, an expression of the particular system of dominant values which operates in such societies. It represents the capacity of those in dominant positions to persuade the rest of society that the attributes *they* consider admirable, and *their* evaluations of worth, are somehow the 'right' ones. Indeed, Parkin goes on to suggest that the functionalist theory of stratification itself is an expression of the same value-system: no more than a rather sophisticated mechanism for providing a justification of unequal rewards. In his view, then, the functionalist approach to *inequality* is nothing else than an ideology designed to legitimate this same inequality.

This criticism echoes our general argument in this chapter. Any explanation of structured inequality which concentrates on normative factors to the exclusion of material ones is inadequate. The failure of the functionalist theory of stratification is ultimately its failure to locate normative and cultural dimensions of stratification within a framework of material inequality; indeed, this reflects the complacent neglect of relations of domination and subordination characteristic of functionalist theory generally.

Yet it is not only functionalism that can be criticised in this regard, for popular conceptions of inequality often suffer from the same deficiency. In the following chapter we examine the way in which four particular forms of subordination have often been the subject of such academic and popular misinterpretation.

REFERENCES TO CHAPTER 2

Abel-Smith, B. and Townsend, P. (1965) *The Poor and the Poorest*, London, Bell.

132 *Introductory Sociology*

Atkinson, A. B. (1974) *Unequal Shares*, Harmondsworth, Penguin.

Coates, K. and Silburn, R. (1970) *Poverty: the Forgotten Englishmen*, Harmondsworth, Penguin.

Corrigan, P. (1979) *Schooling the Smash Street Kids*, London, Macmillan.

Davis, K. and Moore, W. E. (1945) 'Some Principles of Stratification', *American Sociological Review*, vol. 10, pp. 242–9.

Diamond Commission (1979) Royal Commission on the Distribution of Income and Wealth, *Report*, 1979.

Galbraith, J. (1958) *The Affluent Society*, London, Hamilton.

Gerth, H. and Mills, C. W. (1948) *From Max Weber: Essays in Sociology*, London, Routledge & Kegan Paul.

Giddens, A. (1973) *The Class Structure of the Advanced Societies*, London, Hutchinson.

Glass, D. (1954) *Social Mobility in Britain*, London, Routledge & Kegan Paul.

Goldthorpe, J. H. *et al.* (1971) *The Affluent Worker in the Class Structure*, Cambridge University Press.

Goldthorpe, J. H. *et al.* (1980) *Social Mobility and Class Structure in Modern Britain*, Oxford, Clarendon Press.

Kay, J. and King, M. (1978) *The British Tax System*, Oxford University Press.

Lipset, S. and Bendix, P. (1959) *Social Mobility in Industrial Society*, University of California Press.

Lockwood, D. (1958) *The Blackcoated Worker*, London, Allen & Unwin.

Miliband, R. (1974) 'Politics and Poverty' in D. Wedderburn (1974).

Miller, S. M. (1960) 'Comparative Social Mobility', *Current Sociology*, vol. 9.

Parkin, F. (1971) *Class Inequality and Political Order*, London, Paladin.

Revell, J. (1967) *The Wealth of the Nation*, Cambridge University Press.

Rogoff, N. (1953) *Recent Trends in Occupational Mobility*, New York, Free Press.

Spicer, C. and Lipworth, L. (1966) *Regional and Social Factors in Infant Mortality*, London, HMSO.

Townsend, P. (1979) *Poverty in the United Kingdom*, Harmondsworth, Penguin.

Tumin, M. (1953) 'Some Principles of Stratification: a Critical Analysis', *American Sociological Review*, vol. 18, pp. 387–93.

Wedderburn, D. (1962) 'Poverty in Britain Today – The Evidence', *Sociological Review*, vol. 10, pp. 257–82.

Wedderburn, D. (1970) 'Workplace Inequality', *New Society*, 9 April 1970.

Wedderburn, D. (ed.) (1974) *Poverty, Inequality and Class Structure*, Cambridge University Press.

Wedge, P. and Prosser, H. (1973) *Born to Fail?*, London, Arrow Books.

Wedgewood, J. (1939) *The Economics of Inheritance*, Harmondsworth, Penguin.

Westergaard, J. and Resler, H. (1975) *Class in a Capitalist Society*, London, Heinemann.

Wilsher, P. (1973) 'How the Wealth is Split', in J. Urry and J. Wakeford (eds), *Power in Britain*, London, Heinemann.

Wright, E. (1978) *Class, Crisis and the State*, London, New Left Books.

Zweig, F. (1961) *The Worker in an Affluent Society*, London, Heinemann.

3

Forms of Subordination: Youth, the Poor, Race and the Third World

3.1 INTRODUCTION

The preceding chapter examined the general features of stratification, particularly with regard to class inequality within contemporary capitalism. The dimensions of inequality were said to be best explained in terms of both Marxist and Weberian perspectives rather than through functionalist theory, which was shown to be both empirically unfounded and ideologically suspect. One of the principal deficiencies of the functionalist approach is its neglect of conflict and exploitation in society, partly derived from its assumption that *moral unity* is the basis of social life. Social phenomena are explained as being the result either of the 'needs of the social system' or of the 'shared values' held by a group.

The notion that the relationship between groups, that their relative economic, political and cultural place in society can be explained in terms of the particular values and attitudes that each holds, has, however, been adopted by a variety of social science theorists. This chapter examines four forms of subordination that popularly, ideologically and/or academically have been attributed to the distinctive 'cultural characteristics' of the subordinate groups concerned. The four patterns of inequality discussed are: (i) that generational division between young and old; (ii) that division between the poor and non-poor of society; (iii) that racial division between 'white' and 'black'; and (iv) that international division between developed and undeveloped countries. We show that these four patterns of inequality have much to do with the general processes of stratification that we outlined in Chapter 2, and that any particular cultural phenomena which may be associated with these patterns can only be seen accurately in the light of such processes. Thus we argue that the subordinate position of groups in each of the four contexts cannot be properly explained by an emphasis on their values and attitudes which allegedly mark them off from the rest of society, or, in the fourth case, the developed world.

3.2   YOUTH CULTURES

Many sociologists and media commentators regard the idea of the existence of a 'youth culture' as reflecting and expressing the experiences, activities and values of young people. The idea of a 'youth culture' — or more accurately a 'youth subculture' — implies that the young are socialised into and committed to a special set of values, standards, expectations and behaviour patterns distinguishable from those of 'adult society', and at its most extreme it implies a fundamental rift between the two age categories — a 'war between the generations'.

Some have gone so far as to suggest that youth has developed as a separate 'class', subordinate to and cut off from the adult world, so that generational division may be an equally significant, if not more important, social barrier than social class, and, furthermore, one which reduces class divisions. Berger and Berger (1972, p. 227) maintain that 'To a considerable degree, the youth culture cuts across class lines ... [It] has created symbols and patterns of behaviour that are capable of bestowing status upon individuals coming from quite different class backgrounds ... The youth culture has a strongly egalitarian ethos.'

This popular idea of generational division as expressed in the form of a youth culture rests on an essentially functionalist or neo-functionalist perspective, involving a conception of a discontinuity between the *value-systems* of adults and youth. In this view the stable interaction of members of different age grades is essential for the working and continuity of the social system. Sugarman (1968, p. 71) maintains:

The survival of society requires that as members go through this phase [adolescence] in their lives, many of them should work hard at acquiring certain knowledge, skills and values. Failing this, important roles that require great expertise and dedication will not be filled adequately. Yet at this phase of their lives the young are undergoing considerable strain . . . and are exposed to the temptation of a youth culture.

These strains of adolescence, it is argued, mean that youth share common problems and interests in handling a difficult period of transition, and a youth culture with its own values and standards arises as a means of adjusting both to these problems and to imminent adulthood.

Age and membership of an age category, then, are seen as specific and fundamental variables, and generational conflict is the product of the complex and ambivalent socialisation processes at work in modern industrial societies, which are neither as integrated nor as coherent as in pre-industrial societies. In the former 'Intergenerational conflict ("the generation gap") is a socialisation dysfunction, resulting from weak integration between society and age groups. Age is the basis of social and cultural characteristics of actors' (Brake, 1979, p. 25).

Eisenstadt (1956) provides perhaps the most extensive functionalist explanation of youth culture. For him, the problematic position of youth in industrial societies rests on the difficulties involved in the transition to adult roles. While the family is the basic socialising unit, the kinship system is not the basis on which adult roles are organised and allocated: the family is based on ascriptive and particularistic criteria and values, while adult roles (particularly occupations) rest on a foundation of universalism, achievement and impersonality. Thus, there exists a sharp cleavage in value-orientations and expectations between the family and the wider society, so that youth becomes a significant social category, and a youth culture emerges to alleviate this disjunction.

This division is said to be intensified by a number of specific features of industrial societies: the extended provision of education means that more young people for a longer period

have to experience status insecurity and an ambiguous transition; a more complex and differentiated occupational structure with increasingly specialised division of labour means that
meritocratic competition for occupation occurs increasingly,
and following in parents' occupational footsteps is less likely;
and increased social mobility and changes in leisure provision
mean that each generation lives qualitatively 'different' lives.
In Eisenstadt's view, primary and early secondary socialisation
does not prepare individuals to adapt to all this, so that their
values are not stable and their identity is insecure. The creation of a youth culture is the response to the discontinuities
created by the failure of the family and school to effect the
transition to adulthood. As Eisenstadt (1956, pp. 43–5) says:

> In universalistic-achievement societies . . . an individual
> cannot achieve full status if he behaves in his work accord-
> ing to the ascriptive particularistic criteria of family life:
> such behaviour would also prove a strain on the social
> system . . . There occurs in such cases a defensive reaction
> in the direction of age-homogeneous relations and groups
> . . . The individual develops need-dispositions for a new
> kind of interaction with other individuals which would
> make the transition easier for him.

While the idea of a 'youth culture' has held considerable
influence within the ranks of sociologists and the mass media,
its accuracy in portraying realistically both youth-adult relations and the internal relations of youth has been seriously
questioned. Essentially, the critique focuses on two basic and
often interrelated themes: (i) that the differences between
'adults' and 'youth' can be easily overexaggerated; and (ii)
that it is seriously misleading to see both young people and
adults as simple homogeneous categories, since this overemphasises the significance of age as a sociological variable
at the expense of more fundamental lines of social division.
Both these themes cast doubt on the existence of a 'youth
culture'.

In the first place, the concept implies a homogeneous adult
world, a *consensual* picture of 'adult society' which is sociologically inaccurate. As we saw in Chapter 2, inequalities of

wealth, income, mortality, etc., *within* the adult population are considerable and persistent: the world of adults is as divided along crucial lines of life-chances as it is united by accident of age, so that an identity of interest and values is highly doubtful. This alerts us to one of the fundamental inadequacies of the concept of a youth culture, and one which more recent analyses of youth, from a neo-Marxist perspective, attempt to rectify. As Mungham and Pearson (1976, pp. 2–3) observe: 'Behind all the talk of "generation" and "generation gap" there is the forgotten question of the class structure of society. It is as if when youth are discussed that social class goes on holiday. But youth are not a classless tribe.'

The neo-functionalist view of youth seems to suggest (apart from the occasional nodding acknowledgement of class variations) that the young are suspended without other fundamental points of identity in a classless world of leisure, where differences in educational and occupational opportunities and experiences disappear. It is no coincidence that the idea of a distinctive 'youth culture' emerged most strongly at a time of alleged embourgeoisement and increasing dilution of class divisions and consciousness: a myth of affluent youth, with time and money on their hands for enjoying mass entertainment and fashion products, reflected the more general myth of working-class affluence. But, as numerous sociologists have stressed, Western societies are still capitalist class societies, in which class position is fundamental in shaping life-chances and life-styles.

Thus, while youth share certain disadvantages in common and are accorded minority-group status, their life-chances are markedly unequal and differentiate them internally more fundamentally and rigidly than any temporary 'unity' engendered merely by being young, minimising the likelihood of a common sense of identity and often generating mutual hostility. As Murdock and McCron (1976, p. 18) observe:

Schools provide an obvious case in point. They are institutions not simply of age segregation but also of class domination. They operate not only to delay adolescents' entry on to the labour market and to reinforce their subordination to adult authority but also to reproduce the existing structure of class inequalities and class relations. Far from uniting youth as a single subordinate 'class', therefore, schools serve to remake and confirm the prevailing patterns of class divisions and antagonisms.

If some sections of society are given an inferior educational experience, are consigned to routine, unsatisfying work (or to no job at all) and to residence in anonymous estates lacking facilities, it is no surprise that they feel little or no identity with those living in residential suburbs and attending private boarding schools which give access to elite positions. The middle-class teenager (both male *and* female) is socialised towards educational and occupational horizons in which youth is seen as a stepping-stone to a burgeoning career, whereas for the working-class teenager it is a prelude to a humdrum existence and hence to be enjoyed 'while you're young' before harsh reality takes over.

The result is that middle-class and working-class youth tend to develop *distinct* and *separate subcultures* (for example, the Teddy Boys and the Beatniks of the 1950s and the Skinheads and Hippies of the 1960s and 1970s), which, even when they manifest 'oppositional' elements, constitute very different responses. For instance, both radical student protest among middle-class youth and racialist 'Paki-bashing' among some working-class youth were political responses to changing economic and socio-political circumstances in Britain, but they were of a very different order, reflecting less about youth *per se* than about the pressures and contradictions of capitalist class society experienced by *specific* subgroups within the two classes.

Not only are middle-class and working-class youth sub-cultures separate entities but they may also be antagonistic. Willis's (1978) 'bike boys' were highly critical of Mods and Hippies as being effeminate and weak in their involvement with drugs, and the hippy counter-culture (1960s) consisted mainly of students and ex-students, evoking little working-class response besides hostility. In fact, some writers suggest that one particular working-class youth subculture group, Skinheads, were to a large extent a reaction to middle-class hippy subculture,

> a reaction against the quiet introspective influence of flower-power; its most obvious symbol was 'bovver boots' ... The Skins adopted a uniform which seems to be, at one and the same time, both a caricature and a reassertion of solid male working class toughness (Mungham and Pearson, 1976, p. 7).

From the neo-Marxist perspective, then, we must abandon the assumption of a homogeneous youth culture and recognise the basic importance of class inequalities in shaping responses. In this view we need to consider youth subcultures and their styles in relation to a system of class domination and to a dominant culture and ideology. Capitalist societies, as Marx stressed, are characterised by dominant and subordinate classes according to their relation to the means of production, and the existence of a dominant culture reflects the position and interests of the economically dominant class. This class attempts to maintain its hegemony (see Chapter 4) to some degree by achieving the consent of the subordinate classes by incorporating them into the key institutions and structures which support its authority.

But subordinate classes develop means of expressing a response to their position through their own distinctive subcultures, which help them to negotiate relations with the dominant class and its culture — that is, to 'win space' from them by virtue of subscribing to alternative cultural definitions and concerns which may reflect resistance, accommodation, pragmatic acceptance, or whatever. As Clarke *et al.* (1976, p. 44) say: 'The subordinate class brings to this "theatre of struggle" a repertoire of strategies and responses — ways of coping as well as resisting.'

Thus youth subcultures are to be seen as particular generational responses to wider problems experienced by their class, reflecting the common experiences of their members in education, employment and rewards, residential provision, neighbourhood and community relationships, and so on. For example, the dominant ideology suggests that Britain is a meritocracy with equal educational and occupational opportunity and political rights, and equality before the law. Black working-class youths on the dole since leaving school and on the receiving end of racist attitudes (at school, in work and in leisure) experience contradictions directly, so that a distinctive subcultural response on their part may be a meaningful attempt to express dissatisfaction at such inequality.

But class does not simply *replace* age as the major variable of analysis since

Clearly age is an important factor in structuring the social situation of young people. Some experiences, noticeably compulsory secondary schooling, are youth specific . . . Age also plays a key role in determining the range of options and choices available within the leisure environment. It is not therefore a case of [simply] substituting class for age . . . but of examining the relationship between class and age, and more particularly, the way in which age acts as a mediation of class (Murdock and McCron, 1976, p. 24).

Class and generation interact dynamically to produce a specific class-generational response: they *coalesce* to produce a distinct subcultural *style*.

However, while seeing youth subcultures as producing something distinctive, their relations with the parent culture − what is *shared* with this culture − cannot be ignored. Although many youth activities appear to be anti-adult, they often actually *exaggerate* aspects of the parent culture (as with the Skinheads).

Youth subcultures, then, constitute more micro-level responses to the changing macro-structural arrangements of capitalist society, particularly those of the post-war era. Changes in national economic patterns, from the relative prosperity of the 1960s to the recession and inflation of the 1970s, the erosion of the traditional working-class community and the development of housing estates, the impact of technological and organisational changes in the work environment on employment and skills, and the growth of mass consumption and mass entertainment industries, all have left their mark on the working class and have evoked some striking responses among certain sections of working-class youth, from the Teddy Boys of the 1950s to the Punkrockers of the 1970s.

For example, the Skinheads of the late 1960s adopted a 'model worker' dress of short hair, clean-shaven faces, industrial work boots, turned-up jeans with braces as a reassertion of working-class culture and values. Their overtly masculine style, their preference for pubs and beer over clubs and pills, their 'queer bashing' and dislike of student 'hippies', and their willingness to fight, re-emphasised their working-class origins. Their racist attitudes and 'Paki-bashing' and their commitment to the idea of territory ('Hackney Boot Boys Rule, OK?') reflected the sense of threat felt by many sections of the working class over immigration and changes in their community.

They were particularly renowned for their attachment to football teams and came to be seen as the stereotypical 'football hooligans'. The fierce commitment of young (and not so young) football supporters, their singing and chanting and occasionally violent behaviour — under the umbrella description of 'hooliganism' — has been a matter of increasing public and media concern and is often presented as being 'mindless' and spoiling the game for the 'true' spectator. But for a number of writers it classically exemplifies the youthful working-class response to the post-war changes in Britain to which we have referred.

Watching soccer has been traditionally a working-class leisure activity, providing a sense of excitement, pleasure and commitment to 'our team', in stark contrast to the indifference and alienation experienced in unsatisfying work and educational experiences. But, as Taylor (1971) and others have pointed out, in the post-war era — and especially since the 1960s — the game has become more 'bourgeois', more professionalised, more commercialised and less traditionally based in the working-class community. Clubs have attempted to cater for a new kind of spectator, the (classless) consumer of entertainment rather than 'the fan', with the introduction of more seating, of restaurants, and so on, so that the working-class supporters on the terraces, having been removed from their traditional neighbourhoods by urban redevelopment, find that the football team is no longer 'theirs'. Football hooliganism represents the working-class youth's attempt to win back control of his class's game and is 'an attempt to retrieve the disappearing sense of community' (Clarke and Jefferson, 1976, p. 154) in its emphasis on territorial loyalty and sense of common identity. As Robins and Cohen (1978, p. 137) observe: 'It's as if, for these youngsters, the space they share on the North Bank is a way of magically retrieving the sense of group solidarity and identification that once went along with living in a traditional working class neighbour-hood.' This means, then, that passionate support of a football team *is* more than watching a game and being entertained: it is a collective response to problems of class experience and cannot be dismissed as mere 'mindless aggro'.

This *remains* a 'magical' solution, however, because it operates only in the harmless area of leisure. This is no solution for those unlucky enough to have monotonous, alienating, low-paid, demeaning jobs, let alone for those unemployed. Dull schooling, dull jobs and the inequalities they embody are not solved by ritual conflict with opposing fans who suffer similar life-chances. These youth subcultures thus constitute partial 'negotiations' with the dominant class culture rather than effective challenges to the subordination they experience.

Thus the phenomenon of youth subcultures illustrates the need for an analysis of institutions which recognises the central importance of *class*. Instead of seeing a universal 'youth culture' as the product merely of the problems of member-ship of an age category, as the functionalist perspective does, it seems more profitable to explore the ways in which the social relations of capitalist society produce distinctive class-subcultural responses and how these are manifested in distinctive youth subcultures.

3.3 EXPLANATIONS OF POVERTY

The prevalent conception of poverty prior to the nineteenth century was that it was 'God-given', part of the natural order of things. Such a view gave way in Victorian times to one of poverty as an individual problem, the product of deficient personal character and morality: the poor were seen as thrift-less, lazy and undisciplined, lacking initiative and moral fibre.

They were to be assisted in coping with their condition of poverty, but any alteration in this condition had to be achieved through their own efforts. Viewing poverty not simply as an individual but also as a social problem to be handled by systematic state action and provision of welfare services is essentially a relatively recent conception.

As in many other areas of sociology, controversies and disagreements exist as to the explanation of poverty. This particular area of controversy well illustrates how different explanations also often generate very different policy solutions. This can be seen by contrasting 'culture of poverty' explanations — which emphasise shared values, as in the functionalist tradition— and neo-Marxist explanations of poverty.

The *'culture of poverty'* thesis suggests that the poor are poor because they have different values and way of life from the rest of society, a culture of their own — a 'culture of poverty' — which prevents them from achieving success and prosperity. A prominent exponent of the thesis is Lewis (1961, 1966). He maintains that the poor possess certain cultural features which mark them off from the rest of society and which are passed on from one generation to another, inhibiting those exposed to them from taking opportunities to escape from poverty.

Lewis identifies a number of 'core features' of this 'culture of poverty', including mother-centred families, a male preoccupation with being tough and masculine, fatalism, an inability to defer gratification, and a narrow perspective on the world, restricted to the immediate environment and condition. For Lewis, such features constitute a distinctive culture of poverty, preventing the poor from attaining the material standards common to the rest of society: in other words, because their way of life is different, they are poor.

The 'culture of poverty' thesis has found favour with politicians and governments in providing a foundation for policy programmes. In the USA in the 1960s a number of government reports (such as the 1965 Moynihan Report) claimed that adverse socialisation of children by black families was the major factor in black poverty in the ghettos: the solution lay with changes in the blacks themselves, particularly in their (inadequate) socialisation and cultural practices. Hence, during the 1960s, American governments emphasised the need for more social work but less direct economic aid for blacks.

Similarly, in Britain in 1972 the then Minister of Health and Social Security, Sir Keith Joseph, made a number of controversial statements which amounted to the view that 'inadequate' parents do not socialise their children properly in the skills, capacities and motivation necessary for taking up educational and job opportunities. A 'culture of poverty' is passed on, exacerbated, according to Sir Keith, by their 'unfortunate' breeding habits of producing larger numbers of children. So, social intervention is needed to change the behaviour patterns of the poor, particularly their child-rearing practices.

Lewis and other exponents of the thesis have been criticised for using evidence collected on *families* to construct a picture of a *culture*, of a whole way of life, i.e. for concentrating predominantly on attitudes and activities within households to the neglect of the wider social group. Furthermore, 'culture of poverty' theorists are accused of engaging in a purely *negative* analysis: by starting with a middle-class model of life, they have identified merely what is 'lacking' in the poor (e.g. family stability, future planning) without giving sufficient attention to the positive aspects of their way of life.

A more fundamental criticism suggests that differences between the poor and the rest of society have been overstressed at the expense of similarities which exist. One might ask, for instance, whether some of the 'core' features which Lewis identifies as constituting a 'culture of poverty' are entirely absent among the non-poor working class; certainly, emphasis on masculinity and a limited social outlook are by no means restricted to the poor working class. Furthermore, critics would argue that there is considerable evidence that the poor *do* subscribe to many of the 'normal' standards and values about security, steady employment, stable marriage, and so on.

The crucial point, however, may be that the *very fact of being poor* prevents the poor from putting these values and standards into action: for instance, poverty makes future planning and deferred gratification a remote if not unattainable luxury — poverty may necessitate fathers moving away to seek work, and so on. As Gans (1971, p. 160) says:

> Many poor people share the aspirations of the middle class, and yet more those of the stable working class. If they could achieve the same economic security as middle and working class people, they would quickly give up most of the behaviour patterns associated with poverty.

Gans and others stress that it makes far more sense to see that many of the features of the 'culture of poverty' identified by Lewis are not *chosen* ways of life but simply *realistic responses* to being poor, to the realities and pitfalls of an insecure and unpredictable economic existence. If a 'culture of poverty' exists, it is a consequence of poverty and not its cause, and the poor's cultural patterns are not the *source* of their poverty but its outcome.

The *neo-Marxist explanation* of poverty accepts such criticisms. Moreover, it has also pointed to the important *ideological* implications of the 'culture of poverty' thesis, whereby emphasis on the apparent internal inadequacies of the poor suggests that their problems are of their own making. As Westergaard and Resler (1975) succinctly put it, 'The blame for inequality falls neatly on its victims.'

The danger in the 'culture of poverty' approach lies in its neglect of the impact of wider economic forces and relationships in shaping behaviour patterns and social structures. The 'culture of poverty' thesis presents poverty as a 'cultural' condition, a by-product of the inadequate culture embraced by certain social groups, rendering them less socially competent and lacking in initiative; the remedy, therefore, is one of limited, localised 'social therapy', involving the re-education of the poor, with little attention or priority given to structural or economic change.

Gans (1971), Miliband (1974) and Westergaard and Resler (1975) reject the idea of viewing the poor as a distinct, culturally homogeneous group, because this is obviously false and because it involves a too narrow conception of the dynamics of poverty, diverting attention away from larger structures of inequality created by the stratification system, and providing wrong-headed solutions to poverty. These critics emphasise that poverty results from the economic arrangements and relationships of society which determine the distribution of material resources and power; in a society where wealth is still heavily concentrated, where speculators in shares and property can make big financial 'killings', where employers can pay low wages to individuals working long hours in unpleasant conditions, poverty for some will be a persistent fact of life.

Furthermore, the economic *ideologies* of our society do little to enhance the poor's position. Capitalist societies have long emphasised the importance of individual effort, self-help and initiative, so that an 'if you don't work, you don't eat' philosophy is strongly ingrained. The result is that we are not quite prepared to do everything we can for the poor: they receive assistance, but this stops short of relieving poverty completely. Nowhere is this better illustrated than in the operations of the Welfare State. The British Welfare State is widely regarded with great reverence, but the fact remains that the major benefits it provides (family allowance, old-age pension, supplementary benefits, etc.), while assisting the poor, do *not* lift them out of poverty: that is, the benefits are not sufficiently generous to guarantee an income above the official 'poverty line'. As Coates and Silburn (1970) say: 'The Welfare State has been no Robin Hood. It has taken little from the rich and given even less to the poor.' Behind the theory and practice of the Welfare State appears to be an anxiety about giving people 'too much' in case their moral fibre weakens and they become too dependent on help from others and abandon self-help.

The limitations of the Welfare State are compounded by the fact that many benefits to which individuals and families are entitled are simply not taken up. 'Serves them right, then' might be the response to this, but there are more powerful factors working against complete take-up of benefits than mere indifference to what is available. First, many people do not *know* what benefits are available to them, and some benefits are not widely publicised. The system rests on individuals *seeking out* benefits to which they are entitled, and not on 'automatic' provision by the state. Second, personal pride inhibits many eligible cases. Many people feel humiliated or embarrassed at accepting what they see as 'charity'. Again such attitudes demonstrate the powerful impact of Western economic ideologies (as well as the hangover from nineteenth-century notions of poverty), and accepting state aid is made no easier for the poor by the frequent outbursts of the mass media (and others) against 'scroungers', 'layabouts' and 'dole kings'. Third, claiming benefit involves problems and difficulties in procedure: entitlement to many benefits depends on a *means test* (i.e. providing information about personal circumstances in order to demonstrate *proof of need*), involving complicated contact with bureaucratic agencies, as well as the often degrading experience of having to divulge personal details to officials. Consequently, many people eligible for means-tested services do not apply for them.

Ultimately, poverty is a product of the unequal distribution of power in society: it is a condition of political as well as economic deprivation. As Miliband (1974) emphasises, although the poor theoretically possess the same civil and political rights as others, their circumstances do not enable them to be effective politically. The low paid, for instance, are often older, in smaller firms, in declining industries, with significant numbers of women workers — circumstances which do not encourage effective political organisation.

Here, then, we have a very different explanation of the existence and persistence of poverty from that of the 'culture of poverty' thesis, one which firmly locates it within the wider socio-economic structure and its patterns of inequality.

3.4 RACE RELATIONS

Theoretical issues

The problems of race and racism loom large in the modern world; in Africa, America, Europe and Great Britain men and women have been, and still are, deprived of basic human rights and dignity because of their 'race'.

Many people see racial discrimination and racist ideologies as the result of blind and irrational prejudice against 'outsider' groups by individuals of intolerant or bigoted disposition, or, less severely, by groups who cannot cope with the 'strange' cultural characteristics of different racial groups. While both of these notions of prejudice may have some reality and engender forms of inter-racial conflict, and are therefore important issues for sociological analysis, they do not tell the whole story. Racial prejudice functions, as we shall see, in ways which indicate that it is inextricably locked into broader structural dimensions of inequality: racial disadvantage is a form of subordination that, like youth cultures and poverty, must be seen in the context of social stratification.

A number of recent sociological approaches to race relations have concentrated on the relationship between race and social stratification. Those who adhere to this position argue that race relations represent a form of class and status relations and that, accordingly, problems of race relations can be dealt with by existing sociological theories. According to this view, inequality in a class society can be traced to some basic structural fact such as the ownership or non-ownership of productive property or the possession of different market capacities. Racial differences, it is argued, may be viewed (in the same way as sex, age and religion) as complicating factors in the dominant system. Race or colour simply makes the groups in question more visible and more vulnerable to class exploitation. Writers as far apart on the political spectrum as the functionalist Parsons (1965) and the Marxist economists Baran and Sweezy (1966) would, in their different ways, support such an interpretation.

On the other hand some writers, such as Rex (1970) and Lockwood (1970), argue that the attempts to explain race relations in class and stratification terms ignore the unique problems raised by race. Lockwood, for example, gives two main reasons why theories of *class* cannot account for patterns of race relations. On the one hand, he says, racial protest movements involve unification across class lines *within* racial groups, and, on the other, certain moral, aesthetic and sexual connotations of colour are built into our language, and have no equivalent in class terminology. Similarly, Rex argues that stratification theories are unable to explain the part played in racial stratification by 'deterministic' belief systems. These beliefs 'explain' and justify the discrimination directed towards a particular race either in terms of its genetic/biological inferiority or in equally deterministic socio-cultural terms.

Against this point of view, Dunning (1972) argues that the distinctive character of race relations from a sociological point of view lies, not in the presence or absence of deterministic theories and beliefs, as Rex suggests, but that the degree of significance of such ideological constructs is a function of the power discrepancies which exist between groups in a society. Groups with a great deal of power are able to impose their definitions of a situation upon the less powerful, who (given their economic and social subordination) do not have the resources to challenge the way in which they are represented. Where there are vast discrepancies of power between groups, deterministic beliefs may arise which perform certain functions for the dominant group. This means that such beliefs are not restricted to the context of race relations; *class* differences, i.e. inequalities, have been rationalised in such terms. For example, in the eighteenth and early nineteenth centuries there were people who believed that the social classes were formed from different streams of heredity and that they possessed distinguishing physical characteristics that marked the superiority of one class over another. This ideology can be found in the context of race relations in South Africa. Whatever their specific form and context, such beliefs help to justify privilege and/or to handle the discrepancy between established practice and egalitarian values — where such values exist. For example, one way in which Christian slave-owners were able to handle the conflict between their beliefs and their actions was by defining black Africans as 'animals' and therefore as beyond the pale. In general, then, as Castles and Kosack (1973, p. 430) say:

In reality, the relationship between discrimination and prejudice is a dialectical one: discrimination is based on economic and social interests and prejudice originates as an instrument to defend such discrimination. In turn, prejudice becomes entrenched and helps to cause further discrimination.

The capacity of subordinate racial groups to organise and resist exploitation and discrimination will be constrained by the sort of economic and political setting in which they are placed, and this may vary from, say, that of slavery to 'free' wage-labour. Furthermore, whatever general economic relationships hold, the success of resistance against exploitation is bound up with specific historical factors such as ease of communication (important for organisation), the ecological setting in which the groups are located (e.g. rural or urban), and the degree and type of interdependence associated with the division of labour. These factors will vary given different economic and industrial frameworks.

The different power balances which arise out of this complex intermeshing of variables will have potentially different psychological effects upon both oppressors and oppressed. Very unequal power balances are likely to have negative effects both upon the self-images and potential for political action of subordinate groups. Under such circumstances deterministic belief systems are likely to flourish. More equal power balances may create the conditions whereby subordinate groups can challenge, with varying degrees of effectiveness, their subordination and the hostile stereotyping to which they are subject. However, all these processes — their extent and efficacy — are constrained by the fundamental character of the economic system within which they operate. In the light of the discussion above, how can we portray race relations in Britain today?

The British case

Race relations in Britain are very different from those in, say, the USA. Unlike the USA and a number of other countries Britain did not have domestic slavery but, rather, a colonial system in which racist theories were used to rationalise and justify the privileges of whites; a hangover from this situation is that coloured immigrants are still thought of as subject 'races'.

The 'problem' of race relations is of relatively recent origin in Britain. It is only since the Second World War that there has been a sizeable coloured population in Britain, though blacks have been resident in England for more than four centuries. Many of these earlier residents will have experienced exploitation and discrimination of a kind not unlike that suffered by present-day blacks in Britain: in this sense the so-called race-relations 'problem' has existed for many years as an expression of the relative powerlessness of blacks as an economic and political group in the face of British capitalism, whether it be in the context of colonialism and slavery abroad or the exploitation of black wage-labour within Britain.

The immigration of coloured people from the British Commonwealth in the two decades after 1945 was only part of a broader phenomenon, in that over 350,000 white Europeans also entered the country between 1945 and 1957. In general, such immigration was a product of the chronic labour shortage in the period of economic expansion which followed the war. Most of the early Commonwealth immigrants came from the West Indies, but since 1961 the numbers of Indians, Pakistanis and subsequently Bangladeshis have also been growing. However, the scale of this immigration is frequently exaggerated by both press and politicians, and the notion that Britain is being 'swamped' with immigrants is completely false (concentration in particular urban areas gives the impression of 'swamping'). In 1976 the resident coloured population was estimated to be 1.8 million, i.e. only 3.5 per cent of the total population. People from the West Indies made up 40 per cent of this total, Indians 26 per cent, Pakistanis and Bangladeshis 16 per cent, East African Asians 11 per cent, and Black Africans 7 per cent. Moreover, while 1,207,000 immigrants entered Britain between 1970 and 1977, more than 1,400,000 left. (Data from *New Society*, November 1979.)

Neither should it be thought that coloured immigration from the colonies occurred haphazardly. These workers were *invited* and positively encouraged to come to Britain. For example, London Transport set up centres in the West Indies to recruit bus crews, and from 1956 the British Hotels & Restaurants Association recruited labour from Barbados. In India and Pakistan, Birmid Qualcast had agents to find workers for its foundries. Ironically, Enoch Powell was centrally involved in recruiting West Indians for the National Health Service.

Racial disadvantage

Most of the coloured immigrants have been recruited to fill lower working-class occupational positions and hence suffer the low-status, material and environmental disadvantages experienced by many white manual workers.

In this regard, Castles and Kosack argue that immigrant workers are part of the working class inasmuch as they occupy the same objective position within the capitalist mode of production as members of the 'proletariat' — they neither own nor control the means of production. However, they also argue that the particular hardship and exploitation experienced by immigrants mean that one should distinguish two 'strata' or levels within this proletariat: on the one hand the relatively better-off indigenous workers, and on the other the immigrants, 'who are the most underprivileged and exploited group of society' (Castles and Kosack, 1973, p. 477). Thus, immigrants fall into the same general category of subordination as 'the poor', who will, logically, include many immigrants in their number.

The disadvantages experienced by immigrants as *workers* are then multiplied through *racial* discrimination. It was suggested in Chapter 2 that the life-chances an individual enjoys are, for the majority of the population, determined by the 'market capacity' or skills that he or she can sell on the labour market, but there are unequal opportunities between groups to obtain such skills. In the case of immigrants racial discrimination not only accentuates disadvantageous life-chances for those without skills and qualifications, but may also deprive those *with* skills and qualifications of the rewards enjoyed by comparable white workers (particularly in the non-manual strata). This is particularly true for Asians. As the Community Relations Commission (1977, p. 11) says:

> The job levels held by minority men are not equal to those of white men with the same level of educational qualification, even when allowance is made for a possible difference of standard between education in this country and in Asia.

As Smith (1977) has shown, even where coloured workers

hold the same job levels as indigenous whites, from professional to unskilled manual, on average whites are paid more. Most coloured workers, of course, are concentrated in the manual occupational strata: whereas only 18 per cent of white males occupy semi- and *unskilled* manual positions, 26 per cent of East African Asians, 32 per cent of West Indians, 36 per cent of Indians and 58 per cent of Pakistanis in Britain are to be found there. Many of these workers are not 'immigrants' in the strict sense of the word. The use of the term 'immigrant' can be misleading because a significant proportion of coloured people in Britain were born in the country and hence are citizens by birth. However, the statistics do not always enable us to distinguish between recent immigrants, long-term residents and other coloured people.

Income level is only one, albeit very important, factor determining life-chances for coloured workers. As the Community Relations Commission argues, a 'cluster of multiple deprivation' can be found. By way of example the Commission (1977, pp. 15–16) refers to Smith's finding that:

> Asians who speak little or no English were found to have low status jobs with few promotion prospects and low wages, to live in an extended family (which led to a high rate of dependants to wage-earners, and tended towards overcrowding in housing), and to occupy poor-quality housing with no, or shared, amenities for which their payments in rent or mortgages were high.

Why do coloured workers experience this disadvantaged position? Racial prejudice against them by indigenous whites clearly exists but it is not the primary factor: it would be naive to suggest that racial disadvantages could be overcome by removing ignorance and language barriers between white and black. Nevertheless, prejudice, as acknowledged earlier, does play an important role in sustaining and legitimating racial exploitation. Prejudicial attitudes tend to be self-confirming, inasmuch as by encouraging discrimination against a coloured group members of this group are forced into subordinate positions which are then taken to be 'proof' of the group's inferiority. A similar process was seen to operate in the case of the poor. As Castles and Kosack (1973, p. 458) remark: 'This vicious circle helps to prevent the group from improving its situation and gaining equality with the dominant group.'

In general, Castles and Kosack argue that prejudice serves three functions: (i) it conceals and yet legitimates the exploitation of coloured labourers by asserting their racial inferiority; (ii) it helps to divert attention from the real economic destructiveness of capitalism that affects all by placing the blame on coloureds for, among other things, job scarcity; and (iii) it may be used by indigenous workers themselves to protect their position in the labour market — employers and government may be supported by indigenous workers in the implementation of discriminatory and exploitative measures against competing coloured workers, as has happened in both Britain and South Africa. In Britain, as in other countries, prejudice has been channelled into organised political movements usually of an extreme right-wing disposition: the National Front party is the prime British example. The Front promotes a fascist political programme through the ideological guise of a fervent British patriotism. It actively seeks the repatriation of all black workers and their families to keep Britain 'truly British'. Coloured workers are quite openly said to be 'inferior to British people', to be 'taking our jobs', or to be 'scroungers'. Such myths have unfortunately been believed by certain sectors of the electorate, in particular unemployed working-class youth, though recently support for the Front has declined because of opposition from people of all classes, young and old, who want no truck with fascism.

Despite the opposition to groups like the National Front, and the inter-racial communication and perhaps solidarity this has generated, coloured workers in Britain still lack adequate support from fellow white British workers. Those coloured people who become low-paid workers concentrated in the public service, textile and foundry industries do so because of their economic and political weakness. However, coloured immigrants should not be treated as a homogenous group: newcomers arrive bearing with them differing socio-economic backgrounds and, as we shall see, enter on different legal terms. Those with qualifications and fluency in English have a better chance of gaining access to higher rewards than others (despite the fact that, as we have seen, the level of their rewards may be lower than that received by white workers in similar jobs). The majority of Commonwealth members, however, who enter Britain lack qualifications, knowledge of welfare rights, and all, since 1971, unless dependants of male immigrants already settled here, are denied 'immigrant' status, being treated now as 'migrant workers' even though they may hold a British passport. Moreover, a large proportion of coloured immigrants have been recruited to low-paid jobs in industrial areas which typically have had weak trade unions: in the textile industry, for example, they are concentrated in the combing and spinning sectors. Furthermore, in industries with traditionally strong trade unions, coloured membership and representation has been relatively low. Trade-union officials and shop stewards are more likely to seek maximum earnings for their own — typically *white* — members. As such they have been able to organise and control the distribution of overtime and shift-work in the interests of their own members' pay packets, as well as using the principle of the closed shop against both white and black non-members.

Changes in the legal status of immigrants

In 1958 serious race riots in Notting Hill, London, and in other British cities were one factor behind the introduction in 1962 of an Act of Parliament restricting immigration from the Commonwealth. The disturbances demonstrated that the economic benefits of importing cheap labour from the colonies or ex-colonies ('cheap' because the host country had not had to bear the expense of supporting or educating the labour force) had to be weighed against the social cost of political and industrial unrest among the indigenous labour force, certain sectors of which saw immigrants as a threat to their own employment and housing opportunities. The 1962 Act was a significant step in the process of redefining the status of the immigrant from that of Commonwealth citizen to that of migrant labourer. Banton (1972, p. 72) has pointed out that the British labour shortage did not need to be met by immigrants from Jamaica or the Punjab:

They could have come from Turkey, Spain, Iran or Brazil. That they did not was due chiefly to the Imperial connection. Britain had given her citizenship to people overseas, conferring upon them the right to enter the mother country freely. They did not ask for this right. They were given it as part of a policy British governments chose to pursue.

The 1962 Act withdrew this right of entry for Commonwealth immigrants, as did subsequent legislation (1968) for black UK passport holders without parents or grandparents resident in Britain.

The 1971 Immigration Act finally put an end to any settlement and put all Commonwealth citizens on a par with aliens. Immigrants could only enter this country on a permit to do a specific job in a specific place for a period, initially at least, of not more than twelve months. The government had to give its permission before the original job could be changed, so immigrants were dependent upon employers' recommendations and were thus severely restricted in their industrial and political activities. Like any other foreigner, they might apply for UK citizenship after four years provided that they had been of good behaviour. However, it was also possible for the Home Secretary to deport them if it was 'conducive to the public good as being in the interest of national security or of the relations between the UK and any other country or for other reasons of a political nature'.

So there is no longer such a person as a 'Commonwealth immigrant'. Those who came to this country from the Commonwealth before the 1971 Act came into force (January 1973) are not immigrants but 'black settlers'. Those who came afterwards are neither settlers nor immigrants; they are simply migrant workers, and their position, correspondingly, is a very weak one.

The government was not just concerned with introducing legislation to curb immigration during this period, but also introduced anti-discriminatory legislation and policies designed to help integration. It has long been assumed that one cannot legislate against prejudice but that one can legislate against discrimination.

The first legislation designed to combat racial discrimina-

tion was the Race Relations Act of 1965, which also set up
'conciliation machinery' to deal with complaints of discrimination. This brought into existence the Race Relations Board.
Under the terms of the Act the practice of discrimination was
made unlawful in public places, e.g. in hotels, restaurants,
places of entertainment or on public transport. It was also
made an offence to place discriminatory restrictions on the
disposal of leases on property, or to stir up racial hatred by
means of speech or written matter.

The Race Relations Act of 1968 extended the provisions
of the 1965 Act to cover a wider field, notably in the spheres
of housing, accommodation and employment, forbidding discrimination generally in the provision of goods, facilities or
services to the public.

Despite being motivationally well intentioned, government
legislation against discrimination cannot overcome the disadvantaged position of the coloured population in Britain: the
law implies that the 'problem' for blacks is racial prejudice,
thereby reducing the cause of disadvantage to cultural, ideological or psychological processes. Certainly such processes
exist in the form of prejudice, but they arise out of, legitimise
and reproduce a structure of inequality that works against
the objective interests of black British men and women. In
theory, anti-discriminatory legislation gives everyone the legal
right to an equal opportunity to be upwardly mobile; but
equal opportunity does not imply equal chance (see also
Chapter 7 on education). Hence those who adopt a radical
perspective in sociology argue that state legislation is simply
a cosmetic device designed to prevent unrest, that divisions
within the working class between white and black work to
the benefit of capital, and thus that racial harmony is impossible until class conflict has been resolved. One need not
adopt this perspective to recognise the fundamental weakness
of government action: it is frequently pointed out that the
anti-discrimination Acts are unenforceable in practice. The
coloured population, for example, may not be aware of their
rights, may not recognise discrimination against them when it
occurs, and if they do may be unwilling to enter into a lengthy
complaints procedure through the courts. Furthermore, it is
probable that the major source of inequality — disadvant-

ageous life-chances — is likely to engender resignation rather than aspirations for upward mobility among blacks; where this acquiesence occurs, the true extent of the structural constraints on black life-chances remains concealed.

Legislation against discrimination is also proposed with a view towards 'integration' and 'assimilation'. But such notions need close scrutiny: Does 'integration' mean a process through which subordinate racial groups come to accept as legitimate the authority and advantages of the dominant group in society? Or does integration imply a coming together of groups culturally and economically through a process of adaptation, conflict, or competition? Perhaps 'integration', if it occurs anywhere at all, involves a combination of all these processes?

3.5   THE THIRD WORLD

As we have seen, racial discrimination is associated with the exploitation of cheap immigrant labour, a process that has some of its roots in the colonial past. While exploitation of coloured minorities has occurred in Britain and elsewhere in Europe, what about the countries they have come from, for the most part countries which are part of that group collectively known as 'the Third World'? This term derives from the following classification: the 'First World' refers to the advanced capitalist sectors of the world economy and conventionally includes the USA, the United Kingdom, Japan and Western Europe; the 'Second World' refers to the communist industrialised countries like the Soviet Union, Poland, and East Germany; and finally, the 'Third World' refers to the poor, virtually non-industrialised countries of Latin America, Africa and Asia.

Just as we have talked about 'life-chances' being unequally distributed within a society — when subordinate groups pay for the rewards enjoyed by the dominant — so there are unequal life-chances of an international order. The gap between rich and poor countries is rarely discussed or examined in the popular media of advanced countries. It is only perhaps when appeals for money are made by groups such as OXFAM or Save the Children that for a brief moment Westerners are

mindful of poverty in the world. Yet three out of every four
people in the world live in poor countries, and these countries
receive only a fifth of the world's income. One in every four
children in poor countries dies under the age of 5. Children
who suffer from acute malnutrition are just one, horrific,
symptom of the chronic *structural* poverty of the Third
World.

The relative position of Third World countries in the
world's 'development' hierarchy is normally assessed by comparing international rates of manufacturing and agricultural
output, the proportion of the labour force employed in each
sector, the level of technology, the development of education,
the ratio between imports and exports, and the distribution
of consumer goods such as motor-cars and radios. Table 3.1
illustrates the sort of statistical information that this type of
quantitative analysis provides.

TABLE 3.1
Economic development by continent

	Average per capita income (US $)		Consumption of energy (kWh) per capita
	1970	1976	1971
Latin America	550	1,110	832
Africa	190	420	343
North America	4,200	7,020	8,080
Western Europe	2,240	4,840	3,996
Asia	400	1,770	527

Source: *United Nations Statistical Yearbook*, New York, 1978.

The figures in Table 3.1 highlight the development gap
between rich and poor sectors of the world economy. Yet
some statistical sources suggest that within the poorer sectors
growth has occurred over the past twenty years, particularly
in terms of gross national product, even to the extent that *as
a whole* their rate of growth has been higher than that of the

developed countries combined. Some interpret this as a sign that Third World countries are finally beginning to win the battle against underdevelopment (Bauer, 1971; Warren, 1973). Yet overall relative growth rates tell us little about the real inequalities in the world: during the 1960s and 1970s, despite suffering some major crises in production and profitability (especially through the 'oil crisis' of 1973-4), the advanced sectors of the world economy continued to *accelerate* away from the less developed regions. In absolute terms the gap between rich and poor is expanding daily.

Crude statistical measures of whatever little growth there has been in the Third World do not tell us anything about the *character* of this growth. As we shall see, the kind of industrial expansion in less developed countries is very different from that which occurred in the industrialisation of the capitalist sector of the world economy. Thus, for example, there is no reason to assume that capital investment, whether domestically sponsored through official or private institutions or originating overseas from foreign corporations or development agencies, promotes economic growth in poor countries. The simple presence of economic resources such as capital, technology and labour within a country is a necessary but not sufficient condition for its development. The poor country needs to be able to *control* these through its state or class institutions: however, usually sufficient control (particularly over transnational corporations) is lacking, a factor which is one of the most important political aspects reproducing the subordination and stagnation of poor countries; it is, in part, an expression of the weakness of *both* the dominant *and* subordinate classes within them.

Does this weakness derive from an inherent incapacity of people in the Third World to develop their societies towards modern industrialisation? There is a popular view that Third World members lack 'planning' and 'know-how' and are unable to channel their energies into useful enterprise, apart from blindly producing more and more mouths to feed. Such a view, however, merely draws attention to superficial and somewhat caricatured features of the contemporary Third World. Despite its inadequacies, however, a more elaborate version of this popular thesis can be found within sociological

theory itself. There is a school of thought, known as 'modernisation theory', which claims that one of the principal reasons
why the Third World is underdeveloped is that many of its
countries have distinctive cultural characteristics that block
or hinder economic growth and political stability. These
societies have been said to be suffused by values of 'traditionalism' that promote backward-looking and fatalistic
attitudes, attitudes that do not encourage innovation, enterprise or achievement. Modernisation theory puts forward the
ideas that less developed societies can become more developed
or 'modern' by being exposed to the values and norms of
advanced societies, through communication, trade, and so
on. Many development economists — such as Rostow — have
argued strongly for the introduction and diffusion of Western
economic, social and political institutions in the Third World
as *necessary* conditions for growth. Rostow (1960) has
claimed that the development of *all* societies can be understood in terms of a logical, continual progression through
'stages' of growth.

Other theorists, such as McClelland (1967) and Lerner
(1964), who adopt a socio-psychological perspective, have
gone so far as to suggest training courses for Third World elites
to ensure that they develop the appropriate entrepreneurial
values and attitudes. In general, this assumes that in the long
term developing societies will inevitably become more and
more like the already advanced industrial countries of the
globe, as their institutions and values are reorganised and
adapted to favour modernity.

Against this, now much criticised, theory there is another
school of thought that argues that one cannot understand
Third World poverty through identifying alleged deficiencies
in poor countries' cultural make-up; instead, it is claimed
that Third World underdevelopment is a socio-economic condition *brought about* by processes associated with the growth
of North Atlantic countries over the past century and more.
This position has been adopted by some neo-Marxist and
radical economists and sociologists such as Frank (1971), dos
Santos (1969), Laclau (1971, 1977) and Kay (1975). They
see the development and underdevelopment of societies as
simultaneously and mutually produced manifestations of the

same global historical process. Not only does the modernisation thesis neglect the imperialism of the last few hundred years but it also seems to present development as a process that takes place within discrete, isolated, social systems. The decisive strength of the radical perspective is its *global* viewpoint. We now examine the historical analysis on which this perspective is based.

Prior to the specifically European origins of capitalism, most societies in the world had experienced a greater or lesser degree of development in their agricultural sectors. The earliest of the socio-economic alterations that took place in Europe were the advent of *herding* and *crop production*. These developments allowed producers for the first time to overcome purely subsistence farming, the prominent form of production in neolithic times. Through crop farming, families and village clans could produce a certain amount of surplus food which could be then traded in a *market*. The later development of the *money* market was an important factor stimulating trade and economic growth. The surplus allowed an increasing population to be fed, clothed, housed, and to remain in relatively stable sites or regions. However, as was seen in Chapter 2, the surplus has normally been controlled and owned by various dominating classes.

These general technological and social transformations developed unevenly in most areas of the 'primitive' and 'medieval' worlds — which were subject to varying degrees of political unification and subordination by a progression of world empires within and across the continents: Roman, Chinese, Mogul, Aztec and Zulu. Yet the greatest power was to assert itself in northern Europe, and initially in Britain: industrial capitalism. Capitalism has proved to be a greater force for global interdependence and domination than any world empire has ever been (Wallerstein, 1974).

Three factors seem to have been crucial in promoting the emergence of the capitalist economy in Europe: private property, the commercialisation of agriculture, and wage labour, which gradually allowed a greater accumulation of surplus through *more productive* work rather than, as in feudalism, through simply *more work* (Fine, 1978). In Britain the capital accumulation that these factors promoted encouraged not only an increasingly productive and profitable agricultural sector but also a more rational and machine-based form of farming. It was a historically short but massively significant step to develop machinery to actually manufacture goods in workshops and factories; the industrial revolution that was to guarantee the dominance of capitalism in Europe was initiated by the British bourgeoisie towards the end of the eighteenth century (Nairn, 1977). British and, later, French and Dutch capitalism rose on the profitability of domestic manufacturing. But this was not all: the financial investment and materials used by European industry derived from external sources as well.

It is no accident that India plays cricket or West Africans speak French: these are just two legacies of *colonialism*. The wealth of West European economies — particularly their mineral wealth — was as much the result of colonial exploitation (especially in southern Africa) as it was a reflection of the 'native wit' of the English, French or Dutch. By military and political domination the capitalist states established a monopoly of international trade that allowed 'merchant capitalism' to flourish and the 'primitive accumulation' of capital to ensue: profits were made by buccaneering on the high seas and the plundering of Africa, Asia and Latin America. This account implies the need to integrate into one historical analysis the development of capitalism that has taken place in the advanced sectors and the destructive consequences of this development for other sectors we now call 'the Third World'.

Colonialism exploited not simply natural but also human resources. The work of Williams (1972), Dumont (1966) and Rodney (1972) catalogues the colonial promotion of the slave trade in Africa. During the seventeenth and eighteenth centuries there developed what is known as the 'triangular trade' system whereby European (particularly British) manufactured goods (often of inferior quality) were exchanged at a profit in the colonies in exchange for African Negroes, who in turn were traded as slaves for produce in the Americas. It is important to note that profits were made at every stage of the triangular transaction and inevitably encouraged capital accumulation in England. It is estimated that between 1450 and 1870 nearly twenty million male and female Africans between the ages of 15 and 35 were sold as slaves. This figure does not take into account the number who died in transit to the Americas on the slave ships. Clearly, the slave trade had a major demographic effect on Africa, draining the continent of its skilled labour power. British, French and Dutch mining in South Africa and the then Rhodesia complemented the drain on Africa's human resources: the gold and copper mines took able-bodied young men from the rural areas, which, consequently populated for the most part by older men, children and women, were unable to sustain any real level of agricultural productivity.

As might be expected, those regions that experienced the full force of European colonialism suffered economic *and* political distortion. Pre-existing tribal boundaries and trade routes in both Latin America and Africa were rapidly destroyed by the slave trade and by the establishment of coastal ports and towns by European merchants and settlers linked together by the shortest possible navigable route that paid little or no attention to tribal territories. Prior to colonial expansion, most Third World societies had political systems that were as complex and advanced as most of those in feudal Europe, giving the lie to the notion of a 'backward', traditional culture.

A case study: the Volta River project

An excellent illustration of the weakness and dependency of the Third World is provided by Lanning and Mueller (1979) in their account of the Volta River project in Ghana. The reader is urged to consult the original text (pp. 429–35) for full details. The project envisaged a great dam on the River Volta which besides providing hydro-electric power for Ghana could be used to (i) power the development of a local alumina smelter and aluminium factory which could use the massive deposits of bauxite discovered nearby, (ii) enable a large-scale irrigation system to be built, and (iii) promote the growth of a fishing industry on the lake formed by the dam.

Relying on foreign investment and technology to initiate the project, President Nkrumah approached the World Bank,

the US government and the American firm the Kaiser Cor-
poration in 1958. Kaiser was chartered to assess the technical
and financial viability of the scheme; its report recommended
that the budget could be cut by £60 million and that the fishing and irrigation schemes be dropped. But as Lanning and
Mueller (1979, p. 430) note, 'most important of all, there
was to be no integrated aluminium complex using Ghanaian
bauxite. The smelter would use imported alumina instead.
Kaiser estimated that alumina would have to be imported for
at least ten years. The Ghanaians were appalled.' Yet Nkrumah
was convinced of the need for the project if Ghana was to
have any hope of developing and so continued to seek funds
from the World Bank and Kaiser. Financial backing for the
project and Kaiser's active participation only came when
Ghana agreed to allow Kaiser to develop an aluminium factory
using *imported* alumina — to be run on very cheap electricity
from the dam. Kaiser agreed that once hydro-electric power
became available it would buy 300,000kW of Volta electricity
per day for thirty years. But the unit costs Kaiser demanded
and won were so low that Ghana's actual income from the
sale was nothing like what had been expected, while Kaiser's
profits were ensured. Electricity is the most expensive part of
the production of aluminium (accounting for 60 per cent of
total cost) when, by electrolytic process, alumina is converted
to aluminium. Hence, the end-result: 'The low cost of the
electricity meant that it was more profitable for Kaiser to
import Jamaican bauxite, process it into alumina in the US,
and then to tranship the alumina to Ghana for smelting into
aluminium, than to develop Ghana's Kibi bauxite deposits.'
In 1980 there was still no alumina plant in Ghana and the
bauxite reserves which could sustain such a plant for at least
250 years remained underdeveloped.

Thus the Volta Dam project gives a good example of the
character of industrial development typical of many Third
World countries reliant on foreign capital: dependent, and
distorted, in the sense of lacking *full* development of the
industrial infrastructure. Without formal political control the
interests of the advanced sectors of capitalism in the world
economy can be sustained.

Most Third World countries want trade rather than aid in

an attempt to stimulate a domestic capital-goods industry, thereby relieving the problems caused by a shortage of foreign currency and overcome the reliance on primary products. However, there is little hope of this happening given the present trading relationship between the rich and poor countries, and there is little likelihood of the capitalist corporations giving preference to *manufactured* goods from the Third World. The formation of trading areas like the EEC tends to compound this problem: rather than opening up markets, the EEC has imposed a higher duty on imports from Third World countries than it has on rich countries within the bloc.

In short, modernisation is not dependent on the gradual unfolding of an evolutionary process of development or on the adaptation of cultural values (important though the latter may be). Rather, the radical perspective's historical foundation lends strength to the view that development is more dependent on the access to, and use of, political and economic power. As this is denied most Third World societies, many of them will remain underdeveloped, and where development occurs it is likely to be highly distorted.

3.6 CONCLUSION

This chapter has examined four forms of subordination, distinct in their concrete expression but sharing a basic similarity by virtue of their being a product of the dynamics of social stratification. All four, as we have seen, have in varying forums, academic and non-academic, been inaccurately depicted as the result of subordinate groups' particular cultural orientations. Disadvantage, whether experienced by the young, the poor, immigrant minorities or Third World countries, will not be overcome simply by attempting to change these groups' *outlook*. Too often the problems of these groups are seen in this way and dealt with on a piecemeal, partial and fragmentary basis via welfare and aid agencies. Instead, a solution can only be social, national and international, a matter of re-assessing and reorganising social priorities, and ultimately dependent on basic changes in socio-economic arrangements and ideologies.

NCES TO CHAPTER 3

(1972) *Racial Minorities*, London, Fontana.

Baran, P. A. and Sweezy, P. M. (1966) *Monopoly Capital*, Harmondsworth, Penguin.

Bauer, P. (1971) *Dissent on Development*, London, Weidenfeld & Nicolson.

Berger, P. and Berger, B. (1972) *Sociology*, New York, Basic Books.

Brake, M. (1979) *The Sociology of Youth Culture and Youth Subcultures*, London, Routledge & Kegan Paul.

Castles, S. and Kosack, G. (1973) *Immigrant Workers and Class Structure in Western Europe*, Oxford University Press.

Clarke, J. *et al.* (1976) 'Subcultures, Cultures and Class: a Theoretical Overview', in S. Hall and T. Jefferson (eds), *Resistance Through Rituals*, London, Hutchinson.

Clarke, J. and Jefferson, T. (1976) 'Working Class Youth Cultures', in G. Mungham and G. Pearson (eds), *Working Class Youth Cultures*, London, Routledge & Kegan Paul.

Coates, K. and Silburn, R. (1970) *Poverty: The Forgotten Englishmen*, Harmondsworth, Penguin.

Community Relations Commission (1977) *Urban Deprivation, Racial Inequality and Social Policy: A Report*, London, HMSO.

Dumont, R. (1966) *False Start in Africa*, London, Deutsch.

Dunning, E. (1972) 'Dynamics of Racial Stratification: Some Preliminary Observations', *Race*, vol. 13, no. 4.

Eisenstadt, S. (1956) *From Generation to Generation*, New York, Free Press.

Fine, B. (1978) 'On Underdeveloped Capitalism', *New Left Review*, vol. 109.

Frank, A. G. (1971) *Sociology of Development and the Underdevelopment of Sociology*, London, Pluto Press.

Gans, H. (1971) 'Poverty and Culture', in P. Townsend (ed.), *The Concept of Poverty*, London, Heinemann.

Kay, G. (1975) *Development and Underdevelopment: a Marxist Analysis*, London, Macmillan.

Laclau, E. (1971) 'Feudalism and Capitalism in Latin America', *New Left Review*, vol. 67.

Laclau, E. (1977) *Politics and Ideology in Marxist Theory*, London, New Left Books.

Lanning, G. and Mueller, H. (1979) *Africa Undermined*, Harmondsworth, Penguin.

Lerner, D. (1964) *The Passing of Traditional Society*, New York, Free Press.

Lewis, O. (1961) *Children of Sanchez*, New York, Random House.

Lewis, O. (1966) *La Vida*, New York, Random House.

Lockwood, D. (1970) 'Race, Conflict and Plural Society', in S. Zubaida (ed.), *Race and Racialism*, London, Tavistock.

McClelland, D. (1967) *The Achieving Society*, New York, Van Nostrand.

Miliband, R. (1974) 'Politics and Poverty', in D. Wedderburn (ed.), *Poverty, Inequality and Class Structure*, Cambridge University Press.

Mungham, G. and Pearson, G. (1976) 'Introduction: Troubled Youth, Troubling World', in G. Mungham and G. Pearson (eds), *Working Class Youth Cultures*, London, Routledge & Kegan Paul.

Murdock, G. and McCron, G. (1976) 'Youth and Class: the Career of a Confusion', in G. Mungham and G. Pearson (eds), *Working Class Youth Cultures*, London, Routledge & Kegan Paul.

Nairn, T. (1977) 'The Twilight of the British State', *New Left Review*, vol. 101–2.

Parsons, T. (1965) 'Why "Freedom Now", Not Yesterday', and 'Full Citizenship for the Negro American', in T. Parsons and K. B. Clark (eds), *The Negro American*, Boston, Houghton Mifflin.

Rex, J. (1970) 'The Concept of Race in Sociological Theory', in S. Zubaida (ed.), *Race and Racialism*, London, Tavistock.

Robins, D. and Cohen, P. (1978) *Knuckle Sandwich*, Harmondsworth, Penguin.

Rodney, W. (1972) *How Europe Underdeveloped Africa*, Paris, Bogle L'Ouverture.

Rostow, W. W. (1960) *The Stages of Economic Growth*, Cambridge University Press.

Santos, T. dos (1969) 'The Crisis of Development Theory and the Problem of Dependence in Latin America', *Siglio*, vol. 21.

Smith, D. (1977) *The Facts of Racial Disadvantage*, Harmondsworth, Penguin.

Sugarman, B. (1968) *Sociology*, London, Heinemann.

Taylor, I. (1971) 'Soccer Consciousness and Soccer Hooliganism', in S. Cohen (ed.), *Images of Deviance*, Harmondsworth, Penguin.

Wallerstein, I. (1974) *Modern World System*, New York, Academic Press.

Warren, W. (1973) 'Imperialism and Capitalist Industrialisation', *New Left Review*, vol. 81.

Westergaard, J. and Resler, H. (1975) *Class in a Capitalist Society*, London, Heinemann.

Williams, E. (1972) *Capitalism and Slavery*, London, Deutsch.

Willis, P. (1978) *Profane Culture*, London, Routledge & Kegan Paul.

4
Power and Politics

4.1 INTRODUCTION: THE STUDY OF POLITICS

Attempts to say what politics is may appear at first sight unnecessarily pedantic: we all 'know' what politics is about. In everyday popular usage, politics is seen as being about 'Parliament', 'the government', 'the parties', 'elections', 'voting', and endless debates and arguments which produce a month of yawns for every day of excitement. Thus, the common-sense view of what constitutes politics is the misleadingly limited and circular one of 'what politicians do'.

This view is particularly prevalent in stable liberal-democratic societies like Britain or America, where its validity often seems self-evident. But purely on a factual level, this view is highly limited, ethnocentric and lacking in historical perspective — politics is also about civil war, guerilla movements, revolutions, military coups and assassinations, as well as about ballot boxes and speeches in the House of Commons or the Senate. All societies have some sort of political organisation or structure which does not necessarily take the form with which we are familiar in the West — a form which, in any case, is of only relatively recent origin.

So, the apparently easy and straightforward exercise of defining what politics is requires more systematic attention if we are to understand political structures and processes sociologically. Indeed, a sociological view of politics is and must be distinguishable from common-sense approaches and from other academic approaches, particularly those of political theorists and philosophers and political scientists. Political theorists and philosophers in the past essentially relied on a deductive approach to politics, in which certain assumptions were made about man's political and social 'instincts' and behaviour, from which theories about the state and the role of the individual in political action were deduced, only rarely supplemented by systematic empirical observation or analysis. This essentially speculative approach can be contrasted with the descriptive approach of the political scientist, who tends to concentrate attention on the systematic description of the formal political framework, the organisation and the operation of the machinery of government: that is, how political and administrative institutions of the state — Parliament, the Civil Service, and so on — work and have developed.

A sociological conception of politics rejects this approach in favour of a much broader definition, one which regards the study of the machinery of government as inadequate and too narrow, not necessarily to be ignored but representing merely *one* variable in the stuff of politics. For example, the politics of the Nixon presidency in the USA are hardly 'understandable' solely by a knowledge of the American constitution and governmental system — quite the reverse, in fact!

Sociological analysis of politics requires, firstly, the study of political behaviour within a *social* context, the relation of politics to the entire social structure in which it is embedded. But more than this, it also involves the recognition that 'politics' is potentially present in *all* social relationships, in that politics essentially involves the *exercise of power*. As Worsley (1964, pp. 16–17) says: 'We can be said to act politically when we exercise constraint on others to behave as we want them to . . . The exercise of constraint in any relationship is political.'

So, political behaviour is essentially 'power behaviour', not by any means confined to particular governmental institutions or forms, but present in any social situation. Thus, political decisions are being made, and hence power is being exercised, not only when taxation laws are changed by parliaments or when Nazis herd people into concentration camps, but also when parents forbid their daughter to attend an all-night party or when an employer sacks his workers. In this sense, then, almost all areas of social life involve potential political elements, so that *politics* cannot be seen as involving merely 'what politicians do', but is to be seen as a *process involving the exercise of control, constraint and coercion in society*. Any unequal relationship has political dimensions, and since unequal relationships exist throughout social life, politics cannot simply be regarded as a separate realm of boring institutions and politicians, and any search for patterns in social life must also involve a search for patterns in the distribution of power. A sociological approach to politics, then, implies the analysis of the operation of power in social contexts and relationships, and its consequences for social action and stability. Of course, while we all have some power, not all power relations are of equal significance, and we shall be discussing power relations at the societal level.

Power to most people seems distant and detached from their lives, 'not my concern'. We have suggested that this is not realistic to the sociologist looking in from the outside, since relationships of domination and subordination exist throughout society. But the very fact that individuals are often unable to see questions of power as permeating their lives is interesting in itself and raises the very important question of why they should accept domination and the limitations imposed on their lives by others.

At first sight, this may seem a foolish question — the obvious answer is that they may have no real choice: employees obey employers because they need to maintain income, peasants obey landlords because they must pay their rents and debts. They conform because of their *dependence* on others and because the powers that be may be able to impose *sanctions* on them: in other words, the powerful may be able to coerce the subordinates into compliance. But this does not necessarily *guarantee* the successful imposition of the will of the powerful, for although they have coercive resources at their disposal, 'naked' coercive power alone may not be sufficient to achieve compliance. They need to generate willing compliance. Hence, the powerful try to claim legitimacy for their power, so that it is acknowledged and accepted in the eyes of their subordinates and institutionalised in social arrangements. Powerful groups in society attempt to influence the ideas of those below them through the dissemination of *ideology*, to persuade the majority that their subordinate position is normal and natural and that they, the powerful, have the right to command power and influence. Such claims may rest on a variety of foundations: that such a distribution of power has always traditionally existed, that it is a divinely ordained arrangement, that the holders of power possess intrinsic ruling skills or superior social status, or whatever.

In this way, then, unequal power relations persist not simply because of the weakness of subordinate groups, but also because of the *perceptions* and *expectations* which these groups have of their relationship with those holding power. These perceptions are not merely abstract, 'philosophical' ideas but are sociological phenomena in themselves, because they are socially constructed and sustained, and because they may shape the behaviour of subordinate groups and hence contribute directly and significantly to power relations and political stability. If a crucial question for sociologists is how conformity can be explained in a context of unequal power relations, then they have to understand the bases on which power is held and how individuals and groups 'see' their political roles.

So, in the first part of this chapter we will be concerned with analysing and explaining the way in which power is distributed in contemporary capitalist society, and with the political behaviour of the powerful and the powerless. Our major concern in the latter part of the chapter will be with the relationship between political consciousness and behaviour, and with the origins of political ideas and beliefs and their effects on political action — whether this be choosing who to vote for, or rising up in revolution.

4.2 THE RISE OF THE MODERN STATE

States and stateless societies

In our kind of society, political activities take place within the framework called the *state*, but the state is by no means a universal feature of all societies, nor has there always been a state in societies which today have one. In analysing the political organisation of primitive societies, anthropologists have generally found it useful to view political systems in terms of a continuum, with well developed states of the sort we live in at one end, and stateless, or acephalous, societies at the other.

Although societies possessing statelike institutions can vary greatly, they tend to exhibit certain shared characteristics. Crucially there is always some kind of central authority which rules over a given territory and which has the power to force those over whom it rules to obey. So whether they be royalty, military leaders, elected leaders or whatever, as Lewis (1976, p. 315) puts it, 'the ultimate test of a ruler's authority is . . . whether he possesses the power of life or death over his subjects'. However, this capacity to coerce is hardly ever directly achieved by the central authority, but by its delegation to the members of some kind of administrative machinery or other, e.g. to military, bureaucratic or religious functionaries. Also, there is usually some kind of established procedure for the transference of power through time, for state rule involves the continuity of office. Again, this can take place on different grounds – leaders can be elected, or can claim divine appointment, or can inherit from their kin, and so on. Finally, the existence of the state usually implies the existence of structured inequality characterised by sharp cleavages between groups not only of prestige and wealth, but of power too. Political control, then, is ultimately achieved by the use of, or the possibility of the use of, force, with the control of the instruments of such coercion in the hands of the occupants of specialised and differentiated political statuses.

Forms of the state in capitalist society

The rise of capitalism in Western Europe is associated with the rise of centralised, specialised state institutions employing increasingly complex and sophisticated techniques of administration and social control. Paradoxically, however, this complex modern state has developed out of a feudal political structure which was extremely primitive in comparison with ancient centralised states such as those of Egypt or of the Incas.

As we saw in Chapter 2, the feudalism of medieval Europe

was characterised by an extreme fragmentation of political power and production. Feudalism was based on the country-side, dependent upon agrarian production, with a dominant class of feudal lords monopolising economic and political control over localised areas. Whilst there was, theoretically, a hierarchy of allegiance from lower to higher lords and ultimately to the king, this was a fluid system of military alliances which allowed no stable centre of political power to exist. Ultimately based on conquest, the power of the local lord depended on his ability to obtain surplus labour or produce from his serfs, and on his ability to defend his area of land. Thus, larger states were only conglomerates of these local areas of domi-nation, and the great empires of Eastern and Central Europe were little more than loose federations of principalities. Only with the pacification of large areas by dominant lords could wider trade and larger markets emerge. The decline of feudal arrangements was strongly associated with the rise of mili-tarily successful monarchs supported by lords sufficiently powerful to claim dominance over large areas, and with the rise of towns as trading centres, which led to the development in importance of merchants and manufacturers. The inde-pendence of the town introduced an economic dynamism which undermined the rural base of feudalism, and paved the way for the emergence of new, economically powerful classes and a landless class of wage labourers.

Thus, by the sixteenth century in Britain and the seven-teenth century in Europe, a far more centralised form of political domination emerged with the development of abso-lutist monarchies, which imposed laws and taxes over their territory and enforced them by the central monopolisation of the use of force. Clearly, this emergent central administra-tion needed functionaries to run it, and initially these were powerful men, trusted as allies of the monarch. Gradually, they were replaced by administrators whose power depended only upon their official position and not upon their personal military power or wealth. Professional lawyers became more important as codifiers and modifiers of a recorded body of law, replacing arbitrary rule by nobles or local customary laws.

These features show the trend towards a *centralisation of*

power and a *rationalisation* of politics. The state comes to be the only legitimate authority in a territory, and its administration increasingly operates on set principles and procedures. The trend to rational administration by officials culminates in bureaucracy and in the constitutional nation-state. As Poggi (1978, p. 93) defines it,

> there is a unity of the State's territory, which comes to be grounded as much as possible by a continuous geographical frontier that is militarily defensible. There is a single currency and a unified fiscal system. Generally there is a single 'national' language . . . Finally there is a unified legal system that allows alternative juridical traditions to maintain validity only in peripheral areas and for limited purposes.

However, this constitutional nation-state need *not* be democratic: European states became 'fully' democratic, that is, with votes for all citizens and free political association, only in the twentieth or the late nineteenth century. This development followed earlier struggles for representation within these states by the new economic groups, above all the bourgeoisie — the merchants, traders and manufacturers. However, such struggles came at different times with varying degrees of success. In all cases, the constitutional nation-state still aided the rise of capitalism because it maintained peace, protected property rights and contracts, protected foreign trade, and often regulated money as a means of exchange, all of which aided trade and the development of markets.

At the same time, the growing bourgeoisie could be threatened by this centralised state if it was not represented in it, and if the monarch tried to tax or regulate trade for his own purposes. In much of Europe, this led to struggles by the bourgeoisie (in alliance with other dissatisfied social groups) to gain political representation or to reverse a slide back to personal absolutism by the monarch. The seventeenth-century struggles in England are often seen as establishing the conditions for capitalist expansion through the winning of dominance for Parliament and the constitutional regulation of the monarchy. In France, the developments came later but perhaps went further with the French Revolution and the construction of a republic and the new constitution.

The contrast between English and German roads to capitalist development is highly significant. The English road gradually established the principles of representative liberal democracy, as first the commercialised land-owners, then the industrialists, and finally the working class gradually won access to state power and slowly established notions of individual citizenship and rights of political expression. This 'evolution' was punctuated by struggle and conflict, but there is still a marked contrast with the German route, where the political failure of the bourgeoisie led to a continuing 'bureaucratic absolutism' lasting until the end of the First World War. The central state made concessions to the growing working class and organised the growth of industrialised capitalism, but democratic institutions and principles were weak and had extremely shallow roots. Thus, in Germany and elsewhere in Europe, one road to capitalist development and expansion in the twentieth century was authoritarian and undemocratic, gaining its ultimate expression in fascism. In Germany, full liberal democracy has only been stabilised in its Western portion since the Second World War; and this form of state is only now emerging in Portugal and Spain after the recent downfall of fascistic regimes. There is no natural and inevitable link between liberal democracy and capitalism, even though it is now the dominant form of regime in Western Europe. Elsewhere in the world, the establishment of capitalism has gone together with very different kinds of state.

Outside Europe and North America, capitalism has normally been imposed or 'grafted on to' a domestic economy by the expansion of the European economies. As producers of raw materials, as recipients of foreign goods, or as sites for the establishment of production, these nations have often experienced political domination as well as economic domination, with a variety of forms of regime imposed, ranging from imitations of the British constitution to foreign-funded military dictatorships. What is not surprising is the degree of instability characterising many such regimes, for they are not normally founded on the internal development of social and economic institutions, but on imported patterns instituted and run by foreign-sponsored elites dependent on the support of an external foreign power. Where politics is founded on the support of social groups in the society, these groups are frequently profoundly divided, not only by economic position but by language, cultures and territorial loyalty.

Thus, from the above discussion we can conclude that the state in capitalist society has no 'natural' or 'normal' form. Liberal-democratic regimes have developed slowly in America and in some European societies and have been stabilised in others only since 1945. It is not inevitable that these will always remain stable, or that liberal democracy will be established elsewhere in the world, particularly in nations with a peripheral position in the world economic system. What *is* established and growing, however, is the bureaucratic, centralised nation-state.

4.3 THEORIES OF THE DISTRIBUTION OF POWER IN MODERN WESTERN SOCIETY

One of the most distinctive features of Western pre-industrial societies was the grossly asymmetrical distribution of power. In feudal and absolutist Europe, power resided preponderantly in the hands of the barons and large landowners, while the mass of the population who formed the peasantry were merely passive pawns, acted upon rather than acting politically: the owners of the means of production monopolised power and effectively ruled unchallenged.

As we have just seen, the gradual development of commercial agriculture and the advent of industrialisation brought with them extensive and profound changes, spawning new systems of production, new socio-economic relationships and the emergence of new classes and interests, and while the French Revolution by no means gave 'power to the people', it seriously undermined the unquestioned legitimacy of power enjoyed by an aristocratic upper class.

The social, economic and political relations of nineteenth-century industrial society, then, rested less and less on the traditional norms and values of a feudal agricultural system: the new industrial bourgeoisie were keen to translate their economic power into political influence, while the industrial working class began to organise themselves to enhance the representation of their interests. In America and Britain and the rest of Europe (though by no means simultaneously or after an identical pattern), the industrial bourgeoisie came to occupy places in the legislatures, the right to vote was gradually extended, mass-based political parties emerged, and the right of groups of workers to organise occupationally for purposes of bargaining and representation was secured. Thus, a gradual process of democratisation was apparently taking place, the end-product of which would eventually be a system of liberal democracy, in which all classes and groups would have equal rights of participation and opportunity to influence — a 'democratic revolution', in fact.

Such an optimistic conception, however, was not shared universally: the early political sociologists largely remained unconvinced that any 'democratic revolution' had occurred or was imminent, despite the changes which were taking place. The reality for, on the one hand, Pareto and Mosca, and, on the other, Marx, was that power was still effectively concentrated in the hands of a few, with little or no diffusion having occurred. While we shall see shortly that their analysis of the fact differed fundamentally, they were united in their view of nineteenth-century European societies as characterised by a concentration of power.

The Marxist view

Marx sees power relationships as being built into the very structure of society, whose principal feature is the existence of opposed classes. Thus, class domination and subordination are the central dynamics and cornerstones of the Marxist conception of politics and the distribution and operation of power. The distribution of power and patterns of political conflict are a reflection of the relationships of domination and subordination determined predominantly by the economic arrangements of society (a condition resolvable only by the restructuring of these economic arrangements).

We saw in Chapter 2 that Marx analyses social structures in terms of the *mode of production*, the central element of which is the particular form of the *relations of production*. For Marx, production is organised socially in ways which have always created classes with opposed interests and un-equal resources of power: one class will dominate others through economic exploitation. For example, in the slave mode of production in the Deep South of the USA, the slave-owner not only took all the profit from the sale of the cotton grown on his plantation, but also maintained complete con-trol over the work process. Not only did he direct the work activities, but he also prevented slaves from working and living elsewhere. This is a very stark example of economic power, but Marx argued that the relation of exploitation and domination merely took different forms in different (pre-socialist) modes of production.

So, economic power and political power are inevitably linked through the prime importance which Marx attributes to the economic base of society in shaping social and political arrangements and forms. The possession of political power is the direct outcome of the nature of the class structure, a function of a group's relation to the means of production — the class controlling the means of production wields effective political power and is of necessity a ruling class.

Power, then, is *class* power, a resource concentrated in the hands of a particular class, which that class can use to main-tain and enhance its dominant position in society, a position achieved by economic exploitation. So, the concentration of political power and a process of political domination and class conflict are inherent in class societies and rooted in the process of economic exploitation, whereby the dominant economic class extracts maximum surplus value from the labour force.

This equation of political power with economic power does not easily fit in with what is popularly regarded by the man in the street as 'political power': that is, the power to legislate and enforce the law, to raise taxes, to declare war, and so on. It is frequently taken for granted that these 'poli-tical' activities take place within a separate institution, the state, which is seen as being set above the conflicts and squabbles of the rest of society. It is an institution where a collective communal interest can be served: the state can pursue the common good and reconcile, or at least com-promise between, opposed interests in society.

Marx's earliest works were directed vigorously against just such a view. He rejected the idea of the state serving as a neutral instrument of all the people, arguing that the ideals of justice, democracy and equality of political influence which such a view presupposed could only be an illusion while society itself was profoundly unequal. Since the important power relations were those built into the economic structure of society, politics in the state could never ultimately be anything other than *class politics*, because pre-socialist society was essentially a class society, whose predominant feature was class conflict, the manifestation of a basically irreconcilable conflict of interests.

Essentially, then, the key to understanding political events and the effects of political decisions was to relate politics to class interests. Under such circumstances it was impossible for the state to be a neutral arbiter satisfying the demands and interests of all. Rather, the political actions of the state were always to be understood as linked to the satisfaction of the economic interests of the dominant class in society. That is, the state is essentially an 'expression' of the class relationships generated by the particular mode of production and unambiguously involved in the class struggle on the side of the dominant economic class. Thus Marx and Engels (1976, p. 486) wrote that, in capitalist society, 'The executive of the modern State is but a committee for managing the common affairs of the whole bourgeoisie.'

In the Marxist view, therefore, the state is not an impartial referee in the power game, but is a vehicle for the realisation of the interests of the dominant class — an agency of class domination which gives the *illusion* of serving the general will, while in reality acting as a cloak for class interests. Attempts by the dominant class to cultivate a picture of the state as being above particular group or class interests constitute an ideological strategy to legitimise its own dominant position, and the state in turn involves itself in a constant exercise of legitimating the existing order through a variety of 'civil' agencies and institutions.

These attempts reflect a further fundamental feature of Marx's conception of power and class domination: while the economic relations of capitalism give the dominant class control over material forces and political power in society, they are also able to control ideas and beliefs. That is, they possess *ideological* power, whereby a set of *dominant values* (as we have suggested in Chapter 1) may be disseminated through major social institutions which justify or legitimate existing socio-economic and political arrangements, and hence their own dominant position. As Marx and Engels (1976, p. 64) say, 'The ideas of the ruling class are, in every age, the ruling ideas . . . The class which has the means of material production at its disposal has control at the same time over the means of mental production.'

In summary, then, Marx saw economic power as the basis for political power: the dominant economic class was effectively a 'ruling class', because the ownership of the means of production largely determines the distribution of political power.

Classical elite theory – Pareto and Mosca

Marx's uncompromising rejection of the advent of a 'democratic revolution' as a myth and his insistence on the reality of a persistent concentration of power were equally shared by the Italian 'classical' elite theorists, Pareto and Mosca. While agreeing with Marx's basic observation, however, they explicitly denied any credibility to his *explanation* of the concentration of power or to his predictions of how that concentration would eventually be eliminated. Their ideas, then, were just as much a reaction to the Marxist conception of power as to the liberal-democratic view.

Pareto maintained that concentration of power in the hands of a few was an inevitable fact of history and social life, so that in any society or political movement power lies with the active few, while the masses remain mere passive, manipulated pawns in the game. In his view, the political elite are possessed of power purely and simply because they are *more fitted* for such a role: they are individuals whose innate abilities and talents make them the 'natural' leaders and holders of power in their society, whereas the masses are less able and hence unfit to wield power.

Pareto saw the dynamics of history as being essentially

characterised by cyclical patterns in elite rule, by a constant 'circulation of elites', involving two distinct but interrelated processes: changes in the personnel of the elite by the assimilation of new recruits from the non-elite (for example, ambitious individuals or members of rising sections of the non-elite), and the supersession of one complete ruling elite by another. The pattern of history, then, is one of the rise and fall of different elite groups.

The distinctive features, however, are the *omnipresence of elite rule* and a concentration of power in the hands of an elite: the internal composition of the elite may change, either partially and gradually or totally and dramatically, but the *fact* of elite rule remains constant. Revolutions are merely the struggles between new and old elites, and though their outcomes may be variable, the basic defining feature of society, the fundamental character of its political organisation, remains the same, namely the concentration of power and rule by an elite.

Mosca's analysis shares the same essential principle of the inevitability of the concentration of power: power and its attendant privileges reside in the hands of an unchallenged minority. It is a 'law of nature' that 'In all societies . . . two classes of people appear — a class that rules and a class that is ruled' (Mosca, 1939, p. 50).

Mosca's use of the term 'class' is not to be equated with that of Marx: his 'political classes' are not distinguishable merely by an economic predominance, but by their *superior abilities* — it is these which account for their political dominance, and particularly their *superiority in organisation and cohesiveness* in the face of unorganised, fragmented masses. Mosca, however, gives greater significance to social and economic forces in the process of circulation of elites than Pareto, recognising more explicitly than him that the rise of new technological and economic forces and interests may spawn new social groups who achieve power and come to form the political elite. But Mosca was keen to dissociate himself from what he saw as the naive economic determinism of Marx, so that he afforded no primacy to economic forces in bringing about changes in the composition of the elite, but stressed the independent influence of new ideas and value systems, such as religious and moral ideas.

Elites or classes?

While their analyses vary at certain points, both Pareto and Mosca share the view that the concentration of power and elite rule in any society is inevitable, regardless of the outward appearance of the particular political regime or ideology of the society. For them, the necessary existence of ruling elites constitutes a scientific law of politics, which is confirmed at every point in history: though they may be of heterogeneous composition, single, cohesive minorities hold power, essentially uncontrolled by the majority, who are politically incompetent, apathetic and, in fact, prefer to be led.

Basic to this interpretation is an insistence on the *inherent inequality* of individuals, which contrasted sharply with democratic and socialist thought, both of which stressed the basic equality of individuals. Both Mosca and Pareto explicitly rejected what they saw as the two major myths of their time: the myth of democracy as government by the people, and the myth of the classless, equal society of socialism. For them, democracy was an illusion, a facade concealing a political reality in which an elite group of power holders held sway, and socialism and the principles of equality and the classless society were merely non-scientific dreams flying in the face of historical fact.

In stressing the inevitability of elite rule and the consequent concentration of power, the 'classical' elite theorists were attempting explicitly to deny the validity of Marxist socialist analyses of power structures. Like Marx, they stressed the unequal distribution of power but saw this pattern as inevitable and necessary (and indeed proper, in that their low opinion of the masses made them unsympathetic to the idea of popular participation). Furthermore, their analysis of the power structures of nineteenth-century capitalist societies was *not* class-based: the holders of power in Pareto and Mosca are not necessarily members of a dominant economic class, but are members of political elites by virtue of their superior (inherent) abilities, regardless of their social origins.

Here, then, is a crucial disagreement with Marx over the primacy of the variables which shape the distribution of power. For Marx, the mode of economic production and its attendant property relations shape the power structure, and the dominant economic class is a cohesive ruling class with common economic interests and a sense of solidarity and self-awareness; and it is conflict between classes which is the principal force producing social structural changes and hence changes in the structures of power. For Pareto and Mosca, on the other hand, the structure of power is not explicable simply in economic or class terms but in specifically psychological and political terms: the power structure is the product of the inherent qualities and organisational abilities of the elite and their psychological relationship with the masses.

The pluralist view − a diffusion of power

Classical elite theory and Marxism, then, both cast grave doubt on nineteenth-century idealist notions of democracy, rejecting the belief in a trend towards an increasingly democratic pattern in the distribution of power and insisting on a persistent concentration of power. Yet neither of these views has become the dominant model for portraying the social organisation of power in the West: rather, this status can be more readily credited to the pluralist model propounded by Dahl, Riesman and others.

The starting point for the pluralists is the equally forthright rejection of the two opposing views of the political process, classical democratic theory and Marxist ruling-class models, as not corresponding to reality. On the one hand, pluralism denies the possible existence of any direct participatory democracy, since modern industrial societies are too large and too complicated for this to be remotely practical; while on the other, pluralists are equally insistent that a number of significant changes in the past century require that we reject notions of a dominant ruling elite, with a strong internal solidarity and shared interests opposed to those of the majority of subordinate citizens. The more accurate depiction of Western power structures is, they argue, that of 'pluralist democracy', in which a *diffusion of power* prevails, buttressed and safeguarded by a number of important mechanisms and institutions.

Now, if the pluralists' view is to hold water, they have to be able to reconcile their analysis of the power structure with the unavoidable facts that elites do exist in contemporary society and that most citizens are not directly involved in decision-making — that is, they have to demonstrate that something which can be meaningfully called 'democracy' and some diffused pattern of power can be identified in Western societies. Indeed, the essence of pluralism is an attempt by liberal theorists to develop, as they see it, a more realistic account of democratic society which accommodates these facts of political life, and which translates or modifies the more philosophical ideals of classical democracy into a practical theory of democracy. Rather than attempt to sweep the existence of elites under the carpet, pluralists recognise their existence in modern democracy, and in fact regard them as a *necessary and integral feature*. Thus, for them, the existence of elites does not compromise the idea of democracy but strengthens it, given certain conditions which we shall outline below.

Many non-Marxists would accept that the nineteenth-century Western capitalist class was the dominant and pre-eminent group socially, both economically and politically. But, for pluralists, such a description of the pattern of power is no longer tenable, since the power structures of modern societies are now crucially different from those of the eighteenth and early nineteenth centuries. Modern societies have developed into more complex structures characterised by increasing social differentiation, with a more heterogeneous network of social and occupational roles, and a greater proliferation of organisations whose members share common interests. The result of this, according to pluralists, is that interests in modern society have become progressively *diversified*, so that a greater number of groups with particular interests and political demands to be satisfied have come to make their presence felt in the political arena.

For the pluralist, power no longer resides in any one centre, and political resources are more widely distributed throughout society. This is not to suggest that a totally egalitarian society has come about: nevertheless, crucial changes have taken place, so that no single elite group exists in Western democracies, but a *variety of elite groups compete for power*. Giddens (1972, pp. 345-7) has summarised the essential pluralist position:

> It seems to be widely accepted . . . that there has been a decisive transformation in the upper levels of the British class structure in the course of the present century . . . part of a generalized process of 'decomposition' of class relationships as they existed . . . in nineteenth century capitalism . . . The decomposition thesis holds the view that the ruling class has ceded place to a more amorphous and differentiated set of 'leadership groups': this is the sort of position taken by the many variants of the theory of 'pluralist democracy'.

The viability of democracy, then, is not compromised by the continued existence of elites, since for the pluralist the distinctive feature of liberal democracy is that it is a political system of *'open' power groups*, participating in the power game. The various elites are located in such institutional areas as business, government administration, politics (in the parliamentary sense), labour, education and culture, and draw their membership from various social strata on the basis of merit and regardless of class, sex, ethnic background, or whatever. As Dahl (1961, p. 91) observes:

> In many pluralistic systems, the political stratum is far from being a closed or static group. In the United States, the political stratum does not constitute a homogeneous class with well-defined class interests . . . it is easily penetrated . . . movement into the political stratum is easy.

Thus, democracy is characterised as a system of *competing elites*, where no single group is able to secure a monopoly of power and manipulate the system consistently to its exclusive advantage. In Dahl's terms, there are 'multiple centres of power, none of which is or can be wholly sovereign'. No monolithic unity exists, since they are by and large nonoverlapping in membership and are often in conflict with one another in policy preferences. Keller (1963) argues that this is an inevitable consequence of the increased social differentiation and specialisation of modern societies, so that any notion of a narrow, unified elite must be discarded. Rather, there exists a system of 'strategic elites', which can influence decisions but are *separate* elites in their own distinctive social milieux, with their own values and interests and without overlapping memberships, thus minimising the possibility of an omnipotent oligarchy.

Furthermore, the very existence of a variety of elites competing to influence decisions safeguards against any narrow abuse of power. This is because the various elites serve as 'veto groups' able to exercise *countervailing power* against each other as and when necessary. As Riesman (1950, p. 222) says:

> It is possible that where an issue involves only two or three veto groups, themselves tiny minorities, the official or unofficial broker among the groups can be quite powerful — but only on that issue. However, where the issue involves the country as a whole, no individual or group leadership is likely to be very effective, because the entrenched veto groups cannot be budged.

The structure of power, then, is multi-centred, with no wielders of disproportionately great power, a pattern reinforced by the fact that power for the pluralist is essentially *situational* and *non-cumulative*. Elites have varying degrees of influence at different times and over different issues, their power being circumscribed and limited by the nature of the issue: sometimes an elite exercises power and sometimes it does not, depending on the issue.

This assumption that different groups only have influence over a narrow range of issues effectively denies the possibility of a cumulative conception of power: that is, it rejects the notion that power in one area of social life will give power elsewhere (for example, an automatic 'translation' of economic power into political power). Rather, politics and power are *tied to issues* which may be of greater concern to some elite groups than to others and which may give differing opportunities of influencing a decision to some groups rather than others, depending on the nature of the issue. Certainly, one cannot assume that one group's interests will always prevail, and the Marxist emphasis on the prime importance of economic power resident in the hands of a small dominant economic class is also rejected, since there have supposedly occurred a number of significant changes in the economic arrangements of Western societies.

Private ownership is, allegedly, no longer as decisive a basis of power in modern society, for a variety of reasons. Firstly, the state has come to play a greater part in the control of economic decisions than in the nineteenth century, and through the development of public ownership and nationalisation the principle of private ownership has been restricted and the 'capitalist class' consequently weakened in the 'mixed' economy. Secondly, in business and industry, there has occurred an increasing separation between ownership and control, since large-scale industrial organisations are now controlled by managerial specialists supposedly less preoccupied with maximising profit. And, thirdly, the growth of joint stock companies with very large numbers of shareholders invalidates the formerly crucial status of ownership. For these reasons, according to pluralists, we can dispense with the search for a dominant class characteristic of the nineteenth century.

But what guarantees do citizens have that power will not be abused and the political elite will serve the interests of the electorate? According to the pluralist, two important features of liberal democracy provide safeguards in this respect. First, there exists a *basic consensus* on norms and goals, so that there are no fundamental cleavages of values in society or in politics — hence there is no justification for assuming, as Marxists do, an opposition of group interests on a whole range of issues. As Dahl (1961, pp. 91–2) says, the political stratum

embodies many of the most widely shared values and goals in the society . . . The apolitical strata can be said to 'govern' as much through the sharing of common goals and values with members of the political stratum as by other means.

Secondly, this consensus is reinforced by the fact that politicians are ultimately *dependent on votes*: thus, though they and not ordinary citizens normally initiate policies and issues, they will pursue vote-winning policies and not those which will lose them support. So, *accountability of decision-makers* is a key element in the pluralist perspective, and it is accorded greater priority than the lofty but unrealistic ideal of maximisation of participation built into classical democratic theory. The contemporary pluralist view stresses the desirability of *indirect* forms of popular rule, through the opportunity accorded to citizens periodically to choose freely among rival political elites in elections. Thus democracy is *not* direct but *representative*, not 'government by the people', but 'government approved by the people'.

In fact, Dahl and others maintain that large-scale regular participation in decision-making is neither necessary nor desirable, and periodic participation is necessary only occasionally to legitimise the authority of decision-makers. The average citizen is neither well informed nor especially interested in politics and is more likely to espouse 'authoritarian' attitudes, and, Dahl maintains, extensive individual participation in decision-making is invalidated on purely practical grounds of efficiency. Essentially, democracy involves public competition for office holding, in which citizens select rival sets of leaders, who have to be responsive to the wishes of the majority, rendering direct and continuous citizen participation unnecessary.

In summary, then, pluralism rests on the idea that power in Western democracies is not and cannot be concentrated, since these societies possess means of influence, representation and redress, and responsiveness of leadership, and politicians (as 'honest brokers') choose between competing policy alternatives, the choice being an outcome of the relative efforts of the various interest groups (and of the politicians' judgement of what is popular). Since we all have the opportunity to mobilise pressure and make our views felt, all citizens have some chance of influencing decisions, with the result that Western societies manifest a fluid structure of power with a diversity of influential groups and 'power units'.

4.4   EVIDENCE ON THE DISTRIBUTION OF POWER

The dominant view — the pluralistic diffusion of power

The mechanisms of influence in liberal democracy

As we have emphasised, the models of politics which assume a concentration of power must inevitably afford at best only minimal significance to any attempts by the mass of the population to organise themselves effectively and thereby to exert power and influence over formal political decision-makers — in other words, the masses must be effectively powerless.

The dominant pluralist view regards such a picture as inaccurate in depicting modern Western democracies, since for them no concentration of power is possible (and hence no 'ruling class' can exist); such political systems provide a number of fundamental safety mechanisms and devices which are not evident in autocratic systems or where a ruling class consistently monopolises power. There exist the democratic mechanisms of competitive mass political parties, regular free elections, and a multitude of pressure and interest groups which inhibit the concentration and enhance the diffusion of power, so that no single group is able to secure a basis of power in order to suppress or deny effectively the demands of others. Let us examine more closely, then, the supposed virtues of these institutions.

Political parties. In democratic thinking, the *mass political party* is an integral element, a central institution linking individuals and groups with the formal power structure, representing and aggregating a wide range of (group) interests and policy platforms in the political process. The development of political parties in the mid-nineteenth century coincided with the electoral and parliamentary changes which were instituted in European and American political systems in that period, involving, particularly, the extension of participation in elections to increasing numbers of the population. Before this time, voting was an exclusive activity, accorded largely only to men of property and substance; elections were haphazardly and casually contested (if at all), with bribery and corruption of voters common. With the growth of democratic ideologies in the nineteenth century and the gradual extension of rights of citizenship to larger sections of the population — notably the working classes spawned by industrialism — the loose, exclusive groupings which existed in parliaments could no longer regard the electorate and the electoral process quite so lightly. In Britain and elsewhere, this resulted in the creation of political parties on a national basis to organise and win mass support of voters, so that by the turn of the century the mass-based party had become a prominent feature of European political systems.

For the pluralist, parties make an important contribution to the diffusion of power in liberal democracy, serving as secondary associations, linking the mass of the people and the political elites. The mass party is regarded as a significant means by which popular interests, demands and grievances can be fed into the formal power structure to influence public policy. Additionally, parties have come to be the main source of recruitment for the political elites. This recruitment, it is argued, has increasingly manifested a meritocratic pattern: political elites have been rendered more socially heterogeneous, unlike in political systems where parties are absent and where ruling groups are drawn from traditional sources like hereditary ruling families, military personnel, and so on.

The existence of competitive parties allegedly acts as an important stabilising factor in democratic politics, since they commit and unite competing groups to the principle of orderly and open competition for power in elections and thereafter to the principle of majority decision by parliament. Thus, while conflict is accepted as a real and important element of the political process, it is formalised and acted out 'within the system', reinforcing the legitimacy of the idea of bringing power to bear through the appropriate democratic channels.

Pluralists, of course, would recognise that every elector is not and cannot be a member of a political party, but that for the vast majority a humbler and more passive role in the political process is preferred, limited to the opportunity to choose between these competing teams at regular intervals. However, parties are involved in the process, both at election times and between, of shaping, educating and clarifying public opinion: that is, they present the public with a choice between policies, by raising issues and taking stands on them. Thus, besides providing a formal opportunity for the populace at large to participate actively in the political game, a competitive party system generates a political awareness which allows the mass to confirm or veto at elections the holding of power by alternative political elites.

There are, however, good grounds for questioning the extent to which parties perform in the way pluralists assert they do. One of the major virtues of party politics is that, theoretically, the electorate chooses between competing and different teams with distinct programmes and philosophies. In Britain, for instance, the Labour Party is projected as committed to the equalisation of wealth, the extensive state provision of social and welfare services, central economic regulation, and public ownership; while the Conservative Party espouses the principles of free enterprise, minimum state intervention, the distribution of wealth by market economic forces, and the increasing of the 'national cake', so that individuals can make their own decisions regarding the provision of certain social services (e.g. medicine and education).

In practice, however, the degree of alternative choice offered is often *more illusory* than real, since fundamental differences in policy between, for instance, the major parties in Britain or in America are few, and on many issues they have moved increasingly closer together: in Britain, over the last fifteen years, the Labour and Conservative parties have embraced immigration policies which have become increasingly similar in principle and practice, they have shared similar views on Britain's EEC entry and subsequent role, and both have adopted platforms stressing the necessity for 'responsible trade unionism'. The specific indistinguishability of the two major British parties merely underlies, however, a more deep-seated similarity — the *largely uncritical acceptance* (despite occasional protestations about its 'unacceptable face') *of the economic and social arrangements of capitalism*. As Lane (1976, p. 52) argues:

> The dominant political parties in Western democratic States do not differ much over *major* questions concerning the arrangements of capitalist societies. No large political party in stable democratic countries can be seen as a threat to

the integrity of capitalist society. It is not inconceivable that the differences which manifest themselves between, say, the British parliamentary Labour and Conservative parties could be accommodated within one single party.

Besides offering little choice to voters generally, parties also offer little opportunity to their mass members to influence affairs directly. The ideal of the political party as an organ of participation and a channel of communication does not appear to manifest itself in reality, since the mass-based parties of Europe assign *very limited participatory roles* to their mass membership. In the two major British parties, for instance, the members are inactive and largely ineffective and subordinate to the parliamentary teams which reign supreme and unencumbered by them. The party members have few, if any, real policy-making teeth, and any 'grass-roots' resolutions which do gain support at party conferences are not guaranteed adoption or inclusion in official party programmes or manifestos — rather, manifestos are drawn up for the approval of the mass membership by the parliamentary parties. Thus, Western parties are essentially 'parliamentary parties' uninhibited by their mass members, whose major role is essentially that of acting as 'work-horses' for the party, particularly at election times, primarily in the task of 'vote-winning' for local party candidates.

Of course, it might well be argued that the interests of members and supporters of a particular party are still represented effectively by the parliamentary 'team', since, as we indicated earlier, a political party is seen by the pluralist as an amalgamation or aggregation of interests. But we must ask how realistically and effectively and in what sense do parties enhance the interests of their members and supporters. For instance, the large majority of Labour Party voters in Britain are of working-class background, and there is considerable evidence suggesting that working-class people form the bulk of those in favour of capital punishment, yet this 'interest' is in no way enhanced by the Labour Party. The parliamentarian would counter this argument by insisting on a distinction between MPs as 'delegates' and 'representatives', that the MP is not merely a passive mouthpiece for constituents, but must exercise initiative and remain true to his or her own political judgement.

We may well concede that the relations between parties in parliament and the electorate are not and cannot be as direct as this, but remain such that voters periodically choose teams of leaders, having been 'educated' by the debates conducted over political issues by these leadership teams. But again we must ask how extensive and profound a political education is provided by parties. Ideally, parties sensitise the public to issues and generate understanding. But it can be argued that this is a highly selective process, in which parties act rather more like *censors* of issues rather than straightforward suppliers. They are able, in the first place, to *define* what areas of potential controversy are to *become* public 'political issues': equally important, they are able to shape the climate in which the issue is to be debated; and they can also select and process what the public receives as 'political information'. (A good example of this is the way in which, in recent years, wage demands have been presented as being the prime agents in inflation and have been used as the rationale for policies of wage control.) It becomes, then, more difficult to sustain an image of parties as educators, as enlightening the public.

Moreover, politicians in Western capitalist societies are not a microcosm of society, but are predominantly drawn from the ranks of the middle and upper classes, with only a small minority of working-class origin. In the USA, despite the ideology of the American dream of rising 'from log-cabin to White House', Democratic and Republican politicians have long been massively bourgeois in origin and background. In Britain, the Conservative Party, traditionally an 'aristocratic' party, has remained solidly bourgeois and public-school educated: the 1979 Conservative government contained twenty-four members who had received their education at one school, Eton. The Labour Party began as a predominantly working-class party — all twenty-nine Labour MPs elected in 1906 were of working-class origin — and between 1919 and 1939 71 per cent of Labour MPs were rank-and-file workers. But like many of Labour's European counterparts, its MPs have become progressively more bourgeois and significantly less proletarian in the post-war period: by 1951, 46 per cent of Labour MPs were professional people; in 1970 only four new Labour MPs out of fifty-four were clearly working class; and by 1974 only eighty-nine MPs out of 319 (about 25 per cent) were of manual worker origin.

Pressure groups and interest groups. But the inadequacies and shortcomings of mass political parties may not deal the fatal blow to the pluralist case, since we have emphasised how they see pressure groups and interest groups as an equally (if not more) important mechanism for articulating the interests and preferences of groups in democratic societies, as 'translators' of 'raw' political demands into political issues. Ideally, the pressure group brings together those with interests or causes in common, in the hope of using their collective strength to transform demands into public policy. For the pluralist, the advent of democracy and diffusion of power go hand in hand with the rise of pressure groups and interest groups: in pre-industrial and pre-democratic society, such groups on any wide scale were essentially non-existent or at best only intermittent phenomena, since politics was the exclusive activity of a small minority. In contrast, in modern Western society, according to pluralists, pressure groups provide an essential chain of influence for the mass of the population, allowing individuals and groups, should they so choose, to participate in political activity for the promotion of their interests, thus involving more people in the power game, with as great if not greater influence than mass political parties.

Pressure groups are said to serve as 'secondary associations' between the mass and the political elite, enhancing democracy as well as acting as necessary bulwarks against autocracy and totalitarianism. Moreover, by virtue of their special concern with particular issues, they often have specialist knowledge and information to offer the political elite for consideration in decision-making. So, according to the pluralists, pressure groups both bring pressure to bear on decision-making and aid political elites in making policy decisions, and may even actively assist in securing members' co-operation in the implementation of policy (for example, the role of the trade unions in Britain in the implementation of incomes policies). As we suggested earlier, an important element in the pluralist view of Western political systems consists in the idea that there exists a certain basic consensus about 'fundamentals': disagreement about large and fundamental issues of social life has declined, so that ideological conflict is becoming steadily less prominent. This implies that there are no longer highly charged debates over ideologies and issues, but rather that the politics of liberal democracy involves the progressive resolution of *specific* problems accommodating specific interests and demands — a politics of 'adjustment' — and that the widespread existence of pressure groups and interest groups reflects this.

In such a situation, a variety of autonomous groups and interests are able to share in the power game, supported by appropriate legal and institutional arrangements, such as the legitimate devices of 'lobbying' legislators and administrators, engaging in public opinion campaigns, supporting 'test cases' in the courts, and so on. Consequently, it becomes impossible for a political elite to solidify into a coherent class pursuing its own interests to the exclusion of those of other groups, or to see the state and political power as 'its' property (or that of a dominant class on whose behalf they may be governing).

This pluralist picture of politics has been subjected to attack on a number of fronts. First, it cannot be assumed that all groups have roughly equal potential for success in pressing their demands: pluralists may recognise that, in practice, some interest groups are more powerful and successful than others, but this is not strongly reflected in their highly optimistic ideas about degrees of equality in influence and benefit. There is no guarantee that simply because a pressure group shouts it will necessarily be heeded: success in influencing decision-making is far less likely to be determined by any abstract 'justice' or 'fairness' in a group's interests or demands than by a number of other considerations, such as its material resources, its position in society, and its size.

Certainly, a group with substantial resources of wealth and manpower has a significantly higher chance of getting itself heard: the Confederation of British Industry, for instance, can mount campaigns for the realisation of its interests on a scale not attainable by the vast majority of groups. Similarly, a group holding a key position in society can hope to exert

more influence, often by threatening to withdraw its services:
such groups as railway workers, doctors and coal-miners provide essential services, so that withdrawal of labour by such
groups may be particularly damaging, and hence may give
them a relative advantage in influencing decisions as compared with other workers. Often more important than sheer
size are the *ease and privilege of access* to formal decision-
makers which a group enjoys: having 'friends in high places'
is distinctly advantageous. While there is no guarantee that
individuals of similar social background, attitudes and associations will necessarily think alike, the fact remains that in
Western societies like Britain, the existence of an 'old boy
network', whereby some groups appear more acceptable to
formal decision-makers by virtue of their similarities in class
and educational backgrounds and social intercourse, inevitably means that such groups' demands receive a far more
ready ear.

But, of course, the pluralist might well suggest that the
ultimate test is 'public opinion', that a group must convince
the public at large that its demands are acceptable and 'in the
public interest'. Here again, however, some groups are more
successful and better able to present their demands as being
in accord with 'the public interest', emphasising how their
interests are consistent with 'the needs of the nation'. Such
an exercise *is* more easily accomplished by business groups
in capitalist societies (epitomised in the famous American
slogan 'What's good for General Motors is good for America'),
as a result of their image as creators of the nation's wealth
and prosperity. Thus, their demands are more likely to be
sympathetically received (and hence their interests more
frequently realised) because they are consistent with the
dominant values of capitalist society. It is important, of
course, to ask where these values come from: pluralists see
them as widely embraced voluntaristically by members of
society — the product of a social consensus — while Marxists
regard them as imposed, the product of ideological manipulation by the dominant economic class, the very class whose
interests they best serve. Capitalist business groups have been
remarkably successful in presenting their demands as providing benefits for all, while at the same time the demands of

labour are frequently presented as 'inflationary', 'damaging to business confidence', 'holding the country to ransom', and so on. The pluralist assumption, then, that all citizens have potentially equal access to influence through the operation of interest groups is naively optimistic. Interests are by no means equally represented in terms of 'one voice, one value'.

Perhaps an even more fundamental question is whether groups are equally free to *form*, or capable of forming, organisations to represent their interests. Deprived ethnic minorities such as Negroes, the rural and urban poor, migrant workers, the old and the handicapped are much less likely to be able to develop organisational structures to enhance their interests, given both the lack of resources at their disposal and the lack of consciousness of having definite interests to be protected in an organised way. The poor are a classic case in point: even if groups like the Child Poverty Action Group mobilise pressure on their behalf, they have no real threats or sanctions they can bring to bear to force the hands of formal political decision-makers. Thus, governments are free to define welfare expenditure as a 'cost' which can easily be cut when public funds run short or are needed to give 'incentives' to the productive.

Pluralist liberal democracy quite simply appears to ignore the isolated, the less articulate, and the unorganised, attending to the claims of (some) organised interests, but giving very little attention to groups not located in traditional institutional spheres. When competition does occur, it is often no more than a 'managed' process between powerful groups in an atmosphere relatively immune from any significant intrusion by broader sectors of the community. This does not necessarily mean that some interest groups are omnipotent on each and every issue, but that unrepresentative concentrations of power do exist, so that the basic interests of these groups are not on the whole *significantly* compromised or subverted. Ultimately, then, pluralist theory devalues the fact that *inequality of opportunity to influence* is yet another aspect of the unequal distribution of *individual and group life-chances* in capitalist societies.

This leads us to a further difficulty with pluralism: while one may concede that opportunities to influence exist, these are frequently only available to groups whose demands and the methods they adopt to pursue them fall within the conventional and accepted 'rules of the game': lobbying MPs or Senators, assembling petitions, rallying public opinion, winning the backing of a political party, or approaching civil servants. Venturing beyond such tactics means that both the group's credibility and ability to influence may well be impaired by violating the bounds of what is considered a 'reasonable' method of attempting to influence decisions: the 'rules of the game' and the built-in assumptions and prejudices of politicians may *systematically exclude* some groups from influence and benefit.

The pluralist would interpret this commitment to the 'rules of the game' as a manifestation of the *consensus* which, they claim, characterises liberal democracies. Undoubtedly a set of societal values does prevail, but we must ask how far such an ideology is *imposed* by powerful groups, rather than voluntaristically embraced, *and whose interests* it serves best. Liberal democracies are not *merely* that: they are *capitalist* liberal democracies in which, as we suggested earlier, business interests profit from and sustain a dominant ideology of materialism, individualism and free enterprise.

A prevailing ideology exists which sets the boundaries within which decisions will be made, influencing the kinds of issues that may develop and limiting the range of possible policy options for consideration, so that a group in tune with this will have a significantly greater chance of influencing decisions. Within such a framework, a group's demands can be weakened or ignored by defining them as 'extremist', 'unpatriotic', 'Reds', or whatever, and the legitimacy of their challenge, or even a demand for basic rights, can be removed or headed off.

In such circumstances, a rather vicious circle emerges: groups denied an effective conventional voice may resort to alternative methods, but the techniques employed become inextricably linked to the way in which their demands are perceived and the extent to which they are granted any credibility and legitimacy. Thus, the actions of groups like the Provisional IRA and the Baader Meinhof group are invariably depicted in parliaments and the media as 'senseless', the work of 'extremists', and 'madmen', with the result that little or no consideration is given to their demands or arguments.

Research evidence — an evaluation

Our discussion of this mobilisation of bias leads us to focus more directly on a crucial weakness of pluralist theory. As we have suggested, pluralists see power as being essentially situational, that is, tied to particular issues, so that, in order to discover whether power is concentrated in a single group or dispersed among several, we must study 'key issues' and *actual political decisions* — who is involved and who wins — to ascertain which group succeeds in having its policy preferences adopted in observable, open contests over policies. This approach can best be illustrated by reference to Dahl's (1961) celebrated study of local community power in New Haven which claims to demonstrate that the political system of New Haven is one of 'dispersed inequalities'. Dahl shows what he means by this by examining in detail three areas of decision-making: education policy, political nominations, and urban development.

Political nominations showed unequal power distribution very clearly. A small number of top party leaders made all the important nominations; however, Dahl sees this as no real problem, because no groups (he claims) were excluded, since no politician could afford to ignore important sections of the electorate. Education policy, according to Dahl, was influenced most by the public education officials, teachers through their representative association, and parents through the parent-teacher associations (PTAs). Again, power was concentrated in the mayor and others in high official positions, but they had to recognise the views of interested parties, as expressed through these bodies. Hence we see again Dahl's view that power is in the hands of office-holders, but in this case they made their decisions with reference to the demands of organised interest groups.

Finally, urban renewal provided an issue where powerful economic interests were far more likely to be significant. Dahl suggests, though, that political office and citizens' interests again played an important role. The mayor and the full-time development administrator were seen as key figures, instrumental in obtaining federal funds and in organising a structure of advisory committees which brought in wider interests on specific areas such as education or harbour development. The senior body, the Citizens' Action Commission (CAC), contained a selection of those considered influential by the mayor — bankers, employers, traders, unionists, university men, and other community leaders. Dahl emphasises that the CAC never actually initiated planning proposals, nor did it ever change any; it constituted a public relations exercise to engender public support for the programme and to forestall disputes. The mayor used the CAC to test reactions. Proposals would be tailored to avoid opposition from powerful interests. These interests were too weak and divided to carry on the task of initiating and co-ordinating redevelopment, but they could have vetoed some proposals. The mayor therefore had to adapt and compromise in anticipation of conflict — and in the process avoided any. Once again, then, power lies primarily with officials, not social groups, but these decision-makers decide on the basis of a calculation of the sum-total of opposition and support from broader social groups.

Dahl concludes that the power to determine policy in New Haven was diffused and widely distributed among a variety of community elites, with no single group dominating and possessing cumulative power. His method of studying the process of active decision-making on key issues may appear sensible and straightforward, but, as Bachrach and Baratz (1962, 1963) have stressed, it is basically inadequate and reveals crucial weaknesses in the pluralist conception of politics and power. Dahl and others uncritically accept the *observable* political process as their object of study — that is, decision-making on 'issues' — but, as Bachrach and Baratz point out, this constitutes *only one* 'face of power' and completely ignores the equally important *second* 'face', '*non-decision-making*'. Here groups have power to the extent that they may be able to *prevent or exclude* issues from becoming public and other groups from articulating their views and demands, so that power is often exerted, *and is just as real*, when groups can confine open decision-making and controversies to relatively safe issues. Thus, power is not just about decision-making but also about *managing* situations to prevent issues from arising for debate, about influencing the *definition* of matters for public debate. The pluralist preoccupation with 'key issues' automatically excludes those areas where controversy is subdued or prevented from reaching the surface in the 'private' face of power.

Thus, the pluralist researcher might well discover no obvious contests over, say, poverty or racial discrimination and (particularly in view of the pluralist equation of non-involvement with satisfaction) would completely miss the reality of a process whereby the interests of the poor and ethnic minorities had been 'organised out' of the political arena.

While Bachrach and Baratz's criticisms are important, in one basic respect the pluralist account is not thoroughly challenged: Bachrach and Baratz take for granted that different groups are aware of their political needs and that non-decision-making is a conscious, deliberate strategy to exclude these groups. Power is still seen only as involving active, deliberate conflict — even if some acts deliberately prevent conflict from gaining expression. If Dahl rejects the notion of a conspiracy by one ruling group, Bachrach and Baratz merely show that the powerful can employ hidden ways of conspiring. Power may benefit groups or classes unequally, *even though* neither the privileged nor the underprivileged fully understand or control this process of domination. It may be that those disadvantaged by political decisions do not realise it, and have no conscious political demands or grievances. The powerful need not exclude any challenge, for it has not arisen. At the same time, powerful groups may pursue policies which they genuinely believe to be in the communal interests but which *objectively benefit* some groups much more than others. Thus, while there may be no discoverable conflict or grievance, some groups are systematically benefited at the expense of others.

We have to recognise, then, the notion of the *objective interests* of a group or class. That is to say, we must be able to judge as observers what will benefit or harm a group — *whether the group recognises it or not*. For example, we may judge that it is against the interests of citizens to be exposed to radiation, even if they do not recognise the problem as serious. The power of the owners of the nuclear reactor may be demonstrated by the fact that they can continue to run it without being challenged by those threatened by it.

Now this is a very different conception of power and interests to that of the models previously discussed. Steven Lukes (1974) calls this the 'third dimension of power'. For pluralists, a group's interests are only its 'expressed preferences' — the demands the group actually is aware of and puts forward. Lukes defends the notion of objective interests as a necessary alternative, for we must be able to judge when power is being exercised, even in the absence of conflict. After all, power that is never questioned or challenged is the most potent of all.

This leads to a particular conception of power which asks *'who benefits?'* and *not* 'who takes or influences decisions?', and allows us to identify those social groups who benefit most from the routine, institutionalised, unchallenged exercise of power. They are therefore the most powerful, even if they do not actually take the decisions. This seems a rather odd notion: how can one be powerful without actually doing anything?

We can explore these questions through a study of local power by Saunders *et al.* (1978) of farmers in East Anglia. The study focused on Suffolk, a rural area which contains some of the most prosperous large farmers employing farmworkers at some of the lowest male wage-levels in the country. Here, apparently, was a clear basis for political conflict, but on examination Suffolk was noticeable for the lack of any real issues on which conflicts were visible, giving the impression of tranquility, stability and harmony.

In fact, the farmers and landowners, although monopolising council positions, claimed to be community servants, engaged in disinterestedly discharging their obligations as councillors. They felt that two important planning policies, preservation of the environment and maintaining low rates, were in the interests of all and therefore desirable for 'the community'. The *practical effect* of these policies, however, was to secure the objective interests of farmers much more than those of workers.

In housing, limitations on residential development to preserve the rural environment meant that private housing was scarce and costly and council house provision was restricted, with the result that agricultural workers were forced into 'tied' housing controlled by the farmers (the abolition of which farmers opposed because of the lack of alternative accommodation!). This further reinforced workers' dependence on their employers.

Similarly, the preservation of the environment restricted the introduction of new industries which might well have paid higher wages than farmers in competing for labour, thus benefiting farmers once more. The obsession with a low rates policy, moreover, meant that Suffolk has some of the poorest social service provision (in education, welfare, public transport, and so on) in the country: those lacking the means to pay for alternative private provision inevitably suffer more in these circumstances.

Now, while the *intentions* of councillors were not necessarily self-interested, the *effects* of their policy decisions were such that *their* objective interests were enhanced, while those of the agricultural working class were adversely affected. This 'non-politics of the status quo', as Saunders *et al.* term it, has to be viewed in the context of its effects on the routine maintenance of the objective interests of an already advantaged group in the community.

How, then, are we to judge the dominant pluralist account of power? Superficially, it seems to offer a plausible account of politics, but on closer inspection major flaws appear. It gives a bland, over-optimistic and uncritical account of decision-making which fails to perceive many of the subtleties of the power game. The distribution of power in Western capitalist societies will *not* be realistically portrayed by a reliance on pluralist theory, simply because, if for no other reason, the conception of power employed is inadequate. The basic proposition of pluralism, if it has one, is that issue-conflicts reveal power structures. But some issues never reach the arena of overt decision-making, and some interests consistently and routinely prosper even without deliberate action — that is, the routine maintenance of an unequal status quo is enough to serve the interests of those who benefit from that status quo.

Pluralism's emphasis on observable events and issues reveals inadequate attention to social structural factors determining and constraining not only actual decisions and policies but the *definition* of the issues lying behind them. The study of the operation of power must encompass not just action by individuals or groups, in a vacuum, but the institutional and ideological frameworks in which action (and the absence of action) is embodied.

Concentration of power

The contrasting theories

The notion that power may be concentrated in a few hands has only come to seem unusual in those modern societies which claim to be democratic and whose governments therefore claim to serve the will of the whole people. Any *diffusion* of power, then, is a new variation away from the normal condition of extreme concentration, so that contemporary pluralists would have to prove clearly that such a shift in power to a wider base has in fact occurred. We have seen in the previous section that such 'proof' is open to some degree of scepticism, for votes, parties and interest groups may not always be effective means to influence policy outcomes in the direction desired. We shall be arguing that such scepticism is well founded, for economic power remains very concentrated and is closely linked to political power. We shall not assume, however, a direct and simple link through the *active exercise* of political power; it is equally important to establish *who benefits* from political actions. It is not always the case that those who hold political power necessarily serve either their own interests or those of their supporters. It should become clear that these questions cannot be finally resolved on the basis of looking at 'the facts', because different sociologists interpret such facts very differently in the light of their own concepts and, in turn, these concepts relate back closely to the initial competing theories. This is not to say, however, that such facts are useless; indeed, close analysis of the evidence remains indispensable.

The primary competing theories stressing the concentration of power were introduced earlier in the chapter through the works of Mosca and Pareto (*elite theory*) and Karl Marx (*ruling-class theory*). A major area of contrast between them concerns the social basis of power — these theories must specify the *position* of the ruling group or class in the *social structure* and identify the special features which allow it to claim a monopoly or near-monopoly of power. Marxian theory is most immediately clear on this issue, taking as its starting point the premise that political power derives from economic power. Since economic power is embodied in exploitative class relations, we can always identify a ruling class by its economic position, and this economic dominance is translated directly or indirectly into political power. Elite theory claims that a closed social group holds nearly all power, and that the social basis of this dominance is the ability of the group to control entry and to define criteria for membership of the elite which excludes the majority.

Elite theory, then, must first demonstrate that an internally connected group of power-holders does indeed exist, but it is also necessary to show that their primary basis for unity is not shared economic interests, for then they would constitute a class. Secondly, it must show that those identified as members of the elite do actually exercise effective power, that there is no 'hidden power' in the hands of others outside the elite.

Ruling-class theory must establish first that there is indeed a dominant economic class, and, second, that this economic power results in political domination. If this political domination is seen in terms of the exercise of power through the holding of important positions and official responsibility for decision-making, then we can simply examine such holders and judge whether they qualify as members of the dominant economic class. On the other hand, many Marxists have argued that the dominant class may remain dominant through the serving of its interests by others who do the hard work of actually governing. If this view is taken, it is much harder to refute the ruling-class model by means of evidence on the personnel in important positions — instead, we have to examine the actual outcomes of policy and judge whether the dominant economic class normally benefits more than others. This *may* be difficult to establish empirically, but even if we can do so, non-Marxists may always reject this interpretation, arguing that there can be no ruling class unless it rules actively and can actually be identified as that group of people who exercise power. (The weakness of such a response has been demonstrated in the previous section on pluralism.) We can now examine the empirical evidence, bearing in mind these questions.

Empirical evidence

The main body of evidence presented here will relate to the British case. This might be regarded as a weakness, since Britain is notoriously 'class-bound', and the power of traditional elites (particularly the aristocracy) might be thought to be unusually strong. Whilst this may be partly true, we will try to show the broad applicability of the argument to other capitalist societies.

Elite recruitment. Generally, sociological evidence on the top levels of the social structure is relatively scarce compared with, say, studies of the working class. Not only are 'top' groups in society unwilling to see their wealth and power exposed, but these benefits also allow them to resist or exclude prying sociologists. It is not surprising, then, that there are few studies of the *actions* of those in important positions: instead, sociologists have generally studied the *social origins* of these groups and inferred from this some judgement on their likely values or motivations. While such a method may involve weaknesses, the fact remains that these studies do still demonstrate that those in important official positions are recruited from a relatively narrow social base and are socialised through distinctive educational routes. This would seem to justify the use of the term 'solidary elite' on the basis of evidence for closure of entry to elite positions and interlocking relationships between elite members.

The easiest route into this elite is by *inheritance*. Inherited wealth may go together with the inheritance of a senior position in the family-owned company or bank. Stanworth and Giddens's (1974a) study of British company chairmen discovered that 26 per cent of those in industry, and 47 per cent of those in merchant banks, had entered the family firm, while at least 66 per cent of all company chairmen came from upper-class origins (89 per cent in merchant banks), with just 1 per cent moving up from the working class. Thus, those with final decision-making power — the board of directors — are predominantly drawn from the upper class, and this transmission of position over generations is a key feature of the propertied class. These people form the core of the elite, but there are other elite positions which appear to recruit on more meritocratic, competitive grounds. Elite positions in the Civil Service, the armed forces and the media are filled at least partly on the basis of qualifications and 'suitability'.

Access to educational advantage is, then, a prerequisite for access to many elite positions: one must gain a privileged education to compete successfully in the contest for elite positions. The form of this privileged route varies significantly between societies, though the effects are rather similar. In the United States, the privately endowed Ivy League universities (such as Harvard and Yale) recruit quality candidates, but on the basis of high fees. In France, the *grandes écoles* in Paris recruit on the basis of rigorous examination of candidates from selective *lycées*, but the successful candidates are thenceforth sponsored through to positions of power in the state, industry and commerce. The British pattern is probably more selective and exclusive than either of these systems, for an educational route has survived which almost entirely avoids contaminating contact with state education. The child of parents with enough income to afford fees of up to £3,000 a year can be sent to boarding preparatory school at age 8 (or younger), then to boarding public school, and then either directly into management or banking or on to university — especially Oxford and Cambridge. This system allows the fortunate minority (public school pupils formed 2.6 per cent of all 14-year-olds in 1967) to enjoy an enclosed educational career within institutions which recruit from an extremely narrow social base and sustain a highly uniform set of values and assumptions about the world and their pupils' future commanding roles within it.

Table 4.1 indicates clearly that public school products are vastly overrepresented in elite positions, in proportion to their actual numbers, and the top six public schools (Charter-house, Eton, Harrow, Marlborough, Rugby and Winchester) provide pupils with the most glittering prizes of all. In 1979, as we saw, the Conservative government contained twenty-four Old Etonians. It is hard to believe that these pupils are so markedly superior in talent to the products of other schools.

TABLE 4.1

	Total number	Percentage from all public schools	Percentage from six public schools
14-year-olds at school in England and Wales	642,977	2.6	0.15
Conservative MPs (1966)	253	76.6	35.0
Labour MPs (1966)	363	19.5	2.4
Conservative Cabinet (1963)	23	90.9	63.6
Labour Cabinet (1967)	21	42.0	15.8
Royal Navy: Rear Admirals and above	76	88.9	—
Army: Major Generals and above	117	86.1	—
Royal Air Force: Air Vice-Marshals and above	85	62.5	—
Civil Service: Under Secretaries and above	301	61.7	—
Ambassadors	80	82.5	—
Judges	91	80.2	28.5
Directors of forty major industrial firms	261	67.8	41.6
Directors of banks	205	78.6	—
Directors of insurance companies	118	83.1	—

The significance of such data could, however, be questioned on two grounds. The first is that these elite members were all educated at least thirty years ago, and that today's recruits will be more representative of the whole population. This may be true to some extent in those fields with competitive recruitment, such as the Civil Service. Kelsall's (1974) study found that in 1929 only 14 per cent of senior civil servants had attended state schools, 70 per cent having attended Oxford or Cambridge University. By 1967 35 per cent had attended state schools and only 51 per cent had graduated from Oxbridge. Of the new recruits in 1968–70, 59 per cent attended Oxbridge and only 38 per cent had been to state secondary schools. These changes are hardly radical, and the importance of attending the universities with the highest social status remains clear.

A second objection to these data might ask whether the recruitment to the most prestigious universities or colleges has in fact broadened, so that more recruits from lower-class origins can employ these routes to high positions. This trend is, at best, limited, with little evidence for 'open elites' as the pluralist view suggests: it is still the case that only 9 per cent of Cambridge University undergraduates have working-class fathers, compared with 31 per cent in 'provincial' universities. Probably more important is the fact that entrants to elite establishments are self-selected (they have chosen to adapt to this institution) and they are strongly socialised once admitted. In Bourdieu's terms, they must acquire 'cultural assets' of appropriate character, outlook and demeanour to capitalise on their training for the elite. Formerly guaranteed by family background, these 'acceptable qualities' are now guaranteed by the character of elite educational institutions. The social closure of elite recruitment now depends upon the inequalities structured within the education system — above all, private schools, but also wider inequalities in opportunity and achievement.

Elite integration.   While evidence on the closure of elite recruitment seems decisive, we cannot automatically assume that this will produce agreement and solidarity within the elite, nor can we tell what decisions will actually be made.

However, it would be extremely surprising if the narrow common social origins did not have effects. The British upper class (and those of other capitalist societies) remains a self-recruiting and self-perpetuating stratum, with shared economic interests and shared political and social outlook. Over the generations, this upper class has become highly experienced and sophisticated in the pursuit of its own general interests. Elite recruitment is a measure of social closure and self-awareness among the upper class. Moreover, it is by no means insignificant that the great majority of those in important positions share a common vocabulary, demeanour and social outlook, for this can not only facilitate communication and solidarity, but also insulate elite members from ideas or values which challenge their taken-for-granted orthodoxy. This shared cultural security remains, then, a valuable asset of the elite, but it may only be of background significance, for there are divisions of power and interest within the elite which may be more significant.

For example, senior ranks in the armed forces may be concerned to compete (indirectly) for state funds against university vice-chancellors; or senior civil servants may wish to raise taxes to pursue state policies while businessmen may desire tax cuts. Clearly, the occupants of important positions have specific duties and interests relating to their particular area of activity or jurisdiction; there is no obvious unity of interest except in times of serious challenge such as war, or in a general strike. Thus, if elite theory or ruling-class theory is to be supported, it must be shown there is either a greater degree of unity than is immediately visible, or that some interests systematically take precedence over others — that is, that a structure of dominance within the elite itself exists. Both of these conditions can, in fact, be supported.

There is considerable evidence for integration through interlocking links at the level of both personal and institutional connections. Prominent individuals commonly perform multiple elite roles, or transfer frequently between institutional spheres within the elite. At one level, celebrities such as Lord Goodman or Lord Rothschild combine personal business and professional interests with participation in government committees, Royal Commissions and quasi-autonomous bodies for the administration of the arts and sciences. More broadly, a high level of interchange occurs between government employment in the Civil Service or other state organs and employment in industry or commerce. This is extremely important in the USA and in France, and is increasingly so in Britain. A recent example at the highest level is Lord Armstrong, formerly head of the Civil Service and then chairman of Midland Bank. Among politicians themselves, Guttsman (1963) has shown that in the 1951–5 British Conservative government, ministers had an average of eighteen links with other elite groups, and nearly half of these were with banks or firms. Guttsman's 1974 study found that in 1970, 32 per cent of Conservative MPs and 12 per cent of Labour MPs had industrial or commercial occupations.

Perhaps the most direct links of all, however, are those through kinship. A privileged social group will normally attempt to practise 'social closure', that is, to exclude outsiders, primarily through limiting marriage partners to others within the group. In addition, kin ties are crucial when position and property are to be inherited. For both these reasons the networks of kin ties between elite members are extremely close and complex, as the work of Lupton and Wilson (1959) illustrated. Whitley (1974) also demonstrated that those controlling economic institutions are predominantly the families who descend from the commercialised aristocracy and gentry. One-third of industrial companies and all but one of the important financial institutions were linked to others by directors connected through kinship ties catalogued in *Burke's Peerage* and *Burke's Landed Gentry*.

Thus it would certainly seem that we should not regard the elite in pluralistic terms, for formal and informal links abound; it does seem justified to characterise the ruling group as a 'solidary elite'. We must not, however, regard this integration as precluding any structured differentiation within the elite, for some areas of institutionalised power are more important and central than others: vice-chancellors of universities are a good deal less important than the chairmen of major oil companies, for example. We must recognise that the state performs a vital regulatory and co-ordinating role for the economy and for other areas of society, and that the relationship of elite groups to the government and Civil Service departments is of basic importance. The crucial variable here is the extent to which the particular elite sub-group is either *dependent* on the state (e.g. university vice-chancellors, the chairman of the BBC) or the extent to which the elite sub-group has an *autonomous* area of jurisdiction on which the state and the society is dependent (e.g. economic elites). If the state pursues policies which damage exports and the value of the currency, much more serious immediate consequences result than if the state cuts back on postgraduate education. This structuring of the elite can be seen in Britain in the pre-eminent importance of institutional links between financial capital in the City, the Bank of England and the Treasury. The Treasury is by far the most powerful department in Whitehall with a primary role in the formation of economic policy. The links between manufacturers and the Department of Trade and Industry are almost as close; but the Department is a good deal less influential than the Treasury, while the Department of Education and Science is far less powerful in determining overall government policy. As we shall see later, more direct links between economic groups and governments have grown considerably, but even these routine and institutionalised linkages show the predominance of 'the economy' in the formation of policy inside the state.

Among the more *direct* links with economic groups are those between the trade unions and governments through incomes policies and intervention in disputes and redundancies. Trade unions do have sanctions available, especially the strike weapon, which provide the basis for a certain degree of influence and occasionally the power to resist unwelcome policies. As a result, economic policies of the state are frequently implemented (and sometimes formulated) with the direct involvement of union leaders in planning and other committees. This is most clearly in evidence with social democratic governments dependent upon working-class support, or when governments wish to claim consensus and representation of all interests.

Clearly, then, the unions cannot be neglected as a basis for economic power, but it must also be emphasised that this power is only *institutionalised* and *legitimate* in particular areas of decision-making: the power of the economic elite has no such precarious status. It is entirely institutionalised in the basic forms of economic organisation, where economic power to decide on growth or liquidation, expansion of employment or redundancies, remains legally and securely in the hands of owners and senior managers. The great weight of economic power lies in the hands of those who own and run firms and banks, not in the trade unions who represent their employees.

We would argue that Britain and other capitalist societies have a clearly defined elite group characterised by relatively closed recruitment and a relatively high level of internal integration and interconnection. Within this elite, there is an unequal structure of power, with state policy-making affected most by those elites with an independent base of power on which the state depends — and this means, above all, the economic elites. However, is this dominant, integrated elite a *dominant class*?

The dominant economic class.   As we emphasised earlier, we must not simply conclude that an identifiable dominant elite constitutes a ruling class. We must first establish that it is, in fact, a *class*, with its power based on economic domination. While some writers see shared education, values and life-style as indicators that the elite constitutes a class, this is, in our view, mistaken, for these can only be indicators of a cohesive *dominant status group*. While this certainly does exist, the real question is whether these status attributes are founded on a basis of economic class position. We must therefore establish the existence of an economically dominant class before we can ask whether this class can translate its economic power into political domination.

Capitalist society, as we have seen in Chapter 2, rests upon the private ownership of productive property. This ownership gives the right to enjoy the profits of such production and the right to direct the productive process, and the most basic economic institution in capitalism is therefore the owner-managed firm. In this basic form, it is clear that the capitalist enjoys economic power in two senses: he owns the product and the profits from its sale, and he controls the workers in the course of his management of the productive process. Thus, if modern Western economies are to be seen as no longer class-dominated, then ownership must be widely spread, and control of production must no longer be in the hands of a small owning class.

Pluralists claim that such developments have taken place, and that this constitutes a diffusion of power. To sustain such a view, they would have to show economic power based on ownership to be in the hands of many individuals dispersed through the society. At the same time, power in the enterprise would have to be seen as exercised by career employee-managers whose motivations and actions were substantially different from those of an owner-manager.

The later twentieth century has seen the rise of complex management hierarchies and the growth of shareholding by insurance companies, unit trusts, pension funds, and so on, so that power is apparently no longer in the hands of the directors, and ownership is shared by all who have insurance policies or small savings. These impressions have very limited validity, however. Shareholdings are still heavily concentrated: in 1970 only 7 per cent of British adults held shares, and 80 per cent of all personal shares were held by 1 per cent of adults (Westergaard and Resler, 1975, p. 117). It is very hard to see how indirect holdings through insurance policies or pensions can make any real difference to the concentration of economic power. On the other hand, the power of these financial institutions may be increasing: Kotz (1979) has argued that up to one-third of the top 200 US firms are controlled by such interests.

The decline of direct owner-control seems rather more evident, but even here the impression is misleading. We must remember that *strategic* control over investment, mergers, redundancies and so on remains at board level. The directors and senior executives must be distinguished from the middle-management structure below them. When directors are studied, owner-management is seen as alive and well.

Chevalier (1970) studied the top 200 US firms and discovered that 113 were directly controlled by dominant shareholders, while only eighty were management-controlled. Barratt-Brown (1973) discovered that in 1966, thirty-eight out of 120 major British firms were owned by families or tycoons, while among the top 250 nearly half are personally controlled (Scott, 1979, p. 66). Similar situations occur in France and West Germany, while in 1963, 80 per cent of Norwegian firms, employing two-fifths of the work-force, were family-owned. Even in the cases where outside control by banks or insurance companies is in evidence, it must be remembered that these financial institutions are themselves frequently owned or controlled by wealthy families or individuals.

Turning to the position of senior executives, two flaws are evident in the pluralist interpretation. First, we have no real grounds to expect senior salaried managers to behave any differently from owner-managers, since they are still constrained to pursue profit because of competition and because the basic operation of capitalism depends upon such profits for reinvestment. Secondly, senior managers are by no means propertyless, so that profit is by no means personally irrelevant. Over 80 per cent of the income of senior US executives depends directly on the firm's profit performance, and sackings at this level usually follow bad profit performance.

In 1972, according to Heller (1973), 45 per cent of the directors of the largest 200 British companies owned shares in the firm worth over £20,000. Moreover, senior executives are drawn from the same narrow social origin as company directors. As Scott (1979, p. 176) has observed: 'Wealthy families hold shares in a large number of companies and they form a pool from which corporate managers are recruited.' But, as he emphasises, a condition for entry to these dominant economic positions is not only birth and inheritance — the required qualifications and social training must be instilled via elite educational routes. Cultural capital is thus important, as well as financial capital. It is clear, then, that the existence of a dominant economic class can be established in all Western societies; the pluralist contention that such a class no longer exists is, to say the least, premature.

The ruling class?

We have so far established the existence of a socially cohesive, economically dominant class which dominates most significant elite positions in Western societies. In the sense that this class has survived and sustained its economic power so securely, it is clear that their material interests have been preserved and realised over time. As Marshall (1950, p. 123) concludes: 'If a class is strong enough to secure or preserve those institutions that favour its activities, it may be said to be governing to that extent.'

This, however, can be interpreted in different ways. On the one hand, we may regard this dominant class as *ruling* in the direct sense of controlling politics in such a way that challenges to its privileges, above all from working-class movements, can be avoided, defeated or diluted. Alternatively, we may recognise the possibility of an economically dominant class ruling, even though it does not actually run the government or state at a particular time, as long as the class that is running the state still serves its interests. After all, the capitalist class still sustains its position in European countries even after decades of government by social democratic parties based on the working class, or by fascistic regimes drawing support from a 'middle mass' of non-capitalist, non-working-class citizens. We must, therefore, examine both these alternative interpretations of the term 'ruling class'.

The first, where the economically dominant class rules directly, has commonly occurred in contemporary and historical societies. The feudal lords ruled their areas of land directly; the commercialised landowners and gentry of Britain in the eighteenth century protected property, trade and colonies on their own behalf, and, more recently, conservative regimes expressly committed to sustaining the existing economic and social order have formed governments with the support of lower-class voters in contemporary Europe. At various points, this dominant class has been in government at crisis periods and has used this position to defend its interests. A clear example of the defeat of a challenge from below was the British General Strike of 1926.

More unusually, a ruling class under threat may attempt to dilute and assimilate the challenge by making concessions, such as universal suffrage and welfare provision in order to prevent more far-reaching changes in the social order. At the same time, this may have the effect of strengthening and legitimating working-class movements. Paradoxically, the labour movements, thus strengthened, may go on to defend and prop up the existing social order (and hence the dominant economic class). At its most extreme, this has taken the form of forcible defeat of workers' protests by 'socialist' governments, such as the action of German Social Democrat leaders using force to put down workers' uprisings at the end of the First World War. Such policies illustrate the point that the interests of a dominant class may be defended by a different class which actually governs.

As we have seen, governments based on subordinate classes have had contrasting characteristics, ranging from socialist to fascist in ideology. Normally, however, they have all *claimed* to be dissatisfied with the capitalist system in its current form. The election of such governments, however, does not *in itself* abolish the prevailing economic system, and existing economic relationships and inequalities are not necessarily changed. Without fundamental change in the economic structure, the *economic* power of the dominant class is not challenged, and their privileges remain unscathed. Hence, we might deduce that any government (whatever its class character) which fails to change substantially the economic structure of capitalism will *inevitably* serve the interests of the economically dominant class. However, we must also recognise the possibility of a powerful political autonomy for the state where political goals are pursued regardless of any other considerations, so that economic considerations become entirely secondary. In these circumstances, the state in capitalist society may *not* serve capitalist interests.

These issues emerge very clearly in the case of Nazism, where the German state gained a degree of autonomy which had awful significance. The Nazis did gain power with some help from certain capitalists, but they were in no sense 'puppets' of big business. Indeed, control of the state was decisively wrenched away from both capitalists and workers. However, in the early stages of the regime, the interests of big business and not those of the mass supporters were served, because the Nazis did not reorganise the economic structure and were therefore dependent on the success of capitalists for the success of their own military policies. This is a point of much more general significance. As a general proposition we can say that any government, whatever the class basis of support for it, that does not reconstruct the capitalist economic system will in general further the power and benefit of the economically dominant class. This is because that government has to attempt to maintain economic strength or 'health' and depends on such strength for the pursuit of its own policies.

However, the Nazi case provides an additional general point of great significance. As the war economy developed, the 'normal functioning' of the capitalist economy was more and more seriously undermined by the intervention of the state. This Nazi state developed a considerable degree of *autonomy* of political power from economic power, founded on its mass base, its coercive methods, and the priority given to military goals. Increasingly, the state imposed policies on firms contradicting their interests as capitalist enterprises. For example, the shortage of skilled labour forced wages up, but Hitler preferred to exterminate Poles and Jews rather than let them work in the factories. This autonomy of political power may not be a normal state of affairs, but given a strong enough social and organisational base, the state *can* fail to serve the interests of the dominant economic class, even though capitalist economic relations are not changed.

In order to gain this degree of autonomy, however, the state requires very strong organisation in extreme circumstances, and it is very unclear how far this can be sustained if the underlying economic structure is not changed. In general, we can certainly say that a principal feature of capitalism in 'normal' circumstances is a separation of power, where political power (in government and state) is separate from economic power (in the owners or controllers of private economic enterprises). Institutional political power may often be held by social classes without economic power, but their dependence upon the economy leads to the maintenance and defence of capitalists' economic power and privilege. This only applies, though, *as long as* that state does not have a sufficient independent basis of power (and sufficient commitment) to allow it to restructure the social organisation of the economy.

In the light of these considerations, we are left with the conclusion that the capitalist class has often secured its own interest through the state and that others have often governed in ways that secure the continued economic dominance of that class. This leads to the conclusion that the normal state of affairs in capitalist society is that the capitalists dominate, even if they do not govern. We may therefore choose to use the phrase 'ruling class', but with the earlier reservations and qualifications in mind. Perhaps it might be preferable to employ an alternative label to convey these complexities, such as the term 'hegemonic class'. Such a label implies a form of political domination much more diffuse than 'ruling class', which does suggest active intervention in government as the principal basis for 'rule'. Our discussion has attempted to show that such direct rule is not necessary, for as long as existing social institutions are defended and sustained, then the independent economic dominance of the upper class remains and their interests prevail. The evidence points clearly to the absence of any real diffusion of power; the propertied upper class of Western capitalist societies constitutes a *hegemonic class* for as long as the state in capitalist society continues to serve their interests.

4.5 POLITICAL CONSCIOUSNESS AND POLITICAL ACTION

Introduction

In both Chapter 2 and our preceding discussion of the distribution of power, we have demonstrated the persistently large inequalities in material resources and rewards, life-chances, opportunities to influence decisions, and symbolic rewards enjoyed by different classes in contemporary capitalist society. The most striking feature of this pattern is the systematically disadvantaged position experienced by the majority of the population, the working class. In terms of income, wealth, health, political power and the like, their middle-class and, more especially, upper-class counterparts enjoy significantly greater advantages, despite the social and political changes instituted in capitalist liberal democracies in the twentieth century. Effective political power remains concentrated in the hands of a dominant economic class, and the social and political supremacy of the working class which Marx predicted has not materialised.

As we have seen, Marx envisaged a situation in which capitalist society would become increasingly polarised into two warring and opposed classes, the bourgeoisie and the proletariat. The latter, gaining consciousness of their common interests and recognising the inherent conflict between their interests and those of the owners of the means of production, would rise up in revolution, destroy capitalism, and establish socialism. For Marx, such a transformation was *not* an 'automatic' certainty, since it depended on the development of a *revolutionary class consciousness* on the part of the proletariat, and while he felt that the contradictions of capitalism would generate such a consciousness, the transition of this class from a 'class in itself' to a 'class for itself' was essentially problematic.

This revolutionary class consciousness would involve the acknowledgement of a fundamental conflict of interests between those of their own class comrades and those of the bourgeoisie, coupled with the realisation of the pervasiveness of class relations and conflicts throughout all areas of social life and of the possibility of constructing a thoroughgoing alternative set of social, economic and political arrangements − in effect, a 'new society'. Workers attaining such a consciousness would act to do away with capitalism and its attendant social relations and establish socialist society.

The nature of working-class political action

In the century since Marx's death, Western capitalist societies have not succumbed to revolutionary transformation. While political conflict and upheaval have been by no means absent and not without far-reaching national and international ramifications (for example, fascism in Italy and Germany in the 1920s and 1930s), and while political action has frequently and consistently been class-based, capitalist liberal democracy as a political system has negotiated the twentieth century with some apparent success, without the solidification of the working class into an active revolutionary force. The primary political activity of the latter is voting in national elections every four years or so, with working-class political action appearing to manifest itself within the constraints of the status quo; even in societies with strong communist parties, an apparent consensus seems to prevail. Thus, while we must not fall into the simple trap of assuming that capitalist liberal democracy is the only possible socio-political arrangement (after all, it is essentially a *recent* structural form and one which was 'laid aside' temporarily in fascist Italy and Germany), we can acknowledge its relative longevity.

As we have suggested, numerous studies of voting behaviour over the decades have demonstrated a consistent support for left-wing socialist and social democratic parties by the majority of the working class in the capitalist societies of Europe. In Britain, for instance, roughly two-thirds of the working-class vote has regularly gone to the Labour Party, constituting three-quarters of the party's support. In Britain, at least, class constitutes the single most important variable associated with voting. Moreover, the middle-class vote in Britain is significantly more class-cohesive than that of the working class, with only about 20–25 per cent at most of non-manuals deserting the 'party of their class' and voting Labour.

Other European societies are not such 'pure' examples of class voting as Britain: in these societies, other sources of partisan division such as religion, ethnic origin, or urban/rural cleavage are often more significant in their cross-cutting influence on voting than in Britain, where class tends to be the only major line of division. But even in this 'purest' example of class voting in Western liberal democracies, the association is nowhere near perfect. If it were, and the British working class all voted Labour, then their simple numerical superiority would mean that there would be no contest. In Britain, the Conservative Party has been able to rely on about one-third of the working class supplying them with half of their electoral support, and the right-wing parties of Europe have benefited similarly — without such support, these parties simply could not hope to win elections.

Thus, the class basis of political action in the form of voting is by no means straightforward, and a closer examination reveals further complications. While the majority of manual workers consistently identify themselves as working class, this may not reflect a uniform homogeneous attitude to other classes: an admiration for and desire to emulate other classes, accompanied by encouragement of one's children to 'get on' and rise to a higher class; a belief in the intrinsic superiority of one's 'betters'; an awareness of a division between 'them' and 'us'; a resigned recognition of subordination; or a belief in the moral necessity of economic redistribution – any one or more of these may underpin the manual worker's class identification.

Similarly, manual workers, when asked to explain their political loyalties, have been found more likely than other groups to reply in class terms. But the detailed content of this perception again may be variable, even among those identifying with the same party. Butler and Stokes (1971), for instance, have argued that manual workers supporting the Labour Party may be motivated by varying perceptions of the class-based nature of politics. They suggest that some working-class Labour voters – a minority – saw politics as an arena of class conflict in which diametrically opposed class interests were locked in struggle; others saw the party as the simple representative of class interests (without any necessarily hostile view of other parties and classes); while yet others saw voting Labour as an element of their class sub-culture, the pervasive political norm of their class.

Examination of the content of specific political beliefs by Parkin (1971), Jessop (1974) and others suggests that, in Britain, working-class Labour voters are significantly more likely to be critical of the ideas and institutions of the dominant value system, but the partisanship is by no means perfect, since many Labour voters appear to embrace 'conservative' values and beliefs which are critical of Labour Party policy. Thus, they may tolerate the social and economic arrangements of capitalism and be critical of nationalisation programmes. Leaving aside the kinds of problems we have identified, we are still confronted with the fact that not only does the majority of the working class support 'parliamentary' rather than 'revolutionary' left-wing political action, but a substantial minority of this class gives its allegiance (at the ballot box, at least) to political parties committed to the maintenance of the existing social and economic arrangements of capitalism and its attendant inequalities. In other words, a large section of the subordinate class of capitalism spurns the adoption of revolutionary action to remedy their disadvantaged position, while a smaller, though by no means insignificant, number appears to endorse conservative ideologies and policies which systematically operate against their 'best interests'. Are they, in fact, simply exhibiting 'false consciousness' in this behaviour?

The structural basis of working-class political consciousness

If we are to explore adequately working-class political action and consciousness in contemporary capitalist societies, we must attempt to locate these phenomena *structurally*, to examine the ways in which manual workers' perceptions are shaped by the organisation of capitalist society both materially and ideologically. Marx's own analysis attempted to do exactly this, but it is not sufficient to dismiss his ideas as 'wrong' or 'worthless', as do many commentators of the right, simply because the working class has not acted as a revolutionary force. His work has prompted a number of attempts to explain why a revolutionary consciousness has not emerged in the working class in capitalist societies.

Consciousness, images of society, and immediate social milieux

Lockwood (1966) has addressed himself to this problem. Like Marx, he argues that developing a revolutionary consciousness (or any other type of consciousness) implies seeing one's society in a particular light, but that actors do not all 'see' the 'same' society, class structure and patterns of inequality. Hence the investigation of actors' images of society and class structure may explain variations in response to the objective facts of inequality. The ideas which individuals have about the societies in which they live and the systems of inequality they experience may not be 'true' or 'valid' in any objective sense (that is, correspond to objective, measurable inequalities), but they can and do have real consequences for action.

Lockwood argues essentially that images of society are largely the product of certain primary social relationships into which individuals are locked, so that *within* any class the *immediate social milieux* in which members of one class find themselves may *not* be identical. As Lockwood (1966, p. 249) says:

> For the most part men visualise the class structure of their society from the vantage points of their own particular milieux, and their perceptions of the larger society will vary according to their experiences of social inequalities in the smaller societies in which they live out their daily lives.

For Lockwood, the most salient of these immediate milieux are the *residential* and *occupational communities* in which individuals are located, and he identifies three distinctive types of working-class environments which throw up their own images of society.

Proletarian traditionalism is typical of working-class groups living in homogeneous communities which are socially and occupationally isolated and characterised by large-scale industrial enterprise. These are typically communities with heavy industries and predominantly working-class populations with low rates of social and geographical mobility, conditions which generate a strong sense of shared work and community experiences. Thus, communities centred on mining, shipbuilding and dock work, employing large numbers of workers in similar jobs of a single-class character, exemplify most clearly Lockwood's proletarian traditionalism. The sense of community is reinforced by the mutual dependence the worker feels for his colleagues (given the often hazardous nature of such jobs) and by the sense of identity felt at 'doing a man's job', and is reflected in the amount of leisure time which is spent with workmates.

These distinctive community experiences, according to Lockwood, produce 'the most radical and class-conscious segment of the working-class', generating a distinct awareness of the class structure and of being 'proletarian', and give rise to a view of the world in which two classes stand opposed in an arena of conflict between 'us' and 'them'. Thus, proletarian traditionalists embrace a necessary commitment to collective action to defend and enhance their interests through their principled, solidaristic support of collectivist institutions like trade unions and socialist parties.

Deferential traditionalism characterises working-class groups living and working in more heterogeneous environments, in effect relatively more isolated from other members of the working class. Their work situations involve them in personal and particularistic relationships with middle-class employers, often of a paternalistic dependent nature. Agricultural workers in rural areas and workers in small-scale industries (e.g. family-run businesses) and in small towns are the obvious example of this working-class type. These particularistic communities where 'everyone knows one's place' generate an image of society as an organic whole, in which all play a necessary but not equally important part, so that inequality of reward is an inevitable and acceptable outcome.

These workers subscribe to a model of society as a legitimate hierarchy, with deference and trust accorded to social superiors by virtue of their possession of intrinsic skills for elite positions. There is, then, an awareness of a class hierarchy, but one which accepts it as legitimate and proper and involves neither antagonism towards superiors nor any desire to be their equals or to imitate them.

Lockwood's third group of manual workers are free of the traditionalist perspectives which distinguish their proletarian and deferential counterparts. The *privatised* manual worker lives in the community milieu of the housing estate and is involved in specialised but routine occupations which are well rewarded but lack autonomy and offer little intrinsic satisfaction. The classic example here is Lockwood and Goldthorpe's 'affluent workers', for whom work is a means to the end of money with little inherent reward: their low job involvement and instrumental attitude to work produce no strong attachment to workmates but manifest themselves in a privatised home-centred existence focusing on a preoccupation with their families and homes. Enduring fairly boring employment is the price they are prepared to pay for the financial rewards they desire for their families. Their community experience is lived out in less well established areas of the newer working-class housing estate, where neighbourhood relations are less cohesive and more loose-knit.

Such circumstances foster, according to Lockwood, a *pecuniary* image of society. Here, work and community experience do not generate deferential or proletarian perspectives: instead, privatised workers, although seeing themselves as working class, give greater salience to social divisions based on income and material resources, with status judged by personal possessions and conspicuous consumption. Their sense of collectivism is more instrumental than solidaristic, so that their membership of trade unions and support for the Labour Party is less ideologically and emotionally founded than that associated with proletarian traditionalism.

Lockwood stresses that this type of worker is the product of the changes of the post-war period in the material circumstances (in the form of improved standards of living), in the nature of work (with the advent of new methods of production and new consumer goods industries), and in the living conditions (particularly the growth of housing estates in urban redevelopments) of sections of the working class. The decline of occupations and communities associated with proletarian traditionalism implies that the potential for radical class consciousness existing anywhere among manual workers has been steadily eroded.

Critics of Lockwood.   Many studies have questioned whether Lockwood's three types are as clearly distinguishable and discrete as he suggests: do the workers he identifies possess coherent sets of social and political values and images of society? Cousins and Brown's (1975) study of Tyneside, Roberts *et al.*'s (1974) study of Liverpool, and Newby *et al.*'s (1979) study of East Anglian farm-workers were unable to find consistent class images among manual workers: while these workers shared an awareness of being working class, they often had more than one image of society and could not be easily located within Lockwood's scheme.

Even if we accept the existence of Lockwood's types, critics have questioned the link between proletarian traditionalism and any radical consciousness. Generally, it has been argued that the consciousness generated by proletarian traditional milieux may be *much more partial* and limited than Lockwood has indicated: they may well encourage occupational and community solidarity and consciousness, but not necessarily any *class* solidarity and consciousness. The link between them is *not* automatic, since occupational solidarity in itself can spawn very parochial conceptions of who constitutes the 'us' group, and may actually *inhibit* rather than encourage commitment to and recognition of shared interests with other manual workers generally.

Moreover, factors other than immediate work and community milieux may shape manual workers' perceptions of society and their place in it, particularly the impact of the macro-structure of inequality and of ideological influences which transcend local environments. We cannot assume that the kinds of immediate and primary relationships in which workers find themselves will have *no* significance for their perception of society and their class images, but it may be equally misleading to give them primacy.

Moore, for instance, in his study of Durham miners (1975), has pointed to the important role of nineteenth-century Methodist religious ideas in influencing miners' perceptions of and responses to the class structure and class relations, and political parties undoubtedly play some part in shaping images of society, by simultaneously propagating and dampening certain conceptions of the existing social order and of the theoretical and practical solutions necessary for its reconstruction. Scase's (1974) studies of Swedish and British manual workers' images of society emphasise how variations in conceptions of the class structure between these two objectively similar groups were in large part attributable to the different ideologies of the class structure propagated by the socialist parties in the two societies.

The essence of this criticism is well reflected and extended in the contribution to our present discussion of Parkin (1971), to whose ideas we now turn our attention.

Dominant values

Parkin shares Lockwood's view that objective class position

does not spawn an automatic and uniform class consciousness. Consciousness is structured according to individuals' exposure or access to *'meaning systems'*, that is, to sets of ideas which interpret reality. For Parkin, members of the working class are differentially exposed to and touched by three meaning systems in varying degrees, and variations in exposure to these systems of meaning structure different types of working-class consciousness. Parkin differs from Lockwood initially, in that he stresses that meaning systems are formed at a more general societal level rather than through the relationship and experiences of the immediate milieux: that is, they are to be seen as directly related to the macro-structure of inequality and its class relationships and interests.

The dominant value system is 'a moral framework which promotes the endorsement of existing inequality ... The concept of a dominant value system derives from Marx's celebrated statement that "the ideas of the ruling class are, in every age, the ruling ideas"' (Parkin, 1971, pp. 81–2). There exists, then, a prevailing set of values and ideas subscribed to and propagated by the members of the dominant class which are successfully disseminated by the major ideological institutions, such as the education system, the mass media, and religious organisations, and which are embodied in Britain in the high esteem accorded to, for instance, the monarchy, the House of Lords, public schools, the ancient universities, and the military elite. These dominant values provide and sustain an 'official' interpretation of class inequalities, endorsing them as the legitimate arrangements of capitalist society, and members of all classes will subscribe to these values unless they find themselves in circumstances which act as a buttress against their influence:

> Members of the underclass are continually exposed to the influence of dominant values by way of the education system, newspapers, radio, TV and the like. By virtue of the powerful institutional backing they receive, these values are not readily negated by those lacking other sources of knowledge and information (Parkin, 1971, p. 92).

Thus, exposure to the dominant value system inhibits any

radical class consciousness in the working class, not through coercive or other unsubtle methods but by fostering acceptance of status quo ideas and values, encouraging manual workers to interpret the world as legitimately arranged, to see that inequality is just, because higher reward is the result of talent plus effort; that the national interest and not group interests is what matters; that some are born to rule, and so on. This evokes either a *deferential* or an *aspirational consciousness* among manual workers: the former shares Lockwood's traditional deferential's world-view, while the latter sees an 'open' hierarchy with opportunities for self-advancement provided one has the ability to rise.

But, of course, not all manual workers are exclusively exposed to the dominant value system. While those living in socially mixed rural or urban communities, those working in close paternalistic relationships with their employers, and those who are weakly organised in trade unions or not unionised at all find themselves with little or no protection from dominant values, many more members of the working class have access to what Parkin calls the *subordinate value system*, generated at the level of the working-class community. Does this value system, then, engender a potential for radical working-class action?

Parkin again differs from Lockwood here in stressing that this system of values should not be seen as exemplifying radical class consciousness, because

The subordinate value system could be said to be essentially *accommodative*, that is to say, its representation of the class structure and inequality emphasises various modes of adaptation, rather than either full endorsement of, or opposition to, the status quo . . . It would be misleading to construe the subordinate value system as an example of normative opposition to the dominant order. Least of all, perhaps, should it be understood as exemplifying class consciousness or political radicalism (Parkin, 1971, p. 88).

So, while Lockwood interpreted these sorts of values as the basis for opposition, Parkin regards them as better interpreted as 'a negotiated version' of the dominant value system, an adaptive rather than oppositional response to the status quo. Inequalities are seen as an unpleasant fact of life which, while neither recognised as legitimate nor enthusiastically accepted, do not produce wholesale repudiation or rejection. Thus, the subordinate value system allows manual workers to come to terms with the reality of inequality by accommodating themselves to it and by concentrating on improving their lot within the existing reward structure.

This adaptive response is reinforced by the fact that the subordinate value system generates an essentially communal solidarity, but of a parochial, partial kind, whereas 'A class outlook . . . is rooted in a perception of the social order that stretches far beyond the frontiers of community' (Parkin, 1971, p. 90). For Parkin, the limited and adaptive nature of the subordinate value system is well reflected in trade-union activities which centre on attempting to win improved wages and conditions for members *without* advocating an alternative set of social and economic arrangements, 'but by working within this framework' (Parkin, 1971, p. 91).

Thus, exposure to the dominant or subordinate value systems affords little or no potential for the development of a radical revolutionary consciousness among manual workers. It is only through exposure to the *radical value system* that an *oppositional consciousness* can emerge, one which emphasises the constant recognition of a division of society into inevitably conflicting classes and an unequivocal commitment to eliminating the existing capitalist reward structure. Such oppositional revolutionary values are the product of the radical socialist party, committed to 'a set of precepts . . . which are fundamentally opposed to those underlying the institutions of capitalism' (Parkin, 1971, p. 97). The absence of such parties, then, represents a crucial inhibitor to any radical consciousness and action among manual workers who are not able to generate an oppositional value system 'on their own'. And, as we shall see shortly, Parkin and others maintain that the continued triumph of dominant values has been in large part the product of a progressive 'de-radicalisation' of European socialist parties and trade unions in this century and their consequent failure to provide a coherent alternative revolutionary ideology to the dominant value system of capitalism.

Pragmatic accommodation

Parkin's analysis of meaning systems suggests, then, that in Western capitalist societies a minority of the working class have absorbed a set of values and ideas which lead them to grant legitimacy to those in elite positions and to acquiesce in their own subordination. The majority, while manifesting neither moral approval nor enthusiastic acceptance of the existing order, are not committed to full-blooded action to rectify inequalities and restructure social arrangements. Many other sociologists agree that working-class consciousness and response to capitalist inequality and concentration of power is characterised by this *pragmatic accommodation*.

Mann (1970, 1973) argues that we cannot successfully account for the lack of revolutionary class consciousness among manual workers either by crude Marxist explanations which attribute working-class compliance to the successful systematic dissemination of dominant values in a process of ideological manipulation by the ruling class, or by comfortable pluralist notions that a radical working-class consciousness has been dissipated by the development of a *value-consensus* resulting from the alleged economic and political changes in Western capitalist democracies. In this view, manual workers have come to accept normatively the fundamental values and institutions of capitalist society, to recognise its essentially harmonious structure, and to accept the rules of the democratic game.

Such interpretations (as well as the crude Marxist interpretation) must demonstrate a consistent commitment to dominant values on the part of the working class. But Mann argues that the working class have adopted, if anything, a response of *pragmatic acceptance* of their disadvantaged position in capitalism — an unenthusiastic, qualified, realistic response to their situation, where they are not convinced that capitalism and its attendant inequalities are morally legitimate, but where they accept it pragmatically as an everyday fact of life and perceive no realistic alternative.

Mann found that manual workers supported simultaneously both 'dominant' values and 'deviant' values, but these sets of values operate on different 'levels'. Manual workers appear more likely to endorse deviant values when they are related to concrete, everyday realities or when they are expressed in simplistic, unsystematically critical terms than if related to abstract political values. They are likely to concur with such statements as 'People in different classes share fundamentally similar interests' and 'Workers and managers should all work together for the common good' (supporting dominant values), while agreeing with 'The rich have always exploited the poor' and 'Managers should not have privileges like separate restaurants and car parks' (supporting deviant values, but on concrete issues or in a vaguely populist way).

Thus, for Mann, there exists 'a disjunction between general abstract values and concrete experience' (1970, p. 429) among manual workers, created by the contradictory nature of their existence. He stresses that exposure to dominant values is a constant and never totally inescapable feature of working-class life, in which a number of important institutions — such as the education system and the mass media — are engaged in assailing manual workers with politically conservative values and attitudes, so that they cannot fail to absorb some elements of the dominant value system. But total ideological manipulation of manual workers does not ensue, because the more immediate settings in which the working class find themselves, such as the family, the work-group and peer-group experiences help 'deviant' critical values to breed. However, they are, according to Mann, of a rather 'raw' variety, not always articulated in the form of abstract principles which allow the manual worker to grasp the *totality* of his subordination and disadvantageous position so as to generate a *systematic* critique of capitalist society.

Consequently, manual workers are confused by the clash between dominant and deviant values but are touched by both. As Blackburn and Mann (1975, p. 155) point out:

> If the workers in our sample are 'confused', then they have every right to be, for that is an accurate reflection of the reality that confronts them . . . This may not take us very far towards a theory of society, but it does enable us to make more sense of workers' thin images of society. For instead

of viewing them as approximations to consistent and coherent images, we should regard them as attempts to grapple with the real contradictions of the workers' situation.

They emphasise that we should not find it surprising, given the contradictory cross-pressured circumstances in which manual workers find themselves, that they do not develop the cohesive and insulated subcultures and images of society of the kind outlined by Lockwood. Experiences in the work environment and in everyday life 'loosen' the potentially monolithic impact of dominant values, so that deviant values and the seeds of dissatisfaction are never completely absent: the ensuing pragmatic compliance leaves room for a 'latent class consciousness' to exist, in which inequalities are recognised, but with only a limited appreciation of the alternative social arrangements possible, so that opposition is at best spasmodic and partial.

Mann recognises the possibility that there may periodically occur 'explosions of consciousness', such as in the events of May 1968 in France, in the strike at Pilkington described by Lane and Roberts (1971), or in the Grunwick dispute, when a strike may spawn a sense of solidarity with other workers and an increase in consciousness may emerge. But he maintains that such explosions tend to be limited, uneven and temporary in their effects, not least because they are not consistently sustained by a pristine set of deviant values.

Ambivalence and acquiescence

An essentially similar position to that of Mann is taken by Hyman (1972, 1975) and by Westergaard and Resler (1975), though they tend to embrace a more 'optimistic' view of the potential for radical working-class action, while stressing the essentially *ambivalent* nature of working-class images of society. For Westergaard and Resler (1975, p. 403) there exists 'a common sense of grievance, a belief that the dice are loaded against ordinary workers', which, while not constituting any completely coherent ideology of dissent, contains the vital seeds of opposition to the capitalist system and its principles and practices. There are signs, then, of a *quasi-ideology*

236 Introductory Sociology

critical of the present social order, which should not be minimised or ignored, since its embryonic existence makes any
notions about complete working-class incorporation *much*
more open and problematic. The 'pecuniary' image of society,
for example, allegedly embraced by Lockwood's 'privatised'
workers, may be much more problematic and open to interpretation than it appears. We must be very cautious, Westergaard argues, of inferring a 'pecuniary' image of society simply
from the frequency with which workers refer to 'money',
'possessions' and so on: such statements may merely inadequately or symbolically express workers' conceptions of
society and their place within it — that is, they may use a
'money' model as 'a convenient way of referring briefly to
the whole range of social differences of which "money" is the
symbol' (Cousins and Brown, 1975, p. 70).

Westergaard maintains that a pecuniary approach may not
automatically produce an uncomplicated dilution of working-
class consciousness. If workers are as instrumental in their
work as has been claimed, committed to their job purely
because of pay (the 'cash-nexus'), then their integration into
capitalism is essentially partial and not total. As Westergaard
(1970, p. 120) observes,

> The cash-nexus may snap just because it is *only* a cash-
> nexus; because it is single stranded . . . And if it does snap
> there is nothing else to bind the worker to acceptance of
> his situation . . . The single stranded character of the 'cash-
> orientation' implies a latent instability of workers' commit-
> ments and orientations.

The institutionalisation of class conflict and maintenance
of working-class acquiescence then becomes conditional
upon capitalism's ability continually to 'deliver the goods'
to manual workers; it 'depends very substantially on the
capacity of the capitalist societies to maintain the rising levels
of real income which they have achieved in the past' (Giddens,
1973, p. 211).

For Westergaard, Hyman and others, then, it is not out of
the question that working-class radicalisation might take
place, particularly given certain changes and crises experienced

by capitalist societies in recent years, such as the decline of the traditional, particularistic, working-class community, escalating wage demands, shop-floor militancy, rising inflation and international economic recession, and falling rates of profit. Thus, the stability of capitalism may be more apparent than real and significantly more fragile than when viewed from the comfort of the 1950s and 1960s.

Much of our discussion so far has inevitably made reference, either directly or indirectly, to manual workers' position in the capitalist system of production, to the *worker's* most direct experience of the socio-economic system in which he lives. We must now give detailed attention to the implications of these work experiences and industrial action.

Trade unions, industrial action and consciousness

Capitalism as a system of economic production is characterised, as we have shown elsewhere, by a relationship of 'free wage labour' between worker and employer. Though workers are formally 'free' in such a relationship, it is not an equal one, since they have to work in order to live, while employers can dispense with labour for a considerable period if necessary and fall back on their wealth in order to live.

The emergent proletariat of the industrial revolution soon came to realise that individually they were virtually powerless against the employer in the production relationship, but that collective organisation could serve to redress some of the imbalance of power. Thus, from early in the nineteenth century, workers attempted to organise into trade unions: the principle of collective action and 'strength in numbers' was established as the most effective antidote to capitalist economic and power relations.

Marx and Engels recognised the considerable potential of trade unions as significant vehicles of working-class political action and consciousness. Unions could serve as instruments for challenging the capitalist system of class domination, and as schools of solidarity generating consciousness for the class struggle, *provided* they retained a role as political movements, aiming and working to overthrow capitalism and its inequalities. Any commitment falling short of that would

inhibit the growth of a revolutionary proletarian consciousness, since such a consciousness requires recognition of the
necessity and possibility of supplanting capitalist production
relations with those of socialism. Thus, organised manual
workers' demands reflecting a truly socialist commitment
would be oriented towards issues of *control*, towards questioning the *principles* of ownership, organisation and the
system of power relations in production rather than being
simply *economistic* in nature — that is, attempting merely to
alter the worker's market position *within* the structure of
capitalism. Action of the latter kind would generate only
'trade-union consciousness', and not the revolutionary consciousness necessary for the overthrow of capitalism.

Lenin (1961), too, argued that, left to themselves, the
working class were capable of developing only trade-union
consciousness and that a revolutionary consciousness would
have to be induced from without by a revolutionary political
party (an idea echoed subsequently, as we have seen already,
in Parkin's stress on an 'oppositional consciousness' as the
product of a radical socialist party). The victories which
unions achieve, while not insignificant in themselves, do not
encourage a revolutionary consciousness but may actually
inhibit it, because they entail the acknowledgement of limited
aims within capitalism. Trade-union consciousness, while
producing some sense of unity which is *necessary* for a radical
class consciousness, is *not in itself sufficient* for such a consciousness, since it lacks a coherent political programme for
the replacement of capitalism.

Economism and sectionalism

Many contemporary writers maintain that trade-union activity
of the twentieth century bears out the misgivings of Marx
and Lenin. Economism has been the dominant motivation
behind trade unions' theory and practice, and only rarely has
trade-union industrial action been geared towards control.
The pursuit of financial improvements and better working
conditions has been the keynote, which, while often involving bitter conflicts and protracted disputes, has essentially
entailed working within the existing structure of capitalism

and not systematically questioning its fundamental assumptions. Economistic trade unionism, then, generates an essentially parochial consciousness, a collectivism limited in its
scope by its lack of independence from the dominant value
system (particularly the values surrounding ownership, production and distribution). A trade unionism geared predominantly to the pursuit of control would be an altogether
different proposition. As Giddens (1973, p. 206) says:

> Any sort of major extension of industrial conflict into the
> area of control poses a threat to the institutional separation
> of economic and political conflict which is a fundamental
> basis of the capitalist state — because it serves to bring into
> the open the connexions between political power in the
> polity as such, and the broader 'political' subordination of
> the working class within the economic order . . . Union–
> management clashes involving economism are in principle
> reconcilable in a way which those over control are not.

Economistic orientations are reinforced and intensified
by the *sectionalism* inherent in a movement composed of
organisations whose individual role is the representation of
the interests of workers in specific occupations rather than
those of a whole class. This 'occupational' consciousness is
partly inevitable, given the structural position of the worker in
capitalism, but its political consequences may be fundamental
and far-reaching in inhibiting the growth of any full-blown
radical class consciousness. As Lane (1974, p. 268) argues:
'The working class was possessed of a collective consciousness
but it was rooted in the workplace, because it was only there
that it came up against capitalism as an immediately experienced reality.'

Trade unions (particularly of the 'craft' variety) have
traditionally been much concerned with guarding their status
and maintaining differentials in reward in relation to other
occupational groups at the expense of any massive class-
based assault on capitalism. Roberts *et al.* (1974, pp. 97–8)
stress that:

> Concern over differentials and relativities are as much part

and parcel of shopfloor life and occupy as central a place in the history of Trade Unionism as the class struggle . . . The factory, firm, and trade union are real entities with which ordinary workers can identify and ideas about a wider class struggle often cannot compete.

Strikes and explosions of consciousness

Much of our discussion so far about unionism would probably not find favour with many political commentators of the Right, for whom union industrial action represents major threats to social stability, challenges to the system which attempt 'to hold the nation to ransom', 'to bring the country to its knees', and so on. Much sociological observation on the political implications of industrial action is strongly critical of such a view. Firstly, one might well make a case for trade unions as arbiters in industrial conflict rather than as generators of militancy and radical consciousness among their members. As often as not, unions are involved in peaceful relations with managers and employers or in smoothing out disputes flaring up at shop-floor level.

Furthermore, many would argue that industrial action in the form of the strike does not represent an alternative to or departure from economism, but a mere extension or reinforcement of it, hence not threatening capitalism or escalating working-class political perspectives. In this view, strike action at best provides a support to trade-union consciousness, but has no necessary implications for a revolutionary working-class consciousness.

Industrial conflict tends to centre on specific industrial situations, to be *localised* in one sphere of production or plant, thus serving to narrow the workers' perception of 'them' to particular employers or particular management. The limitations of strike activity for consciousness are further compounded by the fact that the strike is basically an *economic weapon* which unions use in their bargaining role; and it is a device of fairly limited *negative* potential in the form of withdrawal of labour.

This highlights the fact that trade unions are essentially *defensive* organisations, concerned with attempts to limit exploitation within capitalism rather than to eliminate it, largely fighting a rearguard action with negative weapons like withdrawal of labour, work to rule and overtime bans. They are, as Lane and Roberts (1971) and Hyman (1975) have maintained, 'reactive', responding to the realities of the prevailing power relations of capitalism, 'because of the right accorded to management in capitalism to direct production and command the labour force' (Hyman, 1975, p. 97).

However, as we saw earlier, some writers see grounds for optimism in trade-union industrial action and warn against evaluating it too negatively and unidimensionally. First, industrial action may serve as an important source for 'explosions of consciousness', which, although occurring at the local level and although possibly even resulting in defeat, may well induce consciousness of wider issues and serve as a necessary *preliminary* stage to full class consciousness. Lane and Roberts show how a fairly minor dispute at Pilkington, a traditionally paternalistic and trouble-free firm, led to a bitter and intense strike lasting almost two months: after the dispute, the firm could no longer rely on the work-force's traditionally submissive acquiescence of the pre-strike era. Lane and Roberts (1971, p. 105) observe:

A new dimension of living can thus be revealed to the striker; an existence in which 'ordinary' people are able to control events and command the attention of 'them'. The experience of this new reality can transform the striker's perceptions of normal life.

Furthermore, it has been argued that although most industrial disputes centre on 'economic' issues, conflict over issues of 'control' is not absent in strikes, even if it is not spelt out or even if these are apparently trivial matters. Nichols and Armstrong's (1976, p. 25) contention that 'control is always a latent issue in factory production whether it be explicitly recognised or not' is echoed by Westergaard and Resler (1975), who argue that workers' demands that appear to centre merely on pay may act as *symbols* for other dissatisfactions of a more fundamental nature and may spontaneously develop into issues of control questioning the legitimacy of ownership and the authority structure of industry. They maintain that:

> The line between accommodative and radical demands
> does not run between claims for money and claims for
> control . . . Demands for worker control . . . may result in
> no more than consultation or wage-earner representation
> on the boards of companies . . . Demands for higher wages
> may be taken to the point where they challenge the con-
> tinued viability of private capital (Westergaard and Resler,
> 1975, p. 418).

Thus, working-class incorporation into capitalist production
cannot be complete and perfectly peaceful, because the structurally inevitable conflict between capital and labour is too
divisive and workers' everyday experiences in capitalist industry are too alienating for that to be so.

The historical incorporation of manual workers

While economistic orientations prevail among manual workers,
this accommodative orientation to capitalism should not be
seen as a recent one. Unions have *historically* adapted to
capitalism with a socialist ideology essentially reformist in
nature rather than with one advocating a radical dismantling
of the system. Lane (1974) argues that this has largely been
the consequence of unions seeing capitalism as involving a
series of discrete 'problems' for workers and *not* as a *system*,
the structural product of a historical process. This reformist
orientation has its roots in the mid-nineteenth century when
the 'aristocracy of labour' — the skilled upper strata of manual workers — were in the vanguard of the growth of the
trade-union movement. These workers — relatively well paid,
more 'respectable' and politically moderate — gained recognition for their occupational organisations and set the tone for
the development of a reformist labour movement which rejected the idea of unions as tools of political change and
produced no radical critique of capitalist society.

This historically reformist orientation among manual
workers in their direct experience of capitalism in the work-
place is coupled with the twin process of the *progressive de-
radicalisation of socialist parties*. We suggested earlier that

Parkin and others regard the development of an oppositional consciousness as heavily dependent on the propagation of a radical value system by a revolutionary socialist party, and that the subordination of the working class in capitalism has been due in large part to the progressive retreat of European socialist parties into *reformist* socialism. According to Parkin (1971, p. 127):

> Socialist parties were initially committed to abolishing the system of ownership and rewards of capitalist society and replacing it with a system based on equalitarian principles. All the major social democratic parties in Western Europe have now abandoned this aim.

Parkin maintains that these parties, like the labour movement, have come to embrace a commitment not to destroy and replace capitalism but to modify its inequalities. They have proved, however, singularly unsuccessful in this regard, in that the introduction of welfare state measures, changes in systems of education, and attempts at equalisation of economic reward have made no significant inroads into the unequal distribution of privilege. This is because these parties have gradually forsaken an 'egalitarian' version of socialism (that is, a commitment to the eradication of privilege and inequality) in favour of a 'meritocratic' version (that is, the alteration of the principles by which privileges are allocated), which is *far less threatening* to capitalism, since it does not question the basic legitimacy of the system.

This is well illustrated in the case of the British Labour Party, where reformism set in early, if not at birth. Miliband (1961), Lane and others emphasise that, from its inception, the Labour Party has rested on a basis of *pragmatic* rather than theoretical socialism and has been a political movement lacking a coherent radical critique of capitalism and a programme for working-class liberation. Rather, it has consistently taken a piecemeal, *ad hoc* approach to social and political change as something to be realised through the established political machinery. This pragmatism has been fused with a commitment to what Miliband has called 'parliamentarianism', so that reform would be gradual and partial and not sudden and total.

This, alongside an increasing desire to be seen as a responsible 'national' party fit for government, has meant that the Labour Party's potential role as a vehicle for radical working-class political expression has disappeared.

It is important to note that the pattern of reformist trade unionism and diluted socialist political parties in European capitalist societies is not completely perfect, since France and Italy provide exceptions. There, working-class political parties and trade-union movements are communist-led and have retained a stronger commitment to revolutionary ideals and goals, with a more radically critical perception of capitalist society and with Marxism as a guiding ideology. French and Italian industrial workers, for instance, appear to be significantly less willing to view the worker–employer relationship as 'harmonistic', tending to be much more militant in their actions and attitudes towards employers; and, of course, manual workers played a significant role in the events of May 1968 in France.

A number of writers suggest that specific historical factors shaping the development of France and Italy distinguish them from other European capitalist societies. Giddens and Mann, for example, both seem to explain the continued radical consciousness of French and Italian workers by the idea of uneven capitalist development, where there exists

a 'merging of contradictions'. In France contradictions already inherent in capitalist society converge with others, such as the co-existence of a fairly mature industrial sector with a relatively primitively organised, large agricultural sector (Giddens, 1973, p. 212).

French and Italian rural workers have manifested a historical tradition of resentment and 'pre-radical disposition' which has intensified when they have moved into the industrial sector and experienced contact with communist and socialist political parties. The revolutionary perspective developed by these manual workers has been reinforced, rather than diluted, by their relations with employers, according to this view: employers have retained a quasi-feudal attitude to their workers, hostile to trade unionism and unwilling to compromise with working-class movements.

Thus far, we have argued that the main components of the labour movement, unions and socialist parties, have not provided a clear alternative ideology but have mediated the dominant ideology in a way that renders it acceptable. The result of this has been a gradual process of incorporation of the working class into capitalism and the continued hegemony of the dominant class, though we have questioned the extent to which either of these conditions has been rendered complete, and indeed whether *total* incorporation is in fact necessary for capitalism to survive.

Ideological hegemony and the limits of incorporation

It is tempting but misleading to see manual workers in capitalist society, both historically and contemporarily, as being faced with a straight choice between adopting economistic and accommodative orientations on the one hand or revolutionary action on the other, with the former gaining unambiguous preference. We must remember that there are both *practical and ideological pressures* guiding workers towards economism and away from wholesale radicalism.

First, manual workers are *not only* workers; they also have homes, families and leisure activities as elements of their everyday reality, and the routine and unsatisfying nature of most manual work does much to induce an instrumental approach to work, with only modest expectations of deriving any intrinsic benefit. Life outside work may be accorded greater priority and salience, and the daily grind of labour does not become a central life interest: work and the class struggle may at best represent only *one* dimension of manual workers' everyday reality.

Second, the realities of the worker's position in the capitalist industrial system make economism an essentially realistic response. As Mann (1973, p. 32) observes:

Economism ... is rooted in the worker's very experience. ... Normally confronted by an employer who will budge on economic but not on control issues, the worker takes what he can easily get and attempts to reduce the salience of what is denied him.

But even more significant than these practical pressures, manual workers' demands and any industrial action they take do not occur in a vacuum, but are heavily constrained and influenced by the *ideological climate* of capitalism: that is, the dominant values and ideology of capitalist society penetrate through to manual workers themselves. Hyman, for instance, argues that there exists a strong materialist ethos in capitalism which, systematically propagated by media advertising, persuades workers that the consumption of certain goods and services (washing machines, cars, holidays, or whatever) is the key to 'happiness' and self-fulfilment, so that it is not at all remarkable that economistic demands predominate.

Furthermore, the ideological hegemony of the dominant class is reflected in the way in which prevailing ideology regarding industrial relations and the structure of capitalist industry becomes ingrained in many workers' consciousness. These dominant values legitimise the principle of private ownership of the means of production and the organisation and operation of managerial authority, they stress the ultimate mutual interests of owners, managers and workers in the smooth running of the enterprise, and they sustain an unproblematic conception of the 'national interest', 'fairness' and 'reasonable demands', and of the kinds of action which threaten these absolutes (such as strikes).

As we observed earlier, these values are not easily resisted, and the majority of workers give them at least partial endorsement, since as Nichols and Armstrong (1976, p. 51) say: 'Workers are not born with a socialist consciousness. Nor is it something they naturally arrive at. Nor does the information to sustain them in alternative analysis automatically drop into workers' hands.' The practical effect of this is to blunt or reduce the possibility of a shared feeling of solidarity with other workers in the same structural position and hence to inhibit any *systematically* critical evaluation of capitalism. Thus, workers frequently condemn the industrial action of others (even within the same industry) as 'greed', 'agitation', 'troublemaking', and so on, even though they may regard their own demands and action as the legitimate expression of a grievance felt about their own employment conditions.

We cannot, however, ignore the fact that normative acceptance of existing social arrangements by the subordinate class has to be *achieved*, that is, to be continually reproduced. While we do not need to assume that the subordinate class are deliberately 'conned' into submission, we may regard the social relations of capitalist society and the constraints on change built into them as forming a taken-for-granted reality which is institutionalised in the routine assumptions and operation of capitalist enterprises, the mass media, the education system, the legal system and in the state itself. Under such circumstances, existing economic relations and property rights can come to appear immutable features of a 'natural' world, and this very 'naturalness' implies a moral rectitude for established arrangements. Thus, it is difficult for manual workers to present demands for improvements in wages and working conditions in ways that do not seem excessive or absurd, and challenges can become routinely labelled as 'subversion' which must be suppressed.

There *are* limits to hegemony, if we mean by this a situation where both the dominant position of one class and the subordinate position of another are *totally* legitimated by normative acceptance by the subordinate class. We have attempted to show that the legitimacy of capitalist social and economic arrangements is not unambiguously accepted and hence that the incorporation of the working class is not unproblematic. Elements of working-class dissatisfaction and protest are present in capitalism, agreement with dominant social values is generally imprecise, ambiguous and even contradictory at times, and 'built-in' industrial conflict is a price capitalism has to pay. Workers see the inequalities of capitalism in education, housing, health, and so on. They know that managers and professionals receive more than they do, and they feel that 'you mustn't let the buggers grind you down', such that a sense of grievance and dissent does exist, applying essential limits to the process of incorporation.

But, as we have suggested, such a pragmatic acceptance of the status quo on the part of manual workers stops short of becoming an oppositional and disruptive response, since it lacks a coherent and thoroughgoing ideology necessary for the *systematic* critique of capitalism and for forging a 'link of consciousness' between economic and political issues. As

Nichols and Armstrong (1976, p. 59) comment:

> The real triumph of capitalist hegemony is seen in the fact that, for the most part, these workers do not affirm or deny its values. For them, capitalism is just part of an un-alterable order of things (not necessarily a proper or just one). It is a world they did not choose, nor can make, nor can alter. Because of this, capitalism (like God) is not the sort of thing you should think about too much.

4.6 THE CHANGING ROLE OF THE STATE

It has been argued that liberal democracy has developed into (in Lenin's phrase) 'the one best shell for capitalism' in con-temporary Western Europe. At this stage, we can now ask why this form of the state seems so appropriate to capitalism, and whether there are any changes in the role of the state (particularly relating to the economy) which might under-mine this form of government.

We argued earlier that the most stable liberal democracies were created by the defeat of traditional, rural-based pluto-cracies or autocracies, often through political revolution. The emerging bourgeoisie successfully removed previous restric-tions on trade and manufacture and gained a great degree of economic freedom. At the same time, the state gradually involved itself in developments facilitating the establishment of capitalism, the most important of these being the gradual estalishment of laws of property, contract and employment which differed significantly from their semi-feudal predeces-sors. Land and other productive assets became exchangeable commodities, owned by individuals who had the sole right to profit from the use or disposal of their property. Older regu-lations on wages, prices and employment conditions dating back to guild regulation and feudal rural ties were abolished, 'freeing' the worker and the employer to make a contract for the hiring of labour. In these respects, the state withdrew from intervention in economic activity to a position where it merely provided the legal and institutional framework. The more 'active' aspect of the state's role concerned military expansion to 'pacify' areas of the globe in order to open them to trade free from foreign competition. In addition, the state maintained and developed its monopoly of force, and used it to repress protest or rebellion against the emerging social arrangements.

These trends came to their heyday in Britain in the mid-nineteenth century with the *laissez-faire* state. Here the formal separation between economic activity and political rule reached its height. An ideology developed (far from dead today) where the whole society was seen to benefit from unfettered competitive capitalism. The state should therefore keep its distance and not 'distort' the hidden hand of the market or the vigorous expansion of capital. Out of this philosophy developed the claim that politics was 'above' the economy and could provide a neutral arena for representation of the national interest. As long as the subordinate classes agreed that economic growth and the expansion of empire were for the good of all, they could be accepted as citizens and allowed the vote and parliamentary representation. As we have seen, in Britain, and to a large extent elsewhere, the notion of the separation of 'economic' and 'political' issues was accepted by the working class in their *division* of the labour movement into the trade unions (with purely economic concerns) and the parliamentary party.

Thus, the capitalist state came to claim legitimacy as the representative of all individual citizens, and not just the dominant class. To sustain this legitimacy, concessions were gradually made, and the early part of this century saw the beginning of welfare and educational provision by most such states. Equally important in sustaining such legitimacy was the acceptance by workers' movements of the need for 'patriotism' to fight off competing European nations in the First World War. When (as in Germany) some workers rejected such compromises at the end of the war in uprisings and mutinies, the state acted to quell rebellion and secure the dominance of the social democratic parties over revolutionary rivals. For the communists, the capitalist state could never claim loyalty from the subordinate class, for it was necessarily a class state, serving only the dominant economic class. Real politics was class struggle, not shabby compromises over limited issues. In the crises of the 1920s and 1930s, political developments produced defeat for such movements, either through fascism or through the further incorporation of social democratic parties into the business of managing capitalism.

However, the latter solution was not fruitless for the working class. Major concessions were made with the development of welfare states, expanded education systems and protection for trade union organisation, and states came to accept the responsibility to intervene in the economy to sustain relatively full employment and steady growth. As long as these could be sustained, legitimacy was strengthened, because all classes were seen to benefit, and even those outside the labour market were aided by social provision. The state was drawn further and further into direct intervention in the economy through management of credit and money supply; through national-isation and investment subsidies; through support for research and advanced technology; and above all through the fact that the state owned large sectors of industry and employed signifi-cant proportions of the work-force. While all this coincided with the long post-war boom, the political effects were largely beneficial; but counter-effects also emerged which have be-come most serious in those nations most hit by economic recession. As a result, the 'consensus politics' of the post-war period has come to appear more precarious and fragile.

The changes in the post-war state's role seemed to support such a consensus because the concessions made to the working class in such fields as health, education and regional aid often served the needs of expanding, technically based industry. A stable, healthy, educated work-force was clearly desirable. All this, however, is costly, and can come to seem to employers and their political representatives to be an intolerable tax burden. The pursuit of full employment and protection of workers' representation also created its own problems, since workers became significantly stronger at shop-floor level. (Full employment meant that strikes gained effectiveness, since no reserve pools of labour were available.)

While advances in wage levels and employment conditions could be powerfully defended, when growth falters there is strong pressure on union leaders to follow their social-democratic political rulers into wage-freezes, incomes policies and the like. Part of the post-war compromise involved the incorporation of union leaders into the formulation and implementation of such policies in order to 'manage' the economy. However, the unions are involved in such policy-making precisely because of their power (they cannot easily be excluded or forced to comply), but this power is fundamentally located at shop-floor level, where top-level compromises may well be rejected. In such circumstances, the union action either succeeds in changing unwelcome policy, or the unions become excluded from the arena of political policy. The limitations of union power may then become apparent as the right of managers and owners to impose redundancy or closure is met only by defensive union action. Basic economic power relations have not been changed.

Faced with the breakdown of the consensus politics of growth, European governments have increasingly attempted to erode the social security and union power of workers, while at the same time strengthening the capacity of agencies of law and order to resist 'internal subversion'.

At the same time, Western economies have found themselves faced with an intractable combination of high inflation and recession in trade. Policies based on state intervention and spending come to seem ineffective in combating inflation. The immediate response of governments has been to resort to harsh measures. Wage levels are squeezed through the pressure of unemployment, and state expenditure is curtailed; the goal of controlling the money supply replaces goals of growth and full employment — monetarism became the new cure-all in the mid-1970s. However, it is unlikely that these policies will be long-lasting, for they place intense pressure on industry and provoke hostility from trade unions, while achieving very little effect on inflation. Economic and political consequences will almost certainly force governments to return to economic intervention of a more positive kind.

Until recently, then, the separation of economic and political power has been explicitly rejected by European governments, who have 'politicised' economic activity by intervention in and regulation and planning of their economies. This has generally not led to any real crisis of legitimacy for these states, for workers' movements became closely involved in the management of capitalism. While the fragility of this compromise may have been exposed, there are as yet no signs of any real challenge to the legitimacy of liberal democracy as a form of state, with little likelihood of any serious challenge to the hegemonic class being generated within Western Europe in the long-established liberal democracies, while those with the most recently stabilised states (West Germany, Japan) seem best equipped to survive recession with only mild economic and political effect. Hence, internally generated political change within advanced capitalist societies does not appear to be a likely prospect outside the circumstances of global political crisis.

REFERENCES TO CHAPTER 4

Barratt-Brown, M. (1973) 'The Controllers of British Industry', in J. *Political Science Review*, vol. 56.

Bachrach, P. and Baratz, M. (1963) 'Decisions and Non-Decisions: An Analytical Framework', *American Political Science Review*, vol. 57.

Barratt-Brown, M. (1973) 'The Controllers of British Industry' in J. Urry and J. Wakeford (eds), *Power in Britain*, London, Heinemann.

Blackburn, R. and Mann, M. (1975) 'Ideology in the Non-Skilled Working Class', in M. Bulmer (ed.), *Working Class Images of Society*, London, Routledge & Kegan Paul.

Bulmer, M. (ed.) (1975) *Working Class Images of Society*, London, Routledge & Kegan Paul.

Butler, D. and Stokes, R. (1971) *Political Change in Britain*, Harmondsworth, Penguin.

Chevalier, J.-M. (1970) *La Structure Financière de L'Industrie Americaine*, Paris, Cujas.

Cousins, J. and Brown, R. (1975) 'Patterns of Paradox: Shipbuilding Workers' Images of Society', in Bulmer (1975).

Dahl, R. (1961) *Who Governs?*, Yale University Press.

Giddens, A. (1972) 'Elites in the British Class Structure', *Sociological Review*, vol. 20.

Giddens, A. (1973) *The Class Structure of the Advanced Societies*, London, Hutchinson.

Guttsman, W. (1963) *The British Political Elite*, London, MacGibbon & Kee.

Guttsman, W. (1974) 'The British Political Elite and the Class Structure', in Stanworth and Giddens (1974b).

Heller, R. (1973) 'The State of British Boardrooms', *Management Today*, May 1973.

Hyman, R. (1972) *Strikes*, London, Fontana.

Hyman, R. (1975) *Industrial Relations: a Marxist Introduction*, London, Macmillan.

Jessop, R. (1974) *Traditionalism, Conservatism and British Political Culture*, London, Allen & Unwin.

Keller, S. (1963) *Beyond the Ruling Class*, New York, Random House.

Kelsall, R. (1974) 'Recruitment to the Civil Service: How has the Pattern Changed?', in Stanworth and Giddens (1974b).

Kotz, D. (1979) *Bank Control of Large Corporations in America*, University of California Press.

Lane, T. (1974) *The Union Makes Us Strong*, London, Arrow.

Lane, D. (1976) *The Socialist Industrial State*, London, Allen & Unwin.

Lane, T. and Roberts, K. (1971) *Strike At Pilkingtons*, London, Fontana.

Lenin, V. (1961) 'What is to be Done?', in *Collected Works*, vol. 5, London, Lawrence & Wishart.

Lewis, I. (1976) *Social Anthropology in Perspective*, Harmondsworth, Penguin.

Lockwood, D. (1966) 'Sources of Variation in Working Class Images of Society', *Sociological Review*, vol. 14.

Lockwood, D. and Goldthorpe, J. with colleagues (1969) *The Affluent Worker in the Class Structure*, Cambridge University Press.

Lukes, S. (1974) *Power: A Radical View*, London, Macmillan.

Lupton, T. and Wilson, S. (1959) 'The Social Background of Top Decision-Makers', *Manchester School*, vol. 27.

Mann, M. (1970) 'Social Cohesion of Liberal Democracy', *American Sociological Review*, vol. 35.

Mann, M. (1973) *Consciousness and Action Among the Western Working Class*, London, Macmillan.

Marshall, T. (1950) *Citizenship and Social Class*, Cambridge University Press.

Marx, K. and Engels, F. (1976) *Collected Works*, London, Lawrence & Wishart.

Miliband, R. (1961) *Parliamentary Socialism*, London, Allen & Unwin.

Moore, R. (1975) 'Religion as a Source of Variation in Working Class Images of Society', in Bulmer (1975).

Mosca, G. (1939) *The Ruling Class*, New York, McGraw-Hill.

Newby, H. (1979) *The Deferential Worker*, Harmondsworth, Penguin.

Nichols, T. and Armstrong, P. (1976) *Workers Divided*, London, Fontana.

Parkin, F. (1971) *Class Inequality and Political Order*, London, MacGibbon & Kee.

Poggi, G. (1978) *The Development of the Modern State*, London, Hutchinson.

Riesman, D. (1950) *The Lonely Crowd*, Yale University Press.

Roberts, K. *et al.* (1974) *The Fragmentary Class Structure*, London, Heinemann.

Saunders, P. *et al.* (1978) 'Rural Community and Rural Community Power', in H. Newby (ed.) *International Perspectives in Rural Sociology*, New York, Wiley.

Scase, R. (1974) 'Conceptions of the Class Structure and Political ideology', in F. Parkin (ed.), *The Social Analysis of Class Structure*, London, Tavistock.

Scott, J. (1979) *Corporations, Classes and Capitalism*, London, Hutchinson.

Stanworth, P. and Giddens, A. (1974a) 'An Economic Elite: A Demographic Profile of Company Chairman', in Stanworth and Giddens (1974b).

Stanworth, P. and Giddens, A. (eds) (1974b) *Elites and Power in British Society*, Cambridge University Press.

Westergaard, J. (1970) 'The Rediscovery of the Cash Nexus', in R. Miliband and J. Savile (eds), *Socialist Register*, London, Merlin Press.

Westergaard, J. and Resler, H. (1975) *Class in a Capitalist Society*, London, Heinemann.

Whitley, R. (1974) 'The City and Industry: the Directors of Large Companies, their Characteristics and Connections', in Stanworth and Giddens (1974b).

Worsley, P. (1964) 'The Distribution of Power in Industrial Societies', in P. Halmos (ed.), *The Development of Industrial Societies*, Sociological Review Monograph No. 8.

5

The Family

5.1 INTRODUCTION

The continued existence of every society depends, at a most fundamental level, on the reproduction of new generations of the population. Sexual relations between some women and some men, culminating in the birth of children, are an obvious necessity, but to satisfy the conditions for biological parenthood is not in itself enough. Human infants undergo a long period of maturation before they are capable of surviving by themselves, and during this period they require some form of protection and support. Moreover, an extended period of socialisation is necessary if children are eventually to become fully functioning members of society. In other words, children need not only biological parenthood but a form of 'social parenthood' — socialisation, protection and support — as well.

In our society, we have come to expect that sexual activity, child-bearing, maintenance and support of children, and socialisation will all be focused upon the institution known as the *nuclear family* — a domestic unit composed of a man and woman in a stable marital relationship, with their dependent children. A distinguishing feature of the nuclear family is that only two adults are involved in all the activities concerned with the reproduction of children: that is, one woman and one man are simultaneously sexual partners, biological parents and social parents, and the mechanism that links their various activities is the conjugal or marital tie.

Even in our own society, of course, the reproduction of children often takes place in different circumstances. Occasionally, for instance, we find *extended families*, where more than one generation of husbands and wives cohabit with their offspring; social parenthood in extended families may be more of a collective affair than is the case with the isolated nuclear family. A more common arrangement in Britain is the single-parent family, where a man or a woman carries out the tasks of social parenthood alone; in 1976 approximately 10 per cent of families with dependent children were single-parent ones (Central Statistical Office, *Social Trends 1980*). If we were to include under this heading those nuclear families where one of the adults opts out of parental responsibilities, the figure would obviously be much greater. Other differences from the nuclear family pattern are exhibited by foster families; here the roles of social parents are played for the children by two adults who had no part in the biological process by which children are born. Furthermore, some children, though obviously having, or having had, biological parents, nevertheless are socialised and supported in an institutional setting; children in local authority care or Dr Barnardo's Homes are obvious examples.

So even in our society, the arrangement of kinship relationships we know as the nuclear family is not the *only* way in which the reproduction of children is ensured. However, once we leave our world and look elsewhere, alternative patterns of child-rearing are even more marked. We can use both historical and cross-cultural evidence to demonstrate this.

Before the rise of industrial capitalism in Europe, the nuclear family did not occupy the privileged position it tends to be accorded today. Among property-owning groups, there was concern about inheritance and transmission of property and privileges, and about the social standing of their 'house', and for all classes, the family unit was an important economic unit, involved in the production of goods and services upon which survival depended. But the nuclear family was closely embedded in the community, and not regarded as a special private sphere set apart from the rest of the society.

In *Centuries of Childhood* (1973), Ariès points out that from the fifteenth to the seventeenth centuries the family did not occupy a special place in people's hearts and minds. People married and had children. But, as in other non-industrial contexts, marriage tended to be seen as an alliance, important for the connections it established with others, but hardly the central relationship in people's lives. Marriage did not have the religious connotations it later acquired; as Ariès (1973, p. 345) puts it, 'sexual union, when blessed by marriage, ceased to be a sin, but that was all'. Neither were children creatures around whom their parents' lives revolved. In many European countries it was common practice to send one's children away, at the age of 7 or so, to be 'apprenticed' — that is, to live for up to seven years in another house, where they would be expected to perform menial chores, to be instructed in manners and morals, and perhaps to learn the trade of members of the household. This was regarded as a more suitable preparation for adult life than a coddled existence in the bosom of one's own family. Thus child-rearing was not the prerogative of the child's biological parents and neither were families withdrawn from the wider community.

Ariès argues that the integration of the family into community life was reflected in housing, particularly that of comfortably-off citizens in the towns. Daily life centred on a series of social and business encounters, so that business life, social life and family life overlapped. Houses sheltered a shifting population of servants, apprentices, friends, employees, clergy and clerks, as well as the parents and children themselves; rooms were used interchangeably for eating, sleeping, entertaining and arranging business deals. Many people slept together in one room — parents, children, servants and friends alike. The home was definitely not, as we think of it now, a private place reserved for family and intimate friends; nor did the 'family' have the character of a private and privileged unit devoted to the working through of the conjugal relationship and the rearing of one's own children.

We can summarise this by saying that nuclear families in European history were less *privatised* — less detached from the wider society — than those of today. Since home and work-place were so often identical before industrialisation, child-rearing groups overlapped with productive groups. Children grew up and worked and played alongside a range of kinfolk, acquaintances and friends; socialisation was a sort of natural by-product of community life, rather than a specialised activity taking place in isolation from activities in the public sphere.

In pre-industrial Europe, then, family life was significantly different from the sort we are used to. If we now turn to look at evidence from primitive societies, we can see even greater differences.

Probably the most common kinship arrangement in simpler societies is a system of *unilineal descent*, in which descent groups consist not (as in the case of families in our society) of people related by both blood and marriage, but of blood relations only. Where descent follows *patrilineal* rules, membership of a descent group is acquired through the male line only. People become members of their father's descent group; such groups consist of generations of brothers and sisters, along with the children of the brothers. (The children of the sisters belong not to their mothers, but to their fathers' descent groups.) In the case of *matrilineal* groupings, descent group membership is acquired through the female line. Here people become members of their mothers' descent group; matrilineal groups consist of generations of brothers and sisters, along with the children of the sisters. The crucial point is that in matrilineal or patrilineal descent systems people related by marriage are not considered as kin in the way in which people who are related by blood are. In contrast with our own society, the major kinship groupings are constructed by excluding marriage altogether.

It is usually the case, even in societies with unilineal descent, that the reproductive and child-rearing unit takes a form more similar to the kinds of families with which we are most familiar. Although descent groups consist only of the mother and her kin, *or* the father and his kin, people usually live, nevertheless, in domestic units based on a conjugal tie — as husbands and wives and children. Where residence follows *virilocal* rules, brothers remain in the descent group home and bring their wives to live with them; the sisters of the descent group eventually leave to marry men living in other descent group homes with *their* brothers. In the case of *uxorilocal* residence, sisters remain at home and import men from other descent groups as husbands, while their brothers leave to marry elsewhere. Residence arrangements such as these enable sexual partners to be in regular contact, while meeting the common cultural requirement that men and women must look *outside* certain categories of kin for their sexual partners. (Where unilineal descent prevails, marriage between members of the same descent group is usually forbidden.) Marriage outside the descent group has the additional advantage of enabling descent groups to establish alliances between their own and other such groups.

So although in unilineal descent systems kinship groups are made up of individuals drawn from only one side of the biological parent relationship, it is almost always the case that people live together as husband and wife in residence units in which some kind of conjugal tie features strongly, thus bearing a much closer resemblance to our own kind of family than the structure of descent groups would suggest.

The universality of the nuclear family?

The presence of residence groups such as these in unilineal societies has often been used as evidence to support the theory that the nuclear family *is* a universal social institution. This argument suggests that whatever the *formal* rules of kinship involved, all societies' child-producing and child-rearing arrangements will resemble nuclear family units. Often the argument is couched in functionalist terms.

In all societies, it is claimed, four basic functions must be performed: the reproductive function, involving conception and childbirth; the sexual function, or regular intercourse to ensure conception; the socialisation function, introducing children to their societies' culture; and the maintenance function, providing economic support and physical protection for children while they mature. It is further claimed that the most efficient arrangement for ensuring their performance is the nuclear family. Regularised sexual contact is said to be best achieved, and reproduction ensured, by the permanent residential attachment of men and women in marriage; the most satisfactory and convenient arrangement for child-rearing is for responsibility to rest with its biological mother; and support and protection of the mother and child is claimed to be most effectively provided by her husband — the child's biological father. Thus the argument is that, whatever the kin

group looks like on paper, the requirements of child production and child-rearing mean that in practice the nuclear family
will always form the basis of residence groups. Because the
nuclear family is in this view best suited to performing functions that are essential for societal survival, it is claimed that
the nuclear family *will* always perform these functions — that
it will be a universal social institution.

However, there are often crucial differences between the
organisation of residence groups in which members of unilineal descent groups live, and the organisation and functioning of our kind of nuclear family. First, there are societies
where the conjugal tie is either absent or is not the basis for
cohabitation; this happens in matrilineal societies that exhibit
natolocal residence. Probably the best-known examples in the
literature of societies with natolocal residence are the Nayar,
the Menangkabau and the Ashanti. The Nayar were a warrior
caste who lived in Malabar in South-west India. All Nayar
men of fighting age were soldiers and thus away from home,
either fighting wars or in barracks, except for brief periods of
leave. For a substantial part of their lives, then, and particularly when their reproductive capacity was at its highest,
Nayar men would not be available to be active husbands to
Nayar women. Although a Nayar woman was always ritually
married to a man from a descent group with which her kin
wished to have an alliance, reproduction had to take place by
other means. Having established an inter-group relationship
in this symbolic fashion, the 'marriage' was then ritually dissolved, releasing the woman to bear children for her descent
group through an institutional means not connected with
marriage. Fox (1967, pp. 100–1) describes it thus:

> The impregnation of women was not a random affair . . .
> the woman was free to take as many as twelve 'lovers' or
> temporary husbands . . . [resulting in] relatively imperma-
> nent and non-residential unions . . . The number of lovers
> may seem rather large, but as many of them at any one
> time might be away on military duties, the large number
> gave some reserve strength to the task force. These men had
> visiting rights with their 'wives', and if one of the men on
> visiting found another's spear or shield outside the house,

then he would go away and try again the next night.

In this method of reproduction the descent group — generations of brothers and sisters and the children of the sisters — coincided with the residence group; the roles of sexual partner, biological parent and social parent (played in the nuclear family by just two people) were far more widely distributed. The sexual relationship was not just restricted to two people: for any one person, a large number of members of the opposite sex (up to twelve for a woman, and any number for men) could be sexual partners. Although for purposes of legitimacy (to establish a child's correct caste origins) one of the woman's lovers was obliged to acknowledge biological paternity, paternity had no other significance and certainly no influence on child-rearing. Social parenthood was thus kept completely within the descent group, or, if you like, 'in the family'. Parenting was not restricted to individuals in a conjugal relationship, nor was it restricted to just *two* adults; parental roles were enacted not by spouses but by generations of siblings.

To put the contrast another way, among the Nayar, sex had nothing to do with marriage, and neither of these had anything to do with the domestic unit, whereas in societies with a nuclear family organisation it is expected that sex and biological parenthood will be based upon a conjugal relationship and that the domestic unit will be established through marriage.

The Menangkabau of Malaya and the Ashanti of Ghana operate similar reproductive arrangements: although in both societies men have permanent wives, they do not cohabit with them, but merely visit them for sexual purposes. So even in these less extreme versions of natolocality, despite the existence of a permanent conjugal tie, the fact that husband and wife do not cohabit has crucial implications for the links between biological and social parenthood. Once again, brothers and sisters form the descent group *and* the residence group, with husbands largely excluded from child-rearing.

Moreover, even in uxorilocal and virilocal domestic units in other unilineal societies where husbands or wives have got a residential foothold in the descent group, there are still

significant differences between these child-rearing arrangements and those of the nuclear family. For one thing, they are
often much larger units than our nuclear families, so that although a child's biological parents take most responsibility for
its rearing, some aspects of social parenthood are attended to
by other people. The fact of common residence encourages kin
other than the biological parents to take a more active interest
in child-rearing. Furthermore, it must be remembered that in
unilineal societies only one of the biological parents belongs
to the same descent group as their children; other members
of that descent group may claim the right to a *greater* involvement with the children than the parent who is an 'outsider'.

Ideas about procreation in matrilineal and patrilineal societies often clearly reflect and support this separation of biological and social parenthood. In many matrilineal societies
physiological paternity is either devalued or its role denied
altogether. Among the Trobriand Islanders, for example, the
biological father is considered to have no part in creating the
child; he serves simply to 'open the way' for its eventual birth.
The reverse ideology sometimes operates in patrilineal societies, with *women* considered to have no part in creating their
own children. This is characteristic of the Tikopia of Polynesia,
where the woman is just the 'shelter house' of the child. The
Kachin of Burma extend such ideas into the arena of intra-
familial sexual activity; perfectly consistently, Kachin do not
classify intercourse with one's mother as incest (she is not
your mother after all) but adultery. (Many would argue that
beliefs popular in our society about 'maternal instinct' constitute a similar ideological mechanism designed to justify *our*
child-rearing arrangements, reliant as they are on women subordinating all other activity to the mother–child bond.)

In contrast to our society, then, where it is expected that
families will be formed on a marital tie, in unilineal societies
the marital bond is not the basis for the establishment of
descent groups or even residence groups: it is a mechanism by
which a group *otherwise* defined reproduces itself. This has
direct implications for the relationships which we can take
for granted so far as reproduction and child-rearing are concerned. As Fox (1967, p. 40) puts it:

The basic unit is the mother and her child, however the mother came to be impregnated. Whether or not a mate becomes attached to the mother on some more or less permanent basis is a variable matter. This attachment varies from non-existent, through highly doubtful to fairly stable ... The 'conjugal' tie is variable. There are other ways of dealing with the problems of survival than by the institutionalisation of the conjugal tie, and when we see it firmly institutionalised we should ask why this is so rather than take it for granted.

This excursion into historical and cross-cultural studies clearly demonstrates that it is a considerable oversimplification to speak of the 'universality of the nuclear family'. There are in all known societies social units concerned with child-rearing, with sexual activity and with the daily activities of eating and sleeping; but these social arrangements differ from one society to the next — in terms of composition of the largest cohesive group, the composition of the domestic group, the links with the rest of society, the authority patterns and division of labour within the 'family' — and these differences may often be dramatic.

5.2 CHANGES IN FAMILY AND KINSHIP IN THE WESTERN WORLD

In Europe in the sixteenth and seventeenth centuries the production of most goods and services was organised on the basis of the family or household unit, and usually involved the efforts of parents, children and all members of the household. Since the family unit produced most of the goods and services it needed to survive (and sometimes a little extra for sale in local markets), the family of this period was an independent commodity-producing unit — the basic unit of social production.

Over time smaller farming families and cottagers were displaced from their landholdings, with the result that families became more reliant on outside employment — often selling their services to larger landholders. But the most decisive change came from the late eighteenth century onwards, as production of goods became organised through workshops and factories. People left home each day to 'go to work', and earned wages by means of which they hoped to purchase the goods which formerly the family unit might have produced. This change is sometimes referred to as the 'separation of home and work-place'; from being an integral part of family life, work became a separate external activity.

A popular view of the consequences of such changes involves the proposition that the family has been 'stripped' of some of its functions. From being a unit of both production *and* consumption, it is said that the family has become a unit concerned solely with consumption. Goods and services are purchased primarily for the family unit and often consumed within the home, but the family no longer acts as a unit in the production of goods. Rather, individual family members sell their labour to employers who organise the process of production without reference to the family. In short, the family is alleged to have 'lost' the function of production, a change with profound consequences for the nature of family life. For example, the separation of home and work-place signified the general exclusion of women from social production; many women became, for the first time, 'just a housewife', with their husbands as the principal breadwinners.

There are other functions, too, of which the family is said to have been stripped. Recreation, for instance, is less clearly a family affair, especially where adolescents are concerned; recreational opportunities are offered by commercial organisations, from cinemas and discos to clubs and ski resorts, and are purchased on the open market rather than being 'manufactured' at home. Families are also said to have shed certain responsibilities for welfare, since specialised agencies now exist for the care of the sick and the elderly. Most children are exposed to formal schooling, which may at times contradict rather than reinforce the teachings of the family; while early childhood socialisation remains the province of the family, formal education has become the prerogative of school and college.

Now we must be careful about accepting too uncritically this essentially crude picture of the effects of industrialisation on family life. For one thing, long after wage labour became a prime source of income for most households, many families still continued to produce goods for domestic consumption. Even urban families in the early years of the twentieth century often supplemented their diets by keeping a few pigs or chickens, and growing their own vegetables on small plots. The almost absolute dependence of the family on purchased commodities which we experience today is a relatively recent development, coinciding not with the *emergence* of industrial capitalism, but with its *later* stages. Second, the exclusion of women and children from productive activity took place neither as quickly nor as decisively as many have implied. Leaving aside the fact that housewives (or houseworkers of either sex) continue today to produce goods and services at home for the use of the family, many women and children were occupied in Britain with the production of goods for sale within their own homes right through to the last quarter of the nineteenth century — aspects of what was called 'domestic' or 'cottage' industry continued as essential contributions to the family income in many areas. Finally, the notion that, with the rise of factory production, men kissed their wives and children goodbye and trooped merrily off to work, only rejoining their idle families at the end of the day, is completely mistaken. As Harris (1977, p. 86) points out:

> Industrialisation did not result immediately in a differentiation between domestic and industrial labour tied to gender, and the isolation of the family. On the contrary, all members of the family were employed in the factories and the mines, and women and children were only gradually excluded against the vigorous opposition of the factory owners and very often of the husbands and parents.

Sociologists have also offered objections to the view that the passing of leisure and welfare 'functions' into the hands of commercial agencies and state-controlled organisations has undermined the family as an institution.

First, writers such as Fletcher (1966) argue that the view of the multi-purpose 'pre-industrial' family is a fiction; the harsh realities of everyday life for the majority of people in pre-industrial, and early industrial, periods meant that most of the so-called functions such as welfare, education or recreation were largely neglected anyway — the struggle to earn a living under harsh conditions ruled out all but the most rudimentary forms of nursing, education or recreation. Second, sociologists such as Parsons (1959) assert that the family has become a more specialised institution, and that the loss of non-essential functions enables the family to perform its central responsibilities more efficiently, including basic child care. Third, Litwak (1960a, 1960b) and others point out that the family still lays a foundation for the performance of non-essential functions described above; the most obvious example is education, where the early training provided in the family is an important — even essential — foundation for success in the system of formal education.

Arguments such as these have been useful correctives to simplistic views about the waning significance of the family. However, in an effort to counteract popular notions about familial decline, some sociologists have promoted an equally one-sided view, that of the modern family as uniquely well adapted to meet the requirements of industrial society and the needs of individuals: the changes in family and kinship which resulted from the rise of industrial capitalism have been interpreted as the 'march of progress'. Fletcher, Parsons, Goode, Young and Willmott, and the historian Shorter are among those who appear to subscribe to a 'march-of-progress' model of family change in one version or another.

These theorists tend to isolate two aspects of change in family life as particularly significant. One of these is a marked alteration in relationships between the nuclear family and other kin — a move, that is, away from an emphasis upon extended kinship groupings and towards an emphasis upon conjugally based ties. The second is a radical change in the quality of the conjugal relationship; industrial capitalism is seen to have encouraged egalitarianism in marriage, a fundamental shift from pre-industrial society where the patriarch apparently reigned supreme. Furthermore, although the works of the writers mentioned above differ in emphasis and in subtlety, all tend to see the changes accompanying the transition from 'pre-industrial' to 'industrial' families as *advantageous*. Contradictions and strains inherent in contemporary family life are played down, and the focus is clearly upon the modern family as a vehicle for individual happiness and self-fulfilment, and for effective realisation of societal goals.

'March-of-progress' theorists

Young and Willmott

Perhaps the simplest description of the march of progress is provided by Young and Willmott in *The Symmetrical Family* (1973). They posit three distinct historical stages through which British families have passed. In stage 1 (the pre-industrial phase) the family was stable, it was centred on production, and the family members were linked by economic necessity; by virtue of his control over production, the father was undisputed master of the household. Stage 2 (from 1750 to 1900) is characterised as a stage of disruption, when the process of industrialisation threatened to tear the family apart. As home and work-place were separated, and family members became individual wage-labourers, the interaction between them was correspondingly less intense. Fathers were often absent from the family, driven out by overcrowding and forced out to work. Mothers assumed the burden of care and emotional support for the family as a whole, as well as responsibility for stretching the often meagre wages; the difficulties entailed in mothers' lot drove women in urban centres to seek the aid of female kinfolk, thus giving rise to new types of kinship networks from which men were by and large excluded.

Stage 3 began around 1900, and is still, according to Young and Willmott, spreading from the middle to the working class. Family and society have achieved a new equilibrium, and the family is once again stable after the disruptive effects of industrialisation — though its characteristics differ from those of the pre-industrial family. In the new 'symmetrical family' the conjugal pair and their children are very much centred on the home, and spend much of their time together there; the extended family counts for less in people's social horizon, while the nuclear family has pre-eminence; there is greater equality between women and men, and less role segregation by sex. Young and Willmott emphasise the 'mutual adaptation' between family and economy in the twentieth century.

Cohesive families fuel the labour force of the industrial system, and the domestic goods available for use in the home provide a bond uniting family members:

> The more united family has provided the incentive for people to exert themselves in the new industrial system, and the new system has made the family more united by giving it some elementary rights in property (including the machines built to the scale of the smallest human group) which are held or at least enjoyed in common by its members . . . After a long period at odds with each other, the family and technology have achieved a mutual adaptation (Young and Willmott, 1973, p. 271).

Ronald Fletcher

In *The Family and Marriage in Britain* (1966) Fletcher is concerned to demolish the popular notion that the family is in decline. The notion of a long-gone golden age of family life — with the parents and children gathered harmoniously around the fire in the evenings, with children respectful and obedient, with wife and husband secure in their traditional roles and sticking together through thick and thin — this vision is, according to Fletcher, an unrealistic stereotype.

To correct this romanticised picture, Fletcher emphasises negative aspects of the family in the pre-industrial and Victorian periods. For example, he documents in detail how the majority of families in pre-industrial England had to work unceasingly simply in order to survive, and how this, combined with lack of recreational or educational resources and poor housing conditions, made 'happy family life' on the scale described above virtually impossible. Again, looking at Victorian families, Fletcher emphasises that while the bourgeois Victorian family may have been cohesive, solidarity was often based on the tyranny of the father, the virtual enslavement of the mother ('a decorative bauble', in Fletcher's description), and the repression of the children ('seen and not heard'). Set against this backdrop, the twentieth-century family appears in Fletcher's work as a rewarding institution catering both for the satisfaction of societal needs and for individual self-realisation and autonomy.

Edward Shorter

In a somewhat similar vein, Shorter portrays the 'intimate life' of traditional European society (roughly, the late-sixteenth to late-eighteenth centuries) in wholly negative terms. In *The Making of the Modern Family* (1977) Shorter asserts that courtship was based only on instrumental considerations: that the relationships between spouses were mainly contractual, with male peasants caring more for their animals than they did for their wives; that mothers were indifferent about their children's welfare; and that the community constantly interfered with family privacy, inhibiting the chances of loving interaction between family members.

Shorter argues that the emergence of capitalism broke the bounds of local economies, and hence freed family and community life from traditional constraints. This 'freedom' allowed 'natural' emotion to flourish; wage labour encouraged not only economic independence of young people from their kinfolk but also promoted individualistic values and, eventually, rising affluence. The immediate result was the first great *sexual revolution* (between 1750 and 1850), which began with pre-marital experiment among young people, and only later spilled over into the search for sexual fulfilment in married life; later consequences were equality of sexual and marriage partners, the emergence of maternal love, and domesticity or privatisation of nuclear families.

Shorter believes that capitalism brought about a variety of changes in values and attitudes which transformed the custom-ridden, unfeeling traditional family into the warm affectionate family of modern times. Like Fletcher, then, Shorter paints such a bleak picture of traditional family life that the changes allegedly wrought by capitalism are glorified in contrast. For example:

> The nuclear family was a nest. Warm and sheltering, it kept the children secure from the pressure of the outside adult world, and gave the men an evening refuge from the icy blast of competition. And as the nuclear family rose in the

enth century, women liked it too, because it let them
ack from the grinding exactions of farm work, or
ace at the mill, and devote themselves to child care.
eryone huddled happily within those secure walls,
serene about the dinner table, united in the Sunday outing
(Shorter, 1977, p. 272).

William Goode

In *World Revolution and Family Patterns* (1963) Goode uses
data from many different countries to try to isolate trends
which he views as universal. Industrialisation seems usually
to be accompanied, he argues, by a trend towards a 'conjugal
family system' — relatively isolated nuclear families which
retain links to grandparents and grandchildren — and to greater
equality of status between husbands and wives. The development of free labour markets (where there are few constraints
preventing individuals from selling their labour to a particular
employer), he suggests, makes it possible for individuals to
earn their living without the consent or co-operation of their
kin. In Goode's analysis industrial capitalism resulted in
greater individual freedom — by which he means primarily
freedom from the authority of parents or of more inclusive
kin groups. Economic independence provided the basis for
the realisation of values of individual liberty; for example,
Goode attributes the rising legal and political status of women
in the West during the past fifty years to the extension to
women of notions about individual freedom, though he adds
that this was possible only when the precondition of *economic*
independence was met.

Talcott Parsons

The theory most often associated with the question of the fit
between industrial society and nuclear family systems is that
of Talcott Parsons. His argument — that a nuclear family
system is uniquely well adapted to the needs of an industrial
society — has two prongs. First, he suggests that the economic
differentiation which is so characteristic of industrial societies
(the multiplicity of different occupations, with different incomes and life-styles attached) is incompatible with the main-

tenance of extended families but ideally served by the nuclear family. If the family is restricted to the small nuclear group with a single primary breadwinner who is also head of the family, Parsons argues, potential conflicts between members of an extended family working in different jobs are avoided — conflicts, for example, over where the family should live, or arising from a disparity in the incomes and life-styles associated with the occupations. Here Parsons is suggesting that only a nuclear family system eliminates economic differentiation within the family and thus prevents the competitive elements of industrial wage-labour from undermining family solidarity; at the same time, the nuclear family is a small enough unit to be geographically and economically mobile, as an industrial economy demands.

The second part of his argument concerns the need to resolve a conflict between the values which underpin economic and 'public' activities in industrial societies and those which characterise family relationships. According to Parsons, families must inevitably be characterised by values such as *ascription* (an emphasis upon *who* people are) and *particularism* (priority for special relationships); for example, it is expected that parents should love and care for *their* offspring above all others, regardless of how 'successful' or 'attractive' these children are by public standards. However, Parsons argues, these same values are unacceptable and harmful in the public sphere; for example, in economic life, hiring, firing and promotion are supposed to take place according to individual merit only. In other words, for Parsons, the efficient operation of the public sphere depends upon constant application of the values of achievement and universalism — the opposite of those which characterise kinship relations.

Disruption would occur if kin obligations and occupational obligations overlapped — for example, where one member of the family was a supervisor and another a labourer in the same firm. Such conflicts are avoided, Parsons argues, by (i) segregating the nuclear family from other kin, and (ii) segregating the nuclear family from the public sphere (except for the father being the principal breadwinner). Intrusion of family values into work is thus avoided, and work values do not disrupt the solidarity of the family; people do not have constantly to choose between loyalty to kin and the impersonal standards demanded by their occupational roles.

From this analysis of the connections between family and economy, Parsons concludes that an arrangement whereby the nuclear family is structurally isolated from its kin is functional to the workings of industrial society. The norms governing family life dictate that our first and primary obligation will be to our spouse and dependent children. We *may* decide to care for ageing parents, or to take an unmarried brother into our home, but there are no clear-cut norms saying that we *should* do so — the decision is optional. The sort of relationship we establish with kin, other than our spouses and dependent children, is left largely to circumstances and personal choice.

Parsons's analysis of the 'fit' between family and society depends as much on the accuracy of his portrayal of the economy as on his portrayal of family systems, and it can be questioned on these grounds.

Is it the case, for example, that industrial economies 're-quire' of their labour force a higher degree of geographical mobility than other types of society? Certainly, at specific periods in pre-industrial Europe peasants and landless labourers were forced to move frequently in search of their livelihood, and the common image of pre-industrial populations as geo-graphically static is grossly exaggerated. Moreover, in mature industrial societies it may well be the case that urbanisation reduces the necessity for geographical mobility, by making available to people a variety of jobs, resources or opportunities within a fairly narrow locality. Thus it is possible the contrast between a relatively static pre-industrial population and a relatively mobile industrial population has been greatly exag-gerated. Also, the improvement of mass communications and transportation facilities which often accompanies industrial-isation makes it possible for more people to work at a distance from their home — witness commuters — or to maintain close contact with kin who are geographically dispersed.

It is possible, too, that the emphasis upon *social* mobility is greatly exaggerated. First, social mobility of a short-range variety may have been more common in pre-industrial societies than simple typologies would lead us to expect. Second, there are more obstacles to social mobility than some would have us believe; 'achievement' and 'universalism' in the public sphere are paid lip-service but are mediated by the ability of privileged groups to translate their privilege into 'achievement' for their children — or, as in the case of the propertied upper class, to transmit their advantages to their children directly in the form of inherited wealth. In other words, in capitalist societies social mobility seems to be limited to a level which does not threaten the privileges of dominant groups, and it is not surprising that kinship plays an important part in this process. Lupton and Wilson (1959) show quite clearly how in British society kinship is used as a basis for recruitment to elite positions. The extent to which the economy 'requires' occupational selection on the basis of 'achievement' and 'universalism' can certainly be called into question.

However, these are criticisms of Parsons's model of the economy. What really concerns us here is his account of *family* structure and relationships; we will now look at this account, and those of the other 'march-of-progress' theorists, in the light of historical and comparative evidence.

There are two crucial sets of questions to be asked. First, we must consider whether such theories are, in broad outline, historically accurate. Have industrialisation and capitalism been the motor of family change, and have the changes taken roughly the form suggested by Parsons, Goode, Young and Willmott, Fletcher and Shorter? In detail, we may ask whether the rise of industrial capitalism in Europe resulted in (i) the attenuation of kinship ties, such that extended families of pre-industrial periods have given way to relatively isolated nuclear families in the present, and (ii) a marked change in conjugal relationships in the direction of greater equality between husband and wife, a marked reduction in social distance between the conjugal pair, and a greater sharing of power and authority as well as of household and familial responsibilities. Second, we must consider whether it really is the case that the nuclear family of contemporary societies represents a marked *advance* of individual freedom and social effectiveness, a successful accommodation of family and society.

The accuracy of 'march-of-progress' accounts of family change

Relationships between nuclear families and their kinfolk: does industrialisation promote the attenuation of kinship ties?

One of the foremost sources of data on kinship in pre-industrial Europe is the work of the Cambridge Group for the History of Population and Social Structure, of whom Peter Laslett is a prominent representative. Laslett and his associates emphasise the use of quantitative data in the historical study of the family, and one of their primary sources of data is the quasi-censuses, or listings of inhabitants of communities, compiled in periods ranging from the sixteenth to the nineteenth centuries. After examining such data for one hundred English communities, Laslett launched a profound attack on the view that industrialisation brought about a decrease in average family size. During the period surveyed, his data suggest, average household size in the communities analysed stayed fairly constant at approximately 4.75 persons per household; in other parts of Europe, too, from the late Middle Ages, the predominant form of household was the nuclear family plus servants, with even modest rural families having one female servant living in. As Laslett says: 'There is no sign of the large coresidential family group of the traditional peasant world giving way to the small, nuclear, conjugal household of modern industrial society' (in Laslett and Wall, 1972, p. 126).

This evidence fairly puts paid to the notion that the large, co-operative extended family household preceded the onset of industrialisation in Western Europe. However, the information available from quasi-censuses leaves certain ambiguities. For one thing it seems likely that, for a brief period of the family life-cycle, households may have accommodated other kin, such as grandparents or nieces and nephews, so that a form of extended family household was a common part of each person's experience. For another we do not know — and quasi-census data cannot tell us — whether the prevalence of nuclear family households in pre-industrial Europe was by choice (representing a normative ideal) or an unwelcome necessity, with factors such as patterns of landholding preventing people from living in an extended form which they might have preferred. Finally, this evidence tells us only about the household or residence group, but kin may co-operate with one another, and have close and privileged relationships, even though they do not live together. Nuclear families may, for all we know, have had a warm and vital interaction with kinfolk in nearby or even adjacent households in pre-industrial times — just as we find that nuclear families living in separate households today maintain close contacts with kin outside their home.

In *Family Life and Illicit Love* (1977) Laslett raises the possibility that households became more complex in the course of the industrial revolution. Indeed, a study of Preston in Lancashire, by Michael Anderson (1971), using census and other data for 1851, confirms this suggestion. Anderson notes that the proportion of Preston households in which kin other than the nuclear family members resided was higher than figures available for earlier centuries, or than statistics for twentieth-century Britain. Anderson suggests several factors which may have contributed to the willingness of nuclear families to 'take in' kinfolk. One such factor was the availability of work at more than subsistence wages for women in the cotton mills of Preston; it was financially beneficial for a family with young children to take in a relative, perhaps one from the surrounding rural area, who could be responsible for care of the children and day-to-day housekeeping, thus making it possible for the mother of the family to earn wages worth more than the cost of feeding and sheltering the relative. The presence or absence of kinfolk seemed to fluctuate with employment opportunities and wage levels in ways that implied how important these factors are in influencing family structure. Moreover, the better-paid factory workers, such as overseers, were more likely to have relatives in their homes of working age, suggesting that perhaps jobs were found for these relations by their Preston kin. Anderson's work thus raises the point that, far from inhibiting geographical mobility, kinship networks may facilitate it, by providing a base for newcomers to an area (in this case, probably, a base for rural people coming for the first time to industrial wage-labour) and contacts to assist them with settling in. Anderson's work underlines, too, the significance of kin as a resource to draw upon in meeting recurring life crises — temporary unemployment, homelessness, and so on. He emphasises clearly the effects of material conditions on the range of options that people have at their disposal in the use of kinship.

Kinship in contemporary societies. Post-war studies of Europe and America have demonstrated, in a variety of contexts, the continuing vitality of kinship ties, particularly those linking married couples to their families of origin. In Bethnal Green, the working-class urban community studied by Young and Willmott in the 1950s (*Family and Kinship in East London*, 1962), kinship networks constituted an important basis for community solidarity and sociability. Among married people interaction with kin was frequent and highly valued. Of married men with parents alive, 30 per cent had seen their father, and 31 per cent their mother, within the twenty-four hours prior to interview; of married women, 48 per cent had seen their fathers, and 55 per cent their mothers, within the previous twenty-four-hour period (Young and Willmott, 1962, p. 46). Here, as in the Ship Street area of Liverpool (Kerr, 1958), kinship interaction was skewed towards women. Mothers often helped their married daughters find accommodation, and provided regular assistance with baby-sitting, preparing tea for sons-in-law, taking clothes to the laundry or doing bits of shopping; they were the first source of help and advice in 'crises' such as illness or the birth of a child. Although there was some reciprocal aid in the form of loans or help in acquiring jobs between fathers, married sons, and adult brothers, Young and Willmott were in no doubt that the lynchpin of the entire kinship network was the companionship and domestic help shared by mothers and their married daughters. Because of the residential stability of areas like Bethnal Green, a high proportion of people had kinfolk living within easy reach. Interaction and mutual aid was made all the more likely by the geographical proximity of kin; but, in addition, the affective and material significance of kinship ties may have contributed to the decisions of young married couples to remain as near as possible to their kin.

The relocation of many working-class families in new towns

or overspill estates gave opportunity to consider the effects of geographical mobility on patterns of kinship behaviour. Young and Willmott's (1962) study of families from Bethnal Green who had resettled in the Essex estate of Greenleigh appeared to bear out the view that geographical mobility attenuates kinship ties. Since people were relocated as nuclear family units, leaving most of their kin behind, mobility did indeed herald a reduction in interaction with kin; women seemed to experience particularly keenly the relative isolation from their mothers and sisters. Although some husbands could manage visits to kinfolk on their way to or from work in the East End of London, and although family reunions were arranged when possible, the major impression given by Young and Willmott is of the nuclear family drawing back on itself, from the community-centred life of Bethnal Green to the more privatised, home-centred life of Greenleigh. Goldthorpe and Lockwood's (1968a, 1968b, 1969) descriptions of the 'affluent workers' of Luton offered a similar theme of privatised nuclear families, with interaction with kin curtailed by geographical separation.

However, the attenuation of kinship ties should not be regarded as an inevitable effect of geographical mobility. In the first place, disruption of interaction does not necessarily imply the destruction of the relationship. For example, as Rosser and Harris (1965) note, kinship obligations are often so strong that people will extend hospitality and help to a visiting relative with whom they have only a slight acquaintance. Second, geographical separation becomes less of a barrier to interaction and help when standards of living are higher. In the Woodford area of London, for example, middle-class people were able to counteract the separating effects of distance by their greater access to cars and telephones, and by more spacious housing which made prolonged visits from relatives possible (Willmott and Young, 1971). Third, the geographical separation of nuclear families from their kin in new housing estates may be a temporary phase; if housing conditions permit, as the new residents pass through the family life-cycle, their children may grow up, marry and settle down near them, thus creating a new network of kin in the area. Willmott (1963) argues that at the time of its initial settlement in the 1920s and 1930s, Dagenham may have been much like Greenleigh of the 1950s; however, forty years on, to some of its residents it was 'like the East End reborn'.

Although studies of working-class kinship patterns have demonstrated conclusively that kinship networks can indeed flourish in urban industrial centres, it has sometimes been argued that only middle-class families, with their higher rates of geographical mobility, could provide a satisfactory test of the 'isolated nuclear family' hypothesis. Yet, as has already been pointed out in connection with the study of Woodford, the greater material resources of many middle-class families may make geographical separation from kin less of an obstacle to interaction than it would be for families who are less well off. For example, in Hubert's (1970) study of the north London suburb of Highgate, few of the couples interviewed had kin in the immediate area; nevertheless, both sentimental and practical involvement was strong, with mothers occasionally coming from abroad to help their daughters at the birth of a child. Moreover, the Highgate couples travelled frequently to see kinfolk, though they did so selectively; geographical distance was used as an excuse for failing to visit kin they did not like, while acting as no barrier to visiting kin of whom they were fond.

Studies by Sussman (1953) in New Haven, Connecticut, and by Bell (1968) in Swansea have observed that young middle-class couples assert strongly their autonomy from kin, and that kin in turn agree that the younger people should 'stand on their own two feet'. In both studies, however, parents provided their married children with considerable material aid, tactfully presented so as not to endanger the illusion of autonomy. Bell reports that even such extravagant assistance as central heating, a car or a house — though obviously of importance to the younger family's standard of living — might be delicately presented as Christmas or birthday gifts. Bell also makes the point that while geographical separation does not automatically rupture kinship networks, or prohibit mutual aid between kin, it does make day-to-day domestic help between mothers, daughters and sisters less likely; the balance of aid tends to shift (in families that are well enough off to make this possible) to the father/son or father/son-in-law relationship, and to financial rather than domestic help.

In reviewing the evidence from these studies, three additional points should be noted. First, the difference between middle-class and working-class families can easily be exaggerated. While Bell's research looked mainly at upper-middle-class families, Rosser and Harris's (1965) work in Swansea found little difference in kinship behaviour between those in their sample who were 'working class' and those who could be described as 'middle class'; for both strata the 'extended family' provided a focus of identity, and a living insurance policy, a resource that could be drawn upon — often the first resort — during times of unemployment, money shortage, bereavement, illness, and so on.

Second, while it has been emphasised that extended kinship networks can and do persist in the face of geographical mobility, it should also be noted that kin can and do actually *promote* both geographical and social mobility. As Anderson (1971) argued for nineteenth-century Lancashire, and Litwak (1960a, 1960b) for twentieth-century USA, kinfolk can provide a base for relatives who are newly geographically mobile; moreover, parents may actually help to finance the move of their married children to a more advantageous location or into a more promising career.

Third, the emphasis upon working-class and middle-class families should not be allowed to obscure the relevance of kinship ties to the cohesion of the upper class. For example, the intricate ties of blood and marriage between Cabinet Ministers, Directors of the Bank of England, and Directors of City banks and other powerful institutions traced by Lupton and Wilson (1959) offer some indication of the extent to which kinship links 'top decision-makers'.

The relationship of nuclear families to their extended kin: conclusions. From a consideration of this historical and contemporary evidence our conclusion must be that there is no simple pattern of extended families in pre-industrial societies, and nuclear families in industrial ones. Instead, we find from historical evidence that, prior to industrialisation in both

Europe and America, the majority of the population lived in nuclear family units; the nuclear family was then, as it is today, an important domestic grouping. Furthermore, in terms of the composition of the usual coresident group, the evidence suggests that there has been continuity through from pre-industrial times to industrialisation. In advanced industrial societies extended kin relationships — particularly those between adult offspring and their parents — appear to continue to play an important part in contemporary family life. Such relationships may be disrupted by aspects of contemporary industrialism — e.g. by geographical relocation — but they appear capable of surviving this sort of temporary disruption; indeed, contrary to some views, such kin ties may facilitate geographical and social mobility by providing assistance for individuals and nuclear families who need it.

Conjugal relationships: has there been an increase in egalitarian marriage due to the effects of industrialisation and/or capitalism?

As we have seen, the 'march-of-progress' theorists have, by and large, argued that the later stages of industrialisation have seen the rise of the egalitarian family, in which the roles and power of husband and wife (and, perhaps, of parents and children) are more interdependent, less one-sided. For Willmott and Young, for example, 'the symmetrical family' is one of the characteristics of the 'third stage' of British family development; greater equality between husband and wife is indicated by such factors as the breaking down of the 'traditional' division of labour by sex, such that women take on 'men's work' (especially paid employment outside the home), while men assume responsibility for some of 'women's work' (housework, shopping and child care). They link the emergence of the symmetrical family, especially among middle-class couples, to better standards of living, which make it possible for husbands as well as wives to spend a greater proportion of their time in the home, building a relationship and a family together, and to the demise of the extended family as a significant moral force in many people's lives, such that both women and men are thrown back much more on each other's company and assistance in marriage.

Bott (1957) attempted to develop a framework for conceptualising and explaining variations in the conjugal relationship. She distinguishes two types of conjugal role relationship — *segregated conjugal roles* and *joint conjugal roles* — which are perhaps most usefully imagined as the ends of a continuum, with numerous possibilities lying in between the two extremes. Where couples have *segregated* conjugal role relationships, husband and wife inhabit distinct and separate social and working worlds, linked only by their reciprocal obligations and rights: each spouse will have his or her own set of friends, probably a single-sex peer group which may have survived from the days of courtship. Each spouse will have separate responsibilities, with in many cases the wife being made strictly responsible for housework, laundry, cooking, shopping and child care, and the husband strictly responsible for financial support and for 'heavier' tasks around the home.

Within a *joint* conjugal role relationship, on the other hand, the demarcation between wife's world and husband's world will be far less clear cut. Husbands and wives may do many chores interchangeably, and be perfectly flexible about which sex is responsible for which sort of task. They will share many friends in common, entertain together, usually take their recreation together, and become, as it were, interchangeable units within the household. Power and authority — as expressed in family decision-making — are equally divided between husband and wife.

Bott predicts that segregated conjugal roles will flourish wherever spouses are enmeshed in tight-knit networks of friends and kinfolk — where, that is, their closest relationships outside the immediate family are with people who not only know them but know one another as well and are in regular contact. The existence of such a network acts as a check, a form of social control, on the activities of the conjugal pair and, by informal sanctions such as teasing, prevents the conjugal pair from drifting far away from the 'traditional' division of labour. Moreover, the existence of such a network ensures that both husband and wife will have persons of their own sex to call upon for help with tasks — women friends or kin to help with baby-sitting, male friends or kin to help put up a new garden shed — so that they will have little need to call upon one another for assistance.

Joint conjugal role relationships arise, by contrast, where the couple have a scattered or loosely knit network of friends, friends whose only link with one another is through the central couple. In this situation the couple will be thrown back more upon their own devices, and end up blurring the 'traditional' role distinctions; they will not be subject to the social control of the community which might act as a check on such changes.

At first sight, applying Bott's framework to evidence from industrial Britain would seem to support the 'march-of-progress' contention that industrialisation has promoted a greater egalitarianism in marriage; this evidence does seem to suggest that the process of industrialisation in Britain has produced conditions which promote the growth of looser-knit networks, and possibly, therefore, more joint conjugal role relationships. As we suggested in Chapter 2, early industrialisation typically involves the exploitation of a country's raw materials so that urban centres grow up around these materials. In such communities, where employment opportunities are usually restricted to one kind of manual work — mining, shipbuilding, fishing, or whatever — and where a lack of educational opportunities inhibit any possibility of mobility, a close-knit network of the kind conceptualised by Bott is the near-inevitable result. We saw earlier the effect this has typically had on kinship relations in such communities and the kinds of conjugal role relationships produced in such circumstances are no less typical.

Two studies which illustrate such a pattern of segregated conjugal role relationships are the study of a Yorkshire mining community, referred to as Ashton, and the study of fishermen based in Hull. Both these studies have in common the finding that, largely because of their work, men were involved in tightly knit single-sex peer groups which attracted much of their loyalty and their time.

In *Coal is Our Life*, by Dennis, Henriques and Slaughter (1956), the relationship between spouses was described as highly contractual: that is, both husbands and wives had certain fixed and non-negotiable obligations, and being a

good husband or a good wife consisted almost entirely in fulfilling these contractual duties. Husbands were expected to
provide for their families, by giving a certain fixed proportion
of their weekly pay packet to the wife as housekeeping money
(her 'wages'). Beyond that it appears that little was expected
of the husband. Wives were expected to use the housekeeping
money and their own labour and ingenuity to provide a comfortable and harmonious home for husbands to seek refreshment in after a hard day at work. The wife's life, her schedule,
was almost entirely dictated by the timing of the husband's
commitments; whatever shift he was on, whatever time he
returned home, she was expected to be waiting with a hot
meal and a clean change of clothes.

Husbands spent most of their free time outside the home,
at sports events or clubs with their male friends and work-
mates. Their commitment and loyalty to their workmates is
portrayed as deep and overriding most other commitments; it
stemmed partly from the experience of growing up together
in the same community, and partly from their sharing of the
arduous work of mining, in which not only the size of a man's
pay packet but his very life might depend on the quick-
wittedness and energy of the members of his work-team.
Thus occupation is seen as a major influence on the type of
friendships which cut across the conjugal relationship. The
existence of segregated conjugal roles was reinforced by two
other factors: first, the ideology that women, being 'incapable' of the difficult work of mining, are somewhat inferior
beings not entirely worthy of the same respect as workmates;
and second, the taboo against men showing (at least publicly)
any display of tenderness towards women. The operation of
this taboo during courtship resulted in many young men making up excuses to their friends for seeking out the company
of women — excuses which reinforced the general disrespect
for women, by suggesting publicly that they were only useful
'for one thing'.

Tunstall's study of *The Fishermen* (1962) focuses again on
an exclusively male occupation and the kinds of conjugal
relationships which are encouraged by this occupation. Tunstall describes an interesting dilemma which besets both the
women and the men whose lives were affected by fishing. The

women were forced, during their husbands' periods at sea, to assume total responsibility for the family, including discipline of the children; yet when their husbands returned from sea, the wives were expected to step back into 'traditional' roles and leave the men to resume temporarily the position of 'head of the household'. They wished their husbands could be more regularly at home, possibly resented them going away, and yet were worried when they were 'beached', for this meant an immediate cut in standards of living and possible poverty. The husbands, on the other hand, as well as missing their wives and children during their long absences at sea, sometimes suspected — from the wives' ambivalence about handing over the reins of power when husbands returned, and from their anxiety when husbands chose to stay ashore — that their wives were 'using them'.

The existence of tightly knit networks is amply illustrated in this study. Husbands returning home from sea nevertheless spent a large proportion of their time ashore in the company of their workmates: going out on the town with the boys was one of the compensations for a harrowing life at sea, and fitted most easily with the relationships which the men built up during their working lives. The women, too, had their own network of friends and kin to whom they turned for comfort, company and assistance when their husbands were away.

However, since all industrial societies develop away from such a reliance on basic heavy industry, manual workers increasingly find themselves living in less homogeneous communities. Evidence from studies of new and expanded towns seems to confirm Bott's prediction that looser networks in such towns, encouraged by geographical mobility, tend to promote a greater 'jointness' of conjugal role relationships.

For example, in Greenleigh, the new town housing estate to which many people from the East End of London were rehoused in the 1950s, Young and Willmott (1962) found that one immediate effect of the move was an increase in 'home-centredness', particularly for the men. The absence of their local public house, the lack of new friends and the reduction of spending money caused by more expensive rents and rates encouraged many husbands who previously spent a great deal of their leisure time outside the home with friends to rely instead on the company of their wives and children. The new houses, too, absorbed more time and energy, and encouraged many men into do-it-yourself projects around the home. Both husband and wife were cut off from their earlier closely knit networks; the isolated Greenleigh spouses were, accordingly, thrown back on each other both for company and for help with chores. This example seems most effectively to support Bott's assertion of a connection between mobility, networks and conjugal role relationships. It is confirmed further by Goldthorpe and Lockwood's 'affluent worker' studies, which suggest that workers in Luton, most of whom were geographically mobile and had young families, were relatively 'privatised', preferring to spend their leisure within the nuclear family and steering clear of close commitments outside.

All this evidence so far refers only to manual workers. What about the middle class? Although the research into middle-class family life is less substantial, it is often suggested that middle-class couples, because of their greater mobility, are more likely to exhibit 'joint' characteristics than normal workers. Bott's own small-scale study supports this contention, and Young and Willmott (1973) expressly argue that joint conjugal roles originated within the middle class and are still spreading to the 'lower classes'.

In sum, then, the process of industrialisation has seemed to produce a pattern of increasing 'looseness' of networks, and therefore a greater 'jointness' of conjugal role relationships, with the result that marriage in industrial society seems more equal than ever before.

More recent work on this topic has tended to throw serious doubt on this conclusion, however. One of the major criticisms is that much depends on how the concepts of 'segregated' and 'joint' are *defined*; too often, it is argued, their indicators are too crude or too crudely applied to give an accurate picture, and that it may therefore be illegitimate to equate joint-ness with true egalitarianism in marriage.

For example, although mutuality — the sharing of friends and activities by spouses — is taken almost without question as a sign of jointness and egalitarianism, this is certainly questionable. If mutuality arises because a wife is cut off from her friends — if she becomes reliant on social contacts her *husband* brings home and must join her husband in activities *he* chooses and initiates — mutuality may represent a *decrease* in autonomy for the wife, *increased* dependence on the husband, and greater *inequality*.

We can see similar problems with the application of Bott's concepts by looking at evidence from various research sources. In Gavron's *The Captive Wife* (1968), for example, 62 per cent of the working-class wives, as against all but one of the middle-class wives, did *not* know their husband's income. This is often presented as an indicator of segregated conjugal roles, and would, in this case, suggest that working-class marriages are far more likely to be segregated than those of the middle class. However, a higher proportion of working-class wives also reported that their husbands helped 'in every possible way with the children', and Gavron concludes, overall, that one of the key differences between middle- and working-class members of her sample was that the men in the working-class sample seemed *more* family-minded and home-centred than middle-class men.

Similar doubts regarding the relationship between conjugal roles and class membership emerge from studies of managing directors in Young and Willmott's *Symmetrical Family* and of managers carried out by Pahl and Pahl (1972). Both these studies suggest that members of this occupational group are more likely than any other to spend considerable time away from home (on pleasure as well as business), to expect their wives not to work but to accommodate their lives to fit in with the man's schedule, and to argue that their wives' confinement within the home, and sole responsibility for familial and domestic concerns, is a fair exchange for the high standard of living the husbands' career might purchase. They indicate, in fact, that the relative market power of husband and wife is a crucial factor in determining the quality of marital relationships and that disparity in market power may be at least as great for upper-middle-class women (who, by virtue of sex and class, have not been prepared for work by their parents) as among the unskilled working class, where the women may get a job without qualifications but at a lower rate of pay than their husbands.

Oakley (1972, 1974) is particularly dismissive about conclusions regarding egalitarianism in marriage which rest on Bott's framework. She argues that sociological studies of 'equality' in marriage have often started from the assumption that cooking, cleaning and child care are somehow inherently women's responsibilities and hence that *any* intervention in these spheres by men is regarded as a major breakdown of conventional patterns. While couples may do things 'jointly', she argues, this does not necessarily mean that they do things 'equally'. (For example, while the husband washing up the dishes twice a week *is* evidence of joint collaboration on domestic tasks, it certainly is not evidence of an *equal* division of this labour.) Again, Oakley points out that sharing, or mutuality, or jointness, may in practice characterise some aspects of the marital relationship but is not extended to others: for example, couples may entertain or visit friends together, but that in itself is no guarantee that child care or housework is shared.

In fact, there is little evidence supporting an egalitarian division of labour in the home. Data from both the USA and Britain indicate that while husbands are more likely to perform certain household tasks if their wives work part time than if they are not in paid employment, and even more likely if their wives work full time, rarely does this effort on the part of husbands even approach taking over half the burden of work in the home. For example, in Young and Willmott's study *The Symmetrical Family*, 21 per cent of men whose wives work full time, 32 per cent of men whose wives work part time, and 36 per cent of men whose wives are not in paid employment, give no 'help' at all to their wives, or restrict their helping to occasional washing up. In fact, the authors' evidence for 'symmetricality' with respect to division of labour is, as Oakley (1974) has pointed out, totally unconvincing. For example, according to Young and Willmott, 72 per cent of married men 'help their wife' in the home in some way other than washing up at least once a week. But these data are so vague that we can draw few conclusions from them, and certainly none that support the charge of 'symmetricality'; included in that 72 per cent would be any husband who took his son on an outing on a Saturday afternoon, or who tucked a child into bed and read a story, or who made

Sunday breakfast or flicked a duster over the living-room furniture. The interesting thing, in fact, is that less than three-quarters of husbands can meet even this loose criterion. Oakley (1974, pp. 100–1) concludes:

> As long as the blame is laid on the woman's head for an empty larder or a dirty house it is not meaningful to talk about marriage as a 'joint' or 'equal' partnership. The same holds of parenthood. So long as mothers not fathers are judged by their children's appearance and behaviour . . . symmetry remains a myth.

In the present state of knowledge, then, while it would seem difficult to judge whether working-class or middle-class marriages are, on the whole, more equal, what is certain is that neither of these classes has a monopoly on segregated marriages, *and* that equality of the partners in marriage is certainly not widespread. Inequality shows up in marriage in numerous ways: the prevalent sexual division of labour within the home; the prevalence of the 'dual role' for women in paid employment — but not for men; the assumption (by some sociologists, as well as by many lay people) that when men do housework, they 'help their wives', and that when women go to work their husbands are 'allowing them to do so'; the degree to which, in the course of marriage, a woman's market situation gets worse while that of her husband in many respects improves (a situation which makes women even more dependent on entering or re-entering marriage in order to survive); the degree to which in Britain the taxation and national insurance and social security systems assume a woman to be financially dependent on the man with whom she lives; and so on. These and other factors make it necessary to recognise that much of the literature on nuclear families in contemporary society has been mystifying, in so far as it has described *families* or *marital relationships* without differentiating the specific and different effects upon different members or without examining their relative degrees of power or autonomy. The development of 'home-centredness' may be used to illustrate this point.

The meaning of home-centredness — particularly since

industrial capitalism separated the site of family life and the site of work — has been different for men and women. As the term is used by Young and Willmott, in *Family and Kinship in East London* and in *The Symmetrical Family*, the trend towards home-centred families can mean only one thing — a tendency for *men* to centre more upon the home. Women have, during this period, *been* home-centred all along, or if anything have been moving out into the public sphere to take up paid employment. Thus, in a sense, the term 'home-centred family' equates the character of the family with the activities of the husband; if those of the wife were included, one would have to argue that to some extent husbands and wives are moving in opposite directions. Moreover, Young and Willmott's own evidence for home-centredness shows a marked difference between women and men, though it is one they hardly comment upon; in *The Symmetrical Family*, on a typical weekday, the proportion of total time spent inside the home was 87 per cent for women not in outside paid employment, 71 per cent for women with outside jobs, and only 55 per cent for men. It is clear that if home-centredness literally implies time spent within the confines of the home, then women are, by virtue of their responsibilities for housework and child care, far more home-centred than their husbands.

If the notion of 'joint conjugal roles' or of symmetrical families is of limited usefulness in understanding contemporary marriage, perhaps we should consider Parsons's model. Parsons suggests that most primary groups (of which the nuclear family is one example) tend to throw up not one but two 'leaders' — people to whom others in the group turn for advice and reassurance. One leader — responsible for 'instrumental' performance — takes the lead in achieving the goal for which the group has been set up, while the other — the 'expressive' leader — is predominant with respect to creating and maintaining the conditions for group solidarity — by peace-making, by soothing, by encouragement and moral support. Within nuclear families, Parsons argues, the mother plays the role of expressive leader, with responsibility for group cohesiveness, and father specialises in instrumental activity — quite literally bringing home the bacon. Unlike

Young and Willmott, then, who believe there has been a (beneficial) lessening of differentiation between husbands and wives, Parsons implies that continuing this differentiation, along the instrumental/expressive dichotomy, ensures the efficient operation of the family as an institution devoted to child-rearing and to emotional gratification. It does not in his view necessarily imply inequality but rather a 'separate but equal' arrangement.

However, Parsons's notion of the importance of the expressive/instrumental split in responsibilities can be questioned on a number of grounds. First, it is unlikely that a definite division of labour along these lines is actually very widespread. One study of middle-class couples in Australia which set out to test the thesis (Craddock, 1977) found that both men and women initiated and developed discussions of feelings, emotions, etc., with equal frequency; women did not specialise in this expressive activity. Husbands specialised in some instrumental tasks (such as putting the rubbish out), wives in some (such as giving children pocket money), and many others were performed sometimes by husbands, other times by wives.

Second, if we consider what is sometimes called the 'traditional sexual division of labour', it does not correspond very readily to Parsons's characterisation, particularly with respect to the responsibilities of women; as Oakley asks, in what sense can cleaning the oven, defrosting the fridge, scrubbing the floors or boiling dirty nappies be regarded as an 'expressive' activity? A more serious criticism is that Parsons fails to demonstrate why this particular division of labour is necessary, or in what sense it can be regarded as functional. Certainly, within any group (family or other) there will be certain tasks that can be deemed 'expressive' and others which can be described as 'instrumental'; but there is no clear reason why (i) these must be divided between different individuals — it is clearly possible for each person to undertake both sorts of tasks — or (ii) the woman must specialise in expressive activities and the man in instrumental ones. Expressive activities do not preclude instrumental ones, either *within child-care* tasks or outside them. Moreover, since the characteristics associated with masculinity or femininity vary enormously from one culture to another, the 'expressivity' of women or the 'instrumentality' of men in one particular culture cannot be assumed to be universal.

Contemporary conjugal relationships: conclusions. It appears that the view that industrialisation ushered in egalitarian relationships is greatly exaggerated. Initially, industrialisation may have worsened the position of women relative to that of men, by crystallising a private sphere within which women, and only women, were assumed to be contained, and by limiting women's access to independent sources of livelihood. Furthermore, although in recent years an accelerated trend towards privatisation of nuclear families, combined with lower fertility rates and the return of women to the paid labour force, has indeed altered the character of conjugal relationships, there is no evidence to support the view that marriages are now typically 'egalitarian' or 'symmetrical'.

Family change: conclusions. The 'march-of-progress' description of contemporary families as (i) relatively isolated from kin, and (ii) egalitarian, must be seen as greatly oversimplified. While changes have occurred in relationships with kin and with spouses, these changes cannot be summed up as representing a unilinear movement from extended to nuclear families, or from patriarchal to egalitarian ones. Nor can it be upheld that 'industrialisation' has been the principal cause of any such changes; on the contrary, industrialisation — described by Goode (1968, p. 322) as 'that ragbag of variables' — may take place in different ways, producing different effects and results for families.

Let us now turn to the second level at which this kind of approach to family change can be assessed: to what extent are 'the march-of-progress' theorists right in interpreting the kinds of changes they identify as *progress*?

The evaluation of family change

As we have seen, 'march-of-progress' theorists tend to emphasise the positive reciprocal influence between family and the rest of society; reacting against the pessimistic view that the family is in decline, such theorists have bent over backwards to emphasise the strengths of the modern family. It is seen as effective with respect to child-rearing (and all the more so, since certain non-essential functions have been catered for elsewhere), and as providing a refuge for emotional development for adults, a refuge characterised not by dependence on kin but by autonomy, and by egalitarian rather than patriarchal relationships between spouses. The evaluative character of this theory is fairly obvious: the familial institution is (reasonably) flourishing in modern societies, it is held, and this is beneficial for society.

Morgan (1975) points to four positions that might be argued with respect to the evaluation of contemporary families. Each position combines two elements: a judgement as to whether the family is or is not in decline, and a judgement as to the effects of the family's position on the rest of society. For example, it might be held that the family is weak, and that this is a major source of the ills of our society; or that the family is weak, and that this is to be applauded, since the decline of the family will bring a number of other benefits (freedom for children, perhaps, or for women). The former position is the one often taken by lay commentators, who wish to find a relatively easy explanation for social problems; the latter position is rarely articulated.

The 'march-of-progress' theorists tend, of course, to subscribe to the third of Morgan's four positions, arguing that the family is alive and well *and* that this is all to the good. While certainly the dominant view in the sociology of the family for some time, it should not be thought that *all* contemporary sociologists subscribe to it; for example, writers in the Marxist tradition, while agreeing that the family is relatively strong, complete Morgan's typology by tending to argue that this strength is to the *detriment* of most sectors of society.

The idea of progress: the Marxist critique

Most Marxist analyses draw attention to the ways in which families tend to encourage and reproduce hierarchical inegalitarian relationships, and to act as a safety-valve, dampening down discontent so that it is robbed of revolutionary content.

In providing a place where children can be conceived, borne and reared in relative safety, the family is providing tomorrow's labour force. At the same time, by offering a centre for relaxation, recreation, refreshment and rest, the family helps to ensure that members of today's labour force are returned to work each day with their capacity to work renewed and strengthened. This is what is meant when it is said that the family reproduces labour power on a generational as well as a daily basis. The family also provides much of the motivation that keeps workers at their benches. This happens again on a generational and daily basis. Children are taught the necessity of work and the basic forms of work discipline (punctuality, obedience) in the context of the family, though this is heavily supplemented by the school. Adult men and women are discouraged from 'dropping out' of the labour force, or from turning their backs on work which is less than fulfilling, by the expectation that *good* husbands/mothers/parents must do their utmost to earn enough to buy their children and themselves certain comforts and advantages. Furthermore, this 'incentive' may be all the more compelling, the more that adults feel their own lives to be barren and want to 'live' through their children. The theme of the 'family-as-incentive' comes through in many studies in industrial sociology. In Beynon's *Working For Ford*, for example, a man describing his intense dissatisfaction with assembly-line work finally commented, 'I just close my eyes and stick it out. I think about the kids' (Beynon, 1973, p. 113).

The privatisation of family life is also seen as contributing to the survival of capitalist society. On the one hand, small and fairly self-sufficient family units offer an enormous market for the sale of domestic goods; competition between families with respect to consumption — keeping up with the Joneses — is, of course, encouraged by advertising. On the other hand, the privatisation of family life acts as a barrier to the development of strong, organised and collective opposition to the status quo. It undermines class consciousness, whether at work or in the neighbourhood, by emphasising that one's first loyalty is to the family; the struggles of workmates or friends must be neglected, if joining in would in any way penalise the family. Privatisation thus counteracts class solidarity and, further, reinforces the notion that goodness, or morality, or commitment, are personal matters, to be enacted on a private basis with one's family rather than on a public basis through efforts to create a better society: this, after all, is part of the implication of 'Charity begins at home'.

Finally, from certain Marxist perspectives, the family quells rebellious spirits in two other ways. Through socialisation of children and also through day-to-day relationships (parents and children, older child and younger child, men and women) people are inculcated into patterns of authority, obedience and power. Thus patriarchal relationships outside the family, or the habit of submission to the 'boss', have a foundation in family life. Second, to the extent that family life is satisfying and warm (for at least some of its members) it can help to sustain inegalitarian and unfree structures outside the family, by offering an escape from these and a chance of recuperation — and this will be all the more effective as a dampener of opposition in so far as people come to believe that the family *is* the only possible sphere of emotion, creativity and fulfilment.

Thus, in the Marxist tradition, although the family is seen as relatively strong, this strength is thought of as detrimental to the development of the individual and society. The strong family helps to preserve the fundamentally unsatisfactory and unliberating patterns of capitalism, and therefore serves to forestall the emergence of better, more enriching ways of life. The fundamental irony from this point of view is that the less fulfilling work and life in the public sphere is, the more desperately people cling to their one potential source of satisfaction, the family; but of course, by escaping to the family, they reproduce the very structures of inequality and powerlessness which made them seek refuge in the first place.

In most versions of the 'march-of-progress' theories, the emphasis is upon the fit between 'the family' and 'industrial society'. In Marxist theory, the emphasis is not upon industrialisation in general, but upon industrial *capitalism* and its effects. The nuclear family, at least in its more repressive forms, is thought to persist not because of its inherent advantages, or its effectiveness at satisfying human needs, but rather because of its general structural position in society — a position which helps to protect the status quo from unified challenge. Thus, from many Marxist positions, the solution lies not in any alteration to the family but in wider structural changes — in particular, the destruction of industrial capitalism.

For others, however, this offers no solution, as the real issues in the sociology of the contemporary family concern the consequences of an institutional coincidence of child-rearing and the conjugal relationship, which remains a basic feature of the nuclear family whatever the wider structural arrangements may be. Here we are concerned with representatives of the fourth of Morgan's possible evaluations of the contemporary family: that which sees the family as a weak institution in our society, but, because it considers that an alteration in our child-rearing arrangements is eminently desirable, does not bemoan this weakness. What are the characteristics of our sort of family which give rise to this position?

The idea of progress: an alternative critique

At the beginning of this chapter we argued that it is quite wrong to see every kind of child-rearing arrangement in the world as being like that embodied in the nuclear family, and that one of the principal peculiarities of a nuclear family-based system is the primacy of marriage — the conjugal tie — in the child-rearing unit. This has a number of significant consequences.

Where a society forms its child-rearing groups exclusively on the conjugal tie, the efficiency of such groups depends directly on the nature and permanence of this tie: the family will be as strong as the relationship on which it is based. Now it seems clear that the strength of any conjugal relationship will depend on (among other things) the expectations held by the married couple: *why* people get married will be an important indicator of the potential strength of their marriage over time. Furthermore, the nature of these expectations will vary directly with the degree to which the institution serves the interest of individuals or of groups in a society. Let us explore these connections.

5.3   CONFLICT AND INSTABILITY IN FAMILY LIFE

The group aspect of marriage in non-industrial societies

Much of what we said at the beginning of the chapter demonstrated that in many kinds of non-industrial societies marriage serves *kin-group* interests. We argued that marriage is both a mechanism designed to provide a kin-group with its new members and also a major means of establishing alliances between such groups. In such societies, then, marriage has to be understood primarily as an institution designed to effect rights and obligations between groups of kin rather than individuals.

There are both structural and normative consequences of this. Since a marriage is an arrangement for and between kin-groups there are very many vested interests in its continuance and therefore many potential structural pressures on the individuals involved. In a patrilineal society, for example, where the children of a marriage belong to their father's group, it would be most unlikely that a groom's group would be happy to see a bride for whom they have paid a substantial bride-price wishing to leave her husband, at least if her child-producing days were not yet done. In any case, her own group would hardly be too pleased to be in danger of having claims made on them for the return of bride-wealth already consumed.

This is one of the reasons why divorce is often so difficult to obtain in a patrilineal society. The aim of patrilineal groups is to secure, via marriage, rights over the reproductive powers of a woman from another group: having effected this exchange and having handed over the bride-wealth, it is hardly likely they are going to hand the bride back. Sometimes, of course, there *are* no constraints which can be brought to bear on the individuals involved in order to avert a threat to the permanence of the conjugal tie. For example, what happens if one of the spouses dies before the groom's group has got its 'money's worth' out of the marriage? It is not surprising that on such occasions there are often contingency plans which can be put into operation, and these only appear bizarre if it is forgotten that patrilineal marriages are primarily designed to serve group, not individual, interests.

In the *levirate*, for instance, if a married man dies, his widow is taken over by one of his brothers. There need not be any new marriage: from the deceased's group's point of view, all that needs to be done is for one of its members to do what the dead man now cannot do — provide group heirs. The woman is still regarded as her dead husband's wife and any children she bears to his brother are still regarded as the dead man's. The structural definition of marriage as a group institution is quite clear here. The levirate is not only an expression of the principle that nothing has changed so long as the bride-wealth remains paid, but also that once a patrilineal group has obtained a woman her reproductive capacity belongs to the group, not to any particular individual.

The reverse patrilineal circumstance, of course, is where a man's wife dies prematurely (that is, the group gets a bad deal so far as her child-producing capacity is concerned). In this case, the arrangement — known as the *sororate* — is that the widower is entitled to a replacement wife, usually the dead woman's sister, from the group who received the bride-wealth. Once again the principle is clear: marriage is meant to serve the interests of the group, and so long as the group gets its money's worth the institution is doing its job.

In matrilineal societies, in contrast, divorce is often more easily available than in patrilineal ones. Marriage is just as much of a mechanism designed to serve kin-group interests here, so why should this be? The answer is simple enough. In matrilineal systems women reproduce for their *own* groups. There is no transference of their reproductive powers on marriage; instead, matrilineal marriage involves men from other groups being borrowed, more or less permanently, to do for their wives' brothers what they cannot do for themselves — give them heirs. The group only loses out if a woman remains unattached, not if she changes husbands. Divorce is no problem for a matrilineal group (so long as remarriage is not long in coming), since a woman remains its heir-producer and her children remain its heirs *whoever* her husband is. Here, then, the group aspect of marriage is reflected less in constraints against the instability of a *particular* marriage so much as against descent group women remaining unmarried.

Probably the best-known method of ensuring that women

remained married is that made famous by Hart and Pilling's
(1960) account of life among the aboriginal Tiwi of North
Australia. The method was devastatingly simple. In Hart and
Pilling's words (1960, p. 14):

> The Tiwi took the very slight step from saying 'All females
> *should* be married' to saying 'All females *must* be married.'
> As a result, there was no concept of an unmarried female
> in Tiwi ideology, no need for such a condition in their
> language, and in fact no female in the population without
> at least a nominal husband . . . all female Tiwi babies were
> betrothed before, or as soon as, they were born; females
> were thus the 'wives' of their betrothed husbands from the
> moment of birth onwards. For similar reasons, widows
> were required to remarry at the gravesides of their late
> husbands.

Clearly, these kinds of marital arrangements only appear
strange if looked at from the point of view of our definition,
that marriages link individuals. If marriage is understood as a
structural mechanism primarily designed to serve group interests and establish relations between kin-groups run by men,
they appear much less bizarre.

One of the consequences of marriage institutions whose
primary purposes are child production (for the kin-group)
and the establishment of alliances (between kin-groups) is that
they tend to promote ideologies which subordinate individual
well-being to the benefit of the group. In traditional China,
for example, the family was treated as the most important
institution and family life as sacred, yet people were taught
that they were not to expect romance or happiness out of
marriage, being told instead that at best they might achieve
contentment and peace. The existence of such limited expectations acts as a mechanism preventing marital breakdown, of
course: since people expecting little from marriage are less
likely to be disappointed, the chances of marital stability are
enhanced.

However, it is important not to confuse the notion of
'expectation' with that of 'choice': just because people learn
to expect little from marriage does not mean that such ex-

pectations necessarily match their desires. Thus, although normative definitions such as these might promote 'societal integration' and 'stability', this does not mean that it is *therefore* promoting individual happiness. Moreover, such definitions operate much more in favour of men than women. In societies such as these, where the definition of women as primarily child-bearers and rearers is only one aspect of their subordination, it is not surprising that the consequences for them of the structural location of marriage are far more oppressive than for men. For example, where divorce is hardly possible, it is normally men who tend to have the freedom to take lovers and concubines, while women remain not only subordinate but shackled. In traditional China usually the only way in which women who refused to swallow the ideology could escape their kin-group obligations was to commit suicide, while in present-day India such a fate can meet even those who comply; the well-publicised cases of newly wed brides being burned to death by their husbands' relatives for failing to provide a sufficient dowry are dramatic manifestations of the general exploitation of women in such systems.

Marriage and divorce in Britain

In sum, then, in societies where marriage is subordinated to descent group interests, where there are strong structural constraints supporting it, and where individual men and women's expectations of their married life are undemanding and readily achieved, marital breakdown tends to be inhibited. In our society, however, the marital relationship is potentially much more fragile. Marriage still 'unites' two families, but (with the clear exception of the wealthy) such alliances have little social significance. We tend to view marriage as an arrangement between individuals, entered into for their mutual benefit. Moreover, in our society, the normative emphasis in marriage is upon the emotional and sexual gratification it may provide for the conjugal pair, not upon the heirs that may be provided for descent groups or the alliances that may be effected by the marriage.

What constitutes a 'successful' marriage in our society — with expectations of companionship and romance, as well as a harmonious domestic arrangement — is therefore arguably more difficult to achieve, and consequently more likely to be frustrated, than the objectives of a 'successful' marriage in other times and other places. The emphasis upon personal fulfilment through marriage may justify for many people abandoning an unsatisfactory relationship in order to pursue fulfilment with another partner. Moreover, in the absence of effective pressure from kin-groups, the decision whether or not to remain 'till death us do part' is clearly more dependent upon the circumstances and (fluctuating) emotions of the marital pair.

This may be part of the reason why divorce has been made more available in our society. Lacking the structural and normative constraints which inhibit dissatisfaction with, and severance of, the conjugal tie in other societies, we have instead developed a means of facilitating break-*up* when break-*down* is irredeemable. Not that it was always so, for recourse to divorce is, in Britain, a relatively new 'solution' to the problem of marital unhappiness. In Victorian times, for example, divorces cost on average £700–800 — an incredibly high sum — so it is hardly surprising that the great majority of divorces went to members of the gentry or to men in professional or managerial occupations. Quite simply, the ordinary *men* of Britain could not afford divorce, and sought rather cruder escapes (desertion, physical abuse of wife or children, relationships with mistresses or prostitutes) from unhappy marriages. For women in such marriages the options were even more limited. Their legal access to divorce was more restricted than that of men; for example, it was not until 1923 that it became possible for women as well as men to sue for divorce on grounds of adultery. More important, perhaps, the lack of state support for single-parent families, and the narrow employment opportunities which made it unlikely that a woman on her own could earn a living wage, meant that the great majority of women trapped in unhappy marriages had no choice but to endure them. They effectively remained the property of their husbands, and the marriage contract constituted a principal basis for their subordination.

The increasing availability of divorce in the twentieth century must be explained as much by increasing political and economic independence of women as by general changes in 'ideals' or 'attitudes' to marriage. During this century the grounds for divorce have been extended, and the costs of legal proceedings lowered, in such a way that divorce is less the monopoly of wealthy men. The 1970 Divorce Law Reform Act did away with the idea that one partner had to commit a matrimonial offence (for example, desertion or cruelty) and substituted the notion of 'irretrievable breakdown of marriage' as the sole grounds for divorce. Breakdown can be demonstrated simply by living separately (for two years if both parties wish a divorce; for five if one of them is opposed), though some of the old matrimonial offences can still be invoked as evidence of breakdown.

As laws and procedures regulating divorce have altered, the divorce rate has tended to increase by leaps and bounds; with each new piece of legislation making divorce more readily available, the rate has risen rapidly for a time before levelling off. Today there is one divorce in Britain for every three marriages. (In the USA the rate is one in two.) Many people have suggested that the higher divorce rates reflect an underlying increase in marital instability; the problem with this argument is that we have no way of knowing how many 'unstable' or 'unhappy' marriages existed before legislation made it possible to dissolve them in a public (and recordable) form. Some commentators have gone further, and argued that more permissive divorce laws in themselves *cause* marital breakdown. But we can certainly be sceptical of such a view, suggesting as it does that happily married couples can suddenly be persuaded to abandon their relationship, propelled by the attraction of a new divorce law. A more plausible explanation for rises in the divorce rate after the passage of a law is that unhappily married couples were for the first time given access to a legal solution to pre-existent marital problems; in other words, changes in divorce laws are less likely to cause marital breakdown than to provide new types of solution where breakdown has already occurred.

Contemporary marriage and child-rearing

With divorce now much more readily available than ever

before, it might seem that we are lucky. People appear to get married because they love each other, and, if mistakes are made or feelings change, they can relatively easily go their own way to pursue the ideal of love once more.

But are our *children* so fortunate? What are the implications of our patterns of marriage for child-rearing? Let us summarise the argument so far:

(1) Any society needs to produce children and rear its new members satisfactorily.

(2) Our society tends to do this by using marriage — the conjugal tie — as the sole basis of child-rearing units. In the contemporary nuclear family just two adults, *because* they are husband and wife, are responsible for all the activities associated with reproduction and child care.

(3) This is not inevitable or 'natural': it is only one way of organising things. For example, in an extended family context ties of descent, especially between mother and daughter, can be more significant for child-rearing than the conjugal tie. Other kinds of societies, though usually using some form of marriage, do not rely on it exclusively in the way we do. Ties of descent, whether patrilineal or matrilineal, and blood ties (particularly siblingship) are often as significant as marital ties so far as social parenthood is concerned, and sometimes much more important.

(4) However, if the child-rearing unit is based solely on the conjugal tie, with all responsibilities devolving on only two adults, then this unit can only be as strong as the tie on which it is based.

(5) What affects the strength of the conjugal tie? Although other factors can be significant, two crucial ones are the degree of male dominance and the expectations of the relationship between husband and wife. Marriage will tend to be strongest where wives rely for their survival on their husbands and where expectations of love or romance are absent. It will tend to be weakest where women do *not* have to be married in order to survive and where husbands and wives *do* expect to achieve emotional fulfilment in marriage.

(6) What affects the existence of these sources of stability? A major factor (though not the only one) is whether marriage

serves kin-group or individual interests. Where marriage is primarily a mechanism for reproducing and linking kin-groups, individual interests — and particularly women's — tend to be subordinated in favour of the group. Where marriage primarily links individuals, both husbands and wives tend to be encouraged to expect individual fulfilment in marriage.

In sum, the more marriage links individuals, and the more men and women expect personal fulfilment in marriage, the more fragile the conjugal tie and the greater the need for a means to facilitate break-up. In contrast, the more marriage links kin-groups, and the lower the expectations of individuals (of both women, and husbands and wives), the greater the stability of the tie and the need for divorce reduced.

Since this is so, where child-rearing is based solely, and therefore relies exclusively, on the conjugal tie, it might seem logical to define marriage in such a way as to lower the expectations of the individuals involved, thereby reducing the possibility of instability. Conversely, this might be less necessary where child-rearing is less dependent on the stability of marriage.

However, what *actually* happens is the *reverse* of this. It is in societies where marriage is an institution serving kin-group interests, where the expectations of marital partners are encouraged to be lower, and where the relationship is therefore inherently more stable, that satisfactory child-rearing is *not* dependent solely on marriage. In contrast, the performance of these roles *is* wholly dependent on the conjugal tie precisely in those societies — like ours — where the expectations of those about to be married are encouraged to be high. The irony is that it is precisely in *our* kind of society, where the institution of marriage is so inherently fragile, that we nevertheless *still* expect these unions to form stable, secure and efficient bases for child-rearing. In short, the normative bases of the two institutions of marriage and child-rearing in our society are completely contradictory.

Even given our definition of marriage they *could* still be stable and efficient, of course, but only if it could be somehow guaranteed that husbands and wives will always want to stay together all their lives, *and* that men and women who fall in love with each other and get married will always become good parents. However, since the only provision we operate to ensure the former is to have a ceremony in which spouses say 'till death us do part' — hardly a guarantee of stability and permanence — and since we make no provision at all to ensure the latter, it is only surprising that conjugally based families do not fail more often than at present.

Not that we have any accurate indicator of the extent of such failures, for we cannot assume that husbands/fathers and wives/mothers who actually split their marriages/families up are the only ones who have not succeeded. For one thing, divorce is a solution which is still unequally available to men and women: state support for single-parent families is still too meagre and women still too discriminated against for separation to amount to anything other than a last resort for many married mothers. In any case, although our marriage practices can often spell disaster for child-rearing, it seems reasonable to assume that the demands of child-rearing can often have equally deleterious effects on the pursuit of our marriage ideals as well. Who knows how many husbands and wives would like to split up but are deterred because they are stuck with being father and mother to their children, and must therefore reconcile themselves to marital failure? Or again, who knows how many potentially successful marriages suffer because of the demands made on the couple by their parental responsibilities? These responsibilities impose just some of the practical strains and constraints which contribute to divorce.

Parenting and the contemporary family

However, it is not just the respective ideals underlying the family and marriage which contradict each other in our society. What about the position of women in our families? Traditional nations regarding the importance of the conjugal tie as the basis of the family unit assume not only that marriage will be lifelong and that husbands and wives will be good fathers and mothers but also that married women will above all else wish to spend a large part — if not the bulk — of their lives being full-time mothers.

This 'traditional' view regarding parenting is of fairly recent origin, even in British society, but is so much a part of common-sense thinking about the 'natural' role of women and the 'natural' way in which children should be raised that most of us find it difficult to imagine things being done differently. Yet child-rearing has *not* always had the character we take for granted, and we *can* find reasons why things changed.

Ideas about the nature of children have changed through the centuries, and so, too, have ideas concerning the proper relationship between parents and children. Modern families are often described as 'child-centred'. Viewed in historical perspective, the phrase is apt: not only because parents tend to spend so much of their time and energy on their children, but also because we tend to view the careful nurturing of the young, their protection and their education, and their emotional well-being, as the *raison d'être* of the family as an institution.

However, the family was not always viewed this way. As Ariès (1973) has shown, and as we pointed out at the beginning of the chapter, in pre-industrial Europe family life was much less private and much more a part of community life generally than it is for us. The same applies to childhood. Ariès (1973, pp. 395–6) puts the contrast clearly:

Our world is obsessed by the physical, moral and sexual problems of childhood. This preoccupation was unknown to medieval civilisation, because there was no problem for the Middle Ages: as soon as he had been weaned, or soon after, the child became the natural companion of the adult.

This is not to say that people of the Middle Ages did not love their children; rather, the needs of the children were differently conceived, and hence the interaction of loving parents with their children was different.

The change from the Middle Ages to the contemporary relationship between parents and children occurred very gradually and is too complex to document in detail here. However, what we can notice is the significance once again of the removal of most productive activity from the home with the rise in factory production; this accelerated the isolation of children from the 'real world' (at least after various Factory Acts limited their labour) and encouraged the notion of them (as of women) as somehow uniquely familial creatures. In addition, their removal from most production, as well as the extension of formal schooling, probably reinforced views of the frailty and dependence of children by making them quite literally dependent upon their families for support for a longer period of time.

One of the results of these changed conceptions of childhood has been a systematic increase in the obligations of parents towards their offspring. These include: financial obligations (and not only food and ordinary clothing, but school uniforms, money for school meals, educational toys, journeys, pocket money, and so forth); fairly constant attendance, particularly during the first five years; and not just warmth, affection and protection from harm but also intellectual stimulation, exposure to new learning experiences, and so on. One consequence of this is that despite far lower fertility rates than in the nineteenth century, it is probable that parents, nevertheless, spend more time in active child care than used to be the case. Parental attention is made all the more urgent given certain of the changes, especially in the urban environment, which make a greater degree of autonomous play for children rather more dangerous — busy traffic, lack of commons or green spaces, high-rise flats, and so on.

If the obligations attached to parenting have increased, this burden has fallen disproportionately on women. 'Parenting' connotes an activity involving protection and socialisation, security and affectionate interaction, an activity which is clearly necessary for the physical, moral, emotional and intellectual development of any human child (though it need not, of course, be offered by *biological* parents). However, in our culture, the ideological emphasis is upon mothers: they are regarded as the correct, the logical and the natural people to provide the parenting. This emphasis is reflected in, and supported by, a number of beliefs regarding parenting which refer either to a child's need for its mother or to a mother's predisposition to mothering. For example, beliefs about the importance of breast-feeding clearly do this (though of course the provision of milk is only a tiny part of child care) as does a belief in the existence of a 'maternal instinct'. However, in more recent times the principal belief of this kind has been the widespread but rather vague notion that 'A child needs its mother.'

In Britain this idea has been a plank underpinning many aspects of state policy since the Second World War, including social work objectives (to keep the child with its mother if at all possible) and policies concerning institutional care for children in difficulties. Much of the theoretical backing for this idea came from the work of John Bowlby (1965, 1971, 1975), whose studies on how human beings form attachments, and how they experience grief or loss, have been widely quoted and misquoted in support of the notion of 'maternal deprivation'. Bowlby suggested that human beings have from infancy a predisposition to form a deep and overwhelmingly important attachment to one person — and that person will probably be the mother. Disruption of the relationship with the mother in childhood by, for example, prolonged separation will produce anxiety in the child and effects similar to grief for the loss of a loved one. This experience may colour the child's later emotional make-up, and may interfere with his or her ability to form emotionally stable relationships. Thus, in brief, 'maternal deprivation' in childhood is believed to have effects which are severe and lasting. Bowlby's work has, sometimes unreasonably, been read to imply that even temporary separations from the mother (e.g. leaving the child with a minder while at work) can 'scar' the child for life; in this form the notion of maternal deprivation has been used to castigate mothers even for working in paid employment, or for taking an occasional evening out. Mothering has, in other words, been interpreted as a 24-hour, 365-day-a-year, responsibility, with anything other than this being potentially damaging to the child's welfare.

Thus, reflected in and supported by these kinds of beliefs about the relationships between mothers and children, the conventional view is that only women can perform child-rearing properly and 'naturally'. Now while this may or may not be true (and we will refer to objections to it shortly), the fact remains that it is a view which is entirely incompatible with another contemporary belief — that women should have equality with men. Just as we noted contradictions in our ideal definitions of family and marriage, here we find two directly opposed conceptions of the role of women. So far as conjugally based child-rearing is concerned, we expect that women should get married, have children and devote themselves to raising these children. In contrast, so far as contemporary attitudes regarding women's rights are concerned, the demand is that women should have exactly the same opportunities in life — political, educational and, especially, occupational — as men. The contradiction here is plain to see: given our views about women's role in nuclear families, how is it *possible* for women to have the same opportunities as men? Leach (1968) portrays the conflicts clearly:

> As nuclear families become more isolated, the network of kinsfolk families becomes dispersed. The young mother can still talk to her Mum on the telephone, but she can't ask her to drop in for a few minutes to mind the baby. Ideas about the status of women have been changing; wives are now thought of as companions rather than servants to their husbands, but perhaps they are even more thoroughly enslaved to their children than before.
>
> There is no easy solution. There is a genuine clash of interest between the right of a woman to be treated as a free and self-respecting individual and the right of her child to demand care and attention. But we don't get out of the difficulty by mouthing shibboleths about the eternal sanctity of the family. We have set ourselves noble ideals: social equality of men and women, permanence of the conjugal relationship, life-long love and cooperation between parents and children, but we have created a social system in which it is quite impossible for these factors to co-exist.

Now it is important to remember that these kinds of problems are not simply of academic interest. We must not forget that because we are talking about contradictions and tensions involved with our kind of family, we are also talking about resulting strains and pressures under which people in our society have to live out their lives as husbands and wives, fathers and mothers, and children. Unfortunately, however, because there has been little sociological interest in such issues we have little real evidence about the kind of consequences they have had for people's lives. Certainly there is a considerable body of literature devoted to the analysis of crisis situations in families — coping with the death of a spouse, for example, or with the birth of a severely handicapped child — and with the situation of 'problem families'. But what is less often acknowledged are the strains and tensions which, we are arguing, may well be a fairly routine part of life in 'non-problem' families.

For too long, in our view, many sociologists, eager to counteract superficial notions of the decline of the family, have unintentionally given substance to another myth, the myth of the happy family. Of course, it would be nonsensical to suggest that it is not *possible* for families to provide a haven of warmth and security while allowing an optimum level of individual freedom and contributing successfully to the socialisation of children — but whether they do or not is an *empirical* question. Thus, any adequate conceptualisation of modern families must ask questions about child neglect, battered wives, absentee husbands and problems people face in the transition from adolescence to adulthood — about what Morgan calls 'the dark side of family life' — *as well as* about the warm attachments which many people undoubtedly experience within the family. And in fact, when research into the contemporary family *has* been directed by concern with such issues, a very different picture from that painted by the 'march-of-progress' theorists often emerges.

The dark side of family life

One important facet of the dark side of family life is the incidence of marital violence. A recent study by Dobash and Dobash (1980) indicates that the practice of wife-battering — far from being an isolated act by disturbed or drunken individuals — is widespread, and has considerable cultural and institutional support. One-quarter of all serious assaults in the criminal statistics they analysed were assaults by husbands on their wives — and this figure greatly underestimates the frequency of wife-battering, since this is one of the crimes to be least fully recorded in criminal statistics. Dobash and Dobash report that wife-beating is seen by many as an unremarkable extension of a husband's right to control his wife; in this sense it both demonstrates and results from the asymmetricality of the marital relationship. The reluctance of police and others to intervene in cases of reported wife-battering indicates that domestic violence is regarded as acceptable in a way that other forms of violence are not: 'wifehood' often erases some of a woman's rights to protection by the law from physical injury or intimidation. The low penalties against husbands who plead guilty to charges of wife assault (seldom more than £10 during the period of the study, often only an admonishment) imply that wife-battering is regarded somewhat less seriously than parking offences.

The phenomenon of violence against wives demonstrates in an extreme way that marital relationships are *power* relationships as well as relationships involving (more or less) love and concern. Violence (or the threat of violence) may be only one source of masculine power, but it is a source which gains potency when it is given explicit or tacit support by economic, political and legal institutions. Although the majority of battered women in the Dobash and Dobash study left home to escape their husbands' violence, most were forced to return; major reasons for returning were the social stigma against a wife leaving her husband for *any* reason, lack of child-care facilities, and economic dependence on the husband. The disadvantages facing women in the wider society increase the likelihood that women will have to endure physical violence in marriage. Thus it can be argued that the persistence of wife-battering is not an idiosyncratic phenomenon but the predictable consequence of the inequality of the sexes and of the asymmetrical nature of marriage in contemporary society.

Several psychiatrists have drawn attention to 'the dark side of family life', notably Laing. A typical problem of family life, and a recurrent theme in Laing's work, is the tension between a child's early dependence on its parents and its eventual strivings towards independence. Parents are often depicted as being highly ambivalent about letting go of the child in which so much of their energy has been invested. The striving for independence raises problems for the child, too.

The family has defined for the growing child not only who he or she is but also, simultaneously, what *they*, the world outside, the others, are like; hence the child's sense of identity is so closely bound up with family relationships, and the sense of uncertainty about the outside world ('them') may be so deeply ingrained that breaking free is a highly traumatic process. In Laing's accounts, the process of socialisation is by no means a smooth process of gradually preparing the child to take its place in the adult world: on the contrary, interaction in the family involves all manner of confusions, ambiguities, uncertainties, even deceptions, to which the child is forced to adapt. This may be poor preparation indeed for an independent adult life. As Laing (1960, p. 189) says, 'the total family situation may impede rather than facilitate the child's capacity to participate in a real, shared world'. A central theme of Laing's writings, then, is that loyalty to the family often goes hand in hand with distrust of autonomy and of the outside world.

One serious objection that has often been raised against Laing's work is that his analyses of family life are based, in the main, on the study of schizophrenic patients. Indeed, part of Laing's argument is that many of the more bizarre symptoms of such patients may be understood if we know enough about patterns of interaction in the patients' families. Laing is not simply suggesting that families drive patients to madness; rather, he wishes to argue that familial relationships provide the grammar in which certain disturbances may be expressed. One of the useful aspects of Laing's writings is that since the families in question rarely involve instances of extreme child abuse, neglect or other sensational incidents, these analyses highlight the way in which fairly mundane patterns of family interaction can still confront the developing child or adolescent with severe tensions or contradictions.

However, while Laing's work is very sensitive to the tensions within family life, it fails to consider how these might be shaped or affected by the social context in which particular families are embedded. It is not clear, for example, how social class or ethnic differences, how property ownership or lack of property, or how the emphases of different historical periods, might influence the patterns of leaving home that have been described. In arguing that the family is an *experience* lived by its members, existing only through interaction, Laing may be underestimating the extent to which the family is given a particular structure and form by laws, welfare regulations, wage structures, and so on. To take a simple example, while it is certainly the case that parents have considerable room for discretion in the relationship they aim to construct with their children — and that no two parent–child relationships are likely to be identical — nevertheless the laws which specify that parents or guardians have a right to 'reasonable' physical punishment of a child sets a certain boundary upon the nature of parent–child interaction. In some Scandinavian countries, in contrast to Britain, children have the same rights as others to protection from physical punishment, and the parental relationship does not override this right.

If it is the case that the process of seeking independence from the family which has reared a child often involves tensions, then we must ask why that is: why, for instance, are parents ambivalent about letting go of their children? Harris (1977) argues that the answer must be sought in terms of the progressively degraded character of contemporary life: the exclusion of most people from all but the most superficial involvement in political decision-making, and the gradual routinisation of the majority of jobs, as well as the attenuation of community ties, all tend to mean that men and women are progressively denied the chance for expression of their talents for creativity. This, Harris insists, is the backdrop against which the contemporary child-centred family must be understood. Disappointed and denied in other spheres, men and women load the family with great expectations — the family, it is hoped, will ease the frustrations of life, and will supply the solidarity, companionship and enrichment which are otherwise absent. While the ideology of privatisation, and the image of happy families promoted by the media, may help to encourage unrealistic expectations, the fundamental impetus, Harris suggests, comes from the inevitable frustration and disillusionment with public aspects of life in advanced capitalist societies. The recurring tensions of family life result from 'the attempt to realise within the family household the creative potentials of its members which are denied expression elsewhere' (Harris, 1977, p. 79).

Harris applies this analysis in particular to the emotional investment made by parents in their children; in an effort to compensate for disappointments in their own lives, parents try to live through their children, and to control them. This effort is, by and large, doomed. Ironically, the same division of labour which (by denying fulfilment) leads parents to seek satisfaction by controlling their children also denies parents the power to retain that control. In Harris's account (1977, p. 80) this is one of the central contradictions reflected in contemporary family life:

> the need to control and hence live 'through' one's children increases at the same time as the basis of this sort of control is eroded. The emotional demands made by parents upon children increase at the very point at which the children have least to gain from acceding to them. As a result the fulfilment of the parents becomes incompatible with the autonomous development of the children.

Harris's analysis suggests, then, that many of the agonies of child-centred families are the (more or less) predictable outcome of pressures upon the family in a society which identifies family as the *only* source of solidarity and fulfilment for the majority of the adult population.

5.4 ALTERNATIVES

So what should be done? In essence, it would seem we need a solution to this tangle of institutional contradictions which will, at one and the same time,

(i) encourage loving and efficient child-rearing,
(ii) enable men and women to pursue and achieve love in their personal relationships, and
(iii) enable women to achieve equality with men.

It would further seem that such a change out of our present predicament could occur in one of two ways: either our marriages could be modified in some way to make them a more

suitable basis for proper child-rearing or different child-rearing
institutions could be developed instead.

People who support the idea of a modification of marriage
as a solution tend to see the problems we have outlined as
stemming from a lack of commitment on the part of spouses
which affects their performance as parents. Marriage, they
say, should be taken more seriously, and once entered into
should be difficult to abandon. The argument here, then, is
that strictly limited opportunities for marital dissolution will
discourage all but the most committed and will make the
conjugal relationship, and therefore the parenting built upon
it, more secure and effective. Proponents of such a position
thus tend to support the establishment of quite definite constraints on divorce for those who get married and choose to
be parents.

Pringle (1980), for example, proposes a two-tiered marriage
contract. One tier, appropriate for spouses who do not wish
to become parents, would be a loose arrangement, easily dissolved; the other tier would involve a contract legally binding
for fifteen years, and would apply to those who intended to
have children. At first glance this might appear to adequately
solve at least (i) and (ii) of our preconditions for a satisfactory solution; children would be guaranteed a permanent set
of parents, and if people felt the pursuit of love more important to them than parenthood they could enter into the
first kind of marriage instead. However, critics argue that if
people enter the binding kind of marriage and *then* find out
they are unsuitable for each other, they obviously have no
recourse at all; therefore, it may well be that only those who
want or expect companionship alone from their adult relationships will accept the risk and become parents. But in a
world where love *can* be pursued elsewhere, how many of
these people will there be, and *who* will they be?

The other kind of objection to this sort of 'solution' is that
it makes no attempt at all to cope with our precondition (iii).
Pringle, for example, stresses the importance of an equal division of labour in the family through role reversal by mother
and father, either on a long-term or short-term basis. However, any solution that favours the retention of child-rearing
as it is, *and* that bases child-rearing on the marital bond,

necessarily involves making the traditional assumption that the people best made responsible for the social rearing of children are their biological parents, and that, in particular, women should be primarily responsible for raising their children.

Others reject this, insisting that there is no *necessary* reason why child-rearing should be based on the conjugal tie — why biological parents should always be the social parents. The argument here is that if marriage and the family no longer necessarily implied each other, this might free both institutions from the problems they presently pose for each other. Marriage could be about the 'proper' pursuit of love and, at the same time, children could be protected, since spouses who are unhappy together would no longer automatically be parents who are unhappy together. In addition, women would have a choice about whether to become social parents as well as biological parents.

Of course, this sort of argument is in direct opposition to notions such as 'maternal instinct' and 'maternal deprivation' which underpin popular views of parenting. Such notions have recently come under serious attack. However one defines the 'maternal instinct' — as, perhaps, the instinctive knowledge of what a child needs and how to provide it, or as the instinctive and overwhelming desire to have children, or as the instinctive and irresistible love for one's own child — there are always sufficient women who do *not* know how to care for a child, who do *not* wish to have a child, who do *not* love their children, to demonstrate that a universal notion of maternal instinct in women is a myth which occupies the same sort of ideological status in our society as beliefs about procreation do in patrilineal and matrilineal societies (see p. 262 above).

Moreover, there is considerable evidence which contradicts Bowlby's conclusions about maternal deprivation. Bowlby's work was thoroughly examined by Rutter (1972). Rutter takes Bowlby's point that children form early attachments on the basis of intense social interaction, but notes that interaction leading to stable attachments, play and physical care are three distinct activities which need not come from a single person. In Rutter's view, the evidence suggests that separation

316 Introductory Sociology

need not involve disruption of attachments — children can, and do, maintain close relationships with loved people during those people's absence; and they do so all the more success- fully if play and physical care are adequate in the meanwhile. Finally, Rutter notes that the troublesome effects of separa- tion from mother are mitigated by the presence of other familiar people, such as brothers or sisters. He argues that this indicates that the bond to the mother is not necessarily different in quality from that with other people with whom the child has intense interaction — and hence, the more people to whom the child is attached, the less chance of a sense of loss there is. Rutter (1972, pp. 124–5) concludes:

> Of course in most families the mother has most to do with
> the young child and as a consequence she is usually the
> person with whom the strongest bond is formed. But it
> should be appreciated that the chief bond need not be with
> a biological parent, it need not be with the chief caretaker,
> and it need not be with a female.

It is difficult to gauge the potential success of any kind of child-rearing arrangement which denies the need for any necessary connection between biological parenthood and social parenthood. Where such attempts have been made in the past, they have tended to generate the kind of horror- struck reaction usually only associated with revelations of incest. For example, the Oneida community, founded in New York in 1848, in which children were reared apart from their parents and whose inhabitants were therefore able to enter into complex sexual relationships with one another, en- countered so much hostility from the surrounding society that it only lasted thirty years. Contemporary (but much less dramatic) equivalents — so far as child-rearing is concerned — are communes and the Israeli kibbutzim. Although in Britain and the USA, for example, communes have varied very con- siderably in character, they too have often adopted the prin- ciple that child-rearing should be communal, with the com- munity as a whole taking corporate responsibility for looking after the children. In many cases, however, the continued recognition of ties of blood and marriage between spouses and their own children within the context of community life has meant that traditional notions of child-rearing as the responsibility of biological parents have often overwhelmed the ideal of corporate responsibility.

The same has also become true of an even more celebrated alternative child-rearing arrangement embodied in the Israeli kibbutz. The original notions here regarding parenthood were once again that biological parent–child ties should be lessened in favour of ties between children and the whole community. For example, in the early kibbutzim care of the children was in the hands of a communal nursery, and trained nurses and teachers took over many of the duties performed in the nuclear family by parents, who were encouraged to spend only Saturday and an hour or two each weekday with their children. Once again, however, the continued recognition of blood links as signifying special social relationships eventually began to undermine the ideal: as time passed, conjugal relations became well-established and three-generational ties developed (although recently, in some kibbutzim, extended collective child-care provision has reasserted the old ideals).

These apparent 'failures' have been used to support the idea that the nuclear family is universal — that any attempt to bypass or ignore the supposedly elemental ties between parents and children must be doomed. Whether this is a fair judgement seems open to question. It could well be argued that the commune/kibbutzim evidence serves not to prove that alternative child-rearing institutions *cannot* succeed, but that individuals already socialised into traditional values will find it difficult to reject these totally, especially where the alternative is practised at a micro level only, inside a wider society which is unhelpful or hostile.

In his Reith lectures in 1967, Edmund Leach (1968), as he says himself, 'aroused much public hostility' when he suggested that:

> We should look carefully at experimental institutions, such as the Israeli kibbutz and the Chinese commune in which the local community takes over the parental support role which has been exercised in the past by the family. As in the case of Oneida, these experiments have not worked out

very well but their problem is real. Sooner or later we shall have to devise some variation on the same theme ourselves.

Although it seems doubtful that the commune or the kibbutz should be held up as any kind of model for alternative child-rearing in an industrial society (while such units may work well where they are self-sufficient or constructed around the production of agricultural goods, they are probably too large to suit a world demanding a mobile work-force), it seems likely that Leach's conclusion is correct. The strains resulting from the institutional contradictions we have been describing make it unlikely that people subjected to strain will allow the institutions to remain the same. For example, the pressure for more nursery schools, and the growth of single-parent families and open marriages, might be interpreted as manifestations of the contradictions and the search for a proper solution.

However, such a solution will not come automatically. Social institutions producing strain, suffering and disadvantage have persisted long enough to show that the 'needs' of social groups will not necessarily be served and that 'social integration' will not emerge of its own accord. The isolated individualism that characterises the contemporary family is an enormous barrier to any mobilisation of collective demands for change. Social institutions do not emerge solely through deliberate choice but act back on people in unexpected ways; at the same time, understanding the source of our problems can permit deliberate change. Sociology has an important role to play in providing some of this understanding — above all, through emphasising that the nuclear family system is *not* natural, universal and inevitable. Deliberate social change must be fought for. The fight for women's rights is part of this; the following chapter on sexual divisions in society deals with the social position of women and assesses the potential for full equality and liberation of the sexes.

REFERENCES TO CHAPTER 5

Anderson, M. (1971) *Family Structure in Nineteenth Century Lancashire*, Cambridge University Press.

Ariès, P. (1973) *Centuries of Childhood*, Harmondsworth, Penguin.
Bell, C. (1968) *Middle Class Families*, London, Routledge & Kegan Paul.
Beynon, H. (1973) *Working for Ford*, Harmondsworth, Penguin.
Bott, E. (1957) *Family and Social Network*, London, Tavistock.
Bowlby, J. (1965) *Child Care and the Growth of Love*, Harmondsworth, Penguin.
Bowlby, J. (1971) *Attachment and Loss, vol. I*, Harmondsworth, Penguin.
Bowlby, J. (1975) *Attachment and Loss, vol. II*, Harmondsworth, Penguin.
Craddock, A. (1977) 'Task and Emotional Behavior in the Marital Dyad', in N. Glazer and H. Y. Waehrer (eds), *Women in a Man-made World*, Chicago, Rand McNally.
Dennis, N., Henriques, F. and Slaughter, C. (1956) *Coal is Our Life*, London, Eyre & Spottiswoode.
Dobash, R. and Dobash, R. (1980) *Violence against Wives*, London, Open Books.
Fletcher, R. (1966) *The Family and Marriage in Britain*, Harmondsworth, Penguin.
Fox, R. (1967) *Kinship and Marriage*, Harmondsworth, Penguin.
Fox, R. (1975) *Encounter with Anthropology*, Harmondsworth, Penguin.
Gavron, H. (1968) *The Captive Wife*, Harmondsworth, Penguin.
Goldthorpe, J. H., Lockwood, D. and colleagues (1968a) *The Affluent Worker: Industrial Attitudes and Behaviour*, Cambridge University Press.
——(1968b) *The Affluent Worker: Political Attitudes and Behaviour*, Cambridge University Press.
——(1969) *The Affluent Worker in the Class Structure*, Cambridge University Press.
Goode, W. J. (1963) *World Revolution and Family Patterns*, London, Collier-Macmillan.
Goode, W. J. (1968) 'The Theory and Measurement of Family Change', in E. Sheldon and W. E. Moore (eds), *Indicators of Social Change*, New York, Russell Sage.
Harris, C. C. (1977) 'Changing Conceptions of the Relation between Family and Societal Form in Western Society', in R. Scase (ed.), *Industrial Society: Class, Cleavage and Control*, London, Allen & Unwin.
Hart, C. W. M. and Pilling, A. R. (1960) *The Tiwi of North Australia*, New York, Holt, Rinehart & Winston.
Hubert, J. (1970) 'Kinship', in E. Butterworth and D. Weir (eds), *The Sociology of Modern Britain*, London, Fontana.
Kerr, M. (1958) *The People of Ship Street*, London, Routledge & Kegan Paul.
Laing, R. D. (1960) *The Divided Self*, Harmondsworth, Penguin.
Laslett, P. (1977) *Family Life and Illicit Love in Earlier Generations*,

Cambridge University Press.

Laslett, P. and Wall, R. (eds) (1972) *Household and Family in Past Time*, Cambridge University Press.

Leach, E. (1968) 'The Family as an Instrument of Women's Enslavement', *Sunday Times Magazine*, 10 November 1968.

Litwak, E. (1960a) 'Occupational Mobility and Extended Family Cohesion', *American Sociological Review*, vol. 25.

Litwak, E. (1960b) 'Geographical Mobility and Extended Family Cohesion', *American Sociological Review*, vol. 25.

Lupton, T. and Wilson, C. S. (1959) 'The Social Backgrounds and Connections of "Top Decision Makers" ', *Manchester School*, vol. 27.

Morgan, D. H. J. (1975) *Social Theory and the Family*, London, Routledge & Kegan Paul.

Oakley, A. (1972) *Sex, Gender and Society*, London, Temple-Smith.

Oakley, A. (1974) *The Sociology of Housework*, London, Martin Robertson.

Pahl, J. M. and Pahl, R. E. (1972) *Managers and their Wives*, Harmondsworth, Penguin.

Parsons, T. (1959) 'The Social Structure of the Family', in R. Anshen (ed.), *The Family: its Function and Destiny*, New York, Harper & Row.

Parsons, T. (1964) *Essays in Social Theory*, New York, Free Press.

Parsons, T. and Bales, R. F. (1956) *Family: Socialisation and Interaction Process*, London, Routledge & Kegan Paul.

Pringle, M. L. K. (1980) *The Needs of Children*, 2nd edn, London, Hutchinson.

Rosser, C. and Harris, C. C. (1965) *The Family and Social Change*, London, Routledge & Kegan Paul.

Rutter, M. (1972) *Maternal Deprivation Reassessed*, Harmondsworth, Penguin.

Shorter, E. (1977) *The Making of the Modern Family*, London, Fontana.

Sussman, M. (1953) 'The Help Pattern in the Middle Class Family', *American Sociological Review*, vol. 18.

Sussman, M. and Burchinal, L. (1962) 'Kin Family Network', *Marriage and Family Living*, vol. 24.

Tunstall, J. (1962) *The Fishermen*, London, MacGibbon & Kee.

Willmott, P. (1963) *The Evolution of a Community*, London, Routledge & Kegan Paul.

Willmott, P. and Young, M. (1971) *Family and Class in a London Suburb*, London, New English Library.

Young, M. and Willmott, P. (1962) *Family and Kinship in East London*, Harmondsworth, Penguin.

Young, M. and Willmott, P. (1973) *The Symmetrical Family*, London, Routledge & Kegan Paul.

6
Sexual Divisions in Society

6.1 INTRODUCTION

In Chapter 1, it was pointed out that many of our common-sense notions about 'natural' differences between the sexes do not stand up to scrutiny. The more informed we are about other cultures, and other periods in history, the more we are forced to recognise that men or women can be active or passive, aggressive or conciliatory, sexually voracious or sexually timid, depending upon the society in which they are born (and, to an extent, their position within that society). However, there are a number of important points to recognise about sexual difference and sexual divisions.

First, we can clarify our thinking by adopting Oakley's (1972) distinction between *sex* and *gender*. Sex refers to the most basic physiological differences between men and women — differences in genitals and reproductive capacities. Gender refers, on the other hand, to the culturally specific patterns of behaviour, either actual or normative, which may be attached to the sexes. When speaking of *sexual* differences, we are distinguishing between males and females; when speaking of *gender,* between masculine and feminine. The content of the male/female distinction is genetically determined and largely universal; the content of the masculine/feminine distinction is culturally determined and highly variable.

Second, most societies do prescribe different activities and characteristics for males and females; these may come to be perceived as 'natural' by the people concerned. In this way the fairly limited range of biological differences between male and female are heightened, or compounded, by culturally prescribed gender differences. As Mathieu remarks, thinking of the French language which assigns a gender to objects such as books, streets and rocks, 'We must therefore try to understand that each society *uses* the biological sexes to construct a sexual grammar ... just as arbitrary as the grammatical genders of the language' (1977, p. 2). One of the things we will consider later in this chapter is the way in which patterns of socialisation in our own society encourage females to become feminine and males to become masculine. The amount of attention paid to shaping the personalities and interests of males and females along lines deemed appropriate by our culture is in itself an indication that masculinity and femininity are socially constructed; as the irate girl in the cartoon (Figure 6.1) emphasises, if femininity were biologically induced, then much of the process of socialisation and social control would be superfluous.

FIGURE 6.1

Cartoon from Liz Mackie, Jo Nesbitt, Christine Roche and Lesley Ruda, Sour Cream, *published in 1979 by Sour Cream, 136 Florence Street, London N1*

Third, sexual divisions cannot be subsumed under the question of gender differences. While masculinity varies — for example, tenderness is sometimes allowed, sometimes tabooed — in most societies, males, whatever their gender characteristics, have more power and more authority than women; more than that, they have power *over* women. Men and women are, then, not merely *different* but in a relation of subordination and domination. The structure of subordination and domination is called *patriarchy*. Although there is a great deal of controversy about the precise connotations of the term, at the least it implies a hierarchy of social relations and institutions in which and through which men are able to dominate women.

In Chapter 2 we saw that inequality is not explicable in terms of the individual attributes of property-owners or of workers. Stratification inheres in relations — to understand wage labour we have to understand capital. Similarly, the inequality of males and females is not something that can be explained by reference to the qualities of one or the other sex. Sexual inequality or oppression inheres in the relations between women and men.

6.2   THE SIGNIFICANCE OF FORMAL OR LEGAL EQUALITY

The campaign for social and political equality for women appears as one of the great success stories of the past one hundred years. Women gained full voting rights in 1928. A number of important legal rulings and administrative decisions restored or extended to women the right to hold public office, to enter the professions, and to own and administer property. Laws governing family life gradually circumscribed husbands' exclusive rights over wives and children, so that women were enabled, for example, to sue for divorce on the same terms as men. In the past decade two important pieces of legislation — the Equal Pay Act (1970) and the Sex Discrimination Act (1975) — 'outlawed' certain categories of less favourable treatment to men or women on the basis of their sex.

'You've come a long way, baby!' quipped an advertisement for Virginia Slims in the 1970s, and (if we ignore the implication that cigarette smoking represents the ultimate in liberation) most people would probably agree. Yet the notion that the traditional domesticity and dependence of women in the nineteenth century yielded to complete equality with men in the twentieth century needs to be qualified in the light of sociological and historical evidence. On the one hand, the Victorian period may have represented a low point in the history of the relations of the sexes, and it may not be correct to characterise the Victorian situation as the 'traditional' one. It has been argued that three centuries earlier women enjoyed a more prominent position in public life; before the end of the sixteenth century women had, according to Sachs (1978, p. 37), 'voted in Parliamentary elections, acted as attorneys, held leading positions in trading guilds, and even occupied high military office'. A comparison of the sixteenth and nineteenth centuries should warn, therefore, against too readily accepting Victorian standards as representing the 'traditional place' of women. Such a comparison should also make clear that a view suggesting steady, progressive advance in women's position throughout the ages is unfounded; the history of the sexes is one of shifting balances of power, sometimes in the direction of greater equality, and at other times away.

On the other hand, the notion that there is complete equality between women and men today, even in the narrow sense of formal rights, does not stand up to scrutiny. Despite the high proportion of married women who have an income of their own (or who need one), the assumption that married women are not, and should not be, financially independent of their husbands continues to be a cornerstone of the administration of the welfare state. As described by Land (1976), this assumption has been used to justify different pension and disability entitlements for married women. It underlies the payment of the taxation subsidy for married persons specifically and exclusively to the husband. A most important consequence of the assumption that wives are dependent is that wives (and female cohabitees) are thereby not entitled to draw social security benefit in their own right, regardless of their financial circumstances or employment history; the self-fulfilling prophecy element of this regulation is neatly summarised by Wilson and her associates (1974, p. 274): 'The Social Security scheme starts with the assumption that women are dependents of men. Because of this expectation, it almost forces them to be so.' Since the passage of the Sex Discrimination Act (1975) it is sometimes assumed that any remaining discrimination based upon sex is vestigial, and will fade away of its own accord. However, far from a situation of continuous movement towards equality, new legal and administrative distinctions in the treatment of women and men have been introduced *since* the Sex Discrimination Act came into effect. Under the provisions of the 1980 Immigration Rules, for example, many British women will be denied the right to bring their foreign-born spouses to live with them in Britain, though all British men will retain that right. This rule has in practice been particularly disadvantageous to black women; it is thus racist as well as sexist, and as such is an indication of the shortfall of legislative attempts to establish racial and sexual equality.

What, then, of the Sex Discrimination Act? In a recent assessment of this legislation Coussins (1980) argues that the main impact of the law was educational: the Act provided an impetus for people to recognise that sexual inequalities are neither natural nor inevitable, but man - (and woman - ?) made. On the other hand, in terms of ensuring non-discriminatory treatment in employment, education and other spheres, Coussins describes the Act as 'feeble'; difficulties of proof and enforcement have limited its usefulness. In her view the crucial areas excluded from the Sex Discrimination Act demonstrate governments' *lack* of commitment to equality of the sexes:

Tax, social security, pensions, nationality and immigration are the most important exclusions. The Government was clearly not prepared fundamentally to challenge the position of women's dependency on men, whether it be for money or for status; and it did not intend to do anything which meant spending money on achieving equality (Coussins, 1980, p. 10).

It should be clear, then, that the legal status of women and men is far from equal; women continue to be regarded as adjuncts of their husbands. But formal or legal equality is in any case an inadequate index for assessing the structural position of different social groups; as we have seen in earlier chapters, manual workers have *legal* equality with others in our society, but this equality goes hand in hand with persistent and severe inequalities in life-chances and power. Before examining the distribution of income between women and men, a few points can be raised for consideration.

First, an assessment of movements towards or away from equality, and of the consequences, must not ignore the absolute condition of the groups being compared; in certain circumstances equality for women would involve a worsening of their life-chances. For example, women have at present certain protections in law which are not available to men; protective legislation, for instance, gives women and not men the possibility of resisting shift-work and night-work, while some women are entitled to retire and draw a pension five years earlier than men. Whether women's lot would improve or deteriorate by attaining equality with men on these issues depends largely on whether change involves removing the protections and earlier retirement eligibility from women, or extending similar protections and opportunities to men.

Second, it should be borne in mind that equal opportunities legislation *does not guarantee* equality of condition. Just as the freedom to dine at the Ritz rings hollow if you lack the money to pay the bill, so too the freedom to pursue a career is illusory unless appropriate training, encouragement and advice, and — in the case of those in charge of children — suitable help with child care are widely available. There is, for example, no legal disability which prevents women from assuming directorships in industry; yet a survey published in 1978 of the twenty largest firms in the United Kingdom (including BP, Shell, Unilever, ICI) revealed a total of 288 men on their boards of directors, and not a single woman (*Guardian,* 11 September 1978).

The third reservation to bear in mind is that formal equality tells us little about informal social relations between men and women, the sphere about which legislation is relatively silent. Having the vote, for instance, does not ensure that women will be treated as politically important or politically responsible. In fact, many discussions of the legal status of women contain an implicit assumption about the powerlessness of women, as when it is said that 'Women have been *allowed* to vote', or that 'Women have been *given* the right'. Such statements imply, perhaps unintentionally, that whatever rights women have are due to the goodwill of others, and that women are not active political agents with the capacity to influence their own destinies.

Patterns of inequality: the male earnings advantage

The right to work does not guarantee earnings which most people would see as a living wage. According to the *New Earnings Survey 1979* (see Table 6.1), almost 30 per cent of women in full-time employment (41.1 per cent of manual and 25.7 per cent of non-manual), but less than 3 per cent of men (2.7 per cent of manual and 2.1 per cent of non-manual), were earning less than £50 gross per week. Women constitute a disproportionately high percentage of low-paid workers in Britain today.

Our analysis in Chapter 2 highlighted the fact that manual workers — men or women — are systematically disadvantaged in comparison with their non-manual counterparts. Yet, as can be seen below, there is greater similarity of earnings between workers of the same sex *across* the manual/non-manual boundary than there is between women and men within a single occupational class. In order of their average gross weekly earnings the incomes of women and men (full-time employees only) in April 1979 were as follows:

Male non-manual workers	£113.00
Male manual workers	£ 93.00
Female non-manual workers	£ 66.00
Female manual workers	£ 55.20

The excess of men's earnings over those of women (the 'male earnings advantage') was £47.00 among non-manual employees, and £37.80 among manual workers. The relatively privil-

TABLE 6.1

*Earnings and hours worked by women and men in April 1979:
adult employees in full-time employment whose pay was not
affected by absence*

	All women	All men	Manual workers		Non-manual workers	
			Women	Men	Women	Men
Average gross weekly earnings (before tax or other deductions)	£63.0	£101.4	£55.2	£93.0	£66.0	£113.0
Proportion whose gross weekly earnings were:						
less than £50	29.9%	2.4%	41.1%	2.7%	25.7%	2.1%
less than £60	53.3%	8.1%	66.6%	9.6%	48.8%	6.1%
Average hours worked, of which:	37.5	43.2	39.6	46.2	36.7	38.8
overtime hours	0.6	4.5	1.1	6.3	0.4	1.6
Average gross hourly earnings, excluding overtime pay and overtime hours	£1.66	£2.32	£1.39	£1.98	£1.77	£2.90

Source: Summary Tables of *New Earnings Survey 1979*, in *Department of
Employment Gazette*, October 1979, vol. 87, no. 10, p. 971.

eged women who are in non-manual jobs earn on average £27
less a week than male manual workers.

Moreover, these data, concentrating as they do on full-
time workers' cash earnings, underestimate the disparity in
income between women and men. Approximately 40 per
cent of women in the labour force are employed on a part-
time basis; they experience poorer prospects for training and
promotion, greater insecurity and reduced fringe benefits, as
well as lower hourly rates than full-time colleagues who
might be doing identical work. Furthermore, like other low-
paid workers, women are likely to be awarded less in the way

of fringe benefits than those whose cash income is relatively high (Low Pay Unit, *Low Pay Bulletin,* June 1976). If comparisons of male and female earnings included the value of fringe benefits, and took part-time as well as full-time workers into account, then the male earnings advantage would be greater than it appears in Table 6.1.

Why are women's earnings so much lower than those of men? In part this is due to longer hours worked by men; male workers are able to boost their basic rate earnings by overtime, as well as by shift premiums and bonus schemes, to a far greater extent than female workers.

However, in April 1979 non-manual men earned £47 more than non-manual women, even though men's working hours were a mere 2.1 hours longer than the women's. Moreover, a look at gross *hourly* pay reveals that — even with the effects of overtime excluded — there is a male earnings advantage of 66 pence per hour (59 pence among manual workers and 113 pence among non-manual workers).

The male earnings advantage is in large part accounted for by the segregation of women into occupations to which lower pay and status is attached, and by their restriction to the bottom end of the career structure within each occupation. Sexual divisions in employment will be examined in more detail in the next section of the chapter. But it must be recognised that these are crucial in explaining not only the male earnings advantage but also the very limited successes of the 1970 Equal Pay Act.

The explicit aim behind the Equal Pay Act was to eliminate differentiation based on sex with respect to pay (or terms and conditions of employment) between women and men doing *like* work (or work judged to have equal value according to job evaluation) at the same or associated work-places. Employers were allowed five years, until 1975, to make sure that their payment practices accorded with the Act.

An immediate effect of the Equal Pay Act was a significant narrowing of the male earnings advantage (see Table 6.2). Women's gross average hourly earnings rose from being 63.1 per cent of men's earnings in 1970, to 75.5 per cent in 1977. Since 1977, however, the trend has been reversed. Women's earnings sunk to 73.9 per cent of men's in 1978, and further

TABLE 6.2

*Women's earnings as a proportion of men's, employees
aged 18 and over, 1970–9*

	Average gross hourly earnings, excluding effects of overtime (%)	Average gross weekly earnings, including effects of overtime (%)
1970	63.1	54.5
1974	67.4	56.4
1975	72.1	61.5
1976	75.1	64.3
1977	75.5	64.9
1978	73.9	64.8
1979	73.0	63.6

Source: Equal Opportunities Commission., *Fourth Annual Report,
1979*, London, EOC, 1980, table 4.2, p. 79, and table 4.3, p.80.

to 73 per cent in 1979. Most commentators agree that
although the Act may continue to offer a legal remedy to a
handful of women and men who experience discrimination in
pay or conditions, it is unlikely to occasion equal incomes
between male workers and female. Women's earnings were 27
per cent lower than men's in 1979 (36 per cent if reckoned in
terms of gross weekly earnings) and, apparently, falling.

The limited effectiveness of the Equal Pay Act is not surprising given that men and women, prior to 1970, had generally been discouraged from doing like work; in many firms
women were assigned to different jobs than men, so that
there was no basis for comparison for a claim of equal pay. In
addition, during the five-year implementation period many
firms (sometimes but not always with the collaboration of
trade unions) took steps to *ensure* that the earnings of their
male employees would continue to outstrip those of female
work-mates. Snell (1979) documents several such 'minimising
actions': introducing new job segregations by sex where previously there had been a mixed work-force; hiring a handful of
men for very menial tasks at exceptionally low pay, so that it
could not be claimed that women were earning less than the
lowest-paid man in the firm (although they might be earning
less than the vast majority of men); introducing new systems

for grading work, such that the traits associated with 'male' jobs (e.g. lifting heavy loads) were given greater weighting than those associated with 'female' jobs (e.g. manual dexterity). The last 'minimising action' has important implications; it raises the general possibility that the classification of occupations according to 'skill' or similar criteria may, as Braverman (1974) argued, tell less about the actual content of jobs and more about the power of different groups negotiating over the classifications.

There are some general points worth noting about data on sex differences in earnings. First, women's average earnings may be small in comparison with men's, but they can no longer be regarded as 'pin money'. Setting out to challenge 'the myth of the male breadwinner', Land (1975) reports that in 1971 at least one household in six, excluding pensioner households, was dependent to some extent upon a woman's earnings or benefits. The wages of married women, then and now, often staved off poverty for their families. A 1970 Department of Health and Social Security (DHSS) analysis cited by Land indicates that the number of two-parent families with incomes below the official poverty line would have *trebled* were it not for the contribution made by the wife's earnings. The chances of a family in Britain living in poverty are almost one in three when wives do not take paid employment; but the risk sinks to one in fourteen when wives do no out to work (Royal Commission on Distribution of Income and Wealth, *Research Report,* vol. 6, 1978).

Second, women themselves are more likely than men to experience poverty. Townsend's extensive study of poverty in the United Kingdom indicated that 57.2 per cent of those in households in poverty (by the most stringent, official, definition) were women. The 'proportion of women in poverty', Townsend notes, 'was higher than of men at all ages except under 15' (Townsend, 1979, p. 285). Women are particularly vulnerable to poverty in several respects: they are more likely than men to be single parents with sole charge of children, and reduced possibilities for employment; women live longer than men, and spend a greater proportion of their lives beyond retirement age, and yet are less likely than men to be entitled to occupational pensions. The Government

Actuary estimated that in 1971 only 28 per cent of female employees, as against 62 per cent of male employees, were covered by an occupational pension scheme (cited in Equal Opportunities Commission, *Women and Low Incomes,* London, 1977). The male earnings advantage is likely, therefore, to be carried over into old age.

It should be added that assessments of poverty which rely on analysing household or family income undoubtedly underestimate the number of women who actually live in conditions of severe material deprivation. There may be many families or households where the total income is just above the poverty line but where the woman's share of that income is very much less than equal. An investigation into the circumstances of large families in London emphasised that the financial burdens of extra children, and the strains of 'family' poverty, fall disproportionately on the mother. Land (1972) pointed out that mothers often deny themselves cooked meals, new clothing and fuel so as to save these scarce goods for their families. There is a growing body of evidence, too, which suggests that in periods of high inflation the standard of living of mother and children may be eroded while that of the father is preserved; a sizeable minority of husbands fail to pass on the value of wage increases to their families, and those in the poorest households fare worst. These studies (e.g. *The National Consumer Council Survey,* 1975) suggest, therefore, that it may be a mistake to treat the family as an undifferentiated unit as far as standard of living is concerned.

A third point concerns the implications of inequalities in pay for the autonomy of women. If women are less able than men to command a 'living wage', then they will also be more dependent on men for economic survival; and, of course, this is particularly true where women have primary responsibility for the care and protection of children. Thus the structure of income and reward reinforces the dependency aspect of marriage, and makes other options less viable for women than for men.

Any attempt to understand gender divisions must take us beyond a simple check-list of inequalities. It is necessary to examine the different structure of men's and women's lives, an examination which will touch upon the consequences of income (and other) inequalities and upon some of the institutions and practices that reinforce those inequalities. We have broken this discussion down into four areas, areas which overlap but which are analytically distinct: employment; domestic labour or housework; reproduction; and sexuality.

6.3 EMPLOYMENT

Some form of division of labour based upon sex has been a feature of virtually all societies and periods in history of which we have knowledge. But the characterisation of women as 'non-productive' homemakers is relatively specific to the later stages of industrial capitalism.

It is useful to put the return of married women to the paid labour force since the Second World War into some historical perspective.

As we saw in Chapter 5, the existence of most families in Western history has been a somewhat precarious one. Before the changes wrought by the emergence of industrial capitalism, all the members of most households had to work. Whether they were engaged in agricultural labour, or cottage industry such as weaving or spinning, none but the very youngest children would be exempt from making a contribution to the economic survival of the family. Moreover, when families were forced to take factory employment because other forms of livelihood were curtailed, often the entire family of mother, children and father entered the factory together. The notion that only men should support the family — that they should provide the income for wives and children as well as for themselves — was not only impracticable (their earnings would not have been sufficient) but in many cases abhorrent, involving an unwelcome precedent.

However, as we know, many children and many married women were in fact gradually excluded from factory labour in the course of the nineteenth century. The notion that they thereby stopped working (leaving aside the issue of whether housework is work) is open to doubt. Probably the vast majority of single working-class women worked — in factories or sweatshops, in domestic service, and so on. Many of them continued to contribute to family income even after the birth of children forced them to spend more time in the home; they took in laundry, for example, or did sewing, or made buttons and lace. Many middle-class women similarly worked in the family business, ran small lodging houses, or acted as governesses or nurses to the children of the well-to-do. As Land (1975) points out, much of the labour of these women was simply rendered invisible to official eyes by the practice of collecting census data in such a way that only the labour of male members of a household was classified as 'employment' or 'economic activity'.

The First and Second World Wars wrought vast changes in people's lives. During both wars, in the absence of male labour to run munitions factories and steel works, public services and engineering firms, notions of a 'woman's place' were temporarily swept aside. Women were cajoled and instructed to enter these industries in vast numbers. To make it easier for women with family obligations to take up a job during the Second World War, nurseries and crèches were provided in abundance and British restaurants offered cheap meals. After the war, in spite of evidence that the majority of newly employed women wished to keep their jobs, these facilities were largely withdrawn; women were encouraged to return home 'where they belonged'. From this brief sketch it should be clear that the 'male breadwinner/female homemaker' dichotomy does not offer an accurate summary of the traditional division of labour between women and men; rather, it has the character of an assertion that obscures a complex reality, and justifies particular patterns of exploitation of women.

In the 1960s, during a period of economic expansion, women were again acknowledged by industry and by the state as a large reservoir of effort and talent, but by then women had already begun to re-assert their right to jobs and careers. However, women's rapidly increasing presence in industry and commerce (from 32 per cent of the labour force in 1951 to over 40 per cent in 1980) did not mean the dismantling of the gender hierarchy which had been reinforced by the earlier denial to women of independent sources of income. On the contrary, some of the privileges accorded to men within patriarchal family structures were reproduced, with modifications, in the relationships of women to men in the work-place.

Gender divisions in employment

Gender is a fundamental feature around which the labour force of contemporary Britain is fragmented. In the first place, female workers tend to be heavily concentrated within a narrow range of occupations. Of twenty-seven occupational orders listed in the 1971 Census, almost two-thirds of female employees are contained in three groupings: clerical workers (29.1 per cent of female employees); service workers (23.2 per cent), professional, technical workers and artists (11.9 per cent). Within these three groupings women tend to be further restricted to jobs that have come to be defined as 'women's work'. In the broad category of professional, technical workers and artists, for example, the largest occu-pation for women is nursing, where 91.6 per cent of employ-ees are female. Women who are classified as 'service workers' are predominantly (i) charwomen, office cleaners, window cleaners, chimney sweeps (91.7 per cent are female); (ii) maids, valets, and related service workers (96.9 per cent); (iii) canteen assistants and counter hands (96.8 per cent). Evi-dence such as this indicates that women are much more circumscribed than men in their choice of work, and em-ployed men are dispersed over a far greater range of indus-tries, sectors and occupations than are women. The return of women to the labour force has not resulted in a fundamental challenge to demarcations between men's work and women's work, or in women moving across the boundary into 'men's jobs'.

Second, women are overwhelmingly concentrated at the lower levels of the occupational hierarchy in terms of wages or salary, status, and authority. As can be seen from Table 6.3, although women are more likely than men to be found in non-manual occupations, far fewer women than men are in the top stratum of professionals, managers and employers.

Moreover, Westergaard and Resler (1976, p. 163) have argued that within the professions, on 1966 census data, the vast majority of women (93 per cent) are located in the *minor* professions (schoolteaching, librarianship, social work), while the majority of men can be found in higher-status professions such as dentistry, accountancy, architecture and law. Women comprised 89 per cent of nursing staff in 1974, but only 14 per cent of GPs, 9 per cent of dentists, and 8 per cent of consultants (Wainwright, 1978). In the teaching profession women are more likely to be in the primary than the secondary sector, and are far outnumbered by men in university posts. A recent report by the National Union of Teachers showed that although women constitute 44 per cent of the staff of secondary schools, they occupy only 1 per cent of the headships (NUT, 1980).

Again, Table 6.3 indicates that women are heavily underrepresented, compared with men, in skilled manual work; within manual work they are concentrated in the jobs that attract lower pay and carry fewer chances of promotion. Furthermore, the concentration of women at the bottom of the ladder has become more acute in the course of this century: while the proportion of *unskilled* manual workers who are female has risen (from 16 per cent in 1911 to 28 per cent in 1966), the proportion of *skilled* manual workers who are

TABLE 6.3
Socio-economic group of people in employment, 1977

	Distribution of employees (%)	
	Male	Female
Professional, managers and employers	23	6
Other non-manual	18	53
Skilled manual	39	8
Semi-skilled manual	13	24
Unskilled manual	8	9
Total	101	100

Source: Central Statistical Office, *Social Trends* (1980 edn, London, HMSO, 1979, table 5.9, p. 125.

female has shown quite a dramatic decline, from 24 per cent to 15 per cent, during the same period (Department of Employment, 1974, p. 22).

These patterns of employment help to account for the vastly different earnings of women and men; however, the analysis cannot stop here, for these patterns of employment themselves require explanation. One level of explanation emphasises the relationship between wage labour and child-rearing. It is often observed that with lower rates of fertility, the possibility of bottle-feeding, and longer life span, the period of their life cycle spent on average in pregnancy and lactation by women today is a fraction of what it was at the turn of the century. Although this means that the number of years in which women are 'free' to take on paid employment is greatly increased, it does *not* mean that child-rearing has no bearing on sexual divisions outside the family.

Women who attempt to combine paid employment with child care are particularly vulnerable to exploitation by employers. As we have seen, part-time employees typically receive lower hourly rates, as well as reduced chances of security, training or promotion, than full-time employees, even when the work they do is virtually identical. Part-time employees are overwhelmingly female; approximately 40 per cent of women in the labour force, but only 5 per cent of men, are employed on a part-time basis. In a major survey of women's employment, responsibility for husband or children, or for other domestic duties, was cited by almost 90 per cent of women as their reason for accepting part-time rather than full-time work (Hunt; cited in EOC, 1977).

An even more marginal group of (largely) female workers are the homeworkers, those who manufacture items ranging from dresses to lampshades to pens in their own homes, on piece rates, for an outside employer. A report by the Low Pay Unit (1979) revealed that there were at least 150,000 homeworkers in Britain in 1979, nearly half of whom earned less than 40 pence an hour; this was at a time when the average gross hourly wage of the *poorest* 10 per cent of female manual workers was £1. Moreover, homeworkers are rarely entitled to such basic employment rights as holidays (paid or otherwise), pensions and compensation for industrial accident. The vast majority of homeworkers are married women with one or more children, for whom the isolated grind of homeworking is the only way of supplementing family income while looking after their children and their home. The authors of a study of homeworkers in North London conclude:

> The homeworker is a casual labourer exploited on the basis of her ascribed role as a woman/wife ... *The economic and social situation of the homeworker is in effect an extreme instance of the situation of women in general* (Hope *et al.*, 1976, pp. 103 – 4; our emphasis).

Child care is a social activity the major costs of which are borne by individual families; within families the burdens as well as the pleasures predominantly fall to women. The sweated labour of homeworkers demonstrates in an extreme form the way in which the assignment of child care to women gives rise to multiple disadvantages; formal equality is a sterile concept, it has been said, as long as women are left on their own, holding the baby. A number of delicate issues are raised by the recognition that women's exclusive responsibility for child care presents a stringent obstacle to sexual equality.

First, there is the question of why women/mothers, as opposed to men/fathers, are the ones who are assumed to devote themselves to child care on a full-time basis – or, more often, to forge a precarious compromise between child care and employment. There is no compelling psychological, physiological or social reason why primary responsibility for the intimate and long-term care of children should rest exclusively with women – although ideologies of motherhood would try to persuade that either the yearnings of women ('maternal instinct') or the needs of children (the dangers of 'maternal deprivation') demand that the mother–child relationship be virtually full-time and relatively exclusive. An equal contribution from the father would require drastic changes in the organisation of work and home life which few employers – and as yet few male employees – seem prepared to contemplate. At a recent TUC Conference, Anna Coote, speaking from the platform, received a somewhat unsympathetic reception when she argued that a commitment to sexual equality would have to embody personal changes by male union members in the sexual division of labour in their own homes. The issue of whether mothers and fathers accept mutual responsibility for 'their' children is simultaneously a *personal* issue and a *public* one.

A second issue concerns the absence of a material infrastructure which would offer to women, and to men, a greater degree of choice by making it feasible to combine a responsible involvement in child care with paid employment, full-time study, or unpaid community service. This might involve, on the one hand, the provision of viable forms of collective child care — day nurseries, nursery schools, crèches in public places, children's centres — for those who wished or needed them. The policy of the government in recent years has been to offer day-care facilities only to children in dire need — and need has not been taken to include children both of whose parents are employed.

In 1973, although at least one million under-fives (29 per cent of the age group) were estimated to be in some form of day care, only 0.7 per cent were in full-time attendance at a local authority day nursery (Tizard *et al.*, 1976, p. 92). Indeed, in 1977 there were 28,000 *fewer* maintained day nursery places than there had been in 1945; the decision to close nursery places after 1945 was based on an explicit endorsement of the view that the mother's place was in the home. 'The Ministers are of the opinion that, under normal peacetime conditions, the right policy to pursue would be positively to discourage mothers with children under two from going out to work' (Ministry of Health Circular, 221/45, 1945). While the most well-to-do of professional couples may be able to draw on the services of au pairs, professional nannies, or relatively expensive private nurseries, mothers and fathers on more modest means are forced to rely on make-do arrangements, often with unregistered childminders (who are themselves frequently women who work for very low wages in accommodation unsuitable for the job).

A third issue confronts the organisation of work itself. Why should wage labour be structured in such a way that it is often impossible for adults of either sex to combine deep day-to-day involvement with child care with responsible and fulfilling employment? Many developments stemming from the intensification of labour — the extension of shift-work, for example — raise this problem in an acute form.

Misconceptions about women and employment

Many of the attempts to explain, or to justify, sexual divisions in employment over the years have invoked essential differences between the sexes in abilities, interests or motivation as the major explanatory factor; such hypotheses rarely stand up to scrutiny. The evidence mentioned earlier about the importance of two wages for keeping family incomes above the poverty line puts paid to the notion that married women work only for pin money. But a more fundamental issue is why, where the combined incomes of wife and husband are ample for the family's needs, should it so often be assumed that it is the woman's job that is secondary to, or of lesser importance than, the man's? It could as easily be argued that the husband's income is for luxuries, and the wife's for essentials; or that both partners earn partly for luxuries, partly for basics. Gender inequalities in the sphere of work may encourage the view that married women's work is secondary; where women are allocated jobs with lower incomes and less responsibility than those of men, it is not surprising if they come to think of their careers as of lesser importance than those of their husbands — but, of course, lesser importance does not mean *no* importance. To use this as a basis for explaining gender divisions in employment is, however, a totally circular argument: women define their jobs as 'secondary' because they are lower paid and less secure, and women are given lower-paid and less secure jobs because they define their work as 'secondary'.

To argue that there are no obvious grounds for viewing women's work as secondary to that of men is not to imply that all women enjoy and cherish their jobs; many women find their work monotonous and regard it as drudgery — and so do many men. But with women, as with men, paid employment is often a necessity in two senses: first, it is almost the only route to financial independence; and second, in a society in which status and social participation are closely linked to occupation and earning power, a job is for most men *and* women important for social acceptance, involvement and respect.

Another common misconception is that the subordination of women in the labour force can be attributed to their inferior strength; a standard riposte to demands for women's rights used to be, 'Women will get equality the day they are prepared to work in the mines!' The reply to this is straightforward. First, women (and children) used to work in the mines, indicating that they are not incapable of doing so; the last of the 'pitbrow girls' retired in 1953. Second, the vast majority of men neither work down the mines, nor even consider mining as a career; moreover, men who work in other, particularly professional occupations, are higher paid and better rewarded in other ways than miners. This raises a more general point. Women's physical strength, their ability to lift heavy loads unaided, is on average less than that of men in our society, whether through genetic make-up or differential physical training. However, the sort of 'sheer physical brawn' in which men excel is not generally a basis for superior reward in our society; one of the recurrent justifications for paying non-manual workers more than manual ones is that the latter 'merely' use muscle power, while non-manual workers allegedly use the more important qualities of intelligence, judgement and skill. The ideological nature of *both* assertions (about women, and about working-class people) should be clear.

Most of the other attempts to justify sexual divisions in employment by reference to essential differences between women and men are equally contentious. For example, the claims that women are less reliable employees than men (that they are more prone to absenteeism, that they have higher rates of turnover) turn out to be unfounded when like is compared with like — that is, when the women who are chosen for study are in jobs as rewarding as those of the men with whom they are compared, or when the men who are studied have as many domestic responsibilities as the women. However, inaccurate as these views are, they still exert an influence, in so far as they are used by the state to justify the reduction of 'manpower' (*sic*) training schemes for women, or by employers to exclude women from appointment or promotion. Hartnett (1978, p. 83) concludes that these misconceptions 'are still espoused by "gatekeeper" males in personnel departments who are in a position to exert a powerful influence on selection and promotion procedures'. It is not only men (and women) in authority but also some of those on the shop-floor and in the office who may resist attempts at radical improvement of women's employment opportunities. Men and women are sometimes in a competitive relationship in the labour market: that is to say, better promotion prospects for women may mean reduced promotion prospects for men, particularly in periods where the more attractive jobs are contracting. Sometimes it is said that by returning to the labour force in large numbers in recent years women have thrown men out of work; the implication is that a 'solution' to unemployment is the return of women to the home. A somewhat similar argument is that women, by 'agreeing' to work for lower pay, undercut men's wages, thereby leading employers to hire women in place of men, or forcing men to accept lower wages in order to remain competitive with women workers. How justified are these claims?

On the one hand, to the extent that women's jobs are segregated from those of men, the charge cannot be substantiated. Women cannot take 'men's' jobs; they take (and lose) jobs which are anyway specially reserved for women. On the other hand, it is clear that the competition between men and women workers is sometimes used in an exploitative way by employers. The availability of women workers (presumably at lower wage rates) means that it is possible to threaten male workers with possible replacement by women. (The same threat is of course used against women: 'If you ask for equal pay, you will price yourselves out of a job; in short, we will give these jobs to men'). But the more crucial issue concerns the structural arrangements that cannot provide jobs for all who want or need them, and cannot guarantee a tolerable standard of living to all who are prepared to contribute to production. It is precisely these structural arrangements which are the subject of theoretical attempts to make sense of gender divisions in employment.

Dual labour market theory

Some economists and sociologists have suggested that capitalist countries like Britain or the USA give rise to not one, but two, markets for labour. The jobs available in the primary sector are relatively secure, well paid, and tend to have good long-term promotion prospects; those in the secondary sector are more precarious and less well rewarded. According to dual labour market theory, those workers who are preferred by employers (on the basis of certain personal characteristics) in the primary sector will tend to accrue greater rewards than those of identical ability or qualifications who are absorbed into the secondary sector. Moreover, because of the nature of jobs in the secondary sector, those who enter there will, over the course of their working lives, receive less on-the-job training and be more frequently made redundant, so that their disadvantageous position in the labour market will be reinforced. Thus the likelihood of movement of workers from the secondary to the primary sector is small.

Access to primary-sector employment is controlled through the operation of internal labour markets: that is, training for jobs of skill and responsibility, and promotion to and selection for these posts, takes place not on the open market (e.g. through advertisements in newspapers, so that anyone can compete) but within firms themselves. Many firms take in young, relatively inexperienced workers (whether into manual jobs, or clerical/managerial streams) and train them to be good company men and women over a number of years. Those who appear most promising (and who are lucky enough to find themselves in a firm with good prospects in the first place) may be promoted to relatively high positions. Because selection and training takes place within the firm there is little workers can do when initially seeking employment to ensure their chances of ultimate success.

Now, it can be argued that internal labour markets work to the disadvantage of women in at least two ways. First, firms are less likely to recruit women to promotion-stream jobs in the first place, due to stereotypical beliefs about the unsuitability of women. Second, promotion streams have been

structured over the years in ways that match the life experiences of men better than those of women. Thus workers are
recruited fairly young; and the fundamental prerequisite for
promotion is several years *continuous* service, in the late
teens and early twenties. Women who leave for even a few
years to have children find themselves out of the running for
posts of responsibility when they return. Any rigid career
structure which demands continuous application during the
twenties will, in the absence of alternative child-care arrangements and generous maternity/paternity leave schemes, work
to the disadvantage of women.

There has been heated argument over the applicability of
this model to the British context. Barron and Norris (1976),
drawing upon data from the early 1970s, analyse the characteristics of the social position of women in Britain — particularly dispensability — and confirm that this leads to their confinement to the secondary market. Blackburn and Mann
(1979) add that the emergence of a dual labour market
depends to some extent upon the maintenance of an institutional framework (a legal system allowing, or endorsing,
discriminatory practices, etc.) which permits easier segregation of different sectors of the labour force. They too conclude that (1979, p. 284):

> Women manual workers, unlike any of the male groups we
> have considered, are probably a 'secondary' labour force in
> the sense of the dual and radical labour market theories.
> The internal labour market and other defences against in-
> security exist on the backs of a secondary labour market,
> and in this country, that means largely on the backs of
> women.

The strength of this argument (and of the 'reserve army of
labour' view that we will examine in a moment) is that it
avoids two pitfalls common to discussions of women's disadvantaged position in the labour market. First, it avoids
attributing divisions in employment purely to *individual* cases
of 'discrimination' or 'prejudice' without specifying the institutional demarcations which make such discrimination advantageous in the first place. Second, it negates the assumption
that better qualifications for women, or greater ambition,

would automatically dismantle gender divisions in employment; this is a view which fails to give due attention to the facts that even women with the same qualifications as men are disadvantaged in terms of wages and promotion, and that although qualifications may be used as 'screening' devices by employers in choosing between candidates, such qualifications do not actually determine the structure of occupations or the number of rewarding jobs available.

There is, on the other hand, considerable debate as to the processes that give rise to dualism in the labour market. Emphasis is given in some theories to technological developments which encourage firms to train their own employees in relatively specific skills; under such conditions it is in the interests of firms to offer better-than-market rates and conditions in order to maintain a stable labour force, while other firms (or plants) can tolerate higher turnover. The 'radical' version of dual labour market theory emphasises instead the development of stratified labour markets (within the primary and secondary sectors, as well as between them) as an attempt by employers to counteract tendencies towards the homogeneity of the labour force — a strategy of divide and rule in order to inhibit the possibility of unified class action. Finally, the contribution of workers' collective efforts to protect themselves from the most damaging effects of labour market competition by extending areas of job security and improving wages is seen by some as a factor in the development of primary-sector employment (Rubery, 1978).

Reserve army of labour

Other analyses of gender divisions in employment, particularly those deriving from Marxist traditions of thought, identify women as a crucial constituent of the reserve army of labour. This theory suggests that, as capitalism develops, it has an inherent tendency to throw up a large and growing body of people who are available for work but who are only marginally incorporated within the main labour force. One source of the reserve army stems from the permanent and progressive decline in the size of the agricultural labour force — which 'frees' workers for employment in the industrial or service sectors. Another source is the mechanisation and de-skilling of manual and non-manual jobs, deriving from on-going attempts to intensify the labour process; mechanisation either throws people out of work, or pushes them into labour-intensive sectors where they may be under-employed or irregularly employed.

The creation of a reserve army of labour — of a body of people who, though available for work, are unemployed, under-employed or insecurely employed — is thus seen as a consequence of capitalist development, but also as a pre-condition for *continued* development. First, the reserve army can be drawn upon by prosperous firms in times of rapid expansion but can be expelled again when recession sets in and production and costs have to be cut. Second, more labour-intensive firms, whose fortunes are tied to those of the larger corporations and which are often engaged in providing cheap goods and services for the larger firms, can draw upon the reserve army, can pay these workers at lower rates, and can, as above, sack them in a recession, or when rising labour costs make capital investment a more viable proposition. Third, the existence of the reserve army of labour, unemployed or working for lower pay, helps to discipline other workers and to regulate wage demands. Thus, in this view, unemployment and under-employment are not accidental or pathological features of the industrial scene but more or less predictable by-products of the capitalist process of accumulation.

The reasons why women in particular become part of the reserve army of labour is a matter of continuing debate. There is a technical argument which suggests that the employment of *married* women lowers the 'value' of their husbands' labour power, and therefore cheapens the cost of labour to employers (Beechey, 1977). More simply, it has been suggested that women's suitability for the reserve army is a consequence of ideologies that locate women in the home, and therefore diffuse the political strains that arise from cyclical unemployment of women; moreover, the un-employment — at least of married women — can be disguised more easily than that of other workers. ('She's not unem-ployed, she has gone back to being a housewife'.) Bland and her colleagues (1978) add that women in different circumstances may be vulnerable to inclusion in the reserve army of labour for different reasons: women of child-bearing age may, because of their reproductive life-cycle, experience periods of 'voluntary' unemployment; Asian and West Indian women, and unmarried mothers, may be among those women who for social and economic reasons are forced to take work when and where they can.

The reserve army of labour theory has been criticised for failing to take account of the distinct uses to which male and female labour is put. However, empirical support for the theory — or at least for that aspect of it which proposes that women would be expelled from production more readily than men — comes from a paper by Bruegel (1979). While acknowledging the severe difficulties in analysing unemployment figures for men and women, Bruegel notes that between 1974 and 1978 the official rate of unemployment among women rose three times faster than that of men. Moreover, in industries where there was a decline in levels of employment the decline was most acute for women; thus women appear to be more vulnerable than men to recession. A most important point is that the rate of employment decline for part-time women workers exceeded that for full-time workers of either sex: 'It is part-time women workers . . . who conform most closely to the model of women as a disposable reserve army' (Bruegel, 1979, pp. 18–19). On the other hand, Bruegel notes, women's overall employment prospects have not declined in recent years as rapidly as those of men because of women's segregation into the expanding service industries; had women workers been evenly distributed throughout industries, Bruegel argues, their overall employment prospects would have been further diminished compared with those of men. However, as the growth of the service sector ends, and as rationalisation — including the introduction of micro-processing — eliminates many of these jobs, female workers will increasingly be in danger of redundancy.

6.4   DOMESTIC LABOUR

It is often said that 'Women are rejecting their traditional role as housewives, and are entering the labour force.' Apart from questioning whether the housewife role is traditional, we can ask whether it is indeed the case that, on entering the labour force, women reject or abandon housework. The evidence indicates, overwhelmingly, that they do not. In Chapter 5 it was noted that — despite frequent claims of the emergence of egalitarian marriages — the sexual division of labour within the family, with women having responsibility for housework as well as child care, has scarcely been bridged. When women enter paid employment it is generally in addition to (not in place of) 'their' responsibilities within the home. Oakley (1972, p. 152) emphasises the extent to which housework is part of the feminine gender role: 'One basic occupation in particular, that of housewife, is exclusively feminine. In Britain, 76% of all employed women are housewives, and so are 93% of non-employed women.' Housework is indeed treated as indissolubly 'feminine'. Men do some housework, of course, particularly if they are living on their own. But when a woman enters the scene it is assumed that she will take over many of the mundane tasks for him, freeing him to return to his 'proper' spheres. Many a wife has been chagrined to see that when her husband goes away on business or pleasure she is left at home, looking after the children and watching television; but when *she* goes away her husband is besieged with offers of meals and general assistance — it is assumed that he cannot (and should not) cope on his own. Similar assumptions operate at the level of the state. When women were drafted into war duties, for example, they would be excused if it were shown that they were the only woman in a household of men; in that case, it was assumed, their presence was needed to cook and clean. Even in the early 1980s the taxation regulations allow a man without a wife to claim an allowance to pay a female housekeeper; the housekeeper *must* be female. A woman worker on her own cannot make a similar claim.

Is housework a lark, as some would have it, simply involving a quick flick with the duster and a comfortable coffee morning with friends? Or is it, as others suggest, the most dull, monotonous work in the world? The forty housewives interviewed by Oakley (1974) describe some aspects of housework, such as washing up, ironing or cleaning, in terms reminiscent of assembly-line workers; in fact, they more often reported experiencing monotony, fragmentation and excessive speed in their work than had the assembly-line workers in the affluent-worker studies (Oakley, 1974, p. 87). On the other hand, many housewives regarded cooking as potentially satisfying, though the difficulty of cooking imaginatively with restrictions of time and money, and with children in the way, contributed to frustration.

Oakley discusses the variety of skills and responsibilities lumped together under the heading of 'housework', and argues that the refusal to acknowledge housework as *work* is both a cause and a reflection of the lower status of women in society. She analyses housework in the same way that sociologists might analyse automobile assembly work, clerical labour or deep-sea fishing: as a set of tasks done by a particular group of people, within a specific set of social relations. These relations are crucial for understanding housework: domestic labour is usually not directly supervised, and is often done invisibly without other adults watching; it is performed largely on the basis of personal, rather than contractual, relationships; and it is unpaid, with no fixed remuneration linked to the number of hours put in or the quantity of goods or services produced. All three of these conditions contribute to the fact that the effort expended in housework is largely undervalued and unrecognised; in particular, *unpaid* labour is largely regarded as 'not-work'.

Moreover, the view that housework and child care are not work, but merely part of the feminine role, has tended to obscure the links between the sexual division of labour in the home, and sexual divisions in employment:

In an economy in which a person's capacity to work is bought and sold in exchange for a wage, labour which is performed on the basis of personal relations rather than on the basis of monetary exchange is not recognised as labour. Consequently women's work in caring for children and husbands does not appear as necessary labour; it appears as a natural part of family life ... Since domesticity appears an inherent part of being a woman ... the inequalities facing women have appeared to be the inequalities they face when they enter the world of men; there has been no need to explain why this world is a 'man's world'! (Wainwright, 1978, p. 160).

Contrary to popular belief, the introduction of labour-saving devices into the home has not reduced the time spent on housework. Domestic appliances have eliminated some of the heaviest physical demands of housework, but standards of hygiene have risen along with expectations concerning the 'home beautiful' and 'creative homemaking'. The average time spent on housework by a sample of urban housewives (some of whom had paid employment) in 1971 was seventy-seven hours, compared with seventy hours in 1950 (Oakley, 1974, table 5.4). On the other hand, something which has not yet been fully explored is the extent of polarisation within the category of houseworkers. For example, wide-spread car ownership and the emergence of hypermarkets make it possible for *some* women to complete the bulk of the weekly shopping in one journey; the same development makes shopping much more difficult and time-consuming for those who have no access to a car, or who have insufficient cash to spare for a massive once-and-for-all expenditure.

The different demands of housework on women in different economic and personal circumstances is just one of the features of housework militating against a sense of solidarity among women. First, in our society, housework is a largely solitary activity. The design of houses, the location of laundry facilities within the home rather than at some community wash place, and so on, all mean that women spend a large part of their day isolated from one another. Even the act of meeting for political purposes may be inhibited by family responsibilities. Second, women are tied to their work through bonds that few other workers experience — the bonds of love and identification. It is easier to go on strike against a boss you hardly know than it is to refuse to get the children's tea. Third, most people like to feel they are reasonably 'good at their job'. Houseworkers are no exception. But often, in the absence of clear universal standards or praise from 'employers', women use other

women as standards against which to judge their own performance in a competitive light. Hence, as presently organised,
housework has a tendency to divide women rather than unite
them.

The recognition that domestic labour is indeed *work* — and
not simply a natural part of being a woman — has raised the
question of why this aspect of the sexual division of labour
persists. Often this question is posed in terms of asking who
benefits from such an arrangement.

The first type of answer stresses the benefits which men of
all social classes reap from sustaining a system in which
women, regardless of other demands on their time, are expected to look after men, to take care of their daily needs, to
soothe and comfort them. Men have to work hard to earn a
living, it is argued; but they can expect not only an income
but personal service as well, at a cost to themselves (in terms
of maintenance of the woman) far less than the market value
of the goods and services provided. Since men benefit from
the services provided by their wives (or daughters or sisters or
mothers), they have an interest in maintaining the sexual
division of labour. They may express that interest in a variety
of ways: by resisting (or failing to support) legislation that
might truly give women equal opportunities outside the
home; by supporting, through professional organisations and
trade unions, protectionist policies which restrict women's
access to rewarding occupations; by 'allowing' wives to go
out to work, while insisting that the house be kept as efficiently as before; and, finally, by refusing to give more than a
token gesture of help in the home.

A second view is that it is not men but the capitalist
system that is the prime beneficiary of women's unpaid
domestic labour. Attempts to trace the route by which
capital appropriates domestic labour as 'surplus value' (the
'domestic labour debate') have been less than satisfactory. On
the other hand, it is the case that women's domestic labour
contributes to the maintenance of tolerable standards of
living, and may therefore reduce political pressure for radical
change. In periods when wages are rising more slowly than
prices women's efforts and energies may stretch the household income that little bit further so that the drop in stan-

dard of living is not apparent to men. As a result, 'bread-winners' are less likely to be pressed to open revolt. (Of course, women also cushion the effects of falling standards of living by taking jobs, however poorly paid, to boost the family income.) Moreover, women expend much effort on housework and emotional support that rejuvenates their older children, their husbands, their fathers for each day's work.

Although the two approaches to explaining the persistence of the sexual division of labour are not wholly incompatible — in the second, for example, women's efforts protect both men and the capitalist relations of production — the two versions do have different emphases. One limitation of the former (male-benefit) view is that it does not so readily encompass the benefits which female domestic labour offers to children, the elderly and invalids, as well as to men, while the latter version is somewhat less effective in explaining why *women* should be designated to these particular tasks.

6.5   REPRODUCTION

The single most far-reaching difference between men and women lies in their reproductive capacities. Genetic contributions from both a woman and a man, in the form of egg and sperm, are biologically necessary to begin the process of creating a human child. But only women have the physiological capacity to nurture the foetus through the months from conception to birth; only women can bear children.

This simple fact sometimes leads people to assume that the divisions between men and women in society are biologically determined: that 'biology is destiny'. Such arguments are sometimes developed by drawing analogies between women and the females of other species. The comparison between women and cows, for example, is explicitly drawn in this celebration from *The Imperial Animal* of the qualities of women:

The human mother is a splendid mammal — the epitome of her order. Her physiology is more highly developed for suckling behaviour — with permanent breasts, for example

— than any of her cousins, except domestic ungulates bred specially for milk-giving. But more than this, she is like any other mammal, emotionally programmed to be responsive to the growing child (Tiger and Fox, 1974, p. 86).

This quotation implies a direct continuity between the human and animal worlds which is unwarranted. Of course, humans, like other animals, reproduce; and women, like other mammals, bear the growing infant. But in the case of human beings all behaviour surrounding reproduction — from the decision to engage in heterosexual intercourse, to the forms of contraceptive knowledge available, from the taboos and obligations surrounding pregnancy, to the manner and place of birth — is meaningful in social (rather than biological) terms, and is heavily influenced by social custom and social structure.

There have been many societies in which child-bearing was regarded as the principal duty of women. They have been trained from infancy with this goal in mind, being discouraged from any pastimes other than those that would make them more pleasing wives and more devoted mothers. Married women who remained childless (whether through their own, or their husband's infertility) might be regarded as social failures, to be cast aside, divorced or replaced by other wives. Child-bearing was the only way in which women could gain a degree of security and acceptance in the community. In such societies there would be some truth in the statement that 'biology is women's destiny' — but the thing to notice is that the importance of biology in defining women's position rests upon *social* mores and *social* structure which forbid women other sources of security and esteem, and not on natural laws.

In Western Europe there have been remarkable changes in the social conditions surrounding reproduction in the past one hundred years. One such change is what Oakley (1975) refers to as the 'medicalisation of pregnancy and childbirth'. In Britain and the USA (unlike, for example, the Netherlands) the vast majority of babies are delivered in hospital, often with the use of surgical techniques and procedures such as the clinical induction of labour. Many pregnant women welcome advances in health care which have made childbirth safer for themselves and their infants; and medical advice is all the more sought since, with the decline in family size, fewer women have knowledge about childbirth through sharing the experience of pregnancy and labour with their mothers, sisters or neighbours. Nevertheless, argues Oakley, the medicalisation of pregnancy and childbirth has other important implications.

First, in the course of medicalisation the management of childbirth has passed from the control of women to that of men. At the beginning of the twentieth century childbirth and pregnancy in Britain were largely the province of experienced 'handywomen', local specialists in childbirth. As the successors to female healers who had once provided health care for the bulk of the population, handywomen represented, in a sense, the last bastion of female-controlled health care. Their activities were, in the twentieth century, increasingly circumscribed and finally forbidden. Professionally trained doctors and obstetricians — the majority of whom are men — established control over the management of pregnancy and childbirth.

In addition to the transfer of control from women to men, medicalisation makes of reproduction a scientific enterprise, from which mothers-to-be may feel increasingly alienated. Reproduction has been, Oakley argues, redefined; from an everyday if delicate process it has become 'a medical condition fraught with all sorts of dangers: a condition that can only be "cured" by the authoritarian benevolence of professionalised medicine' (Oakley, 1976, p. 18).

The use of techniques for regulating pregnancy is another factor which has dramatically altered patterns of reproduction. The development and diffusion of safe, comfortable and effective ways or preventing or terminating unwanted pregnancies offers great potential for women to control the course of their own lives. But their widespread use only followed after bitter struggles by women in the nineteenth and twentieth centuries against state suppression of information concerning birth control. In an early sociological study of the area, Banks and Banks (1964) argued that practices of family limitation became increasingly widespread among middle-class families when, in the last quarter of the nineteenth century, the rising cost of living made the regulation of births one of the few acceptable ways of maintaining their preferred style of life. Often, too, working-class women, exhausted by child-bearing and child-rearing, took matters into their own hands. One woman, writing in the late nineteenth century (Davies, 1978, letter 33), tells of the effects of having seven children in ten years of marriage:

> During pregnancy I suffered much. When at the end of ten years I was almost a mental and physical wreck, I determined that this state of things should not go on any longer, and if there was no natural means of prevention, then of course artificial means must be employed, which were successful, and am happy to say that from that time I have been able to take pretty good care of myself, but often shudder to think what might have been the result if things had been allowed to go on as they were.

The contrast between the experience of this woman and others of her generation, and women in the second half of the twentieth century, has been highlighted by Richard Titmuss (1958, p. 91):

> it would seem that the typical working mother of the 1980's, married in her teens or early twenties and, experiencing ten pregnancies, spent about fifteen years in a state of pregnancy and in nursing a child for the first year of its life. She was tied, for this period of time, to the wheel of childbearing. Today, for the typical mother, the time spent would be about four years.

And, of course, that four years represents a considerably smaller fraction of a typically longer life-span. Yet the notion that women are now free to exercise complete control over their reproductive processes is somewhat short of the truth:

> The current acceptance of birth control, shown for instance in the provision of free contraception within the NHS, obscures the number of ways in which women's right to choose whether or not to have children is still to be

won. The safety of the Pill is highly controversial . . . The two most efficient methods of contraception, the Pill and the coil or IUD, are not acceptable to all women and are not always physically tolerated. Availability, including sympathetic and informed medical advice, is still a problem, for instance for young girls and women in rural areas. Research into male contraception lags far behind investment in female hormonal alternatives to the monthly pill. Furthermore (and aside from recent attempts to *restrict* the 1967 Abortion Act) abortion is *not* widely or freely available. Indeed the NHS has provided a decreasing proportion of all abortions since 1967 (Bristol Women's Studies Group, 1979, pp. 161–2).

Moreover, the technical possibility of fertility control coexists with a strong ideology of motherhood – a belief that motherhood is the natural, desired and ultimate goal of all 'normal' women, and that women who deny their 'maternal instincts' are selfish, peculiar or disturbed. Evidence suggests that many members of the medical profession share this view (Barratt and Roberts, 1978).

While many women wish to have (and cherish) their children, the views of medical personnel are not merely a reflection of that fact; the idea of a maternal instinct is sometimes used as an excuse for overriding women's expressed wishes with regard to child-bearing. A woman who does not wish to become pregnant may be regarded as deviant. Some of the inconsistencies – and the distressing effects – of medical ideology are revealed in McIntyre's (1976) study. Medical personnel and social workers, she found, tended to view pregnancy in healthy married women as a welcome and completely unproblematic event. Such pregnancies did not require explanation: women became pregnant because of their 'maternal instinct', their biologically based desire to have babies. Evidence to the contrary was often disregarded. Women who wished to terminate the pregnancy, or who were ambivalent about it, were advised that their reaction was a temporary depression brought on by hormonal changes: 'Of course you want the baby.' On the other hand, *unmarried* women who wanted to keep their babies were regarded with suspicion and dismay, and attempts were often made to persuade them to accept an abortion or have the baby adopted. Here the 'maternal instinct' of women was not invoked as an explanation for pregnancy; instead, explanations were sought in some disturbance which propelled unmarried women to become pregnant 'against their nature'. (One may wonder whether a man who time after time got women pregnant would be regarded as having a strong paternal instinct!)

Perhaps the medicalisation of most aspects of reproduction is a mixed blessing for women. On the one hand, medical facilities offer the potential for increased health and safety, for greater freedom for women to decide when, and whether, they will have children. On the other hand, the domination of reproductive technology by the medical profession has enabled others to have an even greater capacity to exert control over women's lives. Moreover, it should be noted that the state always has an interest in the number of children born, as well as in their rearing, and policies fostered in this regard have their most direct impact on women rather than on men.

Intervention by the state to regulate reproduction has followed different policies at different times. An interest in lowering the birth rate of Third World countries has involved policies as diverse as the seemingly compulsory sterilisation programme pursued by Indira Gandhi, and the recommendation by Robert McNamara, the then President of the World Bank, that the governments of developing countries could, by raising the status of women, encourage them to limit their family size. Where the aim is to *increase* the birth rate, incentives such as family allowances or medals for fertile mothers have sometimes been offered, and abortion and contraceptive facilities have been restricted to the well-to-do. Eugenicist policies of selective breeding (encouraging births from favoured groups, discouraging or disallowing those from disfavoured groups) have been frequently recommended, though fortunately less often adopted. Nevertheless, they were used on a compulsory basis in Nazi Germany, and to a lesser extent in the USA in the 1930s. These issues raise the important point that 'technological' or 'scientific' knowledge is seldom neutral either in its usage or in its effects. The state may use the availability or withdrawal of reproductive technology as an instrument of policy, but may thereby curtail, in dramatic ways, women's control over their own destinies.

6.6 SEXUALITY

The dominant assumptions about male and female sexuality in contemporary society emphasise the different sexual needs and desires of women and men, with women generally seen as the more passive partners and men the more active. Men, it is believed, *have* more sex because they *need* more sex. Specifically, the male sexual drive is seen as stronger and less easy to control than the female, so that it leads men to make sexual initiatives, while women's sexual urges are reactive, aroused primarily in response to advances from men; male sexuality is thought to involve a more indiscriminate need for gratification, while women's sexual needs are allegedly more closely governed by their total relationship with a particular partner; men, it is assumed, seek sex primarily for the intrinsic pleasure, while women are more likely to use sex as a means to an end — a route to winning affection or specific favours from a man.

McIntosh (1978) argues that there is little evidence to support these assumptions about the specificity of male sexual needs, but she points out that such assumptions are implicit, none the less, in many analyses of such phenomena as prostitution. Often, for example, female prostitutes are seen as serving a necessary social function in catering for the sexual needs of unattached or unattractive men; but female sexual needs are not seen as requiring an analogous institution. Moreover, many writers find it puzzling that female prostitutes are able to engage in a casual sexual act, apparently without emotion; but no surprise is expressed at the ability of their male clients so to do. The implication is that sex outside an emotional relationship is in keeping with the masculine character but not with the feminine. Hence, McIntosh argues, the ideological assumptions about differences in male and female sexuality underlie, and reinforce, a double standard of sexual morality.

Any notion that the assumptions about male and female

sexuality prevailing in our culture are universal must be rejected in the face of comparisons with other cultures and other historical periods. Albert reports that among the Zuni Indians of North America, women are expected to be sexually aggressive, and men sexually timid. It is men, and not women, who approach their wedding night with trepidation. Henry describes a tribe in the Brazilian highlands where both males and females engage in 'open, ribald and aggressive onslaughts' on members of the other sex, and both sexes take precautions to avoid rape (cited in Oakley, 1972, p. 55). In Europe a frequent male complaint in the seventeenth century was, according to Rowbotham (1974, p. 6), about the 'sexual insatiability' of women; popular folklore retained the notion of the sexually voracious female through to the nineteenth century.

These examples demonstrate the pitfalls of attempting to draw generalisations about the 'essential' or 'fundamental' sexual natures of men or women by examination of contemporary sexual practices. They also illustrate the necessity of trying to understand how assumptions about sexuality, and different sexual practices for men and women, are created and reproduced.

In contemporary society heterosexuality is defined as an important part of gender; men and women whose primary sexual relationships are with members of their own sex are severely sanctioned, and it is often implied that they cannot be seen as 'real men' or 'real women'. To a lesser extent, a similar attitude is taken towards those who are celibate. The sanctions against people who are not in a socially approved heterosexual relationship indicate just one facet of social control over human sexuality in contemporary society.

Control over heterosexual relations tends to incorporate the double standard of morality referred to above: the assumption that sexual 'promiscuity' is natural and even laudable in boys and men (sowing their wild oats), but shameful, 'unfeminine' and disruptive of social order in girls and women. These social controls can be seen to operate at two levels, as Smart and Smart (1978) suggest — the level of informal group processes, and the level of institutional procedures.

Informal group processes include the social pressures which

are brought to bear by neighbours, family and peer groups
on males and females who appear to deviate from the usual
gender roles. In *Learning to Labour*, Willis (1977) describes
the centrality of the double standard for 'the lads' — working-
class boys who evolved a distinct counter-school culture —
and highlights the effects this has on their perception of girls.
A hallmark, Willis says, of being one of the lads is 'to have
either sexual experience or at least aspirations which are exploitative and hypocritical. Girls are pursued, sometimes
roughly, for their sexual favours, often dropped and labelled
"loose" when they are given' (p. 146). The lads expect to be
'promiscuous', but 'promiscuous' girls are despised:

> 'The lads' are after the 'easy lay' at dances, though they
> think twice about being seen to 'go out' with them. 'The
> girlfriend' is a very different category from an 'easy lay'.
> She represents the human value that is squandered by
> promiscuity. She is the loyal domestic partner. She cannot
> be held to be sexually experienced — or at least not with
> others (Willis, 1977, p. 44).

It is not only boys who penalise sexually active girls; Wilson
(1978) reports from her study of teenagers' sexual codes that
the girls regard sex as acceptable only when it takes place in
the context of a steady relationship; girls who have sex without proclaiming their love for the man are regarded as 'lays'.
But while 'lays' were ostracised and penalised, 'promiscuous
boys apparently did not suffer any loss of prestige or status'
(Wilson, 1978, p. 71). These studies illustrate the pervasiveness of the double standard. Open sexuality is acceptable for
girls, it seems, even in this 'permissive society', only in the
context of love and domesticity. For boys, open sexuality
is part of the process of 'being a man'. Many writers have
pointed out that even our language enshrines the double
standard; against the multiplicity of insulting names for
sexually active females (scrubber, lay, whore, slag, slut, etc.)
are laudatory terms for men who are sexually active.

At the more formal levels of social control over sexuality,
assumptions of male/female differences in sexuality are reproduced and, sometimes, enforced. The more enlightened and

open discussions of sexuality which are said to characterise modern schooling still often represent female sexuality as essentially reproductive (about having babies, rather than having pleasure) and as submissive:

> Of course things have changed over the years; we don't just endure sex any longer. It has been converted into a wonder of the world . . . 'It's the most beautiful thing that can happen to you', said one of my teachers. Precisely, it happens to you. You don't do it, it's done to you (Campbell, 1974, p. 102).

Again the ideology of male needs (and of girls' responsibility for controlling them) is explicitly endorsed in a recent (1977) report on health education from the Department of Education and Science:

> Girls should understand that they may inadvertently impose great stress on boys by arousing sexual reactions in them which they do not fully comprehend and may not be able to control (cited in Rance, 'Going all the Way', *Spare Rib*, October 1978, no. 75, p. 15).

The schools help to transmit certain attitudes towards sexuality, but the courts and judicial authorities take a more direct part in enforcing the prevailing definitions of male and female sexuality. In studies of delinquent behaviour it has been suggested that the courts take an interest in the sexual record of girls brought before them for other offences, while generally considering that the sexual behaviour of delinquent boys is immaterial. As Shacklady Smith (1978, p. 82) found, 'there is every reason to suppose that offences by girls are sexualised, in fact non-sexual offences are overlooked in favour of sexual (mis)-behaviour'. This has two implications: first, that girls are penalised for acts which are considered unworthy of attention when committed by boys; second, that the complexity of female deviance is disguised by an undue interest in the sexual content of women's lives.

Our emphasis so far has been upon adolescents, but one area where strong societal control of sexuality is asserted over women and men of all ages is in the area of social security regulations. In cases where a woman is judged to be married or cohabiting she is not entitled to claim supplementary benefit. The assumption officially made is that where a man and woman sleep together the man will support her. Thus, at least in the case of women who are poor, the state insists that active heterosexuality cannot coexist with financial independence; nor can a man sleep with a woman without being assumed by the state to support her.

These regulations provide a striking example of the social control of sexuality in everyday life. More generally, it can be noted that coming to terms with personal feelings and cultural expectations regarding sexuality is a delicate part of the process of growing up. It involves timidity, anxiety and self-consciousness for both sexes. But for boys sexuality represents an extension of the masculine role — boys prove their masculinity (and reassure themselves of their attractiveness) by sexual exploit and adventure. The situation prescribed for girls is very different: girls are expected to be as sexually attractive as possible without being sexually active — femininity involves a suppression of sexuality. The strong demands placed on teenage girls by the media, peer groups and family to be attractive, combined with the strong condemnation of girls who are straightforwardly sexual, implies a built-in tension in the feminine role. It has been suggested by several writers that the appeal of 'romantic' magazines and films (with their emphasis upon courtship and glamour) is that these provide a way of resolving the contradiction between being, as Willis (1977, p. 45) puts it, 'sexy but not sexual'. At the same time, Willis argues, the romanticism espoused by many working-class girls reinforces boys' sense of male superiority:

> The contortions and strange [romantic] rituals of the girls are seen as part of their girlishness, of their inherent weakness and confusion. Their romanticism is tolerated with a knowing masculinity, which privately feels it knows much more about the world (Willis, 1977, p. 45).

Other authors — notably McRobbie (1978) — see romance

as a lubricant which eases for girls the passage from adolescence to adulthood. The teenage working-class girls whom she interviewed did not have starry-eyed ideals about marriage; they saw the realities of marriage through the experiences of their neighbours, mothers and elder sisters, and many recognised the humdrum, exploitative and even brutal aspects of marriage. On the other hand, most of the girls expected to get married, seeing few alternatives for women within their own community. Romance offered the prospect of a little glamour, fun and attention before coming to terms with somewhat harsher realities.

Rape

At first glance cases of rape might appear to be far removed from everyday sexual encounters. The view of rape as an isolated act perpetrated by disturbed individuals is promoted by fictional accounts of rape and by sensational reports in the media which often give disproportionate attention to that small minority of rapists who are apparently 'psychopathic', and whose crimes seem like a spontaneous act provoked by the presence of an unknown (attractive) woman. Such an image of rape is at odds with analyses of rape cases in the USA and in Britain. Research indicates that few rapists are seriously disturbed, that many plan their crimes carefully, and that victims are often attacked by friends, kin or acquaintances within their own home. These studies have also disproved many of the most common myths about rape (that women enjoy rape; that only young, attractive women are vulnerable; that rape cannot succeed if the victim resists). From analysis of police files of rape cases over a five-year period, for example, Wright (1979) concluded that the widespread use of physical violence and of threats of injury or death meant that for most victims the rape was undoubtedly perceived as a 'life-threatening' situation.

When rape is analysed in terms of its relationship to cultural expectations and to the socially structured subordination of women in contemporary society — rather than being viewed as an idiosyncratic act by disturbed individuals — then we can begin to make some headway in understanding the incidence of rape and its social implications.

First, it can be suggested that the likelihood of rape may be enhanced by social pressures on men to 'prove themselves' and to adopt a dominant/aggressive stance in their encounters with women. Such pressures may, in turn, be reinforced by the portrayal of women in the media, not as complex human beings, but as passive objects to be admired, enjoyed and 'consumed'. Finally, the double standard which embodies the notion that women who are sexually active (unlike similar men) are deviant and forfeit the respect of others should be considered; in many court cases the sexual history of rape victims has been discussed (and echoed in news reports), with the clear implication that women who engaged in sex voluntarily had no right to refuse their 'favours' to others, and placed themselves, in some sense, beyond the protection of the law. (This was dramatically apparent in 1979, when after the brutal murder of ten women alleged to have been involved in prostitution the killing of a girl of 'good reputation' prompted the announcement that the 'Yorkshire Ripper had claimed his first *innocent* victim'. The word 'innocent' is of course ambiguous; but many people complained that *either* the police and media were introducing information irrelevant to the crime (the women's sexual history), *or* they were implying that the earlier victims were in some sense guilty victims – as if murder were justified when the victim was a 'promiscuous' woman.)

The number of rape cases known to the police has been increasing in recent years. There is no way of determining whether the *actual* rate of rape is rising or whether, alternatively, in the light of increased publicity surrounding rape and the development of supportive networks to help victims to overcome their fears, more victims are reporting their rapes to the police. But whatever the actual (unknown) incidence of rape, the significance of rape may spread far more widely than its effects on individual victims. An argument pursued by Hanmer (1978), by Smart and Smart (1978) and by Brownmiller (1976) is that rape, and other forms of aggression against women (ranging from minor assaults to 'sexual harassment' – the frequent advances made by men to women in pubs, on the streets, or at work), act as implicit forms of social control upon women. This is not to say that all women are, or feel themselves to be, under constant threat, or that all women live in fear of sexual attack. On the contrary, most women learn from an early age strategies for insulating themselves from such dangers. At home with their families, shopping in town, at work, surrounded by people, they feel themselves (and rightly) to be, on the whole, safe. The forms of vigilance which serve as their protection become 'second nature' to women at an early age; this vigilance involves such things as care with clothing (not to appear too 'provocative'), care where they go (avoiding certain pubs and gathering places, avoiding walking alone at night), care what they do (lowering their eyes; avoiding hitchhiking or striking up conversations with strangers), and care to enlist wherever possible the protection of a man, be he brother or boyfriend, husband or father.

Thus women learn to behave in ways that minimise the chances of sexual assault and give a feeling of security and safety; but the crucial point is that these protective techniques involve a greater degree of restriction on the freedom of women than on the freedom of men. Women learn 'voluntarily' to limit their mobility, their travel, their territory, their range of encounters with other people; the alleged lack of adventurousness of women, their supposed timidity, is at least partly a result of conditioned responses to the atmosphere of physical danger of which they are warned from girlhood. They therefore have much less autonomy than do men. Coote and Gill (1975) have pointed out that rapists have a higher chance of being acquitted if the defence can argue that the victim lived an autonomous life: that she lived alone, for example, or went into pubs without a male escort. This suggests that the public find it more reasonable that women should accept restrictions on their autonomy than that greater efforts should be made to protect women from harassment or assault however they choose to live. The notion that women should seek the protection of a man in order to be safe is particularly interesting: it can be argued that the protection afforded by a man is not merely a function of his (possibly) greater physical strength but also because women 'alone' (even if in twos or threes) are considered to be fair game for advances, aggressive or otherwise, from men — while women with a man are more likely to be considered his 'property', and therefore 'out of bounds'.

The aim of this section has been to explore the cultural expectations surrounding sexuality in our society. It has been emphasised that (although certain physiological drives may be innate) the ways in which human sexuality are expressed are socially controlled and socially constructed. Although the physiological basis of sexuality is given through our biology, the way in which that potentiality is given expression (how, what, where, with what obligations, and with whom) is *not* determined by biological sex. The structure of sexual encounters must be seen in terms of the broader relationships of women and men in our society.

6.7   EXPLAINING GENDER DIVISIONS

It may seem premature to attempt an explanation of gender divisions. After all, systematic sociological research into this area is still in its infancy. The task of describing the complex ways in which sex, gender and sexuality are intertwined has only just begun. Although many aspects of male/female relations that were previously treated as unproblematic have been subjected to analysis, and in spite of the collapse of certain untenable stereotypes, the complexity of men's and women's lives, and of the structures which constrain them, have not yet been fully explored.

The social constructions of gender differentiation through socialisation

How far do parental actions, and the routine organisation of home life, push little girls and boys in the direction of socially prescribed gender roles? Gender-related expectations have been recorded at early stages in parent/child relationships. Goldberg and Lewis (1972) found, for example, that mothers of six-month-old infants expected their girl babies to be relatively quiet, clean and restrained, while their boy babies were expected to be more noisy and adventurous. Expectations such as these might, of course, be the first stage in a self-fulfilling prophecy.

On the other hand, a persistent problem in this area of research is to establish whether parents simply treat their children in a sex-stereotyped fashion, or whether their actions represent a response to initial differences in behaviour between girls and boys. One reviewer notes

> a tendency for parents to begin differential sex role socialization at a very early age, thus obscuring the nature–nurture issue. For example, it was found that newborn girls are spoken to and smiled at more than boys at feedings, and that boys are touched more than girls at this very early stage. It is hard to know whether these differences have been preceded by real differences in the infants themselves or arise through the transmission of sex role expectancies (Weitz, 1977, p. 64).

Parents may sometimes be unaware that they treat their sons differently from their daughters; at other times they may find themselves doing so against their own intentions. A set of interviews with feminist mothers revealed that — despite their avowed intentions to allow children to develop with minimal regard to conventional gender roles — boys (though less so girls) were often raised in sex-stereotyped ways (Van Gelder and Carmichael, 1975). The fact that mothers in this instance found less difficulty in encouraging their daughters to break free of stereotypical roles is consistent with a range of studies suggesting that 'tomboy' girls come in for less criticism, and less pressure to change, than 'cissy' boys. It is possible that, in so far as 'masculine' traits such as assertiveness are more highly valued, parents may be more distressed to see their sons 'stepping down' than their daughters 'reaching up'.

On the other hand, parents are often more protective of their daughters than their sons. Newson and Newson's (1976) study of child-rearing patterns mentions several respects in which 7-year-old girls may be more closely supervised than boys of the same age. Mothers were more likely to fetch daughters from school, less likely to allow daughters to roam outside or play in the street, and more likely to intervene when daughters became involved in 'unsuitable' friendships than in similar cases with sons. Protectiveness towards daughters appears to extend into adolescence. On the basis of interviews with Ealing schoolgirls, Sharpe (1976, pp. 213–14) comments:

> Despite the so-called permissiveness of society today, girls are still kept under quite a strict family control which has consequences beyond the simple one of their protection. Parents fear for the safety of their daughters if they are out at night. But rather than equipping them with knowledge and confidence about the 'facts of life' many of them prefer a method of strict control.

This control — combined with the tendency to give daughters rather than sons domestic chores which centre on the home — may serve to restrict girls' range of experience and to limit their self-confidence.

There are many indications that sexual divisions are reinforced, rather than challenged, by current educational practice. As pointed out in Chapter 7, in spite of efforts to break down curricular barriers between the sexes in recent years, schooling continues to channel girls and boys towards different occupational niches. Moreover, the content of teaching materials, staffing arrangements in schools, and patterns of interaction in classrooms all tend to reinforce expectations of male dominance and of a sexual division of labour. An analysis of British reading schemes in use in the 1970s (Lobban, 1975) found five central male characters for every one female; the author comments elsewhere (1976, p. 42) that the world portrayed in teaching materials is not only sexist but 'more sexist than present reality'.

The world portrayed within such books often has a counterpart in the staffing arrangements of schools. The overrepresentation of men among teachers of mathematics or science, and more generally in posts of authority, does little to undermine pupils' beliefs that scientific or technical subjects are 'unfeminine' and that women are unsuited to positions of power.

Classroom encounters, too, act as a venue where 'appropriate' relations between the sexes are constantly defined. Wolpe (1977) describes how teachers in a comprehensive school encouraged girls to adopt a coquettish manner with men, by, for example, advising them to smile when approaching a male member of staff. Teachers in mixed classes tend to devote a disproportionate amount of their time and attention to male pupils; this is partly a response to more demanding and often disruptive behaviour on the part of boys, who are in fact more frequently criticised for misconduct, but may lead unintentionally to neglect of girls and to the undermining of their confidence. Stanworth (1981) found that the apparent prominence of boys in A level classes led both sexes to underestimate girls' academic performance, and to regard boys as the more capable and more intelligent sex.

The family and schooling by no means exhaust the social agencies involved in the transmission of conventional gender roles. Our earlier discussion of sexuality pointed to the importance of adolescent peer groups in promoting and enforcing acceptable 'masculine' and 'feminine' behaviour. However, socialisation, and the promotion of gender-related views of the world, is an on-going process, and its very pervasiveness may make it difficult to pin down. The mass media, for instance, have been criticised for casting women mainly in domestic or sexual roles — important less in terms of what they do or say, and more in terms of whom they love or nurture. Partly in response to such criticisms women have increasingly been placed in starring roles, as detectives, doctors, and even newscasters; but as one of the newscasters, ITN's Anna Ford, pointed out at a news conference, these women are still presented more for their beauty than for other qualities, and are reacted to in those terms.

The pervasiveness of gender stereotyping is particularly apparent in the case of language. Phrases in common use — such as 'managers and men', or 'scientists and their wives', or 'athletes, some of whom were women' — convey the impression that workers, scientists and athletes are normally, typically, properly male. The use of the terms 'man' or 'mankind' when men *and* women are intended has similar effects. In one study (cited in Miller and Swift, 1979) American college students were asked to illustrate chapters of a forthcoming sociology textbook. Those who were given headings such as 'Industrial Man', 'Political Man' and 'Man and Society' overwhelmingly produced pictures of adult males. Other students, given headings like 'Industrial Life', 'Political Behaviour', or 'Society', offered illustrations of girls as well as boys, women as well as men.

While it is important to recognise the variety of influences by which individuals are socialised, the internalisation of gender roles by men and women constitutes only a partial explanation for the persistence of gender divisions. Three important reservations must be borne in mind.

First, some people have argued that our gender identities and our sexuality are so deep-seated that a thorough understanding must involve psychoanalytic explanations. Theorists such as Mitchell (1975) and Chodorow (1978) have tried to explore the complicated process of the construction of sexual identities through the psychological processes of interaction within the family.

Second, in looking at socialisation processes we have touched upon the family, schooling, peer groups, mass media and language. Some, but only some, of these processes create an expectation of inferiority or submissiveness in women, and of superiority or dominance in men. Others merely enhance *differences* between the sexes; and how those differences come to be evaluated as inferior or superior, or how they come to be unequally rewarded, requires another type of explanation, one venturing into the realm of the creation of ideology and the exercise of power.

Third, it is crucial to avoid adopting what Wrong (1980) calls 'the over-socialised conception of man' (*sic*). We must avoid the notion that people comply with convention, or that structures of inequality persist, because of normative commitment based on internalised values. The number of dissenting women (and men) would suggest immediately the error of such a view. Women and men who try to counteract in their own lives some of the aspects of sexual divisions which they find oppressive are confronted by structural obstacles and by forms of social control, many of which have been discussed in this chapter. It is precisely these obstacles, and forms of social control, which are challenged by collective campaigns, particularly those deriving from the Women's Liberation Movement. Many trade unions have also addressed themselves to issues of sexual divisions; the massive TUC support in November 1979 for the campaign to resist restrictions on abortion was an example of an effort which extended beyond narrowly defined concerns with conditions and terms of employment.

One inhibiting factor in such political struggles, however, is the extent to which women have been systematically deprived of power. Of 635 MPs elected in the United Kingdom in May 1979, only nineteen (or 3 per cent) were women. As of May 1979 women constituted 20.7 per cent of the British Medical Association, 9.4 per cent of the Law Society, 2.2 per cent of the Institute of Directors, and 0.4 per cent of the Institute of Electrical Engineers (Equal Opportunities Commission, 1980, p. 76). In 1972, at a time when 59 per cent of the membership of NUPE, 52 per cent of USDAW and 66 per cent of CPSA were women, women constituted only 1.1, 2 and 0 per cent respectively of full-time union officials (1972 data; cited in Wainwright, 1978).

These statistics indicate the lack of formal power women have with respect to defining issues, influencing legislation and affecting the course of trade-union struggles; they can be taken as both a reflection of, and a contributing factor to, women's continued subordination.

The apparent imperviousness to change of some of the practices and institutions that embody and reproduce male dominance is, in part, explained by the extent to which women are systematically deprived of power. However, there is, in turn, a need to account for powerlessness itself. Theories that try to elaborate the fundamental structures underlying female subordination or oppression are very much in the process of development, and hence very incomplete; that is, perhaps, a reflection of how recently intellectual attention has been directed to the problem of sexual divisions.

6.8   THE UBIQUITY OF MALE DOMINATION

The most promising attempts to construct a workable theory are those which attempt to take account of the ubiquity of

372 *Introductory Sociology*

male domination – its persistence through different historical periods and across different cultures – *and* its variety. Efforts are made to trace, on the one hand, the diversity of ways in which men exercise power over women (and the social and material circumstances that favour more or less rigid hierarchies) and, on the other, the course of sexual antagonisms – the forms of resistance mounted by women, and the circumstances in which such challenges are likely to be successful.

There are disagreements as to whether the male oppression of women has been characteristic of all human societies (and may, in some way, have been connected with the rise of civilisation or human society itself), or whether, on the other hand, an egalitarian sexual division of labour characterised the simplest human societies, with male domination only emerging under certain conditions. It is, however, fairly widely accepted that particular material and political changes served to increase the power of men *vis-à-vis* women: changes of decisive importance included, for example, changes in production techniques that denied women independent control over subsistence production, often combined with the reorganisation of women's labour around the family rather than the community or more inclusive kin-group; and, crucially, the emergence of the state, which consolidated and sustained the power of male heads of households over 'their' women and children. Anthropological and historical evidence suggests, then, that while most known societies have been characterised by female subordination, the rigidity of the hierarchical sexual division of labour became more acute as societies became more complex.

These considerations point to the conclusion that the systematic subordination of women in advanced capitalist societies involves two sets of interrelated structures. The first of these, patriarchy, is defined by Hartmann (1976, p. 138, n. 1) as 'a set of hierarchical relations which has a material base and in which there are hierarchical relations between men, and solidarity among them, which enables them to control women. Patriarchy is thus the system of male oppression of women.' Although it is recognised that some men are in a position to exercise more decisive power than others, the concept of patriarchy emphasises the benefits accruing directly to all men from the domestic, labouring, reproductive and sexual subordination of women.

The second structure implicated in the subordination of women in contemporary society is capitalist relations of production; these exacerbated the hierarchical nature of the sexual division of labour, and encouraged sexual antagonisms at the expense of class solidarity. One source of evidence that capitalism exploits and aggravates sexual divisions comes from anthropological research; studies of economic, social and political change in areas as different as the Dominican Republic, Columbia and Nigeria (see Reiter, 1975) indicate that in the process of capitalist penetration patterns of male domination over women become even more pronounced. Another source of evidence derives from historical analysis of changes in the sexual division of labour consequent upon the emergence of capitalism and the industrial revolution in England and the USA. In particular, Hartmann (1976) argues that in the transition to wage labour and the accompanying class struggle, patriarchy and capitalism were mutually reinforcing; each structure influenced the direction the other took. On the one hand, the actions of capitalists enhanced competition within the ranks of labouring people, and exploited (and reinforced) patriarchal relations within the family by offering women and children lower wage rates. On the other, male workers used trade-union organisation not only to protect their own position *vis-à-vis* capitalists but also to secure advantages over female workers, and to segregate women within the labour market so as to preserve patriarchal privilege at home. Hartmann (1976, pp. 167–8) concludes:

The present status of women in the labour market and the current arrangement of sex-segregated jobs is the result of a long process of interaction between patriarchy and capitalism. I have emphasised the actions of male workers throughout this process because I believe this to be correct . . . Capitalists have indeed used women as unskilled, underpaid labour to undercut male workers, yet this is only a case of the chickens coming home to roost — a case of men's cooptation by and support for patriarchal society, with its hierarchy among men, being turned back on themselves with a vengeance. Capitalism grew on top of patriarchy; patriarchal capitalism is stratified society par excellence.

Hence the oppression or subordination of women in contemporary societies is neither simply an offshoot of the development of capitalism, nor to be understood independently of it. The dismantling of sexual divisions would depend — if Hartmann's analysis is correct — on struggles both to transform the social relations of production and to construct radically new relations between women and men.

REFERENCES TO CHAPTER 6

Banks, J. and Banks, O. (1964) *Feminism and Family Planning in Victorian England*, Liverpool University Press.

Barratt, M. and Roberts, H. (1978) 'Doctors and their Patients: the Social Control of Women in General Practice' in Smart and Smart (1978).

Barron, R. D. and Norris, G. M. (1976) 'Sexual Divisions and the Dual Labour Market', in D. L. Barker and S. Allen (eds), *Dependence and Exploitation in Work and Marriage*, London, Longman.

Beechey, V. (1977) 'Some Notes on Female Wage Labour in Capitalist Production', *Capital and Class*, Autumn 1977, no. 3.

Blackburn, R. and Mann, M. (1979) *The Working Class in the Labour Market*, London, Macmillan.

Bland, L., Brunsdon, C., Hobson, D. and Winship, J. (1978) 'Women "Inside and Outside" the Relations of Production', in Women's Studies Group, Centre for Contemporary Cultural Studies (eds), *Women Take Issue*, London, Hutchinson.

Braverman, H. (1974) *Labour and Monopoly Capital*, New York, Monthly Review Press.

Bristol Women's Studies Group (1979) *Half the Sky*, London, Virago.

Brownmiller, S. (1976) *Against Our Will*, Harmondsworth, Penguin.

Bruegel, I. (1979) 'Women as Reserve Army of Labour: a Note on Recent British Experience', *Feminist Review*, issue 3.

Campbell, B. (1974) 'Sexuality and Submission', in S. Allen, L. Sanders and J. Wallis (eds), *Conditions of Illusion*, Leeds, Feminist Books.

Chodorow, N. (1978) *The Reproduction of Mothering*, University of California Press.

Coote, A. and Gill, T. (1975) *The Rape Controversy*, London, NCCL.

Coussins, J. (1980) 'Equality for Women. Have the Laws Worked?', *Marxism Today*, January 1980, p. 10.

Davies, M. L. (1978) *Maternity Letters from Working Women*, London, Virago (first published 1915).

Department of Employment (1974) *Women and Work: a Statistical Survey*, Manpower Paper No. 9, London, HMSO.

Equal Opportunities Commission (1977) *Women and Low Incomes*, London, EOC.

Equal Opportunities Commission (1980) *Fourth Annual Report*, London, EOC.

Goldberg, S. and Lewis, M. (1972) 'Play Behaviour in the Infant: Early Sex Differences', in J. Bardwick (ed.), *Readings on the Psychology of Women*, New York, Harper & Row.

Hanmer, J. (1978) 'Violence and the Social Control of Women', in G. Littlejohn *et al.* (eds), *Power and the State*, London, Croom Helm.

Hartmann, H. (1976) 'Capitalism, Patriarchy, and Job Segregation by Sex', *Signs*, vol. 1, no. 3, pp. 137–69.

Hartnett, O. (1978) 'Sex-role Stereotyping at Work', in J. Chetwynd and O. Hartnett (eds), *The Sex Role System*, London, Routledge & Kegan Paul.

Hope, E., Kennedy, M. and de Winter, A. (1976) 'Homeworkers in North London', in D. L. Barker and S. Allen (eds), *Dependence and Exploitation in Work and Marriage*, London, Longman.

Land, H. (1972) 'Large Families in London', in E. Butterworth and D. Weir (eds), *Social Problems of Modern Britain*, London, Fontana.

Land, H. (1975) 'The Myth of the Male Breadwinner', *New Society*, October 1975.

Land, H. (1976) 'Women: Supporters or Supported?', in D. L. Barker and S. Allen (eds), *Sexual Divisions in Society*, London, Tavistock.

Lobban, G. (1975) 'Sex Roles in Reading Schemes', *Educational Review*, vol. 27, no. 3.

Lobban, G. (1976) 'Sex Roles in Reading Schemes', in Children's Rights Workshop, *Sexism in Children's Books*, London, Writers and Readers Publishing Co-operative.

Low Pay Unit (1979) *The Hidden Army*, London, HMSO.

McIntosh, M. (1978) 'Who Needs Prostitutes? The Ideology of Male Sexual Needs', in Smart and Smart (1978).

McIntyre, S. (1976) 'Who Wants Babies? The Social Construction of Instincts', in D. L. Barker and S. Allen (eds), *Sexual Divisions in Society*, London, Tavistock.

McRobbie, A. (1978) 'Working Class Girls and the Culture of Femininity', in Women's Studies Group, Centre for Contemporary Cultural Studies (eds), *Women Take Issue*, London, Hutchinson.

Mathieu, N.-C. (1977) *Ignored by Some, Denied by Others*, London, Women's Research and Resources Centre.

Miller, C. and Swift, K. (1979) *Words and Women*, Harmondsworth, Penguin.

Mitchell, J. (1975) *Psychoanalysis and Feminism*, Harmondsworth, Penguin.

National Union of Teachers (1980) *Promotion and the Woman Teacher*, London, NUT.

Newson, J. and Newson, E. (1976) *Seven Years Old in the Home Environment*, London, Allen & Unwin,.

Oakley, A. (1972) *Sex, Gender and Society*, London, Temple-Smith.

Oakley, A. (1974) *The Sociology of Housework*, London, Martin Robertson.

Oakley, A. (1975) 'The Trap of Medicalised Motherhood', *New Society*, vol. 34, no. 689.

Oakley, A. (1976) 'Wisewoman and Medicine Man: Changes in the Management of Childbirth', in J. Mitchell and A. Oakley (eds), *The Rights and Wrongs of Women*, Harmondsworth, Penguin.

Reiter, R. (ed.) (1975) *Toward an Anthropology of Women*, New York, Monthly Review Press.

Rowbotham, S. (1974) *Hidden From History*, London, Pluto Press.

Rubery, J. (1978) 'Structured Labour Markets, Worker Organisation and Low Pay', *Cambridge Journal of Economics*, vol. 12, no. 1.

Sachs, A. (1978) 'The Myth of Male Protectiveness and the Legal Subordination of Women', in Smart and Smart (1978).

Shacklady Smith, L. (1978) 'Sexist Assumptions and Female Delinquency', in Smart and Smart (1978).

Sharpe, S. (1976) *Just Like a Girl*, Harmondsworth, Penguin.

Smart, C. and Smart, B. (eds) (1978) *Women, Sexuality and Social Control*, London, Routledge & Kegan Paul.

Snell, M. (1979) 'The Equal Pay and Sex Discrimination Acts: their Impact in the Workplace', *Feminist Review*, issue 1.

Stanworth, M. (1981) *Gender and Schooling*, London, Women's Research and Resources Centre.

Tiger, L. and Fox, R. (1974) *The Imperial Animal*, London, Paladin.

Titmuss, R. (1958) 'The Position of Women', in *Essays on the Welfare State*, London, Allen & Unwin.

Tizard, J., Moss, P. and Perry, J. (1976) *All Our Children*, London, Temple-Smith/New Society.

Townsend, P. (1979) *Poverty in the United Kingdom*, Harmondsworth, Penguin.

Van Gelder, L. and Carmichael, C. (1975) 'But What About Our Sons?, *Ms.*, October 1975; cited in Weitz (1977, p. 62).

Wainwright, H. (1978) 'Women and the Division of Labour', in P. Abrams (ed.) *Work, Urbanism and Inequality*, London, Weidenfeld & Nicolson.

Weitz, S. (1977) *Sex Roles*, New York, Oxford University Press.

Westergaard, J. and Resler, H. (1976) *Class in a Capitalist Society*, Harmondsworth, Penguin.

Willis, P. (1977) *Learning to Labour*, Westmead, Saxon House.

Wilson, D. (1978) 'Sexual Codes and Conduct: a Study of Teenage Girls', in Smart and Smart (1978).

Wilson, L. *et al.* (1974) 'The Independence Demand', in S. Allen *et al.* (eds), *Conditions of Illusion*, Leeds, Feminist Books.

Wolpe, A. (1977) *Some Processes in Sexist Education*, London, Women's Research and Resources Centre.

Wright, R. (1979) Paper presented to the British Psychological Society, London, December 1979.

Wrong, D. (1980) 'The Oversocialized Conception of Man in Modern Sociology', in R. Bocock *et al.* (eds), *An Introduction to Sociology*, London, Fontana.

7
Education

Sexual Division in Society   377

7.1   INTRODUCTION

On most weekdays in the 1980s, several million British young-sters will be sitting in schoolrooms under the watchful (or harassed) gaze of a teacher. Whether reading aloud in front of the class, or waiting their turn for the big scissors, revising anxiously for a biology test, or hoping to 'have a laff' with their friends when the teacher's back is turned, each pupil will spend at least 15,000 hours of childhood and adolescence in school. Small wonder that formal education is regarded as a major agency of socialisation in advanced industrial societies. Socialisation is, however, a continuous process: individuals are subject to its influence before, alongside and after their school career. Education differs from other forms of social-isation in that it involves instruction which is deliberate, con-ducted within formal organisations set aside for that purpose, and relatively standardised; there is probably less variation in what children learn from schooling (whether through the official or the hidden curriculum) than in what they learn as a result of informal interaction with family, friends and work-mates.

We tend to regard education as a necessary way of preparing children for adult life, in terms of certification (labelling people as 'eligible' for particular positions) as well as social-isation. Yet in many pre-industrial societies, young people learn by involvement in the life of the community, with deliberate, systematic instruction often confined to particular rituals. Ariès points to the marked contrast between our views of schooling and those prevalent in France and Britain in the

Middle Ages, in his book *Centuries of Childhood*. Medieval schools were places where individuals went, at any age of their life and for any period of time. Education was a matter of *academic* learning; schools were not concerned with moral training or character building, nor were they specifically for the young. In fact, Ariès argues, the notion of 'childhood' as a special period of life requiring a systematic programme of training did not exist in medieval society. People passed from infancy — when little notice was taken of them — to full participation in adult life. From the age of 7, most young people were expected to work, learn or play alongside adults, and the performance of children and adults was evaluated by much the same standards. From the fifteenth century onwards, attitudes towards young people began to change, as did views on the nature of schooling. The emergence of a concept of childhood as a time of innocence and vulnerability seemed to justify the isolation of children from adult society in the specialised institutions of schools: 'Henceforth it was recognised that the child was not ready for life, and that he had to be subjected to a special treatment, a sort of quarantine, before he was allowed to join the adults' (Ariès, 1973, p. 396). Of course, the provision of schooling proceeded very slowly and selectively. Notions of the vulnerability of children did not prevent their employment on a wide scale in heavy, dangerous work in factories and mines. In Britain, as late as 1870, only 2 per cent of children aged 14, and 40 per cent of those aged 10, were receiving full-time education. Nevertheless, Ariès does help us to understand how culturally and historically specific many of our ideas of schooling are.

Ariès's research has had a great influence on many of those who argue for the abolition of compulsory schooling. Illich, for example, echoes Ariès when he writes, 'The school system is a modern phenomenon, as is the childhood it produces' (1973, p. 34). Both the spread of schooling, and the 'childhood it produces', are, in Illich's view, to be deplored; childhood robs young people of the right to be independent and responsible beings, and school compounds their indignity and degradation. Those who attend school are, in Illich's view, robbed of creativity, and taught to bow to the wisdom of others. Those who do *not* attend are still conditioned to doubt their own capacities:

> Half of the people in our world never set foot in school. They have no contact with teachers, and they are deprived of the privilege of becoming dropouts. Yet they learn quite effectively the message which school teaches . . . School instructs them in their own inferiority through the tax collector who makes them pay for it, or through the demagogue who raises their expectations of it, or through their children once the latter are hooked on it. So the poor are robbed of their self-respect by subscribing to a creed that grants salvation only through the school (Illich, 1973, p. 36).

While Illich's description of the experience of schooling accords with many of the criticisms offered by others, including those writing in a Marxist tradition, his solution (starting as it does with the transformation of individual consciousness) and his analysis (which takes little account of the relationship between schooling and economic and political power) are not so readily endorsed. Simply, it is worth observing that the notion of children free to enjoy the benefits of adult life may be as much an idealisation as the notion of children cherishing with delight their golden schooldays. Whatever faults we locate in schools, they also offer people opportunities which might otherwise be absent. In the following passage from *Letter to a Teacher*, a group of Tuscan schoolboys describe their reaction to studying seven days a week in a small school set up by Father Milani for peasant children who had been discouraged by the state schools:

> There was no break. Not even Sunday was a holiday. None of us was bothered by it because labour would have been worse. But any middle-class gentleman who happened to be around would start a fuss on this question. Once a big professor held forth: 'You have never studied pedagogy, Father Milani. Doctor Polianski writes that sport for boys is a physiopsycho.' He was talking without looking at us. A university professor of education doesn't have to look at schoolboys. He knows them by heart, the way we know

our multiplication tables. Finally he left, and Lucio, who
has thirty-six cows in the barn at home, said, 'School will
always be better than cow shit.' That sentence can be en-
graved over the front doors of your schools. Millions of
farm boys are ready to subscribe to it. You say that boys
hate school and love play. You never asked us peasants
(School of Barbiana, 1970, pp. 19–20).

7.2 THE EXPANSION OF SCHOOLING IN INDUSTRIAL SOCIETIES SINCE THE SECOND WORLD WAR

While the Education Act of 1870 laid the groundwork for the
provision of elementary or primary education for all children
in England and Wales, it was not until the implementation of
the 1944 Education Act that all girls and boys were entitled
to a secondary education. Indeed, the decades immediately
following the Second World War saw such a rapid increase in
educational provision – in the USA, and many countries of
Western and Eastern Europe, as well as in Britain – that some
writers refer to the 'educational explosion' of the 1950s and
1960s. The minimum school-leaving age was extended from
14 to 15 years (in 1947) and raised to 16 (in 1971–2), but
the proportion of people choosing to pursue their studies
beyond this age hurtled upward; by 1971, 30 per cent of 17-
year-olds were in full-time education in schools or colleges,
compared with 2 per cent in 1902, 4 per cent in 1938, 18 per
cent in 1961 and 22 per cent in 1966. The Robbins Report
(1963) undermined the view that there was a finite 'pool of
ability' – a limited number of people who could benefit from
advanced education – and provided ammunition for the expansion of higher education. This expansion took place
through the establishment of new universities and growth
of existing ones, as well as through the conversion of colleges
into polytechnics which could offer degree courses, and the
founding of the Open University. In 1970, 17.5 per cent of 18-
year-olds entered further or higher education on a full-time
basis (compared with 1.2 per cent in 1900, 2.7 per cent in
1938, 5.8 per cent in 1954, and 8.3 per cent in 1960); another
three million people enrolled for part-time day classes, evening
classes or sandwich courses.

This 'educational explosion' reflected a commitment by successive governments, both Labour and Conservative, to educational growth (at least in times of economic prosperity). By 1968, education claimed 5½ per cent of total public expenditure, compared with 3½ per cent a decade earlier. Educational reformers, including those who supported the expansion of colleges and universities, expressed two major objectives. The first was to create a fairer educational system, and possibly thereby a fairer society, by giving greater opportunities to working-class children for advancement through education; widening access to secondary and higher education was seen as an important step towards a meritocratic society, based on equality of opportunity. The second objective was to use education more effectively to develop the skills of the nation's future labour force; from this standpoint, educational expansion and reform were seen as ways of exploiting the human resources on which national prosperity may depend. Since a large untapped reservoir of ability lay in the talents of working-class girls and boys, the two objectives were seen to be interlocked. Both the target of economic efficiency, and that of social justice, would be met, it was hoped, by educational reform.

The growth of educational provision throughout the 1950s and 1960s was paralleled by an explosion of research within the sociology of education. The bulk of this research was aimed at monitoring the effects of educational expansion on equality of opportunity, and much of it was informed by a functionalist perspective. However, in recent years, many writers in the sociology of education have found a Marxist perspective useful for exploring the connections between education, the economy and social inequality. We will outline the two competing accounts of the relationship between education and inequality before proceeding to consider the evidence, since both perspectives draw on similar bodies of data, but interpret them in radically different ways.

7.3 THEORETICAL PERSPECTIVES ON THE LINKS BETWEEN EDUCATION, ECONOMY AND SOCIAL EQUALITY

A functionalist account

From this perspective, the expansion of formal schooling is seen as a precondition for efficient economic growth and for the development of a meritocratic society. The changes connected with industrialism give rise to specific 'functional imperatives' — needs which must be met if society is to survive and prosper. The education system plays a crucial part in meeting at least three of these needs, performing three vital functions on behalf of society.

First, the education system is a vehicle for developing the human resources of an industrial nation. In pre-industrial society, the range of 'occupations' is relatively limited, and new recruits can usually learn all they need to know to do the job adequately by working alongside their parents or by apprenticing themselves to a skilled practitioner. But industrialisation brings with it marked changes in the occupational structure. New, highly specialised occupations emerge; the number of jobs requiring sheer muscle power is reduced by mechanisation; new forms of technology give rise to occupations requiring higher levels of human judgement and expertise; and the need for white-collar, technical, professional and managerial workers increases.

The expansion of mass schooling, and of higher education, is seen as a direct response to these changes. Through schooling, each new generation is provided with basic skills which will enable them, as the future labour force, to respond to complex technical instructions and to adapt to constantly changing occupational requirements. In addition, those children who are sufficiently clever and motivated can be instructed in the more specialised forms of knowledge necessary for work in professional, managerial or technical occupations. In sum, the provision of a highly developed system of education is a response to the general *technical* requirements of industrial production — the need for a labour force in which skills and talents are developed to the full, and matched to the complexity of jobs in a modern industrialised world.

Second, the fact that industrial societies have a multiplicity of occupations, with differing skill requirements and varied levels of responsibility, means that a sophisticated mechanism is necessary to select individuals according to their talents, and train them for the jobs they can most effectively fill. Education therefore has a vital selection or allocative function. As well as developing the talents of pupils, schools and colleges monitor or evaluate their performance by means of grades, school reports, references, and examinations. Educational attainments (reflected in grades or certificates) are widely used by employers to select the most able candidate for each vacancy. While education determines, then, through its selection function, who will be allocated to humdrum occupations, and who to the more rewarding posts, inequality is not a consequence of the education system itself but of the scarce distribution of skill in society, and of the necessity of attaching greater rewards to more demanding occupations so that individuals have the incentive to devote their energies to competing for these positions. But the selection of individuals through the education system ensures, more or less, that those who come to occupy the more highly rewarded jobs are those who deserve them on the basis of their greater achievement, and, presumably, their greater capacity.

In sum, schooling as we know it is taken (from a functionalist point of view) to be the 'inevitable' consequence of the general technical requirements of industrial production — requirements for technical training, and for allocation of 'the right man or woman' to the job.

Third, it is argued from a functionalist perspective that schooling contributes to the cohesion of society, by transmitting to new generations the central or 'core' values of that society. A standardised curriculum, at least in primary school, exposes all pupils — whether their parents were Jamaican, Irish or Polish, whether they are working class, middle class or upper class — to their 'common cultural heritage'; aspects of British history and political institutions, for example, will be discussed, and 'fundamental values', such as honesty, individualism, achievement orientation and a respect for parliamentary democracy will be imparted. The effect of the transmission of a core culture through the education system is to promote consensus on the basic values of the society, to ensure a fundamental level of agreement despite the diversity of individuals' life-experiences.]

In recent years, the functionalist approach to education has come under attack from several quarters. The assumptions on which it is based appear to be highly problematic. Firstly, the degree of 'fit' between the technical and cognitive skills taught in school, and the technical requirements of efficient production, is far from clear; many pupils are well aware that the material on which they are examined and certified — be it algebra or Latin, sociology of education, or human biology — has little direct connection with the tasks which they undertake when they enter employment in a factory, shop, hospital or office. Berg, in *Education for Jobs: the Great Training Robbery* (1970), offers data which suggest that more highly qualified workers, in educational terms, are not necessarily more productive workers; educational certificates may be necessary to make you *eligible* for certain jobs, but it is unclear whether they make you *proficient* in those jobs.

Second, though schools do undoubtedly select certain pupils as successes or failures, and play a part in allocating them to unequally rewarded positions in the social structure, it is not clear whether the selection and allocation is related to some intrinsic merit of the pupils themselves, or to ascriptive characteristics such as their ethnic or social class backgrounds, or their sex. Some would argue that schools, in the main, *confirm* pupils in the status to which they were born, rather than acting as 'neutral' selection agents indifferent to the background of pupils. Moreover, the notion that the education system encourages pupils to compete for 'the glittering prizes', and hence raises their ambitions and aspirations, is contentious. In practice, many aspects of the education system (whether intentionally or not) seem to dampen down the aspirations of particular groups of pupils, persuading them that they have set their sights 'unrealistically high'.

Third, the notion of a core curriculum is difficult to sustain. Are the values and ideas promoted by the schools equally subscribed to, and equally emanating from, all sectors of society? As King (1977, p. 3) puts it, 'There are many different ways of being British.' Many content-analyses of curricular materials show racist, ethnic, social class and sexist biases; moreover, it can be argued that the values and knowledge selected for transmission within schools will be more familiar, more compatible and more beneficial to some groups in society than to others. Within sociology of education, a renewed emphasis upon the curriculum in recent years has replaced the notion of 'transmission of core culture' with a question: how is it that, out of all the knowledge, ideas and values which are available in a society, only certain ones are selected? The question of the criteria behind the selection of *partial* curricula, and the question of which groups in society benefit most from a particular selection of knowledge, have come to the forefront.

A Marxist account

Partly in response to growing dissatisfaction with the prevailing functionalist account, many analysts have turned to conflict perspectives in search of a more adequate account of the relationship between education, economy and society. One of the best-known conflict models is that proposed by Bowles and Gintis in *Schooling in Capitalist America* (1976). Bowles and Gintis, like the functionalists, see an intimate link between schooling and the economy; but, unlike the functionalists, it is the specific requirements of industrial *capitalism*, rather than the general needs of industrialism, which in their view shape the nature of educational systems.

The social relations of production under capitalism are characterised by rigid hierarchies of authority (shareholders and directors; managers; professional and technical staff; white-collar workers; manual employees), and by an increasing fragmentation of tasks. The diversity of occupations referred to earlier means that, apart from a small proportion of professional and executive personnel, the majority of the labour force are increasingly required to perform mundane tasks allowing small scope for initiative, responsibility or judgement. Because of the hierarchical pattern of work, and its fragmentation, most people have minimal control over what they do and how they do it. The explanation of this lies not in the demands of technology itself, but in the capitalist need to control workers more closely in the interests of greater profits.

Bowles and Gintis argue that schooling operates within the 'long shadow of work': that is, the education system reflects the organisation of production in capitalist society. For example, the fragmentation of most work processes is mirrored in the breaking up of the curriculum into tiny 'packages' of knowledge, each subject divorced from all others; lack of control over work processes is reflected in the powerlessness of pupils with regard to what they will learn in school or how they will learn it; and the necessity of working for pay when jobs seem pointless and unfulfilling in themselves is paralleled by the emphasis in schools on learning in order to gain good grades, rather than learning for its own sake. Therefore, Bowles and Gintis claim there is a *correspondence* between the nature of work in capitalist societies, and the nature of schooling.

While stressing those aspects of schooling that inhibit critical capacity and independent judgement, Bowles and Gintis (1976, p. 42) also point out that schools are not uniform in their patterns of organisation and instruction:

But schools do different things to different children. Boys and girls, blacks and whites, rich and poor are treated differently. Affluent suburban schools, working-class schools, and ghetto schools all exhibit a distinctive pattern.

For example, in schools (or streams, or tracks) which cater largely for working-class children, the emphasis may be placed on docility, obedience, 'rule-following'; pupils may be closely supervised, and subjected to the same sort of discipline, and the same criteria for evaluation, which they will experience in their working lives in factories and shops. In educational institutions that cater for children from wealthy backgrounds, the emphasis will be on encouraging the leadership abilities considered suitable for a future elite. Thus, while it is not denied that schools teach a variety of technical skills and cognitive abilities, the emphasis in Bowles and Gintis's account is on the personality characteristics — particularly patterns of authority and control — that the schools foster and reward.

They also stress that capitalist societies are class societies; they are characterised by great and persistent inequality and by relationships of subordination and domination between social classes. These inequalities cannot be explained, they argue, by reference to the scarce distribution of ability or intelligence in the population; instead, the inequalities are the inevitable result of capitalist relations of production, in which the means of production are privately owned and all other people must compete in the market-place for rewards in the form of income. Thus class inequality is a *necessary* feature not of all societies, but of capitalist societies, and schools play an important part in transmitting inequality between generations. The occupations of future members of the labour force are to a large extent predetermined by the social class from which they come. The majority of girls and boys from working-class backgrounds, for example, are destined to follow in their parents' footsteps. Schools play a part in ensuring that this comes about, by assigning pupils to a school, or track, or stream that is 'appropriate' to their future position in the labour force. There they will be socialised into the habits of thought and practice that will be required of them in their future work. In this way, schools take an active part in 'reproducing' — or creating anew each generation — people who have been moulded in order to slot into their place in a labour force that is divided along lines of social class, sex and ethnicity.

At the same time that education creates the conditions necessary for recreating inequality, it also helps to legitimate that inequality: that is, education helps to justify in people's minds a system of inequality, and to reconcile them to their own position within it. How does schooling do this? As long as most people believe that education gives everyone a fair chance to prove their worth and as long as privilege and disadvantage are widely believed to stem from fair competition in the educational arena, then inequality *appears* to be justified by different levels of educational achievement. The successful ones view their privileges as a well-deserved reward for ability and effort, while subordinate groups are encouraged to 'personalise' their 'failure': they are encouraged, that is, to treat poverty or powerlessness as the inevitable outcome of their own individual limitations — lack of intelligence, ambition or effort.

A brief comparison of functionalist and Marxist approaches

The two competing approaches that have been outlined here are in fact similar in some respects. Both emphasise the macro-level of analysis (the relationship between, for example, education, the economy and social inequality) and devote correspondingly less attention to the day-to-day interactions of teachers and pupils. Both concentrate more on the form or structure of education than on its content, the curriculum. Both approaches have, furthermore, a tendency to give enormous weight to the power of education to shape pupils' minds and their lives. Consider, for example, this statement from Bowles and Gintis (1976, p. 265): 'Through the educational encounter, individuals are induced to accept the degree of powerlessness with which they will be faced as mature workers.' This does not merely suggest that pupils submit, willingly or otherwise, to discipline, but that they are persuaded to *accept* their powerlessness. It has been argued that Bowles and Gintis, like many functionalists, tend to adopt what Wrong (1980) referred to as an 'oversocialised conception' of humankind: that is, a view of women and men as almost entirely conformist, entirely moulded by the socialisation processes of society, rather than seeing men and women as active agents who perceive, interpret, react and innovate in ways neither predicted nor welcomed by the system. The functionalist vision of pupils who internalise core values of society and compete to display newly acquired technical skills would be as alien to many secondary schoolteachers as a Marxist vision of pupils moulded into passivity, conformity and docility.

If the functionalist and Marxist approaches have certain emphases and certain weaknesses in common, they do differ radically in their conception of the relationship between schooling and inequality. Some of the most important differences are summarised by Karabel and Halsey (1977, pp. 34–5):

While some functionalists, for example, may take for granted that the superior technical knowledge of the highly schooled is responsible for their higher earnings, Marxist-oriented conflict theorists conclude that cognitive differences offer at best only a partial explanation for their visibly superior status, and point instead to personality factors . . . Moreover, where functionalists have tended to look at the socialization process as one of those common *values* that hold a society together . . . [conflict theorists] have examined the *interests* that underlie these values and have noted that socialization differs systematically by social class. Finally, where functionalists have often viewed the educational system as offering opportunities for *mobility for individuals*, conflict theorists have generally stressed the role of education in *maintaining a system of structured social inequality*.

7.4 EDUCATION AND SOCIAL STRATIFICATION: THE MERITOCRACY THESIS

Until the Second World War, education in Britain clearly had limited impact as a vehicle of social mobility. The education system did not provide a ladder of mobility but was, rather, 'the stamp put on the social character of individuals whose jobs and life-styles were predetermined by social origin' (Halsey, 1977, p. 176).

Educational reformers and sociologists alike saw the promotion of *equality of opportunity* in education as the key to a new, more egalitarian society — a meritocracy, in which people could move freely up and down the occupational hierarchy according to personal merit. In a meritocracy, the education system would act ruthlessly and impartially to allocate individuals to a station befitting their ability; being born into a humble home would be no barrier to success, and being born into a wealthy or powerful family no cushion against failure. In short, equality of opportunity in education would be the instrument for severing the old links between family background and adult success.

Before examining the evidence regarding the success or failure of this programme, we should note two points about

the linked concepts of 'meritocracy' and 'equality of opportunity'. First, in most versions of the meritocratic thesis,
social inequality is assumed to be a more or less inevitable
outcome of individual differences in intelligence or talent,
given the 'need' in industrial societies to offer incentives to
those of higher ability. This assumption is the basis of the
argument put forward by Herrnstein, in *IQ in the Meritocracy*
(1973, p. 60):

> If virtually anyone is smart enough to be a ditch digger, and
> only half the people are smart enough to be engineers, the
> society is, in effect, husbanding its intellectual resources
> by holding engineers in greater esteem and paying them
> more.

The parallels with the functional theory of stratification,
which is elaborated and criticised more fully in Chapter 2, are
immediately apparent; what is also clear is that the meritocratic thesis addresses itself only to those rewards stemming
from *occupational* position, and therefore completely ignores
the significance of a propertied upper class.

Second, a meritocracy is by definition a society with structured social inequality; all it promises is equal opportunity to
pursue unequal power and reward. Milner (1972) describes
meritocratic ideals as a half-hearted (and unsatisfactory)
compromise between a commitment to equality and a commitment to achievement; what is offered by meritocracy is
inequality allocated according to ability. Thus in a meritocracy the education system is not expected to reduce or
eradicate privilege and disadvantage: it merely offers a new
sorting mechanism for recruiting people to subordinate or
dominant positions. In fact, several writers have argued that
this limitation is part of its appeal: 'Education has always
seemed one of the most acceptable ways of using the national
wealth to provide opportunity for the poor without offending the comfortable' (Hodgson, 1973, p. 353).

Are modern industrial societies meritocratic?

A meritocratic society is one in which social rewards are
allocated not according to 'accidents of birth', but according

to talent, where there are no social barriers to the translation of talent into educational achievement, and thereby into occupational success. Floud and Halsey (1965, p. 4) give an apt summary of the relationship between talent, education and occupation in a meritocracy:

> Ideally, runs the implication, talent should find its own level in the market, and the only guarantees that it may possibly do so lie in a high rate of social mobility and the minimising or elimination of social factors in educational selection and occupational recruitment.

This emphasis upon mobility is, however, open to doubt. It has been argued (by Herrnstein (1973), and in Young's (1961) satirical novel, *The Rise of the Meritocracy*) that an established meritocracy would have increasingly *low* rates of social mobility. *If* social factors were eliminated from educational and occupational selection, very minor hereditary differences in ability would gradually become the basis for class recruitment — thereby fostering the emergence of quasi-hereditary classes. Consequently, a fully developed meritocracy, in which the allocation of unequal rewards was purely on the basis of ability, could be less 'open' than many other stratification systems.

On the other hand, the 'elimination of social factors in educational selection and occupational recruitment' is clearly a precondition for the establishment of a meritocratic society. To demonstrate that Britain, or any other society, qualifies as a meritocracy, it would be necessary to meet two conditions:

(1) Social status and reward must be determined largely or solely by educational achievement (possibly in combination with other demonstrations of accomplishment or merit).

(2) Educational achievement must be determined largely or solely by merit.

This requires equality of educational opportunity, such that the chances of educational success for an individual or group are the same as those for any others of similar ability, regardless of social origins, colour or gender.

Is the distribution of status and reward determined by educational achievement?

We must first make clear that we are only considering whether, *given* the existence of structured social inequality, access to more highly rewarded positions is determined by educational success; we are *not* implying that educational achievement might determine the structure of rewards. The structure of rewards (the division between, for example, challenging jobs and those that are deadly dull; occupations which last for a lifetime, and those under constant threat of redundancy; between jobs with good pay and promotion prospects and those without) is determined by factors outside the educational system. Increases in the number of female, or working-class, graduates, for instance, might enhance equality of *educational* opportunity, but there is no reason to suppose that there would be any direct resulting change in levels of unemployment, in the ratio of highly paid to poorly paid jobs, or in the overall hierarchical structure of occupations (although the political and economic ramifications of such a change might be interesting). Although people with degrees may be better placed than others to move into a rewarding occupation, the existence of highly educated people does not directly determine the shape of the social division of labour.

Empirical evidence that patterns of inequality are not tightly linked to educational achievement comes from the work of Jencks *et al.* (1973). After extensive analysis of data relating to the educational and occupational histories of American males, they conclude that, although years of schooling affect the jobs men get, there are within each occupation vast income differences; men with equal educational achievement and similar occupations often earn vastly different incomes. Moreover, these income differences appear to be closely related to family background:

> the biggest single source of income differences seems to be the fact that men from high-status families have higher incomes than men from lower-status families, even when they enter the same occupation, have the same amount of education, and have the same test scores (Jencks *et al.*, 1973, p. 216).

The relatively small part played by education in determining people's life-chances is further diminished if we look beyond the minority group of white males. Our discussions of sexual divisions and race relations earlier in the book document multiple obstacles facing women and black people in the labour market; evidence of earnings merely confirms what we would expect. In Britain in 1977, of adults in full-time employment, 40 per cent of males with degrees or equivalent qualifications had gross annual earnings of £6,000 or more; only 13 per cent of females with identical qualifications were in that income bracket (*General Household Survey 1977*, HMSO, 1979). In the USA, in 1970, the average annual income for black male college graduates was only 69 per cent of that of white male college graduates (Jencks *et al.*, 1973, ch. 7). We should also remember the importance of inheritance, not only for the distribution of wealth but also for income inequality, as documented in Chapter 2.

To summarise our argument so far: the occupational structure, and the rewards available in society, are not determined by outputs from the educational system; furthermore, given an unequal structure of reward, educational qualifications do not determine an individual's success or failure. It follows (as emphasised by Jencks) that equalising educational achievement would not of itself equalise incomes (or other forms of reward). Equality of opportunity *within* education may be sought as a valuable end in its own right, but it would not guarantee even meritocracy, let alone equality, in society.

Is there equality of opportunity within education?

Everyone can point to an instance of the working-class boy-made-good, but this no more demonstrates equality of opportunity in education than the abdication of Edward VIII represents the abolition of the monarchy. Adequate assessments of the extent of equality of opportunity in education must compare the educational chances of one group (children of manual workers; women; black people) with those of another. But on what criterion should comparison take place? Of all the criteria that have been proposed, three stand out:

(1) The provision of differentiated schools, with entry on

a meritocratic basis. It was on this criterion that equality of opportunity was claimed to have been established following the 1944 Education Act in Britain. With the removal of fees from secondary schooling, and the eventual provision of student grants, certain financial barriers to educational success were minimised. The claim was bolstered by the enlistment of batteries of 'objective' tests (IQ tests; aptitude tests; the 11-plus examination), which allegedly selected the most able for entry to the more prestigious sectors of the tripartite system (grammar school or technical school) or for university.

(2) The provision of similar schools, with similar teachers, resources, and range of curriculum, for everyone. Proponents of comprehensive education — pointing to the very real problems of early selection in the tripartite system — were among those who insisted that separate schools could not be equal, and that equality of opportunity could arise only from the provision of common schools for all the secondary population. This is the basis for the claim to educational equality in most American school districts too; and, although it often goes unnoticed, in the state primary sector of British schooling the idea of differentiated schools is never seriously entertained.

(3) Similar rates of educational success and failure for different social class, ethnic and sexual groups. While the first two criteria call for *equality of access* (either competitive or universal), the third demands *equality of results*. This more stringent index of educational equality has, as Coleman (1973) points out, been increasingly adopted by investigators. It is the most appropriate criterion, in our view, because it acknowledges that what happens to children once they enter the educational system is as important as official policies governing access; it is only on this criterion that schools are assigned some responsibility for the success or failure of their pupils. Moreover, the emphasis on equality of *access* was tenable only in so far as children's performance (on, for example, an 11-plus exam) was held to be a pure reflection of their individual ability and effort; however, sociological research has indicated that a range of social factors linked to social class, ethnic group, and sex influence performance in tests and exams. In sum, the most stringent interpretation of 'equality

of opportunity' involves the recognition that *social* variables intervene between ability considered in the abstract and an individual's actual educational performance.

Whether we measure equality of access or equality of results, however, the overwhelming weight of evidence confirms that social class origins are strongly and clearly implicated in educational success or failure. Halsey, Heath and Ridge (1980), in a study of 8,529 males educated in England and Wales, found that a boy from the 'service class' (employers, professionals, and managers), compared with a boy from the working-class, had:

40 times more chance of attending a public school (independent school aligned to the Headmasters' Conference)
18 times more chance of attending a minor independent school
12 times more chance of attending a direct grant school
3 times more chance of attending a grammar school

Of all the types of secondary school, technical schools were the only ones to admit a representative cross-section of the male population. The pattern of unequal access to the more prestigious secondary schools remained, in the words of the authors, 'depressingly constant over time'. Despite the educational reforms of the post-war era, 'the likelihood of a working-class boy receiving a selective education in the mid 'fifties and 'sixties was very little different from that of his parents' generation thirty years earlier' (Halsey, Heath and Ridge, 1980, p. 203).

The degree of class inequality grows more severe as children move up the educational ladder. For example, a boy from the service class, compared with a working-class boy, had:

4 times more chance of being in school at age 16
8 times more chance of being in school at age 17
10 times more chance of being in school at age 18
11 times more chance of entering university

By comparing the oldest cohort of men in their sample with the youngest and most recently educated cohort, Halsey and his colleagues refute popular notions that the working class have 'caught up' with other groups — or at least narrowed class differentials in educational attainment — over time. They echo the conclusions of Little and Westergaard (1964), and of the Robbins Report (1963), that the expansion of university places has resulted in greater absolute gains for middle-class than for working-class men. During the period being analysed, the proportion of working-class boys entering university increased by 2 per cent, but that of boys from the 'intermediate class' (clerical workers, small proprietors, foremen) and from the service class increased by 6 per cent and 19 per cent respectively. The greater gains of boys from higher social class origins, combined with their initial advantage, meant that differentials between the classes were preserved. Halsey and his colleagues (1980, p. 210) conclude:

> the 1944 Education Act brought England and Wales no nearer to the ideal of a meritocratic society . . . Secondary education was made free in order to enable the poor to take advantage of it, but the paradoxical consequence was to increase subsidies to the affluent.

This conclusion is all the more persuasive because it is consistent with a range of other investigations, not only in Britain but in other capitalist countries as well. While there is, as we shall shortly see, disagreement about the *explanation* for persistent social class inequality in education, the *fact* of that inequality is not in dispute.

The meritocratic thesis, it will be remembered, is concerned not with equality *per se*, but only with equality for those of similar ability. It could therefore be argued that the influence of parental social class on educational success or failure merely reflects a larger proportion of pupils with high IQ in the middle and upper classes. Apart from questions about the validity of IQ data — which will be pursued later in this chapter — other evidence indicates that this argument is in error.

To begin with, there are numerous studies to show that the educational disadvantages of working-class children persist even when their IQ is identical to that of middle-class children.

In a classic longitudinal study, the educational careers of 5,362 girls and boys in England and Wales were charted through primary school (Douglas, 1967) and secondary school (Douglas, Ross and Simpson, 1971). Tests of 'measured ability' (analogous to IQ tests) were made at several points in pupils' careers. Two examples show the way that social class inequalities persist even when measured ability is controlled. Of primary school children who scored in an above-average ability band, 51 per cent from the 'upper middle class', 34 per cent from the 'lower middle class', and 22 per cent from the 'lower working class' were awarded grammar school places at the age of 11 (Douglas, 1967, p. 77). Of secondary pupils judged to have high measured ability, 50 per cent of those from the lower working class had left school by the end of the academic year in which they became 16, compared with only 10 per cent and 22 per cent respectively of pupils from upper middle and lower middle class homes (Douglas, Ross and Simpson, 1971, p. 37). Children from lower working-class backgrounds suffer, Douglas (1967, p. 80) concludes, under a double handicap:

> Their performance in tests of mental ability and school achievement shows a relative decline between eight and eleven years, and their chances of going to grammar school are low even when allowance is made for the level of their measured ability at the time of the selection examination.

Recent studies have used sophisticated techniques in an attempt to assess the *relative* contributions of IQ and social class origins to educational success or failure. If correlations between social class background and educational success were merely a reflection of the distribution of IQ in the population, then an analysis of people of similar IQ would show no social class differences in educational attainment. However, a study by Bowles and Nelson (1974) indicates that class-linked differences in educational success are only marginally reduced when IQ levels are statistically controlled.

Table 7.1 is based on Bowles and Nelson's analysis of the US *Population Survey* for 1962, and refers to white males aged 25 to 64 years. A glance at the left-hand column con-

TABLE 7.1

The relationship of educational achievement to socio-economic background, for men of different IQ and men of the same IQ

Educational achievement: average years of schooling received by men from each socio-economic background group	Socio-economic background (a measure combining parental income, occupation, and educational level)	Educational achievement for men from each socio-economic background group with IQ controlled*
15.3	10 (highest)	14.8
14.5	9	14.0
13.7	8	13.4
13.0	7	12.9
12.5	6	12.4
12.0	5	12.0
11.5	4	11.6
11.0	3	11.1
10.3	2	10.6
9.5	1 (lowest)	9.9

*Average number of years of schooling received by men from each socio-economic background group, but including only men of identical IQ (i.e. only those whose IQ scores correspond to the average for the sample as a whole).
Source: Bowles and Nelson (1974); reprinted in Bowles and Gintis (1976, p. 31).

firms the expected relationship between socio-economic background and educational achievement; each 'jump' up the socio-economic ladder is matched by a corresponding rise in average years of schooling for men from that background. Looking at the right-hand column, it can be seen that even among men with identical IQ scores educational success rises for each socio-economic category. Amongst men of identical IQ, those from the top socio-economic group received 4.9 more years of schooling than those from the bottom group. This study strongly supports the view that the educational success of children from higher-class origins is due more to material and social advantages conferred by their backgrounds than to their IQ levels. Moreover, research which shows that IQ levels themselves are systematically influenced by social and material advantages conferred by social class suggests that studies like Bowles and Nelson's *underestimate* the contribution of social class to educational attainment.

The consideration of the meritocracy thesis so far has been

focused almost exclusively on social class; studies of a similar breadth for girls and women, or comparisons of the influence of gender as against ability on educational attainment, are few. However, it is possible to argue that gender offers a case at least as convincing as that of social class for the failure to realise meritocratic claims. Data from official HMSO publications (*General Household Survey 1977*; DES, *Statistics of Education 1976* and *1977*; *Education Statistics for the United Kingdom 1976* and *1977*) indicate that, in some areas of educational performance, girls in Britain have overtaken boys in the past decade: a higher proportion of girls to boys now attempt CSE or GCE O-level examinations, for example, and fewer of the female candidates fail. The way in which females are disadvantaged in the educational system shows itself clearly, however, in other respects.

The first of these concerns A-level results and higher education. Although girl school-leavers in England and Wales were, in 1976–7, slightly more likely than boys to attain one or two passes in A-level subjects, only 14,800 girls, compared with 21,200 boys, left school with strong qualifications for university entry (i.e. 3 or more good passes at A-level). Only 35 per cent of undergraduates at UK universities in 1977 were women; women comprised 29 per cent of those reading for science degrees, 11 per cent of those on physics courses, 18 per cent of those studying business management, and 4 per cent of engineering and technology students. In polytechnics and similar colleges, 30 per cent of the students reading for CNAA first degrees, and only 18 per cent of those on HND and HNC courses, were women. Moreover, women formed an even smaller proportion of postgraduate students than of undergraduates — only 17 per cent of those in science subjects, for example. Even in subjects such as education, English or psychology — where women constituted 70 per cent, 60 per cent and 62 per cent of undergraduates respectively — they formed a minority of students at postgraduate level.

Further education is another area where there is strong evidence of gender inequality. According to the *General Household Survey 1977*, among 'economically active' adults, 49 per cent of men, but 60 per cent of women, possess no educational qualifications whatsoever. Yet of people aged 21 and over who had left full-time schooling, 3½ times as many men as women were enrolled for day-release.

By far the most significant area where gender influences educational success or failure is not in the amount of schooling, but in its content. Although a higher proportion of girls than boys goes straight from school into further or higher education, many of the women are concentrated in secretarial courses or teacher training — stereotypically feminine career paths. The foundations for this are laid earlier in school, with far fewer girls than boys studying mathematics, physics, chemistry or technical skills to examination level. Of good O-level passes in England and Wales in 1977, the proportion going to males was 61 per cent in Mathematics, 78 per cent in Physics, 68 per cent in Chemistry, 98.2 per cent in Technical Drawing, and 99.4 per cent in Woodwork. Although there are differences in the scores attained by girls and boys on certain ability tests (for example, boys score better on average on tests of visual–spatial perception), the differences are by no means large enough to account for the polarities in educational achievement; furthermore, such different test scores are themselves influenced by gender-related styles of upbringing and early school training. Patterns of attainment for males and females do not support the meritocratic claim that our education system is indifferent to gender.

Conclusion

The myth of meritocracy — the view that our schools stimulate individual talents and, without regard for ascribed characteristics such as social class or gender, reshuffle children according to ability — is one of the most cherished myths of our time. The overwhelming evidence is that the British education system, like that of many other countries, favours those who are already privileged, and puts further obstacles in the path of those who are disadvantaged.

While recognition of inequality of opportunity in education is an important step towards clearer understanding of the complexities of our society, it is only a beginning. Conventional measures of equality of educational opportunity (comparisons, for example, of the proportion of working-class to middle-class boys who reach university) tend to focus attention on that small minority of the population that arrives at the upper levels of the educational hierarchy. Such measures may, inadvertently, encourage 'elitist' research perspectives; they may distract attention from what might be happening to the majority of the population, who are condemned to inadequate forms of schooling. The weakness of a concern with equal opportunity is not that it expects too much, but that it expects too little.

Similarly, while an overemphasis on documenting (in)-equality of opportunity in education may focus attention on the effects of schools in awarding certificates to pupils, and allocating them to particular niches within the social structure, it may also *distract* attention from the effects of schools in shaping their consciousness. What kinds of understanding, what world-views, are promoted by our schools? What aspects of social and natural reality are illuminated, and which obscured? Or, as Davies expressed it, 'Look what they've done to my brain, ma!' (in Hopper, 1971, p. 133). Davies was among a group of sociologists of education who argued forcefully, in the late 1960s and early 1970s, for a re-orientation of the discipline. Their view was that the concern with equality of opportunity — with 'who goes where' — had been allowed to overshadow a more important question regarding the forms of knowledge that are validated and reproduced through the schooling system. A lasting contribution of these proponents of 'the new sociology of education' was, in fact, to demonstrate that selection and consciousness must be studied side by side. An effective understanding of education depends on knowing not merely who goes where, or what is taught, but 'who is taught what' — and when, and how, and why.

7.5 EXPLAINING THE SOCIAL DISTRIBUTION OF ACHIEVEMENT WITHIN THE EDUCATION SYSTEM

Sociologists have long been preoccupied with the need to determine why particular groups (the children of unskilled manual workers, girls, black children in the USA) are disproportionately among the 'failures' of the education system —

why, that is, these groups tend to 'under-achieve'. Three types of explanations will be considered: those emphasising intelligence as a possible genetic basis for patterns of attainment; those centring on the home and family environment of pupils; and explanations focusing on the process and organisation of teaching and learning within the school.

Education and intelligence

There is no doubt that some people perform certain tasks better than others. Some consistently lose at 'Monopoly', become tongue-tied in discussions, and write incomprehensible English essays, while others accumulate hotels on Park Lane, make fluent and forceful arguments, and are praised by teachers for original and stylish essays. We often summarise these differences by suggesting that some people are 'more intelligent' than others. But what does 'intelligence' actually mean? How useful are 'intelligence' tests in explaining performance in school, or in other areas of life?

To begin with, however we choose to define 'intelligence' — as a capacity for abstract thinking perhaps, or an ability to learn quickly and accurately — there is no method for determining or measuring individual differences in intelligence in isolation from what people may have learned to do through their upbringing and education. In other words, there is no way of measuring *innate* or inborn differences in intelligence. Imagine, for example, that we are investigating newborn infants, who have been less exposed than adults to the effects of the environment. We could measure differences in their eye movements, the frequency of their cries, the strength with which they grasp a nurse's finger; but there is no reason to suppose that the differences we record are in any way related to 'intelligence'. By the time our infants (or some of them) can take a few halting steps, utter words, or build towers of blocks, they will already have been exposed to a variety of environmental factors — ranging from the adequacy of their diet, to the way their parents handle them — which will have had important effects on their development. Not all the environmental factors to which children are exposed will be equally stimulating or equally likely to encourage 'intelligent activity'. Even within the same family, for example, first-born children may receive more of their parents' undivided attention in their early years than do their younger brothers and sisters, and so first-born children may show more rapid intellectual development.

Many environmental factors, including those related to material resources, may influence the pace and direction of a child's intellectual development. Poverty poses many obstacles to intellectual development; in an overcrowded house with open fires and poor sanitary facilities, for instance, infants may have to be confined to a cot or a pram for much of the day to prevent them from exposing themselves to danger. Compared with other children who have carpeted floors to crawl on, safe wooden or plastic toys, and a warm, comfortable physical environment, children in unsatisfactory housing may lack the 'psychological space' to explore the world around them, and thus to extend their skills and their understanding. These examples should serve to demonstrate that, while there *may* be such a thing as innate differences in intelligence, there is certainly no way of measuring such differences. At best, IQ tests (or tests of 'intelligence') measure the way in which innate intelligence has developed in interaction with the environment. Moreover, there is no way of separating out the portion of an IQ score which is innate (or due to genetic inheritance) from the portion which is a consequence of learning, or cultural or environmental factors.

Nevertheless, IQ tests have been increasingly employed in the last forty years as an aid to 'objective' assessment. A variety of tests have been developed. Some are designed for very young children, others for adolescents or adults; some are administered to individual candidates, others to large groups; some tests or portions of tests use language and depend upon verbal skills, while others emphasise shapes or patterns or numerical symbols. By interpreting the results of such tests, skilled test administrators may conclude that, for example, Sarah performs better (gets more correct answers) than Rob; or that Sarah performs better than many people of her own age on the mathematical parts of the test, while Rob's strength lies in the area of verbal skills. But what must be emphasised about these results is that they do not tell us about the *poten-*

tial (or abstract capacity or ability) of Rob and Sarah. On the contrary, the tests are measures of *performance* or of *achievement*. 'Intelligence tests' are no different in this respect from other examinations. An A-level Sociology examination, for instance, measures your performance on a specific set of questions at a particular point in time, and not your capacity or potential to comprehend or adopt a sociological approach.

Furthermore, just as your performance in a Sociology examination may depend on a range of factors apart from your understanding of Sociology (whether you care about the exam, how confident you are of passing, whether you ate three Mars bars beforehand and gave yourself an upset stomach), so, too, performance on IQ tests reflects variables which are independent of intelligence itself. Experiments have shown time and again that the average IQ score of groups varies according to their reaction to the test situation itself; distrust of the person administering the test, lack of familiarity with tests in which speed is required, anxiety or fear of failure, are examples of the many variables which can lower the IQ scores of a group. For instance, black American undergraduates do less well on IQ tests when they think that their scores will be compared with those of white students, than when they are told that they are competing only with members of their own ethnic group; culturally induced expectations of failure in comparison with whites gives rise to nervousness which interferes with test performance (Katz *et al.*, 1964). It is particularly important to bear these reservations in mind when comparing the average IQ scores of different social class or ethnic groups, whose positions in the social structure, and whose experience and cultural values, may diverge.

Complaints about IQ tests often focus on items which clearly discriminate against certain social groups. One notorious example (now removed from tests) required children to say which of three pictures showed the prettiest person; those who chose a black person, rather than a Caucasian, were counted as 'incorrect'. This item is clearly culturally biased, but the removal of such glaringly discriminatory questions does not in itself produce a 'culture-fair' or 'culture-free' IQ test. In fact, it is difficult to see how tests which *necessarily* draw upon people's familiarity with objects, shapes, words, and testing procedures — tests, that is, that draw upon experiences that are more readily available to some groups than to others — can ever be 'culture-free'.

What, then, is the relationship between IQ scores and schooling? Whatever IQ is, we can say with certainty that it does not *determine* an individual's educational achievement. Girls and boys with low childhood IQs can achieve excellent results in school and even go on to college or university; this is all the more likely to happen, of course, if they receive support and encouragement from parents and teachers, or if their parents are sufficiently well-off to buy them a place in an independent school. Conversely, people with high childhood IQ scores may, through lack of resources (having to go out to work), rejection of school ('drop-outs'), or lack of effort, leave school with minimal qualifications (Douglas *et al.*, 1971).

Several researchers have tried to calculate the *statistical* relationship between IQ scores and educational achievement. Jencks and his associates (1973, appendix B), conclude that the average correlation of IQ scores with highest grade completed in American schools is 0.68 (the IQ scores used in this calculation were taken near the time when the pupils left school; scores taken in childhood show a much lower correlation with length of schooling). A correlation of 0.68 indicates a reasonable likelihood that people who complete more years of school will also have somewhat higher IQ scores. But the correlation in itself tells us nothing about the *reasons* why high IQ scores and lengthy schooling tend to be found together. The problem is to try to *explain* this statistical relationship. At least four different explanations are possible:

(1) Perhaps IQ scores do represent some deep-seated capacity for learning or reasoning which in turn has a marked causal influence on people's achievement in school. This has not been demonstrated; in fact, there is widespread uncertainty — even among proponents of IQ testing (Eysenck, 1962, p. 8) — about what the tests actually measure.

(2) The major lines of influence may operate in the opposite direction; in other words, the longer you stay in school

and the more you learn, the more your IQ goes up. There is some support for this viewpoint in that those who remain in college or in academically demanding occupations show a slower adult decline of IQ than other people.

(3) Another possibility is that IQ and educational knowledge are roughly the same thing. The correlations between IQ scores and educational achievement may reflect only the fact that IQ tests duplicate material and skills called for in school; whether or not these skills represent intelligence is another matter entirely.

(4) Fourth, teachers and educational administrators may treat pupils with high IQ scores in ways that favour their educational progress.

In short, the correlation between IQ and school attainment could be explained in several ways. Since it is not at all clear to what extent IQ tests measure intelligence apart from cultural skills and experience, the correlation probably arises through a combination of the last three explanations offered above.

A long-standing controversy about race and intelligence was revived when Jensen (1969) claimed that, in particular, the average 15-point difference in IQ scores of black Americans and white Americans was largely attributable to genetic differences. This controversial claim has stimulated an acrimonious debate, with important political and educational implications. It was reported in a recent court case that while only 10 per cent of California's school population are black, 25 per cent of pupils who are classified by IQ tests as 'mentally retarded' are black. The judge found that these pupils are segregated into 'dead-end' classes and given inferior teaching; this treatment causes them to lag further and further behind their school-mates as the years go by. After hearing expert testimony from a variety of witnesses, Judge Peckham concluded that the reason for the disproportionately high number of black children in classes for the retarded was due to the use of 'racially and culturally biased' IQ tests which discriminated against black children. He deplored the unwarranted assumption of many educators that black children were intellectually inferior to whites, and saw this assumption as 'all the more invidious when "legitimated" by ostensibly neutral scientific IQ tests'. He banned the use of IQ tests on minority children, a ban later extended to all children in California (*The Economist*, 8 December 1979).

Whatever the details of this particular case, the judge's decision seems to be reasonable in several respects. First, the evidence for a largely genetic basis to group differences in IQ scores is highly unsatisfactory. Kamin (1977) has shown that most of the evidence used by Jensen and his supporters comes from studies with severe methodological shortcomings. Even Herrnstein — a supporter of Jensen in other respects — argues (1973, p. 118) that his information about black Americans is inadequate.

More fundamentally, we can question the *implications* of Jensen's emphasis on heredity. If we do not know precisely what IQ measures, or how IQ scores influence (or are influenced by) schooling, then the question of whether or not group variations in IQ are partly hereditary seems largely irrelevant. The objective of education is clearly not the raising or equalising of IQ scores *per se*; and it is equally clear that a group's comprehension and skills can be increased without any necessary alteration in IQ scores. The concentration on IQ may therefore distract us from more fundamental issues of learning and education. Furthermore, while some people have assumed that a large genetic component to IQ would necessarily entail the curtailment of educational spending on 'low IQ groups', or their allocation to less academic courses, or the withdrawal of funds from programmes of compensatory education, such suggestions should be seen as political judgements and contentious ones at that. Even if it were the case that certain groups were genetically disadvantaged in respect of IQ, *and* that IQ represented 'intelligence' — neither of which has been demonstrated — this could provide a powerful argument for devoting *extra* resources to developing these groups' potential to the full.

IQ differences cannot then be used as an explanation for patterns of educational achievement. The pseudo-objectivity of IQ tests disguises much more complex processes, putting a seal of legitimacy on differences in achievement that are, in fact, socially created.

As we shall see in the following two sections, sociological research over the last fifty years has produced a wealth of data concerning the relationship between social factors and pupils' educational progress. For clarification, we have categorised them into those that focus on the effect of home background and those that focus on school experience. But it must be emphasised that these aspects of experience cannot be seen in isolation. The social distribution of achievement depends upon the interaction between what the child brings (or fails to bring) to school, and what the school offers (or fails to offer) to the child.

Causes of under-achievement located in the home

Income and material circumstances

Despite the elimination of fees in state schools, material inequality continues to play an important part in determining who is successful, and who less so, in the educational system. This is especially so at the extremes; for the wealthiest children and the poorest, school career may depend as much on finance as on 'ability', 'attitudes' or 'ambition'.

The Child Poverty Action Group has consistently emphasised the costs of ostensibly free state schooling — from compulsory uniform and sports kit, to stationery and craft materials — and the failure of welfare provisions to make good these expenses for parents who cannot afford them. They document numerous cases of children being kept away or sent home from school, or excluded from certain activities, for lack of money to provide prescribed equipment or clothing, and of the stigma suffered by children who are set apart (for example, during school meals) because of poverty.

However, the effects of inadequate income on children's educational careers may also stem from the adversity of living conditions at home. Douglas (1967) showed that unsatisfactory housing was associated with lower achievement in the primary school, and that its effects were more permanent for working-class than for middle-class children. Overcrowding, Douglas suggests, may deny children a quiet and private place to do homework, a handicap mentioned also by some of the working-class grammar school pupils in Jackson and Marsden's

(1966) study. A report of the National Child Development Study (Davie, Butler and Goldstein, 1972) revealed that children from overcrowded homes are, by 7 years of age, nine months behind their school-mates in reading attainment.

Wedge and Prosser (1973) summarised the cumulative handicaps of the large minority of children in England and Wales (approximately 6 per cent) who, as well as suffering from poverty and poor housing, were in one-parent families, or in families with five or more children. In particular, they noted that the medical history of these children was hardly conducive to educational success (compared with other children, they were more likely to be off school with illness, to suffer serious diseases such as tuberculosis or rheumatic fever, to have home accidents, hearing problems and speech difficulties), while at the same time they received less medical attention than other children. Moreover, these disadvantaged pupils had less often enjoyed pre-school facilities such as nursery schools or playgroups. By the age of 11, on reading scores alone, they were 3½ years behind their peers. The title of Wedge and Prosser's study, *Born to Fail?*, is an apt summary of the effects of extreme material disadvantage on educational achievement.

However, it would be wrong to give the impression that it is only children in extreme poverty who are educationally disadvantaged by their material circumstances. Halsey, Heath and Ridge (1980) point out that a real crunch-point in achievement comes at the minimum school-leaving age: three-quarters of their working-class respondents left school at this point, whereas three-quarters of the number of boys from the 'service class' stayed on. A major factor in explaining this class difference is the cost of supporting offspring for an additional year or two until the time when they might become eligible for student grants. Indeed Halsey and his colleagues (1980, p. 202) identify the lack of maintenance grants for secondary pupils beyond school-leaving age as one of two major obstacles to equality of opportunity in England and Wales. This may prove an even larger obstacle to working-class girls than to boys: many writers from Douglas and his colleagues (1971, p. 47) onwards have emphasised that parents tend to accord a lower priority to their *daughters'* education.

Families who are financially hard-pressed may well give sons, rather than daughters, priority when it comes to financing post-compulsory education.

Poverty and low income, then, influence educational achievement; but it would be wrong to think these are isolated factors, for they are fundamentally related (as shown in Chapter 2) to the general distribution of inequality in society. This generates not only poverty, but also great wealth and privilege. In the educational world, this is manifested in the continued existence of the private sector of education, at primary as well as secondary level. Although the academic standards of independent schools tend to vary considerably, such schools may provide extra attention and supervision for flagging middle and upper class pupils and a cushion against failure — at a price.

Attitudes, values and achievement

In the fifteen years after the Second World War, there was a dramatic upswing in the number of studies concerned to examine socio-cultural, as opposed to financial, obstacles to educational success. This may be seen partly in the context of pervasive but erroneous beliefs in the disappearance of poverty and the embourgeoisement of the working class; but explanations that emphasised parental attitudes, and the value placed upon education by parents and their children, also had empirical support. One investigation monitoring progress towards equality of educational opportunity found that levels of income and housing standards continued to distinguish successful from unsuccessful grammar school candidates within each social class in Middlesbrough, but in the more affluent area of south-west Hertfordshire, parental attitudes towards the education of their sons, and family size, were more important variables than income and housing (Floud, Halsey and Martin, 1956). Moreover, the Report of the Plowden Committee (1967) identified parental attitudes as more important than material circumstances of the home or variations in schools for educational success, while Douglas (1967) laid considerable emphasis upon 'parental interest' as a factor governing children's chances of being awarded a grammar school place.

Discussions of the connection between values and attitudes and educational achievement employ a range of conceptual devices. For example, Kluckholn discusses the importance of 'value orientations' defined as 'principles . . . which give order and direction to the ever-flowing stream of human acts and thoughts' (Kluckholn and Strodtbeck, 1961, p. 4). Some researchers have described one set of value orientations (including a desire for control, an emphasis upon the future and upon activity, and preference for individuality) as more characteristic of middle-class people, and another (including fatalism, emphasis upon the past or present and on passivity, and preference for collectivism) as characteristic of many working-class people; the orientations associated with working-class life are said to be less conducive to high motivation, to individual striving in school, and generally to educational success. Other studies have suggested that the desire to 'get ahead', rather than contentment with 'getting by', may help to explain the over-achievement of middle-class children, and to distinguish successful from unsuccessful children in the working class (Kahl, 1965). Thus it has been suggested that by socialisation into general sets of values which are conducive to ambition, *and* by continued encouragement and support, middle-class parents may provide their children with the types of attitudes that underpin educational success.

While it does seem likely that a commitment to higher education will be less 'automatic' — that is, less a taken-for-granted fact of life — in working-class families, and therefore, that such a commitment would require *more* effort (and more encouragement and support from teachers), certain reservations must be made about the alleged connection between values and educational achievement.

First, it is important to examine critically the measures used to identify (for example) 'parental interest' or 'high aspirations' or 'emphasis upon the future'. Douglas, for instance, used a measure of *parental interest* that included teachers' comments on the parents' attitudes, and records of the number of times parents visited the school:

The middle-class parents take more interest in their children's progress at school than the manual working-class parents do, and they become relatively more interested as their children grow older . . . the most striking difference is that many middle-class fathers visit the schools to discuss their children's progress whereas manual working-class fathers seldom do so (Douglas, 1967, pp. 81–2).

As we have seen in other chapters, manual workers work longer hours than their middle-class counterparts, and they are less likely to be allowed time off with pay; the lesser 'interest' of working-class fathers may simply reflect this fact (as Douglas is aware). Thus the criterion used to measure attitudes may not so much indicate lack of interest, ambition, concern or encouragement by working-class parents for their children, but simply the constraints preventing translation of interest into practical help. What we might emphasise, rather than attitudes, is the social distribution of knowledge and power that may make it easier, for example, for middle-class parents to 'work the system', to hold their own in disagreements with middle-class teachers about treatment of their child, to fight sexual discrimination on behalf of their daughters, to know what books and periodicals to buy – and to have the money to buy them. The emphasis upon values and attitudes may, at its worst, produce an ideological cover for differences in material privilege: for instance, where it is claimed that parents displayed sufficient 'interest' in their children's education to 'scrimp and save' to send them to public school, we may note that, with independent school fees running, on average, at over £2,000 a year in 1979, this kind of 'interest' is a luxury few parents could afford (Rogers, 1980, p. 10).

Second, it must be emphasised that ambitions and expectations may *reflect* pupils' levels of attainment in school, as well as influencing attainment. A study of secondary school pupils by Banks and Finlayson (1973) revealed that the expectations and aspirations of unsuccessful boys and their parents moved downward as a *result* of their poor reports from school. The school does not merely receive 'inputs' of children with varying levels of ambition, but plays a part in shaping that ambition. Furthermore, an investigation of students who had made their way to university from comprehensive schools argued that working-class parents and children, more than the middle class, look to the school for indications of how far the pupil should aim; as Neave (1975, p. 142) points out, success at O-levels may trigger for working-class pupils the hope of a university career.

Third, the terms in which debates about the effects of attitudes or values on school performance are couched (especially in popular formulations) often present attitudes as though they were simply individual attributes — rather than phenomena generated by the shared experiences of working and community life. It is important to emphasise (as, for example, Bernstein and Davies (1969) have done) that attitudes of parents — which the Plowden Report treated as the very opposite of material conditions — may grow out of and indeed express adjustment to these conditions.

We are not arguing that attitudes are of no importance in explaining educational achievement, but rather that the generation of those attitudes, their roots in the social (and sexual) division of labour, and the effects of the school upon them must be explored. It must be understood that attitudes towards education are not likely to be part of an arbitrarily acquired (and as easily dropped) 'life-style'. At the same time, we are particularly sceptical of those approaches which imply that child-rearing patterns result in children internalising rigidly established psychological traits, which then colour the whole of their school career. For example, it has been argued that working-class children and those reared in conditions of poverty may internalise a propensity to live for today, whereas their middle-class peers are taught to 'defer gratification' — to postpone current pleasures and enjoyments in order to reap greater rewards in the future. This concept has been used in particular to 'explain' the greater proportion of middle-class children at college in the USA. Its limitations are readily apparent. To regard attendance at college by middle-class offspring as the result (and the indicator) of their greater ability to defer gratification appears nonsensical as soon as we recognise that (i) the alternative may be humdrum labour — hardly a form of pleasure or enjoyment, and (ii) many, although not all, middle-class students may be subsidised by their parents to the extent that their standard of living and certainly their opportunities for gratifying leisure are better than those of many employed (or unemployed) working-class counterparts. In addition, continued attendance at school or college may itself be gratifying, if pupils are receiving praise, encouragement from teachers, and 'success'. The experience of working-class children may *create* a realistic refusal to wait for success which they doubt will be forthcoming. An experiment in the USA found that the tendency *not* to defer gratification was unrelated to social class or ethnicity, but arose as a reaction to unfulfilled promises: children who chose to wait a fortnight on the promise of getting two candy bars instead of one, but who were never given *any*, did not make the error of 'deferring gratification' the second time around!

While we have expressed reservations about the extent to which studies of attitudes can explain social class (or other) differences in achievement, other types of research into home environment, which focus on the acquisition of skills and socio-linguistic competencies, on experience and modes of social control, may have a more direct applicability to the problem. The socio-linguistic theories of Bernstein will be considered in the discussion of language and deprivation; for the moment, a simple example from the research of Bernstein and his colleagues may help to make the point. They find that, while many working-class mothers regard play and learning as separate activities (a view that may reflect the nature of manual occupations), middle-class mothers tend to view toys and play in general as vehicles for their children to 'find out about things'; it is possible that middle-class mothers enable their children to take explicit educational advantage from play.

This suggests that middle-class children may arrive at school with advantages in two respects: they may indeed have learned more as a result of their form of socialisation, and their expectations may be more in line with those of the school. These environmental advantages may be reinforced throughout the school career. Availability of books, travel, exposure to 'quality' papers — these and other experiences may mean that middle-class children may be already familiar with, and attuned to, many of the phenomena that will be explored in school. School may greet them as an extension of home life, and they may appear to the teachers as more sophisticated; they may also — although this is a separate point — be more intellectually advanced. It is useful to conceive of the competencies and experiences that may be more prevalent in middle-class and upper-class households as *resources*, resources that are differentially distributed throughout the class structure, and that may be of concrete advantage to children who receive them; inheritance, it has been said, can be 'cultural' as well as financial. (See the discussion of 'ruling class' in Chapter 4.)

However, a shortcoming of this type of formulation is that it tends to take for granted a single model of the 'educable' child — primarily middle class. The educational failure of certain groups is then 'explained' by the degree to which they deviate from this model. But instead of asserting that children who do not conform to the model are less well prepared for school, we could as easily argue that the school is unprepared for them — that the educational system is not oriented to their gifts and their needs.

One of the attractions of Bourdieu's theory of cultural transmission is that his depiction of the family–school relationship appears to evade the dilemma described above (see, for example, Bourdieu and Passeron, 1977). Each class, according to Bourdieu, possesses its own set of meanings or cultural framework, which is internalised initially through socialisation within the family; henceforth this *habitus* shapes perception, thought, taste, appreciation and action. Although one culture is not intrinsically superior to another, the power of the dominant class enables them to impose their own framework of meanings on others (and on the school) as the only legitimate culture. Through this capacity for *symbolic violence*, the dominant class succeeds in defining which topics are worthy of consideration, and the appropriate relationship to those issues — in effect, the dominant class defines what counts as 'intelligent' or 'knowledgeable' activity.

As pupils move up the educational ladder, those from the *dominated* class are progressively eliminated, or shunted into less prestigious forms of education; on the other hand, the *habitus* of children from the *dominant* class provides them with *cultural capital* which is translated into academic (and eventually, occupational) success. The education system acts 'neutrally', in the sense that it evaluates *all* pupils according to their mastery of, and their relationship to, the dominant culture. But those who have inherited a cultural capital that accords with the school will appear 'naturally' more gifted. Thus, schooling reproduces the relations of inequality between the classes; in the process, schooling validates the superiority of dominant classes, and confirms for the dominated their own worthlessness, their distance from 'what really counts'.

However, Bourdieu's theory also has its limitations. First, we are left with the unresolved difficulty of whether certain forms of knowledge or skill are superior in themselves, or whether (as is claimed) they appear superior *merely* because they are imposed. Second, as there are many different groups seeking to define the content of educational knowledge, we require a great deal more information about the processes by which powerful interests may be translated into educational programmes. Third, there are empirical questions about the usefulness of the notion of 'cultural capital'. Bisseret (1979) produces a strong case that in France, where the theory evolved, Bourdieu and his colleagues have not demonstrated the primacy of cultural capital over income in explaining educational success.

For England and Wales, Halsey, Heath and Ridge produced an ingenious analysis (1980, ch. 9) which reflects not only on Bourdieu's work, but on the other socio-cultural approaches we earlier discussed. They constructed a hypothetical variable called 'family climate', which stands opposed to the family's 'material circumstances'. Since *family climate* would measure parental values and encouragement, and family-based motivation as well as 'cultural capital', this procedure would reveal the *maximum* importance of social and cultural benefits deriving from the family, relative to material benefits. Halsey and his colleagues found (i) that both material circumstances, and family climate, influence whether or not a boy goes to a selective secondary school (grammar, direct grant, independent); (ii) that boys of identical IQ, family climate, and material circumstances did substantially better at secondary level if they went to one of the more prestigious types of school — this indicates the influence of school itself, rather than home, on this aspect of educational success; (iii) most importantly, within any particular type of secondary school, for boys of identical IQ, family climate seemed to exercise no influence over a boy's success; material circumstances did, however, continue to play a part in determining length of school career, examination results and so on: 'The results are clear. Cultural capital influences selection for secondary school, but thereafter its importance is minimal' (Halsey *et al.*, 1980, p. 200). This analysis suggests that equality within education might be furthered more by redistribution of wealth and power than by attempts to augment the 'cultural capital' of disadvantaged groups.

Causes of under-achievement related to the organisation of teaching and learning within the school

So far, our discussion has centred upon the factors that shape what children of different social class and gender bring to the school. Schools, however, do not merely react to children with varying qualities and capacities in a neutral way: they play an active part in creating children who are more or less educable, more or less knowledgeable, more or less manageable.

This is perhaps most obvious if we consider some aspects of the tripartite system, the division of secondary schools into grammar, technical and secondary moderns that was the typical arrangement in Britain until the 1970s. Opponents of tripartite schooling often pointed to the inaccuracy of the 11-plus examination, which resulted in approximately 70,000 children being allocated to the 'wrong' type of school each year (Yates and Pidgeon, 1957), and to the fact that these errors disproportionately penalised children of the working class; Halsey and his colleagues (1980) estimate that about 6,000 working-class boys each year were denied grammar school places which, on the basis of ability, should have rightfully been theirs.

The argument that selective schooling was inaccurate appealed strongly to meritocratic ideals. The more crucial evidence to emerge, however, from often heated debates, concerned the ways in which the tripartite system placed a ceiling on the eventual performance of the *majority* of pupils, those who were allocated to secondary modern schools. Despite the existence of many excellent secondary moderns, the overall performance of their pupils was depressed by several factors: assignment to a secondary modern ('failure' of the 11-plus) led many pupils to lower their aspirations and ambitions, a reaction to the judgement made on their capacity, and to realistic assessment of what the school had to offer them; secondary modern schools often offered a less challenging curriculum, so that whatever pupils' *capacity* for academic work, their *opportunity* was restricted; such schools less often prepared pupils for, or even allowed them to sit, national examinations (although by 1959 one-third of secondary moderns were entering pupils for O-level examinations, thus demonstrating forcibly the capacities of their pupils); many secondary modern schools suffered, in comparison with grammar schools, fewer resources, poorer facilities for special subject work, and fewer specialist teachers. Secondary modern pupils were indeed less successful by the end of their educational career than grammar school pupils; but with such a gap in provision and prestige, it is difficult to say whether differences in ability, or in educational advantage, account for inequality of results. Claims that academic standards are lower within a comprehensive than a tripartite system often overlook the fact that comprehensive schools aim to cater for pupils who would otherwise be condemned to secondary moderns, as well as for that minority who previously entered grammar schools. (See Wright (1977) for a detailed analysis of 'standards' in the two systems.)

The main point is that schools can — and do — make a difference, not in terms of the extent of inequality in society, but in terms of 'who gets what' within the education system. The discussion of tripartite schooling merely emphasises that in stark form. But the same principles, we have argued, that tended to depress the performance of pupils in secondary modern schools, operate on other levels. Consider the way resources and facilities are distributed. While independent schools do not necessarily provide 'better' education than state schools, they tend to offer advantages such as a higher teacher–pupil ratio; in addition, independent schools receive considerable subsidies from the state in such forms as tax relief – subsidies estimated at £350 million in 1979 (Rogers, 1980) – so that their resource advantages do not derive entirely from fees paid by pupils' parents. For the state sector, Byrne (1976) argues that the way local authorities allocate educational resources gives priority to the needs of 'academic' (disproportionately middle-class) pupils, to those in urban areas, and to boys, while providing less generously for the needs of less academic pupils, those in rural areas, and girls. Another study found that the higher the social class composition of an area, the more was spent on schooling – and the higher the average levels of achievement. The authors (Byrne, Williamson, and Fletcher, 1975) argue that broad social class differences in attainment may be accounted for (partly, we would say) by higher standards of resource-provision in largely middle-class areas. This sort of evidence is regarded as controversial, especially as it seems to contradict findings that the differences in achievement between pupils who went to well-endowed schools in the USA, and those who went to poorly endowed ones, were not much greater than the differences between pupils *within* one school or school type. But the contradiction is less severe than it appears at first glance. As soon as we recognise that *within* a school (whether well endowed or poorly endowed) not all pupils are given the same treatment, or the same access to resources, we are part of the way to solving the problem. To put it crudely, working-class pupils (or black children, or girls) may be less favourably treated than others in a 'good' school, just as middle-class (or white, or male) pupils may be more favourably treated in a 'poor' one.

Comprehensive reorganisation has made investigation of the processes that influence success or failure *within* schools (rather than *between* them) all the more urgent. Reorganisation could simply disguise educational inequality, by locating working-class and middle-class pupils within the same school (Westergaard and Resler, 1975). Similarly, the gradual merging of single-sex into coeducational schools makes it important to examine how the experiences of girls and boys may differ even within the same establishment.

As Jackson (1968) illustrated vividly in his analysis of classroom life, one of the 'problems' facing all pupils is the necessity of adapting to constant surveillance and evaluation. At all times, teachers are unavoidably involved in judging pupils and in classifying them as bright or dull, lively or withdrawn, model pupils or problems. Many investigations — especially those informed by symbolic interactionist or phenomenological perspectives — have explored the way teachers arrive at such judgements, and the effects their evaluations have on the pupils. Brandis and Bernstein (1974), for example, note that infant school teachers in working-class areas tend to judge pupils on their reactions to questions, comments or commands from the teacher. In middle-class areas teachers express more interest in initiatives made by pupils themselves. The authors speculate that, because infant school teachers are in sympathy with the spontaneous styles of middle-class pupils, they concentrate on encouraging further independence; many working-class pupils, on the other hand, do not fit teachers' ideas of the good pupil, and so teachers direct attention towards pupils' capacity to react to given signals, and thus towards reshaping and 'civilising' the children's conduct. Although the study was not backed up by classroom observation, Brandis and Bernstein (1974, p. 607) argue that 'the judgements of the teachers and the implicit model which these judgements may presuppose ... give us some idea of what is relevant to the teacher ... that which is relevant to the teacher eventually shapes the behaviour which the pupil learns to offer'.

Several studies have shown that teachers' expectations can colour their assessment of pupils' performance. Teachers (like other people!) tend to give the benefit of the doubt to pupils whom they already judge to be good, and to overlook or regard with scepticism superior performances by those they believe to be bad. One result of this 'halo effect', as the process is called, is that pupils may become typecast on the basis of earlier impressions — a child who has been dubbed a 'skiver', for example, may be suspected of cheating or copying when he hands in an excellent piece of work. But what determines first impressions?

Often, it seems, early impressions in the infant school are

linked to pupils' appearance and clothing, their manners and speech, and to information from school records about home background. In Goodacre's (1968) study, infant school teachers rated children whom they thought came from middle-class and skilled manual backgrounds as better able to read than those whom they believed to be from working-class homes; however, standardised tests did not reveal such a marked difference in the reading levels of these groups of children. In cases such as this, teachers' assessments of pupils reflect their views of what middle-class and other pupils *should* be capable of, rather than their actual performance. There is an ironic possibility that sociological evidence demonstrating a link between working-class origin and under-achievement may have led teachers to expect their working-class pupils to perform poorly:

> The idea that the working-class child is ineducable is all too pervasive. Those who think like this tend to hold one of two attitudes. Either they believe that nothing can be done for working-class children (the right wing position) or they put their faith in preschool programmes and compensatory education (the left wing position). Both are wrong and for similar reasons ... All genetic and sociological factors are mediated and realised through the interaction between the teacher and the child in the classroom. If, for working-class children, the outcome of these interactions is a sense of failure, then the responsibility is as much that of the teacher as of the child (Nash, 1973, p. 123).

There are two obvious ways in which low expectations may affect the progress of working-class, or any other children. They may lead, as we have seen, to lower assessments of performance, such that the child may appear from the records to be doing worse; and teachers may, because of low expectations, make fewer attempts to stimulate. Pidgeon (1970) argues that the widespread use of IQ tests (on which, as we have seen, working-class children and black children tend to do poorly) may well discourage teachers from stretching pupils to the full; some teachers, he concludes, 'will be satisfied with a relatively low level of achievement from many of their pupils simply because their test results tell them that the children are "working up to capacity"' (Pidgeon, 1970, pp. 32–3). Classroom observation studies in a variety of settings testify that, on the whole, teachers do tend to expend more of their time and energy on pupils they believe to be 'bright'; it may be partly the case that 'bright' children learn more than their classmates *because* of this extra attention.

Even in 'progressive' infant schools, where child-centred ideology puts a premium on minimising evaluation and allowing children to develop at their own pace, pupils are categorised and stratified by the teachers. In Mapledene infant school (Sharp and Green, 1975), teachers used vaguely defined notions of the 'readiness' of children for intellectual advance to justify inequality of treatment; all children, they claimed, are equally valued as individuals – but some are more ready, and these tend to get most of the teachers' attention. The progressive ideology allowed teachers to ignore children who were not developing, on the grounds that they were 'not yet ready' for intellectual growth. Sharp and Green stress the process of stratification within each classroom, with teachers categorising pupils as 'normal' or 'peculiar' or successful, and meting out different treatment to each group.

A poignant example of stratification within the classroom comes from a study of an American kindergarten (similar to nursery school) (Rist, 1970). Within eight days of the children's arrival, using sketchy information about home background, appearance and demeanour, the teacher had divided them into three streamed workgroups. Those she guessed to be fast learners, the Tigers, were constantly shown signs of favour, such as being invited to the front of the room for 'show and tell', and they were seated at a table nearest the teacher where they could claim her attention more readily. The others, the Cardinals and the Clowns, were seated at tables further away. Because the Clowns and Cardinals had low-level workbooks and were expected to read as a group, there were few opportunities for individual children to demonstrate to the teacher their capacity to move to more advanced work. Rist argues that the teacher set in motion a 'self-fulfilling prophecy'; by predicting that the Tigers would be fast learners, and then by encouraging them and giving them signs of favour, the teacher almost ensured that the prediction would come true.

The notion of a self-fulfilling prophecy (which clearly has much in common with the labelling theory discussed in Chapter 10) implies that differences between 'dull' and 'clever' children, or 'good' ones and 'deviants', may be heightened, or even created, by classification. Pupils may gradually feel 'persuaded' to bring their own self-image in line with that of the teacher (what is the point of trying if the teacher *knows* you're hopeless at maths?). But even when pupils are resilient enough to maintain a good opinion of themselves, they may face — as did the Clowns and Cardinals — a withdrawal of the assistance that would enable them to prove their capabilities.

Both these processes are likely to occur where pupils are streamed into different 'ability' groupings. The fact of being placed in a low stream may damage pupils' confidence, and discourage them from trying. Even where *pupils* are not disheartened, *teachers* may attempt less with lower-stream children than they would with others. Although streaming is sometimes justified as providing an incentive for pupils to work their way up, in practice transfers between streams are rare (according to Douglas (1967), less than three children in a hundred changed streams in a year). One explanation for this is that streaming boosts the performance of top-stream pupils, but lowers the performance of those at the bottom (Pidgeon, 1970, p. 105). Since streaming is often linked to social class — the higher a pupil's social class, the greater the chance of being allocated to a top stream — streaming and its effects may well contribute to the under-achievement of working-class pupils.

Two studies of English boys' secondary schools suggest that the effects of streaming on performance may be enhanced where it contributes to formation of pupil subcultures opposed to the ethos of the school. Hargreaves (1967) found that lower-stream secondary modern boys tended to reject the academic values and behavioural norms of the school that had labelled them as failures; they evolved a counter-culture, which, in its emphasis upon feats of daring and defiance, could be seen, Hargreaves argues, as 'delinquescent' — that is, providing justification and encouragement for certain forms of delinquent behaviour. Similarly, Lacey (1970) traces the changes in grammar school boys after their first year in school, when all tended to be committed and compliant. Once streaming had occurred, the values of the pupils and their views of the school became less homogeneous. An 'anti-group culture' — involving less emphasis on attainment and conformity, and more tolerance for slacking, copying, lateness and playing-up the teacher — began to emerge in the lower streams, and hardened as the years went by. The emergence of this subculture can be seen partially as a group response to failure: pupils dissociated themselves from the school that devalued their efforts. However, the subculture contributed to further failure. Boys in lower streams who tried to remain conformist to school rules lost popularity with their classmates; they were swimming against the tide. Streaming seems then to contribute to the disaffection of certain pupils from the education system. By a complex process involving the practices of schools and their personnel, and responses and actions of pupils, certain children are propelled towards success and others towards failure.

Even without streaming of course, or in situations where pupils have apparently free choice, some pupils may be 'sponsored' by school personnel in ways that heighten their chances of success, while others may be dissuaded from aiming 'too high': for example, teachers may persuade a girl that physics is 'not for her', or gently nudge working-class pupils towards CSE rather than O-level examinations. Cicourel and Kitsuse (1963) discovered that many pupils in an American high school who wished to go to college (and whose test scores and grades made them suitable candidates) were gradually steered by counsellors towards courses that closed off their chances of qualifying for college entry. Interviewing methods suggested that school personnel evaluated pupils according to tacit judgements about their family, emotional stability, level of maturity, and 'citizenship'. This sort of investigation suggests that processes of stratification in schools that are more subtle than streaming may be all the more effective; where pupils can be persuaded that certain courses of action are not for them — where they can be induced to drop out or opt out, without being selected or failed in an obvious way — then pupils may be left with the conviction that it is not the 'system' that is at fault, but themselves. Clark (1960) terms this the 'cooling-out process'. In his case-study of a community college in America, he noted a range of techniques regularly used by college staff to persuade students to opt for short courses of vocational training, instead of the university degrees to which they aspired. The 'operational speciality' of the college was, according to Clark, to ease a great many ambitious students out of the education system, while leaving them with the feeling that they had had their chance. Some educational practices, on Clark's account, do not serve simply to fail people (that could be done more straightforwardly), but to convince them that failure is an individual, rather than a structural, problem.

This brief account of the cooling-out process should not be taken to imply that academic staff consciously set out to 'con' particular pupils, or to legitimate a system of inequality. Rather, teachers do their job as best they can under conflicting pressures from pupils and parents, from colleagues and superiors, from local education authorities and employers. They try to uphold standards, while doing their best by their pupils. But — and here is the crux of the matter — notions of what pupils 'are' and what is best for them, views of what is possible and views about standards themselves, clearly influence the treatment that is accorded to individual pupils or to an entire class. Perceptions and expectations, beliefs regarding the nature of knowledge and academic standards — all of which have roots outside a teacher's individual consciousness — bridge the gap between 'good intentions' and 'bad effects'.

This process is relevant not only to social class differences in achievement but also to the recreation of gender differences through schooling. Where teachers believe that boys are noisier, more independent, or more mechanically inclined than girls, they may, by their actions and comments, heighten any such differences as initially existed. Moreover, the downturn in girls' achievement during adolescence, which is particularly marked in mixed schools, may owe as much to the effects of teachers' expectations in the classroom as to the ways in which boys exert their claims to dominance. In a study of teachers and pupils in urban comprehensives, for example, teachers' commitment to sexual equality went hand in hand with the acute distinctions made about the capacities of girls and boys:

> The teachers almost with one accord wanted to encourage absolute parity between boys and girls in timetabling, in curriculum and career opportunities, and even games. Surprisingly, however, they were then willing to make quite sweeping generalisations about boys and girls . . . Boys . . . were seen as more logical, more enthusiastic, quicker to grasp new concepts and better on the oral side. Girls' complaints about receiving less attention in class could well be justified if teachers do reveal their appreciation of the boys' dynamic personality characteristics. Moreover . . . 72 per cent of teachers said they would prefer to teach boys (Davies and Meighan, 1975, pp. 174–5).

In our discussion of schooling to this point, we have seen that stratification — along lines of gender and social class, as well as ability — is a feature of virtually all classrooms and schools. Studies focused on home environment tend to ask: what types of upbringing promote intellectual development, or fit the child to the school? Many studies of the school, by contrast, ask not what makes a good pupil, but what must a pupil do to *appear* worthy or able in the judgement of the school. Keddie's (1971) study of the humanities department in a comprehensive school offers an intriguing analysis of this issue. She found that even teachers who believed streaming to be a harmful and misguided pedagogical practice tended to make distinctly different types of material available to 'A', 'B' and 'C' stream pupils. They assumed, for example, that 'A'-streamers did not require illustrations and examples, while 'C'-streamers could *only* grasp issues in a concrete, descriptive way. Furthermore, questions from 'C'-streamers were viewed as disruptive, while similar questions from 'A'-stream pupils were taken as confirmation of their eagerness for knowledge. Keddie argues that pupils deemed 'bright' are not necessarily those with the greatest capacity for abstraction and generalisation (as many teachers assume) but rather those who are least sceptical of the teachers' definition of 'important' versus 'irrelevant' knowledge — those who, even when they do not understand the issues, are willing to 'accept the teacher's presentation on trust . . . It would seem to be the failure of high-ability pupils to question what they are taught in schools that contributes in large measure to their educational achievement' (Keddie, 1971, pp. 151, 156). A similar conclusion arises from Sharp and Green's study of child-centred infant classes, where 'dull' or 'problem' children are often those who do not, of their own accord, involve themselves in activities considered important by the teacher. By contrast, 'The bright ones are the "biddable", easily controllable ones who are on the teacher's wavelength' (Sharp and Green, 1975, p. 121).

An issue raised by studies such as these is the extent to which schooling involves a suspension of critical sensitivities, even (or perhaps especially) for successful pupils. Bowles and Gintis (1976), it will be remembered, argued that habits of thought and practice, such as submission to authority, discipline, and acceptance of the status quo, were in many ways more important outcomes of contemporary schooling than the fostering of cognitive skill. While this would be difficult to demonstrate, discussions of the 'hidden curriculum' provide some support. Attempting to take a pupils' eye view of the situation, for example, both Jackson (1968) and Hargreaves (1972) argue that the pressures of evaluation lead many pupils to adopt a strategy of 'pleasing teacher'. Pupils develop a range of techniques for concealing ignorance or idleness (from guessing what teacher wants them to say, to mastering an appearance of rapt concentration that enables them to daydream undetected). While these individual adaptations indicate that pupils are still alive and well, and not 'brainwashed by the system', they may also inhibit learning, in so far as approval (or avoidance of punishment) rather than knowledge becomes the primary objective.

Nevertheless — surprising though it may seem after our emphasis upon stratification and achievement — pupils are exposed to knowledge in schools, and they do, sometimes, learn. The question of what they learn (or, as we suggested before, of who learns what) is pursued in the sociology of the curriculum. Out of the vast stock of knowledge and skills available in a complex society — from how to cure warts, to motorcycle maintenance; from the thoughts of Marx, to those of Mrs Thatcher — only a fraction is selected for transmission in schools.

What is selected, and what left out, has consequences for patterns of success and failure. The study of music in school, for example, often excludes 'pop' and 'reggae'. This increases the discontinuity between school and everyday life for working-class and black pupils. It may also increase the chances for pupils from privileged backgrounds who are familiar with classical music to succeed (Vulliamy, 1976).

What is selected, and what left out, also has consequences for social control. Schooling may help to sustain the status quo not only by stratification of pupils but also by the images of society it promotes. Examination of the content of science textbooks, for example, and observation of science lessons, indicate that the existence of uncertainty and disagreement about important issues is disguised; knowledge is portrayed as external, objective — and therefore unnegotiable — and the existence of conflict is downplayed (Apple, 1971). As a result, the forms of 'knowledge' that come to be valued may be those that appear to reveal uncontroversial facts, and in so doing suggest that the real nature of the status quo is fixed. (Certainly many sociology students initially complain that 'sociologists cannot agree even among themselves': ambiguity seems to be experienced as threatening.)

Most pupils come to see knowledge as something which must be presented to them by experts; for it is only at the higher levels of education that students are encouraged to use their own critical faculties, and are enabled to take part in the questioning of tradition and the creation of new knowledge. As Bernstein argues, only those who have shown themselves to be successfully socialised may be permitted to explore the potential of knowledge as an *activity* for 'creating new realities':

> only the few *experience* in their bones the notion that knowledge is permeable, that its orderings are provisional ... For the many, socialisation into knowledge is socialisa-

tion into order, the existing order (Bernstein, 1975, pp. 97-8).

Additionally, the manner in which knowledge is taught and assessed in schools may encourage pupils to regard knowledge not as the evolving product of a social activity, but as private property, to be acquired and hoarded: 'Children and pupils are early socialized into this concept of knowledge as private property. They are encouraged to work as isolated individuals with their arms around their work' (Bernstein, 1975, p. 97). These examples illustrate the ideological dimensions of the curriculum, and the way in which the organisation of knowledge may operate as a subtle and effective form of social control.

In the view of writers such as Young, Bourdieu and Bernstein, the organisation of knowledge in schools is inextricably bound up with the distribution of power in society. Knowledge is not merely organised in the descriptive sense (in the sense that it falls into discernible patterns) — it is *managed*. Analysing the curriculum may offer a way of arriving at a better understanding of education *and* of social control.

It would be unrealistic to expect in any complex society complete consensus on the kinds of knowledge to be transmitted in schools. However, powerful groups may be in a better position to impose *their* definition of educational knowledge — in short, to define the curriculum. Moreover, where knowledge is stratified (where certain subjects such as pure sciences are accorded higher status than others such as sociology or domestic science), possession of knowledge deemed 'superior' represents a gain. Hence, powerful groups may have an interest in restricting access to the more valued forms of knowledge. This view of the way knowledge may be managed is aptly summed up in a ditty:

I am the great Professor Jowett
And what there is to know, I know it
What I don't know isn't knowledge
And I am Master of this College.

(Halsey, in Hopper, 1971, p. 265)

To say that powerful groups may have an interest in defining the curriculum is, however, to risk grave oversimplification. For example, it is no advance simply to assert that 'everything which is taught in schools represents the interests of the bourgeoisie'. For one thing, this ignores the efforts of parents, of the labour movement and of student movements to influence the content as well as the structure of the education system. For another, groups with a vested interest in educational curricula include not only an abstractly defined dominant class, but also teachers and academic researchers — subject specialists whose careers and statuses are at stake. However, teachers themselves are checked by professional codes that can affect their careers (for example, the emphasis upon a 'non-political' stance); material constraints (over-large classes, inadequate textbooks); and by the pressures exerted by examination boards. It is worth remembering also that curricular changes seldom occur in a revolutionary fashion. As Bourdieu suggests, there is a gradual process of renewal — the old persists alongside the new. Hence some elements of the curriculum will be explained by reference to interest groups which were *formerly* powerful.

Considerations such as these are behind Williamson's warning, part of a review of the 'new' emphasis upon sociology of the curriculum: 'It is not enough to be aware only of the fact that the principles governing the selection of transmittable knowledge reflect structures of power. It is essential to move beyond such suspicions to work out the precise connections' (Williamson, 1974, p. 10). We cannot stay at the level of sweeping generalisations about education, such as 'cultural transmission' (as functionalists might have it) or 'reproduction of dominant ideology' (as some Marxists see it). The processes which shape both the organisation and content of schooling are complex and ever-changing; there is always, therefore, *potential* for reconstruction within the education system.

Theoretical perspectives

Our discussion of the inner workings of schools, and of the

organisation of school knowledge, has drawn on research which is informed by a variety of theoretical approaches. The influence of symbolic interactionism (with its emphasis upon the way identities are shaped by everyday processes of inter-action) can be seen in the writings of Hargreaves and Lacey on the emergence of 'anti-school' cultures. In Keddie's study 'Classroom Knowledge' (1971), which aims to disclose the processes whereby ordinary actors ascribe meaning to their world, phenomenological sociology is put to good effect. The sociology of knowledge, with its interest in the way that knowledge may be generated from particular social and eco-nomic conditions, clearly underpins many writings on the curriculum — as does the Marxist tradition, which itself has contributed so much to a sociology of knowledge.

It is difficult to sustain the claim that these diverse per-spectives represent a 'new sociology of education', since the boundaries between new and old are far from clear-cut. How-ever, it is the case that since the early 1970s, these perspec-tives have been much more influential in British sociology of education than before; in addition, there has been an accom-panying shift towards ethnographic accounts of classroom encounters along with a de-emphasis on the survey techniques that earlier dominated the field.

The shift of emphasis has in many ways enriched the socio-logy of education. Insights have been gained into the mechan-ism whereby schools produce the selection and legitimating outcomes discussed in the section on meritocracy. Moreover, by questioning notions such as 'ability' and 'standards', and by asking how views of these as 'objective' phenomena are sustained, recent work has helped to make problematic many aspects of educational theory and practice that were pre-viously neglected.

On the other hand, some of the recent writings on the inner workings of schools and the organisation of knowledge raise problems of both a practical and a theoretical nature. First, some analyses of classroom encounters fail to show how classroom life is shaped by the wider social context. Therefore, these writers may exaggerate the degree to which teachers and pupils are free to re-interpret the world in new and independent ways. This can create the impression that educational change is merely a matter of transformation of individual consciousness; by revealing the prejudices underlying assessment, for example, we do not remove the power of the examination system over pupils and teachers. Second, one of the points made most insistently by recent work in the sociology of education is that the curriculum is partial, that educational knowledge is less than objective, that the world-views of working-class (and other) pupils are not given the respect they deserve, and that the nature of prevailing assumptions about ability, standards, and education itself can justifiably be questioned. This still leaves us, however, with the problem of whether there are any forms of knowledge or skill that might be intrinsically superior, or that might increase pupils' capacity for understanding and hence create one of the conditions for change.

7.6 LANGUAGE, DEPRIVATION AND KNOWLEDGE

We have tried to emphasise that slogans about education reproducing inequality are insufficient; on the contrary, it is necessary to elaborate the processes linking the class structure (and patriarchy) to the school through its effects on individual pupils. Bernstein's theory of socio-linguistics attempts to do just that; his writings have had considerable influence on educational policy and practice, and have become the focal point for major controversy concerning the links between home, school, deprivation and inequality.

For Bernstein, social structure, especially class structure, generates specific linguistic forms; these forms in turn reinforce cultural differences, and help to channel behaviour into certain patterns. Bernstein suggests links between experiences at work, and community and family interaction, which influence the way in which children learn to relate to language. For working-class (especially unskilled or semi-skilled working-class) people, wage-labour involves slotting into prescribed work roles that minimise individuality, but may maximise solidarity with work-mates; these qualities are echoed in the cohesion, based on homogeneity of background and experience, that may characterise traditional working-class communities, and also in the family, where roles may follow traditional patterns and be fairly non-negotiable (called by him *positional families*). Modes of control over children in positional families lean towards commands with little explanation (Do it because I said so!), or towards 'positional appeals', involving reminders of the obligations and rights of mothers, fathers, boys, girls, older children, younger children, etc. (Daddy doesn't want to hear that sort of talk from little girls!). In short, rules are transmitted in such a way that children are reminded of what they share in common with others; children's similarity with others is constantly underlined, reinforcing the sense that what they feel, or see, or do, is what everyone in their group sees, or feels, or does. In Bernstein's view, these circumstances promote a particular relationship to language, in which language (speech) is understood as a way of enchancing solidarity; speech occurs against an assumption of shared experience with others, therefore minimising the felt need to make one's meaning explicit.

Briefly, the position of middle-class and especially professional people is thought to generate a very different relationship to language. Relative autonomy in work, freedom to plan and organise tasks and schedules, combines with the lack of tight-knit community structure, to encourage a premium on individual development with reference to shifting standards and objectives. This is echoed, according to Bernstein, in *person-oriented* families, where greater discretion in role performance requires more frequent use of language to explore the meaning of individual actions in the face of ambiguity about appropriate behaviour. For the child in such a family, 'personal appeals', which emphasise individual motives and actions, and their consequences for other individuals, are likely to be the predominant mode of control (I know you don't like kissing Grandpa, but he is unwell, and it makes him very happy when you kiss him). Moreover, since middle-class parents may be more likely to punish for bad intentions than for bad consequences, children are encouraged from an early age to verbalise motives, and to express experience and emotion in verbal rather than other forms. These circumstances promote, in Bernstein's view, an understanding that language is the major means of expressing and interpreting emotion, and a vehicle for exploring and bridging the gulf between oneself and other people who are assumed to be different.

Bernstein identifies a *restricted code* (a form of speech in which meanings are relatively implicit, linked to a particular context, and particularistic) which can be fully understood only by those who have already shared the experience or emotion being verbalised. Restricted code is said to be more characteristic of the working class; although the middle class have access to this code, they tend to reserve it for use among peers (playmates, close friends or work colleagues). Against the restricted code, Bernstein sets the *elaborated code*, the usual mode of speech for the middle class. An elaborated code tends to make meanings explicit, to be universalistic in the sense that most English-speaking people can catch the meaning, and to be relatively independent of the context in which it is used. The differences between the two codes are not easy to grasp. An admittedly extreme example might be the difference between the speech of lawyers in a courtroom (elaborated code), and a chat with a best friend, where it is almost understood what is meant before it is said — where phrases like 'God!' or 'Same with George and me' can communicate a world of (implicit) meaning.

Bernstein's argument is that lower working-class children, whose socialisation has given them easy access only to a restricted code, face several disadvantages in the schooling system. First, schools demand that children communicate in a universalistic way that can be understood by everyone, and this demand becomes more intense at the later stages of schooling. Children who have been reared with the restricted code are not used to projecting their separate experience, and their speech and written work will appear to teachers and middle-class school-mates as difficult to understand, incomplete, and inadequate. Second, the linguistic barriers between working-class children and teachers may compound misunderstandings. Teachers who express emotions through purely verbal means may appear to the child as cold and unfeeling, while teachers may regard a child who speaks to them in restricted code (seen by middle-class people as suitable only for conversations with peers) as rude or aggressive. Third, while school represents to middle-class children an extension or refinement of earlier experience within the home, there are for working-class girls and boys severe discontinuities between home and school — discontinuities not only in language-use but also in modes of discipline, or ways of cementing personal relationships — with the result that success for working-class children does not merely involve learning more than they knew before, it means *unlearning* aspects of previous experience. Fourth, Bernstein emphasises that children cannot be taught elaborated code in the way they might be taught vocabulary: the use of restricted code is rooted, for working-class children, in the structure of their community and their family. They may feel uneasy with an elaborated code because it implies roles and relationships that are fluid and ambiguous, and that play upon a foundation of individual difference; the elaborated code is not simply *new* to many working-class children, it is an alien means of expression. Criticisms of restricted code seem to be attacks on the child's actual way of life.

The codes are not, in Bernstein's view, equivalent to differences in dialect, or accent, or vocabulary, nor are they simply arbitrary ways of speaking, which can be altered by providing models of 'good' speech. In order for working-class children to be judged successful in school, they must change their very identity, and radically alter a way of perceiving the world that is rooted in the realities of working-class life.

Since Bernstein's theory is so ambitious, embracing work relationships and forms of class solidarity, as well as modes of control and language-use both in home and school, it is not surprising to find that only fragments of the theory have as yet been put to the test. Questions remain as to whether there are two, or more, codes in the English language, whether codes are genuinely distinct from dialects, and whether the codes are actually linked to social class in the manner hypothesised. Years of further research might be necessary to produce a body of evidence that would finally support Bernstein's theory or lay it to rest.

It is interesting to note, however, that Bernstein's views have often been counterposed to those of another socio-linguist, Labov (in Keddie, 1973). Labov examined the form of speech (called NNE or Negro Non-Standard English) used by some black children in the USA — children who, like those from working-class backgrounds, tend to under-achieve in the education system. He observes that children who are extremely reticent in a formal research setting become highly verbal when placed in a less threatening situation. More importantly, he concludes that though NNE differs from other forms of speech, it has a coherent inner logic and a complex structure, and is perfectly capable of being used to articulate complicated or abstract ideas. These observations have been taken to imply two fundamental deficiencies in work such as Bernstein's: first, the methodological error of eliciting speech from working-class people in formal contexts, which inhibit them from displaying their full range of verbal virtuosity; second, the false assumption that different forms of speech reflect superior or inferior patterns of cognition or reasoning. Labov's formulations are frequently claimed to be more promising than Bernstein's (Stubbs, 1976; Edwards, 1976). However, the debate does not end with this assessment; the controversy centring upon these figures extends into areas of educational research and educational policy, raising many questions of continuing importance for our understanding of education.

The argument that surfaced with the publication of *Tinker, Tailor* (Keddie, 1973) involved a telling condemnation of attempts to explain educational under-achievement by reference to children's cultural and linguistic heritage. Children in Britain and America have been identified as 'deprived' because of cultural or linguistic inadequacies in their upbringing, when in fact, Keddie and others contend, they are merely different — not inferior or superior, just different; the notion of cultural and linguistic *difference* replaces that of cultural or linguistic *deprivation*. The view that certain children are deprived is seen as not only mistaken but also politically reprehensible. They offer several reasons. First, to define the culture or language of working-class or black people as 'deprived' or 'inadequate' involves a lack of respect for those people, and an ethnocentric refusal to recognise their cultural richness and strength. Second, to suggest that children are deprived because of the inadequate heritage they have received from their family or community implies that these children are doomed to failure because of their *own* inadequacies — a position similar to that of 'blaming poverty on its victims' (see dis-

cussion of the *culture of poverty* in Chapter 3). Thus notions
of cultural or linguistic deprivation may be similar in their
effects to (equally mistaken) notions of the genetic inferiority
of low-achieving groups:

> Liberals have eagerly seized upon the social pathology
> model as a replacement for the genetic inferiority model.
> But both the genetic model and the social pathology model
> postulate that something is wrong with the black American.
> For the traditional racists, that something is transmitted by
> the genetic code; for the ethnocentric social pathologists,
> that something is transmitted by the family (Baratz and
> Baratz, 1972, p. 189).

Third, by locating the 'problem' in the family, a justification
is produced for neglecting such children in schools. In illustration of this, Fuchs (in Keddie, 1973) describes how a teacher
in a slum school was induced by her colleagues to stop worrying about the poor quality of teaching offered to the children,
and to accept instead that they were already destined to fail.
The notion of cultural or linguistic deprivation may trigger
low expectations for children so labelled, leading to a self-
fulfilling prophecy. Fourth, at the level of sociological research, an over-emphasis upon 'deprivations' which have their
origin in family or community may limit research into the
shortcomings of the schools themselves, where the real explanation for failure may well lie. Finally, we are urged to consider the possibility that the knowledge made available in
school, which admittedly does not 'fit' with the orientation
of many 'under-achieving' children, may be an inappropriate
curriculum, favoured only because of its close association
with dominant or 'mainstream' culture.

These criticisms of cultural and linguistic deprivation have
been extended to include critiques of 'compensatory education' — the diverse programmes of remedial help, counselling,
and 'educational enrichment' that were, in the 1960s and
early 1970s, introduced ostensibly to improve the educational
chances of young children who had been identified as 'deprived' or 'disadvantaged'. The charge was made that projects
such as Headstart in the USA, and the Educational Priority

Areas programme in England and Wales, were mistaken in aiming to 'compensate' for deprivation that did not exist. Moreover, they were denounced as politically misguided in so far as they institutionalised the 'deficit' view of working-class or black children, with the consequences, such as labelling or avoiding fundamental changes in schooling itself, that were outlined in preceding paragraphs.

The time has come to consider these arguments, to explore some of their implications, and to look at alternative views. While accepting some of these arguments (especially those concerning the failure to focus on inadequacies in the schools), there are others we reject: two issues seem to us to be central. The first concerns programmes of compensatory education. There are many valid grounds, in our view, for criticising the *particular* compensatory programmes of the past two decades. Many of the schemes were ambitious in outline, but inadequately implemented; not enough resources were made available; sometimes teachers were unclear about the objectives of the schemes, and unprepared for their part in the programme (Gross, Giacquinta and Bernstein, 1971, pp. 2–7). Furthermore, many of the projects had a hit-and-miss quality, since there was little evidence available about the precise kinds of intervention that would most effectively help children in need. But in spite of these and other defects, the limited success of *certain* compensatory education programmes in no way demonstrates the inevitable failure of all such programmes to improve the skills of children in need. The principle of positive discrimination in favour of disadvantaged groups seems highly desirable; one of the remarkable features of our education system is that so much (at the level of national resources *and* classroom attention) is channelled towards a privileged few. However, to refer to positive discrimination (or even equal shares of resources) as 'compensatory education' may well be misguided. The issue is why schools do not, as part of the general run of things, orient themselves to the needs of children who do not fit a straightforward middle-class model of educability. 'It is an accepted educational principle that we should work with what the child can offer; why don't we practise it? The introduction of the child to ... public forms of thought is not compensatory education − *it is edu-*

cation' (Bernstein, 1971, p. 199).

The second issue concerns the educational implications of the view that groups of children who systematically under-achieve are not 'deprived' but merely 'different'. One implica-tion is that respect for the cultural heritage brought to school by working-class children, by girls, by children of Asian or West Indian origin in Britain, by black Americans, should be a basic tenet of educational practice; this respect should be reflected in the books they read and in the materials they study, while their view of the world should be a starting point for explorations of other issues. Our earlier discussion of causes of under-achievement indeed suggests the importance of reducing the discontinuity between home and school for many pupils.

More controversial suggestions to arise from the insistence on cultural *difference*, however, are for the provision of dis-tinct curricula for children from working-class or ethnic minority backgrounds, and for the rejection by teachers of all efforts to 'substitute' their ideas for those of the pupils. These suggestions are certainly well-intentioned, but they could have unfortunate consequences. A consequence of special curricula for special groups could be to place children in 'educational ghettoes': that is, to confine their knowledge of the world to their immediate circumstances. Far from liberat-ing them, this might foreclose options by denying them the chance to understand alternative realities. An insistence on equality of *cultural* status could distract from inequality of power and resource. Differentiated curricula could help dis-advantaged groups to build 'positive identities and lots of pride' (Valentine, 1968, p. 151), while leaving unchallenged the structures of inequality and powerlessness that led to the denigration of their culture in the first place.

What conclusions can we draw from this discussion of lan-guage, deprivation and educational achievement? First, we would argue that deprivation does indeed exist. Its source is not, as some have alleged, in the family, but rather in the class structure and the patriarchal structure which deny to many people not only a reasonable share of material resources and decision-making power, but also the chance to develop their capacities for learning.

Second, deprivation that has its roots in inequality cannot be 'defined out of existence' by simply insisting on the *cultural* equality of the privileged and the disadvantaged; it can only be tackled by a strategy that involves redistribution of effective power in society, as well as efforts to forge a more just and more liberating form of education. For schooling itself, this requires the recognition that education is about the development of skills and understanding. If that education is inadequate, it may be only marginally (as the peasant boy at the beginning of this chapter remarked) 'better than cowshit'. The central questions raised by the sociology of education are about curriculum, pedagogy, and the relationship between society and schooling. In short, what kinds of skills can enable people to penetrate reality and increase their capacity for control over their world, *and* to what extent can these be realised or anticipated in present unequal society? While educational change cannot on its own transform that society, strategies for equality cannot afford to ignore the educational system. Arguments over knowledge and ideas are also arguments about the future of society.

REFERENCES TO CHAPTER 7

Apple, M. (1971) 'The Hidden Curriculum and the Nature of Conflict', *Interchange*, vol. 2, no. 4, Spring 1971.

Ariès, P. (1973) *Centuries of Childhood*, Harmondsworth, Penguin.

Banks, O. and Finlayson, D. (1973) *Success and Failure in the Secondary School*, London, Methuen.

Baratz, S. and Baratz, J. (1972) 'Early Childhood Intervention: the Social Science Base of Institutional Racism', in Open University Language and Learning Course Team (eds), *Language in Education*, London, Routledge & Kegan Paul.

Berg, I. (1970) *Education for Jobs: the Great Training Robbery*, Harmondsworth, Penguin.

Bernstein, B. (1971) 'A Critique of the Concept of Compensatory Education', in *Class, Codes and Control*, vol. 1, London, Routledge & Kegan Paul.

Bernstein, B. (1975) 'On the Classification and Framing of Educational Knowledge', in *Class, Codes and Control*, vol. 3, London, Routledge & Kegan Paul.

Bernstein, B. and Davies, B. (1969) 'Some Sociological Comments on Plowden', in R. S. Peters (ed.), *Perspectives on Plowden*, London, Routledge & Kegan Paul.

Bisseret, N. (1979) *Education, Class Language and Ideology*, London, Routledge & Kegan Paul.

Bourdieu, P. and Passeron, J.-C. (1977) *Reproduction in Education, Society and Culture*, London, Sage.

Bowles, S. and Gintis, H. (1976) *Schooling in Capitalist America*, London, Routledge & Kegan Paul.

Bowles, S. and Nelson, V. (1974) 'The "Inheritance of IQ" and the Intergenerational Transmission of Economic Inequality', *Review of Economics and Statistics*, vol. LVI, no. 1, February 1974.

Brandis, W. and Bernstein, B. (1974) *Selection and Control*, London, Routledge & Kegan Paul.

Byrne, D., Williamson, W. and Fletcher, B. (1975) *The Poverty of Education*, London, Martin Robertson.

Byrne, E. (1976) *The Rationale of Resource-Allocation*, Milton Keynes, Open University Press.

Cicourel, A. and Kitsuse, J. (1963) *The Educational Decision-Makers*, New York, Bobbs-Merrill.

Clark, B. (1960) *The Open Door College*, New York, McGraw-Hill.

Coleman, J. (1973) 'The Concept of Equality in Educational Opportunity', in J. Raynor and J. Harden (eds), *Equality and City Schools*, London, Routledge & Kegan Paul.

Davie, R., Butler, M. and Goldstein, H. (1972) *From Birth to Seven*, London, Longman.

Davies, L. and Meighan, R. (1975) 'A Review of Schooling and Sex Roles, With Particular Reference to the Experience of Girls in Secondary Schools', *Educational Review*, vol. 27, no. 3, pp. 165—78.

Douglas, J. W. B. (1967) *The Home and the School*, London, Panther.

Douglas, J. W. B., Ross, J. M. and Simpson, H. R. (1971) *All Our Future*, London, Panther.

Edwards, A. D. (1976) *Language in Culture and Class*, London, Heinemann.

Eysenck, H. (1962) *Know Your Own IQ*, Harmondsworth, Penguin.

Floud, J. and Halsey, A. H. (1965) 'Introduction', in A. H. Halsey, J. Floud and C. Anderson (eds), *Education, Economy and Society*, New York, Free Press.

Floud, J., Halsey, A. H. and Martin, F. M. (1956) *Social Class and Educational Opportunity*, London, Heinemann.

Goodacre, E. (1968) *Teachers and Their Pupils' Home Backgrounds*, Slough, NFER.

Gross, N., Giacquinta, J. and Bernstein, M. (1971) *Implementing Organizational Innovations*, New York, Harper & Row.

Halsey, A. H. (1977) 'Towards Meritocracy? The Case of Britain', in Karabel and Halsey (1977).

Halsey, A. H., Heath, A. F. and Ridge, J. M. (1980) *Origins and Destinations*, Oxford, Clarendon Press.

Hargreaves, D. (1967) *Social Relations in a Secondary School*, London, Routledge & Kegan Paul.

Hargreaves, D. (1972) *Interpersonal Relations and Education*, London,

Routledge & Kegan Paul.
Herrnstein, R. (1973) *IQ in the Meritocracy*, London, Allen Lane.
Hodgson, G. (1973) 'Inequality: Do Schools Make a Difference?', in Silver, H. (ed.), *Equal Opportunity in Education*, London, Methuen.
Hopper, E. (ed.) (1971) *Readings in the Theory of Educational Systems*, London, Hutchinson.
Illich, I. (1973) *Deschooling Society*, Harmondsworth, Penguin.
Jackson, B. and Marsden, D. (1966) *Education and the Working Class*, Harmondsworth, Penguin.
Jackson, P. (1968) *Life in Classrooms*, New York, Holt, Rinehart & Winston.
Jencks, C. *et al.* (1973) *Inequality*, London, Allen Lane.
Jensen, A. (1969) 'How Much Can We Boost IQ and Scholastic Achievement?', in *Environment, Heredity and Intelligence*, Harvard Educational Review Reprint Series no. 2.
Kahl, J. (1965) "Common Man" Boys', in A. H. Halsey *et al.* (eds), *Education, Economy and Society*, New York, Free Press.
Kamin, L. (1977) *The Science and Politics of IQ*, Harmondsworth, Penguin.
Karabel, J. and Halsey, A. H. (eds) (1977) *Power and Ideology in Education*, Oxford University Press.
Katz, I. *et al.* (1964) 'Effect upon Negro Digit-Symbol Performance of Anticipated Comparison with Whites and Other Negroes', *Journal of Abnormal and Social Psychology*, vol. 69, pp. 77–83.
Keddie, N. (1971) 'Classroom Knowledge', in M. F. D. Young (ed.), *Knowledge and Control*, London, Collier-Macmillan.
Keddie, N. (ed.) (1973) *Tinker, Tailor*, Harmondsworth, Penguin.
King, R. (1977) *Education*, London, Longman.
Kluckholn, F. and Strodtbeck, E. (1961) *Variations in Value Orientations*, New York, Row & Peterson.
Lacey, C. (1970) *Hightown Grammar*, Manchester University Press.
Little, A. and Westergaard, J. (1964) 'The Trend of Class Differentials in Educational Opportunity in England and Wales', *British Journal of Sociology*, vol. XV.
Milner, M. (1972) *The Illusion of Equality*, London, Jossey-Bass.
Nash, R. (1973) *Classrooms Observed*, London, Routledge & Kegan Paul.
Neave, G. (1975) *How They Fared*, London, Routledge & Kegan Paul.
Pidgeon, D. (1970) *Expectation and Pupil Performance*, Slough, NFER.
Plowden Committee (1967) *Children and their Primary Schools*, London, HMSO.
Rist, R. (1970) 'Student Social Class and Teacher Expectations: the Self-Fulfilling Prophecy in Ghetto Education', *Harvard Educational Review*, vol. 40, no. 3, pp. 411–51.
Robbins Committee (1963) *Report on Higher Education*, London, HMSO.
Rogers, R. (1980) 'The Myth of Independent Schools', *New Statesman*, 4 January 1980.

School of Barbiana (1970) *Letter to a Teacher*, Harmondsworth, Penguin.

Sharp, R. and Green, A. (1975) *Education and Social Control*, London, Routledge & Kegan Paul.

Stubbs, M. (1976) *Language, Schools and Classrooms*, London, Methuen.

Valentine, C. (1968) *Culture and Poverty*, University of Chicago Press.

Vulliamy, G. (1976) 'What Counts as School Music?', in G. Whitty and M. Young (eds), *Explorations in the Politics of School Knowledge*, Driffield, Nafferton.

Wedge, P. and Prosser, H. (1973) *Born to Fail?*, London, Arrow Books.

Westergaard, J. and Resler, H. (1975) *Class in a Capitalist Society*, London, Heinemann.

Williamson, B. (1974) 'Continuities and Discontinuities in the Sociology of Education', in M. Flude and J. Ahier (eds), *Educability, Schools and Ideology*, London, Croom Helm.

Wright, N. (1977) *Progress in Education*, London, Croom Helm.

Wrong, D. (1980) 'The Oversocialized Conception of Man in Modern Sociology', in R. Bocock *et al.* (eds), *An Introduction to Sociology*, London, Fontana.

Yates, A. and Pidgeon, D. (1957) *Admission to Grammar Schools*, London, Newnes.

Young, M. (1961) *The Rise of the Meritocracy*, Harmondsworth, Penguin.

8
Work

8.1 INTRODUCTION

For most employees work has a generally unpleasant quality. If there is little Calvinist compulsion to work among propertyless factory workers and file clerks, there is also little Renaissance exuberance in the work of the insurance clerk, freight handler, or department store saleslady . . . Such joy as creative work may carry is more and more limited to a small minority (C. Wright Mills, 1953, p. 219).

It is often suggested that boring, mundane work is part of the price that people living in industrial societies have to pay for their high material standards of living. Moreover, it is argued, these standards can only be attained by the systematic utilisation of machine technology, and this requires both rational, bureaucratic forms of administration and a complicated division of labour. Consequently, *any* industrial society, because it *is* industrial, will incur certain costs — including the degradation of work — in order that sufficient surplus be produced to allow opportunities for leisure, diversification of interests and high mass consumption.

However, work and production are not just physical activities, they are social activities which can be organised in a variety of ways. Britain's industrialisation process — and that of most of Western Europe — occurred on a capitalist basis, a fact of crucial importance for understanding how work is organised and experienced.

In this chapter we shall examine the distinctive nature of capitalist social relations and the various strategies used by management to control labour and to justify that control. We shall also analyse the methods used by employees to resist this control, both at the point of production and in the wider society. Finally, we shall make a few brief observations about the possible future of work in societies such as ours.

8.2   THE CAPITAL–LABOUR RELATIONSHIP

General features

Capitalism means that much of the productive system is privately owned, usually concentrated in relatively few hands, and organised for profit. Work has the status of wage-labour, and jobs are located within a labour market, where prospective workers must find employers willing to pay a wage or salary in return for the use of their skills, knowledge or physical strength. We shall argue that it is the *capitalist*, and not merely the industrial, nature of Western society that is primarily responsible for the way the organisation of work has developed.

Industrialisation involves basic changes in the structure of a society. A fundamental change is that, in industrial societies, most people become employees. This is in marked contrast to non-industrial societies, where three-quarters or more of the occupied population are either employers, self-employed, or family workers. The change to a society dominated by wage-labour is a relatively recent one which is associated with the emergence of the factory system of production, which became dominant in Britain as late as the nineteenth century.

The factory system developed alongside craft and domestic systems of production and took some time to supersede them — never replacing them entirely. The modern worker is often compared with the craftworkers of earlier centuries, so we must be wary of romanticising such workers' position. The craft system operated within a society marked by poverty, deprivation and brutal exploitation. There was, nevertheless, a difference in the nature of the relationship which existed between craft employers and employees, in that it was a *personal* relationship in which both employer and employee had mutual obligations much broader than anything expected today. Furthermore, the craftworkers owned their own tools and place of work, bought their raw materials and sold the finished product direct to the consumer. However, much more important was the skill and knowledge that they controlled:

> From earliest times to the Industrial Revolution the craft or skilled trade was the basic unit, the elementary cell of the labour process. In each craft, the worker was presumed to be the master of a body of traditional knowledge, and methods and procedures were left to his or her discretion. In each such worker reposed the accumulated knowledge of materials and processes by which production was accomplished in the craft ... The worker combined in mind and body, the concepts and physical dexterities of the specialty (Braverman, 1974, p. 109).

However, factory production was to involve basic changes in the social situation of *all* workers with far-reaching implications for craft skills and employment relations. It meant the concentration of labour in one workshop or factory and the separation of home and work. Workers were subject to the discipline of employers who required that they worked regular hours with regular intensity. Although legally free, they were subordinate and dependent both economically and socially.

The factory system also made possible much greater division of labour and specialisation as machine power was introduced. The introduction of the machine meant that greater amounts of fixed capital were required for manufacture, and that much factory work came to involve the performing of semi-skilled or unskilled tasks, fragments of the total process, in which the intrinsic satisfactions derived from the task itself and from the completion of a finished product were diminished. Increasingly employees lost a good deal of contact with their employer — sometimes *all* personal contact was severed. Finally, workers lost most of their rights over materials, tools, and the product of their labour.

The development of the factory system represents a division of labour between agriculture and manufacture which allows food and goods to be produced more efficiently. The technical division of labour and the development of new technologies are *potentially* liberating, in that both permit greater control over the environment and the possibility of producing a surplus. However, the technical division of labour — which separates work into specific tasks and which can create greater efficiency — is also accompanied by a crucial *social* division of labour between factory owners and those who work for them, and by the *intellectual* division of labour between manual labourers and clerks and administrators. (Such a division is important because when a market for labour exists, different skills become defined as more or less important, more or less valuable, more or less prestigious.)

Moreover, the technical efficiency of the division of labour and its rational organisation does not necessarily work to the benefit of all workers. Under capitalism, production is organised for the benefit of the owners of private property, for the few, and control over production is enforced *downwards* by the owners' managerial agents and functionaries. The labour force is not just co-ordinated by the division of labour and rational production processes, it is also *controlled*. People at work have *power* exercised over them.

The reduction of labour power to the status of a commodity under capitalism has two very important implications for the nature of this control. The wages and conditions forming the basis of the employees' existence are a *cost* to the employer to be taken out of profits; consequently it is in employers' interests to resist improvements in these, just as employees are bound to press for them. Because employers must regard labour as a cost to be minimised, they will only employ people while it is profitable to do so. Therefore, workers are always at the mercy of economic and technological developments and constantly threatened by unemployment. Consequently, technological developments which cause redundancies are not always welcomed with enthusiasm.

Furthermore, when *marketable* skill becomes the basis of reward, it is imperative that those who possess such skills attempt to control the conditions under which they are offered for sale. They must strive to maintain the scarcity and utility of their skills. Conversely, it is in the interests of capital to reduce its reliance upon skilled personnel, for skill is expensive. The simplest way of cheapening labour power is to break it up into its simplest elements and to divorce the labour process from special knowledge and training. In fact, the history of manual labour may be seen as a process in which workers have gradually lost control or possession of their knowledge and skills. (Arguably, the development of micro-computer technology poses a similar threat to intellectual skills.)

The same principle which breaks down work into routine and meaningless tasks means that management, by organising and co-ordinating the fragments, can gain a virtual monopoly of knowledge and therefore control over the work process itself.

Let us examine, then, some of the theories of management consultants, industrial psychologists and sociologists which have been used to explain and justify strategies of management control over labour.

Scientific management

The move towards deskilling the labour force and establishing control over the knowledge necessary for production was well under way by the end of the nineteenth century, but reached its modern form in the work of F. W. Taylor and the school of thought known as 'scientific management'.

Taylor, a management consultant, was initially concerned with achieving higher productivity in the steel industry, and furthered this end by introducing what has become known as 'work study'. The techniques he developed included the methodical study of work to devise the quickest, most efficient way of doing a job, and an emphasis on piece-work — linking an individual's pay directly to his output — so that workers had incentives to produce as much as possible in a given period. More significantly, he insisted that management should assume responsibility for deciding how work was to be performed, leaving to workers the task of obeying orders to the letter.

In 1899 Taylor's methods were utilised at the Bethlehem steel works where they were responsible for raising pig-iron production by almost 400 per cent per day. This was accomplished by offering financial incentives to workers and then specifying every detail of their work: when to load, when to rest, when to walk, the size of the shovel, and the arc of the swing. Most of the scientific management studies initiated during the 1920s and 1930s were concerned with finding the 'best' way of doing a job — the best pattern of rest periods, the best level of heating and lighting for indoor work, and so on. Taylor maintained that if workers could be brought to a level where they were operating at optimum efficiency, they would find this intrinsically satisfying.

In *Principles of Scientific Management* Taylor (1911) argues that, left to their own devices, workers will do as little as possible and engage in 'soldiering' — working more slowly together in order to keep management ignorant of their potential. Similarly, left to plan their own work, workers' output is further lowered. They will do things in the customary way rather than the most efficient way. The solution is for management to 'relieve' workers of the necessity of planning their own tasks, particularly those with a mental component. Workers will learn from management how best to increase their output to the benefit of both. The best inducement, he believed, is *money* or *economic reward*. People are primarily interested in achieving a level of pay commensurate with the effort they have expended and expect a fair day's pay for a fair day's work; and piecework ensures that individual effort is rewarded.

Many of Taylor's assumptions — especially that people are primarily motivated by economic rewards — have since been questioned as oversimplifying the complex nature of human motivation. Similarly, exactly what constitutes a 'fair day's pay for a fair day's work' is subject to a continuous process of formal and informal negotiation between management and workers. Also, within a capitalist market, the price of labour depends upon a variety of factors such as scarcity, demand, economic conditions, and so on. However, the assumption most severely criticised was that people seek individual satisfactions in work, and necessarily value these above the satisfactions of solidarity with work-mates.

It is often argued that Taylor's methods of organising work 'failed' or that his ideas were superseded by those of the human-relations school that 'followed' scientific management. Others — such as Braverman (1974) — have suggested that his techniques of work study have simply been refined and extended and his principles implemented in a range of settings, if in modified form. Braverman regards scientific management not as an objective 'scientific' study of the difficulties of performing and organising work in a complex society but as a means of *adapting* labour to the needs of capitalism and of *exerting control* over the labour process. Various means of control, such as gathering people together in factories, dictating the length of the working day, supervising workers to ensure diligence, had all been instituted before. Taylor, however, raised the concept of *control* to new heights by his insistence that management dictate to workers *the precise manner in which work was to be performed.* Braverman claims that scientific management operated with three main principles which still operate today.

The first he calls the *dissociation of the labour process from the skills of the workers,* which, as Taylor himself observed, means that 'the managers assume ... the burden of gathering together all the traditional knowledge which in the past has been possessed by the workmen and then of classifying, tabulating and reducing this knowledge to rules, laws and formulae (Taylor, 1967, p. 36).

The second principle he calls *the separation of conception from execution.* Here, the unity of the labour process is broken up by the capitalist, who separates mental from manual labour, and then further sub-divides both. Taylor argues that the full possibilities of his system 'will not have been realized until almost all of the machines in the shop are run by men who are of smaller calibre and attainments, and who are therefore cheaper than those required under the old system' (Taylor, 1903, p. 105). The study of work processes is reserved to management, who pass on to the worker simplified job tasks divorced from the overall logic of the process.

The third principle is *the use of the monopoly over knowledge to control each step of the labour process and its mode of execution.* Under 'ordinary' management the worker had become more skilled and knowledgeable than anyone in management, so the details of how work could best be done had to be left to him or her. By contrast:

> Perhaps the most prominent single element in modern scientific management is the task idea. The work of every workman is fully planned out by management at least one day in advance and each man receives in most cases complete written instructions, describing in detail the task which he is to accomplish, as well as the means to be used in doing the work. This task specifies not only what is to be done, but how it is to be done and the exact time allowed for doing it. . . Scientific management consists. . . in preparing for and carrying out these tasks (Taylor, 1967, pp. 63, 39).

Braverman argues that the most important part of this process was not the written instructions but the systematic pre-planning and pre-calculation of the labour process, which took away from workers the responsibility for conceiving, planning and initiating their work tasks thus leaving the imaginative task of creation to management.

He suggests that the process of deskilling and degrading work has been steadily advancing in modern capitalist societies among both manual and white-collar workers and that its extent is disguised by the categories used to classify skill levels. The designation of occupations as 'skilled' or 'unskilled' is frequently arbitrary, and a rise or fall in either category may merely be the result of changing standards or methods of classification. For example, many contemporary 'semi-skilled' jobs may be learned in a few weeks — the level of skill required is miniscule — and cannot meaningfully be compared with semi-skilled jobs of even fifty years ago.

Although Braverman provides a range of stimulating insights into work in modern societies, we must not assume that employers' attempts to control the labour process in its entirety — despite evidence of deskilling and the degradation of work — occurred without resistance. Taylor himself recognised the existence of 'soldiering' as a tactic for resisting management control, and (as we shall see in our discussion of human relations in the next section) this tactic survived his methods and was instituted against them. We shall argue that management, in its attempts to gain control of the work-force, has proved to be both more sophisticated and more pragmatic than Braverman allows. Various methods have been used, ranging from the 'carrots' of high wages, profit-sharing, fringe benefits and job enrichment, to the 'sticks' of speed-ups and lay-offs.

Similarly — as the human-relations school also recognises — workers do not face management as isolated individuals, but as members of integrated work-groups with their own ideas about work-loads, pace and 'fairness'. Furthermore, they have methods for resisting management encroachment upon these norms which operate both at the point of production and at the broader societal level by means of trade unions and political parties.

The human-relations school

The human-relations school attempted to use the ability of work-groups to establish their own norms and values as a way of integrating employees into the industrial enterprise without basically altering the structure of capitalist social relations. The school's ideas are often presented as a radical alternative to Taylorism, but they share Taylor's emphasis on controlling the worker. The informal work group was to be turned back upon its creators.

The approach is most closely associated with the name of Elton Mayo, who publicised the ideas of the school after the 'success' of a series of industrial studies carried out at the Western Electric Company in Chicago in the 1920s and 1930s — the famous 'Hawthorne Experiments'. The experimenters were attempting to test some of Taylor's principles by invest-igating the effects of temperature, lighting, humidity, rest-breaks, incentive schemes, and so on, upon worker productiv-ity. They had been experimenting with illumination, expect-ing production to rise with increased levels. Unexpectedly, they found that output went up, or remained relatively stable, *both* when lighting was improved *and* when it was drastically reduced. Upon redesigning their experiments, the researchers reassessed their preconceptions of the importance of economic and physical conditions, concluding that the *attitudes* of the workers and their *feelings* about their work were of strategic importance. Good relations with supervisors, and the positive atmosphere inadvertently introduced into the experimental situation by seeking the workers' co-operation, were deemed responsible for the high morale that helped maintain output despite worsening conditions. Thus, the researchers rejected a largely *physiological* interpretation of worker behaviour for a more *psychological* one.

Moreover, another study of a small group engaged in assembling switches for telephone switchboards — the Bank Wiring Room Experiment — revealed that the workers shared a set of 'unofficial' norms which ran counter to the rules and expectations of management. Management had established as a normal day's output the figure of 6,600 wiring connections, while the workers defined a reasonable day's work as only 6,000 connections. It was expected that no one should work too hard and become a 'rate-buster', even though the group as a whole might profit by the increased output through the operation of group piecework.

Human-relations theory rested upon the recognition that the influence of group norms and values on individual attitudes and behaviour was a resource which management could turn to its own advantage, if the allegiance and leadership of the informal work-group could be diverted into management hands. The possibility of achieving this required an alternative model to that used by the scientific management school. 'Economically' motivated workers were replaced by 'socially' motivated workers to accommodate the existence of the informal group. This group fulfilled social needs for 'belonging' and engagement in worthwhile activities that management neglected, and hence embraced norms and values different from those of management.

Proponents of human relations believed that the development of more efficient communication and the training of front-line management in the art of winning workers' allegiance could break down the 'artificial' barriers between managers and workers. The skilful manager, having generated the commitment and identification that workers need and wish to offer, could use this in the service of the formal organisation.

The human-relations approach has been heavily criticised, most notably for its assumption that 'normal' organisation involves consensus in the work-place, with management and workers sharing the same end. The essential rationality of industrial conflict is denied (Mayo himself described workers who criticised management as 'neurotic' and 'obsessive'), while unions are depicted as essentially mischievous agencies with an institutional interest in sowing and aggravating distrust. Conflict is defined as pathological, and may be attributed to failures in communication which can be overcome by enlightened management.

Critics have pointed out, however, that far from exacerbating industrial conflict, poor communications have probably contributed a major part in its alleviation. Allen, for example, in drawing attention to the way in which information about job changes, planned redundancies, profit ratios and directors' salaries is not communicated to workers, comments: 'for those who believe that there is a correlation between communications and industrial unrest, perhaps it is well that communications are faulty' (1966, p. 109).

The human-relations approach has been accused of seeing the work process purely from the viewpoint of management and of regarding workers as pawns to be manipulated in pursuit of managerial goals. It is seen as an attempt by management to retain the benefits of hierarchy, extreme division of labour and elaborate authority structures, while at the same time attempting to avoid their 'costs', such as the indifference or outright hostility of the people exposed to them. It tried to use the 'social' needs of workers to involve them in an integrated community of purpose without altering the basic structure of reward, decision-making or job design within which they were situated.

Thus the theories of scientific management and human relations are not only inadequate as explanations of the experience of work but are ideologically slanted in their uncritical justification of the capital/wage labour relationship.

8.3   THE EXPERIENCE OF WORK: SATISFACTION AND FULFILMENT

Marx and alienation

The schools of scientific management and human relations both recognised that work in industrial societies was not very satisfying. However, their views of economic motivation (gaining limited satisfactions from extrinsic material rewards and operating at peak efficiency) and motivation (seeking satisfaction in their work-group) — derived from management-inspired studies of work which were mainly concerned with fitting workers into a system of work over which they had little control. Marx, on the other hand, saw humans as potentially creative creatures who express their basic humanity — and differentiate themselves from other animals — in and through work. This led him to argue that the industrial worker was *alienated*, and that the source of this alienation was the structure and social relations of production under capitalism.

For Marx, alienation had four main dimensions. First, workers in a capitalist society are divorced from the products of their labour. People put themselves into the goods they produce, but under capitalism the goods are then expropriated and sold for profit. Instead of creating what they need workers are forced to create property for others — who then use it to enslave them. The more the workers produce, the more they create the conditions of their own domination.

Second, the process of production becomes fragmented; labour becomes an uninteresting chore, meaningless, unfulfilling and unrewarding — a means to an end rather than an end in itself.

Third, at the social level people become alienated from others, as relationships come to be dominated by the market. The nature of capitalist social relations is such that actors, in their economic roles, find themselves in situations of mutual hostility, relating to one another not on the basis of their common humanity or as whole beings but as worker to employer, or as one worker in competition with another for a job or promotion. Consequently the co-operative nature of human enterprise is obscured.

Fourth, humans are alienated from their 'species-being', for manual work is made mindless and uncreative. Human beings differ from other species by their ability to conceive of ideas and plans before executing them. Capitalist production relations deny this by seeking to separate design and planning (mental labour) from routine manual labour. This reduces manual work to a bestial, inhuman level.

It should be stressed that Marx was not a critic of technological advance or of the machine. It was not the machine to which he objected but the way it was used under capitalism:

> Machinery considered on its own shortens the working time, whereas when it is used for capitalistic purposes it lengthens the working day; when on its own it is intended to lighten work, its capitalistic use increases the tempo of work; intrinsically it is a victory of mankind over the forces of nature, but used for capitalistic ends it employs the forces of nature to enslave men; on its own, it increases the operative's wealth, used capitalistically it impoverishes him (Marx, 1962, p. 465).

Similarly, Marx insisted it was misleading to define 'capital' merely as physical assets such as machines, factories or buildings used for the production of goods or services. Machinery only becomes capital when it has the status of a commodity, owned and controlled by individuals who can oblige others to work for them. It is capital when it is an integral part of a social relationship in which some men and women are subordinated in their work to the dominance of others.

Thus Marx argued that the nature of work in capitalist societies — its fragmentation, specialised division of labour, confinement of workers to narrowly defined aspects of production — was alienating. But, apart from the physical and technological conditions of work itself, alienation also stems from the organisation of productive activity in a much broader sense. The social relations of production established under capitalism mean that workers are denied control over what is produced and why it is produced. Work is organised for profit rather than the satisfaction of collectively determined needs. Labour power becomes a commodity like any other. Therefore, even those individuals who are fortunate enough to be performing satisfying and creative work in modern society may still be alienated, since, for Marx, alienation is an objective condition which exists even if the workers are not subjectively aware of their condition.

Empirical studies of alienation

One of the most oft-quoted empirical studies of alienation in modern industrial society, by Blauner (1964), departs almost immediately from the framework established by Marx. Blauner, though believing that certain relationships and work arrangements are objectively satisfying, starts from the assumption that it is the technology itself, rather than the social relations of production within a capitalist economy, that is the 'cause' of alienation. He argues that not all workers are equally alienated, because they are exposed to a range of different technologies. Alienation is 'a general syndrome made up of a number of different objective conditions and subjective feeling-states which emerge from certain relationships between workers and the socio-technical settings of employment' (Blauner, 1964, p. 15). Blauner then attempts to define 'alienation' in such a way that degrees and types of alienation may be *measured*. (The theoretical and methodological issues which this attempt at measurement raises are examined in Chapter 11.) He suggests that:

> Alienation exists when workers are unable to control their immediate work processes, to develop a sense of purpose and function which connects their jobs to the over-all organization of production, to belong to integrated industrial communities, and when they fail to become involved in the activity of work as a mode of personal self-expression (1964, p. 15).

Blauner identifies four dimensions of alienation: powerlessness, meaninglessness, isolation and self-estrangement.

Individuals are *powerless* when they cannot control their own actions or conditions of existence. There are three modes of powerlessness: separation from the ownership of the means of production and the finished product; inability to influence managerial policies; and lack of control over employment conditions and over the the immediate work process. The latter, in turn, relies upon three freedoms: freedom of movement, freedom of choice, and freedom from oppressive constraints. Human-paced, rather than machine-paced, work is likely to be characterised by such freedoms.

Meaninglessness occurs when job specialisation and bureaucratisation reduce workers' organic connection with the work process and they experience difficulty in locating their contribution to it. Modern manufacturing, with its standardised production and extreme specialisation, increases tendencies towards meaninglessness.

Isolation arises when workers feel no sense of belonging in the work situation and are unable or unwilling to identify with the organisation and its goals.

The final dimension, *self-estrangement,* stresses the *subjective* experience of work and thus departs from Marx's conception of alienation as an objective condition. The individual gains no intrinsic satisfaction from work, is not involved or engrossed in the activity, and experiences boredom, monotony — even disgust.

Blauner, following his basic assumption about the importance of technology, then examines four different US industries, in order to assess how alienation varies with the type of technology. Printing is used as an example of craft technology, textiles as machine-tending, car production as assembly-line and chemicals as an example of continuous-process technology.

Besides stressing the importance of technology for alienation, Blauner recognises the influence of three other variables: the division of labour, the social organisation of the industry, and the economic structure within which it operates. He suggests that whereas technology sets limits on the organisation of work, it does not fully determine it, since different arrangements of the work process are possible within the same technological system. And while industrial development has brought about an increasingly elaborate division of labour within the factory, the four industries studied displayed different forms of the division of labour which, in turn, directly affected the amount of meaning and purpose the workers could experience in work. Similarly, work may be *socially organised,* either along bureaucratic lines, as in the car industry — with the emphasis on rules and rational procedures, or — as in printing — it may be organised on more traditional lines and involve more personalised practices and procedures. Finally, industries also differ in their *economic structure,* and factors such as competition in product markets, trends in demand, growth rates and profitability will indirectly affect alienation. When an industry is economically profitable and progressive, workers are less subject to pressure, more free from fears of unemployment and have opportunities to advance. Thus economic prosperity furthers a climate in which the worker becomes more integrated in the company.

However, despite these qualifications, Blauner is still essentially a technological determinist, given the overriding significance he attaches to technology:

Since technological considerations often determine the size of an industrial plant they markedly influence the social atmosphere and degree of cohesion among the work force. Technology also structures the existence and form of work groups, in this way influencing cohesion. Even the nature of discipline and supervision to some extent depends on technological factors. And technology largely determines the occupational structure and skill distribution within an enterprise, the basic factors in advancement opportunities and normative integration (1964, p. 8).

Blauner concludes that the four industries he studied — *because* of their different technologies — produce very different alienating tendencies.

Alienation levels in *printing* were low because the craft technology allowed workers access to traditional skills and relatively high degrees of control over tools and techniques. The unique nature of the product makes standardisation difficult, and a strong union, together with steady demand for the industry's products, induces a sense of security. Consequently powerlessness, so far as employment conditions are concerned, is slight. Similarly, the skills necessary to produce high-quality printed products mean that printers have considerable control over the pace, quality and quantity of their work, and must be free to move around the print shop — so powerlessness in the work process is also slight.

Meaninglessness is reduced because the broad craft-training allows printers to appreciate their contribution to the whole productive process. Isolation is also low, not only because lack of pressure and freedom of movement allow friendships to be made in the course of work, but also because the work itself also carries respect and status, both in the work-place and the wider community. Furthermore, the work is intrinsically satisfying and offers more than simply money, so the boredom and monotony characteristic of self-estrangement is seldom experienced.

The *textile* industry, on the other hand, employs a machine-tending technology producing standardised products for which there is a falling demand. The minimal skills required and the industry's concentration in the Deep South of the USA (where labour is cheap and plentiful) mean wages and unionisation levels are low.

The workers' control over the immediate work process is also minimal. The machine controls pace, output and the operatives' freedom of movement, so powerlessness is high. Meaninglessness is also quite high, because jobs are highly specialised, lack variety and involve only part of the process. However, the small size of many mills allows some workers to comprehend the full production process.

Social isolation, however, is fairly low because the industry's 'small-town' nature means that workers share common kinship and religious affiliations, and have personalised relations with management, which helps integrate them in their firms.

Similarly, self-estrangement is not as high as might have been expected given the lack of involvement implied in machine-tending; very few textile workers found their jobs dull or monotonous. Blauner suggests that they do not expect variety or interest in work and so do not define repetitive tasks as monotonous. However, textile work — especially for men doing what is regarded by them as 'women's

462   Introductory Sociology

work' for low wages — does not provide a favourable self-identity, and this encourages self-estrangement.

Blauner presents the textile worker as an example of the way objective tendencies to alienation may be overcome or lessened by the integration of work with family, religious and community life.

According to Blauner, the technology most likely to give rise to alienation is assembly-line technology, epitomised in *motor-car production*. The vulnerability of the car industry to fluctuations in the business cycle means that workers have little job security, and this powerlessness is only slightly off-set by the existence in the USA of a strong car workers' union. However, in the work process itself powerlessness is at a maximum. The worker follows a set routine at an exhausting and constant pace; the line controls both the quantity and quality of the product with physical movement restricted to the few feet of one's 'station' on the line. Meaninglessness is encouraged by the standardisation of the product and extreme fragmentation of work tasks. The implications are brought home by Beynon in *Working for Ford:* 'In the last minute or so a man working on the high line. . . in Fords. . . has fitted a petrol tank into the shell of a car and is starting to fit another' (Beynon, 1973, p. 11). Under such circumstances a worker cannot take personal pride in the job or feel that a unique contribution to the final product has been made.

Isolation is also high because the line's speed, and the workers' separation from one another, inhibit conversation and the establishment of personal relationships. The social organisation of large, bureaucratically administered factories discourages any sense of loyalty to the company or its products — most car workers insist they would never buy their companies' cars — and encourages isolation. Car workers are likely to be self-estranged and experience their jobs as dull and monotonous. The work itself provides no source of satisfaction: it is merely a necessary evil and a source of income. In a study by Chinoy a worker remarks: 'The things I like best about my job are quitting time, pay day, days off, and vacations' (Chinoy, 1955, p. 85).

Blauner's final example is the continuous-process technology found, for example, in the *chemical* industry, which, despite being the most highly mechanised of the four technologies surveyed, reverses the tendency towards alienation.

A key characteristic of this technology is that it restores the workers' sense of control over the work process. In chemical manufacture the raw materials flow through pipes from one stage of the process to another without being handled by the workers: temperatures, pressures and speeds are automatically regulated. It is the workers' responsibility to check that all is functioning smoothly, so that in contrast to the typical one-minute job cycle of car workers, chemical workers take a round of readings every two hours, checking perhaps fifty instruments in different places. According to Blauner, continuous-process production liberates workers from the rhythm of the machine, allowing them to set their own pace. It gives them freedom to move around the plant and to plan their own work schedule. Control is also restored in that they become free to use their own initiative. The jobs are much less standardised and repetitive than in mass-production industry, offering more interest and allowing workers to choose their own techniques and to experiment with different ways of doing the job. It also restores the meaningfulness of work. In assembly-line technology the work process is fragmented and workers cannot connect their fragment with the whole, but in automation meaning is restored in two ways. On the one hand, the workers gain an increased understanding of the overall process because they are no longer tied to specific work posts but can move around the plant and appreciate the complete sequence of operations. On the other, automation reconstructs the collective nature of work and encourages workers to think in terms of the whole rather than the part.

Blauner further suggests that in automated settings the work-team takes over responsibility for supervising the quality of work, consequently developing a more dignified and co-operative relationship with management. The dividing-line between manual and non-manual workers is broken down, encouraging the feeling of being part of a unified community.

Finally, because numbers of workers have been reduced to the lowest levels compatible with safety and efficiency (because output is determined by the equipment and not by

worker effort, and profit is relatively assured by high demand
for chemical products) employment is secure and unpress-
ured. Management can afford to adopt a more humane
approach — higher profit depending more on technological
development than on increased exploitation of the work-
force — in which greater account may be taken of workers'
own needs. Hence powerlessness, meaninglessness, isolation
and self-estrangement are all low.

Blauner suggests that because developments in technology,
division of labour and industrial social structure have affected the various dimensions of alienation in more or less the
same direction, the history of alienation may be seen as an
inverted U-curve (see Figure 11.1 in Chapter 11). At an early
historical period dominated by craft technology alienation is
at its lowest level and the worker's freedom at a maximum.
Freedom then declines and levels of alienation rise sharply
with the introduction of machine technology, and continue
rising until an extreme point is reached in the assembly-line
industries of the twentieth century: 'Thus ... a depersonal-
ized worker, estranged from himself and larger collectivities,
goes through the motions of work in the regimented milieu
of the conveyor belt for the sole purpose of earning his
bread' (Blauner, 1964, p. 182). In Blauner's account the
different industries may be seen as stages in the development
of technology, with the modern age characterised by continuous-process technology which increases the workers' control
over the work process, checks the further division of labour
and growth of large factories, and provides meaningful work
in a more cohesive, integrated industrial climate.

Blauner's study, although a central one which stimulated
further research, is flawed. His attempt to examine the
effects of *both* social organisation *and* technology upon the
experience of work would seem to qualify him for a place
among the *socio-technical systems theorists* who have
attempted to analyse the interdependence of technology and
a range of other factors in work and the wider society. However, his insistence on the primacy of technology — often in
defiance of his own data — disqualifies him.

Undeniably the technology of an industry can affect the
experience of work, but it has been argued that greater im-

portance should be attached to the *organisation* of that technology. We suggested earlier that technology is potentially liberating, and *could* be used to remove the drudgery from human labour, but, as Hyman (1972, pp. 100–1) argues:

> whether the consequences of technology are in fact liberating or enslaving depends on *how* it is decided to use the machines and on *who* makes these decisions. To attribute unpleasant social consequences to inanimate machinery is to evade examining those *human* actions which — deliberately or by default — are in fact responsible.

Even Blauner's own data emphasise the importance of non-technological factors in work satisfaction. In the case of chemical workers enlightened or progressive management policies, plus high wages, are cited to explain low levels of alienation. Printers are able to resist technological changes affecting their work satisfaction through union strength, while textile workers are cushioned against alienation by integration into the local community and its dominant institutions of kinship and religion.

Beynon's (1973) study of assembly-line car work supports this criticism. The technology of car assembly is internationally uniform, and yet levels of job satisfaction appear to differ from firm to firm and society to society. It is important to recognise that the *speed* of the assembly line is usually controlled by management. Consequently, workers wishing to maintain high standards of work may be prevented from doing so as much by management policy as the technique itself: 'The bad thing about the assembly line is that it keeps moving. If you have a little trouble with a job, you can't take the time to do it right' (Walker and Guest, 1952, p. 51).

Similarly, Beynon explains the *isolation* of Ford workers not only in terms of the technology but also in terms of management policies and the way in which manual workers are treated. One man pointed out the contrast between Ford executives and office workers, and the men on the assembly line: 'It's different for them in the office. They're *part* of Fords. We're not, we're just working here, we're numbers' (Beynon, 1973, p. 121). Another commented: 'Ford class you more as machines than as men. They're on top of you all the time. They expect you to work every minute of the day.'

Blauner, then, underplays the way in which power operates in the work-place itself and the importance that the
workers' lack of formal control has for their experience of
work. In addition, his contention that under automation the
worker is no longer dominated by the technology but is lib-
erated by it and allowed a new dignity, responsibility and
sense of function has been questioned by more recent
research, by Nichols and Beynon (1977) on the
chemical industry and Gallie (1978) on oil-refining.

Both these studies stress that continuous-process technology requires *shift-work,* which imposes very real constraints
on the workers' overall pattern of life. It is intensely disliked
by those subjected to it and is seen as damaging to health,
family and social life — dominating rather than liberating.

Furthermore, both studies contradict Blauner's contention
that automation reduces the exploitation of workers, because
management no longer has any need continuously to reduce
manning levels already reduced to levels compatible with
safety and efficiency. Gallie points out that one of the distinctive features of continuous-process technology is the
difficulty in defining what constitutes a satisfactory level of
manning, even from the viewpoint of technical efficiency.
Managers and workers in his French and English refiner-
ies had very different ideas about satisfactory levels, and this
led to considerable conflict. Whereas managers wanted to
reduce costs by reducing manning levels, workers wanted to
maintain existing levels, or increase them, because these influenced the intensity with which they were required to
work, the quality of team life, the degree of inconvenience
caused by shift-work, and their job security.

Similarly, Gallie suggests that — despite automation
reducing much of the hardship and unpleasant features of
traditional mass-production industry — Blauner's description
of the typical work task was based on a very small section of
the work-force, and that the tasks of most refining operatives
were substantially less advantageous than he suggested.
Nichols and Beynon, too, stress the negative side of chemical
production for the majority of workers. They comment: 'as
we walked around the site what struck us most strongly was

. . . the noise, the heat, the dust and the large number of men who were paid to hump one-hundred-weight bags of fertilizer' (Nichols and Beynon, 1977, p. 11).

Most work in the plant was unskilled 'donkey work' (ibid, p. 12) and not the demanding, dial-checking work emphasised by Blauner. Even control-room work — despite being easier than the humping and loading of sacks — was not so satisfying as Blauner implies. It was *not* teamwork — most of the control-room operatives worked alone — it *was* stressful, and it *was* noisy: 'You just listen to this noise. It's just a steady drone isn't it? Well, imagine having to sit in this hour after hour watching everything go OK' (ibid, p. 20).

Finally, both studies suggest that it is mistaken to see automation as *necessarily* leading to higher levels of satisfaction, social integration and more harmonious class relations. Automation is perfectly compatible with very different systems of power and organisation within the work-place and wider society, and these will help determine the relationships between managers and workers and the quality of the work experience.

Orientations to work

Technological-determinist and socio-technical systems approaches tend to attribute alienation or satisfaction in work to the effects of experiences of the work environment *on* the worker — that is, to a predominantly unidirectional process. However, it is possible for workers to find jobs boring and monotonous and yet be 'satisfied' with them if they do not believe they have the opportunity or right to enjoy work. Some workers may define an 'acceptable' or 'satisfactory' job as one which is reasonably well paid, clean and safe, only rejecting 'alienating' work if they *expect* to find interest, involvement and self-expression in work.

Such an attitude may indicate, therefore, that we need to consider the *orientations* which workers bring to their work. These may well vary from individual to individual in the same occupation, in such a way that reference merely to technological arrangements, and other work conditions, may be insufficient to explain workers' satisfaction or dissatisfaction.

Reference to actors' orientations constitutes an important element of the *social-action* approach to work satisfaction.

In Britain the 'affluent worker' studies conducted by Goldthorpe and Lockwood in Luton provide one of the best-known examples of this action approach (see also Chapters 2 and 11 for a further discussion of this work). Their study of car assemblers, process workers and machinists found that most of the workers bitterly disliked many aspects of their work — its monotony, pace, fragmentation, stifling of initiative, and so on. This, of course, would have been sufficient for Blauner to label these workers 'alienated' and to seek the primary cause in the technology employed (though, of course, this uniform dissatisfaction embraced workers in different types of technology). However, despite *disliking* the nature of the work, they were on the whole firmly attached to their jobs, having made few concrete attempts to find alternative work. How can this paradox be explained? Goldthorpe and Lockwood maintain that the explanation lies not only in the nature or conditions of the work itself but in the attitudes and values which the men brought to their work from outside. They argue that the Luton car workers came to work with an *instrumental* orientation, not looking to work for emotional, creative or social satisfaction but merely as a means for providing the wages which would allow them to live the kind of life they valued *outside* work. Work, then, is regarded as an *instrument* valued only for its use in satisfying other needs, a means to an end rather than an end in itself.

The affluent worker studies, then, would appear to demonstrate that for some groups of workers work can be a depriving experience and yet still be tolerated in return for the extrinsic rewards in which they are primarily interested.

The value of Goldthorpe and Lockwood's contribution lies in their rejection of attempts to explain work behaviour and attitudes purely in terms of the working conditions themselves. Work-places are *not* closed systems, and attempts at explaining work behaviour *must* range outside the factory gates, and particularly beyond the influence of technology on worker behaviour and attitudes.

However, a one-sided emphasis on an action approach also has its dangers, particularly in underestimating the force of objective and material constraints upon workers and in overestimating the degree of *choice* they have in determining the conditions under which they have to work. As we have seen, Braverman argues that, objectively, the work that most people are asked to perform in capitalist societies is highly fragmented, offers little chance to exercise skill or initiative, and has, in his terms, been deskilled and degraded. As Blackburn and Mann observe:

> the *absolute* level of skill of all but the very highest jobs is
> — to say the least — minimal. Eighty-seven per cent of our
> workers *exercise less skill at work than they would if they
> drove to work*. Indeed, most of them expend more mental
> effort and resourcefulness in getting to work than in doing
> their jobs (Blackburn and Mann, 1979, p. 280, our
> emphasis).

Furthermore, various studies — Goldthorpe and Lockwood's among them — demonstrate that a high proportion of people actually *experience* work as tedious, monotonous and unfulfilling: that is, their subjective experiences are in line with the objective nature of the work.

Goldthorpe and Lockwood suggest that their workers willingly accept deprivation at work in order to satisfy their material aspirations in other spheres of life. However, it is the *willing* nature of this acceptance that must be questioned. We must beware of seeing the identification of instrumental attitudes towards work as in any way a unique 'discovery'. Instrumentalism is better regarded as an *unsurprising* consequence of the capitalist organisation of work, in which the survival and standard of living of an individual is dependent upon the selling of labour in an open and competitive market, and upon the kind of bargain that one can strike with an employer. The degree of choice that one can exercise given such a structure is necessarily limited.

Blackburn and Mann attempt to modify Goldthorpe and Lockwood's position by introducing a conceptual distinction between *strong* and *weak* orientations. A 'strong' orientation indicates a situation in which concern with one type of work reward dominates to the exclusion of all others (Goldthorpe and Lockwood's instrumental orientation would fall into this category), while a 'weak' orientation indicates a situation where a worker may have a whole set of expectations and priorities about work which have to be reconciled in some way.

They argue that orientations can only guide behaviour if the individual has sufficient knowledge of all the job conditions likely to influence his choice, in both the external job market *and* the internal market of the individual firm. The strong form of orientation would obviously simplify the problem of job choice for the worker, while the weak form would create greater difficulties.

However, Blackburn and Mann found very little support for the notion of strong orientations and very little for the weak form, or for orientations generally. They were not particularly surprised by this because the objective labour market so limits the choices available to workers that there is little scope for orientations — which implies choice — to develop.

Their workers did make choices, but these involved them in sacrifices. They point out that a manual worker cannot actually choose to work in one of the professions even if his 'orientation' is to do so, and it is only in the manual working class that people *have* to sacrifice — more or less completely — other work rewards in order to receive that which is most salient, such as relatively high wages. Blackburn and Mann argue that while the importance of money wages may appear to dominate (given lack of opportunity to choose other rewards), a distinction may be made between 'alienated instrumentalism' — where other rewards are not seen as significant and the aim is to make enough money at minimum cost to non-work life — and the direct concern with high wages which may be a temporary response to the financial burdens experienced at particular periods in life.

Goldthorpe and Lockwood's own data would seem to indicate that most workers took on depriving work because of family pressures, especially after the birth of the first child, when financial commitments were greatest. Similarly, Beynon (1973) suggests that the degree to which workers *choose* car-assembly work is highly debatable. It was one of the few decently paid jobs in an area of high unemployment, and most workers only expected to do it for a few years.

However, with mortgages and family commitments their chances of changing jobs grew more and more remote. (The Personnel Department at Ford were aware of this and preferred to take on mature workers, with home, family and hire-purchase commitments.)

Goldthorpe and Lockwood were right to broaden the debate about job satisfaction and alienation to encompass the world outside the factory gates. However, the same sorts of criticism may be directed against them as have been directed at Blauner's over-reliance upon 'self-estrangement' and workers' subjective experiences of the work situation as indicators of alienation. Blauner regards the subjective satisfactions of textile workers as a factor offsetting their objectively depriving work conditions, and thereby reducing their levels of alienation, but it could equally well be argued that their apparent acceptance of work deprivation — far from reducing alienation — is an indication of just how greatly alienated they are. The same thing may be said about 'instrumental orientations' to work. Marxists would argue that alienation is an objective condition inherent in the structure of capitalist society and that it cannot be 'measured' by probing subjective experiences and feelings which are themselves the product of that structure: one does not have to *feel* alienated to *be* alienated.

8.4   WORKER RESISTANCE

So far we have attempted to indicate ways in which capitalist employers try to exert control over labour. We turn now to the various ways in which workers attempt to resist this control and examine how far the organisation of workers into trade unions serves to rectify the unequal balance of power that employers enjoy in relation to their employees.

We have argued that one of the fundamentals of capitalism is that work has the status of wage-labour. Jobs are located within a labour *market,* and individuals wanting to work must first find an employer willing to pay a wage or salary in return for the disposal of their skills, knowledge or physical strength. Labour, under capitalism, is a commodity like any other, and its price depends upon conditions in the market.

Legally, of course, relations between employers and workers are governed by a contract of employment which, theoretically, is freely agreed between them. In reality, however, the notion of a free contract is dubious. The concentration of economic power in capitalism means that employers can virtually dictate the broad outlines of the employment contract. This contract is indeed free, in that people are not physically forced to work, but as we pointed out in Chapter 2 the alternative to not working for workers is very much more drastic than it is for employers.

Admittedly, market forces may occasionally work to the benefit of labour, with workers able to wring concessions from employers when their skills are scarce or in demand. Moreover, workers who organise themselves into unions or associations are far less vulnerable than isolated individuals. This recognition of the inherent weakness of the individual worker and of the advantages to be gained by *collective* action lay behind the early development of the trade-union movement, which helped workers offer or refuse their services collectively rather than individually. Consequently, it is often argued that collective bargaining lies at the heart of the trade-union movement as the means by which workers might counteract the power of the employer.

However, collective bargaining must not be seen as restoring a balance of power between workers and employers. For Hyman (1975) and Fox (1974), collective bargaining represents one way of challenging certain management decisions on issues which unions see as of immediate or special importance. But other equally important decisions could be challenged if they *did* possess decisive power. Most union/management disputes centre upon wages, or who does what work and under what conditions, or who should join what union — issues which are of obvious significance to both sides, but not ones which touch the fundamentals of the capitalist system. Most of the time trade unions are striving to effect marginal improvements in the lot of their members and attempting to defend them against arbitrary management action. What they do not do is to challenge management on such basic principles of the social and industrial framework as private property, the hierarchical nature of the organisation, the extreme division of labour, and the massive inequalities of financial reward, status, control and autonomy in work. Similarly, they have little or no say in decisions made within an organisation on issues such as management objectives, markets, capital investment and rate of expansion. Moreover, rarely do they challenge such principles as the treatment of labour as a commodity to be hired or dispensed with at the convenience of management.

As suggested in Chapter 4, one effect of collective bargaining is to oil the wheels of capitalism and make it work more smoothly. As Clarke argues:

> collective negotiation may secure better terms for the sale of labour power — but it does not begin to question the acceptability of wage slavery. Thus workers' organisations, which were created in opposition to capitalist control, may have come to serve as an element in that control structure (in Clarke and Clements, 1977, p. 16).

In this view the bureaucratic structure of large unions works against fundamental change at the societal level and prevents unions from presenting a radical alternative to the status quo. They have been moulded according to the contours of capitalist industry through their acceptance of the sectionalism encouraged by capitalism, of skilled versus unskilled, carpenter against electrician. For example, commitment to maintaining wage differentials has blurred awareness of the common problems of workers inherent in capitalist work relations. Crucial in the development of such tendencies was the growth of union bureaucracy, with official leaders who institutionalised sectionalism and consolidated oligarchical control. The voice of the individual member has tended to become lost in these large, impersonal, union machines.

However, despite the difficulty of direct membership control of nationally organised unions, this does not exclude worker participation and control at other levels. In Britain shop-floor trade unionism and shop-floor resistance to managerial prerogatives exist as an embarrassment to unions and management alike. Workshop organisation, often led by shop-stewards, has increased earnings at factory level, and eroded management control *at the point of production*. It is at this level that workers can be most effective in determining the conditions under which they work.

Before we examine some of these techniques, and the extent of their effectiveness, we must examine the employment contract more closely. The obligations of employers are relatively precise and specific: they agree to pay a specified wage or salary, provide holidays, pensions and other fringe benefits, and to observe certain legal requirements. Here, their obligations to employees ends. On the other hand, the obligations on workers are imprecise and elastic. It is normally impossible for workers to agree to perform a certain amount of manual or intellectual labour, and employers never know how much work is available or how much labour they need at any particular time. Consequently, they need to be able to make flexible use of their labour force, and the contract of employment allows them to do just this. Rather than agreeing to expend a measured amount of effort, employees *surrender their capacity to work;* and it is the job of management, through its power of control, to transform this capacity into actual productive capacity. Here again the 'equality' of the employment relationship gives the employer the right to issue orders, while imposing on workers the duty to obey.

Yet there are limits to what employers can reasonably ask, and limits to what employees have to obey. The law often defines such limits (for example, through safety regulations), but an informal limit, tacitly acknowledged by manager and worker, often prevails, just as there is a tacit agreement about the level of effort which will be accepted by both as a reasonable equivalent for a given rate of wages. However, these understandings are imprecise and fluid, and such things as production speeds, manning levels, job allocations, performance standards, and the whole gamut of practices governing workers' relations with one another and with management, may depend upon a shifting set of understandings and traditions which are never identical in any two work situations. The power of employers may be substantial but they are still dependent, to a certain extent, upon their work-force. In most work organisations the commitment and co-operation of the most ordinary employee is necessary because constant supervision is impossible and a disaffected labour force can easily sabotage production. The vulnerability of employers to hostile action by employees increases as the work process becomes more technically sophisticated or the functions of the labour force become more strategic. As Hyman (1975, p. 26) puts it:

> in every work place there exists an invisible frontier of control, reducing some of the formal powers of the employer: a frontier which is defined and redefined in a *continuous* process of pressure and counter-pressure, conflict and accommodation, overt and tacit struggle.

It is at this frontier that workers are most successful in controlling their conditions of existence, though still remaining vulnerable to the forces of capital.

Management attempts to set certain goals for workers and expects a certain rate of work and quality of product for what is defined as 'a fair day's work'. These standards may be extremely rigid and be resented and resisted by workers. Beynon (1973, p. 135) shows how the imposition of these standards and the timing of jobs which often accompanies them, is questioned on both ethical and scientific grounds by workers subjected to them:

> They decide on *their* measured day how fast *we* will work. They seem to forget that we're not machines. . . The standards they work to are excessive anyway. They expect you to work the 480 minutes of the eight hours you're on the clock. They've agreed to have a built-in allowance of *six minutes* for going to the toilet, blowing your nose and that. It takes you six minutes to get your trousers down.

However, in some cases workers deliberately avoid working to management's standards, if the machine allows and if they can do so without breaking their contract. Sometimes these 'restrictive practices' mean that workers' potential wages are cut (as we saw in our discussion of the Hawthorne experiments). It is misleading to view this behaviour as sheer bloody-mindedness — rather, it represents an attempt by workers to exercise control over the work process and to carve out some autonomy for themselves. It is also a rational attempt to protect a job over which they only enjoy a very fragile hold:

> Workers who restrict their output, who 'malinger' at work, frequently justify themselves by their need to regulate the supply of labour. 'If we all worked flat out it would be dead simple what would happen. Half of us would be outside on the stones with our cards in our hands' (Beynon, 1973, p. 133).

Beynon points out that in car-assembly work the method of work and the strategic position of a particular section in the overall plant assist workers' attempts to make significant gains in job control. Similarly, market conditions affect workers' ability to influence control over line speeds, manning levels and work allocation. During periods of market boom advantages may be pressed home. During one such period Beynon found that the strategically placed small-parts section was able to establish manning levels almost twice as high as those considered reasonable by management. But, as shop stewards recognised, such advantages are often short-lived.

The same applies in the case of demarcation disputes. The media and other commentators frequently publicise occasions when five men with different trades are involved in a simple task capable of being performed by any one of them. These disputes are frequently attacked for their triviality, but they have an entirely rational basis. It is perfectly understandable, given the insecurity of employment with which ordinary workers are faced, that they should attempt to establish some form of property rights in their jobs by drawing demarcation lines around them.

The organisation of work around systems of payment allows us to demonstrate how the 'frontier of control' is 'defined and redefined'. Systems of payment by results — 'piecework' — were often introduced by employers as a means of intensifying the pace of work and of getting employees to agree to a rate for the job *as individuals* rather than collectively. However, in certain industries this system of control was turned against its instigators. The spread of piecework encouraged the growth of work-place union organisation, which in turn brought the piecework bargain under collective control through the mediation of the shop steward. The rate for a job would often be determined after a battle between workers and stewards on the one hand, and first-line management on the other. The latter would often be willing to make concessions rather than risk halting production. When jobs or production methods are constantly changing many bargaining opportunities arise which can have two main consequences: bonus earnings may be achieved far in excess of formally negotiated basic wage rates, and a strong shop-steward organisation can emerge with an influence over the labour force based on concrete bargaining achievements.

Workers' success in turning piecework to their own advantage may depend upon the *internal control system* of management. Junior managers often have aims and interests which conflict with those of top management, and are often allowed to override the decisions of, for example, personnel departments, in order to ensure that production quotas are met. This allows the union at shop-floor level to win improvements in conditions and establish precedents valuable for subsequent negotiations. However, firms with more sophisticated systems of internal information and control can limit the autonomy of first-line management and hence the ability of workers to apply pressure in a fragmented way. Such developments as productivity bargaining, measured day-work and the reinforcement of work study as the basis of payment by results are unified by their concern with the elaboration of management cost controls and consistently applied industrial-relations policies. The aim of employers is to present workers with a more uniform front by centralising negotiations, over all but the most trivial and routine issues, at the level of senior management. Important tactical decisions — such as when to 'take on' workers over threatened strike action — can then be made within the framework of a conscious long-run strategy. In this way managements attempt both to increase their control over labour costs and labour utilisation, and to reduce the effectiveness of shop stewards and their influence over their members.

8.5   THE EFFECTIVENESS OF POINT-OF-PRODUCTION RESISTANCE

Implicit in our discussion so far has been the important role played by shop stewards in point-of-production bargaining and control strategies. National collective bargaining only provides the bare framework, leaving plenty of scope for local interpretations and modifications, the relevant location for which is the work-place. Here, the activities of shop stewards help fill the gaps left by the formal operations of the trade-union/management structure. Although shop stewards are often presented in the media as 'trouble-makers' and the instigators and leaders of unofficial strikes, most managements tolerate — if not actively encourage — their existence, recognising that they *prevent* more disputes than they cause by helping to iron out local difficulties. They also provide a means by which shop-floor workers can make their voice felt in an era of large-scale bureaucratised trade unions.

However, the part played by shop stewards in the overall system of industrial relations — and the attempts to influence manning levels, piecework rates, job demarcation, and so on — illustrate the *relative* ineffectiveness of the piecemeal struggles that take place within the structure of capitalist industry.

Managements are often able to emasculate shop stewards by using managerial power to encourage 'reasonable' demands. Beynon (1973, p. 158), for example, reports a manager as saying:

> It's difficult to say what type of steward does best for his members. A militant may well force a few concessions, but we'll always be waiting to get them back or to make life difficult for him. While a quiet, more reasonable bloke may be less dramatic he'll probably get more for his members because if he's in any trouble we'll help him out. We make concessions to him that we wouldn't make to the other bloke.

So, while workers and stewards may 'destroy' the occasional supervisor, work in a factory means working, to a very large extent, on management's terms: 'While a shop steward may find himself in a situation where he has to challenge management's authority on the shopfloor, he is more often in situations where he is forced to play the game management's way' (Beynon, 1973, p. 158).

The policy of rewarding 'reasonable' shop stewards and punishing militants is pursued by many managements, and it subjects those affected to intense pressure to conform to accommodative relationships. Such accommodation becomes particularly important the more the stewards' preoccupations centre on the routine problems and day-to-day issues of the work-place. Here, the *personal* relationship between management and union representatives can exert a major influence on the outcome of negotiations. This reliance on personal considerations, however, must be seen as weakness when one considers the wider issues of the exercise of power at the societal level:

> when strategic interests of workers and employers are at stake, the *mobilisation of power* becomes of critical importance; and union representatives who are accustomed to rely on a 'reasonable' relationship with management may find themselves disarmed (Hyman, 1975, p. 109).

Similar qualifications apply to nearly all the tactics operative at the point-of-production level. Herding, for example, while recognising the necessity of, and reasons for, such shop-floor tactics, also comments that:

> Gains made in collective bargaining or through grievance processing and pressure tactics on the plant or shop level normally tend to strengthen the better situated plant, or the more strategic group within the plant at the expense of others (in Clarke and Clements, 1977, pp. 261–2).

Similarly, Hyman, while recognising the rationality of demarcation disputes, questions their long-term effectiveness, suggesting that 'It might show a higher level of rationality were workers to devote their collective energies to resistance to the employment status which condemns them to permanent insecurity' (1972, p. 134).

Nichols and Beynon, reviewing the methods open to process workers to control their work conditions, including sabotage, point out that:

> Jacko spoiling clean product, his mates practising their version of 'job rotation' [sharing out work and rotating jobs informally], regulating the size of their work teams and maximising the time they spend in the rest room — what these and other activities have in common is that they are entirely *covert*. They take place outside of established union—management relationships. *The significance of this is that while in certain circumstances management is prepared to turn a blind eye to them, it may also — quite arbitrarily and with a monopoly of right — choose not to do so* (Nichols and Beynon, 1977, p. 136, our emphasis).

However, the limited efficacy of *all* piecemeal attempts at job control becomes apparent in the face of that everyday feature of contemporary capitalism: redundancy. Efforts to combat employers at the point of production are emasculated if the intention is to cease production altogether.

8.6   PROFESSIONALISATION: AN OCCUPATIONAL STRATEGY

Although much of our argument so far has concerned manual labour, it has much wider applicability. In capitalist societies *all* non-owners of the means of production have to offer their labour or services for sale on the market. However, some groups are able to do so on more favourable terms than others. For example, in the division of labour a distinction is made between manual and intellectual skills, with intellectual skills generally commanding both greater material and symbolic rewards. Consequently, white-collar workers tend to enjoy certain advantages compared with manual workers. One group of white-collar workers has been particularly successful in controlling the conditions under which they have offered their skills for sale: these are the *professions*. Given our theme of *control,* we can examine the argument that professionalism may be viewed as a device — and a very effective one — by which certain occupations attempt to establish control over occupational expertise and reward.

A precise and unambiguous definition of a 'profession' is difficult. Most people could probably name occupations which they consider to be professions, without being able to abstract the general characteristics behind their choice, apart from a vague feeling that professions differ from mere 'jobs' in being more respectable, prestigious and highly rewarded.

Academic writers on the professions have faced similar problems in isolating *the* characteristics of professions. Millerson (1964) has amalgamated the most frequently mentioned characteristics into a model profession, without insisting that *all* professions will display *all* the characteristics. These include: skill based on theoretical knowledge; an extensive period of education; the theme of public service and altruism; the existence of a code of conduct or ethics; insistence upon professional freedom to regulate itself; and the testing of the competence of members before admission to the profession.

However, professionalism is not an in-built or fixed quality of particular occupations. Many occupations are constantly attempting to attain the status of a profession because they are aware of the advantages of doing so. In the USA, for example, undertakers have tried for years to achieve professional status in the eyes of the public. To this effect they have changed their name (to 'funeral directors'), emphasised their belief in service to the public, and have tried to insist on college degrees for entry to the occupation. Thus over the years an occupational group may attempt to move itself, with greater or lesser success, towards professional status. Consequently, at any one time one may be able to distinguish between established, marginal and new professions.

To varying degrees, professions have been able to claim high status, high monetary and material rewards, and considerable autonomy, and there are conflicting sociological explanations of why they have been so successful in these respects. For many years the generally accepted interpretation of the professions was that provided by *functionalism*.

The functionalist interpretation of professionalism

Functionalists take as their point of departure the unique role of the professions in society and the special relationship that exists between the professional practitioner and the client.

They argue that work performed by professionals involves 'central values', such as health, justice and education, and is therefore of functional importance for all social groups. Consequently, this work commands both high material and symbolic rewards.

Furthermore, since the situations in which clients consult professionals are so crucial, and since professional expertise is so much greater than the clients, the latter, irrespective of their status, must be persuaded to submit unquestioningly to professional authority (to follow doctor's orders, for example).

However, this means that clients may be vulnerable to exploitation by the professional. Therefore, it is necessary that professions institutionalise various procedures and norms to *protect* clients. These protective mechanisms include: the socialisation of prospective professionals during the prolonged training period; a formal code of ethics; the ideal of public service; the disciplinary procedures of the profession; and, most importantly, the testing or qualifying process by which the competence of each professional is ensured.

Hence the functionalist interpretation claims to explain *both* the high status and high incomes accruing to the established professions, *and* (in addition) many of the specific characteristics of the professions.

An alternative interpretation: professionalism as control

The alternative view of the professions, as expressed, for example, in the work of Johnson (1972), claims that the characteristics of professionalism function as a means of occupational control and work to the benefit of *professional practitioners themselves* rather than the public. Similarly, the *image* of public service, altruism, and the disinterested pursuit of a vocation propagated by professions, is an *ideology,* used to *justify* the higher incomes and prestige of the professional.

Many of the long-established and most influential professions are those that have professional bodies which have a legal right to test the competence of prospective members. These, which Millerson (1964) calls the 'qualifying associations', include such bodies as the British Medical Association and the Institute of Chartered Accountants. They control the right of individuals to practise the profession and are able, by their control over entry, to control the number and type of practitioners in a particular field. Such control eliminates, or drastically reduces, competition from those who have not received the profession's seal of approval and creates an *artificial* shortage of practitioners. By controlling the supply of practitioners in this way the profession is able to command high salaries and comfortable working conditions for its members. As Ben-David (1964) puts it, commenting on the medical profession, 'control of entry into the medical societies boosts the income of doctors out of all proportion to that of comparable professions the same way as monopoly increases profit'.

One of the major implications of this perspective is the implicit parallel drawn between the occupational strategy of the professions and that of certain craft unions. Craft unions have traditionally attempted to control their market situation by insisting on long periods of apprenticeship for prospective craftsmen, and, by limiting the ratio of apprentices to journeymen, have been able to maintain an artificial shortage of craftsmen. Studies of apprenticeship claim that this is not very effective as a means of education, but *is* relatively successful so far as its regulatory functions are concerned. Liepmann (1960), for example, argues that apprenticeship regulates entry to the occupation, and protects jobs, by establishing demarcation lines between skills and by obtaining agreements with management to the effect that in a time of recession non-apprenticed labour is laid off before craftsmen. Moreover, 'skilled' craftsmen may use this fact to negotiate higher wages. As we shall see, professional associations use essentially similar strategies.

Some professions not only restrict entry to their occupations but, unlike craft unions, have secured a *legal* monopoly of the right to perform particular tasks. For example, it is illegal for a person not on the General Medical Council register to accept money for the diagnosis and treatment of medical problems. During the past century physicians in Britain have used their influence to ensure that many new medical occupations — dieticians, physiotherapists, chiropodists, for example — do not pose a serious threat to the dominance of doctors. Doctors have succeeded in obtaining legislation which ensures that professions 'supplementary to medicine' may only carry out treatment after prior diagnosis by a doctor, thus subordinating them to the authority of doctors. Lawyers, too, have retained a virtual monopoly over such areas as house conveyancing. Illich (1973) has referred to this process as 'occupational imperialism': a process of carving out an occupational territory and preventing even the competent outsider from practising the skill. So, while the practices of job demarcation and the closed shop by trade unions are often roundly condemned, essentially similar practices by professional bodies are accepted as the norm.

Again, then, the alternative interpretation of the professions presents this particular element of professionalism as a strategy protecting the interests not of the public but of the profession itself. In fact, the *Report on Professional Services* by the Monopolies Commission (1970) concluded that 'a number of the restrictive practices carried on by professional groups and justified on the basis of community welfare looked . . . rather like arrangements for making life easier for practitioners at the expense of their clients'.

But how can the ethical codes and disciplinary procedures, characteristic of the professions, be explained using this alternative perspective? Three basic points are crucial.

First, professional ideology emphasises service to the client, but in fact the client is rarely given the opportunity to express satisfaction or dissatisfaction with the service received. Professionals usually insist that only fellow professionals are qualified to assess their performances, but their own ethical codes usually prohibit one professional from criticising another, at least in public.

Second, ethical codes are often concerned with preventing internal competition, rather than guaranteeing the quality of the service or protecting the public. Many professions, for example, restrict advertising so as to prevent attempts at fee-cutting which might adversely affect overall professional remuneration.

Third, studies by Carlin (1966) in the USA and Elliott (1972) in Britain reveal that the disciplinary committees of professional bodies deal mainly with cases where professionals have brought *adverse publicity* to the profession — being cited as co-respondent in a divorce case or being found guilty of drunken driving, for example — or where they have 'competed' with fellow practitioners. Few professionals are disciplined, and those that are tend to be the least influential.

Moreover, although most professional associations deny any affinity with trade unions, condemning many aspects of trade-union activity as 'self-interested', many professional associations do engage directly in collective bargaining, as well as acting as pressure groups lobbying Parliament for improvements in salary and working conditions. For example, the British Medical Association (BMA) tries to avoid all links with the trade-union movement and attempts to cultivate the image of doctors as neutral professionals. But its General Medical Services Committee negotiates very effectively with the National Health Service on behalf of doctors, and another organisation, the British Medical Guild (BMG), collects and administers a fighting fund for doctors in case of strikes or overtime bans. The BMG has no members, and is merely a puppet organisation used by the BMA for some of its trade-union-like activities.

We have argued, then, that all occupations seek to control the conditions under which they offer their labour; and professionals seek to do this as much as manual workers. Like trade unions, professions engage in collective bargaining, control entry to the occupation, and seek a monopoly of the right to practise so as to create a scarcity of licensed practitioners. In these ways the profession attempts to protect its skills and to improve its bargaining position in a market economy. As Parkin (1971, pp. 21–2) puts it:

> Although long and costly training is usually defended as an essential preliminary to ... professional work, there is little doubt that much of it is of little practical value and is

simply a device for restricting the supply of labour. The persistent efforts of many white collar occupations to become professionalized may be understood ... as an attempt to enhance their market scarcity, and so increase their power to claim rewards.

And Johnson (1972) defines professionalism as a special means of occupational control whereby both the needs to be provided for, and the manner in which they are to be dealt with, are defined by the producer. At the same time, he argues, the notion of professionalism as involving public service and lofty ideals is still fostered, because it is an *ideology* which helps to justify the privileges of the professions. (For a discussion and critique of the functionalist approach, see Chapter 2.)

8.7   INDUSTRIAL CONFLICT

Probably the most publicised area of industrial relations and the most criticised area of trade-union activity is the *strike*. The media and politicians often encourage the belief that the problems of British industry and its economy may be laid at the door of strikers and the unions, who make Britain a particularly strike-prone society suffering from its own peculiar 'disease'. Furthermore, strikes are presented as the pathological breakdown of normally smoothly functioning systems of industrial relations. We shall examine both these viewpoints shortly, after analysing the patterns of strikes revealed by official government statistics. The pattern of strikes in Britain in recent years is shown in Table 8.1. Until about 1970, despite the greater frequency of strikes, most were of considerably smaller scale and shorter duration than previously. However, over the last ten years the trend seems to be towards longer and larger strikes.

However, despite the recent upward turn in working days lost, it is still incorrect to see Britain as a particularly strike-prone country. This myth was exploded by Turner (1969), who demonstrated that six major industrial countries, plus Eire, had higher rates than Britain, and that rates for the USA and Canada were almost five times higher than in Britain. Figures for 1973–7 show that six countries — Canada, Italy,

TABLE 8.1
British strike statistics: annual averages 1965–78

	Number of strikes	Workers involved	Working days lost (000)
1965	2,354	868	2,925
1966	1,937	530	2,398
1967	2,116	731	2,787
1968	2,378	2,255	4,690
1969	3,116	1,654	6,846
1970	3,906	1,793	10,980
1971	2,228	1,171	13,551
1972	2,497	1,722	23,909
1973	2,873	1,513	7,197
1974	2,922	1,622	14,750
1975	2,282	789	6,012
1976	2,016	666	3,284
1977	2,703	1,155	10,142
1978	2,471	1,001	9,405

Source: *Department of Employment Gazette*, July 1979, p. 731.

India, Denmark, the USA and Eire — have higher strike rates than Britain (Central Statistical Office, *Social Trends 1980*).

Turner argued, moreover, that whatever inconvenience and expense may arise from strikes, the extent of economic damage involved is often exaggerated by both media and employers. It is frequently claimed, for example, that disputes in the motor industry 'cost Fords £x million a day'. However, such losses are often presented in terms of the selling price of the cars, and not simply lost profits. In fact, most of manufacturing costs comprise fuel, wages, power and materials — which are *not* lost during a strike. Also — partly because of the morale-boosting effect of strikes — lost production is often made up after the strike ends. In some cases, that production could not have been sold anyway: many strikes occur during recession periods, when production is not needed and managers are more willing to 'push' their workers to strike action.

Finally, many authorities have pointed out that production lost through industrial stoppages is far less than losses due to industrial accidents and illness:

> The number of working days lost through industrial disputes — 10.4 million in 1977 — is still small compared to losses through sickness. Sickness benefit was paid for 310 million lost days in 1974/75. Total days lost . . . must have been considerably more than that because sickness benefit is not paid for short absences and is not paid at all in public service jobs with entitlement to sick pay (Central Statistical Office, *Social Trends 1979*, pp. 92–3).

And Knowles (1952, p. 271) comments: 'the loss of time and output through managerial inefficiency . . . may sometimes be considerable, but while the time lost by workers is measurable, that lost by management is not'.

Interpreting the absence of strikes as an indication of 'good' industrial relations must also be questioned. Strikes are only one way in which industrial discontent is expressed — other manifestations of conflict include absenteeism, high rates of labour turnover, political action by both sides of industry, sabotage, pilfering, inefficiency, restriction of output, and so on. Industrial conflict may in fact be regarded not as a 'malfunction' but as an integral part of capitalist society where there is a permanent conflict of interest between employers and workers. At the very least, this corresponds to the characteristic market conflict in a capitalist economy between buyer and seller: the buyer wants to buy cheap and the seller to sell dear. Conflict, then, is built into the labour/capital relationship, and strikes are but one expression of wider class divisions in society.

Indeed, strikes may be seen as 'functional' for society, in that they confine discontent within manageable limits. Dahrendorf (1959), for example, has suggested that the potentially violent and revolutionary class conflicts of nineteenth-century Britain have been tamed by the development of formalised systems of industrial relations separate from the 'political' sphere. Strikes, unlike·revolutions, can be contained within this institutional framework. This, in large part, helps explain the hostility to *unofficial strikes*.

TABLE 8.2
Official and unofficial strikes

	Total	Stoppages official	% official
1970	3,906	162	4.1
1971	2,228	161	7.2
1972	2,497	160	6.4
1973	2,873	132	4.6
1974	2,922	125	4.3
1975	2,282	139	6.1
1976	2,016	69	3.4
1977	2,703	79	2.9
1978	2,471	89	3.6

Source: *Department of Employment Gazette*, July 1979.

As Table 8.2 indicates, unofficial strikes account for approximately 95 per cent of all recorded disputes, and those not recorded would make this figure larger still. The majority of strikes in the motor industry, for example, last less than a day, and these, by their very nature, are unofficial. Conversely, many unofficial strikes are unofficial in name alone, beginning unofficially but later receiving union backing and qualifying for retrospective strike pay. Many others may be described as quasi-official, in that union leaders give tacit support but not formal backing — which may be prevented by rule-book or procedural restrictions. On other occasions official support may be withheld from a strike simply in order to save union money. So, many unofficial strikes are not *anti-*official and may simply represent a more effective way of settling spontaneous local grievances without recourse to the formal and cumbersome union machine.

However, we suggested earlier that because unions have accommodated themselves to, and been integrated into, the structure of capitalist society, it is to be expected that dissatisfaction with capitalist social relations may be expressed in dissatisfaction with, and hostility towards, formal, bureaucratised trade unions. In many instances the unofficial strike is the only way in which rank-and-file unionists may exercise *any* degree of control over their working lives and over full-time union officials.

Thus strikes — official or unofficial — may not necessarily be about money or working conditions but may be concerned with exerting control over work and over distant, institutionalised trade unions. This may be illustrated by analyses of the 'causes' of strikes. Knowles (1952), for example, attempted to analyse changing causes of strikes in Britain by classifying all disputes during the period 1911–47 into one of three categories. He called those concerned with issues of principle or with trade-union recognition 'ideological', those concerned with wages or hours 'basic', and those revolving around manning arrangements and matters of work routine 'frictional'. He concluded that the *proportion* of all disputes due to ideological or to basic causes had decreased over the period, while the proportion due to frictional causes had increased.

Knowles's analysis has a certain plausibility and coincides with the belief that the rapidity of technological change in the post-war period and accelerated changes in administrative and organisational procedures have produced more issues of a frictional kind over which conflict can occur. Hyman (1972), however, questions this analysis, not least because of the distorting influence of disputes in the mining industry, in which the majority of strikes occurred up to the 1960s. In mining, prior to the introduction of the basic day rate, most disputes were frictional, which skewed the national pattern of strikes in Knowles's analysis. Hence, in other industries excluding mining in the post-war period, demands for straightforward wage increases precipitated the majority of strikes; Hyman cites the 1970 statistics in which 70 per cent of strikes were due to wage disputes, with 'frictional' disputes comprising a mere 15 per cent.

However, his main criticism is of Knowles's *use* of the statistics, not his conclusions. Although Hyman agrees that economistic reasons are behind many strikes, and that money *has* to be important to most workers, he warns against accepting the actual demands made in a strike at face value (as Knowles appears to do). For example, in Gouldner's 1954 study of the *Wildcat Strike* a group of American gypsum miners, striking for the first time in the history of their plant, demanded a considerable wage increase as a condition for resuming work. They had been previously content to work for low wages for years, and Gouldner argues that the strike was more the result of a whole range of changes in the management and organisation of the plant which had destroyed the traditional understanding previously existing between workers and management. Thus, according to Gouldner — and Hyman would agree — the underlying motive behind wage demands may be frustration about working arrangements and specific aspects of managerial control; demands for higher wages may be seen by workers as the only legitimate, or realistic, compensation for their frustration. This, in turn, may be because many aspects of working life other than wages are often treated by employers as non-negotiable. In other words, the reasons why people down tools and refuse to work may be very complex, but the terms they demand as a condition of a return to work may be governed by what is traditional in collective-bargaining procedures, and by what they can reasonably hope to get. As Hyman (1972, p. 131) puts it, 'demands may be formulated during the course of the strike simply because, conventionally, strikes have to focus around some demand: they can only be settled if there is something to negotiate about'.

Strikes are invariably more complex than they appear on the surface and may have a wide range of causes, with not all the participants sharing the same motives for action. And once under way a strike may develop its own momentum. We can be fairly sure, however, that the 'causes' sometimes suggested by the media (which tend to trivialise strikes) are very seldom the real reason for strike action.

The study by Lane and Roberts (1971) of the dispute at the Pilkington glass works in Lancashire in April 1970 illustrates both the complexity of strikes and some of the general themes pursued in this chapter. Pilkington had historically attained a dominant position for itself as the major employer of labour in the area, and as a family firm had obtained the acquiescence of the work-force by instituting various welfare measures and by stressing a paternalistic concern for its em-

ployees. However, the firm's national and international expansion, and the consequent employment of new managerial
staff, gradually and inevitably lessened its dependence upon
paternalism and upon the local area and work-force. The
strike which occurred provided an opportunity to withdraw
from an outdated relationship — it was partly *due* to the
changing relationship — which was no longer of direct
economic utility to the firm.

The strike itself was 'unofficial' — neither organised nor
sanctioned by a trade union — and lasted seven weeks. It
began in a spontaneous and unexpected manner and, on the
surface, appeared to be about money. A wages error in one
department — a bonus was missing — led to a stoppage while
shop stewards conferred with management. However, quite
spontaneously, some workers decided to press for a small rise
in pay before returning to work. Gradually, over a period of
days, workers from other shifts, departments and plants were
contacted and most decided to back the strike.

Three main points emerged from Lane and Roberts's detailed account of the strike which are relevant here. Primarily,
despite the 'spark' of the wage discrepancy and the demand
for an increase, the strike represented a challenge to managerial authority, particularly that of the new career managers
who were gradually replacing the Pilkington family in the
day-to-day running of the firm.

Second, however, the strike also brought to light the
contradictory attitudes of manual workers towards the firm:
a combination of 'exaggerated deference' on the one hand —
for Pilkington so dominated the local labour market that
people feared to offend them — and 'dull resentment' at their
dependence on Pilkington on the other:

> Everything was bubbling away and sooner or later it had to
> explode. It wasn't just the young workers. . . it was some
> of Pilkington's long serving and 'most trusted servants'
> who were most militant. Their children had grown up,
> they'd paid off their mortgages, and it was a chance for
> them to make up for the suffering they had endured in the
> past (Lane and Roberts, 1971, p. 187).

Finally, the strike provided a challenge to the General and

Municipal Workers Union (GMWU), the established union at Pilkington, which should have been representing the workers' interests. By the end of the strike the nucleus of a sizeable breakaway union had been created. The GMWU was taken by surprise when the strike broke out, but local union officials then attempted to persuade the men to resume work and leave negotiations over pay to the normal channels (the Joint Industrial Council). The local officials only reluctantly agreed to support the strike when the determination of the rank and file became apparent, and furthermore their support only involved declaring the strike 'official at branch level', a meaningless phrase which served to alienate the strikers further when they later learned that official support had, in fact, been withheld.

Lane and Roberts, by emphasising that unofficial strikes are always likely to be frowned upon by union officials, raise two issues of basic importance to our discussion. First, the role played by unions in contemporary society is often one of taking the heat out of conflict situations and of trying to reduce conflict to predictable routine; and second, such a tactic may not always be successful, in so far as workers see their interests differently and have the opportunity to pursue them.

Earlier we raised the question of whether the existence of a strong union movement escalates industrial conflict or reduces it. Some authorities — the 1968 Report of the Donovan Commission on Trade Unions and Employers' Associations, for example — have urged the strengthening of trade unions as a means of reducing the outbreak of industrial conflict and particularly unofficial strikes. However, as Lane and Roberts (1971, p. 56) point out, in such reports, 'the "unions" have been narrowly defined in terms of the union apparatus, and the consequences of this narrow definition have been recommendations aimed at increasing the power of the officials over the membership'.

Therefore, 'strengthening' the trade unions has often involved the appointment of more full-time officials drawn from the union hierarchy rather than the shop-floor. This can imply increasing the power of trade-union officials to discipline members who deviate from official policy, and can also involve the incorporation of union officials into the 'establishment' and the formation of close consultative relationships with government and the civil service.

However, these same processes which make the union apparatus stronger and more efficient also increase the likelihood that a disparity of viewpoints will develop between the union hierarchy and rank-and-file members. Hence, 'revolts' by members of the union become an increasing possibility. These, as in the Pilkington case, may in fact lead to an *escalation* of conflict and to its abatement. Such 'revolts', however, may force 'responsible' 'statesman-like' union officials into articulating their members' demands rather than lose all influence over their actions.

8.8   ATTEMPTS TO INTEGRATE THE WORKER

The abandonment of paternalism by Pilkington may be seen as a recognition that such methods of control were unlikely to pay dividends when production is organised on an international level. However, it also raises the point that when workers are threatened by unemployment, or when control is relatively secure, the 'problem' of job satisfaction need not delay management long. In fact, general recognition of the need to be concerned with job satisfaction only began to develop in most advanced capitalist countries in the late 1960s at the tail end of a 'boom' period in their economies. It was recognised that under the conditions of the 'affluent society' the threat of unemployment was no longer real enough to motivate workers, and yet the demands of international competition required greater productivity and reduced costs. At this time the ideas of management consultants (like Herzberg), advocating job-enrichment, job enlargement, job rotation, participative management styles, and so on, increased in popularity. From the 1960s onwards the upsurge in worker activism and militancy also occurred, along with the growing influence of shop stewards and the increasing incidence of 'unofficial strikes' to which we have referred. As Braverman (1974, p. 29) puts it, 'Clearly . . . the problem does not appear with the degradation of work, but only with overt signs of dissatisfaction on the part of the worker.'

It has long been recognised that workers suffering boredom or frustration do not always produce to their full potential, and this frustration may be expressed in a variety of
ways which create problems for management. Wherever possible, workers will try to 'escape' from the job, and (as we
have noted) absenteeism, job-changing and high labour turnover represent 'concealed' forms of industrial conflict. For
example, in car-assembly work — despite studies such as
Goldthorpe and Lockwood's which show that a high percentage of workers with instrumental orientations stick with the
job — rates of absenteeism and labour turnover tend to be
very high. Beynon observed high labour turnover at Fords,
despite lack of alternative job opportunities and managerial
policies rejecting men aged under 20 and preferring family
men with mortgages. In 1966 the paint, trim and assembly
plant lost 1,140 manual employees out of a total labour force
of 3,200, in 1967 about 800, in 1968 1,160 and in 1969
1,800 (Beynon, 1973, p. 90).

Sabotage — in management's eyes — represents an equally
damaging alternative to escaping from the job. Sabotage may
be used as a tactic for winning better working conditions and
as a means of control, but it may also arise out of sheer
frustration and dislike of the work. It can be very expensive
for management: 'In some plants worker discontent has
reached such a degree that there has been overt sabotage.
Screws have been left in brake drums, tool handles welded
into fender compartments, paint scratched and upholstery
cut' (*Fortune,* July 1970). Taylor and Walton tell of the half
mile of Blackpool rock which had to be thrown away at one
firm: instead of the customary motif running throughout its
length, it carried the terse recommendation to 'Fuck Off' (in
Cohen, 1971, p. 219).

Consequently, management has had to seek ways in which
the advantages of job specialisation, bureaucratisation and
mechanisation can be maintained while reducing their unpleasant consequences for workers *and therefore for profits.*
They have been aided in this task by social psychologists and
management consultants such as Herzberg and Argyris.

Herzberg, in assessing the impact of job improvement
schemes such as job rotation (where workers move from one

sub-divided job to another, allegedly adding variety and increasing their knowledge of the overall process) and job enlargement (the combining of several sub-divided tasks), has argued that the combining of 'two or three meaningless activities [does] not add up to a meaningful one' (Herzberg, 1968, p. 113). He recommends 'job enrichment' as the solution to unsatisfying work: that is, providing jobs which challenge the intellect and which allow people to exercise initiative and responsibility.

In 1966, for example, he was commissioned to reorganise work at American Telegraph & Telephone (ATT), where labour turnover and inaccurate work characterised the claims and invoices department. Errors had been consistently high for years, and checkers had to be employed simply to duplicate earlier work. This work was broken down into ten separate operations. In reorganising it Herzberg made each clerk responsible for a particular section of the town so that she would always be dealing with the same clients and could feel responsible to them. 'Flexitime' was introduced and supervision relaxed. Subsequently, errors fell to 3 per cent, the checkers were no longer required, and over half a million dollars saved annually.

'Successes' such as this have given credence to the theories of those social psychologists who argue that human beings have 'needs' — such as that for self-actualisation — which need satisfying in work. However, the criteria for measuring the success of such schemes tend to be highly selective and loaded. Management's criteria for 'success' are usually reduction in costs or improvement in productivity, while the effects upon workers themselves are often ignored, except for the assumption that 'they worked harder, so they must be more satisfied'. So, for example, in the case of ATT, the checkers' redundancy was not regarded as a disadvantage of the scheme, though this could hardly have enhanced *their* job satisfaction.

The well-publicised schemes introduced by car manufacturers Volvo and Saab further illustrate the lack of altruism in management's concern with job satisfaction. In Sweden assembly-line work — because of labour turnover, absenteeism, rejection rates and high costs of supervision — is no longer a paying proposition. Both Volvo and Saab have introduced the team method of car assembly and have tried to make their factories more pleasant places in which to work. Volvo, for example, has attempted to reduce noise levels and has introduced joint management/worker canteens, saunas, coffee shops and picture windows. Productivity has not increased, but faults are fewer, and stand-by teams necessary to fill the gaps left by absentees can be smaller.

Both firms were *forced* to alter their methods because, in Sweden, car production failed either to attract or retain the kind of labour needed for smooth, high productivity. Attempts to exploit migrant labour from Turkey, Yugoslavia and Greece were inhibited by the trade unions and government policies. However, the better-educated Swedes were not prepared to accept the work as it was, and welfare measures which allowed four paid days off work without medical certification meant high absenteeism levels. The firms, then, were constrained to behave as they did and concern for the welfare of workers was not a primary consideration. Volvo has recently opened a plant in Norfolk, Virginia, a poor part of the USA with few alternative employment opportunities and an acquiescent working population. The new methods are *not* used here. It would appear that traditional assembly-line methods, in circumstances where potential employees have few alternative employment opportunities or limited welfare support, can be cheaper than the costs of providing more satisfying work.

Similar doubts may be expressed about the nature of more 'radical' attempts to involve workers in decision-making, such as those recommended by the Bullock Report (1977). It has been argued that most such schemes for the extension of industrial democracy simply involve the absorption of workers into capitalist forms of control rather than the elimination of these control structures.

In Britain one such form of industrial democracy — joint consultation procedures — enjoyed considerable popularity after the Second World War in both government and management circles. It was hoped that employee consent could be strengthened, and work motivation improved, through the voluntary adoption of formally constituted committees representative of management and employees meeting regularly to discuss common problems and interests.

Joint consultation, however, was to prove a disappoint-ment, for, as Blackburn and Mann (1979, p. 293) emphasise,

> Co-determination is rather different [from job-improvement schemes] for it does provide a second channel of decision-making to the formal chain of managerial, bureaucratic hierarchy, but despite the claims made by its proponents it is a *second* channel. It does not replace the hierarchy. Nor does it alter anything in the market.

Moreover, whatever the effects of joint consultation upon the perceptions and satisfactions of the worker representatives, it does little for those of the shop-floor workers whose jobs remain unchanged, and who remain subject to hierarchical authority and control.

Furthermore, many union officials regard joint consulta-tion as a device by which management hopes to undermine rank-and-file loyalty to their collective organisations and thereby to weaken them. In fact, it has been argued that the general orientation of managerial proposals on industrial democracy of this type is to take the initiative away from the labour movement and to restrict conflict by *containing* it within joint regulatory institutions. This in turn tends to blur the divergent interests of management and workers, erode the basis of independent worker organisation, and thereby inhibit the capacity of workers to take defensive action.

Similar criticisms have been levelled at attempts to incor-porate workers through the medium of employee director-ships. Although worker directors may benefit both sides, in reducing mutual suspicion and gaining some influence for workers in policy-making, the rationale behind such schemes is still one of making the *existing system* operate more smoothly. Usually worker directors have no real effect on decision-making and have no sanctions or power at their dis-posal to enable them to make an impact at board level.

It can be argued that capitalist economic relations are essentially exploitative and hierarchical, with little possibility of employers voluntarily introducing elements of industrial democracy, except as a manipulatory device designed to incorporate workers more fully into the control structures of capitalism. As we shall see, some of the discussions of the way in which work affects non-work activities such as leisure — that by Rigauer (1969), for example — suggest that these attempts at incorporation extend well beyond the field of work itself.

8.9 WORK AND NON-WORK

Many analyses of the relationship between work and leisure take the form of polarities in which contrasts are drawn between leisure which duplicates work, and that which compensates for it. On the one hand, there is the 'spillover' leisure hypothesis, in which alienation from work becomes alienation from life, and in which the mental stultification produced by work permeates leisure. Wilensky (1960, p. 545), in a vivid caricature of this position, describes the worker who

> goes quietly home, collapses on the couch, eats and drinks alone, belongs to nothing, reads nothing, knows nothing, votes for no-one, hangs around the home and street, watches the late-late show, lets... the TV programmes shade into one another, too tired to lift himself off the couch for the act of selection, too bored to switch the dials.

This is contrasted with the *compensatory leisure hypothesis,* where leisure beomes an explosive compensation for the deprivation of work. Wilensky (1960, p. 545), in another caricature, describes the car-worker who

> for eight hours gripped bodily to the main line, doing repetitive, low-skilled, machine paced work which is wholly ungratifying, comes rushing out of the plant gate helling down the super-highway at eighty miles an hour in a second-hand cadillac Eldorado, stops off for a beer and starts a bar-room brawl, goes home and beats his wife, and in his spare time throws a rock at a Negro moving into the neighbourhood.

Similar ideas are expressed by those writers who suggest that urban industrial society involves the segmentation or separation of the various spheres of life, such that work is separated from leisure, production from consumption, work-place from residence, and politics from recreation. Conversely, there are those who see a reversal of this trend towards the segmentation of life, and hypothesise the fusion of work and leisure. According to this view, work is becoming more like play, and vice versa.

Parker (1976) suggests that the 'fusion versus polarity' argument has been conducted at the societal level instead of the sub-cultural level of particular occupations and work milieux. He suggests that 'fusion' occurs when we refuse to divide up our lives into work and leisure, 'polarity' when such a division is insisted upon. The corresponding functions of leisure may be labelled 'spillover' and 'compensatory'. According to Parker, work may be said to spill over into leisure to the extent that leisure is the continuation of work experiences and attitudes; leisure is compensatory if it seeks to make up for dissatisfactions felt in work. Parker adds a third function, distinguishing between extension, opposition and neutrality. With the *extension* pattern, the similarity of at least some work and leisure activities and the lack of demarcation between work and leisure are the key characteristics. Parker suggests that this pattern is typically shown by social workers, successful businessmen, doctors, teachers and similar people. The key features of the *opposition* pattern are the intentional dissimilarity of work and leisure and the strong demarcation between the two spheres. Those with tough physical jobs, like miners and oil-rig workers, may either hate their work so much that any reminder of it in their off-duty time is unpleasant, or they may have a love— hate attitude to it, such that it still constitutes a central life interest. He suggests a third pattern of *neutrality* consists of having leisure activities which are generally different from work but not deliberately so, and of appreciating the difference between work and leisure without always defining the one as the absence of the other. It is often associated with jobs which have been described by Berger (1964) as 'grey' — neither fulfilling nor oppressive, such as routine clerical or semi-skilled manual work. Such workers, he claims, tend to be as passive and uninvolved in their leisure as they are in their work.

From his own and other research Parker suggests that each of these patterns of the work–leisure relationship is associated with a number of work and non-work variables. People with high autonomy in work are likely to manifest the extension pattern, and those with low autonomy the neutral pattern. Extension is usually accompanied by a feeling of being 'stretched' by the work, neutrality by being 'bored' with it, and opposition by being 'damaged' by it. The likelihood of having some work colleagues among one's close friends seems to be high among those with the extension pattern and low among the neutrality group. Level of education varies. Those with the extension pattern are characterised by the highest education levels, while those with the opposition pattern manifest the lowest. Parker also suggests that in the extension pattern leisure functions mainly to develop personality, in the neutrality pattern 'chiefly as relaxation' and in the opposition pattern 'chiefly as recuperation from work'.

Basic criticisms of this whole approach are made by Elias and Dunning (1969). They are more narrowly concerned with establishing a theory of *leisure*, but their arguments carry implicit criticisms of Parker and similar theorists. They suggest that there has been an over-concentration in the literature on the work–leisure relationship, arguing that the characteristics and functions of leisure activities cannot be appreciated if discussion is confined simply to establishing the relationship between leisure and work. They disagree with Parker's assertion that, 'While it is possible to make statements about the nature of work and leisure separately, they have full sociological meaning only in relation to one another' (Parker *et al.*, 1967, p. 158).

Elias and Dunning argue that many theorists of the work–leisure relationship commit the basic conceptual error of equating spare-time activities with leisure activities. They suggest that in the conventional polarisation of work and leisure the term 'work' usually refers only to a specific type of work: that which people perform in order to earn a living. In our societies this is a strictly time-regulated and, in most cases, highly specialised type of work. However, we also have much unpaid work to do in our spare time. Only a portion of this spare time can be devoted to leisure *in the sense of a freely chosen and unpaid occupation of one's time — chosen primarily because it is enjoyable for itself.* So, although all leisure activities are spare-time activities, not all spare-time activities are leisure activities. Parker (1972, p. 24) recognises this when he argues that 'It is . . . necessary to distinguish leisure from allied concepts, particularly that of free-time.' However, by the time he comes to discuss work—leisure relationships he has apparently forgotten this distinction and is including work-related reading under his extension pattern.

Elias and Dunning distinguish five different spheres in people's spare time which shade into one another and overlap but which nevertheless represent different classes of activities. These are (i) the spheres of private work and family management; (ii) rest; (iii) catering for biological needs; (iv) sociability; and (v) 'mimetic' or play activities. Of central importance to their classification is the degree of *routinisation* involved in the various spheres. By 'routines' they mean recurrent channels of action enforced by interdependence with others and/or one's own bodily needs. These interdependencies and needs impose upon the individual a fairly high degree of regularity, steadiness and emotional control of conduct to which leisure provides the counter.

They argue that the specific functions of sport, theatre, racing, parties and all activities and events usually associated with the term 'leisure' have to be assessed in relation to this ubiquity and steadiness of emotional control. Hence their concern with distinguishing 'spare-time' from 'leisure'. They suggest that in a society where most activities are routinised leisure activities provide opportunities for emotional experiences which are excluded from the highly routinised parts of people's lives. In leisure — as they define it — the routine restraint of emotions which occurs in *all* spheres of life, and not just occupational work, can be relaxed publicly, with social approval and without danger to oneself or others.

Hence they would not agree with Parker, and those who argue similarly, that the function of leisure is necessarily that of providing 'relaxation from tension' or 'recuperation from the strains of work'. Rather, they suggest that the basic function of almost all leisure events is that of *arousing* tensions and that when they fail to do so boredom or disappointment can be created, as (for example) in a 'poor' football match.

They argue, then, that theoretical propositions which concentrate upon the value of leisure for occupational work or vice versa, or the relationship between work and leisure, block enquiries into the wider question of the intrinsic function of leisure for people in societies like ours — functions in relation to all aspects of their social life, including non-occupational aspects.

Such an approach — and that of Rigauer that follows — raises the question: Is the nature of work *and* leisure in societies such as our own the direct result of capitalism and capitalist social relations, or are they both the result of processes general to industrialised societies?

The Marxist Bero Rigauer (1969) has no doubt about the function of one particular leisure activity — sport — in capitalist society. He argues that an activity which once served as a counter-agent to work for the upper classes has now taken on characteristics which closely resemble those of work. The division of labour, mechanisation, automation and bureaucratisation which have produced 'rational' but dehumanised work have helped, he suggests, to determine the form, content and organisation of sports activities.

He argues that the gruelling training techniques thought necessary for achievement in modern sport mirror the alienating and dehumanising character of assembly-line production. Furthermore, the individual has been swamped by whole teams of experts and — particularly in team sports — is expected to comply with a prescribed tactical plan and fit into a fixed division of labour that he has played no part in working out. Consequently, just as in work, he has minimal scope for the exercise of initiative. (The American footballer required to perform moves called by the coach epitomises this development.)

Moreover, the bureaucratic administration of sports means that full-time officials, and not sportsmen themselves, decide on policy. So, despite his admission that room for exercising initiative is larger in sport than most forms of work, he claims that the gap is constantly narrowing. Sport has become a demanding, achievement-orientated and alienating area of behaviour. Consequently it follows that sport loses its potential for relieving the strains and tensions of work. The belief that sport can still fulfil this function, he argues, is still widespread, but such a belief serves as a 'masking ideology', hiding from the participants its real function — that of reinforcing in the leisure sphere an ethic of hard work, achievement and group loyalty necessary for the operation of an advanced industrial society. According to Rigauer, it helps maintain the status quo and bolster the dominance of the ruling class.

Rigauer is probably right to suggest that in many ways sport in industrial societies has come to assume a work-like character. However, his analysis is not entirely adequate: there are a *variety* of internal and external constraints which form the pressure to participate in sport and a *variety* of reasons why it occupies such a high place in the scale of values of modern societies. Just as in the work sphere, there is *resistance* to the attempts to bureaucratise, commercialise, professionalise and systematise sport — 'fun runs', for example. Different groups are proponents, on the one hand, of achievement-orientated values and, on the other, of values which stress the pleasure-giving leisure character of sport. Rigauer, however, paints a blanket picture which asserts that all sports in all industrial countries have developed work-like characteristics and hence function to serve ruling interests to the same extent (see Dunning and Sheard, 1979).

8.10 THE FUTURE OF WORK AND WORK SATISFACTION

What changes may be expected in the nature and meaning of work in industrial societies such as ours, and what is the role of trade unions likely to be in the struggle to provide more satisfying work?

Recent years have seen the growth of huge international corporations and conglomerates, seemingly committed to policies detrimental to the interests of ordinary people. These policies include the intensification of capitalist 'rationalisation', which is shorthand for widespread redundancies, greater work intensity and stricter wage controls. Under the changed economic circumstances of recent years, in which economic growth and near full employment have gradually given way to stagnation, inflation and decline, it may no longer seem necessary to buy off worker discontent with high wages and job-improvement schemes.

The new concentration of power by employers requires similar concentrations of power on the trade-union side. And, at first glance, union strength and organisation would appear to be increasing. The figures in Table 8.3 show that union membership has increased dramatically this century, both absolutely and as a percentage of the labour force, and that there are now fewer but larger unions. The *density* of unionism is also indicated — the number of potential members in the union — because number of unions and membership figures are not adequate in themselves. However, such figures cannot, of course, show the *character* of the various unions — which may range from 'mild' staff associations to

TABLE 8.3

Trade-union membership and density in the United Kingdom

Year	No. of trade unions	Total union membership (000)	Labour force (000)	Membership density (%)
1892	1,233	1,576	14,126	11.2
1901	1,322	2,025	16,101	12.6
1913	1,269	4,135	17,920	23.1
1920	1,384	8,348	18,469	45.2
1933	1,081	4,392	19,422	22.6
1945	781	7,875	20,400	38.6
1954	711	9,566	21,658	44.2
1964	598	10,079	23,706	42.5
1970	540	11,179	23,446	47.7
1974	498	11,755	23,689	49.6
1975	488	11,950	23,502	51.0

Source: Clarke and Clements (1977, p. 8).

much more militant trade unions — and without some knowledge of this the social significance of membership cannot be estimated. Both density and character are of particular significance so far as the unionisation of white-collar workers is concerned, as we shall see.

A further development hidden by these figures is that the industrial unions, once the areas of greatest strength in such industries as coal, cotton, railways and shipbuilding, are now declining in size, while the general unions, which developed after the craft unions as craft skills were degraded into semi-skilled machine work, are growing.

The most significant development, however, has been the growth of white-collar unions, several of which feature among the largest unions (for example, NALGO, ASTMS and the NUT.) Between 1948 and 1964 the numbers of white-collar unionists rose far more rapidly than those of manual union members, such that the proportion of all trade unionists who were white-collar workers increased from about one-fifth to about one-third. However, membership roughly kept pace with the growth of the white-collar labour force itself — that is, the *density* of white-collar unionism remained fairly stable at about 29 per cent. Since 1964, however, the situation has changed markedly, and the increase in white-collar unionists has outstripped the growth of the white-collar labour force, such that density has increased from 29 to 38 per cent.

A major factor in this growth has been the concentration of clerical and technical workers in large offices, providing conditions in some ways similar to those on the factory floor. However, the *character* of white-collar unions is of utmost significance here, since it has been argued that their activity has been more instrumental and less ideological than that of manual workers and that commitment to trade unionism may merely reflect a short-term goal of raising immediate wages. There are also grounds for believing that the support for unionism among clerical and technical workers is motivated by a desire to restore their previous status and differentials.

We have implied that changes in the work environment *may* wait upon changes in the structure of society more generally, and that concerted action by all employees is necessary to bring about such change. The development of the white-collar unions *may* represent a source of weakness so far as this concerted action is concerned. The weakness of unions generally is already exacerbated by the increasing employment — in both business and commerce — of professional managers. This means that ownership has become more impersonal and remote, and is rarely seen to be involved in the actual direction and management of the huge commercial and industrial undertakings that have come to dominate the economies of Western industrial nations. Moreover, the larger the conglomerate, the more likely it is that banks and finance houses will be involved in ownership.

These developments create two major problems for union power and union attempts to control conditions of work. On the one hand, dominant shareholders tend to spread their investments over a number of companies, which means that strikes and other traditional forms of resistance are less effective than those directed at individual owners. Consequently, strike action, in many circumstances, may do more damage to the economy than to the 'employer'.

Moreover, the development of multinational corporations means that strike action at a particular plant or directed against a particular national firm does not necessarily do serious harm to a particular giant organisation, which can simply step up operations elsewhere. Again, however, such action may affect the economic welfare of Britain generally — by reducing the export of cars, for example — thus drawing governments even more directly into the industrial arena with serious implications for the balance of power between employers and workers.

In the past governments have avoided *direct* intervention in the industrial sphere, though the state has always supported the institutional framework within which capitalism operates. However, as a large investor and employer of labour the state has an interest in keeping labour costs low. Moreover, government involvement with incomes policies in recent years, and its increasing intervention in collective bargaining, place unions in apparent conflict with governments as well as employers. In fact, it has been argued that governments' re-assertion of their right to intervene in determining the outcome of strikes, for example, has led to a renewed awareness on the part of workers of the political and class nature of the confrontations between employers and trade unions.

The huge, bureaucratically organised unions necessary to combat the power of state and employers almost inevitably run the risk of losing touch with the members they were created to represent. Furthermore, the attempts of union officials to co-operate with government in making incomes policies 'work' — against the interests of their members — lead to an ever-widening split between leadership and membership which finds expression in a variety of unofficial actions, including strikes. However, despite sporadic bursts of protest by shop-floor workers, they have been weakened by unemployment, redundancy, pressure to reduce manning levels and increase productivity, and technological innovations designed to decrease reliance upon labour power and to eliminate traditional skills. Even workers in high-level white-collar occupations, once relatively safe from degrading and deskilling tendencies, face a potential threat from micro-chip technology, and it remains to be seen whether their unions — faced with such a threat — can prove more effective, given their greater proximity to control structures, than those of manual workers.

8.11 CONCLUSION

In speculating about the future of work in societies such as ours we have offered rather pessimistic forecasts about the inability of unions and their members to exercise really decisive control over their working environments and lives. The declining profitability of capitalism in manufacturing industry, and large-scale unemployment in the traditional craft industries of Western Europe as a whole, does not augur well for moves to increase work satisfaction. The attempts by industry to cut costs in the absence of long-term growth would apparently increase the necessity for higher levels of state expenditure to help sustain 'acceptable' levels of employment. Instead, monetarist policies such as those of the British Conservative government necessarily involve cut-backs in such expenditure.

Optimistic predictions about micro-chip technology issuing in an 'age of leisure' — the twenty-hour week and substantial increases in holidays have been mentioned — would be amusing were not the implications of these, and other developments, so serious. Enforced idleness, redundancy and unemployment cannot, by any stretch of the imagination, be called *leisure*. There is no guarantee that under capitalism the fruits of technological advance will be shared out equally among the population, given that such technologies, and related developments, have had weakening effects upon traditional means of resistance.

This being said, we have to recognise that the relationships between technological innovation, social control and job satisfaction are very complex. Even in avowedly socialist societies the task of constructing satisfying and democratically organised work has hardly begun and remains a problem for the future.

REFERENCES TO CHAPTER 8

Allen, V. L. (1966) *Militant Trade Unionism*, London, Merlin Press.
Ben-David, J. (1964) 'Professions in the Class System of Present Day Societies', *Current Sociology*.
Berger, P. (1964) *The Human Shape of Work*, London, Macmillan.
Beynon, H. (1973) *Working for Ford*, Harmondsworth, Penguin.
Blackburn, R. M. and Mann, M. (1979) *The Working Class in the Labour Market*, London, Macmillan.
Blauner, R. (1964) *Alienation and Freedom*, University of Chicago Press.
Braverman, H. (1974) *Labour and Monopoly Capital*, New York, Monthly Review Press.
Bullock Report (1977) *Report of the Committee of Enquiry on Industrial Democracy*, London, HMSO.
Carlin, J. (1966) *Lawyers' Ethics*, New York.
Chinoy, E. (1955) *Automobile Workers and the American Dream*, New York, Beacon Press.
Clarke, T. and Clements, L. (eds) (1977) *Trade Unions under Capitalism*, London, Fontana.
Cohen, S. (ed.) (1971) *Images of Deviance*, Harmondsworth, Penguin.
Dahrendorf, R. (1959) *Class and Class Conflict in Industrial Society*, London, Routledge & Kegan Paul.
Dunning, E. and Sheard, K. (1979) *Barbarians, Gentlemen and Players*, London, Martin Robertson.

Elias, N. and Dunning, E. (1969) 'The Quest for Excitement in Leisure', *Society and Leisure*, December 1969, no. 2, pp. 50—85.

Elliott, P. (1972) *The Sociology of the Professions*, London, Macmillan.

Fox, A. (1974) *Man Mismanagement*, London, Hutchinson.

Gallie, D. (1978) *In Search of the New Working Class*, Cambridge University Press.

Goldthorpe, J. H., Lockwood, D. and colleagues (1968a) *The Affluent Worker: Industrial Attitudes and Behaviour*, Cambridge University Press.

——(1968b) *The Affluent Worker: Political Attitudes and Behaviour*, Cambridge University Press.

——(1969) *The Affluent Worker in the Class Structure*, Cambridge University Press.

Gouldner, A. W. (1954) *Wildcat Strike*, London, Routledge & Kegan Paul.

Herzberg, F. (1968) *Work and the Nature of Man*, London, Staple Press.

Hyman, R. (1972) *Strikes*, London, Fontana.

Hyman, R. (1975) *Industrial Relations: A Marxist Introduction*, London, Macmillan.

Illich, I. (1973) 'The Professions as a Form of Imperialism', *New Society*, 13 September 1973, pp. 633—5.

Johnson, T. (1972) *Professions and Power*, London, Macmillan.

Knowles, K. G. J. C. (1952) *Strikes: A Study in Industrial Conflict*, Oxford University Press.

Lane, T. and Roberts, K. (1971) *Strike at Pilkingtons*, London, Fontana.

Liepmann, K. (1960) *Apprenticeship*, London, Routledge & Kegan Paul.

Marx, K. (1962) *Das Kapital*, vol. 1, Harmondsworth, Penguin.

Millerson, G. (1964) *The Qualifying Associations*, London, Routledge & Kegan Paul.

Mills, C. Wright (1953) *White Collar*, Oxford University Press.

Monopolies Commission (1970) *Report on Professional Services*, London, HMSO.

Nichols, T. and Beynon, H. (1977) *Living with Capitalism*, London, Routledge & Kegan Paul.

Parker, S. (1972) *The Future of Work and Leisure*, London, Paladin.

Parker, S. (1976) *The Sociology of Leisure*, London, Allen & Unwin.

Parker, S., Brown, R. K., Child, J. and Smith, M. A. (1967) *The Sociology of Industry*, London, Allen & Unwin.

Parkin, F. (1971) *Class Inequality and Political Order*, London, Paladin.

Rigauer, B. (1969) *Sport and Work*, New York, Columbia University Press (English edn 1981).

Taylor, F. W. (1903) *Shop Management*, New York, Harper & Row.

Taylor, F. W. (1911) *Principles of Scientific Management*, New York, Harper & Row.

Taylor, F. W. (1967) *The Principles of Scientific Management*, New York, Harper & Row.

Turner, H. A. (1969) *Is Britain Really Strike Prone?*, Cambridge University Press.

Walker, C. R. and Guest, R. (1952) *Man on the Assembly Line*, Harvard University Press.

Wilensky, H. L. (1960) 'Work, Careers and Social Integration', *International Social Science Journal*, vol. 12, pp. 543—74.

9

Belief-Systems

9.1 INTRODUCTION

Most people live out their lives in a fairly stable pattern of daily encounters with others, whether in the home, at the shops, school or work. In these settings, actions can seem automatic and unthinking, and conversation accompanying them is normally carried out in terms of well-worn commentaries about the weather, the price of goods, the latest record, 'last night's result', 'the good news, the bad news', and so on. Much of the time these exchanges do not convey new information, since they are more devices for sustaining 'normal' patterns of social interaction. There is, then, a considerable amount of social 'patter' in 'public' that changes little from day to day, like the patter of the market tradesman. Everyday interaction tends to be most successful when 'short', 'sweet', and role-bound.

Despite its superficiality, the culture of everyday interaction in all societies bears the imprint of more articulate and critical social myths and ideologies, knowledges and beliefs, whether they be drawn from the institutions of religion, magic, science, politics, education as primary sources of ideas, or from secondary sources such as the media. In this chapter we examine the way in which these ideas are formed into what we call 'belief-systems'.

All people are more or less committed to a range of beliefs, attitudes, or opinions. Strongly held ideas are usually those that have been institutionalised among a body of like-minded people. The stronger and more persuasive a set of ideas becomes, the more it is likely to become an all-embracing system

of belief and ideology governing members' actions and interpretations of the world. Some of the strongest belief-systems
are those which have been formally instituted with specific
ends in mind, such as the major religions or political philosophies of the world. Belief-systems work because the actors
involved take account of others' ideas, intentions and behaviour. *What* we do and *why* we do it are comprehensible to
others.

At the same time, however, one need not assume that
accountability and comprehension necessarily imply social
consensus. Given that in any society there are different groups
with different social, economic and political interests, it is
likely that specific belief-systems will be associated with each
group. Specific ideas and beliefs may contradict other sets of
beliefs, so that controversy and conflict develop between
groups, as, for example, occurred in the struggle between religion and science in Europe in the eighteenth and nineteenth
centuries. It would seem that science won the battle: it is said
that we now live in a 'scientific age'.

Before proceeding further, however, we need to make some
general comments on the concept of 'belief-systems'. First,
to speak in terms of a belief-*system* is not to imply that the
beliefs making it up are fully articulated, clearly worked out
ideas ordered and arranged in a systematic, consistent fashion.
Rather, people may hold beliefs without any clear reason
why they do so (perhaps they are simply ideas that have been
passed on by custom and tradition). Similarly, people may
unwittingly hold contradictory beliefs simultaneously without this being in any way difficult or worrying for them.
Second, to proclaim a belief is to assert that one holds something to be true. This may be an assertion like 'I *personally*
hold X to be true, but don't require that you must as well';
or it could involve an assertion such as 'I believe that X is
true, and you should as well'. As we shall see, the second
assertion tends to figure more prominently in institutionalised belief-systems. Third, different belief-systems — say
those of magic and religion — will invoke different criteria in
measuring what is held to be 'right' or 'true'. If this is so,
then sociology must not make any quick and easy judgements about the truth or falsity of belief-systems which are

not based on the same type of assumptions that are used in 'modern' industrial society. In other words, we should not deride or denounce, say, witchcraft and magic as products of a 'primitive mind', expressions of stupidity and childishness. Instead, sociology should examine these belief-systems on *their own terms*, that is, in terms of the way they are used and described by *the very people who act* on them. This approach accepts that, as far as the actors who profess them are concerned, their beliefs do form a stable and rational set of ideas.

In short, then, belief-systems refer to those ideas that people hold to be right and true, which provide not only guides and rules for action, but also justifications for actions by which behaviour is made accountable to the self and to others.

Finally, as propositions that claim to be in some way true, beliefs imply access to 'knowledge': they can be treated as 'knowledge-claims', whether they be made generally or within the institutional contexts of science, magic, witchcraft, or religion. These institutions are deliberately established to give 'answers' to make the world (variously) accountable; they are also made up of people who claim to have special talents and abilities for discovering these 'answers' — 'scientists', 'magicians/witches', 'theologians'. If the 'layman' accepts this expertise, then these knowledge-specialists are in a very favourable position, enjoying power, prestige and perhaps material reward. Clearly, however, this has important implications. 'Experts' may maintain ideas which support their position, refuse to consider, reject, or even squash non-orthodox, competing ideas from other groups outside the institutional framework who challenge the expertise and ultimately basic livelihood of the incumbent professional experts. Vested interests may then operate to varying degrees and with varying effects in belief-systems, indicating that what is accepted will depend on power relations as well as cognitive considerations. In as much as this is so, knowledge-claims may have ideological dimensions in serving the interests of different groups; we shall develop this point later, particularly in our consideration of the mass media.

9.2 MAGIC AND SCIENCE AS BELIEF-SYSTEMS

Although European anthropologists have long since distanced themselves from any covert beliefs about white man's racial superiority, a considerable number of them did suggest that 'modern' — not so much 'white' — society is superior to, more evolved than, 'primitive' society. Some anthropologists, such as Frazer and Lévy-Bruhl, argued that primitive society's belief in magic, witchcraft, and totemic rites derived from the 'pre-logical' mentality of its people, a mentality that was essentially defective. It lacked the capacity to account for phenomena in terms of a logical, natural causality, a capacity enjoyed by people at a more developed stage of social and cognitive evolution: magic was seen to be crude, mistaken, suffering from inherent logical weaknesses that would be gradually acknowledged and displaced as 'primitive man' seeks and is shown the way to modern 'rational' thinking.

Few, if any, anthropologists would subscribe to this (ethnocentric) evolutionary thesis today. The belief-systems of modern industrial society are no longer given a privileged position at the top of some evolutionary tree: instead, belief-systems of whatever cultural origin are examined in their own right. Though they may be different from Western science in terms of *how* they account for the world, it is accepted that the account they use displays logical and rational characteristics just as Western science does. This change in perspective was in part due to the influence of the foremost British anthropologist of the last fifty years, Edward Evans-Pritchard (1902-73).

His major texts published in the 1930s are extensive ethnographies of three African tribes, the Nuer, Azande, and Bedouin, based on a number of years fieldwork living in their villages and camps and learning their languages. This use of participant observation was crucial: Evans-Pritchard insisted that one could only understand alien belief-systems by immersing oneself in their language, culture, and everyday activities. The anthropologist must seek out the assumptions and accounts of the world that underpin different systems, and be ready to accept that there is more than one way of constructing a rational and coherent belief-system. We can consider, for example, Evans-Pritchard's famous account of the Azande of Sudan in Central Africa.

Life among the Azande is built on a belief in witchcraft and magic. Whenever misfortune falls on someone, he or she consults a magic oracle which reveals the source of the witchcraft that has caused the mishap in the first place. To consult the oracle, a chicken is fed with a specially prepared potion ('benge') and is asked whether a particular person could be held accountable as the source of witchcraft. The diviner tells the potion to kill the chicken if the answer is 'Yes', and then, with a second chicken, to kill if the answer is 'No'. In the end the poison oracle provides an answer as to who is to blame for the misfortune. The sufferer can then go to the accused and publicly demand that the witchcraft stop. This public accusation is considered sufficient to prevent further trouble from the accused.

Witchcraft is not a source of great terror or fear for the Azande but is invoked as an everyday explanation for unaccountable events which are put down to the workings of 'fate' or 'chance' in the West. Witchcraft answers the question 'why *me*?', a question left unanswered in Western culture. Not all mishaps are attributed to witchcraft: as in any society, certain events are put down to technical incompetence — for example, cracks in pottery are seen to be caused by poor craftsmanship. Furthermore, the Azande are well aware that, for instance, there are diseases which make people sick, or that hippos may overturn boats and so cause people to drown. Yet the Azande asks, 'Why should *I* be sick while everybody else is well?'; or again, 'Why did the hippo attack *my* father, today, when he's been down the river a hundred times before?' Western science would simply say that it was coincidence that someone happened to meet an angry hippo in mid-stream on a particular day, and offer no further explanation. But the Azande are more curious than this and explain such apparently coincidental occurrences as witchcraft.

Witchcraft accusations — having been directed and confirmed by the poison oracle — are made against someone believed to be a jealous or envious neighbour. Normally, it is only neighbours who live together who accuse each other, since they are close enough physically and socially to envy one another, to quarrel, to compete and plan to hurt each other. The princes of the Azande, the Zande ruling class, are immune from accusations of witchcraft. At their personal courts, each prince owns an oracle which is used as final arbiter in maintaining peace and order, by confirming or rejecting witchcraft accusations made by one commoner against another after initial consultation with subsidiary oracles. Their immunity from witchcraft charges results primarily from the belief, reinforced by tradition and myth, that only they possess and control the magic of the major oracle whereby witchcraft may be detected. Such tradition and myth help to legitimate the privileges enjoyed by the aristocracy of Zandeland. The special status given to the knowledge-claims of the princes' oracles not only serves to maintain the social order but also the inequality of that order. As Evans-Pritchard (1967, p. 15) says, 'privileges invested in one class in society require the halo of myth'.

An accusation of witchcraft does not necessarily mean that the suspect will suffer great social opprobrium. The Azande believe that witchcraft is a *psychic* power emanating from a physical substance located in the intestines. A person may have witchcraft without using it intentionally to harm other people. This belief allows the accused to proclaim shock and amazement, to apologise and to promise that future be-witching will stop. This means that neighbours are encouraged to behave in an extremely courteous manner towards one another so as to minimise the likelihood of accusations. Hence, the belief in (non-deliberate) witchcraft ensures that good relations between neighbours in the homesteads can be maximised; small misfortunes can be accounted for, accusations made and acknowledged, and good will restored. As Douglas (1980, pp. 51–2) argues, 'The witchcraft belief-institution had a lubricating effect on community life. Grudges would not be allowed to fester . . . The air was cleared, and social life would go on.'

Major misfortunes, such as the death of a relative, are attributed to witchcraft being used in a deliberately malign manner by an evil witch. Deaths were, until stopped by British colonials, to be avenged by the death of the witch. When the witch was accused, he would be 'tried' by the final authority, the prince's poison oracle. He would be required to imbibe the poison ('benge'), and if death followed, the accusation was vindicated, and if not, the accuser would have to find another guilty party. If the accused refused to drink the poison, the court would administer it to a chicken to evaluate the charge, which (if proven) allowed the relatives of the deceased to spear the witch to death.

A correct accusation of witchcraft creates problems for the witch's kinsmen, since the Azande believe that witchcraft is inheritable, passing from male witch to son, or female witch to daughter. Hence, the immediate kin are suspected as witches. To allay witchcraft accusations against them, kin resolve to clear the name of their father or mother. This is done by the institution of the post-mortem, wherein the intestines of the deceased are examined by the court. If the court finds the accused to have been rightly charged and killed as a witch, his or her relatives may go so far as to deny that the person was a true member of their clan, that the witch was conceived and born illegitimately: if the mother is still alive she is forced to confess to adultery. This confession thus removes all suspicion of inherited malicious witchcraft from the living.

The Zande belief-system of magic and witchcraft institutions appears to serve two purposes:

(1) It works to relieve anxiety created by worry and frustration over unforeseen and inexplicable events by pinning blame on an accountable member of the village.

(2) Such accountability is typically required of people who are believed to be in competition, to be envious or spiteful: witchcraft accusations thus help to dissipate potential conflict between rivals and so reduce the level of enmity within the community. One cannot then dismiss Zande beliefs as 'foolish' or irrational: in many ways they are a reliable set of ideas that work well once one accepts certain assumptions.

Nevertheless, Evans-Pritchard recognised that Zande beliefs about witchcraft did not form a perfectly consistent body of ideas. Inconsistencies do not undermine the Zande faith in witchcraft, because the analytical questions bringing them into relief are never considered by the Zande. Such questions would presuppose assumptions and a perspective that is not part of what Evans-Pritchard (1937, p. 338) calls 'the idiom of their beliefs': 'They reason excellently in the idiom of their beliefs, but they cannot reason outside, or against, their beliefs because they have no other idiom in which to express their thoughts.' Thus, for example, there would be no point in asking the Azande how a man can be proven innocent of witchcraft by post-mortem when witchcraft is also believed to be present in all, and inheritable through descent. Again the Azande would laugh at a European who asked whether the poison would kill the chicken without any accompanying address. As Evans-Pritchard (1937, p. 315) says, 'If the fowl died they would simply say that it was not good "benge". The very fact of the fowl dying proves to them its badness.' Any such 'test', then, would actually reinforce rather than undermine the Zande belief-system. Within its terms, the Zande reason logically and coherently. If an oracle contradicted itself it would simply be said to have been addressed or prepared improperly, once again reaffirming the basic assumptions of the belief-system. These assumptions are used as interpretative resources, drawn on to account for the world, and establishing the point at which reasoning and further questions come to an end. As we shall see shortly, science itself relies on unverifiable assumptions, commitments towards certain perspectives that may encourage scientists to *ignore* evidence that appears to contradict their beliefs.

Evans-Pritchard's sympathetic treatment of the Zande culture not only made a more fruitful anthropology but also led to philosophical debate about the logical form of magic compared with that of science, and the sense in which *both* can be construed as belief-systems. Polanyi, for example, believes that it is possible to identify an idiom of belief operating at the heart of all scientific knowledge, albeit in a covert form. Implicit beliefs and assumptions have been screened from our eyes by the ideology of 'objectivism' in modern science, an ideology that insists that scientific truth is a matter of objectivity and not faith. This assumes that scientific theories are built on the observation of empirical 'facts' and the systematic consideration of evidence. Peering behind this curtain of 'objectivism', Polanyi (1958) brings to light a number of features common to both witchcraft and science.

There are, he says, three features working together to ensure that any belief-system is sustained as right and proper (for those who profess it) despite 'evidence' challenging its validity: their combination guarantees that questions, problems or issues not covered by the belief-system's assumptions will be 'unhesitatingly ignored'. First, Polanyi points to the 'circularity' of the ideas that constitute any belief-system: each idea in the system is explained through reference to another idea, the validity of which is never doubted. This other idea, however, only makes sense itself through reference to the original idea. All languages as symbolic systems embody this circular aspect. Thus, for example, a dictionary presupposes a literary circularity of meaning and legitimation; the definition of a word may itself be explained in terms of the original word — 'marriage' may give 'wedlock' which in turn is defined as 'a state of marriage'. This circularity promotes the stability of a system of ideas and beliefs: if one belief is doubted, it is justified through reference to a different belief, which, if challenged subsequently, is justified in terms of the original belief. Hence, as Polanyi (1958, p. 289) says, 'So long as each doubt is defeated in its turn, its effect is to strengthen the fundamental convictions against which it was raised.'

Second, Polanyi suggests that all belief-systems hold in reserve a supply of 'subsidiary explanations for difficult situations'. For the Azande, for example, failure of the oracle could be accounted for in terms of incorrect use of the device; similarly in science, certain events or phenomena not conforming to expectation may be explained away in terms of some auxiliary hypothesis. Thus conflicting evidence is often discussed in science as 'anomalous findings', quirks of investigation that can be ignored. In physics or chemistry many experiments are designed to show constant relations between two phenomena, which can then be plotted as a straight-line graph. Sometimes, one point on the graph is consistently out of line with the rest: students may be told to ignore this apparent anomaly, which is frequently dismissed as the result of incorrect method at some point in the experiment, an explanation which an Azande student would find most appropriate!

Third, belief-systems reject alternative views of the world by refusing to grant any legitimacy to the assumptions on which rival conceptions depend. This may mean that new ideas challenging orthodox knowledge-claims are suppressed from their first appearance, and those making them denied any respectability within the community of 'experts'.

According to Polanyi, then, these three features explain how, in practice, contradictory evidence or inconsistent findings do not normally lead to the overthrow of a set of ideas, be it Zande magic or European science. Such evidence can be explained away, denied any validity and meaning, or simply ignored. Hence all systems of knowledge rest on basic premises which are sustained by virtue of actors' *commitment* to them as 'true': ideas are reaffirmed as much by faith and trust as they are by any 'methodologically correct' procedures: 'believing is seeing, as much as seeing is believing'.

Polanyi's commentary forces us to reconsider the way in which scientific knowledge-claims are certified as correct by scientists. Most importantly, we are required to abandon the customary view that regards science as an activity which, by unbiased, neutral observation, accumulates evidence from which the universal laws of nature are derived. It would seem, then, that an intrinsic feature of scientists' work is their selective inattention to evidence or knowledge-claims which do not conform to their picture of reality.

Recent contributions to the area known as 'the sociology of science' have extensively documented the way in which the production and acceptance of scientific ideas depend on social and cultural factors (see, for example, Mulkay, 1979). The growth of this area of sociological research was partly due to the influential work of Kuhn (1970). Kuhn (1972, p. 82) identified what he called 'the dogmatism of mature science', which he defines as 'a deep commitment to a particular way of viewing the world and of practising science in it'. As a scientific field such as physics becomes more mature or developed, as the number of practitioners increases, as education courses are established and textbooks produced, so those working and training within it adopt common ideological commitment to what it is 'to be a physicist and study physics'. This dogmatic commitment provides the scientist with 'the rules of the game', *what* is to be treated as a scientific puzzle and *how* it is to be solved. These rules constitute what Kuhn (1972, p. 93) calls 'the paradigm' of a scientific field or speciality:

> Their paradigm tells [scientists] about the sort of entities with which the universe is populated and about the way the members of that population behave; in addition, it informs them of the questions that may legitimately be asked about nature and of the techniques that can properly be used in the search for answers to them.

Kuhn's notion of paradigmatic science can, then, be set against the misleading notion that scientists test their theories by collecting observable 'facts' which exist 'out there' in nature, awaiting observation and classification. Instead, scientists 'go out' armed with their respective paradigms seeking evidence, dealing with problems, that *confirm* it. As Kuhn argues, 'the challenge is not to uncover the unknown, but to obtain the known'. This clearly parallels Polanyi's concept of the 'circularity' of belief-systems, in as much as it suggests how scientific research operates in terms of a relatively closed system of ideas that are self-confirming. If counter-evidence to the paradigm does appear, it is typically ignored as an anomaly, and, says Kuhn, for good reason. An anomalous finding or unexpected discovery is, by definition, potentially subversive: it threatens to change the 'rules of the game' by which the paradigm works. Hence, the paradigm is a source of resistance to innovation in science. But if one stopped here, major innovations in science that have occurred — such as the shift from Newtonian to Einsteinian physics — would remain inexplicable. Kuhn explains that innovation takes place when anomalous findings become 'particularly stubborn or striking' such that they force scientists 'to raise questions about accepted beliefs and procedures'. When the paradigm consistently fails to deal with an increasing number of anomalous results, the scientific field experiences a period of major intellectual and social crisis, overcome by the formulation of a new paradigm.

Kuhn's analysis of the paradigmatic nature of science extends the general ideas raised by Polanyi. Polanyi was concerned to show how the *conceptual logic* of science is very similar in form to that sustaining the Zande belief-system; Kuhn indicates the way in which aspects of the *social institution* of science — textbooks, curricula, research communities — continuously sustain the conceptual commitments of its practitioners, guiding their activities, interpretations and accounts of the natural world, and reinforcing the stability of their scientific belief-system.

A commitment to a particular scientific interpretation of the world is therefore an ever-present interpretative resource that scientists use to justify their knowledge-claims, and encourages resistance to new ideas or 'deviant' interpretations. A considerable body of literature in the sociology of science examines the way in which non-orthodox knowledge-claims are received and evaluated by orthodox science (see, for example, Wallis, 1979). Case studies — for example, on parapsychology (Collins and Pinch, 1979), on acupuncture (Webster, 1979) — show how 'fringe' groups that threaten the conceptual and social status quo of science have been dismissed, but not on the basis of open-minded impartial scientific theorising and experiment: instead, many scientists have simply asserted from the outset that the existence of the kind of phenomena proposed is inconsistent with known reality, and therefore any findings, however carefully presented, must be the result of fraud or experimental error, and thus need not be taken seriously. Hence, as Mulkay (1979, p. 91) comments on parapsychology:

> For the critics of parapsychology, the central assumption that paranormal phenomena do not exist was never in question. Rather it pervaded and gave meaning to the whole armoury of formal arguments which they employed. It ensured that, for these critics, every item of evidence and every claim of reasoning provided further grounds for rejection of the deviant views.

This once again draws our attention to the circularity and self-confirming nature of orthodox science as an idiom of belief: as Polanyi argues, the stability of a belief system is apparent by 'the way it denies to any rival conception the ground in which it might take root'.

We see, then, that not only magic and witchcraft but also science can be regarded as belief-systems. We now want to focus attention on the institution of religion. As with science, we shall begin by comparing it with magic.

9.3   RELIGION

Religion may be said to be a system of belief about the individual's place in the world, providing an order to that world and a reason for existence within it. It has been institutionalised over the centuries, so that powerful religious organisations and ideas have arisen, like the Catholic, Islamic and Hindu churches. As such, it has a major influence in societies, affecting non-religious institutions specifically, such as the family or conjugal ties, as well as bringing about general social change, indicated by the great religious wars, the contemporary Islamic revolution(s), and so on.

We cannot merely define religion as a system of belief(s) that guides social action, since, as we have seen, this is also true of magic and science. One must go further and suggest that the beliefs are supported by a community which we call a 'church'. Moreover, a defining feature of religious belief has been said to be its concern to venerate 'the sacred', or the 'holy'. In 1945 the British anthropologist Radcliffe-Brown (1881–1955) defined religion as 'an expression in one form or another of a sense of dependence on a power outside ourselves, a power of which we may speak as a spiritual or moral power'. The dependency on supernatural powers is expressed in the importance of religious rituals, through which such powers are revered and supplicated, asked for direction, forgiveness, blessing, or vengeance. Durkheim's analysis of religion led him to define it as 'a unified system of beliefs and practices relative to sacred things, that is to say things set apart and forbidden — beliefs and practices which unite into a single moral community called a church all those who adhere to them' (1965, p. 47). Natural objects, such as minerals, animals, or plants are given a divine significance as symbols through which supernatural entities — gods, angels, or spiritual ancestors — are worshipped. Ritual is important in both reinforcing and expressing the solidarity of believers and establishing a distinction between what is to be treated as 'sacred' as opposed to 'profane' (the everyday, earthly concerns of life).

Though the veneration of 'the sacred' and the mystical is a hallmark of religious faith, something like this also goes on in magical rituals. Hence, it may be inappropriate to distinguish firmly between the two. Thus, Horton (1960) and Worsley (1968) argue that *religious* ritual may have a *magical* power for those taking part, and conversely, magical beliefs and actions normally presuppose some notions about gods, spirits, mystical forces, and so on. Those who maintain the distinction between magic and religion do so primarily because of their functionalist interpretation of belief-systems. That is, magic and religion are said to serve distinct functions in society, the former allowing the individual some control over events, the latter strengthening social values and attitudes through community ritual.

This functionalist perspective was developed in detail by Durkheim, principally in *The Elementary Forms of the Religious Life* (1912). He argues that belief in a supernatural realm cannot have any foundation in reality, since 'religious experience' has led to conceptions about 'the spiritual' which have 'varied infinitely'. The myths and 'imaginary forces' that religion creates are in fact inspired by the collective sentiment and shared morality of people in society. It is the *moral* order and not some mythical God that is held in reverence and awe by the individual. Although individuals may think that they are worshipping the divine, in reality the only thing that transcends individuals, that has a permanence outlasting them, is society itself: it is society that we really worship. Durkheim is interested in how religion 'binds man to society' through helping him to (i) understand the reality of social relations; (ii) communicate with other men; and (iii) establish obligations between men. Religion thus gives a 'sacred authority to society's rules and values'. In maintaining social solidarity religion is, for Durkheim, an essentially conservative force: when it fails to perform this function for social groups, new groups and new ideas emerge which become the new religions. Durkheim sees Nationalism and Communism, for example, as the new religions of industrial society, taking over from Christianity, giving the members of society an image of an ideal world. Politics and the rituals associated with it — flag-waving, parades, and doctrines — become the new form in which collective sentiments are symbolically expressed: collective ritual must be performed regularly to strengthen the moral codes and order of society. Thus the Durkheimian theory of religion suggests that religion, in one form or another, is a necessary and essential feature of society.

Durkheim's analysis of religion has a number of similarities to that developed by Marx. Like Durkheim, Marx believed that the 'supernatural' realm had no reality: God did not create mankind; instead, mankind had created God, as well as much of the physical world, and the social and political institutions that order it. But the illusion of religious belief turns all this upside down, making God (or gods) the supreme being, whose authority passes downwards through earthly rulers who order the affairs of ordinary mortals in 'the great chain of being'. Religion thus serves to legitimate the power and material advantage enjoyed by the dominant groups and rulers of society: rulers promote the myth that their position is given by God; hence 'the divine right of Kings'. Again, like Durkheim, Marx argues that religion serves a social function: it hides the real basis of power and exploitation in class society and hinders the development of class consciousness and a materialist politics that would show that the world is pro-duced and reproduced through man's — not God's — labours. In hiding this reality, religion alienates man from his true self, and yet is the means by which man can — albeit by delusion — escape the suffering and oppression brought about through the conflict of economic interest. It is in this sense 'the opium of the people'.

Both Marx and Durkheim, then, explain the origins and functions of religion in terms of *social* factors. But neither believed that one could reduce religious ideas to either purely economic or purely moral factors respectively. Both believed that once religion was institutionalised, it gained a relative independence from its underlying social bases. One cannot, for example, explain the opposition between Catholic and Protestant in Northern Ireland, or Jew and Palestinian in the Middle East, simply in terms of an economic or moral opposition between competing social groups.

This belief in the partial independence of religion from its material/social foundations was shared by Weber. As he says:

> However incisive the social influences, economically and politically determined, may have been upon a religious ethic in a particular case, it receives its stamp primarily from religious sources . . . [It] is at least usual that religious doctrines are adjusted to religious needs (Weber, in Gerth and Mills, 1948, p. 270).

Weber was interested in the way in which religious ideas varied and how they could effect social change rather than being simply a defence or justification of the status quo. His general concern was to explain the development of capitalism, which had only reached full maturity and dominated the world economy from within the social and economic climate of Western Europe. He examined the differing religious traditions of the West and the Orient and tried to show that the former was especially well suited to promoting the development of capitalism in the West, while the latter had the opposite effect in the East.

Weber showed that the ideas and practices of Protestantism were particularly conducive to capitalist development because of their general convergence with the 'spirit of capitalism' (Weber, 1952). He argued that the most significant feature of this spirit in Western Europe was the desire to be productive and accumulate riches continually. Elsewhere in the world, production was geared much more to the provision of exotic and luxurious material for immediate consumption. In the West, investment, hard work, and steady accumulation were seen as the correct and proper activities for working people: idleness and immoderate consumption of riches received harsh judgement. Such an attitude is by no means naturally adopted by individuals: people may just as easily produce sufficient for their needs and then stop working. Yet the continual accumulation through disciplined and controlled labour is a necessary condition for the growth of a truly capitalist economy. Capitalism could not have developed if the labour force worked erratically or only when they felt they needed to. Therefore, something peculiar to Western Europe must have encouraged people to work regularly, continuously, and in a disciplined manner. This, for Weber, was what he called the 'Protestant ethic', which found its most complete expression in the Calvinist doctrine.

The principal tenet of Calvinism is the belief in 'predestination': that God has selected those who are to be saved and those who are to suffer damnation. No individual can know whether he or she is one of the chosen few, nor can God's selection be altered in any way: salvation cannot be earned, but is given (or withheld) by God. Weber argued that those who believe in predestination are bound to suffer from 'salvation panic', a terrifying anxiety about whether one has been chosen, throwing the believer into psychological turmoil. In practice, the only way to cope with anxiety was to bend the Calvinist doctrine slightly, to believe that, like the good tree that cannot bear evil fruit, if one behaved in a Christian manner, performed 'good works', and was moderate in all, then these were *signs* that one had been elected for salvation.

Hence, the believer had to ensure that *everything* he or she did was for the 'greater glory of God' and a confirmation of election. Any slip, any brief lapse into immoderate or sinful behaviour was enough to show that one could not be among the chosen few, and that there would be eternal damnation. The pressure therefore to be highly disciplined and righteous in all one's daily activities was intense, with one's place of business or occupation being no exception. Here then we can begin to see the seeds of Weber's argument.

The Protestant ethic that derives from the doctrine of predestination demands the faithful to be diligent, disciplined, and fully committed to their 'worldly' obligations. The 'spirit of capitalism' encourages the view that hard work is an 'activity' which is good in itself, something to be admired as honourable and fruitful. Thus Weber believes that there is a convergence of attitudes and orientations here, an 'elective affinity' between the religious ideas of Calvinism and the spirit of capitalism, a reciprocal relationship only found in the society of Western Europe.

Weber's analysis illustrates one of his central beliefs about the relationship between ideas and the economic or material foundations of society. It is apparent that the 'ethic' is no simple reflection of the economic interests of any specific class group, nor even a direct mirroring of the capitalist spirit. Instead it derives from the rational solution to a psychological anxiety generated by belief in a religious doctrine. The solution — to behave as though one were chosen — had far-reaching consequences for other, non-religious, social institutions, particularly for the promotion of the economic institutions of capitalism.

Weber's thesis has been questioned on a number of points. For example, Samuelson (1961) points out that a number of places in Europe have had flourishing Calvinist communities yet have not been quick to develop along capitalist lines — Scotland is one case mentioned. Furthermore, the decisive role of the Protestant ethic in the growth of capitalism is challenged by some critics who argue that the accumulation of investment capital in, say, Britain, Holland, Huguenot France and New England, was as much the result of profiteering through trade, piracy, and plunder as it was of careful saving by frugal Calvinist craftsmen and traders. Marxists argue that the Protestant ethic served as an ideological legitimation of *laissez-faire*, free-market capitalism. Others question Weber's portrayal of Oriental belief-systems as obstacles to the development of capitalism, unlike Calvinism (Rodinson, 1977). Why is it, they argue, that a religion such as Hinduism could quite happily accommodate, even promote, the development of trade, a legal and monetary system, a division of labour, and yet apparently, as Weber claims, prevent further development in economic growth along capitalist lines? These critics suggest, then, that the lack of development in Hindu or Islamic societies must be attributed to factors distinct from the particular belief-systems of their respective religions, and so, by implication, cannot be explained in terms of their lack of a Protestant ethic.

While these criticisms must be taken seriously, and imply that continued historical and theoretical analysis is required if we are to understand the relationship between religious values and social change, Weber's analysis cannot be accused of being theoretically simplistic. He stated quite clearly that his thesis was *not* that Protestantism *caused* capitalism, but was one contributory factor in a highly complex process of economic and social change.

Rationalisation

One of the central features of this process identified by Weber is the dimension of *rationality* that underpins the Protestant ethic and the development of capitalism. Calvinists were being highly rational in seeking to maximise evidence of their 'calling' through adopting a disciplined and methodical approach to all their worldly concerns. Such an approach encouraged the likelihood of success, taken to be a clear sign of election. This rational religious ethic encouraged the Calvinist entrepreneur to be more and more calculating and efficient. This led to the growth of book-keeping, accounting, and an orientation that sought a continual, controlled return on investment. Hence the rationality of the religious ethic paralleled the rational characteristics of the organisation of capitalist enterprise.

Rationalisation of both religious belief and economic activity is the main feature of modern society in which the twin forces of rationalisation and intellectualisation lead to 'the disenchantment' of the world. The world becomes less and less an 'enchanted', mystical or 'sacred' place: all things in principle can be mastered by calculation, by reason. Weber insists that this does not imply an *increased* knowledge about the world, simply a different way of interpreting it. Nevertheless, this different interpretation has been seen to have great significance by a number of social theorists, some of whom argue that in as much as the 'holy', the sacred, and the mysterious no longer hold any meaning for members of a society, then that society can be said to be experiencing the process of 'secularisation'.

Secularisation

The argument that society is becoming increasingly secular seems fairly straightforward. 'Everyone knows' that religion is not as strong as it used to be. But clearly this begs the question as to how we are to measure the 'strength' of religion. Depending on the indices we use, a society could be defined as being more or less 'religious', or conversely, less or more 'secular'.

An account of the secularisation process depends on the definition of religion adopted in the first place. Many sociologists define religion, and hence secularisation, in *institutional* terms. Glasner (1977, p. 7) summarises this approach:

> The assumption is that, since a common usage definition of Christianity for example, is concerned with church attendance, membership and presence at rites of passage, these constitute significant elements of a definition of religion, and that any move away from this institutional participation involves religious decline.

Wilson (1966), for instance, defines secularisation as the process through which religious thinking, practice, and institutions 'lose their social significance'. He then provides 'statistical evidence of secularisation' for both English and American Christianity which measures 'the decline in organised religious participation'. While admitting that falling baptism and membership numbers in England may in fact be interpreted as people voting with their feet and seeking alternative religious vehicles, he still believes that such figures show how the institutionalised Christian *Church* is 'losing direct influence over the ideas and activities of men'.

Statistical information about membership of and participation in the Christian religion must be treated carefully, since it is provided by denominations — Catholic, Anglican, Non-Conformist — that use different criteria of membership. It is estimated that about 60 per cent of the adult British population are counted as members of the Anglican faith, roughly 30 per cent of the population split between Catholic and Non-Conformists (such as Methodists, Unitarians, etc.), with about 5 per cent belonging to small 'sects'. On average only 10–15 per cent of the adult population attend church on any one Sunday; baptism or 'christening' takes place in about 90 per cent of births, although the number baptised in the Anglican

Church dropped from 623 per 1,000 live births in 1885, to 531 per 1,000 in 1962. Wilson comments that while institutional religious duties such as prayer, mass, and communion, have lost much of their importance for members of the Church of England and Roman Catholic Church, they still provide a number of ceremonial services that form the *rites de passage* for members, particularly marriage and burial. While the number of church weddings declined from the turn of the century till the 1950s, they are now much more constant and account for approximately 70 per cent of all marriages each year. Wilson argues that this need not be taken as a sign of renewed religious commitment among Church members: rather, Church weddings may give people a dramatic sense of occasion lacking in registry ceremonies. The continued use of religious funerals similarly need be no indication of religiosity: 'The control of funerals is so much more professionalised than the control of baptisms, confirmations and weddings that religious officiation becomes almost a matter of routine' (Wilson, 1966, p. 17).

Generally, however, the predominance of religious institutions has given way to new social institutions, in the realms of politics, education, social policy and morality, and the pulpit has lost out to the power of the mass media. Religions no longer wield the political or economic power that they once enjoyed, and have modified their doctrines in the face of pressure from secular society. Some sociologists, such as Parsons, claim that this process whereby the extent of the institutional influence of religion is narrowed, leads to a stronger church, since it is a purer one, less distracted by secular cares and so more able to concentrate on matters 'sacred'. This view may be challenged, however, in as much as such a process would seem more likely to increasingly isolate religious observance and participation, and the values on which they depend, from a widening majority of the population.

Wilson argues that the gradual development of 'denominations' within Christianity in competition and in conflict with the Church of England — such as Calvinism and Methodism — is an additional indicator of secularisation. Both these developments within Christianity have been linked to specific

social strata and their experience of the early period of industrialisation. Calvinism, with its emphasis on election, was
particularly suited as a religio-social ethic and belief-system
to a privileged merchant class. Methodism, however, based on
Wesley's doctrine that all men were equal before Christ and
were free to choose salvation, appealed to the 'new mass
society' of industrial England, and, as Marx might claim, was
perhaps better equipped as a theology to provide the poor
working class with some relief from their suffering. Indeed,
some of the early offshoots from the Anglican Church – the
Adventists for example – expressed through their religious
solidarity a critique of their poverty and suffering, although
this was channelled into *religious* fervour rather than class
protest against capitalism. Later, however, members of various
denominational groups – especially the Non-Conformists –
came to regard their lot in life as a necessary burden in the
heavenly order of things. As Calvinism encouraged this ethic
among the wealthier merchants, so Methodism, for different
reasons, provided a corresponding work ethic and set of values
that could bring 'dignity' to the working class, whose lives
had been radically disrupted by the wage-labour demand of
industrialisation. Indeed, to some extent Methodism became a
vehicle of social mobility for some, in as much as a religious
'working man' was seen as a 'respectable man', a 'law-abiding
man', above the 'common rabble' of the working class. But a
religion closely associated with a subordinate group in the
way Methodism was could, if tolerated, be an agency of
dissent and *protest* against the dominant economic classes.
Something like this occurred in the nineteenth century when
a broad alliance of dissenters from within the ranks of the
Methodists and the Liberal Party criticised the links between
the Tory Party, the landed aristocracy and the 'established'
Church of England.

The notion of an 'established' Church highlights the major
distinction between a 'Church' and a 'denomination'. The
'Church' of England, for instance, claims to command loyalty
and respect, not simply because people have chosen to become
Anglicans, but also because they become members of a Church
traditionally recognised as the national and ethnic religious
body, formally regarded so by the state. A denomination,

such as Roman Catholicism, need not have this political or social status, and is usually a smaller body within a broadly defined belief-system such as Christianity. A third type of religious organisation, the 'sect', is a highly exclusive group. All members are required to conform to clearly defined rules and regulations. Sects, such as the Jehovah's Witnesses or Christadelphians, do not typically have some form of ordained clerical or ministerial group at their head, being run instead by the laity themselves. The sect tends to reject any liaison or ties with the wider society, unlike an 'established church'. Stark (1967) has described the sect as 'typically a contra-culture', indicating its tendency to reject the prevailing social values and norms. Wilson (1966, p. 181) describes the selective quality of the sect thus:

> Whereas the Church represents itself as the religious organisation of the nation or the society, to which men are come at birth as members, the sect regards membership as an achievement, proved by one's capacity to live up to certain standards. The sect member both chooses and is chosen.

As Churches appear to lose their institutional pre-eminence, they may in fact become more like sects, small and somewhat cut off from the dominant culture. Conversely, there are a number of religious groups that have now become considerably church-like but which were initially conceived as sects, such as the Quakers. These different patterns of development indicate that there is no simple chronological passage from Church to sect, or vice versa. Moreover, within particular social contexts, the *same* religious group may be perceived quite differently: thus the Mormons have a churchly status in America but a very sectarian one in Britain.

Secularisation has been characterised as a process accompanying the increasing rationalisation and industrialisation of society, and the expanding authority of the state over all areas of life, reflected by the separation of Church and state. Theorists like Parsons regard this separation as an expression of the increasing 'structural differentiation' of society, as it develops from a relatively simple to more complex form.

Even if one accepts that the religious institution has adapted to changes in its environment, one need not assume that the industrialisation process has the *same* influence on religious practice whatever society one examines. So, for example, while British institutional religious participation and membership has declined, the level of American religious practice is at least constant if not climbing. One explanation of this contrast has been given by Herberg (1967). He argues that three factors peculiar to the USA have encouraged sustained religious practice within the context of increasing urbanisation and industrialisation: the effects of massive immigration from Europe; the ideology of equality of opportunity; and the absence of an 'established Church' of any kind in the USA. Immigrants, and especially ethnic groups, shared in a religious community in which they found stability and identity in a vast, new, ever-changing 'land of opportunity'. At the same time, all religions enjoy the same social and legal status within the USA, there being no privileged established church. They are, then, a living reflection of the American dream of equality, freedom, and tolerance. Religious practice in America is a symbolic celebration of the urban, middle class, affluent community's life-style and values. Hence the American pulpit is a religious soap-box championing the values and standards of American society, a forum for preaching *secular* values. Thus it appears that a form of secularisation has occurred *within* American religion as a result of and not despite the sustained religious participation and affiliation. As Scharf (1970, p. 174) comments: 'In America there is secularisation within the churches; in England there is secularisation by withdrawal from the churches.'

Secularisation has also been explained in terms of the impact of science and technology on religious beliefs (see, for example, O'Dea, 1966, p. 82). The development of increasingly sophisticated technology means that human needs can be met not only with greater ease, control and efficiency but also to an increasingly higher standard. Thus if one believes, like Malinowski, that human powerlessness and anxiety are the root cause of reliance on religio-magical beliefs, then technological developments may make religious faith redundant. 'Mysteries' can now be understood as manageable 'problems', dealt with by the precision of scientific method rather than the fervour of religious prayer.

The growth of science over the past fifty years has been massive, not only in terms of the amount of money spent in the area, but also in terms of the number of people, publications, and specialties that can be counted within it. Large-scale research centres — the new 'cathedrals' of today — have become the norm. The pace of scientific development and its application in the industrial sector is encapsulated in Cooley's (1976, p. 76) comment that: 'In the 1930s machinery was obsolete in about twenty-five years, during the 1950s in ten years, and at the moment computerised equipment is obsolete in about three to five years.' This process clearly threatens to make certain machinery and many human skills obsolescent, and it has also meant that more and more inventions are made and used by 'ordinary' people who increasingly have less and less knowledge about how things work. Modern science, then, plays a major role today as a system of ideas and understanding, but frequently only does so in a way that is quite baffling and incomprehensible to laypersons. Yet the advance of science, while often unintelligible for the individual, is nevertheless held to be the major achievement of modernity. The predominance of the scientific culture is suggested by the comment made by the editor of the journal *Nature* in the 1930s: 'My grandfather preached the gospel of Christ, my father preached the gospel of Socialism, I preach the gospel of Science.'

Critique of secularisation

A number of criticisms have been made of the secularisation thesis, most of which are discussed at length by Glasner (1977). We shall focus on two aspects of the thesis: the first concerns the institutional decline in religious participation and affiliation; the second, the alleged displacement of religion by science.

We can question firstly the extent to which a drop in levels of institutional practices indicates a decline in religiosity. Could we not ask, as Glasner (1977, p. 34) suggests, 'whether religion continues to flourish outside the structures which have conventionally embodied it'? Might not an extra-institutional

religious commitment be possible, even in a highly industrialised, scientific era, as suggested by the increasing importance
of sectarianism in today's society? Sects indeed demand a
level of commitment and involvement which would be 'above
and beyond the call of duty' for members of the traditional
faiths.

Conversely, we could ask to what extent is public participation in religious institutions necessarily an indication of
religious commitment? Thus, as Demerath (1965) argues,
participation may not indicate any deep-rooted religious concern: elite members of a local community may feel obliged
to attend Sunday services to sustain their image as public
notables whose fortunes are blessed by God. Furthermore,
we can also challenge the notion that there was some time in
the past when religion was (institutionally) of central concern
for the majority of the population of Western societies. Even
using statistical evidence as a measure of religious concern,
some studies (for example, Hill, 1964; Thomas, 1971) indicate that a past 'Age of Faith' is more myth than reality.

In short, the institutional definition of religion may be
historically suspect and sociologically narrow. Some sociologists insist that a broader definition of religion is required.
One of the broadest is given by Berger and Luckmann (1963),
who claim that people only have a sense of identity, meaning
and purpose in their lives because of a deep-seated religious
dimension in their personal lives. According to Luckmann
(1967), the decline in institutionalised religious practices has
meant that personal forms of religion are beginning to emerge,
and the 'specialists' and 'experts' of institutionalised religion
(priests and theologians) are less able to control, interpret and
speak with legitimate authority about this private religion.
Whether or not this non-institutional private religion exists,
we do need to look more carefully at activities that social
actors regard with some sort of 'religious' significance — be
it drug-taking, popular demonstration, political rallying, or
rock music.

What, then, of the second aspect of the secularisation thesis,
that science has dispelled the myths and irrationality of religion? Two issues need to be considered here. First, *has*
religion really given way to science? As we have seen, much

depends on how one defines religion, and possibly, on how one defines 'science', since one could argue that science is 'the new religion of today'. Second, even if we agree on a definition of religious belief, does the secularisation thesis propose that religion is weaker today than in the past, because people have consciously evaluated the relative explanatory powers of religion and science, and in the end have favoured the latter? If so, such a proposition would need to be challenged, since it implies that ideas and beliefs are judged independently of the social context in which they are found. As we saw with both magic and science, beliefs are sustained not so much for their conceptual veracity but because of the way they express and recreate the collective solidarity of various social groups — be they the Zande or the scientific community. Hence the shift away from a religious to a scientific interpretation of the world is as much a shift in the community in which one lives as it is in the ideas one has. This shift may occur very gradually, by meeting and living with a new group of people, and, crucially, *talking* to them in a language which has little reference to 'the sacred' or other conventionally defined religious dimension.

Nevertheless, science has of course developed as *an institution* over the past two hundred years. A principal reason for this growth has been its success in serving industrial development and profitability through technological innovation. Industrial capitalism not only disrupted the long-standing pre-feudal and feudal traditions that had allowed stability for centuries, but it also initiated change of an order and at a pace never seen before. The division of labour that it set in motion meant that the task of discovery and invention was itself institutionalised, and the occupational role of being 'a scientist' was gradually established in academic, governmental and industrial contexts in Western Europe and America, most especially in Germany (Ben-David and Zloczower, 1962).

By providing answers to technical problems of industrialisation, the practical pay-off of science afforded it an ever-increasing prestige within administrative and economic circles, as it was, as Marx suggests, 'pressed into the service of capital'. This social and economic enhancement of the status of scientific inquiry, rather than any direct conceptual superiority it might have over religion, posed the real threat to the pre-eminence of religious orthodoxy and its specialists — the archbishops, clergy and theologians. Conceptually speaking, science and religion are, arguably, not necessarily incompat-ible, in as much as they pose different types of questions about, and give different answers to, the environment. There-fore, many scientists and many theologians may feel quite happy to sustain both religious and scientific conceptions of the universe. Indeed, over the last fifty years many theo-logians have sought to reassert the importance of religious ideas, not by debunking or attacking scientific discoveries, but by welcoming them as illuminating the immense know-ledge behind the divine design of nature.

If anything, then, it was the development of science as a *profession* that may have led to a relative decline in the power of the established religions. Scientists have carved out an area of expertise for themselves which has claimed and received considerable material and symbolic reward through govern-ment and industrial patronage. Though public and private funding is crucial in sustaining the material viability of the institution of science today, the practitioners of science have sought to ensure that they be free from public scrutiny and control. The public or government are said to be unable to assess professional work competently. Whereas religious pro-fessionals, such as theologians and Popes, may be able to justify their claims on the basis of their privileged access to revealed truth or 'infallibility', the 'imprimatur' of scientific knowledge-claims is in part a reflection of the exceptional degree of autonomy enjoyed by science, and the mystifica-tion of expertise this promotes.

Normally, in societies utilising belief in magic and witch-craft as a means of social control, as we saw with the Azande, the dominant groups — the monarch and princes — claim to have special powers and ultimate authority over the use of the magic, and as such, cannot be charged with witchcraft by subordinate diviners. In societies where religious institu-tions have been established with their respective experts and specialists, the latter try to ensure that religious ideas and be-liefs which give them their *raison d'être* are under *their* con-trol. Luckmann (1967, p. 66) points to 'The vested interests of the religious experts in the recruitment and training of their successors, in the exclusion of laymen from the "higher" forms of sacred knowledge and in defence of privileges.'

The institutionalised scientific enterprise has similarly created its own mythology: this is the notion that rewards only go to those scientists who have merited them by producing results which other scientists have evaluated and accepted through impartial, universally adopted criteria. Any inequality within the scientific community seems to be meritocratic: rewards and privileges only go to those who have fairly and honestly achieved them. Elite members of science can claim that their reputation 'speaks for itself'. Yet there are good grounds for questioning this view of the relationship between reward and the value of scientific findings: it appears that the value of knowledge-claims is much more dependent on the highly variable context of negotiation between competitor scientists than on any alleged standard criteria of evaluation. Thus some groups may be in a weaker 'negotiating position' because of their *structural* position in the institution of science: as Mulkay (1979, p. 26) says, 'women and the members of other social categories in science are systematically prevented from . . . establishing that their work is of high quality'. Thus while the low rank of women in science may be explained by participants in terms of the low quality of their work, we should not necessarily regard this as indicating objectively inferior work by female as compared with male scientists; instead, it is best regarded as an ideological justification for sexism in science. A similar type of argument applies with regard to the treatment given by scientific orthodoxy to deviant knowledge-claims that challenge the conceptual and social status quo, as suggested in the earlier reference to parapsychology and acupuncture.

These comments on the institutions of magic, religion, and science refer to the way in which elite practitioners *within* them can legitimise the privileges they receive over and against other members. In terms of their relationship to the wider society, professional experts, be they magicians, bishops, or scientists, will strive to ensure that the conceptual and social bases of their expertise will be publicly valued, either by restricting recruitment to their ranks or by mystifying their skills (see Chapter 8 on work). But dominant groups in society are not only, or even necessarily, constituted by trained 'experts' of one form or another. Thus there may be additional ideological resources that are drawn upon to help sustain the socio-economic status quo and cultural belief-systems, which may have their roots in religious or scientific conceptions of the world, but which have become generalised political conceptions about 'what's right and what's wrong', 'who should get what', and so on. Some of the more prevalent of these conceptions can be examined by considering the role played by the mass media in the construction of social ideologies in Western capitalism.

9.4 THE MASS MEDIA

What are commonly called the 'mass media' are those institutions which use the increasingly sophisticated technological developments of industrialism for the communication of ideas, for the purposes of information, entertainment and persuasion, to large-scale audiences, whether this be by means of newspapers, radio, television, books, magazines, advertising billboards, or whatever. Compared even with the nineteenth century, the mass media in industrial society have become hugely expanded both in terms of the *scope* of the audiences they reach and in terms of the *range* of the media available to those audiences.

Exposure to and consumption of media products has become an integral part of the daily lives of the majority of the members of Western societies, occupying a considerable proportion of their leisure time, and, as we shall suggest shortly, providing them to a considerable extent with their picture of social reality. Television, for instance, represents the major and most pervasive mass medium of today. It is the principal leisure activity of most adults and children, the 'organiser' of their entertainment and social life, missed when unavailable, and a source of information and ideas widely regarded as authoritative and trustworthy.

Given these high levels of exposure, the media constitute potentially strategic socialisation agencies, since they serve as sources of information and ideas for the large numbers of people consuming their products. As Golding (1974, p. 78) says, 'The media are central in the provision of ideas and images which people use to interpret and understand a great deal of their everyday experience.' More specifically, they represent an institutionalised channel for the distribution of *social knowledge* and hence a potentially powerful instrument of *social control* (as well as *social critique*) sustaining or challenging the status quo. As we have suggested elsewhere, there exists a variety of agencies disseminating ideas and values, and shaping actors' perceptions — the family, the school, the peer group, the ethnic group, and so on — so that the impact of the media on behaviour and attitudes cannot be seen as simple and unambiguous. For instance, the short-term effects of television on voting preferences during election campaigns appear limited, but its general long-term role in legitimating a system of parliamentary democracy may be much more fundamental and profound. Our discussion of the media, too, will focus not on the 'immediate' effects of media messages, but on their more pervasive role as a source of social knowledge, ideas, and beliefs for those exposed to them.

The media as providers of 'experience' and 'knowledge'

While modern industrial societies provide their members with access to a range of material resources, cultural artefacts and opportunities unavailable in former times, the nature of these societies is such that they are characterised by social differentiation and segregation, rather than social homogeneity and integration. This means that 'the world' has become much larger and more fragmented for most of us, no longer encompassed or measured solely by the immediate community in which we live. But this larger world is normally *not directly* experienced by us, despite greater national and international mobility. The media provide us with much indirect experience of events and processes happening beyond our own social experience. We increasingly 'know' more, and are encouraged to do so, through the mediated experiences of TV, films, radio, the press, books and magazines. The media have, then, become steadily more influential in defining 'reality', in encouraging a common image of society among its members. As

Cohen and Young (1973, p. 342) observe:

> The mass media provide a major source of knowledge in a segregated society of what the consensus actually is and what is the nature of deviation from it. They conjure up for each group with its limited stock of social knowledge, what 'everyone else' believes.

The popular image of the mass media — particularly of TV and the press — and one perpetuated by media personnel themselves, has a strong pluralist flavour about it. In this view, the media are important agencies within the democratic process of a 'free society', ensuring an unrestricted public airing of differences of opinion on issues of public interest and concern; in the ideal healthy democracy, the opportunity for free expression of a wide range of voices and opinions is a fundamental prerequisite. According to this pluralist conception, the media in Western societies contain a diversity of opinion and information, they are independent and not state-controlled institutions, presenting a variety of 'definitions of reality'.

Furthermore, the media allegedly act as neutral autonomous servants of the public: besides providing entertainment, they inform and educate the public and, more importantly, raise issues, act as watchdogs of the highest and lowest, and as guardians of the public interest against violation of generally accepted standards and patterns of behaviour, or abuse of power. The 'grilling' of politicians in TV interviews, the 'digging' of the investigative reporter, and the identification of disturbing new 'problems' all allegedly bear testimony to the media's public service role in social critique and democratic public enlightenment.

Such a view is buttressed by the argument that the media maintain above all the *sovereignty of the consumer*, attempting to satisfy consumer demand by 'giving them what they want', be it news, fiction or entertainment: the audience decides, and media owners and personnel respond to their wishes. Thus, any accusations that the media resort to a 'consensus' portrayal of the world are, according to this view, fundamentally misconceived, since the media are said to be merely *reflecting* ideas existing in society among the mass of the population, freely arrived at and accepted by them as 'sensible'.

The media and the construction of reality and consensus

But this view of the media as merely neutral or 'open' vehicles has received much critical sociological scrutiny. The mass media do not simply provide information and reflect a social world — rather, they *structure* it for us, not simply increasing our knowledge of the world but helping us to 'make sense' of it. Topics of conversation among workers, children at school, pub-drinkers and so on, are not only generated by what they have seen, heard, or read in the media, but the *content* and *context* of these conversations will be greatly shaped by media exposure. More fundamentally, the media represent the major means by which such individuals, groups and classes construct an understanding of the lives, meanings, practices and values of *other* individuals, groups, and classes, and acquire a picture of how the whole of 'social reality' hangs together.

While there may exist in newspapers or in TV news an explicit propaganda position which deliberately aims to further particular views, ideas and values, such direct activity represents only a part of the media's influence. More subtle, less overt, but none the less important processes are at work in which implicit frameworks or guidelines for interpreting social reality, for 'making sense' of a problematic world, are provided, which encourage certain lines of thinking and perception, and discourage others. Reality, then, is constructed by imposing a *selective* framework which may exclude alternative interpretations or meaning systems.

One of the most important implications of this process is the media's reliance on an apparently prevailing *consensus* for the framework in which ideas and issues are presented, and in which action is interpreted: that is, they work within a climate of opinion which they themselves have played some considerable part in constructing — they both *utilise* a consensual image of society and help to *reproduce* it. This assumes that the majority of, if not all, members of society are in agree-

ment on a wide range of norms, values and ideas, and therefore on what are 'reasonable' and 'acceptable' patterns of
behaviour. The news media select and interpret events within
the terms of this pre-existing consensus. This may not necessarily be consciously done — in fact, often in trying to be
unbiased and objective, in attempting to examine a particular
issue 'rationally', journalists draw on consensual values un-
consciously. As Hall *et al.* (1978, p. 55) observe of news
reporting:

> This process of 'making an event intelligible' is a social
> process — constituted by a number of specific journalistic
> practices which embody (often only implicitly) crucial
> assumptions about what society is and how it works. One
> such background assumption is the consensual nature of
> society; the process of signification — giving social meanings
> to events — both assumes and helps to construct society as
> a consensus. We exist as members of one society *because*
> — it is assumed — we share a common stock of cultural
> knowledge with our fellow men . . . This 'consensual' view-
> point has important political consequences . . . It carries
> the assumption that we also all have roughly the same
> *interests* in the society, and that we all roughly have an
> equal share of power in the society . . . The media are
> among the institutions whose practices are most widely
> and consistently predicated upon the assumption of a
> national consensus.

Thus there supposedly exist no fundamental conflicts of
interests between groups and classes; there are legitimate
institutionalised means for resolving conflicts that do occur,
and members of society enjoy equality before the law and
equal access to decision-making opportunities by means of
the conventional institutions of parliamentary democracy.
Since legitimate political activity is seen to be conducted only
through parliamentary democratic channels, the media tend
to regard any activity going beyond this as not permissible,
and its perpetrators as consequently less *credible* actors. Thus
non-consensual opinions receive more critical attention, or
no attention at all; where such dissenting views do appear,

they are frequently made to appear peripheral, fanatical delusions, or mere fads; they are commonly portrayed as embracing a world view which is unreal and unnatural — literally a *misunderstanding* of reality. Thus in the news media, spokespersons expressing 'legitimate' opinions and values will be much less likely to have their basic assumptions questioned (because they echo the prevailing consensus), while those of 'non-legitimate' persuasion will be pressed to justify theirs. Those not operating within the rules of the game, that is, those who disregard the rules about what is considered 'reasonable' disagreement, are portrayed as marginal to, or outside the debate, because they are 'extremist' or 'irrational'.

Deviant values are regarded as restricted to a minority, and the likelihood of dissent being widely felt is generally perceived as too remote for consideration. As Westergaard (1977, pp. 110–13) observes:

> The possibility, for example, that large wage-claims, strikes and go-slows, direct action of other kinds, may reflect popular clamour for equity in a society where inequality is entrenched . . . is not so much rejected as, simply, never more than momentarily entertained. When the media publicise dissent, in short, the effect of their interpretation is to minimise its sources and objects, to magnify its fragmentation and incoherence . . . The eddies and currents of dissent in popular consciousness find virtually no representation in media interpretations of the world.

The media, then, constitute crucially important vehicles of basic social and political values, with a central role in creating and sustaining a consensus, and in structuring its *style*. Media personnel would probably maintain that they are merely portraying the world and its values 'as they are', and *reflecting* public opinion and conventional wisdom. This assumes that 'public opinion' is some supra-social entity in whose construction social actors play no part. But what comes to be accepted as conventional wisdom and public opinion is likely to be determined more by some actors and institutions than others — that is, opportunity to influence the production of ideas is unequally distributed.

But even at this point, those who regard the media as mere neutral and faithful reflectors of social reality might well point out that there exist some media outlets for non-conservative, even critical, social and political values (for example, in newspapers like the *Daily Mirror* and the *Guardian*, and in television documentaries and dramas). But in the 'popular' press this expression of 'alternative' values takes an essentially mild form, with support for a 'moderate' Labour party, but not one which might effect a thoroughgoing socialist challenge to the power of capital. The popular press

> takes a 'radical' editorial orientation no further than to a
> blend of vacuous populism with support for political
> moderation and social compromise . . . [they] blow a care-
> fully tuned populist trumpet. Their tone is 'matey' and
> aspires to plain speaking; they pride themselves on talking
> for as well as to ordinary men and women . . . When they
> attack and 'expose', their targets are not the routine power
> of capital, property and profit in common affairs; occasion-
> ally, of course, business malpractice . . . but far more regu-
> larly officialdom (Westergaard, 1977, p. 103).

Furthermore, while the output of the media as a whole is not blatantly and uniformly consensual, it remains true that critical ideas and opinion do not amount to a *systematic* critique of existing social arrangements, but are essentially spasmodic and exceptional in their appearance. The critical character of the media is then severely restricted not so much by deliberate censorship − although this does occur − but by the routine practices of media production.

The manufacture of news

The dominant thrust of our argument so far has been that the media constitute a major source of knowledge and beliefs for members of industrial societies, helping to structure their perception of social reality and its constituent elements. One of the realms of media output particularly central to this process is that of *the news*. While it is a popular cliché that 'you shouldn't believe everything you read in the newspapers or see on TV', most people, reading the newspaper or watching a TV news broadcast, expect that they will obtain a picture of what significant events are occurring in the world, of 'what's happening'.

But as media researchers have increasingly observed, the news doesn't merely 'happen' — rather it is *made*, it is a *socially manufactured product*, the result of a social process with a distinct order to it. Thus items included in a TV broadcast or in a newspaper are not in reality the *only* events of that day, but are *defined* as 'news' by the media. In other words, the news is not merely a faithful account of events whose significance and interest is intrinsically obvious and unproblematic, but it is a socially constructed form of know-' ledge dependent upon a whole host of factors: media personnel's notions of what is important and interesting; the contexts in which the news is produced and the sources from which it comes, and so on. As Hall *et al.* (1978, p. 53) stress:

> The media do not simply and transparently report events which are 'naturally' newsworthy *in themselves*. News is the end-product of a complex process which begins with a systematic sorting and selecting of events and topics according to a socially constructed set of categories.

This process of selection — or 'agenda-setting' — does not occur randomly: on the contrary, it is the systematic product of a number of forces, as we shall see shortly.

Constraints on media news

What becomes 'news' is shaped not only by material and economic pressures, by cultural and normative constraints, but also by 'internal' organisational pressures within the media, which are equally potent contributors to the reproduction of the status quo. As Golding and Elliott (1979, p. 18) observe:

> The content of broadcast news portrays a very particular view of the world that we can label ideological . . . This is not the result of a conspiracy within newsrooms or of the

inadequacies, professional or political, of broadcast journalists. It is a necessary result of the structure of news-gathering and production, and of the routines and conventions built into broadcasting practice.

More specifically, the frameworks of perception which media news employs to interpret events and issues are partly 'internally' generated through editorial practices and procedures, technical restrictions, professional ideologies about journalistic objectivity and impartiality, and so on. A number of practical constraints, such as time limits (working against the clock), the desire to produce visually interesting material, pressures to obtain 'hot' news, as well as the standard size of a newspaper or length of a news broadcast, structure the need for a constant 'amount' of news to be regularly available, in more or less constant portions (foreign news, sports, industrial news, and so on) and often consigned to specific sections of the paper or programme. Therefore, for these reasons alone one cannot regard news reporting as merely recounting faithfully 'what happens in the world'.

The media operate with definitions of what is significant and 'newsworthy', with 'a set of institutional definitions and meanings . . . commonly referred to as *news values*' (Hall, in Cohen and Young, 1973, p. 87). Journalists claim that their professional training, and expertly acquired 'nose' for a story, give them a special capacity for recognising what events and individuals are 'news' by virtue of their unusual or humanly interesting nature. Thus, for instance, stories which can be made dramatic and visually attractive (with suitably available photographs or film), those which can be reduced to the level of personalities and individuals, those which are immediate and presentable as completed accounts of discrete events or issues, those which are supposedly entertaining, quirkily diverting or titillating, or especially those which involve 'bad news' or the disruption of the normal pattern of events, are more likely to be considered newsworthy by media personnel.

As a result, certain areas of social life are given greater attention by the news media, and a particularly vital aspect of this agenda-setting process is the tendency for those in powerful and advantaged positions to be *more frequently consulted* for information and opinion. As Hall *et al.* (1978, p. 58) say:

> This is what Becker has called 'the hierarchy of credibility' — the likelihood that those in powerful or high status positions in society who offer opinions about controversial topics will have their definitions accepted, because such spokesmen are understood to have access to more accurate or specialised information on particular topics than the majority of the population.

While it would be too simple to suggest a conscious process of collusion between the news media and those in dominant positions in society as bringing about these circumstances, it is nevertheless the case that particular *structures of interpretation* are established which serve as given frames of reference within which issues can be 'naturally' located. Alternative interpretations have to be able to operate within this framework or have to face a struggle for recognition and legitimacy with the cards stacked heavily against them.

While it is obviously important to recognise the constraining effects and influence of technical and organisational aspects of media production on the nature of the end product, we cannot ignore or minimise a fundamental material constraint, that of the *pattern of ownership and control*. Quite simply, the media are big business, owned by or linked to some of the largest capitalist enterprises in society, so it would be surprising to find them adopting a consistently critical perspective on society and/or embracing a framework of interpretation and explanation at odds with that of the dominant value system — revealing social inequalities, offering radical solutions, and so on.

But the media are not a mere component of capitalist society: they are increasingly a part of capitalist commercial conglomerates. The growth of monopoly capitalism in the second half of the twentieth century is graphically reflected in the mass media, with their progressive concentration in the hands of a few large companies as a result of mergers and takeovers. In 1970, for instance, in Britain, five companies were responsible for 65 per cent of record sales, 70 per cent of paperback books, 78 per cent of cinema audiences and 71 per cent of daily newspaper sales, and the top five commercial TV companies accounted for 74 per cent of TV audiences.

Thus, the media have increasingly become parts of powerful capitalist interests through a steady concentration of control. There has occurred a progressive *interrelation* of different sectors of the media, with large corporations coming to accumulate control in several sectors simultaneously: in Britain, ATV for instance has interests not only in television but in feature films, commercial radio, theatres and music; Granada TV's television interests are supplemented by holdings in music, films, commercial radio, books and bingo; Thames Television, controlled by EMI, one of the world's biggest record producers, have sports facilities, films, commercial radio and theatres under its control.

The major motivation for this diversification and conglomeration appears to be the desire on the part of large enterprises to find ways of maintaining and expanding their profit potential. The acquisition of interests in a range of media outlets allows these companies to spread their risks, to minimise the possibility of being trapped in a sphere of the media which experiences a down-swing in popularity, and to cushion the effects of having to reduce their control in any particular media sphere as a result of possible government limitations on concentration. But such diversification also facilitates certain very profitable production strategies, one of which has recently become highly prevalent — that of the 'spin-off'. If a large organisation controls a variety of media outlets, then a single media product — say, a film — can generate a great variety of associated profitable 'spin-offs'. Audiences who have seen a film are persuaded to buy the book of the film, the special glossy magazine, the music from the soundtrack, the book recounting the making of the film, and so on.

A number of important implications follow from the nature and pattern of media ownership. The goal of maximum profit and the need to maintain advertising revenue, to attract the widest audience, to appeal to everyone and offend no one, increase the likelihood of an attempt to find the 'lowest common denominator' at which to direct output. Furthermore, an equally vital consequence is implicit in concentration, as

Murdock and Golding (1977, p. 105) point out:

> Concentration limits the range and diversity of views and
> opinions which are able to find public expression. More
> significantly, it is those views and opinions representing
> the least powerful social groups which are systematically
> excluded by the process of concentration.

Thus the 'ownership and control of the means of mental production', as Marxists such as Miliband (1973, p. 203) put it,
becomes increasingly concentrated also.

The Marxist view of the media is very different from that of
media personnel and the pluralist conception to which we referred earlier, in emphasising that the media and their products
cannot be seen outside the context of the material interests of
capitalist society, its system of production, and relations of
domination and control. For the Marxist, the media constitute
a fundamental instrument of control possessed by the dominant class, who, besides controlling material production, also
control the production of ideas through ownership of the
communications media. The media serve, along with the
family, the education system, religion, and so on, as part of
the ideological apparatus used by the dominant class to reproduce the system of class domination.

The media, according to Marxists, systematically reproduce
the ideology and so hegemony of the dominant class, and
disseminate these ruling ideas into the consciousness of subordinate groups, thus shaping the form and impact of the
value systems of these groups. They provide justifications and
legitimations for prevailing socio-economic and political
arrangements, excluding radical critiques and challenges to
the system of material and power inequalities. Thus the
presentation of a whole range of institutions, events and
behaviour patterns in society (for example, patterns of inequality and poverty, deviants, women) is systematically
distorted, since they take bourgeois capitalist society as their
given base-point for interpreting social reality and for understanding social relations within it.

Ethnic relations, deviance and the media

A good illustration of our arguments about the socially produced nature of media news, and more particularly of its role
in defining the issues and the scope and area of the debate,
can be seen in the reporting of ethnic relations. Studies suggest that while the media do not necessarily encourage racial
prejudice, their style of reporting defines the *presence* of
ethnic minorities as an objective problem for society — that
is, ethnic relations are a matter of the problems created by
coloured people merely being here. Hartman and Husband's
study (1974) found that in areas without large immigrant
populations, children obtained their knowledge, ideas and
opinions about immigrants predominantly from the media
rather than through personal contact, and moreover, as a result
of this exposure, immigrants were seen as causing trouble and
conflict, as being a 'social problem' in themselves.

Coverage of ethnic minorities in the media tends to be disproportionately unfavourable, focusing particularly on the
immediate social and political tensions of the presence of
ethnic minorities, with little real analysis of their structural
position — for instance, in the early 1970s, black 'mugging'
received considerable media coverage, but the economic,
social and educational deprivations of blacks did not. The
absence of *background exposition* by the media of events and
issues is particularly noticeable in the case of ethnic relations:
in their reporting, the news media give little consideration to
the long-term and more immediate historical contexts in
which ethnic relations have evolved. As we have seen in
Chapter 3 when discussing race relations, British colonial
history has had crucial implications for the way in which
those of Asian and African descent are perceived, though the
widely exploitative nature of this period of British capitalist
expansion is rarely discussed in the media. Perhaps even more
pertinently, analysis of the *context* in which post-war immigration from the Commonwealth into Britain occurred is
largely neglected in discussion of ethnic relations. Commonwealth immigration was encouraged by governments and
employers to satisfy post-war demand for labour in jobs of
low pay and inferior work conditions and hours; the media

'silence' on the economic functions of immigrant labour contrasts sharply with their frequently strident attacks on newly arrived groups of immigrants, such as Ugandan, Malawi and Kenyan Asians, or the dependants of already resident immigrants. Sensational and exaggerated headlines condemning their supposed exploitation of welfare services can only serve to generate negative connotations around those of minority ethnic background and to confirm their presence as a 'problem'.

This confirmatory effect also appears in the reporting of deviance and crime, where the media are crucial agents in the defining of groups as deviant, as violators of prevailing social norms. They shape public knowledge about crime, and infuse that understanding with particular interpretations, so that the framework of what exactly constitutes 'the problem of crime' as a matter for public debate is set not by any objective criteria of frequency, seriousness, or whatever, but by the 'picture' of crime portrayed by the media. In Chapter 10 on deviance, we shall examine at greater length how the attachment of a deviant label to some actors and to some behaviour is very much a social process, with distinct implications for those on the receiving end and for their subsequent interaction with the rest of society: here we wish to emphasise that a particularly vital element of the media's role in this defining process serves to reinforce and sustain a dominant consensual morality.

As Cohen (1973), and Hall *et al.* (1978) have stressed, the media are frequently prime contributors to the creation of 'folk devils', around whom 'moral panics' take root, exaggerating the incidence of a phenomenon, increasing the likelihood of it being noticed, whipping up concern over its supposed epidemic proportions, and mobilising society against the perceived threat. This process of manufacturing 'folk devils' occurs particularly in periods of social, economic or political crisis or upheaval, and the responsibility for this state of affairs is directed at groups whose marginal structural position makes them ideal scapegoats. The exaggeration and stereotyping of their behaviour as 'mindless', 'wild' and irrationally founded simultaneously places them outside acceptable boundaries and depicts them as threats to social order, so that any explanation which locates their behaviour structurally, and critically analyses the contribution of existing social arrangements to their actions, is rendered irrelevant and easily dismissed.

Thus Teddy Boys, Mods and Rockers, Hippies, Skinheads, 'drug-takers' and 'football hooligans' have been prime targets for media identification as 'folk devils', and the subsequently created 'moral panic' has served to reinforce dominant social norms and to legitimise increased formal social control in the shape of 'law and order' campaigns.

The media and industrial relations

While such areas of behaviour are never far from the headlines of media news, pride of place in this respect is more regularly accorded to the reporting of industrial relations and economic affairs. In recent years, there has been a considerable amount of sociological investigation into the presentation of industrial and economic news, casting grave doubt on the notion that the news media present impartial and authentic records of events, of 'what's happened'.

The general conclusion to be drawn from such research is that trade unions, workers and strikers tend to be portrayed unfavourably as the root cause of national economic problems and under-performance, of industrial trouble and disruption, and of harm and inconvenience to the lives and interests of their fellow-citizens. Specifically, industrial relations tend to be discussed around notions of a unifying 'national interest', so that the range of images and interpretations employed by the media are contained within a set of *consensual assumptions* about the relations between capital and labour. Thus strikes are located within the context of their impact on *our* national economy, from whose smooth running we all benefit equally, and from whose disruption we all suffer equally, regardless of the disproportionate concentration of ownership of wealth and property and the unequal distribution of the capitalist cake. The state is presented as the neutral overseer of the national interest in handling the economy and in industrial disputes, working disinterestedly for 'the public good'; 'sectional interests' are equated with the shortsighted demands of greedy workers and/or the dubious political motives of a minority of activists, rather than as arising from the structure of inequality within capitalist society.

Accordingly, strikes are invariably 'bad news' and to be deplored, regardless of any inherent justice in the strikers' grievances or demands, or in the principles on which the action is based. They are always disruptive because they interrupt the production of goods and services that are equally beneficial to all. The 'national interest' is the ultimate barometer against which action is to be measured, so that trade-union action is reported and analysed primarily within the context of national economic performance, its impact on trade and foreign customers, and only incidentally, *if at all*, within a framework which assesses the inherent validity or justice of their actions.

In fact, union leaders are invariably asked to provide justification for industrial action *vis-à-vis* society with little regard or consideration for the internal merits of their case. As a matter of *routine*, 'There is the constant assumption of the correctness of the managerial argument, that strikes achieve nothing and are basically irrational' (Walton and Davis, 1977, p. 129). Workers, then, can have little hope that their actions will be interpreted as matters of legitimate grievance, or still less as expressions of a fundamental conflict of interests in the work-place or the wage-labour relationship: their actions are more likely to be seen as disrupting the orderly patterns which management are seeking to maintain, as threatening national economic health, or as the misplaced, inexplicable bloody-mindedness of workers led by the nose by minority elements.

Disputes and poor economic performance, then, unequivocally become problems caused by the *work-force* in a particular industry, with little reference to the inadequacies of management, investment strategies or international recession. The outcome of this is the distortion and simplification, not necessarily by conscious design, of industrial and economic matters in media news. A striking example in recent years has been the way in which the news media have tended to present inflation as unambiguously linked to wage increases, so that 'the problems of an economic system are thus reduced to the irresponsible actions of trade unionists' (Philo, Beharrel and Hewitt, 1977, p. 20). Yet, as these writers note, even *The Times* acknowledged that, during the first six months of 1975, average earnings rose by 6.1 per cent, while retail prices rose 17.3 per cent.

Now the successful dissemination of a particular explanation of a fundamental economic problem like inflation is not merely important for the way in which it attributes responsibility and to whom, but also for the acceptability and legitimacy accorded to *policies* for its *solution*. If wage rises are presented as 'causing inflation', policies controlling wage increases, irrespective of their effects on the distribution of wealth and patterns of inequality, may come to be regarded as right and proper, so that 'Rationality and hard "realism" are thus presented as being the prerogative of those who are in favour of wage restraint and of allowing unemployment to rise' (Philo, Beharrel and Hewitt, 1977, p. 13).

These processes of distortion and simplification are also manifested in the picture of the incidence and patterns of strikes presented in the news media, and in the *angle of emphasis* adopted in their interpretation. The *Bad News* team (Glasgow University Media Group, 1976) observed consistent 'over-reporting' of disputes in some British industries, notably car manufacture, and transport and communications, to the neglect of others, and a systematic tendency to report disputes with the emphasis on such themes as 'inconvenience to the public' and the 'threat to national economic interest'.

Furthermore, the partial nature of media news is reflected in the tendency to indulge in sensationalised reporting, which concentrates on *consequences* and *effects*, on incidents and personalities, at the expense of analysis of causes and of structural background and context. Thus interviews with commuters affected by a transport strike, films or photographs of jostling picket lines or of housewives in supermarket queues, are given greater prominence, not least because they correspond with 'news values' of what constitutes 'good television' or 'good copy'. While this may satisfy media personnel, it frequently means that the real issues at stake in an industrial dispute become lost, and the dominant interpretation of strikes as disruptive and irrational, embraced by owners and managers, is sustained.

In fact, the importance of the internal construction and presentation of news items, while superficially appearing non-problematic, cannot be underestimated. The *Bad News* study points to the TV news media's tendency to seek 'facts' and information from official management sources, and to rely on workers to provide filmable 'events', while the *location* of filmed interviews may give authority to or discredit those involved: official spokesmen and management are far more likely to be interviewed in the quiet and comfortable surroundings of a studio or office, while workers' representatives more frequently have to put their case outside factory gates, surrounded by vociferous colleagues, background traffic, or whatever. Moreover, the *language* in which disputes are reported is an integral part of the framework of interpretation provided by the media. The use of such terms as 'moderates', 'militants', or 'extremists', of 'wildcat' or 'lightning' strikes, of 'violence on the picket-lines', constitutes a symbolic code which grants implicit legitimacy to managers' and owners' actions and opinions, while simultaneously denying it to those of the workers. But occasionally, of course, the news media are faced with the problem of high-status occupational groups involved in disputes but not fitting the stereotype of 'revolting workers'. In such circumstances these disputes receive rather different treatment, so that the grievances of, say, doctors are presented in a more sympathetic light, worthy of more legitimate consideration, and are reinforced by the use of more 'gentlemanly' language ('industrial action' rather than 'strike', 'representatives' rather than 'leaders', and so on).

Ultimately, then, our argument is that the news and the media generally present a systematically partial account of social reality, drawing on particular sets of values to interpret action and events. As we have stressed, it is neither merely a question of any deliberate, purposive, conspiratorial process of manipulation, nor a question of the expression of bias in *particular* news items or on the part of *particular* media personnel. More fundamental are the kinds of assumptions *regularly* invoked in interpreting the world, so that the content of the media is *organised around* particular explanations and solutions. In this sense the ideological character of the media resides in their creating and reinforcing acceptance of dominant social and political values, which take as given, and accord legitimacy to, the socio-political and economic status quo. The provision of this 'social knowledge' by the media serves to shape the ideas and beliefs and hence the consciousness of actors, and as such constitutes an important dimension of the mechanisms of social control in society.

9.5 CONCLUSION

This chapter has suggested that ideas and beliefs may not only be used to assist members of society in understanding their world, but also as resources serving a variety of groups. Since the structural position of these groups may be unequal, it is more likely that those in advantaged positions will obtain greater benefit from the successful dissemination and institutionalisation of a particular system of belief. As Evans-Pritchard (1967, p. 21) says 'any section of society enjoying special privileges, whether magical or otherwise, produces its own mythology, the function of the myth being to give sanction to the possession of the exclusive privileges'.

REFERENCES TO CHAPTER 9

Beharrel, P. and Philo, G. (eds) (1977) *Trade Unions and the Media*, London, Macmillan.

Ben-David, J. and Zloczower, A. (1962) 'Universities and Academic Systems in Modern Societies', *European Journal of Sociology*, vol. 3, pp. 45—84.

Berger, P. and Luckmann, T. (1963) 'The Sociology of Religion and the Sociology of Knowledge', *Sociology and Social Research*, vol. 47, pp. 417—27.

Cohen, S. (1973) *Folk Devils and Moral Panics*, London, Paladin.

Cohen, S. and Young, J. (eds) (1973) *The Manufacture of News*, London, Constable.

Collins, H. and Pinch, T. (1979) 'The Construction of the Paranormal', in Wallis (1979).

Cooley, M. (1976) 'Contradictions of Science in Advanced Capitalist Society', in H. Rose and S. Rose (eds), *The Political Economy of Science*, London, Macmillan.

Demerath, N. (1965) *Social Class in American Protestantism*, Chicago, Rand McNally.

Douglas, M. (1980) *Evans-Pritchard*, London, Fontana.

Durkheim, E. (1965) *The Elementary Forms of the Religious Life*, New York, Free Press (first published in 1912).

Evans-Pritchard, E. (1937) *Witchcraft, Oracles and Magic Among the Azande*, Oxford, Clarendon Press.

Evans-Pritchard, E. (1967) 'The Morphology and Function of Magic', in J. Middleton (ed.), *Magic, Witchcraft and Curing*, London, Natural History Press.

Gerth, H. and Mills, C. W. (eds) (1948) *From Max Weber: Essays in Sociology*, London, Routledge & Kegan Paul.

Glasgow University Media Group (1976) *Bad News*, London, Routledge & Kegan Paul.

Glasner, P. (1977) *The Sociology of Secularization*, London, Routledge & Kegan Paul.

Golding, P. (1974) *The Mass Media*, London, Longman.

Golding, P. and Elliott, P. (1979) *Making the News*, London, Longman.

Hall, S. (1973) 'A World at One with Itself', in Cohen and Young (1973).

Hall, S. *et al.* (1978) *Policing the Crisis: Mugging, the State, and Law and Order*, London, Macmillan.

Hartman, P. and Husband, C. (1974) *Racism and the Mass Media*, London, Davis-Poynter.

Herberg, W. (1967) 'Religion in a Secularized Society: the New Shape of Religion in America', in R. Knudten (ed.), *The Sociology of Religion*, New York, Appleton-Century.

Hill, C. (1964) *Society and Puritanism in Pre-Revolutionary England*, London, Secker & Warburg.

Horton, R. (1960) 'A Definition of Religion and its Uses', *Journal of the Royal Anthropological Institute*, vol. 9, pp. 201–26.

Kuhn, T. (1970) *The Structure of Scientific Revolutions*, University of Chicago Press.

Kuhn, T. (1972) 'Scientific Paradigms', in B. Barnes (ed.), *Sociology of Science*, Harmondsworth, Penguin.

Luckmann, T. (1967) *The Invisible Religion*, London, Collier-Macmillan.

Miliband, R. (1973) *The State in Capitalist Society*, London, Quartet.

Mulkay, M. (1979) *Science and the Sociology of Knowledge*, London, Allen & Unwin.

Murdock, G. and Golding, P. (1977) 'Beyond Monopoly – Mass Communications in an Age of Conglomerates', in Beharrel and Philo (1977).

O'Dea, T. (1966) *The Sociology of Religion*, Englewood Cliffs, N. J., Prentice-Hall.

Philo, G., Beharrel, P. and Hewitt, J. (1977) 'One-Dimensional News – Television and the Control of Explanation', in Beharrel and Philo (1977).

Polanyi, M. (1958) *Personal Knowledge*, University of Chicago Press.

Radcliffe-Brown, A. (1945) *Structure and Function in Primitive Society*, New York, Free Press.

Rodinson, M. (1977) *Islam and Capitalism*, Harmondsworth, Penguin.
Samuelson, K. (1961) *Religion and Economic Action*, London, Heinemann.
Scharf, B. (1970) *The Sociological Study of Religion*, London, Hutchinson.
Stark, W. (1967) *The Sociology of Religion*, London, Routledge & Kegan Paul.
Thomas, K. (1971) *Religion and the Decline of Magic*, London, Weidenfeld & Nicolson.
Wallis, R. (ed.) (1979) *On the Margins of Science*, Sociological Review Monograph No. 37, Keele University Press.
Walton, P. and Davis, H. (1977) 'Bad News for Trade Unionists', in Beharrel and Philo (1977).
Weber, M. (1952) *The Protestant Ethic and the Spirit of Capitalism*, London, Allen & Unwin.
Webster, A. (1979) 'Scientific Controversy and Socio-Cognitive Metonymy', in Wallis (1979).
Westergaard, J. (1977) 'Power, Class and the Media', in J. Curran *et al.* (eds), *Mass Communication and Society*, London, Arnold.
Wilson, B. (1966) *Religion in a Secular Society*, London, C. A. Watts & Co.
Worsley, P. (1968) *The Trumpet Shall Sound*, London, MacGibbon & Kee.

10

Deviance

10.1 INTRODUCTION: THE NATURE OF DEVIANCE

In our first chapter we pointed to a popular view which denies
validity to sociological explanation by asserting the unique-
ness and individuality of human beings — in simple terms
'we're all different' — so that generalisations about behaviour
cannot be made. Furthermore, this recognition of individual
differences is also reinforced by an *approval* of the fact: again,
the casual observer often maintains that 'it would be boring
if we were all the same', and generations of men and women
have supported the principle of 'vive la différence!'

But by no means all the people we encounter who are 'different' from us are as easily accepted; foreigners, for instance,
may cause us embarrassment and irritation by their peculiar
inability to speak our native language or to abide by our
'sensible' practices like queueing, and some categories of
people who are physically different through no fault of their
own — whether by infirmity or deformity — can cause us to
feel uncomfortable.

So, the toleration of differences between human beings is
highly provisional, and this is equally so in the case of individuals and groups whose behaviour patterns generally — or
particular aspects of them — differ from what is considered
'normal'. Such individuals or groups are engaging in 'deviant
behaviour': that is, 'behaviour which somehow departs from
what a group expects to be done or what it considers the
desirable way of doing things' (Cohen, 1971, p. 9).

Assuming for the moment that there exists in a social group

some set of shared expectations about what is 'normal' behaviour, we have here a conception of deviance as the violation of the accepted norms or social rules of a group or society, and of a deviant as someone who transgresses these (apparently) taken-for-granted standards. Thus nude-bathers, bank-robbers, alcoholics, suicides, shoplifters, adulterers, Marxists, tramps, rapists, 'tomboys', skinheads, feminists, murderers and female wrestlers are deviants because they indulge in behaviour which the rest of the society or group regards as socially different, odd, or undesirable.

Most people's direct experience of or contact with such individuals is often highly limited, yet despite this the reaction to them is invariably one of disapproval, fear, suspicion, hostility or outrage. Why is this? Essentially, deviants are disturbing because they disrupt our picture of reality by behaving in a way which questions our expectations of what 'normal people' do — 'normal people' only drink in moderation, 'normal' women do not indulge in anything so unfeminine as wrestling, 'normal people' *pay* for goods in supermarkets, and so on. Thus our social expectations about behaviour structure for us a conception of stable, orderly, understandable social life. Deviants are awkward people who disturb this, but by identifying them as 'deviant' we can place their behaviour in a category outside normality which makes it comprehensible to us and stabilises our perception of social reality.

Our observations so far on deviance have emphasised the reaction of others, and this in itself indicates one very important feature of deviance: what is regarded as deviance is very much a matter of *social definition* imposed by a community or by groups within that community. Thus a particular pattern of behaviour is not deviant *per se*, whether it be murder, lesbianism, belching, or whatever, but is defined as such by a social group. In the sociological sense, then, deviance is indeed *social* behaviour (despite being frequently described in everyday terminology as 'anti-social behaviour'), since it involves reaction by some actors to the behaviour of others with some kind of sanction such as social disapproval, ostracism, imprisonment or execution.

The socially defined nature of deviance is highlighted even

564 *Introductory Sociology*

further when we recognise that what is regarded as deviance
in one society may not be so (or not so seriously regarded) in
another: that is, deviant behaviour is often *culturally relative*.
While sexual intercourse between black and white individuals
is, in certain circles in Britain, merely frowned upon, in South
Africa it is a criminal activity. Similarly, incest among those
of high birth in Ancient Egypt was considered vital for the
preservation of the lineage stock, while in modern societies
such behaviour is both illegal and a matter of almost universal
public revulsion.

Furthermore, within a particular society variations occur
over time in what is held to be deviant or criminal: many
activities regarded with disapproval in Victorian times (particularly for women) are now commonly accepted with little or
no controversy — mixed bathing on beaches is a matter of
comparative indifference to even the most ardent moralist in
the 1980s. Similarly, professional boxing attracts considerable
public interest, yet it was illegal in New York State as late as
1920.

Most societies, too, suspend or modify temporarily their
definitions of deviance in particular contexts and circumstances. In Western societies killing is ordinarily regarded as
the most serious of offences, but in the defence of the nation
it may become an act of heroism and deserving of honour or
reward, and even peacetime killing is hedged about with qualifications like 'self-defence', 'manslaughter', 'justifiable homicide', and so on. Similarly, in many pre-industrial societies
and traditional rural areas in industrial societies, killing to
avenge family honour may be a duty which members are
expected to fulfill. Thus deviant behaviour cannot be conceived as something which is absolute or universal but must be
seen as socially variable and dependent on what a particular
society or social group at a particular time defines as deviant.

Reference to the definitions and reactions of 'society' in
the application of the label of 'deviance' to behaviour must
not lead us into the trap of simplistically positing an unambiguous or voluntaristic consensus on what is considered
normal or deviant in any society. There may exist a widespread consensus on what is deviant in certain spheres of
behaviour, but no such straightforward agreement prevails in

all other areas. While child-battering or bigamy would be un-equivocally viewed as deviant by the vast majority of people in Western societies, other activities such as the consumption of soft drugs or the use of contraceptives before marriage evoke no clear-cut consensus as to the extent of their 'deviant' nature. Such examples as these may sensitise us, therefore, to the fact that the characterisation of some patterns of behaviour as deviant may ultimately depend on the ability of certain groups to *impose their definitions* of 'normality' and 'deviance' on the rest of society and hence to manufacture an apparent consensus about what is proper and improper behaviour.

In this chapter we concentrate our attention on two major areas of deviance: crime and suicide. While an analysis of such kinds of non-conformist behaviour is worth while by virtue of their intrinsically interesting nature, they also reflect very significant theoretical debates in sociology, particularly that between positivist and anti-positivist explanations of social phenomena.

10.2 EXPLANATIONS OF CRIMINAL BEHAVIOUR

If one accepts a conception of crime or deviance as being the behaviour of individuals who are not like normal or law-abiding citizens, then it follows that there must be some characteristics or propensities which mark off criminals or deviants from non-criminal or normal actors. Thus their behaviour can be seen as a sign or product of some personal or social trait(s) which make them different from the rest of society. Such a conception is certainly sustained in the mass media, where football hooligans, muggers, drug-takers and others are often portrayed as different to the point of being demoniacal. At best, many areas of deviant behaviour, and especially crime, are seen as *social problems*, about which something should be done, and a basically similar view has traditionally prevailed within the academic study of crime.

Positivist criminology

The study of crime has been a major meeting-point for several academic disciplines, all of which have taken the idea of crime as a 'social problem' as given: they have accepted that it is something which has to be eradicated or brought under control, and that any attempt to *explain* the phenomenon necessarily involves a commitment to a belief in the *application* of knowledge to practical ends. Thus criminology, according to this view, cannot be simply a matter of 'armchair theorising' but must involve putting analysis and explanation to use in developing policies and programmes to combat crime and to 'reform', 'resocialise' or 'treat' the criminal.

This correctionalist stance, with its prevalent emphasis on order and control, is a product of the fundamental assumptions underpinning much of the study of crime. The bulk of this study has been preoccupied with what Matza (1964) has called 'the search for differentiation', based on the premise that there is something 'wrong' with the criminal, or at least something very different about him as compared with law-abiding citizens, generating his criminal behaviour and inhibiting conformity to conventional norms and legal rules. Thus 'criminality' resides in individuals or social groups and can be identified and explained by examining personal biography, background events or circumstances of criminals.

The criminal, then, is someone whose behaviour is *determined*, the product of some constitutional defect, of some physical or psychological condition or abnormality, or of some social circumstances or subculturally specific experiences. Such explanations of criminality have traditionally centred on the common principle that it is possible to identify causal forces or factors fundamentally distinguishing criminals from the rest of society: that is, that an explanation of criminal behaviour within a *positivist scientific tradition* is an attainable goal.

Gibbons and Jones (1975) suggest that we can broadly differentiate explanations into three types.

(1) *Biogenic explanations* of crime identify motivations to criminal behaviour in the physical or constitutional make-up of individuals. Thus early explanations which posited a link between criminality and physical degeneracy, or which ascribed criminal propensities to personalities or temperaments associated with particular body types or shapes, served

as precursors to apparently more sophisticated explanations such as chromosome theories, in which criminality has been linked to the existence of an extra chromosome in the genetic constitution of some males.

(2) *Psychogenic approaches* identify a causal link between criminal tendencies and psychological characteristics and processes. Freudians argue that very early childhood experiences which disturb or distort the development of a stable personality may result in later childhood and adulthood in anti-social tendencies in behaviour manifesting themselves specifically in criminal activity. Thus the causes of criminal behaviour lie in defective primary socialisation of the child, so that his or her innate anti-social motivations are not brought under control. Notably the failure to develop a warm, loving relationship with one or both parents — as the result of physical separation, deprivation, or harsh or inconsistent treatment — is seen as distinctly criminogenic, and subsequent criminal behaviour constitutes the 'acting out' of the feelings of guilt and frustration engendered by these early experiences.

Behavioural psychologists such as Eysenck (1970) suggest that criminal behaviour, like other patterns of behaviour, is the product of an individual's receptiveness to a process of psychological conditioning, and that a specific genetically determined personality type, the *neurotic extrovert*, is less conditionable and hence more prone to criminality than others. Deviant behaviour, then, is a product of the individual's psychological incapacity to respond to the social training experienced in childhood and adolescence which conditions 'normal' individuals away from anti-social conduct.

Both biogenic and psychogenic explanations attempt to answer the questions 'What kinds of people commit crime?' and 'How do they get like this?' They attempt to identify types of 'maladjusted' individuals with some defects or pathological characteristics which predispose or impel them towards involvement in criminal activity.

(3) *Sociogenic theories*, on the other hand, see criminal behaviour as socially acquired and hence focus on the ways in which cultural and/or social structural factors are crime-producing. Thus social environmental influences or subcultural socialisation experiences in family, class and peer group make

it likely that some social groups will be involved in criminal activity.

Now, while we can identify fairly easily, even from such a brief résumé as this, major points of divergence between these differing types of explanation, they share a fundamental similarity which we need to reiterate and bear in mind: that is, the belief that a meaningful distinction can be drawn between 'criminals' and 'non-criminals', and a commitment to the utility of formulating a theory to account for this distinction. This implies, then, that these types of explanation make certain assumptions about the phenomena under investigation — not only about the *actors* involved but also about the *behaviour* in which these actors engage.

They assume particularly that their criminal behaviour can be meaningfully viewed as homogeneous and therefore subsumed under some single explanatory umbrella, and that the causes of this behaviour lie outside the actors' control in peculiar genes, defective personality, distinctive subcultural norms, or whatever. Individuals or groups commit offences because of the peculiar forces acting upon them.

In popular belief and in the eyes of the media, politicians, moralists, and indeed of many of those involved in what we may broadly call 'social work' with criminals, non-sociological explanations of criminal behaviour have held sway and continue to do so. While it is our task here neither to examine in detail such explanations nor to account for their relative popularity, we must briefly consider how and why sociologists have found them unsatisfactory and have felt the need for a sociological explanation of crime.

Most sociologists would reject non-sociological explanations of criminal behaviour as being inadequate and incomplete rather than for being necessarily 'wrong'. Fundamentally, the phenomenon under investigation — crimes — are unavoidably violations of *legal statutes*, which are not ethereal and absolute but are socially defined rules and hence part of social structural arrangements. Furthermore, even though crime may be individually enacted (which is not always the case anyway), we cannot assume that it is merely individually motivated. We must see criminals as located in a social structure and subject to specific conditions, opportunities and experiences, so that we must ask what it is about social structures which generate criminality and its preponderant incidence *within* certain groups in society. That is, criminal behaviour is not randomly distributed by genes or personality but follows a consistent *social pattern*, which must be explained by examining the different structural positions of criminals and non-criminals.

While such explanations vary in emphasis on the key explanatory factors they identify, there is a basic acceptance of the idea of *social forces* as causal in criminal behaviour. Before considering them in detail, however, we must examine the extent to which crime is socially patterned.

10.3 THE PATTERN OF CRIME

The patterns and trends in criminal behaviour are usually constructed by using official criminal statistics. We shall present a critique of these statistics later in the chapter, but at this stage we shall accept them more or less uncritically and merely suggest some of the difficulties to which they give rise. It should be noted, however, that the figures to which we refer are those relating to *indictable* crimes that are *known to the police*. Indictable offences are those which may be tried by jury and are usually considered to be more serious than non-indictable offences which are often ignored in discussions on crime trends. However, not only are non-indictable offences more numerous but they include behaviour that is often regarded as quite serious, for example common assault, drunken driving and taking away a car without the owner's consent.

The pattern of indictable offences for the years 1971–6 in England and Wales is shown in Table 10.1. The fact that these figures refer only to known offences means, of course, that they tell us absolutely nothing about the *actual* level of crime in our society. Many factors can produce rises in the level of recorded crime: better and more efficient policing, increased police resources, changes in the law, changes in public co-operation, and so on.

As well as examining the volume of crime, we also need to identify its *social incidence*. Generally, crime appears to occur most frequently among *young working-class males*, and is

TABLE 10.1
Indictable offences known to the police

1971	1,666,000
1972	1,690,000
1973	1,658,000
1974	1,963,000
1975	2,106,000
1976	2,136,000

Source: Central Statistical Office, *Annual Abstract of Statistics*, London, HMSO, 1979, p. 101.

primarily located in *urban areas* and committed *against property*. Let us examine the figures that appear to support this pattern.

Sex and age

The ratio for the *conviction* of male and female offenders over the last thirty years or so has remained fairly constant at approximately 7 to 1, and in both sexes criminal activity appears to peak in adolescence and early adulthood. (See Table 10.2.)

TABLE 10.2
Conviction per 100,000 population (England and Wales)

Age	Males 1972	Males 1975	Females 1972	Females 1975
Up to 14	1,229	1,291	124	150
14–17	4,597	5,229	490	660
17–21	5,475	6,428	639	830
21–30	2,427	2,714	368	460
30+	567	642	137	170

Source: CSO, *Social Trends*, London, HMSO, 1976, p. 185.

Although the age distribution is the same, it would appear that women and girls commit fewer offences than men and boys. It has been suggested that this pattern may be partly explained by the fact that girls have alternative ways of protesting against conformity and the adult world, and that these are not usually defined as 'delinquent'. For example, the dual standard of morality which condemns early sexual behaviour in girls but tolerates it in boys, which we have already noted in Chapter 6, means that sex can serve as a protest for girls in a way it cannot for boys. As West (1967, p. 15) puts it: 'It has been pointed out with justification that troublesome boys go in for crime, whereas troublesome girls merely go with boys.'

On the other hand, the law often operates in a sexist way by treating the sexual adventures of girls as delinquent when the same behaviour by boys might be ignored. So, when girls *are* brought before the courts it is very often for sex offences and for 'incorrigibility' or 'running away', which equally often are euphemisms for sex-related behaviour. The police may also be more 'chivalrous' when choosing between arresting or cautioning females than in their contact with male offenders. Similarly, the role that females play in criminal activities — such as a 'look-out' or receiver — may not be as easily detectable as that played by men.

Social class

The published statistics do not provide information on the social-class background of offenders, but other types of data would seem to indicate that a larger proportion of working-class people than middle-class people are convicted of crimes. Estimates based on such studies conclude that the sons of manual workers are four times as likely to be found guilty of offences as the sons of businessmen and professionals. Again, this does not *necessarily* mean that working-class boys and adults *commit* more crime than members of the upper and middle classes but that they are more likely to fall foul of the official judicial system. Their offences may be defined as more serious by police, magistrates and judges, and they are less likely to benefit from informal means of social control.

Geographical location

In most societies crime rates appear to be significantly lower

TABLE 10.3

*Known indictable crime per 100,000 population according
to size of town and police area (1965)*

Greater London	3,378
Large cities (over 400,000 population)	3,327
Large towns (200,000—400,000)	3,333
Medium-sized towns (100,000—200,000)	2,795
Small towns (less than 100,000)	2,544
All urban police forces	3,176
County police forces	1,747

Source: McClintock and Avison (1968).

in rural areas than urban areas. (See Table 10.3.)

Various factors may account for this pattern. Large urban
areas afford greater opportunity for criminal activity, with
the availability of department stores, warehouses, and so on,
and their police resources are more extensive. In rural areas,
too, more informal methods of social control may be employed by police officers, who may be more integrated into
the immediate local community than are their urban counterparts.

Types of offence

Even though the rate of known crime appears to increase every
year, the general *pattern* of offences has remained remarkably
stable over the years. Consistently, the vast majority centre on
the theft of property or other types of dishonesty involving
small amounts of money or property, as Table 10.4 indicates.

'Professional crime' makes up a very small proportion of
the total, as do sex crimes and violent offences. But for this
very reason popular confusion frequently abounds. Because
the number of such offences is small, a modest numerical increase in reported crimes of violence is often distorted by the
media into a spectacular *proportional* increase. Crimes of
violence are a very minor proportion of all crimes and their
typical form is not the 'mugging' of some defenceless old

TABLE 10.4

Crimes known to the police, England and Wales (1976)

Theft and receiving	60.2%
Fraud and forgery	5.6%
Robbery	0.6%
Burglary	24.1%
Criminal damage	4.3%
Sex	1.0%
Violence against the person	3.7%
Other	0.5%

Source: CSO, *Social Trends*, London, HMSO, 1977, p. 201.

granny but a fight among friends, neighbours or relatives or a public brawl, and the apparent rise in such crimes may reflect not a more 'violent' society (a dubious description if historical comparisons are made) but a greater *willingness* to call in the police when violence does occur.

From the statistical evidence, then, it would appear that, generally, most crime is committed in urban areas against property by young, working-class boys. Consequently, much sociological research on crime has concerned itself with analysing and explaining the social pattern of juvenile delinquency, and, implicitly, with finding a *cure* for delinquency.

As we suggested earlier, sociologists traditionally started from the basic premise that the delinquent was not an isolated individual but was the product of a particular social world, and that criminal behaviour might best be explained by identifying the different structural positions of criminals. Consequently many sociological explanations have operated with the assumption that certain environmental conditions such as poverty, economic insecurity, poor housing, and so on, are more conducive to crime than other, more favourable conditions, and hence that most crime is committed by working-class people who are more likely to face these harsh social and economic conditions. Moreover, it has been claimed, the children of these families are more likely to be socialised into ways of coping with their environment which are criminal. Such assumptions led to the development of 'subcultural' explanations of delinquency.

10.4 THEORIES OF THE DELINQUENT SUBCULTURE

Traditional positivist sociological explanations take the view that delinquency is a social activity like any other, *learned* in association with others in much the same way that more conventional behaviour is learned. Furthermore, they suggest that certain norms, values and standards of behaviour become traditional among delinquent groups and are passed on and perpetuated within the group. That is, there exists a delinquent *subculture* in which certain types of delinquent or potentially delinquent behaviour are approved of or condoned. The more extreme versions of this thesis posit delinquent activity as a *requirement* for membership of the subculture.

There are certain problems associated with the concept of a delinquent subculture and, in fact, with the concept of subculture itself. The main problem concerns the nature of the relationship between the 'subculture' and the wider society in which it is located. What *are* the distinguishing characteristics of the norms and values of the wider society and how distinctive are subcultural values? Who adheres to dominant values and subcultural values? Who propagates them? How far do dominant values penetrate into 'subcultures'? These questions have not only been the concern of the critics of subculture theories but they have also been at the centre of the 'internal' debate among subculture theorists themselves.

We can broadly identify two competing conceptions of the nature of the relationship between the subculture and the larger culture which we can call 'independent' and 'reactive'. The *independent* conception sees the delinquent subculture as a discrete and self-contained set of norms and values which, while not consciously in opposition to the prevailing (largely middle-class) values of the wider culture, are the *independent* product of and solution to the group's particular way of life. The *reactive* conception, on the other hand, sees delinquent subcultural values and behaviour as a *response* to the values and opportunity structures which prevail in the wider society.

The 'independent' delinquent subculture

An example of the 'independent' variant in delinquent subculture theory is provided by Miller (1958), who argues that delinquency is, in fact, conforming behaviour. For Miller, delinquent activity is motivated by an attempt to live up to the values of the lower-class community itself and is not a reaction to, or turning away from, the values of the wider community. If a subculture exists, it does so only in the wider sense of there being different *class* subcultures, and one cannot suggest that the working-class subculture as a whole is committed to delinquency. Delinquency arises because young boys who are exposed to lower-class culture *over-conform* to its standards. By conforming to the norms of this culture they *automatically* violate middle-class norms, but this does not necessarily imply that these are maliciously or deliberately flouted.

Miller supports this interpretation by arguing that lower-class life, in common with all distinctive cultural groups, is characterised by a set of 'focal concerns'. These focal concerns, together with their opposites, are:

(i)   a concern with trouble rather than law-abiding behaviour;
(ii) toughness and masculinity rather than weakness and effeminacy;
(iii) smartness or achievement by mental agility as opposed to gullibility or achievement through routine;
(iv) excitement and thrill, as opposed to boredom and safety;
(v)   belief in fate, fortune or luck rather than control over the environment; and
(vi) autonomy and freedom, contrasted with dependency and constraint.

Miller argues that young males 'overconform' to the focal concerns of *adult* lower-class culture because of *status insecurity*, which occurs because lower-class culture is characterised by female-based households in which the significant relationships are between mature females and children. The children often have different biological fathers who may play an inconsistent and unpredictable part in the family, so that the family is not organised around the expectation of stable economic support provided by an adult male.

This type of household, Miller argues, generates delinquency, because the intensity of the mother-son tie creates an equally intense desire to demonstrate masculinity on the part of the boy. He is driven out into the adolescent street-corner group in search of the type of experiences his family cannot provide, and here he is more fully exposed to the focal concerns that *may* make him delinquent. His need to belong to the street-corner group and to gain and maintain status in it leads him to overconform to the values of lower-class culture, and to commit offences in so doing.

Miller has been criticised for appearing to stress the homogeneity of lower-class culture, which is, in fact, subject to wide regional and ethnic variation, with only blacks having any history of female-based households in the extreme form he describes. Furthermore, critics argue, his focal concerns are more likely to be found among the inhabitants of slums in large cities than elsewhere. Moreover, his reliance upon these concerns in his explanation has been criticised as tautological, in that they are *derived* from observing behaviour and then used to *explain* that same behaviour. He might well have done better to look in more detail at the structural factors giving rise to the focal concerns such as the prolonged instability of employment and the whole uncertainty of the lower-class way of life.

The delinquent subculture as 'reaction'

The 'reactive' conception of delinquent subcultures is illustrated by two explanations which, although different in emphasis and detail, can both be differentiated from that of Miller.

Cloward and Ohlin (1960) build on the foundations provided by Merton's (1938) reworking of Durkheim's concept of *anomie*. Merton argues that anomie results when there is a disjunction between the valued cultural goals of a society — in the American case, economic success — and the legitimate means of reaching such goals, such as hard work, education, or speculating on the stock market. Deviance is caused by the fact that large numbers of people at the lower levels of the social structure *accept* the dominant values and cultural goals but are unable to realise them by legitimate means, and so they 'innovate'. Thus, for example, if monetary wealth is stressed as the goal towards which each must strive, then it will be sought by illegitimate means such as robbery or fraud.

However, Cloward and Ohlin argue that not all boys who find their legitimate avenues for advancement blocked are able to utilise *illegitimate* means because these are not evenly distributed either; for instance, not everyone has the opportunity to learn how to crack safes. Moreover, the subcultural form which develops depends upon the illegitimate means available. According to Cloward and Ohlin, *criminal subcultures* devoted to theft, extortion and other means of securing an income are most likely to occur in more stable slum neighbourhoods which provide a hierarchy of criminal opportunity. Adult criminals exercise social control over the young to make them desist from expressive, non-utilitarian actions that might attract the attention of the police to their own activities. Similarly, *conflict subcultures* tend to arise in disorganised areas with high rates of geographical mobility and social instability that provide *no* organised hierarchy for criminal development. These boys turn to violence, gang warfare, the defence of 'turf', as alternatives. Finally, the *retreatist subculture* emerges as an adjustment pattern for those lower-class youths who have failed to find a position in either the criminal or the conflict subcultures because of lack of access to either legitimate or illegitimate opportunity structures. These 'double-failures' tend to move into a retreatist pattern of behaviour revolving around the use of drugs.

Our second illustration of a 'reactive' conception of delinquent subcultures is to be found in the work of Cohen (1955), who argues that Merton's innovation adaptation cannot account for the distinctive content of the delinquency of juvenile working-class gangs. Cohen points out that far from being an attempt to achieve material success by means of rationally calculated property theft much delinquency is non-utilitarian, malicious and negativistic in character. Boys do not steal in order to get their hands on valued objects, they steal for the hell of it, taking a malicious pleasure in the discomfort of others and in breaking the rules of middle-class society.

Cohen explains this by constructing an 'ideal type' of middle-class standards which he contrasts with the values of delinquents. He argues that subcultural values are at one and the same time in opposition to and a reaction to, those of the middle class. Cohen, then, reaches a conclusion which is almost diametrically opposed to that of Miller. How does he do this?

He maintains that a collective way of life — a subculture — develops when a number of people with a *common problem of adjustment* are in effective interaction. The common problem of delinquents derives from their working-class socialisation, which does not prepare them adequately for successful functioning in middle-class-dominated institutions such as schools, youth clubs and work-places. However, these institutions reward and punish the boys by reference to a middle-class set of standards: a 'middle-class measuring rod'. This set of standards or values stresses the virtue of ambition, the ethic of individual responsibility for actions, deferred gratification, the control of aggression, good manners, the importance of respect for private property and the enjoyment of wholesome recreation. Because the working-class boy is ill-equipped to measure up to these standards, he inevitably suffers disapproval, rejection and punishment. The delinquent subculture provides a way of *adjusting* to the resulting problem of status deprivation which lower-class youths share. This sense of deprivation stems not only from the negative evaluations of others but also from self-derogation: the working-class boy shares in the poor evaluation that others make of him. This is partly because there exists 'the democratic status universe', whereby everyone is expected to strive and everyone is measured against the same standard. But it is also because the boy's parents may have projected their own frustrated aspirations upon him, and because the existence of a certain degree of upward social mobility seems to indicate that it is possible to 'get on'. (That is, dominant values permeate through.)

According to Cohen, then, the young working-class male has partly accepted the values of the middle class as being a legitimate or even superior set of values. This creates status problems for him and a sense of ambivalence about his position in the world, for he not only knows that he is accorded low esteem in the eyes of the wider society but he also suffers from low *self-esteem*. Cohen's explanation of the nature of the boy's reaction to this feeling of inadequacy rests on the Freudian psychoanalytic concept of 'reaction formation'. (Basically this is an unconscious way of denying that which one really wants, exemplified by those disappointed in love claiming: 'I never fancied him/her anyway!') Cohen claims that the working-class boy has such a strong desire for status in the middle-class world — a desire which can only be frustrated — that the reaction formation is instituted against it. It is this which helps to explain the *content* and *spirit* of the delinquent subculture, as characterised by 'versatility, short-run hedonism and group autonomy'. Gang delinquency is an ambivalent denial of and opposition to the middle-class values and standards for which he has a grudging respect. The delinquent's conduct is right by the standards of his subculture *precisely because it is wrong* by the norms of *middle-class culture*, and his low status in the middle-class world is compensated by adherence to a different, antithetical set of status criteria which he *is* able to meet.

There have been many criticisms made of Cohen. Rabow (1966) questions the proposition that working-class boys accept middle-class success goals, and Short and Strodtbeck (1965) found little evidence that members of delinquent gangs reject either middle-class values or those who administer the middle-class measuring rod. Cohen stresses too strongly, it is claimed, the non-utilitarian aspects of delinquency, and his emphasis on malice and negativism leads him to miss some of the more 'positive' aspects of delinquent activity — much behaviour that is labelled 'delinquent' is not reactive or defiant but simply done for fun, for kicks. It is behaviour that, if engaged in by middle-class youngsters, would be called 'youthful high spirits'. He is also accused of relying too heavily on official statistics and therefore accepting too readily that working-class delinquency is more of a 'problem' than middle-class delinquency.

Perhaps the greatest flaw in Cohen's argument, however,

is the rather crude distinction drawn between middle-class values and those which he claims characterise the delinquent subculture. His analysis, that is, is based upon a gross, undifferentiated concept of middle-class values and an equally gross and undifferentiated characterisation of those of the delinquent subculture. This is an issue to which we shall return.

The utility of 'subculture' explanations

Our discussion so far has centred on the specific content and merits of particular subculture theories, but this should not be construed as implying that one merely has to 'choose the "best" one', for the *general* utility of explaining delinquency by recourse to subcultural theories has also been the subject of much criticism.

Various authorities question the stress that subculture theories put upon the existence of the delinquent *gang*. Much British evidence, for example, indicates that structured gangs with a leader, definite and enduring membership, and a territory are most unusual. Most delinquent acts are not committed by organised delinquent gangs but by small, fairly transient, loosely structured friendship groups. Scott (1956) found that when members of the teenage street-corner *groups* that he studied committed offences they did so as individuals, or with close friends or kin. Downes's (1966) study of East London supports this interpretation. Instead of utilising the concept of a subculture in which delinquency is a central norm, he sees working-class boys being led into delinquency by a process of 'dissociation' from the middle-class-dominated contexts of school, work and leisure. For the lower levels of the working class *leisure* becomes a central goal — the only means of achieving self-realisation — and yet leisure opportunities open to them are dull and unexciting. Delinquency is the 'solution', providing the thrills missing from conventional leisure and life generally.

These findings represent a significant critique of subculture theories, for such theories *depend* upon the existence of permanent structured gangs, since it is only via such established gangs that the transmission of specific subcultural norms and values becomes a feasible proposition. If the gang is rare, or absent, then the idea of the subculture becomes difficult to sustain.

Matza's (1964) criticisms not only throw doubt on the validity of subcultural accounts of delinquent behaviour and motivation but also raise important questions about the positivist assumptions underlying them. He argues that subcultural theories fall into the same trap as some orthodox positivist approaches in that they present a highly deterministic view of the subcultural delinquent and hence a distorted picture of delinquency.

The concept of delinquent subculture implies that working-class adolescents are committed to and organise their activities around the central value of delinquency so that illegal behaviour is widespread, collective, persistent and salient. Most working-class youth, however, do not engage regularly in criminal activity, and of those who do many apparently 'give it up' in early adulthood. How, then, can there exist delinquent subcultures of the type posited by Cohen, Cloward and Ohlin, and others?

Matza maintains that the over-deterministic assumptions of delinquent subculture theories generate a fundamentally erroneous portrayal of the nature of delinquent activity. He rejects the notion of the 'delinquent subculture' in favour of the less deterministic idea of the *subculture of delinquency*, in which the commission of offences, although common knowledge among a group of juveniles, is neither a condition of membership of the group nor a full-time activity of its members. In his view, adolescents *from time to time* act out delinquent roles rather than engage in permanent violation of the norms of conventional society. Their delinquency is casual and intermittent, they are predominantly occupied with the mundane, non-deviant activities of conforming society. They 'drift' into and out of delinquency periodically and temporarily without embracing it as a 'way of life'.

Law-breaking, according to Matza, results from the fact that male working-class adolescents' leisure time is peer-orientated and focused on asserting masculine identity and gaining acceptance by friends. They are under pressure to conform to the norms of the group because not to do so would threaten their position within it. So, when an activity is suggested which involves law-breaking, each individual adds his support, thinking that the others are in favour of it. However, Matza suggests that this is a 'comedy of errors', with each individual misapprehending the motives of all the others. These 'shared misunderstandings' are not challenged because adolescents want to appear 'one of the boys'. Their activities centre on delinquency not because of any fundamental value conflict with conventional society but because much adolescent activity is geared towards finding something to do, towards solving their 'leisure problem'. Leisure, if it is to be satisfying and exciting and at the same time a way of asserting toughness and masculinity, carries the risk of law violation.

Matza also rejects the 'absolutist' conception of values contained in subculture theories (in the form of 'conventional' societal values and 'deviant' subcultural values) in favour of a position which views commitment to values as a more problematic and relativistic process. Rather than assuming that law-abiding individuals subscribe unambiguously to a discrete set of values, he suggests that coexisting with the 'official' values of society are series of 'subterranean' values distributed throughout the various social classes and which, for the middle classes, find expression in leisure, sports and other ritual events. Values supposed to characterise delinquency, such as the search for excitement and masculinity, may be given expression on these occasions with social approval. British Rugby Union players who are predominantly middle and upper class regularly violate middle-class values and standards of behaviour relating to violence, drunkenness, obscenity, and so on, and yet this behaviour is often condoned as 'excusable high spirits', whereas similar activities by soccer supporters are condemned as 'hooliganism'.

Among working-class youth, Matza argues, this simultaneous acceptance of 'official' values and 'subterranean' values is also apparent, in that they often experience and express guilt over their law-breaking. But they, too, are able to call upon subterranean values which, particularly when activated at 'improper' moments, in inopportune circumstances and accentuated beyond an acceptable limit, take the form of delinquency. In Matza's view most rules are not categorical imperatives but qualified guides for action which are limited in terms of time, place, persons and social circumstances. The law itself recognises this with its allowance, for example, of 'justifiable homicide'. Similarly, one can avoid *moral* culpability for criminal actions if one can show that criminal intent was lacking.

He maintains that the male delinquent extends this by justifications for deviance seen as valid by himself but not by the legal system or society at large. These 'techniques of neutralisation' allow the delinquent to justify his offences to himself in particular circumstances while knowing them to be wrong. By denying responsibility for his actions, by denying any real injury to the victim, by denying that the victim deserves consideration, by condemning those who condemn him, or by appealing to higher loyalties like 'family solidarity' or 'friendship', he deflects in advance the sense of guilt which in other circumstances may have inhibited or constrained him.

Thus Matza's overall critique of subculture theorists, and his own explanation of delinquency, may be described as weakly anti-positivist, in that he does not entirely abandon the search for the structural location of delinquency or its 'causes'. However, he does raise important questions about deterministic explanations of crime, about the provisional nature of rules and values, and about the meaning of action for both actors and the rest of society. Such questions form the basis for a more thoroughgoing anti-positivist critique — which we shall examine in detail shortly.

The official crime statistics: a critique

We have already suggested that the official criminal statistics may not in fact tell us very much about the patterns of crime, trends in crime or the type of person who commits crime. This does not mean that official statistics cannot be profitably used by sociologists but that the use made of them will have to differ from that made by traditional sociology and criminology. Much recent writing on deviance suggests that, rather than assuming that these statistics represent 'hard' data which tell us something 'real' about patterns of crime within a society, they should be seen as arising out of complex processes of social interaction between offenders, victims, members of the public and formal agencies of social control, and these processes *in themselves* constitute the real problem for sociological investigation. Thus official statistics on crime may only be useful in so far as they tell us something about the activities of official agencies and about the way 'crime', the 'delinquent' and the 'criminal' are socially constructed phenomena which emerge in 'solid' form from a variety of sifting and selecting processes.

Of course, once one accepts that the dimensions of crime cannot be measured accurately by means of the official statistics, then the validity of traditional theories purporting to 'explain' crime — including subcultural theories — must be called into question, as we shall see later in this chapter.

A major limitation of the statistics is that they concentrate on the number of *'crimes' known to the police* (the CKP index). Considerable evidence indicates that this figure probably represents the tip of an iceberg and that the 'dark figure' of hidden or undetected crime is very much larger, as we shall illustrate shortly.

Furthermore, as the statistics concentrate on known *offences*, they tell us little about the number of offenders or the type of persons they are. In addition, the clear-up rate, even for known crimes, seldom rises much above 45 per cent, which leaves open the possibility that the other 55 per cent of *known* offences are committed by very different criminal 'types' from those who come before the courts.

The problems associated with the CKP index become even clearer if we divide indictable crimes into three main types, according to the nature of the victims:

(i) Crimes with identifiable victims, such as offences against the person and most property offences.
(ii) Crimes without victims, e.g. certain homosexual and drug offences.
(iii) Crimes against public order, such as drunkenness and disorderly behaviour.

These different types of offence have a variable chance of appearing in the statistics or becoming known to the police.

Most crimes with victims become known because they are reported to the police, but crimes in the other two categories usually have to be detected by the police themselves before they appear at all. Even crimes with victims differ in the degree to which they are reported. Violent crime is both more likely to be reported *and* detected; the reporting and clear-up rate for murder is over 90 per cent and that for serious assault over 80 per cent, while petty larceny can only boast a 10–15 per cent clear-up rate.

Offences are more likely to be reported, of course, if the victims are aware that they *have been* victimised, and this in itself may produce an underestimate of the 'real' amount of crime. We all 'lose' objects that may in fact have been stolen. Furthermore, some knowledge of the criminal law is necessary before we are *able* to define certain acts as crimes, and even then we may be reluctant to involve the police in matters we regard as 'trivial'.

In some cases the victim may not report an offence because of sympathy with the offender, who may be a relative or friend. Victims or witnesses may dislike or distrust the police and courts or may reside in a community where reporting crimes is considered deviant. Other communities, on the other hand, such as public schools, universities and army camps, provide their residents with 'institutional immunity' by operating internal systems of social control which often shield offenders and 'silence' victims.

Much crime, too, is not reported because those who witness it (as well as those who perpetrate it) regard it as inconsequential, socially approved, or a legitimate 'perk'. The theft of stationery, pens, building materials, etc., from one's employer is often regarded in this way, as is travelling on public transport without paying.

The statistics for the second category of offences — crimes without victims — are *notoriously* unreliable as an index of the amount of crime of this type. These consensual crimes — such as prostitution, illegal abortion and supplying drugs — usually involve one party providing a service or good that another person requires. Consequently, few offences of this type would appear in the statistics at all were it not for the activity of the police themselves, and this in any case merely scratches the surface. For example, in Britain before the implementation of the 1967 Act legalising abortion under certain circumstances, the annual average number of illegal abortions known to the police during the period 1962–6 was 262. Unofficial estimates based on the reports of social workers and other welfare agencies put the 'real' annual figure at somewhere around 100,000.

A similar situation prevails with the third category of 'crimes against public order'. Only a very small proportion of these are reported by the public, most becoming known through the activities of the police themselves. Hence, as with 'crimes without victims', clear-up figures for this group are virtually identical with figures of crimes known to the police, which again, represent only a small minority of the actual offences of this nature that are committed.

Two main methods have been utilised to highlight the limitations of the official statistics and to provide a rough indication of the 'dark figure' of crime. These are *self-report studies* and *victim surveys*.

Self-report studies usually involve asking people to volunteer their past illegal actions either in response to a questionnaire or interview. Various studies reveal that anything between 50 and 90 per cent of people admit some kind of illegal behaviour, whether trivial or serious, that could result in a court appearance. Wallerstein and Wyle (1947) found that even ministers of religion admitted an average of 8.2 offences committed since the age of 18. In Elmhorn's (1965) sample of Stockholm schoolboys 57 per cent admitted to at least one serious offence, and of these 93 per cent were not caught. The boys admitted to 1,430 serious offences between them, with the culprit being known to the police in a mere forty-one cases, or 3 per cent of the reported total. There may be problems with the validity and reliability of these self-report studies, of course. Respondents may exaggerate or under-report their delinquencies due to dishonesty, bravado or forgetfulness. Be that as it may, these studies nevertheless clearly demonstrate the partial nature of the statistics. Moreover, they also seem to indicate that middle-class individuals are just as likely to commit crimes as working-class people. While some researchers suggest that, on average, convicted offenders do seem to commit a greater number of *serious* offences than unconvicted self-reported offenders, these studies do throw into doubt unambiguous distinctions between 'criminals' and 'non-criminals' and particularly the assumption that working-class individuals have a virtual monopoly of criminal activity.

Victim surveys are designed to investigate the number of individuals who have been victims of crime. They too indicate that official statistics are an incomplete and unrepresentative sample of the actual amount of crime committed. Erickson and Empey's (1963) study of Utah found that only one-third of the burglaries that had been committed were reported to the police and only one-quarter of the rapes. A Washington study showed that 38 per cent of the surveyed population had been the victims of a serious crime within a year compared with the 10 per cent revealed by police statistics (US President's Commission, 1967). Such studies obviously also suffer from limitations, especially the difficulty of remembering how often one has been 'victimised', though this would seem more likely to produce underestimation rather than the reverse.

Even if a crime is reported or detected, there is no guarantee that it will be *recorded* by the police, or that it will be recorded as the type of crime originally reported or detected. The police constantly make discretionary decisions about whether to charge a suspect, on what charge and on how many counts. Where 'clear-up' rates are used as measures of police efficiency, the police may try to persuade a suspect to admit to more crimes than he has been arrested for or even for more crimes than he has actually committed. In return for his co-operation they may promise to press for a lighter sentence or, in some cases, agree to drop charges altogether.

The policies, priorities and activities of different police forces may vary from place to place as well as over time. In such circumstances, of course, the statistics will also vary. For example, Whitaker (1964, p. 30) notes that after the appointment of a new Chief Constable in Manchester, the recorded incidence of the crime of male importuning increased by 1,000 per cent over a four-year period. A change in police policy produced this dramatic increase, of course, and not thousands of new closet doors opening.

The police may also exercise their discretion in the light of what they know to be the priorities of later decision-makers in the judicial process. If they know that the local magistrates take a different line and that this is reflected in their sentencing decisions, then they may not 'waste' time arresting people who are likely to 'get off'.

We have by no means exhausted all the possible influences acting upon the social construction of official statistics. Our analysis, however, does bear out the widely held view that the official statistics on crime, like most statistics, are not 'facts' to be accepted uncritically but are the product of dynamic social processes that involve the activities not merely of offenders but also of numerous decision-makers in the field of law and order. Consequently, sociological theories based upon such data must be regarded with considerable suspicion.

10.5 THE ANTI-POSITIVIST RESPONSE: LABELLING THEORY

We have seen how sociological theories of crime in the subcultural tradition have been the focus of considerable debate and criticism. Much of this criticism has questioned the 'internal' rationale and validity of these explanations, without necessarily questioning the *fundamental assumptions* of the explanations proposed. We must now turn our attention to an approach to crime and deviance which represents a significant departure from, and criticism of, traditional positivist explanations (both sociological and non-sociological) of crime and deviance. This perspective, drawing heavily upon symbolic interactionism, has variously been described as the 'labelling' approach (or simply 'labelling theory'), the 'interactionist' approach, or the 'social reactions' approach. Although there is no single theoretical position embraced completely by the various sociologists subsumed under such designations, there does exist an amalgam of themes and ideas which they share.

The critique of positivist criminology

The distinctive perspective of the exponents of the labelling approach stems from a fundamental criticism: they maintain that traditional positivist criminology employs erroneous assumptions about the nature of the phenomena of crime and deviance and about their explanation. Such theories, they argue, tend to see their subject-matter as straightforward, easily identifiable phenomena, as concrete, easily and more or less unambiguously 'known' to us — 'crime' is behaviour that violates the law, and 'criminals' are those who engage in this law-violating behaviour. By regarding their subject-matter as *objectively given* — out there, and amenable to observation — they too readily take it for granted: for labelling theorists such a stance cannot be justified.

The second major flaw in traditional criminology, according to this view, lies in the assumption that criminals are unambiguously *different* from non-criminals, and that it is possible to identify factors causing the differences in behaviour between them. This entails two difficulties. First, the kinds of behaviour falling under the umbrella of 'criminal' are massively wide-ranging. As Robertson and Taylor (1974, pp. 105–6) remark: 'It becomes difficult to regard crime as a behavioural constant when one is faced with such relatively diverse and novel behaviour as glue-sniffing, vandalism, industrial sabotage and football hooliganism.'

But according to labelling theory the search for causes is essentially misplaced for the second, even more fundamental, reason that it rests on *official statistics* of crime and on studies of *convicted criminal populations*; the former, as we have seen, cannot be taken as reliable indices of the amount of law-breaking, and the latter do not constitute a representative sample of those committing 'officially' known crimes, even disregarding hidden crimes. Self-report studies suggest that law-breaking among adults and juveniles is far more widespread than official figures indicate — very few of us have not broken the law, and many of us do so frequently without these offences being officially known or recorded.

Thus, if everyone commits crime, it becomes difficult to sustain a qualitative distinction between 'criminals' and 'noncriminals', so that attempts to find universal causes of crime like abnormal chromosome structures, inadequate socialisation or distinctive subcultural value systems are inevitably misleading and fruitless. As Pearson (1975, p. 63) observes: 'When the blinds of positivism are pulled away, all men are revealed as potentially law-breaking. The commonsense gulf between "us" and "them", which is supported by positivist criminology to a considerable extent, is dismembered.'

The problematic nature of deviance

How, then, are we to view crime and what is to be our major focus in studying it? Labelling theorists suggest that crime (and any deviant behaviour) is to be best seen as *subjectively problematic*, since the relationship between the commission of a criminal act and the designation of that act and its perpetrator as 'criminal' is by no means a perfect one. Thus we need to ask why it is that behaviour in *some* contexts and engaged in by *some* people comes to be defined and processed as 'criminal', while other behaviour and actors experience no such labelling. If anything, we should not be surprised at the amount of officially recorded crime but should concentrate our attention on how and why *so little* of the criminal activity which occurs is processed by the agencies of social control. We must abandon the search for 'causes' of crime in favour of an analysis of the *social processes* by which the behaviour of some individuals comes to be labelled as officially criminal and look at the ensuing *consequences* and implications for these individuals. Traditional criminology, despite occasionally recognising the inadequacy of official figures on crime, generally proceeded as if it were dealing with the whole 'class' of criminals (or at least a representative section of it), instead of recognising and treating as primary the fact that official criminals constitute a *socially defined* population publicly labelled as 'criminal'.

So, a preoccupation with etiology — a search for causes — is to be dispensed with, in favour of an analysis of the processes of social definition of behaviour, of how some actors and their behaviour come, in certain contexts, to be labelled as 'criminal' or 'deviant'. We cannot categorise behaviour abstractly or non-contextually as criminal or deviant, since definitions of behaviour in those categories rests on a socially conferred judgement. Social rules and the persons and acts which become officially deemed as deviant from them are, then, *socially constructed* phenomena, emerging from the patterns of social interaction in a society. As Becker (1963, p. 14), perhaps the most renowned figure in the labelling tradition, says: 'Deviance is not a simple quality present in some kinds of behaviour and absent in others. [It] is not a quality that lies in the behaviour itself, but in the interaction between those who commit acts and those who respond to them.'

A major implication of such a perception is that the labelling perspective lays great stress on the *dynamic* processes of the labelling of behaviour as criminal or deviant, with the concomitant rejection of the idea that deviance can be seen as a 'present or absent' feature of behaviour. Thus the focus of investigation must be significantly extended to embrace a more micro-sociological perception of deviance and of the ways in which social meanings are imposed on behaviour within specific social settings.

In order to understand crime and deviance as problematic products of a process of social interaction we have to consider *all* the groups involved: rather than unambiguously concentrating on the deviant actor, we must also examine the *social audience* and its reaction to law-breaking, since labels are not automatically imposed on all law-breakers, and some escape labelling altogether.

We must see deviance as having two sides — behaviour and reaction — both of which are problematic but reciprocally and integrally interrelated. More specifically, we cannot understand social deviance *without* understanding social control, in the form of the response of the rest of society, and particularly that of the police and courts, to rule-breaking behaviour.

The study of crime or deviance, then, must encompass analysis of the law-breaker, the law-maker, the law-enforcer and the community at large. Traditional criminology tended to take social reaction for granted or at best to be studied as a discrete afterthought, and not as an integral element. Similarly, official statistics, rather than being a means of research — that is, a resource providing data on the phenomenon to be studied — should be regarded as an *end* of research, a socially constructed phenomenon worthy of study in their own right.

They may tell us more about the *activities of the agencies of social control* than about the extent and incidence of criminal behaviour. We shall consider these activities shortly, but we must first give some attention to labelling theorists' observations on *law-making*, since we have stressed how their approach emphasises a reorientation towards rules and social reaction in the social construction of deviance.

Labelling theorists argue that positivist approaches to crime and deviance tend to regard the norms and values of society as given and absolute, and hence fall into the trap (often unwittingly) of supposing that a consensus on values is more widespread than is the case with the 'norms of society', carrying misleadingly precise connotations of deviance and conformity. Labelling theorists argue that we should not adopt a position of *moral absolutism*, as positivist theories do, but should reject such a consensus view in favour of one of *moral relativism*, seeing rules and values as problematic and not as societal 'givens'. (This is one reason why much work by sociologists within the labelling tradition has centred on behaviour on which no clear-cut consensus exists, such as drug-taking, gambling and homosexuality.)

But why *should* we adopt such a position? Their answer is that social rules and laws have to be seen as essentially *political products*: that some groups in society are capable of creating these rules and laws and hence of deciding what behaviour is regarded as deviant or criminal. Although many areas of illegal behaviour are popularly presented as a threat to widely held core values, laws are not an automatic reflection of 'the will of the people', nor are they invariably directed against behaviour which is universally believed to challenge fundamentally social arrangements. Behaviour is often made illegal even when the majority may not regard it as deviant, criminal or terribly wrong: prohibition in the USA earlier this century was a classic example of laws often vigorously enforced which in no way commanded the support of the majority of citizens.

We need to understand, then, that definitions of 'criminal' and 'deviant' reflect the *power* of groups who have succeeded in having their ideas and values about normality, deviance and wrong-doing imposed on a society and established in social conventions and laws. Becker calls these rule-creators 'moral entrepreneurs' — individuals and groups with particular interests and the necessary resources to define and control behaviour as 'deviant' or 'undesirable'.

Thus, for labelling theorists, the establishment and enforcement of laws are very much bound up with the distribution of power in a society, so that some groups may be more likely to commit 'crime' because their behaviour is more likely to be defined as 'criminal' by those with power. Deviance, then, is 'a consequence of a process of interaction between people, some of whom in the service of their own interests make and enforce rules which catch others, who in the service of their own interests have committed acts which are labelled deviant' (Becker, 1963, p. 163).

Certain groups, then, are in a position to define the dominant social and legal values. But what about laws which exist to curb the behaviour of the powerful? Labelling theorists suggest that such laws are much less frequently activated, that the deviance of the more powerful is less publicly displayed, that these groups have the resources to shield their behaviour from exposure, and that their behaviour is much less heavily monitored by the agencies of social control. This inevitably leads us to a further important element of the labelling perspective — the problematic and selective nature of law enforcement.

Problematic law enforcement

Labelling theorists argue that the agencies of social control employ considerable *discretion* and *selective judgement* in deciding whether and how to deal with illegal behaviour which they encounter, so that an understanding of the organisational practices and perceptions of the police and the courts is fundamental to the study of crime. While such discretion might not be exercised in, say, cases of murder, most criminal activity is of a more mundane nature, in which police and court encounters with illegal behaviour do not result in all cases in similar action.

It is impossible practically and unwise tactically for the police to process *all* criminal activity. They come across all manner of illegal activities, but to deal with it all in a formal way would strain their resources beyond the limit. Tactically, relations with the general public are important, so that vigorous enforcement of laws not enjoying full public support may lead to loss of respect, hostility or lack of co-operation from sections of the community whose support they require. Hence full law enforcement does not occur, and 'criminal' labels are not universally bestowed.

Labelling theorists argue that the police operate in their work with *pre-existing conceptions* of what constitutes 'trouble', what 'criminals' are like, of what areas need heavy policing, and so on: that is, *stereotypical categories* shape their perception and structure their responses to behaviour which they encounter. Thus it may well be that a particular individual committing an offence will be arrested, charged, tried, found guilty and sentenced, while another may be ignored or merely cautioned for the (objectively) same act. Such selective discrimination, labelling theorists argue, may not so much depend on criteria connected with the nature of the *actual behaviour* as on the policeman's personal biases and prejudices about certain groups and offences, his perception of the community's feelings about such offences, the family background of the offender, the latter's attitude and appearance, and so on.

The essential fact is that a problematic process of social interaction occurs between police and offender, the outcome of which — the public labelling as 'criminal' or not — rests on other factors besides the intrinsic nature of the illegal act. A good illustration here is a study by Piliavin and Briar (1964) of a police department in a large American city. They found extensive evidence of policemen exercising discretion in decisions about official action, largely based on officers' assessment of character from juvenile offenders' appearance, accent and attitude: those giving a positive impression on such counts were far less likely to be arrested and charged. The authors observe:

The official delinquent, as distinct from the juvenile who simply commits a delinquent act, is the product of a social judgment, in this case a judgment made by the police. He is a delinquent because someone in authority has defined him as one, often on the basis of the public face he has presented to officials rather than of the kind of offence he has committed (Piliavin and Briar, 1964, p. 214).

Similarly, studies have shown that judicial decisions reveal selective patterns of conviction and sentencing, emphasising that, again, a process of social interaction is at work between offenders and the courts. Those involved in disposing of defendants have ideas about 'typical' offenders and the causes of their behaviour which are sometimes enshrined in the law. In Britain, for instance, the 1969 Children and Young Persons Act encourages the setting aside of a custodial sentence — that is, a 'softening' of the labelling process — if the juvenile offender can be shown to come from a 'good' home background with supportive parents.

Police and court perceptions and practices, then, do not result in the uniform application of the law but often involve highly selective decisions. Thus we should not be surprised to find blacks and working-class people over-represented in the official statistics of crime, since they and their behaviour are more likely to fit law-enforcement agencies' perceptions of 'criminals' and 'crime', and they are less likely to be able to mobilise the material and social resources necessary to convince others that 'they're not like that'.

We have been emphasising how labelling theory is less interested in 'patterns' of crime and deviance than in the process whereby individuals come to be seen as deviant and labelled as 'outsiders'. As we have seen, the application of such public labels is frequently fortuitous, not necessarily dependent on the nature or gravity of the act but on the subsequent behaviour and/or social characteristics of the actor and the attitudes and perceptions of social-control agencies. Selective law enforcement is significant enough in itself, but it is even more important when one considers *what happens* to individuals labelled as 'deviant' or 'criminal'.

The process of labelling

In their view, the application of a deviant or criminal label to actors' behaviour serves essentially as a 're-ordering' mechanism with which to interpret satisfactorily action which may be perceived as dangerous, disruptive, alarming or unsettling. For example, two men seen walking hand-in-hand along the street disrupts many people's 'picture of reality', but the labelling of this behaviour as 'homosexual' and therefore deviant 'makes sense' of it and provides a set of interpretations for future encounters with these individuals. Thus the application of deviant labels is not merely a punitive response or an expression of disapproval but also an attempt by the social audience to produce a sense of order in social relations.

The major implication of this process rests on the fact that the attachment of a deviant label has important effects on how the individual is perceived by others, on how he comes to regard himself, and on the subsequent patterns of inter-action between him and others, since the ascription of deviant or criminal status means that an individual actor and the social group around him must accommodate themselves to his 'spoiled identity'. The critical point in this process is the public exposure of one's deviant activity. As Becker (1963, pp. 31–2) observes:

> One of the most crucial steps in the process of building a stable pattern of deviant behaviour is likely to be the ex-perience of being caught and publicly labelled as a deviant ... Being caught and branded as a deviant has important consequences for one's further social participation and self-image.

A process of *stigmatisation* occurs: getting caught leads to a re-evaluation of one's public identity by others, whereby one becomes labelled as a certain 'kind' of person, to be viewed and treated by others in the light of this label. A new status is accorded to the deviant, and the possibility of retaining a normal identity is made increasingly difficult. This is intensified by the fact that the label *oversimplifies* what the deviant 'is' through its *stereotyping and 'essentialising' effect*. It is not merely attached to his behaviour but to his whole being, so that he is seen as nothing but a deviant. This 'master status' takes over any other conception we may have of him or which he may wish to project. For instance, someone who has been sexually involved with children is not seen as a neighbour, a factory manager or a family man who has committed certain offences, but as a 'sex maniac' or 'pederast'. As Rock (1973, p. 32) says: 'Rule-breaking is not so much regarded as an ephemeral partial aspect of a person's self but as an indication of his essence. A deviant role is not just another role in a varied repertoire; it is a critical and revealing guide to a deviant *personality*.'

What the deviant (occasionally) *does* becomes transformed into what he *is*: his whole identity and existence become questionable. But the re-ordering of present identity is not the only issue at stake — *past* behaviour may also come to be seen in a new (and inevitably negative) light, so that perfectly harmless behaviour is reinterpreted as having reflected sinister and deviant motivations. Similarly, *future* conduct is predicted as likely to be shaped by the present deviant identity — 'he won't change, they never do', or 'once a queer, always a queer', and so on.

Interaction now occurs within the context of the existence of a deviant label, and resisting its consequences becomes difficult, since it may not be possible to convince others that a continuing application of the label is not justified, that 'they've got it all wrong', and so on. Sustaining an alternative image in the eyes of others (and of oneself) is inhibited by the power of the deviant definitions which are being imposed, and the deviant's good intentions of behaving 'normally' may be subverted by the fact that the response of others in very practical ways reduces his chances of 'normal' behaviour — that is, the social support which may enable him to engage in such behaviour (and hence to resist the 'deviant' label) is now denied him. Imagine a 24-year-old male, living in a village, who has a 15-year-old girl friend with whom he has sexual relations: the public revelation of such activity brands him as an 'unlawful-sex' man (even 'kinky'), so that subsequent attempts to establish relationships with older females (i.e. 'normal' behaviour) may be constantly rebuffed, despite his attempts to reassure them that his sexual tastes are not deviantly narrow. He is thrown back, as it were, on younger females, thus 'confirming' his deviant inclinations.

The stigmatising effect, then, of the label places the deviant outside conventional circles and sparks off a sense of uncertainty in him. He feels branded as a 'deviant' despite his denials, and, put simply, becomes bad because he is being defined as bad. That is, a *self-fulfilling prophecy* occurs, in which a self-image and subsequent behaviour result from the reactions of others: the deviant is labelled and comes to live up to his label, because his perception of himself depends to a large part on the perceptions of others with whom he interacts.

According to the labelling view, the long-term effect of this process is to lock individuals into deviant roles and project them along deviant courses or careers, by closing off legitimate opportunities and forcing them to resort to social groups which offer support but perpetuate their deviant activity, thus reinforcing and confirming an 'outsider' status and a negative self-image and precluding the possibility of a withdrawal from deviance. Thus society 'creates' deviance in the sense that the application of deviant labels may produce more deviance than it prevents. As Becker (1963, p. 9) says:

Social groups create deviance by making the rules whose infraction constitutes deviance, and by applying those rules to particular people and labelling them as outsiders ... When the deviant is caught he is treated in accordance with popular diagnosis of why he is that way, and the treatment itself may well produce increasing deviance.

For the labelling approach, then, our focus of analysis must be on the ways in which the behaviour of certain actors comes to be defined as 'deviant' or 'criminal' and the effects of this labelling process on their future behaviour. We must recognise a difference *in kind* between what Lemert (1966) has called 'primary' and 'secondary' deviance and must concentrate our attention on the latter. Primary deviance comprises the widespread acts of deviant behaviour in which we all engage, but which in most cases do not lead to apprehension and public labelling. Lemert and other labelling theorists are not particularly interested in why individuals become involved in such activity: that is, they regard the study of the origins and 'causes' of this behaviour as of comparatively little value for two reasons.

First, a search for causes assumes, as we suggested earlier, a common thread running through illegal acts. Lemert argues that primary deviance arises from a variety of motivations and circumstances — a search for 'kicks', desire for gain, risk-taking, or whatever — which may be of such variation from one individual to another that any meaningful generalisation or all-embracing theory may well be impossible, or at best largely trivial.

Second, primary deviance entails *little implication* for the individual's self-image — it is behaviour engaged in without being incorporated into one's identity, but rather is accommodated easily into a favourable conception of oneself. Such acts are 'merely troublesome adjuncts of normally conceived roles . . . with only marginal implications for the psychic structure of the individual' (Lemert, 1966, p. 17).

It is only when social reactions in the form of public labelling occur that problems come about. Such processes may create numerous difficulties for the deviant, forcing him to embark on a career of 'secondary' deviance, which is crucially distinct in evolving a *self-image* as a deviant. According to Lemert, a spiralling sequence of interaction between the deviant and the community in the form of progressive deviance and penalties ensues, so that the deviant becomes confirmed in his deviant role. Thus the process of what has been called *deviance amplification* is set in motion.

Undoubtedly the rise of labelling perspectives represents a major turning-point in the study of crime and deviance. Labelling theorists have been responsible for confronting many questions which traditional positivist explanations occasionally recognised but rarely made explicit: the problematic nature of the phenomenon of 'crime' and of the process of interaction involved in the definition of behaviour as such; the political and ideological implications of a correctionalist stance; the recognition of the value-laden implications of accepting an official definition of crime; and the stress on the role of power in the defining process. All of these have become central issues in the discussion of crime and deviance thanks to labelling theory.

But we must not assume that labelling theory has gone unchallenged, since it too has been the subject of much critical attention and has sparked off two distinctly divergent approaches to the study of deviance: on the one hand, an even stronger anti-positivist orientation in phenomenological and ethnomethodological approaches; and on the other, the development of a structuralist reaction in the form of recent attempts in 'radical' criminology to apply Marxist concepts and ideas to the explanation of crime and deviance. In this brief outline of the history of the study of deviance, then, the pattern of development of sociology is reflected in microcosm.

10.6 THE CRITIQUE OF LABELLING THEORY

Labelling theorists have received a variety of criticisms from a number of different perspectives. They have been accused of engaging in over-romanticised accounts of deviance which, in their concern to sympathise with the 'underdog', significantly distort the reality of crime. Thus their alleged overconcentration on marginal and often exotic forms of deviant behaviour has produced rich and varied insights into the 'grey' world of homosexuals, marijuana users, and others, but *at the expense of* a complete analysis of mainstream criminal offenders against property and the like. Young (1975, p. 68) says of the labelling perspective: 'Indeed it is engaged in an astonishing accomplishment − the development of a criminology that does not deal with property crime, and a criminology whose subjects live in a world not of work but of leisure.'

A number of critics, such as Akers (1967), Taylor *et al.* (1973) and Box (1971), also question labelling theorists' disregard of the origins of deviant behaviour. Such an omission, they maintain, places *too much emphasis* on the impact of the social reaction and hence on the deviant actor's *present* at the expense of a recognition of his *past*. This particular line of attack constitutes one of the underlying threads of a further criticism levelled at labelling theorists − that they have been guilty of *oversimplifying* the process of labelling, and particularly of minimising the *role of the deviant himself* in the defining process.

Such critics, along with Bordua (1970) and Gouldner

(1968), argue that labelling theory tends to view deviants and criminals as rather too powerless and passive victims of labels about which they can do nothing. For Bordua, the deviant is portrayed as 'an empty organism or at least one with little or no autonomous capacity to determine conduct', they are 'men on their backs ... more sinned against than sinning', a sharp and even contradictory contrast with the free-floating, self-willed primary deviant. Thus the *degree of choice* and *consciousness* of actors, and the *meaning* of their behaviour to them, is apparently devalued by the labelling perspective. And as Taylor *et al.* (1973) and Mankoff (1971) point out, we cannot rule out the possibility that deviants choose to continue in their behaviour simply because they find it *rewarding* in some way, 'because of a positive attachment to rule-breaking' (Mankoff, 1971).

Furthermore, critics argue, if the process of labelling is as simplified as it sometimes appears in labelling theory, then it should be uniform in its effects. Not only should it always produce negative consequences (secondary deviance) but, conversely, such consequences should only be produced by the application of the label. But is this always the case? Davis (1972) and Bordua (1970) suggest that the application of official deviant labels may well result in a *decrease* rather than an increase in deviant behaviour (as a consequence of the shock and shame of the experience). Similarly, it is possible that certain individuals or groups may take on a deviant identity and manifest all the features of a secondary deviant *without* any public labelling of their behaviour occurring — homosexuals, for instance, may see themselves as deviant prior to or in the absence of any public labelling experience simply by virtue of being *symbolically associated* with others so designated. And other deviants may *actively negotiate* labels for themselves in their interactions with others, by encouraging the application of deviant labels or adapting to the labelling process by employing 'techniques of neutralisation' (Sykes and Matza, 1957) or 'fighting-back' techniques (Rogers and Buffalo, 1974).

Much of the preceding critique of labelling theory thus centres on the dangers of not doing justice to the response of deviants and the *meaning* of their behaviour to them. The need to recognise and centralise the meaning of deviant acts to both actors and reactors has prompted the adoption of an even more micro-sociological and anti-positivist conception of behaviour in general and deviant behaviour in particular in the form of phenomenology and ethnomethodology. While a more detailed consideration of these approaches can be found in the last two chapters of this book we must examine briefly their general assumptions and procedures to appreciate their relevance for deviance study.

Phenomenology, ethnomethodology and deviance

Although phenomenological sociology and ethnomethodology share a number of common themes with the symbolic inter-actionist approach, which informs much of labelling theory, there are also significant points of departure between them. Phenomenology starts from the idea that the social world and interaction is essentially fragile and provisional, where the meaning of social situations and behaviour is not 'given' but has to be constructed by members. Stable social interaction rests on the possession of shared stocks of socially constructed knowledge: that is, 'social life' is a matter of the ways in which individuals create shared social meanings. The subject-matter for sociologists, then, is the subjective meanings of actors, and more especially the common-sense taken-for-granted knowledge of everyday life which they employ in effecting the 'practical accomplishment' called 'society'. Sociologists, however, must not *predefine* the members' world with their own concepts or 'second-order constructs', as opposed to the 'first-order constructs' employed by members, since one set of constructs is no more meaningful than the other — there can be no *special* status for sociological general-isations. Thus:

> The investigation of substantive areas should give primacy to the revealing of the shared meanings people attach to their situation, and the rules in terms of which they inter-pret their situation ... The sociologist's accounts are commonsense accounts, as are those of members, and share the same status as members' accounts as documents

of practical reasoning (Phillipson and Roche, 1974, pp. 135, 139).

The study of deviance, from this point of view, is the study of the problematic nature and outcome of 'moral meanings' and their part in the 'production' of social order. Like labelling theorists, phenomenologists accept that deviance is constituted and made meaningful by social interaction, and they commend the former for questioning absolutist conceptions of legal and social rules and for pointing to the problematic and socially constructed definition of behaviour through public labelling and selective law enforcement. But in their view labelling analyses are not thoroughgoing enough. First, while labelling theorists stress the importance of actors' perspectives, they do not present and use members' meanings, but rather rely on *their own* sociological constructions of these meanings, or at least do not indicate clearly how these are derived from the first-order constructs of actors. Second, although they acknowledge the ambiguity of 'crime' and 'deviance', they still accept *official* definitions of deviance (even if they see them as selectively applied) and hence the idea that social norms as abstract rules exist as 'solid' and 'real' entities.

For the phenomenologist and ethnomethodologist the 'moral rules' involved in the production of deviance are inherently problematic and do not correspond (necessarily) with any social norms or 'surface rules', however selectively enforced. These moral rules require 'situational constructions' for their use in everyday life, so that the interpretation of behaviour as 'deviant' does not depend on the application of some normative guideline but on certain 'common-sense' rules embracing notions of, say, responsibility, provocation, and so on — that is, it depends on methods of 'practical reasoning' and decision-making which are highly provisional.

The focus of interest in understanding deviance, then, should be on the *procedures* actors employ to make sense of problematic behaviour, on

the procedures for arriving at formulations of character and biography, for accusing and excusing, for interpreting points of law in specific cases, for bringing an action under the jurisdiction of a rule or law, for ascribing motives, for imputing responsibility, for assessing evidence, and the rest (Coulter, 1974, p. 131).

A number of ethnomethodological studies have demonstrated this preoccupation. Cicourel's (1968) study, for example, focuses on the 'background expectancies' and common-sense constructions employed by law-enforcement agencies, particularly police and social workers, in creating delinquents. He emphasises 'the negotiable character of who comes to be defined as "criminal"', a process which involves clarification of the ways in which formal legal statutes are linked by officials to concrete situations and cases to produce 'delinquents'. So, both official statistics and the 'delinquents' contained within them are artificially 'solid' phenomena of a highly provisional character which particularly conceal the ways in which the police and probation officers deal with cases and events by the use of 'typifications' or 'folk theories' of delinquents and their behaviour to produce a stable logical picture of 'delinquency'.

Similarly, Bittner's (1967) study attempts to show how police activities on 'Skid Row' are a matter of 'practical reasoning' in handling their everyday work with alcoholics. They act in accordance with the demands of the situation, regardless of whether this violates official legal statutes and recommended practices; these are merely *one* consideration, alongside protecting the alcoholics and preventing further trouble, which patrolmen employ in their work. The exigencies of the situation, rather than official rules and norms, prevail.

Radical criminology

Now, while a number of the criticisms made of labelling theory have been characterised by this kind of desire to develop an even more anti-positivist interpretation of deviance and crime, a very different development in the study of crime has sprung out of its analysis of *power*. A number of sociologists have attacked labelling theorists' failure to analyse systematically and fully the structures of power and interests at work in the making of laws and the definitions of 'criminals' and 'deviants'. Gouldner (1968) and Liazos (1972), for instance, maintain that while labelling theorists *raise* questions of power, they fail to deliver a sufficiently coherent and structurally based critique of the operation of the inequalities of power, so that their 'sociology of the underdog' remains a rather romanticised, pseudo-radical liberalism which pays too much attention to the *middle-level* agents of social control (the police, courts, etc.).

For these critics the essentially actor-dominated, micro-sociological level of labelling analysis, emphasising interaction, reaction and identity formation, devalues crucial *macro-sociological* concerns and fails to expose the wider *economic and socio-political forces* operating in the construction and application of 'deviant' or 'criminal' labels.

This particular reaction to labelling analysis has been more fully reflected in the rise in recent years of a 'radical' or Marxist criminology, which, while accepting many of the insights of labelling theory, attempts to relocate the study of crime and deviance in a *structural* context, in the reality of existing social arrangements. The exponents of this perspective (who can be seen only loosely as a 'school') maintain that we can use Marxist frameworks for a theory of crime and deviance by analysing the ways in which particular systems of production and their attendant social relations in both contemporary capitalism and previous historical periods have generated attempts by the dominant class to order societies in specific ways. Thus today capitalist economic systems must be regarded as the central structural framework for analysing crime; in this view one crucial weakness of labelling theory is its neglect of 'master' structural institutions and its failure to recognise that the definition of behaviour as 'criminal' is inseparably bound up with questions of political economy. The potential radicalism in labelling theory is inhibited by a failure to produce a macro-social analysis of capitalist power structures and, particularly, a theory of the state.

Indeed, both traditional criminology — with its highly consensual view of social order and its correctionalism or liberal reformism — and labelling theory are guilty, according to Marx-

ists, of continuing to accept *official definitions* of crime and
deviance in their analyses, as this involves an acceptance of an
existing social order by restricting analysis to a predefined
range of subject-matter and inhibits the questioning of the
propriety of other areas of behaviour. As Liazos (1972, p. 109)
says:

> They concentrate their attention on those who have been
> *successfully* labelled as 'deviant', and not on those who
> break laws, fix laws, violate ethical and moral standards,
> harm individuals and groups, etc., but who either are able
> to hide their actions or when known can deflect criticism,
> labelling and punishment.

He recommends that we should also be prepared to examine
'covert institutionalised violence' such as exploitation, poverty
and imperialism. We must recognise, then, the *political dimension* of the definition of behaviour as 'criminal' and locate the
ways in which the system of legal control regulating such behaviour is related to the structure of capitalism. In this sense
capitalism 'creates' crime in its legal definitions; but it is also
criminogenic in a more *direct* sense, in that the behaviour
itself is an *integral product* of capitalist economic arrangements. It emanates from the class relations between a propertied and powerful class and the propertyless and powerless
classes and is a product of the contradictions and inequalities
of capitalism. Taylor *et al.* (1975, p. 34) maintain that

> Property crime is better understood as a *normal* and con-
> scious attempt to amass property than as the product of
> *faulty* socialization or inaccurate and spurious labelling.
> Both working class and upper class crime . . . are *real* feat-
> ures of a society involved in a struggle for property, wealth,
> and self-aggrandisement . . . A society which is predicated
> on the unequal right to the accumulation of property *gives
> rise* to the legal and illegal desire to accumulate property
> as rapidly as possible.

Crime, in this view, *is* determined, as the positivists say — their
error, however, lies in their failure to locate their explanation

in capitalism's effects on human nature. Radical criminologists stress how the designation of certain kinds of behaviour as 'criminal' is the outcome of the capacity of a dominant economic class to enshrine their definitions of 'crime' and 'deviance' in legal statutes, in definitions which simultaneously legitimise the status quo, proscribe activities which threaten the reproduction of capitalism, and conceal the inequalities of the capitalist system. As Pearce (1976, p. 81) says:

> Concentrating on lower-class criminals . . . is functional in maintaining the . . . class system . . . If the criminals are also the social failures . . . then their criminality is caused by their *inadequacies* . . . and the major social institutions are not exposed to critical assessment.

Thus the study of crime cannot be merely a matter of the uncritical analysis of behaviour which violates ('given') legal norms, since this fails to recognise the political dimension of the phenomenon of crime and perpetuates pluralist myths of impartial laws and an 'arbiter' role for the state. The legal system is an essentially coercive instrument which, while occasionally instituting some laws against powerful groups, is used to secure the interests of the dominant class against behaviour that threatens or disrupts them.

Ultimately, for radical criminologists the study of crime necessarily requires a theory of the state and the legal system in relation to particular systems of production and their attendant class relations and to the legitimation of these arrangements. As Taylor and Walton (1975, p. 234) say:

> What many radical deviancy theorists, Marxist or otherwise, are attempting to do is to move criminology away from a focus on the 'criminality' of the poor, the pathologising of deviant behaviour into categories derived from biology, psychology, or positivistic sociology, and to abolish the *distinction* between the study of human deviation and the study of the functioning of States.

Our discussion so far illustrates well how different theoretical perspectives in sociology have focused their attention on a major area of deviant behaviour, that of crime. The study of suicide, too, has generated similar controversies, and we now turn our attention to these debates.

10.7 SUICIDE

Only a small minority of people deliberately end their lives (only about 1 per cent of all deaths in Britain are officially classified as 'suicides'). This small minority may be regarded as deviant in terms of our earlier definition, in that their action goes against what is regarded as normal behaviour by other members of society. Indeed, it is important to remember that suicide and attempted suicide were *criminal* offences in Britain until 1961 — that is, they were *officially* defined as deviant. Not surprisingly, then, a wealth of sociological literature has been amassed over the years dealing with suicide as an example of deviant behaviour. The study of suicide raises in a readily accessible way many of the theoretical and methodological issues discussed throughout this book, and it spotlights once again the debate about the nature of social reality between positivism and interpretivism.

The divergence in these different approaches to suicide may be illustrated by the starkly different opinions of the worth of what is usually regarded as the 'classic' study of the phenomenon: *Suicide*, by Durkheim, first published in 1897. On the one hand, Selvin (1965, p. 113) claims that 'Sixty years after it first appeared in print, Emile Durkheim's *Suicide* is still a model of social research . . . few, if any, later works can match the clarity and power with which Durkheim marshalled his facts to test and refine his theory.' On the other, the ethnomethodologist Sacks (1963, p. 3) maintains equally categorically that 'in terms of the history of sociology nothing is more tragic than that Durkheim's *Suicide* should be conceived as a model investigation'.

In this section we outline the various premises about the nature of social reality and the sociological enterprise that lie behind these two very different assessments. We begin by presenting an uncritical account of Durkheim's *Suicide* which brings out its firm base in the positivistic tradition. We then briefly consider the kinds of criticisms that have been made by those operating from within the same kind of tradition. Finally, we turn to supporters of the interpretivist, anti-positivistic view, who fundamentally challenge the approach of the Durkheimian school.

Durkheim's theory of suicide

In Durkheim's time (the nineteenth century) there had developed a general intellectual movement seeking a scientific understanding of society. Just as the natural sciences, such as physics, proposed various laws of nature based on scientific observation, so the founders of modern sociology sought laws about society. Durkheim believed that if sociology were to be accepted as a science and an academic discipline in its own right, it must be able to establish that its own special area of investigation, 'society', exists as an object that can be studied and about which laws can be formulated. Sociology must be able to identify and account for *social* phenomena.

To demonstrate the existence of social phenomena, we must be able to identify, says Durkheim, processes which are consistent across a whole range and number of individuals but which cannot be reduced to or explained solely in terms of any one individual's expression of them. These processes allow us to identify a collectivity or society which is greater than its parts, the individuals who comprise it. Durkheim was claiming that society exists independently of its individuals, just as a football team is more than just eleven individual players. Members of society adopt its values, beliefs and traditions in common. This neither happens by chance, nor by individual members of society consciously deciding to support particular values and/or beliefs. Rather, Durkheim argues that these aspects of culture are products of collective interaction: individuals are constrained to adopt their culture precisely because they are members of that culture. So, for example, individuals may behave as members of a crowd or audience, they feel obliged to applaud or laugh at the 'right time', to conform to the feeling of the collectivity. The social group is then a social phenomenon since it can be seen to constrain individual behaviour. All such phenomena Durkheim called 'social facts' which can be observed by the sociologist:

they comprise 'every way of behaving, fixed or not, capable of exercising an outside constraint' on the individual (Durkheim, 1964, p. 13). In *The Rules of Sociological Method* Durkheim (1964) argues that social facts must be regarded as *things* which can be observed existing at the level of the collectivity and are not reducible to the level of individual behaviour or meaning. It then follows that we can identify social (collective) phenomena by identifying situations of social constraint.

Now suicide is, according to a common-sense view, the most individual of actions. If Durkheim could show that, on the contrary, this act is influenced by the social collectivity, then his proposition that we can identify purely social phenomena has passed its most difficult test: that even in this most solitary and individual of acts something external to individual consciousness, namely 'society', has not only been a 'witness' to but also the 'director' of this tragic drama.

To test his general hypothesis, Durkheim sought evidence that would indicate the social nature of suicide. For this he turned to the statistics of suicide recorded for various societies and groups within societies. From these he could determine different *suicide rates* for different populations. Tables 10.5, 10.6 and 10.7 illustrate the suicide rates used by Durkheim, as well as providing more recent figures.

TABLE 10.5
Rates of suicide per million

	1866—70	1871—5	1874—8
Italy	30	35	38
Belgium	60	69	78
England	67	66	69
Norway	76	73	71
Prussia	142	134	152
Denmark	277	258	255
Saxony	293	267	334

Source: Durkheim (1970, p. 50).

TABLE 10.6
Differences in suicide rate across religions
(rates of suicide per million)

Protestant states	190
Mixed states	96
Catholic states	58
Greek states	40

Source: Durkheim (1970, p. 152).

TABLE 10.7

Rates of suicide per million

	1951	1955	1959	1961
Australia	95	103	111	119
Italy	68	66	62	56
England and Wales	102	113	115	113
France	155	159	169	159
Ireland	26	23	25	32
Japan	183	252	227	196
West Germany	182	192	187	187

Source: World Health Organisation, *World Health Statistics Report*,
no. 6, Geneva, 1968.

From his statistical analyses Durkheim drew three conclusions:

(i)   Within single societies the incidence or rate of suicide
      remains remarkably constant over time, e.g. England,
      1866–78.
(ii) The suicide rate varies between societies.
(iii) The suicide rate varies between different groups within
      the *same* society.

The crucial points for Durkheim were that (a) for any society
the suicide rate remained constant over many years despite
the fact that the individuals comprising it changed, and that
(b) between different populations the rate varied consider-

ably. How could such constancy and variation be explained? Having discussed and eliminated factors associated with climate, heredity, alcoholism and the seasons, Durkheim also had to rule out psychological explanations of suicide, which see individual mental states as more or less predisposing some individuals to the pathological states that lead to suicide.

Although Durkheim was prepared to admit that some individuals may have a psychological predisposition towards suicide, he rejected the view that suicide was governed solely by such a predisposition. By considering the variations in the suicide rate across different populations he found no significant correlation or connection between the mental state of individuals and the number of suicides. For example, he found that although there had been a high level of insanity among Jews, it was this same religion that had the *lowest* suicide rate. He argued that 'In this case, therefore, suicide varies in inverse proportion to psychopathic states, rather than being consistent with them' (Durkheim, 1970, p. 72). Psychological explanations of suicide do not then explain the variations in the suicide rate across different populations.

Durkheim was then able to offer a more adequate, sociological, explanation, built on two concepts upon which much of his general sociological perspective depended. These are his ideas of the 'social integration' and the 'moral regulation' of society. Durkheim believed that the order or 'harmony' of any society or group within society — such as the family or a religious community — depends on the extent to which it is 'integrated'. Although Durkheim's definition of 'integration' was somewhat vague, in general the concept describes the sharing of values, attitudes, beliefs and behaviour patterns among individuals in a social group: individuals are (more or less) dependent on their group membership for their social identity. The group provides an ordered world which guides individual action in such a way that it continuously renews the bond between members of the group. An integrated family is one in which individuals share values and expectations, and engage in behaviour that promotes the interests and 'order' of the family as a group.

Durkheim's other central idea, moral regulation, refers not so much to *how* groups or societies in general establish cohesion among their members but more to *why* this process occurs. According to him, individuals have human appetites and desires that, left unchecked, are limitless, so that society needs to restrain humans' unlimited, egocentric desires — otherwise they would be engaged in an endless and ungratified search for satisfaction. Thus Durkheim claimed that society functions to provide control over individual desires, such that individuals are satisfied with their position in society, by not only controlling the means through which satisfaction is to be achieved but also by socialising the individual into accepting that certain ends or goals rather than others should be pursued. In a sense, then, Durkheim believed that individuals only want those things that society tells them to want. While there could not be too much moral regulation in society, Durkheim argued that too much integration could have harmful effects; we shall see later how over-integration may promote the tendency to commit suicide.

Durkheim (1970, p. 44) defined suicide as 'every case of death resulting directly or indirectly from a positive or negative act performed by the victim himself which he knows will produce this result'. A positive act would be to hang oneself, for example. A negative act would be the captain who 'goes down with his ship'.

Durkheim then offers the following proposition to account for the variation in the suicide rate: 'Suicide varies . . . with the degree of integration of the social group of which the individual forms a part.' He follows this by attempting to demonstrate its validity by classifying suicide into three basic types: 'egoistic', 'altruistic', and 'anomic' suicides.

Egoistic suicide

These are the most common, according to Durkheim, and result from 'excessive individualism' among individuals with few social ties — that is, when individuals become detached from the values and expectations shared by those around them. Durkheim says that egoistic suicide is 'inversely proportional to the degree of integration to be found in the groups of which the individual is a part'. In other words, a low degree of integration gives rise to a high suicide rate, and vice versa.

Durkheim argued that particular religious, domestic (family and parental) and political ties act as social integrators and therefore as factors inhibiting egoistic suicide. For example:

(i) Single, widowed and divorced people are more prone to suicide than married people, and in turn, married people with children have even more immunity to suicide, which is strengthened as the number of children increases.

(ii) There are higher suicide rates among Protestants than among Catholics and Jews, and a higher rate in predominantly Protestant countries than in predominantly Catholic ones. All condemn suicide equally strongly, so why should such variation occur? Durkheim's answer is that Protestantism involves a higher degree of religious individualism and is less dominated by a group morality. Protestants are given much more personal freedom in deciding how to express, both intellectually and behaviourally, their faith. The Catholic church, however, has a tightly woven set of beliefs and ritual practices to which the life of individual believers is closely bound. In other words, Catholics are much more protected from egoistic suicide because they are much more integrated into religious life. Similarly, Durkheim argued that Jews have a lower rate than Protestants because they have strong ethnic and family allegiances, and a history of persecution which has bound them together as a highly integrated group.

(iii) In times of political turmoil — e.g. in war, revolution — there is a greater feeling of unity between people, a stronger sense of community: the struggle against a common crisis unites the population and hence increases individuals' immunity from egoistic suicide.

Altruistic suicide

This occurs when individuals are *completely* immersed within their social group, so highly integrated that in effect the individual has little or no value. For example, the Hindu widow in India throws herself on the funeral pyre of her dead husband because it is expected of her by the social group, i.e. she is conforming to the demands of the society without regard to her self-preservation. Altruistic suicide is also found in armies, where the suicide rate is higher among officers than lower ranks. This is because officers are subject to a code of behaviour, or, more correctly, a 'code of honour'. It is honourable for officers to die for soldiers because they are responsible for their safety. Alternatively, they may commit suicide as the honourable thing to do because they have failed in their duty as officers. Durkheim sees this type of suicide as essentially obligatory: that is, the individual has little choice, since he or she has 'little value', but is part of a highly compact and integrated society. As Durkheim (1970, pp. 220–1) says: 'For the individual to occupy so little place in collective life he must be almost completely absorbed in the group and the latter, accordingly, very highly integrated.'

Anomic suicide

An 'anomic' situation exists when society's members have lost the normative order by which their behaviour and expectations are regulated. For some reason or other the established norms cease to operate. According to Durkheim, when the social order is disturbed an increase in the anomic suicide rate ensues. This influences society's capacity for moral regulation: when a society has lost its ability to regulate the moral order, when there is a lack of a clear definition of norms, individuals have little to guide them and no longer derive a sense of satisfaction about their position in the world. Desires and wants at these times are less disciplined, and so, Durkheim argued, 'deregulation or anomie' sets in. A period of social disorder may occur through economic disruption, such as a financial disaster like the Wall Street 'crash' of 1929, or times of sudden and extreme economic prosperity.

In conclusion, Durkheim argues that these three types of suicide (egoistic, altruistic and anomic) are related to one single social factor — the internal cohesion and integration of the social group. Thus the suicide rate in a society depends on the degree to which its institutions produce objectively identifiable states of egoism, altruism and anomie: 'The basic proposition that social factors are objective . . . finds a new and especially conclusive proof in statistics and above all in the statistics of suicide' (Durkheim, 1970).

The 'internal' critique

Durkheim's theory and methodology, as well as many of his conclusions, have been subjected to detailed criticism over the years from within positivism. It is not our intention to examine all of these here, for most are relatively minor ones which do not question the overall adequacy of the assumptions behind Durkheim's pioneering efforts to use empirical data to support a theoretical explanation of the causes of suicide. For example, his student Halbwachs (1930) confirms the relationships that Durkheim establishes between suicide and family structure and suicide and religion, only adding that we should not see these variables as having an independent effect. He argues that several of the factors that Durkheim *isolates* as being associated with a high rate of suicide are in fact *combined* in the conditions of modern urban life, and that perhaps the major explanatory factor in suicide is the difference between rural and urban ways of life. Thus the higher rate of suicide among Protestants than among Catholics may be more a function of Protestants' *urban* location than any independent effect produced by the religion itself. Similarly, he argues, evidence indicating a higher suicide rate among the unmarried, divorced and those living alone could be attributed to a lack of integration in urban areas and the absence of friends or relatives willing and able to hide the evidence of suicide.

From the same kind of perspective Durkheim has also been criticised for not providing an adequate operational definition of one of his key concepts, social integration — without an adequate indicator of what integration is, it is hardly likely that different degrees of integration can be adequately assessed. Gibbs and Martin (1964) attempt to provide such a definition, suggesting that an integrated society exhibits stable and durable relationships and that these are most likely to occur when the individual has compatible statuses. Arguing that status integration exists when the individual's status in one role does not conflict with the status in another (for example, an individual can be said to have compatible statuses when educational status and occupational status are in alignment), they suggest that the suicide rate varies inversely with the degree of status integration.

A variety of other criticisms from within a positivist tradition have also been levelled at Durkheim's work on suicide: for example, it has been claimed that Durkheim ignored contradictory data in his attempts to 'fit' the available data to his theory; that he misinterpreted, often deliberately, other theoretical contributions to the suicide debate; and that he dismissed far too readily the influence of non-social factors in suicide.

However, these kinds of criticisms proceed from a position which essentially accepts the validity of Durkheim's basic approach, only questioning the accuracy and adequacy of specific aspects of his analysis.

The 'external' critique: the interpretivist reaction Douglas.

Interpretivists, on the other hand, provide what we can call an 'external' critique of the approach not only of Durkheim but of all those working in a positivist tradition. The work of Douglas (1967) and Atkinson (1978) exemplifies this kind of criticism.

Interpretivists, as we have pointed out in this chapter and elsewhere in the book, argue that the source of individual attributes and behaviour cannot be seen as external to individual actors, since social reality is consciously and actively created by individuals who *mean* to do things and who attribute meanings to the behaviour of others. Durkheim appears to deny this premise by arguing that suicide rates are social facts which can only be explained by reference to sociological categories of 'egoism', 'anomie', etc., and not by examining the way in which individuals make sense of the situations in which they find themselves by assigning meanings to them. Douglas argues that the social meanings of suicide should be the central concern of sociologists *and* that they were in fact central to Durkheim's *own* analysis; according to Douglas, Durkheim operated with an *implicit* theory of shared social meanings, and these meanings are the real causal agents in his findings.

For example, he stresses that Durkheim's argument that common morality reproves suicide is no more than an *assumption* on his part for which he provides no evidence; he simply assumes that common morality corresponds to his own morality. Similarly, in explaining the different relationship between non-marriage, marriage and suicide rates for men and women he again relies fundamentally upon his own commonsense interpretations of the differences between the masculine and feminine mind and social position which fit his theory but for which he again provides no evidence. In effect, then, Douglas argues, Durkheim contradicts his own rules of explaining social facts only by reference to other social facts.

So, for Douglas, the error in Durkheim's approach lies in its assumption that suicide is a unidimensional and unvarying form of behaviour just waiting to be discovered 'out there' by analysis of official statistics. According to Douglas, we must instead investigate the way in which these statistics are *themselves* socially constructed — an analysis of those processes of interpretation by which acts come to be *defined* as suicide.

How and why do such interpretations vary? Douglas argues that we must examine both the way in which different *societies* operate with different cultural conceptions of what sort of action constitutes suicide and also, within the *same* society, the way in which the interpretations of a variety of interested parties (often influenced by the wishes of the deceased) can transform a death into a suicide.

Douglas shows how the act of taking one's life, and in fact the very concept of 'death', may have very different meanings for the members of different societies. For example, among Trobriand Islanders attempted suicide is used as an acceptable sanction in matrimonial disputes and is 'meant' as an indictment of an offending spouse. Again, in Japan, suicide may be regarded as a *honourable* death, which constrasts with the shame accorded it under the Christian tradition.

However, Douglas's most significant emphasis — and the focus of much of Atkinson's work — is on the way in which particular deaths within particular societies come to be defined as 'suicides'. Both agree that from an examination of this process it becomes clear that suicide, far from being a 'social fact', is instead very much the product of meaningful categorisations by officials investigating certain kinds of act, and that it cannot be assumed that these officials share the *same* meanings on which they base their interpretations. Officials, no less than all other members of society, necessarily operate with their respective stocks of common-sense knowledge which they cannot help but use to make sense of the reality which they encounter — in this case suspicious death. Let us examine more closely the implications of these interpretivist assumptions for the sociology of suicide.

In Western culture suicide is regarded as an unnatural form of death, and suspected cases have to come under the scrutiny of a wide range of officials, including doctors, the police and coroners. Consequently, what eventually appears as a 'suicide' in the official statistics results from a very complicated process of inference and the application of common-sense notions on the part of all the people involved in the process.

Furthermore, despite the fact that there may be some general agreement that 'intention to die' is in some way a necessary distinguishing characteristic of suicide, there are likely to be considerable differences of opinion among officials of different countries, and among officials of the *same* country, as to how such an intention may be inferred.

Both Douglas and Atkinson provide numerous examples of this. Douglas (1967, p. 185) cites an American coroner who refused to label a death as suicide unless a note was found with the body, while Atkinson (1971) shows not only that coroners can be crucially influenced by the *mode* of death — road accidents, for example, are very seldom classified as suicides, whereas hangings almost invariably are — but that they also often take into account other significant factors such as the location and circumstances of the death. There is, however, no consistency among coroners in their selection of those factors which they regard as significant indicators of the intention to die.

Furthermore, they argue, different coroners' offices — and indeed *all* the officials concerned — use different *search procedures* in their efforts to obtain evidence of *cause* of death, and different degrees of thoroughness in looking for indications of *intent*. For example, some officials approach more informants than others in their search for socially defined motives for suicide (such as unhappiness). These different informants thus add to the cumulative process by which suicides are socially constructed by using *their* own stocks of common-sense knowledge and assessments of the victim's character and state of mind in making their own sense of his or her action. One official may read private diaries and letters in the search for clues, whereas another official might define such actions as violation of basic rights of privacy that even the dead possess. There is, of course, no way of knowing whether the biases introduced into the statistics by these practices are systematic or random.

So, according to Douglas and Atkinson, whether the official cause of death is designated as 'suicide' or 'accidental' is very much a *social* product, the result of a complex interaction process involving the physical scene, the sequence of events leading up to the act, the significant others of the deceased, various officials such as doctors and the police, the public, and finally the official who must impute the 'correct' category. It is this final categorisation that produces an apparently 'solid' suicide out of what can in fact be a much more imprecise, and problematic, situation. (Cicourel's (1968) analysis of the way in which a stable, logical picture of delinquency is produced by the activities of the police and other official agencies shows similar processes at work.)

All of this clearly demonstrates the interpretivist emphasis on the way in which definitions of deaths as suicides are *social* constructions. Quite simply, the argument is that since the accomplishment of *all* social interaction necessarily involves the application of a meaning by one actor to the action of others, there can be no reason why things should be any different so far as the interaction between the living and the dead is concerned.

Yet interpretivists also emphasise that we should not think that the interpretative procedures employed by those whose job it is to apply a meaning to a death are the *only* meanings involved; like all other pieces of social interaction, the social construction of suicide is not simply a one-sided activity. Although (except in the case of suicide notes) suicides lack the usual means which actors employ to communicate meaning — language — this does not mean that individuals who have taken, or intend to take their own lives cannot *by different means* try to structure the interpretations of this act by others.

We suggested in our discussion of crime that interpretivists see individuals not just as passive recipients of labels but as having a role to play in actively negotiating their own identity, and so it is with suicide. For example, someone wishing his or her death to appear an accident can accordingly arrange the scene in order to influence those involved in the categorisation process to interpret things in this way. Furthermore, as Douglas argues, the individual may be aware that his or her action, if defined as 'suicide', is likely to be interpreted in two basic ways by the various other actors who become involved: they will either see the individual as the cause of (or 'responsible' for) his or her own actions, or will see him or her as having been 'driven' to it by circumstances or by other people. Douglas suggests that the individual therefore often attempts to place one of these two general constructions of meanings upon his or her action by employing various devices indicating to others how they should interpret the cause of the act. However, individuals cannot simply use *any* means of attempting this but must make use of those meanings *likely to be accepted by other members of the society*. He suggests that in the West the most common patterns of meanings of this sort are those involving 'revenge', 'the search for help', 'sympathy', 'escape', 'repentance', 'expiation of guilt' and 'self-punishment'. Consequently, Douglas argues that these societal conceptions of suicide must be studied, because they exert a crucial influence on both the actor and the other participants in the drama. This is not to say that individuals are necessarily successful in having their intentions defined in the way that they would like (of course, the *living* very often fail to do this in their interactions as well) but simply that all these considerations influence whether a death comes to be labelled as suicide or not.

Douglas suggests, then, that priority in suicide research must be given to the manner in which suicides are socially constructed. He argues that it is necessary to look at detailed case studies of deaths defined as 'suicide', suggesting that by examining the construction of meanings in particular contexts it should prove possible to classify different patterns of suicidal meanings. If suicide is a matter of social definition, and if these definitions vary — if there is nothing 'out there' with the intrinsic meaning 'suicide' — then the only course for the sociology of suicide is to analyse the meanings that the various actors involved in suicides attach to the world. Douglas argues that to do this an in-depth analysis of their words and actions, in all its qualitative detail, is required, and in fact by using such a method he is able to produce a provisional classification of meanings, ranging from 'transformation of the soul', 'escape', 'expiation of guilt', through to 'revenge'.

Conclusion

The study of suicide, then, encapsulates clearly the problem of 'structure' and 'action' in sociological analyses — of providing an explanation of social phenomena which takes sufficient account of structural forces acting on individuals, while at the same time doing justice to the meaningful choices and responses made by actors. While explanations like Durkheim's have been subjected to considerable criticism, it would be foolish to deny the influence of the social environment upon individuals and the reality of the structures within which they operate. A study of suicide which concentrates almost exclusively on the interpretative procedures by which individuals attribute meanings to the actions of others remains essentially partial.

At the same time, however, interpretivists are justified in insisting upon the recognition of individual motives for suicidal behaviour, since individuals do play an active part in creating their own social world through the meanings they employ in social interaction. Such a view provides a valuable counter to a model of humans in which a passive creature responds to the pulls and pushes of social forces in a mechanical and deterministic way.

A synthesis of theoretical perspectives which emphasise on the one hand 'structure' and on the other 'action' would seem, then, to be a necessary exercise for the explanation of suicide and, indeed, of any sociological phenomenon. Giddens (1977) makes some preliminary suggestions as to how this might be effected in the study of suicide, though he and others, such as Willis, have attempted to explore the dialectical relationship between structure and action in a more complete theoretical way elsewhere (Giddens, 1976; and Willis, 1977). For, in fact, the resolution of such issues is ultimately a theoretical and methodological, not substantive, problem. We now turn to such issues in our final two chapters.

REFERENCES TO CHAPTER 10

Akers, R. (1967) 'Problems in the Sociology of Deviance: Social Definitions and Behaviour', *Social Forces*, vol. 46, pp. 455–65.

Atkinson, J. M. (1971) 'Societal Reactions to Suicide: the Role of Coroners' Definitions', in S. Cohen (ed.), *Images of Deviance*, Harmondsworth, Penguin.

Atkinson, J. M. (1978) *Discovering Suicide*, London, Macmillan.

Becker, H. (1963) *Outsiders*, New York, Free Press.

Bittner, E. (1967) 'The Police on "Skid-Row": a Study of Peace-keeping', *American Sociological Review*, vol. 32, pp. 699–715.

Bordua, D. (1970) 'Recent Trends: Deviant Behaviour and Social Control', in C. Bersani (ed.), *Crime and Delinquency*, London, Macmillan.

Box, S. (1971) *Deviance, Reality and Society*, New York, Holt, Rinehart & Winston.

Cicourel, A.(1968) *The Social Organization of Juvenile Justice*, New York, Wiley.

Cloward, R. and Ohlin, L. (1960) *Delinquency and Opportunity*, New York, Free Press.

Cohen, A. (1955) *Delinquent Boys*, New York, Free Press.

Cohen, A. (1965) 'The Sociology of the Deviant Act: Anomie Theory and Beyond', *American Sociological Review*, vol. 30, pp. 5–14.

Cohen, S. (ed.) (1971) *Images of Deviance*, Harmondsworth, Penguin.

Cohen, S. (1973) *Folk Devils and Moral Panics*, London, Paladin.

Coulter, J. (1974) 'What's Wrong with the New Criminology?', *Sociological Review*, vol. 22, pp. 119–35.

Davis, N. (1972) 'Labelling Theory in Deviance Research', *Sociological Quarterly*, vol. 13, pp. 447–74.

Douglas, J. (1967) *The Social Meanings of Suicide*, Princeton University Press.

Downes, D. (1966) *The Delinquent Solution*, London, Routledge & Kegan Paul.

Downes, D. and Rock, P. (1971) 'Social Reaction to Deviance and its Effect on Crime and Criminal Careers', *British Journal of Sociology*, vol. 22, pp. 351–64.

Durkheim, E. (1964) *The Rules of Sociological Method*, New York, Free Press.

Durkheim, E. (1970) *Suicide* (ed. G. Simpson), London, Routledge & Kegan Paul (first published in 1897).
Elmhorn, K. (1965) 'A Study on Self-reported Delinquency among Schoolchildren in Stockholm', in K. Christiansen (ed.), *Scandinavian Studies in Criminology*, London, Tavistock, pp. 117–46.
Erickson, M. and Empey, L. (1963) 'Court Records, Undetected Delinquency and Decision-making', *Journal of Criminal Law, Criminology and Police Science*, vol. 54, pp. 456–69.
Eysenck, H. (1970) *Crime and Personality*, London, Paladin.
Gibbons, D. and Jones, J. (1975) *The Study of Deviance*, Englewood Cliffs, N. J., Prentice-Hall.
Gibbs, J. and Martin, W. (1964) *Status Integration and Suicide*, University of Oregon Press.
Giddens, A. (1976) *New Rules of Sociological Method*, London, Hutchinson.
Giddens, A. (1977) 'A Theory of Suicide', in A. Giddens, *Studies in Social and Political Theory*, London, Hutchinson.
Gouldner, A. (1968) 'The Sociologist as Partisan: Sociology and the Welfare State', *American Sociologist*, pp. 103–16.
Halbwachs, M. (1930) *Les causes de suicide*, Paris, Alcan.
Kitsuse, J. and Cicourel, A. (1963) 'A Note on the Uses of Official Statistics', *Social Problems*, vol. 11, pp. 131–9.
Lemert, E. (1966) *Human Deviance, Social Problems and Social Control*, Englewood Cliffs, N. J., Prentice-Hall.
Liazos, A. (1972) 'The Poverty of the Sociology of Deviance', *Social Problems*, vol. 20, pp. 102–20.
McClintock, F. and Avison, N. (1968) *Crime in England and Wales*, London, Heinemann.
Mankoff, M. (1971) 'Societal Reaction and Career Deviance: a Critical Analysis', *Sociological Quarterly*, vol. 12, pp. 204–18.
Matza, D. (1964) *Delinquency and Drift*, New York, Wiley.
Merton, R. (1938) 'Social Structure and Anomie', *American Sociological Review*, vol. 3, pp. 672–82.
Miller, W. (1958) 'Lower Class Culture as a Generating Milieu of Gang Delinquency', *Journal of Social Issues*, vol. 14, pp. 5–19.
Morris, T. (1957) *The Criminal Area*, London, Routledge & Kegan Paul.
Pearce, F. (1976) *Crimes of the Powerful*, London, Pluto Press.
Pearson, G. (1975) *The Deviant Imagination*, London, Macmillan.
Phillipson, M. and Roche, M. (1974) 'Phenomenology, Sociology and the Study of Deviance', in Rock and McIntosh (1974).
Piliavin, S. and Briar, S. (1964) 'Police Encounters with Juveniles', *American Journal of Sociology*, vol. 52, pp. 206–14.
Rabow, J. (1966) 'Delinquent Boys Revisited', *Criminologica*, vol. 4, pp. 22–8.
Robertson, R. and Taylor, L. (1974) 'Problems in the Comparative Analysis of Deviance', in Rock and McIntosh (1974).

Rock, P. (1973) *Deviant Behaviour*, London, Hutchinson.
Rock, P. and McIntosh, M. (eds.) (1974) *Deviance and Social Control*, London, Tavistock.
Rogers, J. and Buffalo, M. (1974) 'Fighting Back: Nine Modes of Adaptation to a Deviant Label', *Social Problems*, vol. 22, pp. 101–18.
Sacks, H. (1963) 'Sociological Description', *Berkeley Journal of Sociology*, 8pp.
Scott, P. (1956) 'Gangs and Delinquent Groups in London', *British Journal of Delinquency*, vol. 7, pp. 8–21.
Selvin, H. (1965) 'Durkheim's "Suicide": Further Thoughts on a Methodological Classic', in R. Nisbet (ed.), *Emile Durkheim*, Englewood Cliffs, N. J., Prentice-Hall.
Short, J. and Strodtbeck, F. (1965) *Group Process and Gang Delinquency*, University of Chicago Press.
Smart, C. (1976) *Women, Crime and Criminology*, London, Routledge & Kegan Paul.
Sykes, G. and Matza, D. (1957) 'Techniques of Neutralization: a Theory of Delinquency', *American Sociological Review*, vol. 22, pp. 664–70.
Taylor, I. *et al.* (1973) *The New Criminology*, London, Routledge & Kegan Paul.
Taylor, I. *et al* (1975) 'Critical Criminology in Britain: Review and Prospects, in I. Taylor *et al.*, *Critical Criminology*, London, Routledge & Kegan Paul.
Taylor, I. and Walton, P. (1975) 'Radical Deviancy Theory and Marxism: a Reply to Paul Q. Hirst's "Marx and Engels on Law, Crime and Morality"', in I. Taylor *et al.* (1975) *Critical Criminology*, London, Routledge & Kegan Paul.
US President's Commission (1967) *Report on Law Enforcement and Administration of Justice*, Washington, D.C., US Government Printing Office.
Wallerstein, J. and Wyle, C. (1947) 'Our Law Abiding Lawbreakers', *National Probation*, pp. 107–12.
West, D. (1967) *The Young Offender*, Harmondsworth, Penguin.
Whitaker, B. (1964) *The Police*, Harmondsworth, Penguin.
Willis, P. (1977) *Learning to Labour*, Westmead, Saxon House.
Young, J. (1975) 'Working Class Criminology', in I. Taylor *et al.* (1975) *Critical Criminology*, London, Routledge & Kegan Paul.

11

The Production of Sociological Knowledge

11.1 INTRODUCTION: INTERPRETING REALITY

What happens when workers are made redundant? Why is the Third World underdeveloped? How can we explain the origins of crime and delinquency? These are just a few of the many possible questions that face the sociologist. Can such questions be answered? If so, are the answers we select based on sociological evidence and fact? What *is* a sociological 'fact'? This textbook is full of information on the family, education, inequality, power, and so on. But where does it come from, what assumptions lie behind it, how was it collected? Furthermore, how are different *types* of knowledge about the world — e.g. common-sensical, scientific, theological or magical — to be distinguished, and what type of knowledge does sociological research offer?

Common sense is taken-for-granted knowledge derived from and designed to cope with the routine activities of everyday life. However, such knowledge is, as was suggested in Chapter 1, frequently inconsistent and contradictory. This is because it is not a product of deliberate or rigorous thought: it does not develop according to a consistent, systematic and cumulative process. There appear to be no objective criteria for assessing the merits of apparently conflicting common-sense pronouncements: thus, *when* do you 'look before you leap' and *when* do you 'strike while the iron is hot'? Of course, one can only answer this by analysing the particular situation one is in — that is, by going beyond a *ritual* stock of knowledge to an *objective* assessment of the world. Descriptive and explanatory accounts of the world that try to do this claim to be *scientific*, and since sociology claims to be a social 'science' we should begin by considering some general features attributed to scientific inquiry.

To most people science is concerned with 'truth', by which they mean that it provides proven explanations of the way reality works based on the discovery of 'facts'. They would therefore distinguish it from other kinds of explanation of reality – for example, religious or magical ones – on the grounds that these rest on evidence which is not capable of being proved in the way that facts can be, and that they are really more a matter of faith.

Yet in many ways this popular conception of science is too simplistic. First, although there may be 'facts', they do not present themselves directly to us as such; we do not collect facts like the park attendant picks up litter from the lawns. Rather, phenomena only appear to us as facts because we selectively interpret the world about us. This selection works in two ways:

(i)   The individual may perceive and interpret the world according to the particular *practical* interests he or she may have. For example, the artist and the planning officer may selectively perceive the landscape before them in terms of their own concerns – the artist may look more closely at and perceive the colour and form of the area very differently from the planner. Ways of 'seeing' the world are not simply a result of the physical act of 'looking at' the world.

(ii) Second, selective perception of the world also occurs in response to an individual's attempt to *understand* and *explain* the world. The 'facts' of perception are meaningful as facts only because they have been identified and understood in terms of an explanatory model of the world. For example, the 'facts' that a particular piece of wood is a metre long and not just a piece of wood derives not from the wood itself but from a model or idea of *measurement* devised by humans. What is a 'fact', then, is essentially the product of interpretation and selection.

Moreover, it can be argued that the establishment of scientific truth ultimately involves an act of faith not unlike that associated with religious conviction. For example, if we think that knowledge can be gained through observation, we are therefore likely to *believe* that our senses give us an accurate picture of reality. But do we really 'know' that what we see, hear or feel is *actually* there? How do we know we are not dreaming or imagining things? We don't of course; such a belief in the 'truth' of what our senses tell us rests on an act of faith just as a religious belief does.

For many people another feature that marks science off from other types of explanation is the methods it uses. Controlled laboratory experimentation is perhaps the one method most would associate with science, though for some sciences, such as astronomy, direct experimentation with the raw data — the stars — is clearly technically impossible. Yet few would challenge the scientific status of astronomy because of this practical problem. This gives us our first hint that there may be more than one way of going about scientific investigation. There may indeed be different methods for collecting evidence, and more importantly there may be different ideas about what can be accepted as evidence. Many issues then arise, including questions such as: Are propositions only to be accepted if supported by directly observable data? Do explanatory models differ from one another? Can one phenomenon be accounted for in more or less adequate ways? These conceptual and philosophical aspects of scientific inquiry will be discussed in more detail below.

All in all, then, what science is has to be seen as a rather more complex and problematic issue than our common-sense assumptions usually allow. In order to investigate it further we will first consider the question of how we arrive at what we count as scientific evidence of reality.

Any investigation of phenomena, be it in the natural or social sciences, offers answers to questions or problems that have arisen in the course of on-going research. The actual questions we ask about the world, however, do not suddenly appear out of the blue. Rather, our questions only arise within the context of general interpretations of what the world *is*, or according to what Hughes (1976) has called our 'meaning systems'. Different models of reality will lead to different propositions about what reality *is*, and so different ways of *establishing what can be accepted as real*, different ways of *justifying the data relevant to* reality, and different *strategies for collecting* such data.

These four aspects of investigation and understanding are built into all meaning systems. They are respectively designated by four key terms: *ontology, epistemology, methodology* and *methods*. These terms can be understood as follows:

(1) *Ontology*. Ontological issues are concerned with *being* — i.e. with what *is*, what we believe to exist. Here, then, the question may be: 'What is the particular object of investigation or subject-matter of sociology?'

(2) *Epistemology*. Epistemological issues are concerned with *knowing* — i.e. what sort of statements will we accept to justify what we believe to exist?

(3) *Methodology*. Methodological issues are concerned with the *logic* of inquiry — i.e. how are we to discover and validate what we think exists?

(4) *Methods*. Issues of method concern the *technique* for collecting data — i.e. which specific techniques do we use to get at evidence which will support our propositions?

We can illustrate how these aspects differ from one another, and possible variants of each, by constructing two possible accounts about the existence of atomic particles. The (a) and (b) variants within each aspect combine to form an overall interpretation of atomic particles:

Ontological dimension: An atom exists
- (a) in the fourth dimension
- (b) in observable form

Epistemological dimension: I know it exists
- (a) because a clairvoyant told me
- (b) because I can see it

Methodological dimension: I can validate what I know about atoms through
- (a) crystal-ball gazing
- (b) experimentation and deduction

Methods dimension: I should collect data on atomic particles through the technique of

$\left\{\begin{array}{l}\text{(a)   visiting as many authentic mediums as possible}\\ \text{(b)   collecting as much quantitative data as possible}\end{array}\right.$

The crucial point is that all four aspects of understanding are closely tied in with one another. That is, neither methodologies nor methods are constructed or chosen in isolation from ontological and epistemological positions. So the way we get at knowledge and the techniques we use to collect evidence are directly related to our image of reality and the way we think we can know it. Different ontological and epistemological positions generate different methodologies and methods for research.

In sociology, as in the natural sciences, there has been and continues to be considerable debate about the nature of reality, in this case social reality. Although some texts on research methodology often skate over this issue, it is apparent that there is no one undisputed or self-evident research strategy to be adopted.

In short, sociology is characterised by a *methodological pluralism*: there is not *one* style of social research, with *one* method which is *the* method. Nevertheless, all is not complete chaos; it is possible to identify at a very general level the major ontological and methodological perspectives that sociologists have adopted. We can best understand where major differences lie by examining the influence of the philosophy of *positivism* on sociology.

11.2 POSITIVISM

First, we need a basic outline of this philosophy. In very simple terms positivism involves the following assumptions.

Reality is constituted of phenomena which are causally linked to one another. What is 'real' can only be demonstrated to be real by reference to *empirical* evidence of its existence. While other kinds of explanation obviously exist, they are not admissible for the positivistic scientist unless they are based on empirical — observable — evidence. So although it may well be that God made the world in six days, this is not an acceptable positivistic scientific explanation since there is no empirical evidence to verify it.

The establishment of scientific knowledge thus involves the empirical explanation of how phenomena cause other phenomena — and can be expressed in the form 'if *A* happens, then *B* happens'. Now, according to the positivist ideal, science involves the uncovering of such cause-and-effect relationships between phenomena in reality that *always* hold true. Such *universal* statements are called *scientific laws*. However, since the statement *A always* causes *B* means that *B* happens every time and at every place that *A* happens, past, present and future, both philosophical and practical problems follow. For even if we are certain we have solved the practical problems of knowing empirically the results of what happened every time *A* occurred in the past and of knowing what happens each time it occurs in the present, there is no way we can *finally* be sure of what will happen when it occurs in the future, since it has not happened yet. For these kinds of reasons, and others, most cause-and-effect statements established by positivistic science are more likely to be 'probability' or 'tendency' statements, depending on the degree of certainty involved. (Such explanations thus take the form: *x* per cent of the time *A* happens, *B* happens.)

Nevertheless, such statements are indispensable for the positivistic scientist, since it is their existence which enables explanations of events to be arrived at. A famous example of Carl Gustav Hempel demonstrates this very clearly. Upon waking up one morning a man finds that his car radiator has burst. How is he to explain this event to himself? He does so by remembering that he had left his car outside the garage the night before when the temperature had fallen well below zero, he had forgotten to put anti-freeze in the water, the radiator had been filled to the top and that the radiator cap had been screwed on tightly. What is crucial about such an explanation, argues Hempel, is that it rests on the man only choosing *certain kinds* of factors as relevant to his explanation and not others. Why, for example, did he not ask himself whether the moon had been full the night before, or whether someone was practising witchcraft against him, or whether it was the work of fairies? The answer for the positivist is that people are attracted by things they think relevant to an explanation by the existence of empirically based 'scientific' cause-and-effect statements about reality.

So, in Hempel's example, the only reason why factors such as the lack of anti-freeze in the water and the severe drop in temperature are chosen as relevant to the explanation is because the laws of physics — and especially the one which states that the volume of water expands when it freezes — make them so.

Furthermore, since for the positivist *explanation* is facilitated by the existence of such cause-and-effect statements, they are also the reason why events in the future can be *predicted* as well. To use Hempel's example again, it is only our knowledge of the laws of physics that enables us to predict the consequences of leaving a car outside on a freezing night without anti-freeze, etc., etc.

So, for positivistic science, scientific laws or their equivalent perform the double function of allowing both explanation and prediction and as such are obviously crucial.

Next, we must consider *how* such cause-and-effect statements about reality are established, and to do this we must look at what the positivistic scientist means by the *scientific method*. In simple terms, this involves the construction of as yet unproven cause-and-effect statements about reality, called *hypotheses*, and their testing against empirical evidence.

Now since much of the rest of this chapter is a discussion of the applicability of this kind of model of scientific method for the study of social behaviour, we ought first to look at the strategy for scientific research which it implies in more detail.

Positivistic methodology

It will help if we think of this as a methodology which consists of three separate stages:

    (i)   a stage at which *discovery* is made
    (ii) a stage at which *validation* is made
    (iii) a stage at which *explanation* is made

and look at the logic underlying each stage separately.

Logic of discovery

(i) *The categorisation of reality.* All reality has to be conceived of in such a way that it can be talked about — that is, it has to be categorised and its existence given a symbol of some sort. Most of these symbols make up the *language* that we use, for this is what a language is for — it enables us to refer to aspects of reality meaningfully. Normally in our everyday life the application of these linguistic symbols is unproblematic; we can interpret the vocal sounds others make when they speak 'our language' without having to stop and *self-consciously* make the connection between the sounds and their meaning. We do it without, apparently, thinking.

The language of physical and natural science may, however, be much more deliberate in its formulation, employing a very precise terminology which refers to certain aspects of reality in as clear and unambiguous a manner as is possible. Often, of course, the everyday symbols we all use may be adequate; so, for scientists and non-scientists alike, the terms 'rock', 'tree', etc., will do to talk about these aspects of the world. Sometimes, however, the common-sense meaning of a term may not be precise enough for science; for example, a chemist prefers to talk about calcium carbonate rather than chalk because it specifies more clearly the relationship between calcium and carbon than the term 'chalk' does. At other times, however, there are not everyday symbols available. Here the scientist has to *invent* a term — e.g. 'molecules', 'atoms', 'DNA'. Terms which a science uses to refer precisely and clearly to objects in reality are usually called the 'jargon' of that science.

Much of the jargon of a science will also include terms which refer to 'objects' of a scientist's interest which do not have a natural existence — they are not real-world phenomena, e.g. pressure, temperature, volume, etc. Here, then, the linguistic symbol refers to a category in reality which exists only in the scientist's mind; it is a *concept*, part of a *theory* which the scientist has about the world. Now plenty of everyday linguistic symbols also refer to such abstract categories as well — e.g. love, fear, beauty, hate, depression, health, illness, euphoria. And although you could argue that the use of such concepts is in fact an extremely complex activity, in everyday life once again it never seems so; we use these sorts of terms without hardly ever stopping to *think* about what we mean by them, and, even more remarkable, we assume, and are usually right to do so, that others will know what we mean by them too.

But the scientist is faced with a different sort of problem from the layman here. Not only is precision required in the use of *theoretical* concepts, as in the use of terms to refer to real-world phenomena, but also the scientist must be able to show that the phenomena they describe are, in fact, 'real'. So, although a scientist 'knows' that theoretical constructs like pressure, volume and temperature have a *conceptual* reality, it is still necessary to provide *empirical* evidence of their existence so that they can be investigated. This process is called the *operationalisation* of theoretical concepts. It is carried out by translating these theoretical *variables* into *indicators* of their existence which are *observable* — perceivable by the senses; thus, for example, in the case of pressure we measure it by using the reading on a pressure gauge, while in the case of temperature we do so by using a thermometer.

(ii) *Hypothesis construction.* Having categorised reality so that it can be talked about meaningfully and having established indicators by which theoretical concepts can be examined empirically, scientists then proceed by hypothesising about cause-and-effect relationships between the phenomena in which they are interested — their variables — in such a way that these are, in principle at least, capable of being tested.

Logic of validation: testing rituals

Dealing with non-human phenomena the natural or physical scientist relies overwhelmingly on a single method — the *experiment*. Thus one tests the hypothesis 'if X exists, then Y is likely to follow' by setting up an experiment which makes X happen in order to see whether Y happens as a result. One must, of course, *control* the experiment in such a way that variables *other than X* cannot accidentally cause Y. For example, in order to see whether carbon dioxide is produced by the action of hydrochloric acid on calcium carbonate, a chemist will isolate these two variables in a bell jar and collect any gas produced as a result. Furthermore, the chemist can measure

how *much* carbon dioxide is produced by how *much* hydrochloric acid and calcium carbonate. Indeed, it is natural
science's ability to *quantify* and *measure* cause-and-effect
relationships between natural phenomena in this way that
has proved so attractive to positivistic sociology.

Logic of explanation

For the positivist scientist, then, as we said earlier, reality is
thus explained by the establishment of empirical evidence of
the extent of cause-and-effect relationships between phenomena.

Positivism in sociology: an idealised account

A completely positivistic sociology will thus embrace not only
the ontological/epistemological position we outlined earlier
but will follow the logic of natural and physical science research methodology at each of these three stages.

Logic of discovery

(i) *Categorisation of reality.* First of all this means that like
other scientists the positivist sociologist will seek to define
and use terms clearly and unambiguously, to categorise
reality meaningfully, and to allow concepts easy operationalisation so that they can be empirically investigated. (However, as we shall see when we examine the sort of critique
made of positivistic methodologies by anti-positivists, compared with other sciences this is a task fraught with unique
difficulties.)

(ii) *Hypothesis construction.* Having decided what the variables are and how they can best be investigated empirically,
the positivist sociologist then hypothesises a causal relationship between these variables.

Logic of validation: testing rituals

The next task is to measure these relationships by providing
empirical evidence of the extent of their existence. As we
have seen, for the natural or physical scientist this almost in-

variably means setting up an experiment to do so.

However, this type of physical manipulation of variables is usually impossible for the positivist-minded sociologist, not only for practical reasons — for example, how could one introduce the Protestant ethic and wait and see if capitalism is encouraged? — but also ethical ones: one would presumably find it morally reprehensible to test Durkheim's hypotheses about suicide by encouraging the development of those social conditions which he correlated with it. So, instead of physically manipul⸻ ⸻iables, as in the classical experimental method⸻ ⸻ciologists typically construct *symbolic simulatic⸻ ⸻nents using statistical models. Indeed, the estab⸻ ⸻tatistical relations between formally defined va⸻ ⸻as age, sex or occupation — is probably the m⸻ ⸻evidence for testing hypotheses in positivist so⸻ ⸻mple, the positivist may want to examine the⸻ ⸻tween occupation and voting behaviour. Ac⸻ ⸻ariable X defines the particular jobs people may⸻ ⸻ Y the way these same people vote. Experimenta⸻ ⸻easuring the extent to which an hypothesised c⸻ ⸻ip between these two variables exists. Other⸻ ⸻ch as social background, nationality, sex and ⸻ ⸻e held *constant* so that only those actors with⸻ ⸻es in these respects are examined. Any correspc⸻ ⸻ween occupational status

TABLE 11.1

Voting intention by social class 1966
(Gallup Poll figures)

	Upper (5%)	Middle (22%)	Working (62%)	Very poor (11%)
	(%)	(%)	(%)	(%)
Conservative	78	63	30	21
Labour	8	22	57	65
Liberal	9	8	6	6
Other	0	0	1	1
Don't know	5	7	7	9

Source: Blondel (1976).

and voting behaviour is then measured. The results are typically reproduced in a graphical or tabulated form (see Table
11.1 for an example).

Logic of explanation

The logic underlying the positivist sociologist's explanation of
social reality is, then, based on the desire to measure quanti-
tatively the extent of a causal relationship between phenomena, and in so doing to match the rigour of the laboratory
experiment in other sciences, and provide general law-like
propositions about social reality.

11.3 ANTI-POSITIVISM IN SOCIOLOGY

The positivist perspective, depicted in somewhat idealised
fashion above, has been the subject of considerable debate
within sociological theory. In this section we shall present the
major alternative approach to the nature and explanation of
society: anti-positivism. The term 'anti-positivism' is only a
label we have devised for purposes of the discussion here. In
your more general reading, as elsewhere in this book, the
terms 'interpretivism' or 'the social action approach' will
frequently have been used to designate this alternative perspective. As with the preceding section, the following is only
a general outline of the principal arguments involved.

The perspective in sociology we have called 'anti-positivism'
has its primary roots in nineteenth-century German philosophy and social science. The more prominent German academics, particularly those writing at the close of the century,
such as Sombart, Dilthey, Rickert and Weber, were all concerned in varying ways to distinguish the 'human' or 'cultural'
sciences from the natural sciences. Dilthey (1833-1911), for
example, believed that whereas the latter provide causal
explanations of 'outer' events, human science (or 'life philosophy') is concerned with the 'inner' knowledge of 'meaningful conduct', or, as Sombart put it, with 'grasping the meaning'
of an individual's experience of the world.

Max Weber placed probably the most influential emphasis
on sociology's need to understand and interpret meaningful

behaviour: for him sociology should develop the method of 'interpretative understanding'. The German term *Verstehen*, denoting this technique, has been very closely associated with Weber, though he was not the first to develop it. (As we shall see later, Weber does not neatly fit into the anti-positivist perspective outlined below, however, for although he was concerned that sociology should examine the meanings lying behind social action, he nevertheless believed a positivistic type of explanation for such action to be possible.)

Anti-positivism: an idealised account

For anti-positivists the source of individual attributes and behaviour cannot be seen to be ontologically *external* to the individual actor, since for them social reality is consciously and actively created by individuals who mean to do things and who attribute meanings to the behaviour of others. Onto-logically, then, social reality only exists as meaningful inter-action between individuals. Hughes (1976, p. 25) gives the following broad description of the anti-positivist position:

> Human beings are not 'things' to be studied in the way one studies rats, plants, or rocks, but are valuing, meaning-attributing beings to be understood as subjects and known as subjects. Sociology . . . deals with meaningful action, and the understanding, explanation, analysis, or whatever, must be made with consideration of those meanings that make the ordering of human action possible . . . To impose positivistic meanings upon the realm of social phenomena is to distort the fundamental nature of human existence.

Positivist sociology is thus criticised for assuming that society can be described and understood according to an ontology and methodology that is committed to seeing social behaviour as an empirically evident, quantifiable, object of investigation. By implication, the preconceived categories devised by positivism to define social reality are rejected since they are not derived from any understanding of the subjective aspirations, meanings, values and language people have in everyday life. It is the latter, claim the anti-positivists, which must form the basis of sociological understanding. Unlike the positivist approach, then, the meanings and consciousness of the social actor are not seen as a problem to be overcome by a strict adherence to quantitative methods that measure social behaviour. Rather, sociology must treat meanings, values, beliefs and hopes of individuals as its principal data, its primary subject-matter.

Logic of discovery

The anti-positivist discovers or 'discloses' social reality, not, as the positivist does, by imposing observer categories on individual action but by being receptive to and accepting the actor's *own* perceptions and interpretations of the world fashioned through interaction with other actors. Since meaningful human communication depends primarily on language, this is obviously of central interest. Positivists are criticised for believing that it is possible, via the use of observer categories and theories, to provide an 'expert' account of the social world superior to the 'lay' accounts of actors. Instead, anti-positivists insist that the process of discovery in sociology can only involve the attempt to look at the world through the actors' eyes and make sense of it through the means they employ, since there *is* no more to the social world than this. Consequently, not only are the positivist's observational categories rejected but also any preconceived hypothetical statements about causal relations: the latter would impose a totally illegitimate structure on sociological research that would prevent an understanding of the actor's ways of seeing and interpreting the world.

Logic of validation

Validity therefore involves *not* the measurement of alleged causal relationships between variables but the apprehension of the way individuals create reality in interaction with others. In order to contrast this enterprise with the *quantification* typically associated with positivism in sociology, this validating process is sometimes referred to as the establishment of *qualitative* data.

640 *Introductory Sociology*

Logic of explanation

Whether understanding reality as the actor sees it means that it is therefore capable of *objective explanation* is a matter of debate among anti-positivists. There are those who feel that once one has avoided imposing categories on the subject-matter at the discovery and validation stages and has understood the actor's way of looking at the world, one is then in a position to provide an objectively valid explanation of the nature of this socially constructed reality. Max Weber was an important exponent of this view (as we shall see in more detail in the final chapter). However, there are others who claim that such objectivity is impossible. These argue that a sociologist is just another social actor trying to make sense of the world: he or she can only interpret, understand and attribute meaning to the world by virtue of the fact that he or she is capable of engaging in meaningful social interaction with other social actors. Although this capacity allows sociological understanding, there is no reason for assuming that such understanding provides a more objectively true account of society compared with competing accounts from others — be

TABLE 11.2
Positivism and anti-positivism — differences

	Positivist	Anti-positivist
Ontology/epistemology	Social reality exists as objective causal relations between phenomena	Social reality is a product of meaningful social interaction
Methodology		
(i) Logic of discovery	Observational constructs in order to hypothesise about causal relations between variables	Actor constructs
(ii) Logic of validation	Testing of hypotheses by use of quantitative evidence	Understanding through the apprehension of qualitative evidence
(iii) Logic of explanation	Empirically valid statements about law-like causal relationships between variables	Meaningfully intelligible descriptions of how social life is accomplished

they sociologists or non-sociologists. From this point of view the only sort of explanations that sociologists can provide are *subj*ective: reflexive or retrospective accounts of how, as meaning-attributing individuals, they arrived at their particular understanding of some specific social situation. Ultimately, as we shall see later, this can result in the process of 'doing sociological research' becoming the actual topic of inquiry: that is, the research effort itself can be considered a legitimate source of data.

In Table 11.2 we summarise the main positivist/anti-positivist differences suggested above. Having constructed these idealised versions of positivism and anti-positivism, we shall now assess the extent to which they are adopted by the major theoretical perspectives established in contemporary sociology.

11.4   THE RELATIONSHIP BETWEEN THEORETICAL AND METHODOLOGICAL PERSPECTIVES IN SOCIOLOGY

Different theoretical approaches are more or less positivistic in the logic of their research strategy; we should not expect sociological perspectives to either completely embrace a positivistic methodology or completely embrace a non-positivistic one. If we think of the models we have constructed as poles at either end of a continuum, we can properly understand the positions perspectives variously occupy along it by bearing in mind the distinction we have made between the logical stages of discovery, validation and explanation in methodology.

Behaviourism

Behaviourism adopts an extreme positivist position. According to one of the principal exponents of this perspective, B.F. Skinner, *all* of the behaviour of humans is determined by, and is a product of, factors external to them in their environment. This approach argues that an individual's mind or mental state cannot be shown to have, and therefore be understood and be known as having, an independent effect on his or her actions: all mental states involving beliefs, values, motives and reasons can *only* be defined in observable behavioural terms. Hence,

Skinner's ontological and epistemological position is clearly manifested in his 'philosophy of the non-person': 'There is nothing going on in my head . . . talk is just another example of conditioned behaviour.'

Although a number of sociological perspectives insist that external factors may 'condition' behaviour, none share the behaviourist's view of action as being simply a mechanical behavioural response to external stimuli. Indeed, the crudity of the behavioural account of action has meant that it has gained little or no credibility within the sociological community.

The structural perspective

Although there are a number of radically different structural theories in sociology — including structural-functionalism and Marxist structuralism — common to all is an analysis of society in terms of its structural properties and how these combine to form a social system. In more concrete terms this type of analysis may, for example, propose that the investigation of family life reveals the existence of a regular, systematic order governing the relations between and the behaviour of members in the kin group. It might then be argued that one can only understand observable aspects of family life — e.g. forms of residence and marriage — by seeing them as expressions of a more general system of kinship. More abstractly, whether dealing with the family, the economy, politics, or systems of belief, an analysis of the overall system takes precedence over the examination of its constituent elements. The parts are to be explained in terms of the system, and not the system in terms of its parts: in other words, the system is seen as being greater than the sum of its component parts.

Much structural sociology may be characterised as positivist to a greater or lesser extent. Of major importance here is Durkheim's work and that area of research on which it has had great influence — the structural-functionalist school of Talcott Parsons that dominated American sociology from the 1930s to the end of the 1960s. Without denying that individual social actors have values, beliefs, motives and attitudes, the Durkheimian and later Parsonian analyses claim that these aspects of experience and meaning come from *outside* the individual. Individual attitudes and behaviour are first and foremost reflections or expressions of a non-individual collective culture which generates expectations, beliefs and practices. Thus the cultural system is regarded as *external* to individual consciousness, its structural components, in particular its institutionalised set of norms, constraining individuals to behave in a specific way. This type of analysis, therefore, assumes that social structures, as external determinants of behaviour, cannot be reduced to, or defined in terms of, discrete individual actions. Thus religious behaviour, for example, cannot be simply understood in terms of the particular behavioural activity of each of those individuals that engage in it. To repeat, the whole is seen as being greater than the sum of its parts.

Durkheim's idea of the 'social fact' — a 'thing' that can be identified as external to individual consciousness, a phenomenon (like the suicide rate) that indicates the existence of wider social forces — clearly derives from the type of structural perspective outlined above. In developing Durkheim's analysis Parsons not only promoted and carried out research into the structural and systemic character of society, but did so having adopted Durkheim's broad positivist methodology. For example, he states that sociological theory should concern itself with 'the formulation and logical relations of propositions containing empirical facts in direct relation to the observation of the facts and thus empirical verification of the propositions' (Parsons, 1937, p. 49). George A. Lundberg added to the positivist cause in American sociology by claiming that the quantitative methods common to natural science not only could but should be used in sociological research to establish an accurate and objective description of social phenomena. Thus, for example, for Lundberg, from a 'scientific' point of view, intelligence can be nothing else than that which intelligence tests measure. Here, then, actors' ideas, attitudes and beliefs may be counted as data but only as expressions of the external — and quantifiable — social reality.

As stressed earlier, since positivism and anti-positivism are not exclusive categories, but should be seen as the poles of a continuum, structuralist approaches can vary in their positivistic commitment. We can illustrate this variation by comparing the respective methodologies of two basically structural accounts about industrial attitudes and behaviour. These are:

(1) Robert Blauner, *Alienation and Freedom* (1964); and
(2) J. Goldthorpe and D. Lockwood *et al.*, *The Affluent Worker: Industrial Attitudes and Behaviour* (1969).

Blauner: 'Alienation and Freedom'

In this study of alienation in industrial work Blauner adopts a markedly positivistic methodology at all stages.

Logic of discovery (i). First, since alienation is a theoretical concept, it has to be given some means of being measured empirically:

Alienation is a general syndrome made up of a number of different objective conditions and subjective feeling-states which emerge from certain relationships between workers and the sociotechnical settings of employment. Alienation exists when workers are unable to control their immediate work processes [he calls this *powerlessness*], to develop a sense of purpose and function which connects their jobs to the overall organization of production [he calls this *meaninglessness*], to belong to integrated industrial communities [he calls this *isolation*], and when they fail to become involved in the activity of work as a mode of personal self-expression [he calls this *self-estrangement*] (Blauner, 1964, p. 15).

To put this another way, he is saying that if you measure

(i) the extent to which workers feel powerless in their work,
(ii) the extent to which they feel their work is meaningless,
(iii) the extent to which they feel isolated in their work, and
(iv) the extent to which they feel uninvolved in their work,

then what you are doing is measuring the extent to which they are alienated in work.

Logic of discovery (ii). Having operationalised his concept in this way, Blauner then hypothesises that the degree to which it will be experienced by individuals will be causally related to another variable — a material, or real-world phenomenon this time — the nature of the *technology* with which they work and the structure of their work roles. In the hypothesis, alienation is the *dependent* variable (the effect), while technology and work-role structure is the *independent* variable (the cause). Blauner (1964, pp. vii, 166) states:

> I attempt to show that the worker's relation to the technological organization of the work process and in the social organization of the factory *determines* whether or not he characteristically experiences in that work a sense of control rather than domination ... His industry even affects the kind of social personality he develops, since an industrial environment *tends* to breed a distinctive social *type* (our emphasis).

Logic of validation. To test this hypothesis Blauner investigates worker attitudes in different sorts of industries with different sorts of socio-technical systems:

craft — printing
machine-tending — textiles
assembly-line — cars
process — chemicals

Having collected his data (and used other results for secondary analysis), he then attempts to see whether they indicate that the hypothesised relationship between the existence of a particular work structure and a level of alienation holds, as measured by his indicators.

Logic of explanation. From his analysis Blauner (1964, p. 182) concludes that alienation in industry is to be seen as following 'a course that could be charted on a graph by means of an

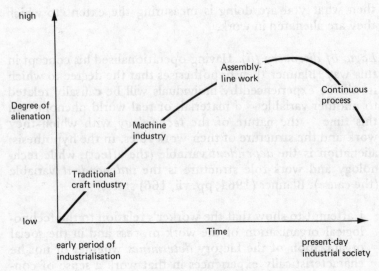

FIGURE 11.1

inverted U-curve', as shown in Figure 11.1. In other words, Blauner believes that at a certain stage of the development of technology (i.e. at the 'continuous-process' stage) mechanisation no longer dominates and alienates workers as before but rather allows workers to control their work process: 'The alienation curve begins to decline from its previous height as employees in automated industries gain a new dignity from responsibility and a sense of individual function' (Blauner, 1964, p. 182).

In general, therefore, workers' attitudes and behaviour are to be explained in terms of the structure of the work roles which they perform; change this, and attitudes and behaviour change also. In order to specify the sort of changes required, the sociologist provides a measure of the extent to which the specific structural factors cause the four aspects of alienation defined above. The correspondence between the ontological assumptions specified by Blauner's theoretical perspective and the logic of his research procedures is thus clear: social attitudes and behaviour are determined by external structural factors, and so the job of the researcher is to measure the strength of these determinants.

Goldthorpe and Lockwood et al. — 'The Affluent Worker: Industrial Attitudes and Behaviour'

In contrast to Blauner's approach, that of Goldthorpe and Lockwood is sometimes called 'weak actionism' since it is based on a theoretical perspective whose ontological position, while still essentially structural, allows much more causal status to actors' meanings and definitions of situations.

They argue that to understand industrial attitudes and behaviour one should not *impose* one's own understanding of reality on the individual workers but instead look at the way they perceive their world. They thus try to move away from using predefined categories — such as Blauner's 'powerlessness' — to classify an individual's experience of work. Rather, they try to understand the meanings the workers attach to their actions and the actions of others, meanings which arise from *both* their non-work and work roles and experiences. The first step in such research, then, they say, 'must be that of establishing empirically the way in which, in any given case, the wants and expectations which men bring to their employment, and the interpretation which they thus give to their work, shape the attitudinal and behavioural patterns of their working lives as a whole' (Goldthorpe and Lockwood *et al.*, 1969, p. 184).

However, they simultaneously want to examine the way in which this 'variety of meanings' is moulded, influenced or 'mediated' by structural factors, such as 'the workers' experience of both social and geographical mobility, their position in the life cycle, and their present patterns of family and community living'. Hence the second research stage involves

demonstrating how any orientation to work which is in question is in fact socially generated and sustained. The values and motivations that lead workers to the view of work they have adopted must be traced back . . . to typical life situations and experiences. In this way, therefore . . . the necessity . . . arises . . . of explaining and understanding the social life which goes on within the enterprise by reference ultimately to the structure and processes of the wider society in which the enterprise exists (Goldthorpe and Lockwood *et al.*, 1969, p. 185).

As we shall see shortly, compared with the approaches of symbolic interactionism and, in particular, ethnomethodology, this has a positivistic orientation.

Here, then, is an attempt to allow for both structural determination of attitude and behaviour while also recognising the existence of 'action' — *meaningful* social behaviour. However, this is a task which produces both methodological problems and, as we shall see in more detail later on, problems of method.

Since in an ontology such as Blauner's, reality is *given* as an *external* structure, the methodological job of the sociologist is to conceptualise this structure, investigate its empirical indicators and produce quantifiable results. But if, albeit only in part, reality is not a *given* — if it is not just a question of conceptualising an objective reality but also of discovering the conceptualisations of actors which are a significant part of the reality itself — then new problems arise. What is to be the logic of discovery? That is, how can one get at the actors' concepts? What is to be the logic of validation? That is, how are you to talk objectively about actors' concepts and show others what they mean? These are problems faced by all anti-positivists at these methodological stages, and we will look at them more closely later, in particular when we examine observation as a research technique. In Goldthorpe and Lockwood's case, however, because their desire to understand actors' meanings goes hand in hand with an ontological commitment to structure, these problems are much greater than is usual. This is because the actors whose concepts, meanings and definitions of their situation they wish to understand are the *same* actors about whom they also wish to make positivistic-type statements concerning structural sources of their behaviour. This combination of interests produces real difficulties for method:

(i) In order to produce generalisations about a large population it is normally the case — often for practical reasons of time and money — that a survey technique will be employed. Although a survey may be suitable for providing data about which quantitative generalisations can be made, it is, as we shall see later, extremely doubtful (though not impossible) that it can be used qualitatively, to uncover properly the subjective meanings of individual actors. So despite the fact that the latter is seen as a crucial element in their analysis, Goldthorpe and Lockwood are forced to use a survey technique in a positivistic fashion to generate quantitative data to measure the relationship between individual attitudes and the structural factors with which they are also concerned. The result is that their partial anti-positivist commitment to the discovery of actors' meanings is endangered by their positivist logic of validation.

(ii) Survey results are necessarily ahistorical — they are a snapshot in time. How can one call an account of social reality based on such results a legitimate account when one's acceptance of the importance of meaning, choice and the possibility of creativity presupposes that this reality is an ongoing historical *process*? Meanings are the product of interaction with other social actors and, as such, can change.

It is *this* consequence of the theoretical pre-eminence allocated by Goldthorpe and Lockwood to structural determinants of attitudes and behaviour that sociologists much further down the anti-positivist road criticise. As Silverman (1970, pp. 184–5), for example, puts it:

By arguing that work orientations are determined by a combination of internal and external factors, one may miss the way in which people's view of themselves and their situation is the outcome of an *ongoing process*, i.e. never fully determined by one or another set of structural constraints but always in the act of 'becoming', as successive experiences shape and reshape a subjective definition of self and society.

This fundamentally anti-positivistic definition of reality as process rather than as a static entity is the hallmark of the next theoretical and methodological perspective we shall consider — symbolic interactionism.

Symbolic interactionism

The principal ontological claim of the symbolic interactionist is that reality is not immutable or fixed but is constantly

being recreated or 'achieved' through the meaningful interaction of individuals; for the interactionist, social actors are
continually engaged in 'negotiating' the meaning of reality
with one another. Major representatives of this approach include Howard Becker and Erving Goffman. Challenging the
Durkheimian and Parsonian analysis, these theorists criticise
the view that behaviour can be perceived as an expression of a
rigid system of normatively defined statuses and roles. Social
identity is much more fluid — being built up and broken
down as a result of interaction; its development is analogous
to that of an occupational career, with opportunities, dangers,
success and failure. A classic study adopting this perspective
is Goffman's work *Asylums* (1968), in which (among other
things) he looks at the 'career' of mental patients and pri-
soners in their respective confining institutions. These characteristic interactionist concerns are examined more fully in the
final chapter.

Methodology

Logic of discovery. Given the interactionist's epistemological
position that social reality can only be known through understanding the point of view of social actors, their meanings and
definitions of their situations, a positivistic logic of discovery
is not followed. That is, the construction of hypotheses prior
to investigation based on predefined observer categories is
replaced by research that asks much more open-ended questions: the usual exhortation is for the researcher to 'tell it
like it is'; such a research enterprise is very often described as
'naturalistic'.

Logic of validation. Once this initial exploratory research has
been accomplished, interactionists are then normally more
prepared to develop tentative hypotheses, though even these
may be reformulated in the light of further evidence. To
some extent, therefore, it is not unreasonable to suggest that
in interactionist research, discovery and validation take place
at one and the same time. The logic underlying this approach
— often formally defined as 'analytic induction' — is that
understanding can only emerge out of the continual interplay

of theory and method in the field. Investigation is thus concerned with the deliberate search for disconfirming, or *negative*, cases, so that hypotheses can be continually refined.

The development of hypotheses and assessment of them against further evidence is one indication that interactionism is not *completely* free from positivist influence. A further indication is that interactionists often try to provide *proof* for their theories. The attempt to prove something presupposes that the subject-matter one is dealing with has an *objective* existence, and that one is capable of *demonstrating* this to be so.

Logic of explanation. This positivist influence carries on through to affect the interactionist's logic of explanation. Thus, although most research reports are largely qualitative in character, interactionists may claim support for their discoveries by using evidence of an implicitly quantitative nature. Phillips (1971, p. 137) makes a telling point here:

> all descriptions and analyses of behaviour are inevitably *both* qualitative and quantitative — although with observational studies the counting and measurement may be implicit. For instance, in observational studies there are assertions that a pattern of behaviour occurs *frequently*, *often*, *sometimes*, *seldom*, or in *many* different situations.

Moreover, *explicit* quantification is not entirely absent either. For example, in his study of college students — *Making the Grade* — Howard Becker numerically tabulates some of his data. We will return to these kind of points when we look in more detail at observation as a technique. Here we can conclude by quoting Cuff and Payne (1979, p. 173): 'It is not the case that structuralists measure, while interactionists do not. Interactionists merely tend to have a distaste for certain ways of measuring.' So the symbolic interactionist goes some way down the anti-positivist road but stops short of its end. Right at the end of the road, however, are ethnomethodologists.

Ethnomethodology

The term 'ethnomethodology' was coined by Harold Garfinkel. It is worth considering its two parts: 'ethno' refers to the stock of common-sense knowledge available to a member of society: 'methodology' refers to the methods or strategies which actors use in different settings to make their meanings understandable, or, in Garfinkel's terms, 'accountable' to others. These methods allow the successful accomplishment of everyday communication and activity.

Ethnomethodologists thus share the interactionists' view that social reality must be seen in terms of the on-going process of 'interaction' by which participants accomplish or achieve meaningful communication with one another. However, ethnomethodology does *not* share the view that the processes through which such interaction is accomplished can be *objectively* described and explained by the 'expert' sociologist. Unlike all those perspectives discussed above, ethnomethodology dismisses the idea that sociology can provide some 'scientific', objective, account of social reality. The sociologist is seen as being just one more actor on the social stage, trying to 'make sense' of the social world. He or she is no more than a 'member' of the world, not a privileged observer rendering 'true' accounts of that world.

Thus 'doing sociology' is regarded as just one more practical activity by which certain actors — sociologists — make sense of their world in terms of a shared 'common' sense. The term 'common sense' is therefore not meant to denote an *inferior* form of knowledge: rather, it must be taken literally — that is, it signifies a meaning system which is common to, or shared by, certain social actors, whether they regard themselves as 'sociologists' or not. However, ethnomethodologists argue that there is one significant difference between the sociologist and the non-sociologist. This is that 'doing sociology' is (or should be) a self-conscious reflexive activity. Unlike the majority of social actors who take for granted or rarely examine the means by which they successfully achieve understanding, the sociologist can actively investigate the ways in which he or she accomplishes his or her accounts of the world. This does not mean that these accounts can be regarded as more objective than alternative ones, but it does mean that they can be treated as topics for investigation in their own right. So it is that sociologists who do not share the ethnomethodological perspective often find themselves and their theories subject to the scrutiny of ethnomethodologists. This can be particularly exasperating for those who believe that their theories are true or objective accounts about social phenomena. Ethnomethodological accounts usually involve the close examination of the way language is used to convey meaning in social interaction — language being the primary symbolic means by which individuals make sense to each other — although, since there are other means, e.g. non-verbal gestures and communications, these are sometimes the object of interest as well.

This tends to mean that the topic for other sorts of sociologist — say crime, or suicide, or mental illness — is important to the ethnomethodologist only in so far as it provides an arena in which to investigate the *real* topic: the common-sense mechanisms through which human beings observe, conceptualise and make meaningful the world they encounter in their everyday life. A critique of the ethnomethodological position we reserve till our final chapter on sociological theory. For the moment the main point we wish to make is that since ethnomethodology denies any possibility of objectivity or warranted explanations about social phenomena, we cannot examine it in terms of our model of the logical stages of research. That is, it does not offer any logic of discovery, validation or explanation.

11.5 INTERIM CONCLUSION

Besides significant methodological differences, the theoretical perspectives we have examined so far can be distinguished in terms of the relative causal status they each give to individual action compared with structural factors in constituting the social world. The relationship between individual consciousness and a 'wider' social reality — between 'action' and 'structure' — is often regarded as the crucial theoretical problem for sociology. We shall consider this issue in greater depth in the final chapter. Here, because of its implications for methodology, it is worth drawing attention to one of the more recent contributions to this debate, Anthony Giddens's *New Rules of Sociological Method* (1976).

Giddens tries to unify the notions of structure and action by giving a causal status to each in the production and re-production of social reality. Not surprisingly, such a synthesis challenges the theoretical division between 'hard' positivism and 'hard' anti-positivism, with their mutually exclusive onto-logies, epistemologies and methodologies. To effect such a reconciliation requires going beyond the conceptual frame-work upon which each of the two perspectives is built.

Against the positivist position, Giddens argues that social reality cannot be envisaged in terms of a 'pre-given universe of objects', open to some 'independent' or context-free observer. Rather, it should be understood as the on-going product of actors consciously creating their world as historical agents. At the same time, however, he argues that actors are constrained by the structural conditions under which they live such that although 'men produce society' they do so 'not under condi-tions of their own choosing'. He is suggesting, in other words, that there is a dialectical relation between structure and action: on the one hand, 'structures are constituted by action', yet, on the other hand, 'action is constituted structurally'. Such a logic seeks to overcome the positivist/anti-positivist split. However, although Giddens has demonstrated that this unifi-cation is theoretically warranted, he has yet to specify the methodological procedures that would follow from it for purposes of empirical sociological research.

Some recent work by Paul Willis, presented in two books, *Learning to Labour* (1977) and *Profane Culture* (1978), adopts a theoretical position which, in many ways, comes close to that advocated by Giddens. Willis (1977) tries to ex-plain why 'working-class boys get working-class jobs'. En-deavouring to unite the processes of structure and action, he argues that while specific structural features of capitalist soci-ety work to restrict the educational, occupational and poli-tical horizons of working-class boys, certain boys themselves actively use such features as sources of meaning to create and recreate working-class culture and life-chances. This process occurs in a variety of ways and may be expressed in apparently insignificant behaviour. For example, Willis argues that it even occurs when the 'lads' — those boys who constitute the 'counter-school culture' — choose to smoke. His perhaps somewhat contentious point is that they 'seize upon' cigarettes — 'one of the three great consumer goods of capitalism' (the other two being clothes and alcohol) — in this way, not simply because it is against school rules, but more importantly because through it they can project themselves into the adult male world of the working class. This 'act of insurrection' thus allows them to separate themselves from the school and to overcome what they experience as the 'oppressive adolescence' of the school; but ironically, Willis argues, it is this very act of liberation which places them more firmly within the constraints of working-class culture.

According to Willis, then, the task for sociology is to examine the way in which people — as individuals or groups — respond to their structural conditions. His commitment to this type of analysis is evident when he writes that

> In the case of job choice amongst the unqualified working class, for instance, we can *predict* final employment quite well from class background, geographical location, local opportunity structure, and educational attainment . . . But . . . to quote [these] larger factors is really no form of explanation at all. It does not identify a chain or set of causalities which indicate particular outcomes from many possible ones. It simply further outlines the situation which is still in need of explanation: *how* and *why* young people take the restricted and often meaningless available jobs in ways which seem sensible to them in their familiar world as it is actually lived (Willis, 1977, p. 172).

We do not intend to assess whether Willis's work answers this question successfully: this would require considerable theoretical discussion going beyond the brief of this chapter. The point that should be taken here is that many sociologists — like Giddens and Willis — are trying to break out of the often sterile debate between positivism and anti-positivism as competing explanations of social reality. As always, however, much remains to be done.

We shall now move on to consider the actual methods that competing theoretical perspectives typically employ to collect 'data' for their research. There are two types of sociological data: 'primary' and 'secondary'. Primary data are those which sociologists collect for themselves. Later on we will look at some of the characteristics of, and problems involved with, the two most often used methods for the production of primary data — asking questions in surveys, and observation. First, however, we will look at the chief source of secondary data for sociologists, which, while apparently unproblematic and neutral, is in fact a renowned arena for the confrontation between the whole range of epistemological positions we have just considered — official statistics.

11.6 OFFICIAL STATISTICS

Most sociology students will at one stage or another be confronted by statistical data. Textbooks, for example, often rely on social statistics describing population, births, deaths, marriages, income and wealth, etc., as documentary evidence to support various interpretations of the social order. The very mathematical, quantitative character of such statistics presented in graphs, tables and figures seem to give the data the scientific, incontrovertible status of being 'hard facts'. The use of social statistics in sociology is not just a recent phenomenon: early British sociologists in particular regarded them as important and necessary sources of information which could be used, both to bolster the scientific usage of the discipline in academic circles, and to develop informed social policy programmes designed to relieve poverty, illness, poor housing, and so on. The more renowned of these early pioneers include Charles Booth, Seebohm Rowntree, and Sidney and Beatrice Webb.

Following in this tradition contemporary British sociologists draw on a wide range of *official* statistics in their analyses. Official statistics are obtained from 'official' sources: that is, government agencies such as the Office of Population Censuses and Surveys (OPCS), and the Home Office. Moreover, the Government Statistical Service publishes more detailed information collected from these two sources in its

Annual Abstract of Statistics and *Social Trends*.

There are a number of reasons why sociologists have been particularly reliant on official statistics as sources of data:

(i)   they are frequently the *only* available source of data in a particular area;
(ii) they are readily available, such that the researcher does not have to spend time or money collecting his or her own information;
(iii) they allow an examination of trends over time – e.g. divorce, crime and strike rates;
(iv) they allow inter-group comparisons to be made, e.g. middle-class and working-class family size, as well as international ones, e.g. suicide rates in different countries;
(v)   they allow 'before' and 'after' studies to be made – e.g. examining the effect that changes in legislation have on divorce patterns.

At the same time, however, there are a number of major drawbacks connected with the use of official statistics. First, they may draw on information which has been collected for completely different purposes than those which the sociologist has in mind. That is, official agencies are normally concerned with gathering statistics to assess specific government policies, and they are unlikely to reflect the particular research problems of the sociologist. Second, the categories used by agencies – the official definitions of households, income groups, or social classes, for example – may differ from those employed by the sociologist.

Apart from these two problems, a more fundamental theoretical issue arises which bears on the positivist/anti-positivist debate examined earlier. This concerns the sense in which statistics can be regarded as objective, 'factual' measures of social phenomena. With regard to this issue let us consider once again Durkheim's use of statistics in his classic study of *Suicide*.

Durkheim drew on information from both official and non-official sources to document the number of suicides occurring in different countries. Accordingly, by comparing such data he was able to prepare differing *suicide rates* (per million) for each country. Crucially, not only was there apparent variation between countries but each country's particular suicide rate appeared to be constant over a number of years. Durkheim believed that such regularity indicated that the suicide rate, and those factors (such as religion) which encouraged its variation, could be treated as 'social facts', objective evidence on which to establish a scientific, positivistic, theory of suicide.

However, those who are critical of Durkheim's positivistic perspective challenge, among other things, his statistical 'evidence': Douglas, in his book *The Social Meanings of Suicide* (1967), and Atkinson, in his work collected in *Discovering Suicide* (1978), argue that if one examines the ways in which individuals — in particular official agents such as coroners — identify acts as 'suicides', one discovers wide variation and inconsistency. Both argue that statistics such as the suicide rate cannot be regarded as objective measures of phenomena precisely because they are the result of complex social processes of meaning and interpretation which eventually define certain acts as 'suicide'. This means that the actual suicide statistics do not record acts which are identical, as Durkheim assumed. Suicide rates cannot, then, be compared since, as Douglas shows, officials use various definitions of suicide. Hence Douglas (1967, p. 235) comments that

> the first task is to examine the different forms of behaviour which a society labels 'suicide' in order to develop a classification of the different meanings associated with what superficially appear to be similar forms of behaviour.

Atkinson provides further evidence of the socially constructed nature of the 'fact' of suicide where coroners *infer intent to have committed suicide* by relying on a wide variety of criteria. Some regard the mode of death as an indicator of suicide — for example, it is conventionally assumed that hanging must be self-inflicted, whereas road deaths are not. The point is that the incidence of so-called 'suicides' is socially constructed. This can be further illustrated in cases of death occurring in more equivocal contexts: for example, in the case of a drug overdose one coroner might be prepared to record a suicide verdict, whereas another may regard the death as the result of a mistake, or absent-mindedness on the part of the person taking the pills.

Indeed, Douglas tellingly shows how Durkheim himself, in order to explain the 'social fact' of the distribution of suicide, also fundamentally relied on such subjective interpretations based on common sense. He argues, for example, that Durkheim was only able to arrive at an explanation of the variations in the suicide rates of, say, Protestants and Catholics, or of those who are single and married, by employing stereotypical images of how Protestants, Catholics, single and married people behave. That these images are gleaned from *his own personal* stock of common-sense knowledge is well illustrated by his characterisation of those female attributes which (in his view) make them poorer candidates than men for inclusion in the suicide statistics. For instance, according to Durkheim, divorced women kill themselves less often than divorced men because the inferior female intellect reduces the traumatic effects of sexual deprivation! He thus argues that 'woman's sexual needs have less of a mental character because, generally speaking, her mental life is less developed'. The point here, then, is the crucial one that not only do processes of interpretation produce statistics but that explanations of statistics thus produced *also* rely on them; for anti-positivists, in fact, suicide statistics can only tell us about the living, not the dead.

The anti-positivistic perspective embodied in the work of Douglas and Atkinson therefore focuses attention on the inevitable role that meaningful interpretation plays in the construction of statistical information about reality, as, indeed, for anti-positivists, it does in the construction of all social reality. However, it should not be thought that the anti-positivist/positivist debate is confined to the use of statistics in sociological explanation. What we have tried to emphasise in this chapter so far is that it should be recognised that *any* decision about how sociological research should be carried out is ultimately a decision about epistemological commitment; as we shall see, decisions regarding specific primary-data collection methods are no exception.

11.7   THE LOGIC AND PRACTICE OF DATA COLLECTION

Asking questions: the survey

Before we see how epistemological commitment affects the choice of question-asking techniques, we ought to be aware of the range of such techniques which are available.

Respondents can either be asked questions which are written down — in a *questionnaire* — or presented verbally, i.e. in an *interview*. Interviews and questionnaires are almost invariably used in the context of a *survey*. The point of any survey of a population is to make comparisons between the responses to the questions asked so that a general statement about them may be made. Surveys vary according to the degree of *structure* involved, for questions can be asked, and answers elicited, in a more or less structured way. In interviews the degree of structure of the questions can vary:

(1) The most *structured* interview is the sort where the order and wording of the questions are predetermined and each respondent is asked exactly the same question in exactly the same way with the questions following the same order every time.

(2) The *focused* interview, as its name suggests, is the sort where the questions are focused on particular topics but where the interviewer can choose the words he/she uses to ask them as well as the order in which they are asked. (Usually, then, this sort of interview *schedule* — as the list of questions an interviewer is to ask is called — simply lists general areas of interest the interviewer is to get the respondent to talk about.)

(3) The completely *unstructured* or *discovery* interview involves the interviewer simply engaging the respondent in conversation, and then following up particular points of interest as they develop.

Structure of responses

In general two types of question may be used:

First, 'closed-ended' questions provide a range of alternatives from which the respondent is asked to choose his/her answer. For example,

Question Please tell me how you voted in the last election:
Tory
Labour
Liberal
Other
Didn't

Second, 'open-ended' questions place no such structure on the answer and allow the respondent to reply in any way he/she likes. For example,

Question Why did you vote the way you did in the last election?

In a questionnaire sufficient space is left for a lengthy answer, while in an interview the interviewer will usually write down the reply verbatim.

Coding

The degree of structure of the response determines the ease with which they can be *coded*. The purpose of coding is to convert responses to questions into symbols which can be easily compared with one another. If a question is closed-ended, the codes can be attached to the range of alternatives during the construction of the questionnaire or schedule; this is called *pre-coding*. Thus, in the case of our earlier example of a closed-ended question, the alternative responses would be pre-coded and the respondent (if included in a questionnaire) or interviewer asked to indicate the answer to the question by ringing the appropriate code in the following fashion:

Question Please tell me how you voted in the last election:
Tory   1
Labour   ②
Liberal   3
Other   4
Didn't   5

662 Introductory Sociology

If a question is open-ended so that the response is not structured in this way, and if coding is desired, it has to take place
after the questioning has finished. This makes things more
difficult, so a list of codes for each question is not usually
drawn up until a number of answers have been examined in
order to see if any patterns emerge. Thus, for example, after
looking at a number of answers to our other question, 'Why
did you vote the way you did at the last election?', it might
be discovered that nearly all of them fit into one or other of
the following categories:

family always vote that way
like the political leader
like the policies
dislikes the others
will improve standard of living

A list of these codes is then drawn up and answers to the
remaining questionnaires/interviews coded from this list
(which can be added to if need be). The advantage of coding
is that the responses can be transferred to a punch card —
nowadays almost invariably a computer card — and almost
any sort of comparison between different sets of responses
can be made very easily.

Before we go on three further points need to be made.

(1) Some open-ended questions produce results that cannot be coded, either because the range of responses is too
diverse or because they are not unambiguous enough and it
would be illegitimate to 'force' them into particular categories. Since such responses cannot be coded, it means that
they cannot be statistically compared and generalised about
in quantitative terms; any comparison of the responses to
these sorts of questions thus usually takes a qualitative form,
typically with verbatim extracts reproduced alongside as part
of the results of the survey.

(2) Where individual questions are unstructured — where
the interviewer can ask a question as he/she sees fit — it is not
only impractical but also illegitimate to make the sorts of quan-
tified comparisons which coding and computation facilitate,

since differences in the way questions are asked of different respondents may well be influential in producing differences or similarities in the answers.

(3) The same restriction obviously applies to an even greater extent to an unstructured interview since it has to be seen as a social encounter of a qualitatively different status from all the others in the survey. As a result, not only can quantitative comparisons not be made for practical (coding) and epistemological reasons but even qualitative comparisons can be made only with the greatest of care.

Obviously, then, there is a direct relationship between the degree of structure of both questions and interviews in a survey and the possibility or legitimacy of comparison, generalisation and quantification of the results. Therefore, we should next consider the way in which surveys are designed to be more or less structured, and how the degree to which they are affects the sort of results they produce. It is here that we begin to consider the relationship between epistemological position and choice of question-asking technique.

Survey design

In designing research of any sort there are two important issues which need to be examined – those of *validity* and *reliability*.

Validity. This is concerned with notions of *truth*, and as such is a *relative* concept, for the validity of the data or methods used depends on the theoretical, methodological and, ultimately, ontological/epistemological position you adopt. Thus, if you think, positivistically, that social reality is external to the actor and can be understood by means of observer categories and can be explained by means of the measurement of relationships between these categories, then techniques designed to do this are valid. If, however, you think reality is subjectively created out of the meaningful interaction of actors, and that you can only understand it by understanding these meanings, then you are more likely to think that techniques that embody observer categories are *in*valid and that only techniques which get at actors' conceptualisations of the world will provide you with valid data.

Reliability. This concerns not so much truth as *replicability*. For a technique of data collection to be reliable, it should produce results which are not affected by the process of collection. For a *survey* to be reliable it must be reasonable to assume that each time the survey is repeated and applied to the same respondents it will produce similar results.

Validity and survey design. Notions of validity in asking questions are intimately bound up with

(i) the ease with which the responses to the questions can be compared, measured and generalised about, and

(ii) the size of the population about whom such comparison, measurement and generalisation can be made.

Validity, comparison and measurement. In general, the more we think we need to understand the meanings of our actors, the less structured our questions and our interviews will have to be. Since this is so, it follows that the more we think we need to understand meanings, the harder it will be for us to compare, measure and generalise about the results of our questions:

(1) *Structure of questions*. For example, if you think that the response to a closed-ended question like

Question Do you think trade unions in Britain have got too much power?
Yes   1
No   2
Don't know 3

is a valid indicator of the respondent's attitude towards trade unions and/or the distribution of power in Britain, then it also means that your results about this topic from your survey population are going to be easily coded (pre-coded in this case, of course), compared and measured. If, however, less positivistically, you think that only questions like

Question What do you think about trade unions in Britain?
Question Who do you think has power in Britain?

are valid — i.e. are likely to allow the actor to tell you what he means — then your results can only be coded, and comparison and measurement made, with great difficulty.

(2) *Structure of interview.* The more one wants to understand the way the actor looks at the world, the fewer preconceptions or assumptions should be made about the general topic of inquiry. Hence unstructured interviews should be seen as unique events since the questions, their sequence, the emphases given by the interviewer and, in fact, everything other than the general focus of the interview can vary considerably from one occasion to the next. This means that it is very difficult to compare and measure the responses of different social actors gained through this technique. For these reasons, unstructured interviews are hardly ever used in survey research where coding and measurement are the primary aims except as an exploratory technique (to discover questions to ask, as, for example, when key informants are used in the early stages of research), or as a means of enabling investigation of a greater depth into areas of interest previously uncovered by more structured interviews. However, this sort of interview can be a major instrument of data collection where an understanding of actors' meanings is the primary aim and where coding and comparison are of minimal importance. The results of such research are usually reproduced in an almost wholly qualitative fashion. In sum, then, the desire to understand actors' meanings in survey research is inversely related to the ease with which coding, comparison and measurement of its results can take place.

Validity and number of respondents. Validity is also inversely related to the number of respondents of whom questions can be asked — for the more unstructured an interview, the more time-consuming it is, and the fewer the interviews that can be carried out.

These relationships concerning validity and survey design are represented in Figure 11.2.

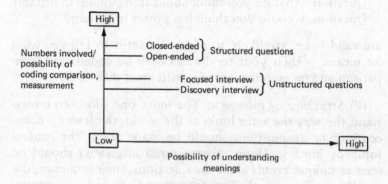

FIGURE 11.2

Conclusion on validity and survey design. These factors concerning validity have a number of consequences for the practice of asking questions in social research:

(i) The tail (method) can wag the dog (aim of the research). Here, while the inverse relationship between understanding and measurability is recognised by the researcher, the desire to come up with 'hard' quantifiable data which can be statistically manipulated in order to produce generalisations significantly reduces the likelihood of registering the subjective meanings of social actors.

(ii) Less extreme is the sort of compromise in what are known as 'attitude scales'. Essentially these are closed-ended questions about a respondent's attitudes which not only purport to get at his/her meaning but which are also, because of the structured nature of their responses, capable of easy coding and measurement. For example:

Question Which of the following comes closest to your point of view?

	Strongly agree	Agree	Neither agree nor disagree	Disagree	Strongly disagree
(a) You can be a good Christian without thinking about God and religion	1	2	3	4	5
(b) You can be a good Christian without being a Church member	1	2	3	4	5
(c) You can be a good Christian without attending Church	1	2	3	4	5

However well intentioned, anti-positivists usually dismiss such questions since they impose rigid observer categories on a respondent's view of reality and are therefore inevitably unhelpful so far as getting at real understanding is concerned.

(iii) The most usual result is that different *sorts* of question-asking takes place, with questions and interviews of varying degrees of structure being used, depending on the extent to which the need for an understanding of meanings is felt to be more important than a desire for quantification.

Reliability and survey design. If a survey is a short cut to observation, then sampling is simply a further short cut. Instead of asking questions of all the people in which we are interested we ask only a fraction of them. Reliable sampling is always concerned with representativeness. The more representative we can make our sample of the population we are studying as a whole in terms of the variables we think are important, the more reliable it is.

But sampling can be a rather difficult procedure. The document listing the parent population from which a sample is to be drawn is called a *sampling frame*. Obviously, the quality of the source of one's sample is crucial to the reliability of one's results, since the sample can only be as good as the frame from which it is drawn. For example, if an electoral register is not up to date, no matter how carefully a sample is drawn, it is not going to be wholly reliable or representative of the actual population concerned. Again, there can be real difficulties in drawing a reliable sample. Say we wanted to investigate students' perceptions of power in a college, and wanted to draw a 10 per cent sample. How can we make this representative? We could put the names of all students on pieces of paper, place them in a drum and draw out the requisite number. Or, better still, we could get a computer to select at random from student records. Or we could choose any other convenient way of obtaining a *random sample*. 'Random' thus does not mean haphazard here — it means that each unit in the parent population about whom generalisations are to be made has exactly the same chance of inclusion in the sample as any other unit. But randomness does not *necessarily* mean representativeness. Thus, drawing a simple random sample from our frame of the student population, we may end up with a disproportionate number of sociology students, or women, or part-time students. To get round such problems we can *stratify* our sample according to factors we believe may be relevant: for example, by full-time or part-time students, subject being studied, sex, or whatever. This would give us several different groups from which to draw random samples in proportion to their numbers in the parent population. Another term for such sampling is *purposive sampling*.

Another sort of sampling technique is *quota*, or *judgement*, sampling. This is a quicker and more convenient way of getting at a sample than other methods but is arguably the least reliable. Typically, before interviewing takes place, the major constituent categories in the population are defined — e.g. categorisation by sex, age, occupation, religion, or whatever. Interviewers are then given a *quota* of respondents from each of these categories to contact, the size of the quota being determined by what it is believed (or, it is hoped, known) is the relative proportion of individuals in each category in the population as a whole.

Much depends on judgement here, however. First, it is exercised before respondent contact is made, in order to decide how many of whom will be interviewed; and second, it is exercised by an interviewer, who has to decide which individuals fit the predefined categories. It has been argued that the bias inherent in this sort of procedure goes a long way to explaining the variance and unreliability of public-opinion and political polls, and it is certainly the case that quota sampling is most effective when representativeness is not needed and where statements about particular groups are the only concern.

Sometimes, of course, a clearly defined sampling frame is not easily available, for in some research – e.g. into deviance – there is no existing information about who constitutes the population (we shall look at Humphreys's problems in this regard later). One way around this is to construct a 'snowball' sample. One begins with a single informant or a few informants among the population in which one is interested and these help one to find more respondents: one contact leads to another, and each of these leads to still more respondents, and so on. Of course, there is no way one can check for bias here, and from this point of view purposive sampling is far better; however, a snowball is better than nothing and may often be quite appropriate if, for example, friendship or kinship networks are being investigated.

Survey implementation

Once satisfied with the design of a survey, the next problem is to implement it. The problems involved with survey implementation are of two kinds: (i) those concerned with making contact with the respondents; and (ii) those concerned with actually asking them questions.

Problems of contact. Although making contact might look straightforward enough, in fact it can be quite problematic. There are a number of issues involved.

Most importantly, the way in which the sociologist approaches respondents almost certainly defines his or her *role* in their eyes. For example, since many people have a stereotyped image of the sociologist as some sort of subversive plotting the overthrow of society, a letter of introduction from the Department of Sociology at some university or other is not going to help establish an immediate rapport between interviewer and respondent. The principle therefore appears to be clear: any method of contact has its own peculiar problems in terms of assigned identities which can affect access to, and indeed the quality of, the data. It is impossible to have a *neutral* identity: any inquiring sociologist will inevitably be assigned a label of some kind. Consequently, where possible we must decide *in advance* the identity we wish to create for ourselves, one which will affect what we are doing least, and play the appropriate role accordingly. However, this is not always possible; sometimes, because we are ignorant of those whom we are studying, we do not know the most useful identity to present and this leads to more or less successful decisions being made on the spot.

No matter how diligent we are there are always those respondents we cannot contact: these are called *non-respondents*. This does not necessarily mean that they have refused to be interviewed but that, for some reason or another, we have been unable to get hold of them.

We need to be fairly certain that non-respondents are not a particular kind of person and that they thus do not differ in any fundamental way from respondents — i.e. that they are equally representative of the sample. The more non-respondents, the less likely this will be a valid assumption to make. A non-response rate of 10 per cent or less is suspiciously good, and in general less than 30 per cent is adequate in survey research. Above 40 per cent, problems of unrepresentativeness arise.

If we suspect real problems, we have two alternatives:

(i) we can weight the replies for some non-respondents in a way which we think will counteract the bias in the sample (this is not very satisfactory); or

(ii) we can replace non-respondents by others chosen in the same way as in the original sample (this is much better and, if done properly, involves drawing two separate samples of the same size so that if, for ex-

ample, no. 83 in the sample proper is a non-respon-
dent, no. 83 from the substitute sample is the replacement).

Problems with interviewing. Assuming we are able to make
contact, we are then faced with problems involved with actually asking our questions. Again, these are of two kinds: (i)
those concerned with the *design* of the interview schedule (as
opposed to the content); and (ii) those concerned with the
interview situation itself.

(i) *The design of the interview schedule.* (The following
points obviously also apply to the design of a questionnaire.)
The questions must be asked sensibly and flow naturally
rather than making sudden changes of direction or of area of
discussion. Furthermore, because respondents often need to
be 'warmed up', we do not start with awkward or embarrassing questions about details of the respondent's sex life, or
his/her income or wealth. Instead we use easy and straightforward questions about variables like age, length of residence,
marital status, etc., at the beginning and leave the more difficult questions towards the end, when the respondent is
more relaxed. Questions must also be both intelligible and
unambiguous. The only way to be sure of this is to try them
out in what is called a *pilot survey*; this is usually carried out
on respondents from the population under scrutiny not in
the sample itself.

(ii) *The interview situation.* Because the interview is itself
an example of social interaction it can crucially affect the
quality of the data collected. It is useful to see interviewing
from a symbolic interactionist viewpoint. The researcher can
define interviews in certain ways in order to reinforce the
role he/she wants to play. Certain gestures, demeanours,
tones of voice, the use of props like a briefcase or a printed
schedule, the wearing of particular clothes, all serve to impose a certain definition of the situation on the respondent.
From this point of view, then, because interviewing involves
structuring our behaviour in order to achieve a required effect,
it in fact involves doing no more than actors do in every social
encounter in which they engage in everyday life, except that

it is a self-conscious process.

However, it is this essential similarity between a social-research interview and a social encounter in everyday life that has led some sociologists to reject the type of data it produces. Their argument is that there is an invalidity inherent in the whole process of asking questions in social research which must cast fundamental doubts on the extent to which we can assume that a respondent's answers to questions actually reveal his or her behaviour and attitudes in everyday life.

The validity of the interview: the congruence of verbal responses and behaviour. We have seen that the primary assumption of the interview is that it is a short cut to observation and that with careful questioning answers given by respondents to questions about their past or future actions will correspond to how they did behave in the past or will behave in the future.

However, there is now much evidence to question the validity of this assumption and therefore the validity of the whole question-asking process in social research. This evidence seems to demonstrate that since asking questions of a respondent is itself an example of social behaviour, involving the meaningful interaction of two social actors, we therefore have to accept that the answers a respondent gives to a question may well be a direct function of his or her interaction with the interviewer rather than anything else, and that (as a result) these answers might not match his or her *actual* behaviour or attitudes.

One of the first demonstrations of this occurred when La Piere (1934) travelled across the USA with a Chinese couple, observing how they were treated by the proprietors at various rest and refreshment places like hotels, camping sites and restaurants. The couple visited 251 places, being accepted at all save one. Six months later, La Piere sent a questionnaire to each one, asking whether it would accept members of Chinese origin as guests: only *one* establishment said it would, a considerable discrepancy between what the respondents said they would do and what they actually did. Phillips (1971) documents similar discrepancies in an examination of a whole range of factors present in an interview situation that can affect the nature of the response elicited. He shows, for example, that the sex, age and race of the interviewer can influence the way a respondent answers questions, as can non-ascribed status characteristics like his or her assumed social status or religious affiliation. He demonstrates in particular how such factors are involved in the well-documented source of bias variously called the 'social desirability effect' or 'evaluation apprehension'. These terms refer to the way in which respondents seek the approval of the sort of person they imagine the investigator to be by answering in ways which may be far from the 'truth'. Hughes (1976) mentions another source of bias, referring to the evidence of a tendency among certain sorts of respondents to answer 'yes' or 'no' to questions irrespective of their content. He also points out that the relatively few attempts to check the accuracy of respondent reports after interviewing have demonstrated that even the response to fairly uncomplicated 'factual' questions cannot be assumed to be free from this sort of bias. For example, respondents have been found to give inaccurate replies with regard to whether they had voted or not, relied on social welfare, used birth-control techniques, and so on.

Of course, some of these discrepancies may well be due to 'faulty memories, attempts to "take a stab" at answering questions which are not fully understood' (Phillips, 1971, p. 28), or a complete misunderstanding of what is being asked. However, interpretivist sociologists stress that by far the more usual reasons for discrepancies stem from the fact that an interview situation is a *social* situation and thus, as in any social relationship, the action of one party to it will necessarily be a direct function of his or her interaction with the other. As Weber (1964) pointed out: 'Action is social in so far as, by virtue of the subjective meaning attached to it by the acting individual (or individuals) it takes account of the behaviour of others and is thereby oriented in its course.'

Given this emphasis, critics of the interview stress that it is, *like any other social encounter*, a potential source of bias, misinterpretation and fakehood. Indeed, Phillips argues that discrepancies between the words and deeds of respondents are not only *as* likely to occur in interview contexts as they are in everyday exchanges but even *more* so. This is because the respondents may be much more sensitive in the interview than in 'normal' interaction to how other people see how they maintain their self-image and respect while having to answer a number of unusually probing questions. This stress, which is not restricted to the interview but possible in *all* social encounters, may encourage an individual to give inaccurate or fake responses. According to Phillips, then, there are two general sorts of lie possible in any social encounter — one to avoid opprobrium, and the other to seek approval — and an interview is no exception.

For these sorts of reasons, critics such as Phillips argue that not only does the validity of the results of such social encounters have to be seen as very much in doubt but so does their *reliability*. Thus, however much care one takes to neutralise the effects of biases on the reliability of one's results, the *main* source of bias — that questions are asked in the context of some sort of social encounter — remains. Phillips concludes that the assumption that social research can be carried out without the researcher (or a representative) influencing what is obtained as data is preposterous. Yet this assumption does seem to underpin fundamentally survey research, at least in its most structured forms, and although it is a technique that has certainly experienced some decline in its popularity, there is evidence that this decline is rather less than significant: for example, more than 90 per cent of the papers in the *American Sociological Review* and the *American Journal of Sociology* in the mid-1960s had used survey-based material. Despite the sorts of serious objections which can be raised against the epistemology on which the technique is based, then, it does seem that at the present time, for many sociologists, the automatic response to coming across any area of ignorance about contemporary society is *still* 'let's do a survey'.

Observation

Subscribing to these objections to the interview involves acknowledging the anti-positivist position that because sociological understanding is essentially the understanding of actors' meanings, this can only be achieved by putting oneself in the actor's place and seeing reality as he or she sees it. Since this is so, participant observation is clearly a far less problematic research alternative for this viewpoint than asking questions.

However, it would be quite wrong to assume that it is therefore a research tool *only* used by anti-positivists for wholly anti-positivistic purposes.

First, its use in no sense implies only the production of data of a totally qualitative character. (We made this point earlier when we referred to the often quite positivistic sorts of results produced by interactionists out of observational studies.)

Second, there is nothing inherently anti-positivistic in observation as a research technique; there is no *necessary* reason why it cannot be used to investigate causal relationships between variables defined in terms of observer categories. To make the same point a little differently: while the more committed one is to an anti-positivistic ontology/epistemology, the more one is likely, for reasons already mentioned, to doubt seriously the validity of the question-asking process and to tend to rely wholly on other methods like observation, this does not mean that all observers in sociological research are therefore anti-positivistic. On the contrary, as we shall see, all sorts of perspectives have made, and continue to make, use of it as a technique of data collection (whether on its own or in combination with other techniques). What matters is the *use* to which sociologists put observation.

Observer roles

The first question we must ask is: *how* is the researcher to join in and observe the actors under study? There is no easy answer, for everything depends on the particular situation being studied and the questions being asked.

The early 'Chicago School' sociologists, inspired by the

interest in social problems of ex-journalists like Park and Burgess, characteristically concerned themselves with the open observation of the social fabric of the huge industrial metropolis that Chicago had rapidly become by the early years of this century. They simply pounded the streets and frequented meeting-places in an attempt to see the city in the raw: 'tell it like it is' was their watchword. This traditional approach is matched by the interests and techniques of the contemporary Chicago School, largely symbolic interactionists with a major interest in deviance.

One issue which is relevant with regard to observational research into any sensitive area of social life, but which is particularly so with regard to the study of deviance, concerns the extent to which observation should be *overt*, apparent to the actors under study, or *covert*, hidden from them. Supporters of covert stances in deviance research tend to argue that because of the very nature of the activities of their subject-matter, the latter would almost inevitably change their behaviour if they knew they were under observation.

The Chicago researchers have consistently rejected this sort of argument, however. As Douglas (1972, p. 6) points out:

> They believe the sociologist becomes a taken-for-granted presence — that is, *if* he establishes trust and rapport, which are, in any case, necessary to his being accepted at all or gaining entrée to the group. Moreover, the Chicago researchers generally argue that defining oneself as a member and trying to do secret research actually makes many things unobservable to a researcher. There are things that members would be willing to expose to a trusted individual who is not a member because he will not use the information against members to advance himself in the organisation, as ordinary members might do.

Ned Polsky, a renowned observer of various deviant activities, adopts a similar position to the Chicago School over the overt–covert issue. Talking about field research in criminality, he argues that you

damned well better *not* pretend to be 'one of them', because they will test this claim out and one of two things will happen: either you will ... get sucked into 'participant' observation of the sort you would rather not undertake, or you will be exposed, with still greater negative consequences. You must let the criminals know who you are and if it is done properly it does not sabotage the research (Polsky, 1971, p. 122).

However, when describing the observational strategy for his study of homosexual behaviour in men's 'tea rooms' (rest rooms/public conveniences), Laud Humphreys (1970, p. 25) takes the opposite line on this issue:

From the beginning, my decision was to continue the practice of the field study in passing as deviant ... there are good reasons for following this method of participant observation.

In the first place, I am convinced that there is only *one* way to watch highly discreditable behaviour and that is to pretend to be in the same boat with those engaging in it. To wear a button that says 'I am a watchbird, watching you' into a tea room would instantly eliminate all action except the flushing of toilets and the exiting of all present. Polsky has done excellent observation of pool hustlers because he is experienced and welcome in their game — he is accepted as one of them. He might also do well, as he suggests, in interviewing a jewel thief or a fence in his tavern hangout. But it should be noted that he does not propose watching them steal, whereas my research required observation of criminal acts.

The second reason is to prevent distortion. Hypothetically, let us assume that a few men could be found to continue their sexual activity while under observation. How 'normal' could that activity be? How could the researcher separate the 'show' and the 'cover' from standard procedures of the encounter? ... a stage is a suitable research site only for those who wish to study the 'onstage' behaviour of actors.

Humphreys thus played an authentic homosexual role — as

voyeur — which allowed him to participate without actually having to engage in homosexuality.

Indeed, William Foote Whyte, in his study of an Italian–American slum gang (*Street Corner Society*, 1943), admits that the actors' knowledge of his presence and intentions may well have changed their behaviour as a result. He quotes the gang leader, Doc: 'You've slowed me up plenty since you've been down here. Now when I do something, I have to think what Bill Whyte would want me to know about it and how I can explain it . . . Before I used to do these things by instinct' (Whyte, 1943, p. 301). As Hughes (1976, p. 119) points out, the implications of this comment are fairly obvious: 'a loss of spontaneity and an increase in self-reflection on the part of the actor concerning what he is doing and why, which may detract from the "naturalness" which the observer wishes to study'.

Another major issue to be decided by the observer concerns the extent to which he or she should *participate* in the activities of the actors under study. Whyte (1943, p. 304) shows how this decision was made for him by his subjects themselves:

> a little later I had to face the question of how far I was to immerse myself in the life of the district. I bumped into that problem as I was walking down the street with the Nortons. Trying to enter into the spirit of the small talk, I cut loose with a string of obscenities and profanity. The walk came to a momentary halt as they all stopped to look at me in surprise. Doc shook his head and said: 'Bill, you're not supposed to talk like that. That doesn't sound like you.' I tried to explain that I was only using terms that were common on the street corner. Doc insisted, however, that I was different and that he wanted me to be that way. This lesson went far beyond the use of obscenity and profanity. I learned that people did not expect me to be just like them; in fact, they were interested and pleased to find me different, just so long as I took a friendly interest in them. Therefore, I abandoned my efforts at complete immersion.

Ronald Frankenburg, when studying the Welsh rural community he called 'Pentrediwaith' (*Village on the Border*, 1957), was allocated an active role in the village of 'stranger', or 'outsider', which, while allowing him to become involved (he became secretary of the local football club, for example), nevertheless meant he could also remain sufficiently detached for an overall view of community life. According to Frankenburg, this is a genuine role in Pentre life (it was not just created to accommodate him) and, he says, is symptomatic of the need any small group or community has to find a means of preventing conflicts and disagreements between interests or groups being brought out into the open, thereby threatening the stability of social life. His argument is that in communities like Pentre 'strangers' or 'outsiders', located as they are outside any of the constituent groupings of the local social structure and therefore peripheral to any conflicts which may exist between them, can be used as scapegoats, in order that blame can be allocated and conflict channelled and contained.

There are literally hundreds more examples we could refer to, all demonstrating that the sorts of roles played by the participating observer can vary a great deal; in fact, the variation is only matched by the variation in the kinds of situations in which observation is used as a research technique.

The next question we have to consider is: How is observation practised? How do we arrive at our observation-based data?

The process of observation

Whether it is subscribed to by positivist or anti-positivist, an emphasis on the need to be involved implies that there is little 'common' sense between observer and observed which the sociologist can take for granted. From any ontological/epistemological standpoint, then, to choose participant observation involves seeing reality as initially unknown — and unknowable until the rules by which the actors play the game are learnt and understood. It thus involves seeing the social behaviour in a Welsh community or a modern urban township or a teenage gang or a hospital ward as just as immediately 'foreign' as the behaviour of a tribe in Africa obviously is.

Not surprisingly, then, all the normative texts stress the importance of immersing oneself properly before any legitimate conception of 'what's going on' can emerge. For example, Polsky (1971, pp. 126–7) exhorts the participant observer to

> initially, keep your eyes and ears open *but keep your mouth shut*. At first try to ask no questions whatsoever. Before you can ask questions, or even speak much at all other than when spoken to, you should get the 'feel' of their world by extensive and attentive listening – get some sense of what pleases them and what bugs them, some sense of their frame of reference, and some sense of *their* sense of language.

This bears out the point we made a little earlier – that observation as a technique should not be confused with a particular type of research methodology, for discovery is a problem for much if not most social research, positivistic or anti-positivistic, and observation at the outset is often the way ideas are first formulated for testing. This is often as true for positivists who write up their results according to the *logic* of the hypothetico-deductive method as it is for anti-positivists whose logic of research strategy – e.g. analytic induction – is more likely to match their practice. Thus although *reports* of positivistic enquiry generally claim that hypotheses have been constructed before any field work was done, this is hardly ever the case in practice, whether in natural or social science.

So it is very often only after this initial stage that the lines between positivists and anti-positivists tend to become more clearly drawn. Now, while the positivistically inclined will tend to use their newly acquired knowledge through observation to construct hypotheses about social phenomena and to draw up a schedule of questions in order to quantify and test these hypotheses, sociologists of a more anti-positivist persuasion will tend to eschew such an approach. For them, since social reality is continuously constructed over time, they hold that testing – validation in social research – must not be a stage or a sequence but a *process*, also carried out over time. This is why they use participant observation so much, since it allows them to understand how the construction of social reality is accomplished by the actors.

This leads us to a rather different issue. Whether observation is used by positivist or anti-positivist, how is one to judge that the interpretations of social activity are adequate and warranted accounts? Is it possible to *demonstrate* that the results of observation are objectively valid? Of course, there are those, ethnomethodologists for example, who deny the possibility of objective knowledge anyway and for whom the problem does not therefore exist. So far as less relativistic epistemological positions are concerned, it is sometimes assumed that the results of observation are completely qualitative, consisting of in-depth descriptions of social life and exhibiting no evidence of a desire to measure or quantify. But we cannot make this assumption, for however anti-positivistic the *stated* position of the researcher is, especially as regards discovery and validation, it is very often possible to discern more positivistic intentions when it comes to the provision of evidence *in order to explain*.

For example, it is common for quantitative data to be provided in order to supplement that gained through observation. Thus Humphreys followed up his role as voyeur with later interviews, selecting a sample of 100 of the participants in the tea-room encounters he had observed. He makes the purpose of this exercise quite clear: 'What verbal research is possible through outside interviews then becomes an independent means of verifying the observations' (Humphreys, 1970, p. 36).

Again, as we mentioned earlier when talking about characteristic symbolic interactionist research, the qualitative results can be given a quantitative form; for example, we mentioned how Becker, in *Making the Grade*, produces tabulated evidence which classifies and counts the number of observed occurrences which support a particular hypothesis.

So observation can be used, either by itself or with other methods, by sociologists espousing very different ontological and epistemological positions. This demonstrates once again that what matters is not the technique itself so much as the uses to which it is put (the questions it is used to ask), and this in turn confirms the importance of seeing sociological research as necessarily carrying specific theoretical commitments.

Problems of observation

What of problems involved with observation? We can identify two distinct kinds. For the positivistically inclined the problem is how the observer can remain objective in order to provide demonstrable proof, while for the anti-positivist it is how to get close enough to the actors to understand their meanings properly. We will look at each of these in turn.

Problems posed for objectivity because of the need for understanding via involvement. One of the more obvious objections to observation is that the participant does not know the extent to which the behaviour of those being observed has changed by his or her presence. We have already discussed some of the arguments used by supporters of overt and covert stances; ultimately, however, even completely covert role-playing by observers cannot *guarantee* that their actors are behaving as they would if they had not been present.

Another objection is that participant observation is always to some extent selective observation, because it is necessarily an account of reality from the point of view of the *particular* role the participant observer has chosen to play. This can have a number of implications for the validity of the research. For example, the role-playing observer can simply cease to be an observer and be 'captured' by his or her subject-matter — a process usually called 'going native'. A possible example of this would be the researcher working in a residential religious community abandoning the project in order to 'join up'. Less drastically, validity may be impaired if the sample chosen does not adequately represent the specific social group under investigation. Bell and Newby (1971) criticise Lloyd Warner's (1960) study of the American town he calls 'Jonesville' from this point of view, quoting Lipset and Bendix's (1967) point that, in his investigation into Jonesville's stratification system, nine-tenths of Warner's informants were upper middle class. According to Lipset and Bendix (1967, p. 162), this bias results in Warner's account of Jonesville stratification revealing only the perspective of the social climbers just below the upper crust of small town society. To people at this level class appears as a matter of interpersonal relations, manners, family and so on. It is not polite to suggest that class is a reflection of one's economic position.

In contrast, the only working-class informant Warner uses refers to class as 'purely a matter of income and power'. Here, then, is a picture of social reality which, because of the concepts and methods used, is incomplete and selective; as Bell and Newby put it, it is a 'social reality primarily as seen from the perspective of the higher strata'.

Even allowing for these problems of producing a valid account of the *particular* setting in which the observer is involved — the *internal* validity of the results — there remains the problem of the extent to which this account is applicable to behaviour *outside* of the particular setting in which it is being observed — *external* validity. That is, how *representative* are participant observation accounts? As Hughes (1976, p. 129) puts it:

How can the observer be sure that the case he has studied, whether a military training programme, a street-corner gang, a group of workers in a factory or whatever are representative of the population about which the inferences are made?

Related to this is the further problem that the validity of participant observation accounts depends in part on their capacity to let the 'facts speak for themselves'. Normative prescriptions for participant observation have a tendency to exhort fieldworkers to have no preconceived notions, to have an open mind and to let reality present itself as it 'really is'.

However, as was suggested at the beginning of this chapter, 'facts' do not present themselves directly to us but rather are only meaningful as facts because they are an empirical representation of a theoretical model adopted prior to observation. Therefore, no one, however hard he/she tries to conform to Polsky's strategy of asking no questions and keeping his/her mouth shut, can avoid looking at the world selectively, if

only because he/she is bound to have some preconceived idea
of what constitutes a fact and what does not.

Where, then, does this leave the objectivity of the participant observer's findings? How do we establish that claims are
demonstrably valid? In community studies in particular it is
usually claimed that this can be done by replication, whereby
one research report is checked by a different sociologist carrying out another study of the same community. However, the
evidence from community studies' replication seems to suggest that ultimate validity is as impossible as is any separation
of theory from methods or from findings. A famous example
of this can be seen in the results of Oscar Lewis's *restudy* of
Robert Redfields' account of life in Tepoztlan, a Mexican
village.

Redfield's study was first published in 1930 as *Tepoztlan
— A Mexican Village*; Lewis returned to Tepoztlan seventeen
years after Redfield, producing his *Life in a Mexican Village*
in 1951. The astonishing difference in their accounts is made
very clear by Bell and Newby (1971, p. 76):

> The impression given of Tepoztlan by Redfield has a Rous-
> seauan quality: relatively homogeneous, isolated, smoothly
> functioning, well-integrated with contented, well-adjusted
> inhabitants. The emphasis throughout his study is on the
> co-operative and unifying factors. He glosses over evidence
> of violence, disruption, cruelty, disease, suffering and mal-
> adjustment, poverty, economic problems and political
> schisms. Lewis, on the other hand, emphasises 'the under-
> lying individualism of Tepoztlan institutions and character,
> the lack of co-operation, the tensions between villages
> within the municipio, the schisms within the village, the
> pervading quality of fear, envy, and distrust in interpersonal
> relations'.

Why such a dramatic set of differences? Although a number of reasons can be advanced, the most important is undoubtedly the selective influence of theoretical perspectives
— the 'blinker-like nature of theory in fieldwork', as Bell and

Newby put it. They continue:

> Redfield's theoretical orientation influenced the selection
> and coverage of facts and the way in which these facts
> were organised . . . Redfield was interested in the study of
> a single social process: the evolution from folk to urban,
> rather than a well-rounded ethnographic account. The
> questions that he asked of his data were quite different
> to those asked by Lewis (Bell and Newby, 1971, p. 77).

*Problems posed for understanding because of the need to be
an observer.* Obviously, the reason why the anti-positivist
chooses participant observation as a research technique is
because of the belief that there is no other way of understanding the principal subject-matter — the actors' definitions
of their situation. Far from seeking to find ways to remain
objective, then, the real problem for the anti-positivist is *how
to become involved enough to understand*, not to worry about
how to remain sufficiently detached. In fact, ultimately, the
real problem faced by the anti-positivist observer is that,
however hard one tries to see the world as the actor sees it,
however involved one becomes, if the observer and his or her
subject-matter are not one and the same person, then, as Hughes
(1976, p. 132) puts it, 'there enters the possibility of bias
and interpretation mediated by the observers' "uncleansed"
experience which he must inevitably bring to the research
setting'.

Some interesting anti-positivist solutions have been offered
as a way out of this problem. For example, Phillips (1971)
makes the point that this is exactly the same problem which
is faced by social actors (ordinary people) in every social
encounter with others. He argues that since this is so — since
no actors in any social relationship can be finally sure of the
validity of their understanding of others' behaviour since they
are not those other people — participant observation-based social
research as an activity is no different at all from social life:
that is, the problems faced by an observer 'trying to understand' are no different from those faced by any actor trying
to understand any other actor. For this reason Phillips suggests that the job of a social researcher should be to become

as much a part of the research setting as possible through participation and observation (to become as much like one of the actors as possible) and then report back, in a sense autobiographically, on his or her *own* experiences – on the problems encountered and the means of their solution, in coming to an understanding of the behaviour of others, in working out 'what was going on', in fact. The point here, then, is that since the process of arriving at understanding in social interaction is precisely what the everyday life of actors involves and is in fact what social life is about, then proper participant observation should be exactly that – *the observation of one's own participation.*

The theoretical consequence of Phillips's comments is that the possibility of objective knowledge by way of participant observation must by definition be denied. This kind of position is completely rejected by those who believe that worthwhile sociological knowledge can only be achieved through the participant observer being sufficiently detached in order to be objective. From this point of view, then, actually being the subject of the research finally denies any possibility of others being able to assess the validity of one's own analysis and 'reduces' the status of such an enterprise to the equivalent of writing novels and autobiographies.

11.8 CONCLUSION

Such a general conflict of views over this specific issue of observation well illustrates the more general conflict in sociological theory and methodology that we have tried to make apparent throughout this chapter. Like any form of production, the production of sociological knowledge depends of course on the use of suitable tools. But, as we have seen, the same tools may be used to create very different images of social reality.

So where does all of this leave the practice of sociology? Having got this far and having seen the way in which the proponents of different epistemological and methodological positions oppose each other's strategies and procedures for research at virtually every turn, you may be forgiven for thinking that actually 'doing sociology', rather than writing about the difficulties involved with doing it, is well-nigh impossible.

But this is only a valid conclusion if it is believed that sociology is, or should aim to be, a single-purpose endeavour — if it is felt that the debates we have been recording are symptomatic of a disordered discipline floundering around seeking some sort of unification of theoretical and methodological intent. But if it is accepted that reality is almost certainly much too complex for any particular human cognitive or intellectual system to apprehend wholly its workings, then it could be argued that the emergence of the multiplicity of 'sociological' approaches to the investigation of reality that has taken place over recent years and that we have been talking about in this chapter actually represents an *advance* for the subject.

This does not mean, however, that the individual sociologist can abrogate the need for making *a* choice; one must decide where one's sympathies lie and pursue one's work accordingly. Such a decision confronts those who work in all areas of research in both the natural and social sciences, and is based as much on analytical reasons for, as on personal commitment to, the greater explanatory power of one approach compared with others.

The existence of methodological diversity should not necessarily be seen as a sign of weakness in an academic discipline, therefore; in fact, it may well be in more danger if its practitioners fail to recognise, or deny, that these choices have to be made. This is not to say that, at present, the choices available are adequate, however. It should be clear from the discussion in this chapter that neither positivism nor traditional interpretivism alone can provide a sociology which adequately confronts the relationship between structure and action; as we shall now see in our final chapter on sociological theories, the task of constructing such a sociology is far from complete.

REFERENCES TO CHAPTER 11

Atkinson, J. M. (1978) *Discovering Suicide*, London, Macmillan.
Becker, H. (1968) *Making the Grade*, New York, Wiley.

688   *Introductory Sociology*

Bell, C. and Newby, H. (1971) *Community Studies*, London, Allen & Unwin.
Blauner, R. (1964) *Alienation and Freedom*, University of Chicago Press.
Blondel, J. (1976) *Voters, Parties and Leaders*, Harmondsworth, Penguin.
Comte, A. (1844) *Discourse on the Positive Spirit*, Paris.
Cuff, E. C. and Payne, G. C. F. (1979) *Perspectives in Sociology*, London, Allen & Unwin.
Douglas, J. D. (1967) *The Social Meanings of Suicide*, Princeton University Press.
Douglas, J. D. (1972) *Research on Deviance*, New York, Random House.
Durkheim, E. (1952) *Suicide*, London, Routledge & Kegan Paul.
Frankenburg, R. (1957) *Village on the Border*, London, Cohen & West.
Giddens, A. (1976) *New Rules of Sociological Method*, London, Hutchinson.
Goffman, E. (1968) *Asylums*, Harmondsworth, Penguin.
Goldthorpe, J. and Lockwood, D. *et al.* (1969) *The Affluent Worker: Industrial Attitudes and Behaviour*, Cambridge University Press.
Hughes, J. (1976) *Sociological Analysis: Methods of Discovery*, London, Nelson.
Humphreys, L. (1970) *Tea Room Trade*, London, Duckworth.
La Piere, R. T. (1934) 'Attitudes versus Actions', *Social Forces*, vol. 13.
Lewis, O. (1951) *Life in a Mexican Village*, University of Illinois Press.
Lipset, S. and Bendix, R. (1967) *Class, Status and Power*, New York, Free Press.
Parsons, T. (1937) *The Structure of Social Action*, New York, Free Press.
Phillips, D. L. (1971) *Knowledge From What?*, Chicago, Rand McNally.
Polsky, N. (1971) *Hustlers, Beats and Others*, Harmondsworth, Penguin.
Redfield, R. (1930) *Tepoztlan – A Mexican Village*, University of Chicago Press.
Silverman, D. (1970) *The Theory of Organisations*, London, Heinemann.
Warner, W. Lloyd (1960) *Social Class in America: the Evaluation of Status*, New York, Harper & Row.
Weber, M. (1964) *Theory of Social and Economic Organization* (ed. T. Parsons), New York, Free Press.
Whyte, W. F. (1943) *Street Corner Society*, University of Chicago Press.
Willis, P. (1977) *Learning to Labour*, Westmead, Saxon House.
Willis, P. (1978) *Profane Culture*, London, Routledge & Kegan Paul.

12

Sociological Theories

12.1 INTRODUCTION

There is no theoretical orthodoxy in contemporary sociology. The previous chapters in this book have all emphasised the diversity of theoretical approaches within the discipline, and they have all attempted to show that differences in concepts, presuppositions and theoretical orientations always produce significant differences in the explanations and accounts of social life offered by sociologists. Ultimately, it is misleading to separate off an area of concern called 'theory', for there can never be any such thing as non-theoretical sociology; no matter how descriptive, 'factual' or apparently 'obvious' sociological accounts may be, sociologists cannot avoid making theoretical assumptions and commitments in the course of their research. By now it should also be clear that many theoretical perspectives are mutually antagonistic and incompatible. We cannot assume that if we simply pursue an honourable compromise between all approaches we can thereby merge and synthesise them into one all-purpose, all-embracing theoretical extravaganza. As we shall see, some theoretical approaches may need to be rejected altogether — and these unacceptable ones are precisely those which have had the most securely entrenched dominance in the history of sociological thought.

That said, it must not be assumed that we have to abandon the quest for a synthesis of those theoretical elements which do appear to be partially acceptable; and we certainly should not jump to the conclusion that there are no criteria for choosing between theories and judging their validity. We saw in the previous chapter that issues of epistemology and methodology remain very problematic — we do not have final agreement on the philosophical grounds for judging the usefulness or uselessness of a particular theory. The quest for such acceptable criteria for knowledge-claims certainly continues, but in the meantime more limited criteria are available. This chapter will assume that provisional judgements of the quality of theories can be made on rational grounds — including standards such as internal coherence and breadth of applicability. This optimism is based on the belief that sociology can and must progress towards more adequate understanding, and that this increasing knowledge can enable people to reshape their society in order to create the conditions for greater fulfilment of human potential. This chapter will argue that sociology has a vital role to play in the active construction of a society better fitted to human needs and aspirations, for humans have the unique capacity to transform their own conditions of social existence. Indeed, people constantly attempt to do this by defending, adapting or transforming their society; a fuller knowledge of the social conditions of existence can only aid this process. What remains problematic, of course, is the goal and direction of such change. We shall see in the course of the chapter that while most great sociologists have been inspired by the concern to improve society, they have differed fundamentally in their definitions of the desirable relationship between humans and their society.

The bulk of the chapter is concerned with three distinct types of social theory which have been significant in the development of sociological thought: *positivist organicism,* where we are concerned with the theoretical approach that dominated for so long through the influence of Durkheim and the functionalists; *structural and historical sociology,* where the contributions of Marx and Weber are compared and contrasted; and *social action* theories of various forms are discussed. We then go on to examine the possibility of moving beyond these orientations to a more adequate general theory of human action in relation to social structures, and then finally to the issue of objectivity and value-commitment in the context of a discussion of the progressive and liberating potential of sociological understanding.

12.2 POSITIVIST ORGANICISM

Organicism is one distinctive version of the holistic approach in sociology, and as such has exerted a dominant influence on sociology for several decades. Although highly contrasting ideas have existed at every stage, which have challenged (or formed a potential to challenge) the dominance of organicism and positivism, this fragmented opposition has only recently succeeded in breaking the claims to theoretical orthodoxy made by these approaches. Effectively, positivist organicism dominated sociology from the early nineteenth century until the early 1960s. The origins lie in the French tradition, but its more general dominance was assured when American sociology came to take the lead. European sociology in the early twentieth century was eclipsed by the massive growth of the discipline in the USA and so the triumph of the perspective was at its height when American functionalism reigned supreme. This functionalism had its deepest roots in the ideas of Emile Durkheim, who in turn extended and developed a general frame of reference inherited from his compatriot Auguste Comte. From Comte came the faith in organic social integration, and in the power of positivist science; uniting the whole stream of theoretical development was the concern for creating the conditions for a harmonious, orderly, integrated society. As we shall see, however, highly contrasting theories were available in American and German universities, and the socialist parties of Europe offered very different social analyses; we therefore need to consider how this perspective rather than others came to have such power. Although the intrinsic quality of an intellectual perspective is only one factor affecting its rise to power, our discussion starts with this aspect.

We saw as long ago as the opening chapter that the holistic perspective was indispensable for sociology — indeed, the reality of sociological explanations can be established by the demonstration that many phenomena (suicide, for example) cannot be completely understood without making reference to the characteristics of the whole social group and the broader social context. The notion that social phenomena cannot be adequately explained by the characteristics of individual actors lies at the heart of sociology. Since for a long period the *only* form of holism widely accepted was organicism, sociology appeared to have no alternative to the analogy. In the course of this section it will be argued that holism is vital, but organicism is a false and misleading version of it.

The distinctiveness of organicist holism lies in its most obvious feature: that a direct analogy is invoked between the living animal organisms and the structure of society. One underlying reason for the attractiveness of such an analogy is that biology as a life-science can thereby provide an exemplar for sociology as a science of the living society. Just as the characteristics of living organisms cannot be reduced to their chemical and physical composition (the organism has 'emergent properties' by virtue of its living organisation), the characteristics of society cannot be reduced to the nature of its component parts. The analogy thereby stresses the interlocking and mutual dependence of specialised 'organs', or elements, within the whole; the central guiding problem becomes the degree to which these parts are neatly and smoothly working together to ensure the 'health' or 'survival' of the social organism. At the broadest level, this leads to the central concern being the so-called 'problem of social order', for an organism is clearly not a real organism at all (or at any rate not a healthy one) if its component parts fight with one another, fail to operate, or drop off. This analogy *must* assume a fairly high degree of integration and co-ordination as 'normal', and it must in turn be able to specify the mechanisms or forces which sustain and reproduce this integration. As we shall see, in most cases this integrating force turns out to be *shared ideas* in one form or another.

Equally important in this general theoretical orientation was positivism. It will be recalled from the previous chapter that the appeal of positivism for social scientists lies in its enticing offer of readily accessible routes to certain knowledge, thus ensuring that sociological knowledge can claim the status of *science* and form the basis for production. Social engineering is therefore made possible, for the neutral scientist can provide the knowledge and tools necessary for social goals to be pursued. Unlike the philosophising, speculating and pontificating on social issues which had for centuries preceded the rise of positivism, the new positive science could provide *certain technical knowledge*. A vital element of such positivism is of course the presupposition that all events are caused, and that these causal relationships occur in regular ways which can be expressed in causal laws. In the field of social behaviour, this therefore implies that individual acts are not explicable by personal 'choices' or 'reasons' but by empirically identifiable external causes. It is an easy step to say that these external causes which derive from society are opaque to individual actors, and determine their behaviour. In the broadest terms, this accounts for the close compatibility of organicism and positivism; organicist approaches seek to *reveal* the 'true' causes of social phenomena by looking behind the naive accounts given by actors themselves, and disclosing the real explanations which lie at the *societal* level. The most familiar example, mentioned in several previous chapters, is Durkheim's account of suicide, which attempts to explain variations in suicide rates without any reference to the intentions or perceptions of actors, and which identifies social causes of suicide that are not 'visible' to the actors concerned. As we shall see, such explanations have come to be regarded as seriously inadequate in their wholesale rejection of the importance of the consciousness and perceptions of the actor; social action theories have led sociologists to regard positivistic social explanations as frequently anti-humanistic in their concern for 'external causes'. Having said that, we must not lose sight of the fact that the early proponents of positivism took its title seriously — they regarded it as a *positive,* progressive, constructive development allowing people to have true knowledge of the world for the first time. Equally important, nineteenth-century positivists were by no means as scrupulous about claiming value-neutrality as their twentieth-century successors — the pursuit of knowledge was for them inseparable from the use of such knowledge to reorder society on rational lines. The quest for the laws governing social organisation, once established as true, were regarded as clearly indicating principles for social reconstruction —

society must be adapted (though not revolutionised) to conform to its ideal healthy condition. At the same time, this positive knowledge derived from a science of social *order* where the whole aim was to discover the conditions for harmonious organic integration. These themes run directly through the development from Comte to Durkheim to functionalism, and so we now turn to more detailed discussion of the way the elements are manifested in their particular theories.

Auguste Comte (1798–1857)

Auguste Comte (1798–1857)

Born: Montpellier, France, 1798.
Education: Ecole Polytechnique, Paris, 1814.
Career: Taught privately.
    Assisted H. Saint-Simon, 1817–24.
Main works: *Course in Positive Philosophy*, 1842.
    System of Positive Polity, 1851–4.

If Comte's birth coincides with the height of revolutionary change in French society, his mature work consists of an attempt to recreate order in that society through the application of true knowledge, as produced by science. The fact that Comte coined the label 'sociology' (previously he had dubbed the subject 'social physics') is not the only reason to regard him as the founder of modern sociology. As conventionally conceived, sociology differs from previous social thought by virtue of its rigorous scientific method and its commitment to holistic explanation; in his *Course in Positive Philosophy* Comte provided methodological prescriptions and theoretical conjectures which attempt to establish precisely these elements. All knowledge, he argued, must be founded upon experimentation or rigorous use of evidence. Knowledge had to be constructed out of the evidence from the senses, out of empirical data, even if there was a role for theoretical conceptualisation to make sense of this data. Truth, therefore, could never be attained through abstract speculation or pure intellectual philosophising. On the contrary, the laws which governed all events in the world (for all were caused in discoverably regular ways) were available to the rigorous observer. The scientist could then formulate these laws in order to subject them to test and verification (or disproof). All this of course was hardly new − British philosophy had said as much for nearly two centuries − but what *was* radical was the application of the positivist faith in discoverable laws to *social* phenomena. The implications were colossal, for positive sociological knowledge could offer the means for peaceful reconstruction of social order by the elite of enlightened scientists and intellectuals − social change need not depend upon revolutionary violence and the manipulation of the mob. As a result, Comte's work came to have an enormous appeal to intellectuals, whose confidence in their own ability to 'engineer' society was bolstered by some of Comte's more specific theories, especially those concerning social development. It should be no surprise to find that social change is explained by Comte in evolutionary terms, since this derives directly from the biological analogy and also implies gradual adaptation rather than transformation.

Human development, Comte argues, is characterised in individual growth and in social evolution by a succession of three stages of thought. The oldest and longest is the theological stage, where humans nestle in a bed of illusions, myths and self-delusions, which shelter them from a harsh reality of military conquest and domination. The metaphysical stage abandons faith in deities for belief in forces guiding life, but it embodies tendencies that move it towards the positivist stage. Here the light of reason illuminates the human mind, as people discover their own real position in the natural order through truths produced by positive science. Since truth has been achieved, the holders and producers of knowledge must dominate social life − that is, the scientists, and above all, the sociologists, who hold the key to social well-being. Such pre-eminence is reinforced by his notion of a hierarchy of the sciences, where the most fundamental − physics, chemistry − form the basis for others dealing with more complex subject-matter, such as biology or (at the pinnacle) sociology. Each higher science builds upon the propositions of those below, for its phenomena obey the laws of more basic sciences but *also* exhibit emergent properties by virtue of their complexity. For example, the behaviour of animals cannot be explained by their chemical composition. In biology and sociology we *must* explain holistically.

However spurious and pretentious Comte's particular 'laws' may appear, they do exemplify *key general features of positivist organicism* which also characterise later approaches in this tradition. Firstly, this approach is *ahistorical.* Evolutionist accounts of this type tend to be very insensitive to historical complexity and diversity and to impose grossly simplistic schemes of 'stages' which are claimed to have universal validity. Secondly, such theories tend to see social development in terms of *cultural* change, rather than in terms of economic or political structures. While the latter are often acknowledged, a change in *ideas* is usually the prime mover. Thirdly, this approach tends to set itself the task of discovering the *general* laws of social integration and social evolution, which are assumed to be universal and invariable. As a result, extremely sweeping generalisations are produced whose grandeur is matched only by their crassitude. A fourth general attribute of positivist organicism is illustrated in Comte's other lengthy work, the *System of Positive Polity*. Here Comte attempted to establish an explicit framework for social reconstruction implied by his positive laws. A prime feature of this was to be the Religion of Humanity (of which he appointed himself High Priest) which would be headed by sociologist-priests. These guardians of the true and the good (for the two are indistinguishable) are able to control and predict social life and help suffuse through society a new moral order. The new industrial order could thus be stabilised, through national control by an elite, and by a new moral order — certainly, conflict was neither inevitable nor constructive. These prescriptions cost him his intellectual credibility (and with it, the credibility of sociology as a subject), but they are only a more extreme version of a theme common to Durkheim and the functionalists, where *moral order* is the key to social health, and thus the stabilisation of industrial society depends upon a civic (non-religious) morality and education, which can teach the citizens that their conflicts are not fundamental, and that social harmony is attainable without radical social change. This fourth theme, then, stresses moral unity as the central integrating force of society, and furthermore, ideas and collective sentiments are regarded as the basic elements of society, the substance from which social order is built. The adaptation of such ideas therefore provides a solution to the conflict-ridden societies of the nineteenth century (and beyond) and opens up a blissful future of harmony, where all perform their allotted roles within a hierarchy of social positions.

It has been argued (for example, by Nisbet, 1967) that these characteristics show the origins of sociology to lie in the classical conservative tradition of social thought, despite the liberal reformism of most sociologists. This claim is based on the contrast between the conservative vision of society and the liberal—individualist version. For the conservative (e.g. Edmund Burke's *Reflections on the French Revolution)* individuals have identity only by virtue of their social position in a hierarchy of social roles, and their position dictates their characteristics, social standing and degree of powerlessness or control. Individuals are civilised only in as much as social rules constrain their bestial selfishness. The key to human happiness, therefore, is a hierarchy of social control with tightly specified rules governing conduct. In complete contrast, the classical liberal view of humanity extols the virtues of unrestrained competition between individuals, and regards the rules and collective aspects of social life as merely the outcome of social contracts, or as the sum total of the individual characteristics of actors. The goal of imposing order by some central authority with specialist knowledge is not alien to the classical liberal, but is decidedly harmful (see Herbert Spencer's *The Man and the State);* only the outcome of competitive free action can be healthy and any modification can only induce ill-health in the collectivity of individuals. Equally, there is no consensus in society but neither is there any fundamental cleavage leading to fundamental conflict. The social organism is invigorated by internal turmoil.

It is clear from this comparison that the classical liberal position is profoundly anti-sociological in that it denies holistic explanations which deal with emergent properties of the social whole. (Despite being influenced by Comte, Mill regarded all social science explanations as ultimately reducible to individual psychology.) Sociology has also wished to stress the prior existence of society, and the extent to which actors are influenced by socialisation and by the constraints on them in their various social positions. At the same time, however, Nisbet is entirely incorrect to assume that sociology *must* therefore be committed to goals of social order, social control and moral integration. These distinctive emphases of positivist organicism certainly do have affinities with classical conservatism, but they do not by any means form the only intellectually viable alternative to the liberal individualism outlined above.

We might note in passing, moreover, that where sociology *was* founded on such a liberal philosophy in Britain by Herbert Spencer, this effectively led to the dissolution of any real sociological development until after 1945. American liberal individualism led towards the development of social psychology, as we shall see later, but British liberalism prevented the development of any real science of social life apart from anthropology.

Emile Durkheim (1858–1917)

Emile Durkheim (1858–1917)

Born: Lorraine, France, 1858.
Education: Ecole Normale Supérieure, 1879.
Career: Schoolteacher in philosophy, 1882–87.
University lecturer, Bordeaux, 1887.
Taught sociology and education,
Sorbonne, Paris, 1902.
Professor of Education and Sociology, 1913.
Main works: *The Division of Labour in Society,* 1893.
Rules of Sociological Method, 1895.
Suicide, 1897.
Elementary Forms of the Religious Life,
1912.

The work of Durkheim is of far more significance for the development of sociology than that of Comte — in fact one of the prime motivations of Durkheim's project was the aim of establishing sociology as a credible and respectable academic discipline within universities. But more than this, Durkheim wished to apply sociological knowledge to social intervention by the state in order to recreate harmony. In these aims there is clearly a direct continuation of the legacy left by Comte. Just like his predecessor, Durkheim regarded himself as a progressive (even a socialist), pursuing reform guided by positivist sociological laws; the goals of these reforms were in each case oriented towards the traditional conservative concerns of moral consensus and stable hierarchy. Progress was towards order above all, rather than towards the emancipation of the individual human being.

Durkheim's earliest work was his doctoral thesis *The Division of Labour in Society* (1893), which provides a key to his earliest ideas on the problems of contemporary society and their possible solutions. In content, the book is purely speculative, imposing a grand conception of the evolution of social institutions reminiscent not only of Comte but also of the Enlightenment philosophers Montesquieu and Rousseau. In this respect, it is remarkable to note the self-enclosed nature of French intellectual thought at this time. Durkheim was an exact contemporary of Max Weber, but the gulf between the philosophical and scientific ferment in Germany and the enclosed development of distinctive French ideas could hardly be more striking.

Durkheim's general thesis in *The Division of Labour* operates with the commonplace distinction (that sledge-hammer of the evolutionists) between 'traditional' and 'modern' society. The diversity and complexity of human civilisations is supposedly encompassed by this simple distinction, which stresses an evolution away from the *mechanical solidarity* characterising primitive societies, to the sophisticated *organic solidarity* which provides the basis for a new harmonious integration within industrial society. Primitive societies, he argues, were 'segmental', in that they were just the aggregation of kin-groups into clans and tribes, where these larger groupings had little real cohesion since each local unit could be self-sufficient as hunters or agriculturalists. Hence, like a worm, the society was divided into similar segments which could survive perfectly well if severed from one another. Even within these 'segments' social cohesion depended upon the power of rigid collective norms governing behaviour in every detail, so that total conformity was enforced; if any transgressions did occur then revenge would be the basic social response. The primary source of conformity, however, was the shared consensus of norms and values, the *conscience collective* which was absorbed and reproduced by every member of society. For Durkheim, *mechanical solidarity* was a phrase which conveyed this rigidity and crudity of social form.

In deliberate contrast to the ideas of writers such Tönnies, Durkheim thus portrays 'traditional' primitive society not as an ideal, harmonious, integrated unity, but as a collection of fragmentary units embodying repressive conformity. Modern society, therefore, is not conceived as the fragmented breakdown of community portrayed by Tönnies; while contemporary society may appear to have this character in its current imperfect form, the evolution of society provides an underlying potential for more stable and sophisticated social cohesion. The key to this potential is the process of social evolution which takes the form of increased *social differentiation,* whereby society develops specialised institutions which deal with particular distinct areas of social life (e.g. religion, production). Just as the evolution of animals produces more sophisticated specialised organs to perform particular functions for the whole creature, society comes to develop a range of distinct institutions which deal more adequately with particular needs of the social whole. Just like anatomical organs, they are mutually dependent for their survival, and correct functioning depends upon the healthy functioning of each other organ, and the maintenance of correct integration of all the organs. The potential, then, built into modern society is for *organic solidarity*. If the component parts of society can be induced to develop 'a lively sentiment of their mutual dependence' then the conflicts and crises so prevalent can be swept aside. Once again, a new *moral consensus* must be constructed to bring forth order; unlike that in primitive society, however, this moral order is flexible and adaptable to allow it to cope with the diverse social roles and positions in a complex society — the individual has more freedom within the social constraints. A prime task for contemporary sociology is therefore the construction of a new central civic morality which will be disseminated efficiently by a state education system. Durkheim was directly involved in the development of precisely these educational aims and techniques in his academic work and in advice given to the French government.

The primacy of value-consensus cannot be overemphasised for, like other organicists, Durkheim conceives of society as primarily a *moral order* constituted by the institutionalised norms and values. At the same time, however, social reform has to have an institutional basis. Durkheim identifies chaotic economic competition as the root of conflict and class struggle; as a result he advocates regulation of the economy and of the worker—employer relationship. He even suggests joint *corporations* or guilds to mediate between worker, industrialist and state.

Equally important, he argues, is the abolition of the *forced division of labour,* where inequality of opportunity denies individuals access to positions to suit their talents. Since unequal rewards should be given to different positions, and since education should be designed to 'get them' to like the idea of circumscribed tasks and limited horizons', then conflict will be created if individuals do not obtain suitable positions. All the other reforms are directed at overcoming the *anomic* division of labour, where economic life is characterised by *anomie* — that is, the lack of regulating norms. As we have seen elsewhere in discussing Durkheim's explanations of suicide (see Chapter 10 on deviance), he regards the lack of sufficient normative regulation as a key cause of social and individual ill-health. Without such norms, humans develop insatiable appetites, limitless desires and general feelings of irritation and dissatisfaction. Modern competitive market society encourages all of this and, despite its claims, condemns people to 'unfreedom'. This 'unfreedom', due to anomie, rests on the conservative assumptions about human nature discussed earlier — humans without normative constraint could only be uncivilised beasts, slaves of their own whims and passions. Individuals must be subordinate to society, they must play their humble part in the functioning of the social organism. The collective consensus may allow them some choice between roles, but once allotted their position they must conform or else become pathological deviants. As Durkheim (1974, p. 72) describes his vision of the correct relation between individuals and society:

> The individual submits to society and this submission is the condition of his liberation. For man freedom consists in the deliverance from blind, unthinking physical forces; this he achieves by opposing against them the great and intelligent force which is society, under whose protection he shelters.

Thus society is outside us and above us; it constrains us and shapes our lives and our psychological responses. What is good for social integration is good for the individual. This emphasis on externality and constraint links directly to Durkheim's conception of scientific explanation as presented in *The Rules of Sociological Method* (1895), an essay which was, as Lukes says, 'at once a treatise in the philosophy of social science, a polemic and a manifesto' (Lukes, 1973, p. 226). The book showed all these qualities, for in it Durkheim developed conceptions of the subject-matter of sociology and of suitable methodology which were dictated by his view of science. Since sociology must be established as a scientific discipline (thus enabling social intervention on the basis of positive knowledge), then the conception of science must *dictate* methods and concepts.

The view of science adopted was, of course, a positivistic one — and a fairly crude positivistic one at that.

Deriving ideas from his contemporaries and teachers, Durkheim assumes that a particular science can only have the status of being a distinct discipline if it has a separate subject-matter not shared by any other science. At the same time, this subject-matter must be empirically accessible (which is why we must 'treat social facts as things'), and variations in the phenomena must be explained by causes which also lie within the scope of that particular discipline. These (false) assumptions led Durkheim to assert that sociology must become the *science of social facts*. These social facts can only be explained in terms of other social facts so that, for example, variations in suicide rates are social facts which must be explained by characteristics of the social group, such as lack of normative control. The claim that there are social facts, then, is important, for it establishes that there is a distinct level of social phenomena which are not reducible to individual characteristics or intentions — indeed they constrain the individual:

> A social fact is every way of acting, fixed or not, capable of exercising on the individual an influence, or an external constraint; or again, every way of acting which is general throughout a given society, while at the same time existing in its own right independent of its individual manifestations (*Rules of Sociological Method*, 1895, p. 13).

Although Durkheim accepted in principle that one could only observe the *effects* of social facts in their concrete manifestations, as in legal codes or in individual acts of suicide, he nevertheless had a marked tendency to *reify* society and speak of social reality as a separate, detached realm from social action. He even writes of 'that conscious being that is society . . . a *sui generis* being with its own special nature, distinct from that of its members' (*Rules*, p. 11). He often referred to social forces such as 'suicidogenic currents' which impose an external causal effect on individual action; this search for external causes is of course part of the general positivistic orientation.

His explicit account of this positive method is naively simple, for he simply advocates a search for correlations between phenomena which indicate *laws*. As long as we 'abandon our preconceptions' we can verify these laws with evidence. Once in possession of these laws, however, we are in a position to identify whether society is in a 'healthy' or a 'pathological' condition, and the sociologist must therefore prescribe the remedies required for social health. This latter assumption is clearly related to Comte's view of science. It demonstrates the distance between the optimistic positivism of the nineteenth century ('the true is the good and the natural'), and the hard-bitten positivism of the twentieth century, which drove a rigid distinction between truth and goodness. Social goals, it was argued, were based on values, and these values could not be derived from science. Such arguments are quite alien to Comte and Durkheim.

Although Durkheim assumes that the necessary starting-point for science is the proposition 'a given effect always has a single corresponding cause', he also accepts the usefulness of *functionalist* explanation. In the latter, phenomena are not explained by preceding causes (e.g. rainfall causes a flood) but by the *useful effects* of their existence. The central nervous system is explained, for example, by its integrating effects on the organism. Similarly, the explanation of the persistence of religion may be in the good effects of religious activity on the level of social integration. At the same time, Durkheim notes, the original causes of the phenomenon are a separate issue from the functions which cause its persistence. The link between the organic analogy and functionalist explanation is thus obvious — we explain elements of the organic whole by their good effects for the functioning of the organism. A closely linked assumption is that institutions only survive if they are useful for society. As in the functionalist theory of stratification (see Chapter 2), this can lead to a justification of existing institutions. This, as Merton (1949) pointed out, neglects the possibility of negative effects (dysfunctions) or 'functional alternatives' where a societal need could be satisfied by another institution. Whether or not these modifications to functionalism are adopted, it is clear that the whole emphasis of positivist organicism centres on the integration (or lack of integration) of the social system, and the effects of social phenomena on this integration.

This organicist perspective is united with exemplary use of positivistic methods in Durkheim's study *Suicide*, which followed two years after the *Rules*. This study has been discussed at length elsewhere (in Chapters 10 and 11) but it is worth emphasising here the extent to which the book embodies Durkheim's methodological principles. Firstly, the methods used exemplify the emphasis on social facts, in that constant suicide *rates* are described, which are established empirically and statistically (even if later commentators criticise his dependence on official statistics). Secondly, these rates concern *group* propensities to suicide and do not involve any attention to individual cases. Hence Durkheim can explain these social facts solely by other social facts — the propensity of the social group to normlessness, egoism or altruism that depends upon the organisation and culture of the group as a whole. Durkheim therefore sticks rigidly to his methodological precepts and attempts to exclude psychological and physiological explanations. Most commentators agree that this is productive only to the extent that it discloses the importance of social factors; it is, however, profoundly mistaken and misleading to attempt to divorce sociological explanations from other complementary ones. Suicide is a phenomenon which must be explained by a range of factors which fall within the fields of many disciplines; this in no sense undermines the scientific status of any one of these sciences. (For one recent attempt at constructing such an interdisciplinary account, see Giddens, 1977.)

Thirdly, the explanations of variations in suicide rates clearly embody the organicist concern for the social cohesion of the collectivity. If egoistic suicide derives from insufficient social integration, altruistic suicide is the result of an excess of it; moral regulation, in contrast, can only be too low (producing anomic suicide), for the 'fatalistic' form of suicide has only a shadowy existence. Thus the two dimensions of the social group that matter are social integration and moral regulation, and the element in society that most strongly influences both is the *moral order* — above all as embodied in religion.

In as much as society is ultimately constructed out of patterns of behaviour (in the organicist view), then norms and values are the ultimate basis of social life. Although related to other aspects of society, its culture remains the key dynamic force shaping individuals and governing their behaviour. Unlike the Marxists, organicists certainly do not regard culture and religion as mere ideologies justifying economic arrangements; instead religion is (as Durkheim put it):

the most primitive of all social phenomena. It was the source, through successive transformations, of all other manifestations of collective activity: law, morality, art, science, political forms, etc. In the beginning all is religious (in Lukes, 1973).

Thus, one explains social organisation and cohesion by reference to a shared normative system (usually religious), common throughout the collectivity. Changes in this structure are not 'reflective' of changes elsewhere; instead, they are the prime movers of social adaptation. This view is common to all positivist organicists and is clearly opposed to all forms of Marxist economic determinism. As such, this approach directs our attention away from a concern with economic relationships, political and economic domination, or variations in class structure. The evolution of culture within the integrated organic society is seen as far more illuminating than the study of concrete structures of power, which vary in historical circumstances. Rather than historical analysis, organicism seeks the *universal laws* governing social order and social evolution.

This concern for the universal significance of religion led Durkheim towards his later ideas in *The Elementary Forms of the Religious Life* (1912). His views here lie outside our scope, but they did lay the foundations for a tradition of speculative anthropology, which attempts to link the basic elements of social structure with the most basic elements in human thought — concepts such as space and time are seen as reflecting the structure of the group (e.g. Lévi-Strauss, *Totemism*). The general notion that shared ideas are a main integrating force in society is reflected in Durkheim's view of religion as the most basic of collective representations: 'Religion is, in a word, the system of symbols by means of which society becomes conscious of itself; it is the way of thinking characteristic of collective existence.' Religion must derive from something 'higher': for Durkheim this must be society. Even though modern society has lost its religious sensibility, Durkheim regarded the construction of a moral consensus to guide and constrain action as a vital necessity. Humans are more civilised to the extent that they can deliberately construct their own moral order and then live by it.

The rise of functionalism

In the course of the first half of the twentieth century, the general orientation developed by Durkheim came to be the predominant perspective in American sociology, and since that nation came to dominate the sociological scene, functionalism seemed for a while to be the only real theory in the discipline. By 1949, Kingsley Davis could claim that functionalism should not be seen as a separate perspective because *all* sociology was functionalist. This never was a valid claim, for although faculties and journals often gave this impression, there were always counter-currents and alternative perspectives surviving alongside. By the end of the 1950s functionalism was beginning to go on the defensive against increasing attacks from these counter-currents — although the criticisms ranged from social action theories to conflict theories with Marxist or Weberian roots.

In that first half of the century, however, functionalism provided a very general perspective which united many sociologists who wished to study the workings of society as a whole (so-called 'macrosociology'), and who wished to provide explanations of social phenomena without looking for anwers in the intentions or consciousness of actors. Functionalism seemed to *reveal* the real significance of social institutions in terms of the way they aided the survival or health of the whole social organism.

One of the main areas for the early establishment of functionalism was the British school of social anthropology. Although British social scientists seemed unable to develop any real theories of the structure of modern societies (they concerned themselves with social philosophy or with the positivistic description of social problems) the Imperial connection did provide fascinating opportunities for studying alien pre-literate societies. In these studies, the necessity of studying these societies as integrated interrelated structures was made clear by the weaknesses of grandiose speculative tours of 'primitive culture' by writers such as Frazer *(The Golden Bough)*. In relation to this, anthropologists saw the need to study each society separately, on its own terms, as a functioning system. The lack of written history in these cultures encouraged the assumption that such primitive societies were stable, unchanging, and fully adapted for survival in their environment. With these assumptions, functionalist approaches (such as those developed by Radcliffe-Brown) are of clear relevance: we must ask how each social institution fits in with others to *serve the needs of the society* and sustain the harmonious integration which is deemed to be the norm. For example, even when conflict is observed, this is regarded as functional for integration if it is ritualistic and institutionalised. As an illustration, bitter arguments are a constant feature among the Makah tribe of American Indians, for they use scandal and gossip to question the purity of ancestry of other tribespeople; it can be argued that this apparently divisive behaviour actually strengthened the group by constantly reminding them of their shared ancestral identity.

Equally important, the functionalist perspective is lent support by the integrating power of shared cultural beliefs in the form of religion, magic and myth. The predominant importance of shared culture often appears self-evident.

These features of pre-literate societies are by no means always present in industrial societies, and so we may be sceptical about the applicability of functionalism; but even in 'primitive' societies this perspective only seems strong as long as we do not concern ourselves too much with change, with wars or with the dissolution of societies. Later anthropologists (including major figures such as Evans-Pritchard) have attempted to deal with these issues; moreover, the functionalists' assumptions of stability and integration have only been applied to modern society by anthropologists when they deal with old-established local communities. In the general European sociological context, few writers wished to transpose to modern advanced societies functionalist emphases on order, harmony, integration and societal health. This is scarcely surprising when one considers the history of twentieth-century Europe with its two world wars, genocide and clashes of class and ideology. What is remarkable is that American sociologists such as Parsons should agree with Durkheim that functionalist perspectives are the most illuminating for a contemporary world characterised by such events. For them, functionalism offered a universal perspective on social structure and in Parsons's case, a universal theory applicable to all areas of social life. Whilst not generated empirically, Parsons's theories pursue the general aim of constructing universal laws of society which are general enough to apply anywhere. Empirical studies should, he thought, validate the explanations generated by the theory.

Talcott Parsons (1902–79)

> **Talcott Parsons (1902–79)**
>
> Born: Colorado Springs, USA, 1902.
> Education: Amherst College, 1920–4.
>   London School of Economics, 1924 – 5.
>   University of Heidelberg, 1925–6.
> Career: Harvard University, USA, 1927–79.
> Main works: *The Structure of Social Action*, 1939.
>   *Toward a General Theory of Action*, 1951.
>   *The Social System*, 1951.
>   *Societies: Evolutionary and Comparative Perspectives*, 1966.

While Parsons's ideas were challenged and rivalled by those of other American functionalists (particularly Robert K. Merton), his enormously prolific output was very widely read and accepted as the most systematic and formalised functionalist theory. His significance for American sociologists was established in the 1940s, but his work began with *The Structure of Social Action,* which aimed to bring more modern European thought on social structure to American attention. In this work he purported to synthesise the European traditions, but the mix was heavily Durkeimian and was free of contamination by Marxian or socialist social theories. As his work developed, the functionalist themes were supplemented by cybernetics (the theory of the working of systems in general) to produce his most abstract and formalistic theory in *The Social System.* Here, Parsons argues that any system of action (a society, an institution, a small group, etc.) has general features, for in order to operate successfully as a system,

certain *functional prerequisites* have to be fulfilled. These
are, in ascending order of importance, (a) adaptation, (b) goal
attainment, (c) integration and (d) pattern-maintenance.
Correspondingly, within the social system as a whole, the
most basic need is for (a), adaptation to the environment
through economic activity, but this only provides the conditions for 'higher' aspects of social life. Actors pursue (b),
socially shaped goals, in ways that are governed by (c), the
norms and sanctions institutionalised in society; ultimately
these goals and norms derive from (d), an overarching cultural system of values, on which there is consensus. Thus the
cultural system *controls* other aspects of society, and if we
wish to explain social change we must look first at changes at
the cultural level. For example, the civil rights riots by blacks
in the USA during the 1960s were explained by Parsons in
terms of the 'core American values' — equal citizenship
rights, equal opportunity —being mobilised by the majority.
Disparities of economic benefit and political power are systematically underplayed as features of the social world that
might cause conflict or cleavage — even when Parsons does
discuss power, it is not portrayed in terms of domination or
oppression. Instead, power is seen as a necessary resource
which members of society collectively agree to allocate to
particular authority positions. The authority-holder then uses
the power selflessly to satisfy particular collective needs.

Parsons clearly gives priority to the 'problem of social
order' and suggests that this problem is solved at two levels.
On the one hand, order in the sense of conformity by actors
is maintained by socialisation and social control. His account
of the personality places great emphasis on internalisation of
socially given norms and values, rather than suggesting any
more active process of negotiating or defining roles by the
actor. Deviance does, of course, occur but this is generally
suppressed by social control agencies. Occasionally, however,
deviance in the form of innovation may aid the survival of
the system of action because some adaption to changed circumstances is needed for the social system. Any action
system needs adaptive mechanisms to bring it back to *equilibrium* — and this need for structural integration is the second aspect of Parsons's solution to the problem of order. It is

argued that the social system operates in such a way as to ensure that its functional needs are fulfilled and that social and system integration are sustained. The ideas of actors are far less important than the functioning and development of the system as a whole. Thus our key explanations lie at two levels — in terms of the cultural system and its effects on behaviour, and in terms of the functional needs of the system as a whole. Thus, the education system may be seen as socialising actors into the prevailing cultural order, but also interlocking with the economy and the political apparatus to aid the functioning of the society.

In addition, Parsons has to give some account of social change, and in his later work he developed the classic solution of the organicist perspective — evolution. Broadly, his evolutionary account lies within the tradition of 'structural differentiation', where modern societies are seen as becoming more complex and internally specialised. Predictably, the major stages of evolution are conceived in terms of cultural change, where modern industrial society is the peak of human achievement towards which earlier societies progressively led. The development of literacy, and then of formalised legal systems, mark the transitions between primitive, traditional and modern society. Thus, what characterises evolution is the development of more sophisticated culture; for those contemporary societies attempting to 'modernise', the problem is not one of economic or political subordination in a world-system, but is instead a question of developing the correct cultural values and orientations (see pp. 159—62). Once again, the organicist tradition betrays its ahistorical and uncritical approach to social development.

Evaluation of positivist organicism

The work of Parsons, then, displays the classic strengths and weaknesses of positivist organicism. He is not afraid to look at society as a structured, interrelated whole, or to attempt to reveal aspects of the operation of that social whole which are opaque to the actors making up the society. Such a perspective, however, can be criticised in three contrasting ways: it can be criticised for being *too* holistic and presenting a derogatory and inadequate account of social action, it can be seen as consistently underemphasising social conflict, and it can be regarded as presenting a false account of social structure.

Criticisms from social action perspectives

The first line of criticism became more insistent in the 1960s, as the old American tradition of symbolic interactionism and qualitative research attained a new prominence, partly through mergers with more philosophical European traditions such as phenomenology.

Their initial line of attack concerns the functionalist conceptions of the self, and of social action. These conceptions are shown to be overly deterministic, allowing individuals to display little or no creativity or originality, and providing little scope for actors to negotiate social situations and social identities. Holistic explanations came to be seen as falsely 'solidifying' social structure by attributing needs or even desires to 'society' as if it were a thinking being.

This leads us to their next line of attack, centring on the functionalist form of explanation. Action approaches rightly emphasise that functionalists commit the 'fallacy of misplaced concreteness': that is to say, society is treated as having a truly independent existence separate from its individual members. By accepting this criticism we do not have to deny all holism, but we do have to recognise that functionalism gives insufficient scope for the continuous development and change in society produced by social action. Such criticisms certainly apply to the perspective on social integration offered by organicists, for they undoubtedly stress the independent power of central values and social control mechanisms. Their account of socialisation seems to imply that the individual is simply a derivative product of the cultural system, and not a real actor at all.

Just as importantly, the structural explanations offered by functionalism *exclude* any connection with action. This is because the second level of functionalist explanation concerns not only conformity to norms, but also the *needs* of the social *system*. The theory claims to explain the persistence of institutions (e.g. the nuclear family) in terms of the functional needs of society, or in terms of the contribution of the institution to social *integration*. This only becomes truly explanatory if the functionalists propose that societies 'act' in such a way as to ensure that their functional requirements are met. Unless there are mechanisms which maintain social survival and integration, functionalist 'explanations' are not explanations at all. To really *explain* in functionalist terms, there must be some theory of *equilibrium mechanisms* which work at the societal level beyond the control (or intention) of any social actors. Functionalists generally fail to provide any real account of the nature of these mechanisms or how they operate independently of social action. Until they can actually demonstrate these things, functionalist accounts (of stratification, for example) will simply be fancy descriptions which tend to justify existing institutions. On the other hand, these criticisms must not be taken too far; action theories wrongly tend to suggest that *any* holistic explanations are inadmissible. It may be argued that structural explanations should not be abandoned altogether, even if the functionalist ones are unacceptable; but any alternative explanations must link up with social action theories, not deny them.

Criticisms from conflict theory

Critics such as Rex and Dahrendorf have accepted the view that models of society must give actors a great role in changing society, but their main emphasis rests on the assumption that social change is linked to actors' conscious activities. Members of society may produce change through individual decisions and actions, but more generally through their conflicts over issues of power and inequality. Functionalism both neglects change and overemphasises conformity — and the two are linked. Conflict theorists deny the assumption that there is a consensus of norms and values or that conflict is necessarily 'unhealthy' for everyone in society. Society may be divided into groups with conflicting interests so that shared general societal needs cannot be easily specified. The growth of conflict over civil rights and the Vietnam war only heightened such criticisms of conservative consensus theories in the 1960s.

Criticisms of the functionalist conception of structure

Other critics however, (e.g. Lockwood, 1964) have argued
that these criticisms from social action perspectives and conflict theories are insufficient. Both of these responses concentrate solely upon Parsons's first solution to the problem of
order — the socialisation and enforcement of a consensus of
values and norms. Those critics are quite right to criticise this
aspect, for Parsons's account of social integration is mechanical and misleading. On the other hand, we must recognise
the importance of the structural or system integration aspect
of social order, for it is vital to know whether there are
points of strain and incompatibility in the structure of
society which might produce change. This level of system
integration is not normally visible to actors and provides
pressures and conditions for change which operate outside
their consciousness. Thus changes in the basic structure of
society (for example, during a period of transition from
feudalism to capitalism) may create the conditions for social
conflict and broader change in social institutions and social
values.

The necessity for *structural* explanations (as well as those
linked to social action theories) is therefore made clear, but
the terms in which structure is conceived are quite different.
In the positivist organicist tradition the basic building-
material for society is cultural — that is, shared norms, values
and world-views. While this aspect cannot be neglected,
Lockwood and many other contemporary theorists would
strongly reject the notion that the general structure of
society and the causes and conditions for change can be
located at the cultural level. In contrast, the basic structures
of society are seen as concerning economic relations and
broader relations of power and domination. The level of culture is instead linked to a concept of dominant ideology,
which expresses the idea that consensus (if it exists at all)
may simply be the forced or artificial dominance of ideas
which justify and take for granted existing inequalities. Such
an approach gives a central place to issues of stratification,
economic power, political domination, and the organisation
(and repression) of resistance from subordinate groups, and
as such can be regarded as a *materialist* structural sociology.

Such a sociology will concern itself with historical changes in the material structures of economic, political and ideological domination.

As we have seen, Durkheimian and functionalist perspectives give a subordinate role to such concerns; where they are discussed, it is in the context of an attempt to demonstrate how contemporary industrial society is potentially ordered, harmonious and integrated. These writers are 'optimistic' in the sense that they see 'modern' society as the culmination of previous evolution, and as potentially perfectible by fairly minor reforms introduced on the basis of positivist knowledge. There is no critique of exploitation or domination in contemporary societies — power and inequality are necessary as long as they are 'fair'. As a result, class conflict or clashes of ideas are pathological deviations from societal health. When these views are linked to the basic assumption that most institutions, most of the time, are functional for the needs of society and all its members, then we have a powerfully conservative social philosophy.

It is deeply ironic that the recent history of Europe should allow the centre of sociological thought to shift to America, for that shift led to the dominance of theories which had little or nothing to say about the most pressing historical issues for the world. The apparent domestic security of America created a 'science of society' which had little or nothing to contribute to the understanding of war, revolution and fascism, and had little room for the creative power of humans to destroy or liberate themselves by their own social actions. As a result, the positivist organicist perspective has lost all credibility through its production of misleading concepts and mistaken explanations, and its conservative political implications. The current task for social theory is to unite social action theory with a material historical account of social structure.

12.3   STRUCTURAL AND HISTORICAL SOCIOLOGY

In contrast to the organicists' pursuit of integration in 'modern' society, the work of Marx and Weber is united by a determination to specify the historical origins, character and

future of contemporary *capitalism*. The distinction lies in the
recognition by Marx and Weber that capitalism is only one
possible form of industrial society, and that the particular
economic relationships which give this type of social structure its character are also vital for the understanding of other
aspects of society. Marx extends this into a general principle
of the primacy of economic relations over other aspects of
social structure which was to apply to all unequal societies.
Weber bitterly opposed any such general theory of history,
and stressed the equal or greater importance of culture and
politics. Despite these disagreements, they share the concern
to distinguish *types* of social structure by specifying material
structures (economic, ideological and political) and thus
avoiding the search for ahistorical sweeping generalisations
about the 'universal' features of society, or of 'modern' or
'traditional' societies. This sensitivity to specific historical
developments and variations allows both Marx and Weber to
have some account (however different) of the role of human
actions in shaping history, even if neither approach can be
seen as fully adequate. However, their conceptions of social
action differ, as does their actual use of structural and historical explanation; consequently we must discuss the extent to
which the ideas of Marx and Weber are ultimately compatible. We shall see that Marx does offer answers to the theoretical problem of system integration and the structural conditions for change, while Weber opposes this account as excessively mechanical. Instead, he regards political, cultural
and economic structures as institutional frameworks in which
social action takes place; ultimately, for him, historical outcomes are the result of the intentional motivated acts of individuals. As a result, Weber gives less account of the 'internal
dynamics' of structures than Marx.

Karl Marx (1818–83)

The influence of Marx on recent sociology can hardly be
overestimated, but his work was not accepted as significant
until almost eighty years after his death. Until sociology became more sensitive to political issues in the 1960s, academically respectable theorists paid little attention to Marx's

---

Karl Marx (1818–83)

Born: Trier, Rhineland, 1818.
Education: University of Bonn, 1835.
University of Berlin, 1836–41.
Work: Editor, *Rheinische Zeitung,* 1842.
Paris, 1843; Brussels, 1845; Germany 1848;
London 1849–83.
Main texts: *Poverty of Philosophy,* 1847.
Communist Manifesto, 1848.
*The Eighteenth Brumaire of Louis
Bonaparte,* 1852.
*Grundrisse (Outline of a Critique of
Political Economy)* 1857.
*Preface to a Contribution to the Critique of
Political Economy,* 1859.
Theories of Surplus Value, 1862–3.
Capital, Volumes 1–3, 1863–7.
Critique of the Gotha Programme, 1875.

---

work. Instead, his ideas have been elaborated and extended within socialist political movements which frequently condemned academic sociology as bourgeois ideology. As a result of this political engagement, Marxist theories have retained close contact with key issues of power and economic domination, and thus provide an alternative perspective for those sociologists who are commited to both historical structural analysis and intervention in social change. This does not mean, however, that sociologists with such interests have been uncritical of Marx's ideas or of the political developments within Marxism.

Perhaps the primary reasons for the great power of Marx's ideas lie in the timing of his work and in the way that he critically drew upon three diverse intellectual traditions — German idealist philosophy, French socialism and British political economy. Marx's theories responded to the establishment of capitalism in the middle years of the nineteenth century, through a critical rejection of all those sources; he rejected Hegel's idealist philosophy in favour of a materialist approach to history, and he attempted to put socialism on a scientific basis by specifying the conditions for socialism created by the structural weaknesses built into the capitalist economic system. As a result, his theory is original and wide-ranging, but also a product of a particular period in the history of a particular part of the world.

In his earliest writings, Marx displays his primarily philo-sophical training by engaging in abstract criticism of the phil-osopher Hegel, whose ideas dominated German intellectual life in the 1840s. For Hegel, the development of human society had to be seen as an uneven and fitful progress towards a state of true, full humanity. The ideal qualities of truth, reason and justice were only imperfectly embodied in the material world at any point in this evolution; but humans gradually recovered knowledge of their true nature through the development of theology and then philosophy. Hegel's system was the culmination of this development of Reason. As a result, once armed with Hegel's solution, the philos-opher could subject the currently existing world to *crit-ique* and discover within it the tendencies moving towards the full realisation of our true humanity. Philosophy was the means by which humanity might discover its real poten-tial, while the state (as the home of law and justice) was the institution which demonstrated these higher qualities in con-trast to mundane 'civil society'. Thus, despite its critical pot-ential, Hegel's philosophy came to justify the existing Prussian state as the closest embodiment of Reason. Radical Young Hegelians — including the young Marx — accepted this role for the philosopher as all-seeing liberator, but wished to stress the critique of the contemporary state. While joining in this, Marx took things much further. Firstly, he drew upon the French socialist ideas which developed out of the French Revolution to suggest that the *proletariat* could be the 'universal class' that would actually bring the philosopher's critique to fruition through revolution. At this stage (1843–4) the role of this class is not derived from real economic analysis, but Marx does make the radical step of rejecting the notion that the state is the embodiment of Spirit or Idea, Hegel's force behind history. Instead, Marx came to see the state as a reflection of class relations in civil society, and he began to see these social relations as shaping human nature.

This constitutes a complete rejection of idealism in favour of a *materialistic* explanation of history in terms of humans' practical actions within the constraints of particular social structures.

However, any imperfection in the structure of these social relations will necessarily create imperfection in people who cannot reach their ultimate human potential. There is no constant 'human nature' but there is a full, ideal human condition which is never reached until social relations are perfected. The faith behind Marx's vision is that society is perfectible by human action, given the historical circumstances which allow the movement to communism. In his mature work, Marx develops economic and political analysis of capitalism in order to provide understanding of the weaknesses in capitalism that will allow it to be superseded by a whole new social order — socialism. Lying behind this, throughout his work, is a vision of what humans could and should be if social conditions would allow, which is expressed in his theory of *alienation*. (Although first elaborated in his Paris Manuscripts of 1844, the basic ideas can certainly be found in his mature works such as *Grundrisse*, his preliminary notes for *Capital*.)

Alienation

The basis for this theory is the notion that what singles out humans from other species is the capacity to control nature by creative activity; they can work out a conception of what they wish to create and then put this into practice. Work can therefore be the expression of human intellect and creative capacity, unless it is *alienated*, by being (a) either concerned merely with survival, or (b) organised socially in such a way that work is debased and made into a burden. The conditions for true humanity are therefore the conditions which abolish alienated labour; these must include abundance, abolition of the current division of production into meaningless tasks, and a removal of all economic domination and exploitation. Alienated labour reaches its worst form, Marx argued, with industrial capitalism, for here workers are tied to the machine in the performance of a meaningless task, only part of a larger process. They are forced to sell their ability to work (their labour-power) to the employer as a *marketable commodity*. Human creativity is therefore turned into an object, bought for the cheapest price. The product of this labour is owned and sold by the capitalist and so the harder workers labour, the more they are exploited by the capitalist. Therefore, since employers own the factory, the raw materials, the labour-power of their workers, and the product, they therefore claim the right to design and control the whole labour process so that the worker's creativity and intellect are constantly stifled and controlled by others (see also the discussion in Chapter 8).

Quite clearly, in order to overcome these aspects of alienation, the basic economic relations which create it must be abolished — by revolutionary means. The whole structure of society must be transformed:

> In a higher phase of communist society, after the enslaving subordination of the individual to the division of labour, and therewith also the antithesis between mental and physical labour, has vanished; after labour has become not only a means of life but life's prime want; after the productive forces have also increased with the all-round development of the individual, and all the springs of cooperative wealth flow more abundantly — only then can . . . society inscribe on its banners: From each according to his ability, to each according to his needs! (Marx, *Critique of the Gotha Programme,* 1875).

Whether communist society really could sustain abundance through high productivity and still abolish alienation is a complex and contentious issue.

As Europe approached its year of revolutions in 1848, Marx became much more closely involved in practical politics through journalism and the Communist League, and he began to specify his account of social relations in terms of the *social organisation of production.* As we saw in Chapter 2, Marx came to see the structure of economic relations as the most basic and important element in society as a whole. We saw in the previous section that organicist social theorists regard economic activity as merely a mundane necessity facilitating the cultural structures which depend upon it; for Marx (and

Engels) this dependance means that the rest of society — more or less directly — reflects these economic relations. The key to understanding a particular society is its predominant *mode of production* which consists of the tools and techniques (forces of production) and the compatible relations of production. The latter constitute *class relations* which in all non-communist societies produce an unequal structure of economic benefit and political and ideological domination. There is no 'common interest' or spontaneous 'consensus' at the level of social integration; fundamental class divisions are one aspect of the inherently unstable system — integration of the mode of production.

Conflicts take infinitely varied forms in society (e.g. religious or territorial) but they ultimately concern benefit or loss to different classes, and the conflicts have consequences for social relations, and hence class structure. In this broad sense then, Marx and Engels argue that 'the history of all hitherto existing society is the history of class struggles' (*Communist Manifesto*, 1848).

Behind these struggles, however, lie the *structural conditions for conflict,* and these derive from the structural features of the economic base. By 1859, Marx argues that 'The mode of production of material life conditions the social, political and intellectual life in general' (*Preface to a Contribution to the Critique of Political Economy*, 1859). Changes occur when structural strains emerge: 'At a certain stage of their development, the material productive forces of society come into conflict with the existing relations of production.' For example, the development of economic progress during the transition to capitalism in Britain came to be *held back* by feudal economic relations. As a result, Marx claims, these social relations must change: 'Then begins an epoch of social revolution. With the change of the economic foundation the entire immense superstructure is more or less rapidly transformed.'

The economic conditions for revolution in social institutions can, Marx claims, be known scientifically, but an apparent element of uncertainty is introduced by the fact that 'men become conscious of this conflict and fight it out'. We might thus conclude that this consciousness may vary, and that outcomes will be unpredictable, but Marx squashes such doubts by arguing that the consciousness of those struggling cannot be taken at face-value; they may delude themselves, and 'this consciousness must be explained from the contradictions of material life' — indeed 'mankind only sets itself such tasks as it can solve'. The main thrust of the *Preface* is, then, the emphasis on changes in the economic base, and these in turn produce ideologies which induce people to fight out social struggles — even if they do not fully understand the real consequences of these struggles. As it stands, this materialist conception of history certainly encourages us to regard the 'evolution' of the economic base as the key to social change — what Engels called 'the law of development of human history' — but we must qualify this in the context of other aspects of Marx's ideas.

Firstly, this 'law' is only a general principle and we should not assume that all historical change can be reduced, simply and directly, to economic factors; on the other hand, the economic level is still seen as determinant in the last instance. In his historical essays, Marx showed no neglect of political and ideological factors but constantly related them to class interests and class divisions. However, no systematic theory is ever developed in general terms and so later Marxists have been led to produce widely varying elaborations which have often been mutually incompatible.

Secondly, the relationship between revolution and class struggle is problematic. We are accustomed today to regard revolution as a sudden seizure of political power, after which radical changes are made — and certainly Marx worked hard as a revolutionary for such a goal. However, the 'epoch of social revolution' Marx refers to in the *Preface* must mean the lengthy process of transformation of one mode of production (and related social structure) into another. According to Marxist historians of the transition from feudalism to capitalism in Britain, this took anything up to five hundred years — a very long revolution! Perhaps the answer is that revolutions as political crises are turning points made possible by the gradually emerging economic changes, which create new classes with an interest in breaking out of old institutional constraints — for example the emerging bourgeoisie extending its political and economic freedom in the French Revolution. The vital difference in the revolution that breaks out of capitalism rests in the fact that for the first time the subordinate class seize power instead of a new ruling class — and so class domination is abolished forever.

This simply raises once again the previous problem concerning ideology and politics, for we need to know not only the material conditions which make possible such change, but also how the working class is to take advantage of its historical opportunity. The material conditions are based in the tendency for capitalism to generate more collectivised and centralised forms of production through monopolies and banks. At the same time, this collectivised system cannot operate for the collective good because it is still tied to the logic of profit and capital accumulation. Eventually, the economy can progress no further until capitalist social relations are swept aside. However, we still need to know whether this consciousness develops inevitably, or whether there are powerful forces resisting the rise of revolutionary political action. Without better accounts of politics and ideology, we are in danger of viewing consciousness as a mere automatic side-effect of material change. The continued survival of capitalism and the defeat of the West European Left have only intensified the pressure on Marxists to give an adequate theoretical answer to these questions. The problem of consciousness remains, however, and Marxists have been bitterly divided over this issue — especially over the role of Party leadership as opposed to 'spontaneous' class consciousness. Marx's own writings gave no real answer to this question, but the structure of his mature writings put so much emphasis on economic analysis that they encourage an almost exclusive concentration on the material conditions for change. The crisis and internal strains generated by capitalism create the conditions for the downfall of the system. Almost inevitably, the three volumes of *Capital,* plus *Theories of Surplus Value,* outweigh all other aspects of his theory, despite Marx's original intention to follow *Capital* with studies of landed property, wage labour, the state, international trade and the world market.

In the event, Marx died with only Volume I completed for

publication and the broader studies were never begun. As a result, it is not surprising that orthodox Marxists have normally placed great emphasis on the economic theory of the weaknesses of capitalism such as the tendency of the rate of profit to fall. It is outside the scope of this discussion to evaluate Marx's economic theory of capitalism (the basic features are discussed in Chapter 2 on stratification), but we can see how the lack of similarly elaborated accounts of politics and ideology paved the way for crude economic determinism in some later Marxist ideas.

More generally, we can also see how the concern for the dynamics and contradictions of capitalism centres our attention on the economy as a separate institutional area of social life. This is possible in capitalism, for here economic activity operates with a logic and dynamic of its own through capital accumulation, expansion and competition. This is much less obviously applicable in pre-capitalist modes of production where economic domination is hard to separate from military, political and ideological relations. When this is the case, it is much harder to see a 'logic of development' for social structure deriving from the economic base. We need a much more complex account of the relations between economic, political and ideological aspects, even if economic relations are seen as the ultimate determinant of social relations. The work of recent structuralist Marxists such as Althusser has been oriented towards such an elaborate theory — though the adequacy of these theories can be disputed.

This leads us to the broader question of the nature of Marx's sociological explanations. If we need material structural explanations as one component of social theory, then we must see what can be drawn from his work.

While bearing in mind the dangers of over-simplified economic determinism, the concept of *mode of production* does provide a foundation for the analysis of *types* of social structure, and it does guide us towards explanations of broader aspects of social structure. The concept is one way to account for *system integration* (and non-integration) in material terms. We can distinguish, for example, capitalist or feudal societies as interrelated systems with particular structural features and dynamics (see Chapter 2 on class theory).

We may also be able to show how potentials for change exist when the system itself generates internal strains or crises (above all, the contradictions of capital accumulation). As such, these structural accounts aim at being revelatory — they show systematic constraints and pressures on actors that those people will probably not understand or control. As Marx wrote, economic relations, once established 'are indispensable and independent of their will'. Despite all this, Marx's account of the rise of capitalist class relations stressed above all the deliberate creation of new economic relations by the capitalist gentry — so we must conclude that only when it is once established as a general dominant system does the capitalist system come to develop dynamics and tendencies that constrain the capitalist as much as the proletarian. At the same time, these structural features create the conditions for a recapture of human control by those who seek to transform the social structure. Thus there is a complex relation between human action and underlying social structures. The real causes lie at a level of structural causation which cannot be seen by looking at individual events or experiences. A theory is needed (as Marx offered in *Capital*) to give an account of the dynamic structures which lie beneath the surface. These structures are, however, constantly changing and developing in uneven, contradictory and crisis-ridden ways. They therefore constantly generate new possibilities for historical change and thus for intervention by groups of actors. This dynamic view of structure is entirely different from the tradition of organicist holism where the organic analogy inevitably produces a static conception of structure; change and development have to be artificially introduced through some notion of evolution.

In contrast, although the Marxian view certainly does see evolutionary progress towards socialism, this takes a historical form, differing markedly in different societies with their particular circumstances. While Marx may have been too ready to generalise the British pattern, and hence underplay the effects of capitalist nations upon each other's development, he certainly never collapsed into the ahistorical speculative generalisations of the organicists. At the same time, we may sustain certain doubts. In particular, the account of underlying economic structures with their dynamics and crises certainly illuminates capitalism, but seems much harder to apply to other types of society; for example, it is hard to see how the transition from Ancient Rome to feudalism can be explained by contradictions between forces and relations of production. The historical primacy of the economic level is clear in capitalism; it is much less easy to employ a simple economic determinism elsewhere. This has led to a number of responses. French structuralist Marxists (above all Althusser) have attempted to develop a rigorous science of social structures out of historical materialism, while some German neo-Marxists of the Frankfurt School (such as Habermas and Marcuse) suggest that culture and politics should be given at least equal weight with economic relations, in the definition of capitalism as the 'main organising principle' of current society. Quite apart from these, other critics have chosen to reject entirely the materialist conception of history as a dangerous fallacy, whilst still undertaking the historical analysis of social structures. One such critic was Max Weber.

Max Weber (1864–1920)

Max Weber (1864–1920)

Born: Erfurt, Thuringia, 1864.
Education: University of Heidelberg, 1882.
University of Berlin, 1884–5.
University of Göttingen, 1885–6.
Career: Teaches Law, Berlin, 1892.
Professor of Political Economy, Freiburg, 1894.
Professor of Economics, Heidelberg, 1896.
Main works: *Methodological Essays*, 1902.
Protestant Ethic and the Spirit of Capitalism, 1902–4.
Economy and Society, 1910–14.
Sociology of Religion, 1916.

Max Weber was a scholar of formidable accomplishment who throughout his work attempted to place modern capitalism in its historical context. Born into an academic family he pursued an intellectual career that spanned economic history, law, sociology, and philosophy. Despite psychological illness he achieved a prolific output, but his body of work has often seemed to others to be fragmentary; Weber does not immediately appear to have any central organising theory to guide his work in the way that Marx did. However, certain guiding interests and theoretical perspectives *can* be seen as unifying the diverse themes within his work.

His first major concern was with the political paradoxes facing German society at the turn of the century. Weber was acutely aware that although Germany had become a strong capitalist state, the bourgeoisie had not succeeded in securing independent political power. As a result, Germany lacked democratic institutions; instead, traditional status groups such as the Prussian Junker aristocracy and their high-born functionaries in the army and state bureaucracies unified and ruled Germany. At the same time, the Germans working class was the most highly organised in Europe and was nominally Marxist. Weber was deeply committed to the pursuit of a liberal-democratic bourgeois regime, but was haunted by the threats from Marxism on the one side and all-powerful bureaucracy on the other. As a direct result, he engaged in passionate debate against the theories of Marx (or more precisely, the Marxists) while at the same time accepting that the contemporary world could only be understood by economic and historical analysis.

His other connected interest concerned the historical conditions for the rise of modern capitalism and science in the West. He posed the question:

> Through what combination of circumstances did it come about that precisely, and only, in the Western world certain cultural phenomena emerged which represent a direction of development of universal significance and validity? (*Origins of Industrial Capitalism in Europe*, 1920).

For Weber, science and modern capitalism were each part of an even broader cultural development: the *rationalisation process.* Unlike other areas of the globe, Western Europe developed from its Ancient civilisations in ways that gradually removed the influence of magic and superstition, and ultimately undermined the basis of spiritual faith. Instead, social institutions and individual action began to show more calculating, instrumental rationality. Law, administration and economic activity became formalised and rationalised, while the connected rise of science undermined the power of religious elites. Only in the West is there true science, and this new situation thereby allows us to look back at history and understand scientifically how we came to this position. The rise of this rational knowledge is, moreover, intimately linked to the rise of rational economic behaviour, institutionalised in the structure of modern capitalism.

For Weber, any pursuit of profit through exchange could be regarded as capitalistic, and so he saw most societies as containing some element of capitalist activity. In the modern West, however, the whole economy comes to be dominated by rational capitalism of a new form. The distinctive feature of this is the 'rational capitalist organisation of (formally) *free labour'*. These 'proletarians' are employed as property-less wage-earners by an industrial 'bourgeoisie'. This employing class pursues capital accumulation (the continual growth of capital through profits) by using *rational calculation,* which Weber argues, is only possible with free wage-labour (as opposed to serfs or slaves). The emergence of this particular form of capitalism is thus 'the central problem in a universal history of civilisation'. It is with this question in mind that Weber embarks upon his vast comparative studies of economic, legal and religious institutions of countries outside the West; he is guided by the question 'Why was it in general that in those countries neither scientific nor artistic nor political nor economic development followed the path of *rationalisation* which is unique to the West?'

At the most general level, the explanation Weber provides is in terms of the institutionalised world-views encouraged by other cultural traditions. The rulers and intelligentsia of other cultures are seen as being prevented from pursuing the road of rationalisation by the nature of the doctrines and intellectual orientations which they themselves produced. For example, the Buddhist monk withdrew from all worldly activity in order to achieve a spiritual elevation, while the Confucian Mandarin engaged in administration on the basis of highly traditionalistic and non-scientific literary knowledge. Only in the West did a cultural orientation emerge which favoured rationalisation. At one level, the non-theological philosophical thought of Ancient Greece and Rome bequeathed an intellectual heritage; this could later fuse with the worldly orientation of Judaic—Christian tradition to provide a basis for rationalistic art and science in the Renaissance. Later still, the Reformation sowed the seeds of a Puritan asceticism which, combined with the worldliness of Christianity, produced a transformation in economic behaviour (*The Protestant Ethic and the Spirit of Capitalism*). This came about because, Weber claimed, Puritanism demanded sober worldly activity — doing one's duty in a 'calling'. If this produced riches it was a sign of God's favour and demonstrated good work. However, this worldly wealth was not to be *consumed* (as the wealthy in non-capitalist societies and eras had all done) but instead the wealth must be reinvested to create the basis for further dutiful work. This was demanded, of course, by the ascetic nature of Puritanism — the demand that the godly should reject all earthly pleasures. This combination of asceticism with worldly work was seen by Weber as a unique cultural development, and one which fitted perfectly with capital accumulation: wealth is amassed but it is continually reinvested to accumulate further wealth. No other religious ethic had ever demanded this combination from the whole population of believers (rather than just from religious 'virtuosos'), none had revered worldly work so highly for its own sake. Therefore, Weber argued, the origins of modern rational capitalism must be seen in Western culture and above all in Puritan Protestantism.

This is not an appropriate context to judge the historical validity of Weber's thesis, even though it has stimulated a long and acrimonious debate among historians. We must concentrate on the form of explanation that Weber employs, and in outline this seems to be based on the opinion that general world-views have a crucial effect on the intentional motivated actions of individuals. These world-views derive most usually from the doctrines produced by religious elites who hold positions of intellectual dominance. Although the content of the ideas and the extent to which they are accepted may be influenced by economic or political interests, these cultural ideas must be accepted as independent causal elements in their own right:

> For those to whom no causal explanation is adequate without an economic (or materialistic as it is unfortunately still called) interpretation, it may be remarked that I consider the influence of economic development on the fate of religious ideas to be very important ... On the other hand, those religious ideas themselves simply cannot be deduced from economic circumstances. They are ... the most powerful plastic elements of national character and contain a law of development and a compelling force entirely their own (Weber, *Protestant Ethic,* p. 277, n. 84).

Weber goes on to suggest that the next most important factors are political and not economic; yet even so, he discounted the importance of any political move towards socialism. Even if Germany did move in a socialist direction, Weber argued, the rationalisation process could not be reversed. As a result, humanitarian goals (whether liberal or socialist) were doomed by inexorable and irreversible growth of rational bureaucratic administration. Sober instrumental calculation would dominate all social life and the individual would be stifled by the constraints of his role within the 'iron cage of bureaucracy':

> More and more the material fate of the masses depends upon the steady and correct functioning of the increasingly bureaucratic organisation of private capitalism. The idea of eliminating these organisations becomes more and more utopian (Weber, 1978, p. 988).

Utopian doctrines of all kinds were pathetic delusions, for rationalisation creates a world of technical efficiency and undemocratic administration that cannot be transcended; the sociologist must not fall prey to such illusions but instead face bravely the 'polar night of icy darkness' that is humanity's inevitable fate. The development of Western culture leads inevitably to a future which derides the very humanistic values which it earlier generated.

This dismal account of contemporary problems demonstrates the opposition to Marxist economic determinism in Weber's perspective, for he is clearly insistent on viewing culture as an independent factor. In consequence, one might think that this places Weber close to the positivist organicists with their stress on the primacy of cultural phenomena. This view cannot be sustained, for Weber always approaches 'culture' in a grounded, historical way as the ideas institutionalised in society by intellectual elites, and so it remains a materialist account of the role of ideas. More generally, it is impossible to reconcile Weber with the organicists because his conception of society is fundamentally different.

It is different because Weber regards social institutions as ultimately reducible to individual acts, although these intentional acts are shaped by this social context. Implicitly the grand historical studies connect with a philosophy of social action which stresses the deliberate intentions and motives of the individual actor (a view we will examine in the next section). As a result, Weber is led away from structural *explanations* in terms of the nature of the social system — a position which distances him from both Marx and the organicists. As we shall see from his approach to power and stratification, Weber only makes reference to social structure and types of social organisation in an *analytical* and descriptive manner — not in terms of structural explanations deriving from an account of the society as *system*.

One source of this perspective lies in his approach to history; Weber refers to the 'meaningless infinity of the world-process'. We only see pattern and order in this infinity of unique events by imposing ordering concepts (the *ideal types* — e.g. 'feudalism') and making comparisons. He rejects any notion of universal causal laws governing society, and is therefore certainly not a positivist. However, as a result of his view of history Weber resists making distinctions between different 'types' of society, and certainly does not attempt to offer analysis of the structural dynamics of any type of social structure. He may have described the basic features of capitalism and acknowledged that competition constrains the capitalist, but Weber is hostile to any attempt to develop theories of the underlying structures and weaknesses of capitalism. Similarly, his account of stratification fails to specify characteristic *sets* of class relations for particular types of society; instead we are presented with a confusing array of analytical concepts that are not even clearly separated from one another. Even though his concept of 'market capacity' is useful for understanding inequality in a market society (see Chapter 2), Weber confuses this account by including property as a form of market advantage, and by illustrating the theory with examples from societies such as Ancient Rome which were clearly not dominated by market relationships. These stratification concepts have achieved popularity because he refused to assume that property classes are the only real divisions, but his alternatives are undermined by the lack of any theoretical effort to distinguish and explain stratification *systems*.

Somewhat similar objections can be made to his account of power and legitimate domination (authority). Power is seen as the ability to achieve one's will, even against the resistance of others, while authority is seen as a phenomenon in which subordinates accept domination by another because they believe that the power-holder has a right to control them. All of this can be seen as excessively concerned with the subjective perceptions of actors, for (as we saw in Chapter 4) power may be institutionalised in objective economic and political relations — independently of the perceptions or wishes of those involved. This is not to suggest that such consciousness is normally absent, but we must pay attention to structures of domination which relate to the basic nature of particular social systems (such as feudalism); Weber generally fails to do this except at the level of historical description.

In summary, Weber's sociology displays a breadth of scholarship which must always remain instructive. However, his explanations of social change in terms of cultural development and actors' motivation would be much more plausible if they were developed in the context of theories of particular types of social system and their dynamics. We shall see in the next section that Weber's methodology stresses social action in a way that seems to exclude structural explanation. Indeed, Weber claims that social phenomena can ultimately be described and explained in terms of individual motivated actions — which seems to preclude holistic theories. As a result of this, as well as his rejection of economic determinism, we can therefore argue that Weber's sociology must remain fundamentally incompatible with that of Marx. Moreover, Marx's ideas will still constitute the strongest model for structural explanations despite the criticisms we have acknowledged. We have argued in this section that such explanations are a necessary part of sociology. As we shall see, however, it is by no means easy to reconcile structural explanation with the social action theories which have so far been produced. There is, at present, no simple compromise between them.

12.4 SOCIAL ACTION PERSPECTIVES

Despite all the other contrasts between them, positivist organicism and Marxian sociology are united by a concern for holistic explanations. In each perspective, the stress is on explaining the causes and unintended consequences of action in terms of features of the social system external to the actor. As a result, the actions of the individual are seen as the effects of social forces (e.g. Durkheim's suicidogenic currents) or of structural constraints (e.g. competition between capitalist enterprises).

Social action theorists (as we saw in Chapter 11) have tended to regard such explanations as misleading in that they fail to take sufficient account of the *consciousness and intentions* of actors, and thus fail to show that the social world is a *meaningful construction* of its members. Actors, it is argued, are thinking, choosing beings who control their own actions through thought. This thought, furthermore, draws upon a stock of shared concepts and assumptions which are held in common by the actor's social group. So we should not look for external causes of behaviour, but instead should attempt to locate meaningful social action in its social context.

As we shall see, however, there are considerable variations in emphasis between particular theories within the social action perspective. We will begin with the widely influential American tradition of symbolic interactionism, then return to the European tradition of Weber and his phenomenological critic, Alfred Schutz, and finally show how the two strands can be seen to interconnect in ethnomethodology.

Symbolic interactionism

This action perspective has been widely influential — especially in the study of small-scale interaction, personality development, and deviant behaviour. It forms a central element in the tradition of qualitative research into the way actors negotiate situations and roles, and gain a social identity. Symbolic interactionism (SI) has come to emphasise the diversity of social roles and subcultures (e.g. how do you learn to be a marihuana-user?) and the way that social rules and social identities are constructed by actors through their interaction (e.g. how does a teenager come to be labelled as a criminal?). The fluidity and diversity of social life and the creative flexibility of social action are central themes of SI.

The origins of the perspective lie in the individualistic orientation of American social science as it developed at the turn of the century. As one might expect from the prevailing ethos of individualistic competition, early American social theories tended to concentrate on individualistic explanations of behaviour, or on moral constraints, neglecting material social structures. In reaction to the earlier emphasis on biologically predetermined behaviour patterns, theorists such as Cooley, Thomas and Mead came to pay much more attention to consciousness and to the social creation of the self. The characteristic approach (directly deriving from the psychology of William James) was on the unique capacity of the human being to develop conscious reflexive thought and symbolic communication. Human beings are not simply driven by innate programming or by learnt behaviour patterns; instead they monitor their own behaviour by conscious thought. This thought, however, takes place through symbols learnt in a social context largely through language. Though we also control our behaviour by reflecting upon our own actions, we can only know our own self, our social identity, through the responses of others. We come to know 'who we are' and 'what we should do' through our interpretations of the responses of others to our actions. Thus our personal identity is created through interaction, and our actions are shaped through our social interaction with others. These general notions develop in sophistication from Cooley's 'looking-glass self' to Mead's conceptions of the 'I' and the 'me', but they all begin from face-to-face interaction. While Cooley's work mainly portrayed society as an interlocking network of small groups, Mead did come to acknowledge more generally institutionalised roles and patterns. For Mead, the development of personality moved beyond a stage where the child responded to the demands of a 'significant other' (e.g. the mother) until the adult knew the demands of the 'generalised other' in the roles he or she played. At the same time, this world of roles remained flexible because actors could always renegotiate the nature of the roles through interaction.

Society, then, comes to be seen as interlocking interactions based on actors' perceptions and expectations of each other. The content of action depends upon the way actors come to define the appropriate patterns of action in the situation: as W. I. Thomas suggested, situations defined as real are real in their consequences. In other words, the nature of the social world ultimately depends on the shared definitions of roles and identities constructed through interaction. Thus, if 'definitions of the situation' (Thomas) and 'imaginations we have of one another' are the 'solid facts of society' (Cooley), then society changes as the definitions change through the interaction between socially created selves. However, some stability and continuity in society is created by socialisation and the institutionalisation of patterns of behaviour into roles. The work of Mead stresses the *social* construction of the self to the exclusion of the biological and instinctual elements that still figured in the work of Thomas. However, both self and society remain essentially fluid and adaptable:

> The individual is continually adjusting himself in advance to the situation to which he belongs and reacting back upon it. The self is not something that exists first and then enters into a relationship with others, but is so to speak, an eddy in the social current and so still a part of the current (Mead, 1934, p. 182).

The real strength of the symbolic interactionism approach lies not so much in its theoretical foundations as in the practical qualitative research that the approach has generated. Writers such as Hughes, Becker, Strauss and Goffman have all pioneered qualitative research methods that aim to 'get in where the action is' and 'tell it like it is'. In other words, we should try to understand the world as seen by our subjects — be they homosexuals, mental hospital patients or 'trainee' marihuana users. The task is to see how they make sense of the world and cope with alien and hostile powers such as the police or the staff of the mental hospital (Erving Goffman, *Asylums*); one therefore needs to use sensitive empathy and participant observation.

Very frequently, the concept of a 'career' guides SI accounts of the way a new social identity (as pot-smoker, physician, etc.) is negotiated. This will involve learning appropriate behaviour, applying initiative, or possibly resisting unwelcome labels being imposed by others. For example, a teenager caught stealing might try to resist the label of 'criminal'. However, undergoing the process of conviction and sentencing to a penal institution may impose such a social identity in the eyes of others. This labelling (and its consequences for employment), together with the skills learnt inside, may help produce an acceptance of the criminal self-identity by the person himself; this would be a completed 'deviant career' (see Chapter 10).

Generally, these qualitative methods are closely associated with sympathy for 'the underdog' and SI often appears as a manual for individual resistance to pressures from powerful social institutions, and a defence of the dignity and rationality of the individual actor.

For all the attractiveness and plausibility of this account of social life, certain problems remain. The first and most obvious is that social structures are effectively dissolved. Social institutions may be acknowledged as a backdrop to interaction but social systems and their related structures of economic and political power have only the most shadowy existence. Indeed, the claim that social life consists *solely* of actors' definitions is not sustainable. The consequences of class (for example) remain real, whether or not the actors define them as real, and the consequences of actions in a complex social structure may be outside the control or knowledge of any actors. In order to understand such consequences we need an account of the structure. However, it is unfair to direct these criticisms only at SI, for they may apply with even more force to other action perspectives. We can also question the adequacy of their notions of self and action since it might be argued that SI overemphasises the degree of conscious monitoring of action and manipulation of situations. Social life seems like a very consciously played game, and perhaps more scope should be allowed for unconscious drives and for social action which is less consciously 'controlled'. Again, though, this issue can also be raised with other action theories, as we shall see.

Despite these reservations, the SI perspective has provided an extremely valuable alternative to holistic theories — especially as it has coexisted with functionalism to produce some alternative to Parsons's over-socialised 'cultural dopes'. As we saw in Chapter 10, however, the *partial* nature of SI has now been generally acknowledged, in that it concentrates so heavily on face-to-face interaction without offering sufficient account of social structure.

Weber's theory of social action

The unique position of Weber's work was stressed in the earlier section on 'historical' and 'structural' sociology. Weber attempted to reconcile large-scale historical comparative studies with a methodology which began from the individual social act. Historical trends and social institutions are ultimately reducible to the unique individual actions from which they derive; at the same time, such actions have characteristic motives and goals which derive from the broader cultural context. The instrumental, calculating rationality of Western individuals derives from a much broader trend of historical development. At the level of abstract methodological statements, however, Weber does not succeed in clarifying this connection, for he concentrated on the problem of how to reconcile this concentration on social action with scientific sociological explanation. He tries to do this by systematising

738   *Introductory Sociology*

the use of *verstehen* (interpretive understanding) — the process by which the sociologist attempts to gain access to the meaning of action for the actor.

In defining action as 'human behaviour when . . . the agent or agents see it as subjectively *meaningful*' (1978, p. 4), Weber emphasises the *motive* present in the mind of the actor which is the 'cause' of the act. Thus, if we see a man chopping wood we may immediately recognise the act (direct *verstehen*). However, we also need to grasp the actor's motive by using empathy and rational judgement (explanatory *verstehen*). When we know the motive, we have explained the act, since 'to "explain", for a science concerned with the meaning of actions, is to grasp the complex of meanings into which a directly intelligible action fits by virtue of its subjectively intended meaning' (1978, p. 9). Weber distinguishes four types of motive: traditional conformity to habit, emotional, rational behaviour oriented to an ultimate value (such as salvation), and rational behaviour oriented to a mundane goal (such as earning a living). Scientific explanation involves using *verstehen* correctly to discern the correct motive. We do this partly by locating the act in its context — we know that a woodcutter chops wood for rational reasons connected with pay. Generally, though, Weber's whole emphasis is on explaining actions by informed guesses about the actor's reasons for acting. This raises issues at two levels.

Firstly, Weber is often seen as trying to compromise with positivism to create a scientific sociology. It is quite clear that explanations in terms of actors' reasons are not at all compatible with the positivist search for external material causes which are empirically discoverable. Even with this perspective, it is difficult for positivists to ignore consciousness entirely, but they will almost certainly attempt to specify outside causes which determine the actor's choices. Weber did accept, in principle, that the choices were caused by social circumstances and by the personality of the actor. However, the causation was so complex that prediction was a practical impossibility. Causal laws were therefore unattainable, and so Weber's compromise with positivism was only partial.

More importantly, perhaps, Weber's theory has been regarded as an inadequate account of action since it remains excessively individualistic, failing to locate thought and action in any real social context. This may seem odd since Weber clearly does pay enormous attention to historical social structure, and to cultures, as contexts for action; but it is true that the connection between these and action is never explained explicitly. This is very unfortunate, because critics of Weber's methodology — above all the phenomenologist Schutz — have radicalised action theory while at the same time abandoning Weber's historical and structural concerns.

Phenomenological sociology

Alfred Schutz, an Austrian philosopher and banker, is best known for *The Phenomenology of the Social World* (1934), a work in which he used the philosophies of Husserl and Bergson to criticise Weber's methodology and construct a radical account of the nature of social action.

In Schutz's view, Weber failed to give any real account of the way in which actions can only be constructed by drawing upon a shared set of social concepts, symbols and meanings. As a result he also presented an overly mechanical account of the relation between actions and reasons or motives.

We saw above that symbolic interactionists acknowledge shared definitions of situations and roles, and that they stress symbolic communication through language. However, they see these societal elements as built up out of inter-action in a creative manner, whereas Schutz's emphasis is rather different. Instead, he argues that the 'life-world' is a precarious set of shared meanings available to the whole social group. It is a shared stock of common-sense knowledge, of taken-for-granted assumptions, about society, other actors, and the world. In this sense, the reality of social life is only created by these shared arbitrary assumptions and conceptions. However, the precarious fragility of this shared 'definition of reality' is not recognised by actors in normal circumstances, because they adopt the 'natural attitude' — that is, they see the world as solid, inflexible and constraining, even though it is really only a product of their shared ideas. It is only by a 'painful effort' that the phenomenologist can suspend this common-sense knowledge to see the real nature of social life. The basic structure of the social world can then be seen, Schutz claims, as resting solely upon 'acts of establishing or interpreting meaning'. Phenomenologists therefore claim that in as much as conventional positivistic sociology 'pretends' that there really is a constraining world of 'social facts', then it is suffering from the same common-sensical self-delusions as any ordinary member of society.

In contrast to other views of action, Schutz rejects the idea that single acts can be associated with identifiable motives. Instead, actors engage in a constant *flow* of action which takes place through a continuous use of 'recipe-knowledge' — practical knowledge of how-things-are-done. We do not constantly reflect on future acts and clarify a goal (though we do have long-term projects); we just use our common sense and do things. Only sometimes do we look back at an 'act' and give an account of our motives. In the course of our action we employ assumptions about society and how it works, and we use *verstehen* in a crude way to predict the action of others. We are therefore *all* amateur sociologists if we are successful social actors. Most important of all, we must understand the socially given meaning of an act in its context. This *socially given meaning* (e.g. of a gesture at an auction) is quite separate from any motive the actor might hold. All actors take part in a social collectivity which primarily consists of *a shared universe of meanings*. Our acts are 'meaningful' not because we have a particular intention or motive, but because other actors interpret our action as having symbolic significance. We act successfully when all share the same set of meanings — if we do not, then an itchy nose at an auction might produce an unwanted acquisition. The fact that we have bought a stuffed elephant has no connection with our intentions, but is a result of the socially given meaning of our act in the context of an auction.

Thus Schutz rightly emphasises the collective, *inter*-subjective nature of meaning, unlike Weber; however a greater problem now arises. Schutz, again unlike Weber, seems to dissolve social life into a *purely* inter-subjective world. Social life becomes a 'mental event': we learn the importance of *shared* meanings, but we are left with no tools to understand social structure or unintended consequences. Our task is now limited to describing correctly the nature of social action. Schutz explicitly rejects any notion of *correcting* the accounts of the world given by actors — the sociologist might be more rigorous and logical than the lay actor but: 'Every social science takes as its goal the greatest possible clarification of what is thought about the social world by those living in it.' Such a conception of sociology removes any potential it might have for revealing the constraints upon action and thus aiding actors to overcome them. Indeed, Schutz's assumption that the universe of meanings is shared by all (and collectively reproduced) comes remarkably close to the consensus which is the key to social order in organicist approaches. Schutz's society is not a 'moral order' but it is a collectivity of *meanings,* not material social relations.

Ethnomethodology

Ethnomethodologists could almost be called Schutz's shock-troops, for their general aim is to demonstrate the truth of his phenomenological arguments by practical experiments. Although only prominent since the mid 1960s, ethnomethodology has its roots in the fusion of symbolic interactionism and phenomenology. Harold Garfinkel is the founding figure and he is responsible for its title; as the previous chapter explained, he intended it to refer to the project of an ethnographic description and analysis of the methods used by actors to sustain social life. In other words, ethnomethodologists work from Schutz's claim that the social world is produced and reproduced by the practical actions of actors, on the basis of taken-for-granted assumptions.

Garfinkel has inflicted many experiments on his students to demonstrate the importance of this common-sense knowledge. For instance, students with problems were asked to try out a new counselling experiment. In fact this was spurious and the 'counsellor' gave random yes/no answers. The victims (who had real problems) suffered anxiety as they tried to *discern some rational pattern* in the responses of the counsellor, and as their taken-for-granted *background expectancies* were disrupted. Garfinkel generalised from his experiments that if securely held common-sense assumptions are challenged, and interaction no longer 'makes sense', then 'ideally speaking, behaviours directed to such a senseless environment should be those of uncertainty, internal conflict, psycho-social isolation, acute and nameless anxiety, acute depersonalization' (1967, p. 55). Garfinkel was correct.

More constructively, ethnomethodologists draw attention to the fact that even the most mundane activities are *practical accomplishments* — the result of the 'organised artful practices of everyday life'. Conventional sociology, they argue, ignores this and therefore fails to recognise the true nature of social action; by searching for patterns and taking for granted skilled action, holistic sociology adopts a rigid and false view of the world in the same way that common sense does. A favourite focus for such attacks is Durkheim's *Suicide,* for as Douglas and Atkinson have argued, the consciousness of the suicidal person is ignored, as is the social process by which the death comes to be defined as a suicide. Durkheim had used official statistics uncritically as a 'resource': ethnomethodology demands that these resources should be made the topic for study. We therefore should treat coroners' decisions as problematic — as outcomes achieved by actors — and we should go further to analyse other areas of social activity which are usually taken for granted. These include the use of language in conversations (Schegloff and Sacks) and even 'doing walking' (Ryave and Schenkein). Turner (1974) provides a representative selection.

Finally, we should note that Schutz's rejection of a revelatory or interventionist role for sociology is also adopted in the concept of 'ethnomethodological indifference'. Ethnomethodologists see their task as revealing the general nature of social processes, *not* helping actors to change the form of any particular society.

Evaluation of social action perspectives

The general emphasis on social action is clearly important; sociology can no longer ignore the meaningful nature of social life, neither can it conveniently forget consciousness and motivation in a mistaken quest for general positivistic laws. Nor can we operate with rigid and simplified conceptions of action where motives precede actions, and where these motives are directly caused by external forces. It must be recognised that society is constantly reproduced and partly modified by the creative acts of individuals in unique social situations. Action theories are surely correct in their view that societies are continually transformed (though usually in a gradual way) by the innovative acts of individual members. Phenomenological approaches place a valuable emphasis on these processes and on the fact that these actions are created in terms of taken-for-granted assumptions characteristic of the particular society. From this it is revealed that the social world is a meaningful construction, created out of the interaction of its members. One profound consequence of this is that the social world is shown to be less solid and impenetrable than it seems to the individual lay actor. Action sociology exposes the potential fragility and *precariousness* of social reality. Instead of viewing society as a solid, fixed entity, we are made to recognise society as a changing flux created out of actors' shared perceptions and definitions (even if we do not accept that this is the *whole* truth about society). This emphasis is certainly a necessary rebuttal of the more 'mechanical' versions of social structure which have been commonplace in both organicism and Marxism (although we should also bear in mind that social arrangements have a good deal of stability in comparison with the power of most individuals). Social action theories are right to emphasise not only that the social world can be changed by actors, but that this is also a constant process.

As a result of this constant intentional and unintentional change, it is very hard to see how positivistic conceptions of *laws* can be applied to social action or social structure. There do *not* appear to be invariable regularities which can be called laws; and where regularities do occur they are open to radical change by the accumulated effects of action. We have seen that we must attempt to specify the principles of organisation of *types* of society, *not* 'society-in-general'; even here there are no fixed laws, but characteristic structures of social relations which constantly generate change. The positivistic conception of sociology seems as unacceptable as the organicist account of structure and action. In general, then, social action theories provide a range of perspectives which are a necessary antidote to the more static and rigid conceptions of structure.

No current action theory, however, successfully combines a convincing account of social action with sufficient awareness of power, conflict and constraint. Schutz provides a better theory of action than either Weber or symbolic interactionism, but one totally detached from any real concern with social structure. Although SI does not provide any theory of system integration or disintegration, it does pay attention to individual responses to *constraints* from the social structure. Phenomenology and ethnomethodology abandon even this. Social life is conceived solely in terms of the negotiation of meanings and the practical accomplishment of routine activities. Society becomes a mere 'mental event' sustained only by the shared definitions and assumptions of actors. In the course of this chapter it has been emphasised that society is more than just this. However much individual citizens today may believe in the existence of liberty or equality, the real distribution of power and economic advantage will constrain their actions; whatever they may intend to do by acting, their actions will have unintended consequences. The nature of these consequences will depend upon the interlocking connections between parts of the social structure, and on the way the social system operates *as* a dynamic system. (For example, the cutting of wages by individual employers to protect their own profits might help to push the economy further into recession, and thereby threaten employers even more.) Although perceptions of society certainly are used by actors in the course of their action, these perceptions are hardly reliable and they hardly constitute the sum total of social reality.

12.5 HUMAN ACTION AND SOCIAL SYSTEM

The most pressing theoretical task for sociology is to construct a theory of social life which acknowledges the fact that human activity embodies *both* social action and social structure simultaneously. Social structures do not inhabit a separate plane of existence, they can only exist through their manifestation in human action. These structures can therefore only be reproduced through such action, and as we have emphasised, social action is creative and innovative. Therefore, action not only *reproduces* structures, but continually *transforms* them to a greater or lesser degree. At the same time, such action takes place within a social system and suffers the *constraints* this imposes as well as employing the *resources* distributed through the social structure. Giddens (1976, p.138) has expressed this two-way relationship in his conception of the 'duality of structure': 'Every act which contributes to the reproduction of a structure is also an act of production, a novel enterprise, and as such may initiate change by altering that structure at the same time as it reproduces it.' Here, and in *Central Problems in Social Theory* (1979), Giddens has made important contributions to the development of a unifying sociological theory.

Most sociologists have stressed the extent to which societies are reproduced rather than transformed; indeed the traditional 'problem of order' sought to explain how society ensured this reproduction. Traditional answers have been in terms of *socialisation* and *social control* (see the discussion in Chapter 1), but it is now clear that both these factors can be exaggerated. Organicism has tended towards an oversocialised conception where actors are simply 'cultural dopes'. Social control may be almost as important as socialisation for explaining the passivity of those who are relatively powerless but the threat of such coercion cannot be seen as the primary source of conformity. The pressures are far more widespread and subtle than this. Instead, we must explore the way that social action relates to an institutionalised structure of constraints and resources. That is, we must identify the way that power, economic resources, and knowledge all constitute resources used by actors in their practical activity in society. Actors are therefore able to act with greater or lesser effectiveness, depending on the extent to which they have access to these resources. At the same time, others may be able to impose constraints on action by holding more political power or authority, more economic power or resources, or by having better access to knowledge. Quite clearly, these constraints and resources are distributed in patterned ways — and our earlier chapters on politics, stratification and belief-systems all tried to show evidence for this unequal distribution.

Those chapters also emphasised the necessity to *explain* the patterns of constraints and resources, and it was argued that the explanation can be found in the *systems of social relations* which characterise different *types* of society. These structures of social relations can only be understood *as* systems and must be regarded as having their own special modes of operating and their own tendencies for dynamic development. For example, feudalism can be distinguished as a *type* of society with a certain basic structure of social relations revolving around the relationships between feudal lords, serfs and the clergy. Distinctive kinds of economic exploitation, relations of domination, and ideological control, all work together to form the particular distinctive social system of feudalism. Basic relationships *cause* a distribution of constraints and resources: feudal lords hold a monopoly of force and demand surplus labour or surplus product, while the clergy hold a monopoly of knowledge. Thus we can see the underlying *system of social relations* as producing *structures of inequality* which both facilitate and limit the practical activity of actors (see Figure 12.1, p. 748). The 'system' box relates to the system of social relations, while 'structure' represents the patterned distribution of constraints and resources which derive from the social system. In previous chapters we have also tried to show how groups can gain or lose in freedom or power as the class structure changes, as political concessions or initiatives are made, or as changes in knowledge and perception develop. For example, we saw how radical changes have occurred in the class position of the clerk, as the job has been de-skilled and feminised, and as some workers have organised in unions. Both the clerks and their employers have different resources they can draw upon to change or defend the clerk's position — in the end, of course, the clerk has more constraints and fewer resources for control. At the same time, the actions of the employer cannot be understood without using explanations derived from a theory of the nature of the social system: the employer may be a capitalist firm forced by competition to lower labour costs, but a liberal-democratic political system may allow union organisation and resistance. Equally, dominant ideology directed towards the workers may well encourage acceptance of the employer's authority as a 'fact of life'.

We can also see the need for a concept of *social system* if we look back at the contrast between Weber and Marx. For Marx, capitalist social relations come to form a system which generates inequalities and has its own 'laws of motion'. He writes at great length in *Capital* on the distinctive way this mode of production operates, and on the crises and possibilities for change that this social system generates by its own imperfect working. In contrast, Weber does not deal with societies as social systems, but only as structures of inequality and power. Weber provides many analytical concepts for describing the distribution of these things but never produces any complete theory of, for example, how capitalism continually generated inequality. Unlike Marx, Weber does not try to establish the structural conditions for social change in terms of changing economic relations, but emphasises the cultural conditions for the development of rationality in every sphere, including the economic. Of course, Weber paid enormous attention to power and conflict, but did not really link this to theories of the way different kinds of social system have interlocking institutions which work together as a whole. Marx, on the other hand, always looked for the roots of historical change in the social system (which in his view meant the mode of production). The social world was *not* static even though capitalism or feudalism (or whatever) had certain fixed system properties. This was because modes of production constantly developed and changed, generating problems, conflicts, and crises. There is therefore no such thing as a perfectly integrated system because: (a) systems may overlap with other systems (for instance, feudal and capitalist modes of production may overlap), and (b) even 'pure' social systems generate problems (for example, the falling rate of profit) and conflicts (especially between classes). Thus, unlike the organicist approach, this system perspective avoids the old split between 'theory of statics' and 'theory of evolution'. Social change and conflict is continuous, but these aspects derive from the underlying changes in the social system.

As we saw earlier, however, there are problems with Marx's approach. Firstly, many have questioned whether the structure of *economic* relations should be seen as the ultimately determining aspect of social systems. The concept of mode of production remains useful and important, but it must be recognised that Marx's accounts of politics and ideology were seriously inadequate. Whether or not economic determinism remains true 'in the last instance', social theories must work from the complex relationship between economics, political and ideological relationships. There is no smooth and perfect integration between them, so the relationship between the underlying social system and actual practical actions are dauntingly complex.

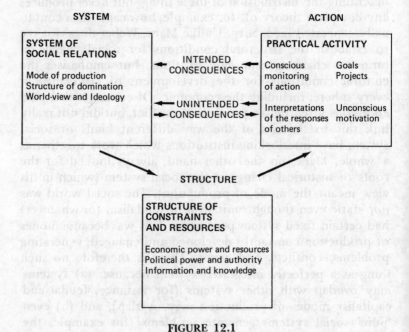

FIGURE 12.1

Figure 12.1 tries to show some of the simpler relationships. Within the 'action' box itself, some of the aspects of motivation and action are briefly suggested. Firstly, action should not be conceived as separate, rigid 'acts' which always have clearly defined motives behind them. Instead, the phenomenological approach rightly emphasises that individuals are constantly engaged in *practical activity* which takes place in a continuous flow of events; it is impossible to wrench acts out of their social context; and this context is defined in particular ways by the actors involved. In very different ways, both symbolic interactionism and phenomenology stress the inter-subjective quality of social life — actors negotiate definitions of situations and build up social identities. At the same time, this symbolic interaction involves the sharing of a universe of meanings taken for granted in the particular social group. Symbolic interactionists have convincingly stressed the ways in which these meanings can vary between groups and can be continually modified during the process of interaction. We should be careful not to assume (as Schutz seems to) that these shared meanings are uniformly available to actors with similar content — this shifts us back towards the 'consensus' theories which we rejected in organicism. We must thus acknowledge that *practical activity draws upon meanings which vary across society and are constantly negotiated.* We must also stress that action draws upon knowledge, information and perceptions of reality. These knowledge resources are unequally available to different groups of actors, and so the effectiveness of their intended actions will clearly be affected by this distribution. The 'structure' box in the diagram summarises these unequally distributed resources as 'information and knowledge'; in fact, of course, all actors employ some common-sense information and understanding about the world. The point is that reliable knowledge is unequally spread, and as Chapter 9 shows, institutions such as schools and the mass media are closely involved in the dissemination of both true and false knowledge. Clearly, since all action draws on such knowledge, the role of science is crucial in that it produces the most reliable and legitimate understanding; the products of science must always have some effect on general practical action and so science can never be divorced from its involvement in everyday life. This intimate connection places a special responsibility on social science to modify the common-sense assumptions used in practical activity; if sociology can produce knowledge, then social actors can gain more control over their own social world.

The diagram also sketches in some aspects of the relationship between the *self* and social action. As the symbolic interactionists emphasise, actors have a unique capacity to monitor their own action reflexively. That is, they can be aware of what they are doing and modify it in the light of their interpretation of the responses of other people. If others react in a hostile manner (as the actor interprets their action) the actor can change his or her action to try to obtain a better response. At the same time, though, we must bear in mind some of the criticisms of SI. We must not assume that all action is as carefully monitored, and unconscious drives and motivations may be highly significant. At the same time, our action is often oriented to long-term goals or projects — such as being a good parent to one's child. Not only will these goals be chosen with the circumstances of socialisation and social control, but what it *means* to be a good parent is a socially constructed definition. For example, in post-war Britain, changes in female employment, family size, and so on, have produced a constant renegotiation of the meaning of motherhood for many women. This is partly in terms of the choices they make in their circumstances, but also in terms of the more general social norms and beliefs which are directed at women. There is a complex relationship (as we have seen in earlier chapters on sexual divisions and belief-systems) between these two aspects of practical activity, and also between them and the subconscious motivations attached to parenthood.

Action, then, is creative and innovative but it never takes place outside social contexts which involve (a) inequalities of power, knowledge and material resources as well as (b) socially constructed meanings, definitions and rules. These constraints upon action need not be recognised by the actor or consciously reflected upon. The circumstances constraining action may be just as opaque to the actors as the consequences for society of the things they do. Even though very often actors do wish to produce particular intended consequences, all actions have consequences which are unexpected and perhaps unrecognised. For example, the imprisonment of offenders may prevent future employment of the prisoner, expose them to professional criminals and disrupt the up- bringing of their children. All this is likely to reinforce deviant behaviour rather than deter it. In addition, *the nature of these unintended consequences is not random − it depends upon the nature of the social system.* This cannot be otherwise, because every event has complex effects because of the patterned interrelations between actors and between social institutions.

This does not mean that all actions unwittingly reproduce the social structure, for the latter will be constantly modified by the complex effects of creative action. We must recognise, though, that an established social system, with established social structures of inequality, will normally possess a con- tinuity which is only marginally affected by particular indi- vidual acts. The potential for change in societies depends upon the degree of system integration, and from this the degree of 'stability' in unequal structures of resources. As we have seen, the political, economic and ideological aspects of systems never fully integrate and indeed generate their own weaknesses and crises. There is always lack of integration, there is always a potential for dynamic change and conflict within society. Social action takes place in the context of social structures which are transformed as they are repro- duced.

12.6 KNOWLEDGE, VALUES AND THE ROLE OF THE SOCIOLOGIST

Two basic goals characterise the project of constructing a science of society. The first is the true understanding of social life − that is, sociological knowledge which can claim the status of *truth*. The second is the goal of expanding human capacity to control our own future by the reconstruction or reform of society. The problem is to establish criteria for the validation of theories as true, while still allowing sociologists to be engaged in the struggle to create a better social world.

To many twentieth-century sociologists, such a combin- ation of goals would seem absurd. It has become a matter of faith that sociological understanding must completely divorce itself from any connection with values — in order that it can claim the status of scientific knowledge. Truth has no connection with values, it is argued, because value-judgements such as 'coffee is nicer than tea' can never be regarded as true or false. Instead, they are personal commitments — neither correct nor incorrect. Therefore, it is argued, since science concerns itself only with *truth*, such judgements must be rigorously excluded from scientific accounts. Thus when Hitler decided that the Jews should be exterminated, this was a judgement based on values, not empirically based theory, and so the scientist had no right to intervene. Many scientists, however, would be uneasy about conceding so much — can we really say nothing with certainty about the rights and wrongs of genocide? The study of society raises such questions acutely, and some answers must be found that are more adequate than simple moral neutrality for the scientist.

In fact, although early sociologists were committed to the pursuit of truth, they saw no conflict between this and the pursuit of the good society. For Comte and Durkheim, the whole point of seeking social scientific knowledge was to find the true principles for a good, ordered, integrated society. The laws of society show the natural and *correct* state to which it should conform; it cannot be doubted that Durkheim saw an extremely active role for the sociologist in creating the conditions for organic solidarity in modern society. This was not imposing the sociologist's values, but simply the pursuit of societal *health*. The latter concept conveys the notion clearly — science can specify a stable state which is also thereby desirable. For Comte, the sociologist-priests should rule; in Durkheim's view the educationalist and the reformer of the economy would create healthy order. Each of these writers, of course, held positivistic views of social science and each saw science as the major force for social progress. The two goals were inseparable until the developments in positivist philosophy during the twentieth century, when a great wedge was driven between truth and values. Before that, though, we should note that such a division was even more alien to Marx. For him it was inconceivable that sociological knowledge could be directed at anything but the criticism of prevailing institutions and the

creation of ideal social relations. Anything else simply justified the existing society and thus could be nothing more than
mystifying ideology. This clearly contrasts with the evolutionary reformism of the organicists and has only come to be
an influential view within academic sociology during recent
years. In general, sociologists have wanted to establish their
discipline as scientific, and have therefore sought to conform
to the dominant conception of science — that is positivism.

Even nineteenth-century positivism contained elements
that threatened the progressive role of sociology. Here the
source of knowledge is, of course, empirical observation;
knowledge consists of generalisations about observed
relations of cause and effect. As a result, speculative philosophy and theology are attacked for claiming knowledge without having any real empirical foundation for their pronouncements. Causes can only be discovered in *this* world: truth can
only be produced by empirical observation of the material
world. For example, Durkheim rejected any explanation of
religious activity in terms of God or the supernatural, for
these could have no place in rational science. Lurking within
this epistemology, then, is a potential rejection of any ethical
commitments, for these can never be justified empirically. It
makes no sense to ask for material proof that genocide is undesirable — you either believe it or you do not. However,
once absolute ethical standards (derived from God or where-
ever) are abandoned, we seem to lose any real grounds for
making any rational decisions on moral or political issues.
Fascist racialism becomes just another opinion, as good as
any other.

These potential consequences of positivism were furthest
developed within *logical positivism,* in the Vienna Circle in
the 1920s. Here, scientists such as Mach and Carnap developed a toughened conception of positivism which rigorously
excluded values from scientific knowledge. Their opposition
to 'metaphysics' went so far that they condemned any statements which did not have direct empirical content (e.g. 'I
think people should be kind') as literally meaningless and
nonsensical. Statements involving values were thus non-
empirical, senseless, and could only be mere emotional outbursts. Scientists must rigorously distance themselves from

754 Introductory Sociology

such distractions and concentrate on producing value-neutral knowledge. Thus two things become crucially, and dangerously, confused. Not only must value-judgements be excluded from scientific *statements* which claim truth, but the *scientist* must also be ethically neutral. This unwarranted claim is contained in the loose instruction to the scientist to 'be objective' — which fails to distinguish (a) the objectivity of knowledge from (b) the objectivity of the scientist in doing scientific work, or from (c) his or her moral responsibility as a citizen. Social scientists should not be 'biased', so it came to be assumed, they must be indifferent to ethical issues. As positivist sociology came to imitate the natural sciences more and more slavishly, the discipline became increasingly divorced from any ethic of social responsibility, let alone any commitment to social reconstruction. American sociology in particular became wedded to this principle of ethical non-responsibility; it reached its nadir in the notorious Project Camelot of 1964. This is worth discussing in detail.

By the early 1960s American social science had successfully established an image of scientific and political respectability, and as Gouldner has argued (Gouldner, 1975), the commitment to value-neutrality was partly motivated by a desire to be seen as 'safe' and non-threatening to the established order. As Lundberg had proclaimed, social scientists were often technicians researching topics defined as 'problems' by others; usually they certainly were not social critics. Such self-defined roles encouraged the US Army to recruit social scientists for a huge research programme in Latin America, designed to discover the causes of social instability. In its natural concern for social order in the lower half of the continent, the Pentagon wished to discover the causes of revolt and remove them. In order to achieve this, they planned to spend up to six million dollars and recruit a huge team of political scientists and sociologists to work in the countries concerned. Their employer made the aims clear in a recruiting letter: 'The US Army has an important mission in the positive and constructive aspects of nation-building in less-developed countries as well as to a responsibility to assist friendly governments in dealing with active insurgency problems.' The aims were equally clear to the South American

governments concerned, and they rapidly forced the abandonment of the project, with accusations of spying and
covert intervention by the United States. All this came as a
shock to those who agreed to take part, for they believed
that they were aiding these countries by advocating policies
such as land reform which would remove the need for revolution. It is a sad comment on social scientists that they could
be so naive about the intentions of the powerful. However
the furore surrounding Camelot added significantly to a
growing tide of dissatisfaction with the dominant positivist
functionalism. We have seen already how this was challenged
on political as well as theoretical grounds; the 1960s saw a
radicalisation of student politics and this was reflected (and
led) by social scientists. A number of American writers insti-
gated furious onslaughts on the bastions of establishment
social science, few more so than C. Wright Mills and Alvin
Gouldner. As we shall see, though, the debate was not always
conducted at a particularly sophisticated level.

Mills (1970, p. 10), for example, states quite baldly that
'there is no way in which any social scientist can avoid assuming choices of value and implying them in his work as a
whole'. On such a view the sociologist *must* have political and
moral concern, and therefore 'value-freedom' is impossible. If
this means, as Myrdal also argues, that we have competing
sociological accounts based on opposed values, then that
must simply be accepted. Sociologists must make their own
stance clear and state their values openly. It is inconceivable
that a scientist can or should be indifferent to ethics and
politics, and so the goal of objectivity must be abandoned.
These writers accept more of the conventional view than they
realise, for they assume that value-commitment and scientific
objectivity must always be incompatible. In doing so, they
merely echo the view that Gouldner (1975, p. 4) summarises:

> The image of a value-free sociology is more than a neat
> intellectual theorem demanded as a sacrifice to reason; it is
> also a felt conception of a role and a set of (more or less)
> shared sentiments as to how sociologists should live.

Gouldner enters the fray in his usual apoplectic manner,
arguing that this principle has dehumanised and demoralised

sociologists: the fact-value distinction 'warps reason by tinging it with sadism and leaves it feeling smugly sure of itself and bereft of a sense of common humanity'. He claims that sociologists have betrayed themselves in this way only to buy a social and intellectual respectability; indeed he acknowledges that this 'did contribute to the intellectual growth and emancipation of our discipline'. This usefulness is long past, however. Today 'it has become increasingly the trivial token of professional respectability . . . the gentleman's promise that boats will not be rocked'. The intellectual poverty of such a stance is only emphasised by the ritual references made to Max Weber's statements on objectivity, for Weber developed a position of more subtlety and complexity than most contemporary writers. Very few of them acknowledge the significance of Weber's telling assertion that 'an attitude of moral indifference has no connection with scientific objectivity'. We need to pay more attention to the real nature of his contribution to the debate.

Weber certainly cannot be seen as adopting a simple positivist position on values. Instead he attempts an uneasy compromise with earlier views (especially those of Rickert) which emphasised the inescapable *relevance* of values to historical and social studies. Weber accepted Rickert's claim that history could only *select* from the seamless web of unique events. These made up what Weber later called 'the meaningless infinity of the world-process'; to discern order or significance in this chaos scientists have to impose pattern by selecting some aspects that they regard as relevant to the values of their time. Weber argued that particular cultural circumstances made some topics (such as the rise of capitalism) relevant for study at a particular time. In this sense scientific activity is guided by values. Unlike Rickert, Weber agreed with the principle that no values can be regarded as ultimately correct; despite this he was convinced that humans (especially scientists) must remain committed to the values they happen to accept. As a result, the scientist must also be a responsible citizen. Ethical and political responsibility cannot be shirked, for arguments over the *use* of knowledge inevitably involve value-judgements. Scientists should not pretend to have priority over any citizen in these decisions but neither should they withdraw from commitment on grounds of objectivity. Weber broadly accepted the view that *knowledge* must be cleansed of values, but the choice of subject-matter and the use of that knowledge are both areas where values must unavoidably be involved. Now this may seem to challenge the positivist position, and indeed it does contradict the simplistic postures adopted by many who followed him. However, it does not logically undermine positivism *if* (and only if) we still have objective criteria for the testing of knowledge. Given neutral testing-procedures, it does not matter whether values affect our choice of topic, because any propositions we produce can be evaluated and modified against independent evidence. However, such a neat solution is dependent on the value-neutrality of this evidence and some of Weber's statements seem to undermine this — his logical solution is weakened by his worries about the availability of 'pure' evidence to prove or disprove our propositions.

Despite these nagging doubts, Weber succeeded in constructing a methodology which sharply distinguishes between the objectivity of *theories* and the value-neutrality of the *scientist*. The investigator cannot and should not be value-free in the choice of topic or the application of knowledge. The fact that Einstein later rejected the use of nuclear weapons in warfare does not invalidate the objectivity of his physics, and certainly does not harm his credentials as a scientist. We thus have a solution to the problems of objectivity available — but only on condition that we possess *neutral testing-procedures*. However, many critics of positivism have questioned the possibility of basing such tests on empirical data, either (a) because sense-data are seen as dependent upon the theories and values used to interpret it, or (b) because non-positivist epistemologies often deny the relevance of empirical observations — many structuralist accounts, for example, seek to look 'beneath the surface' of concrete observable phenomena (such arguments were discussed in the previous chapter). In either case, empirical evidence will not be accepted as a neutral basis for testing-procedures and so the objectivity of knowledge will be under threat.

There are two possible responses to this threat. One is to

accept the criticisms of empiricism and seek a new epistemology with new criteria for truth which still exclude values from theories. At the moment, such an epistemology does not appear to be available. A different response is to accept that values are inevitably built into all theories, *but* to then assert that some values are *correct;* on this view, truth will be reunited with 'the good', and the pursuit of knowledge will be the same as the pursuit of the correct values.

This second alternative sounds bizarre to those trained in positivist assumptions, but it is a position with a long philosophical history. Most obviously, theologians have confidently expounded the 'correct' ethical principles, while more recent political philosophers have defined some political principles and goals (e.g. democracy) as having an ultimate value. For the positivist in the twentieth century, such statements are metaphysical gobbledegook — entirely meaningless; the consequence of such a position is, however, that we have no rational basis for the discussion of ethical and political goals. As argued above, positivists can only condemn genocide on the basis of 'emotional commitment' — and their feelings are logically no more valid than those of Adolf Hitler.

In contrast to such a position, many thinkers have attempted to locate the true goals of humanity in assertions about human nature — for example, the belief that we are born free and equal forms the basis for modern political constitutions in both capitalist and communist societies. Earlier in this chapter, we saw how Marx's vision of human *potential* for free creative labour implied that such a society was possible and desirable: human nature is not fixed but it does embody *capacities* for creativity and control of nature. For Marx, the task is to create a society where social relations will allow such human capacities to develop to the full.

Marx's conception of humans can be criticised, of course, for his stress on human creativity is tied directly to the control of nature in production; and therefore linked to his stress on economic relations. We have argued in the course of this chapter that as a result of this Marx does not provide a satisfactory account of social action and consciousness. However, if we *do* acknowledge the importance of these aspects of social life we are in an even better position to see how sociology must be linked to human goals. This link is unavoidable since humans are uniquely powerful creatures: they have the capacity to transform their social world and thereby their own nature. We have seen in the course of this book that humans constantly change the social world as they reproduce it. Actors negotiate new ways of acting and they consciously try to change things; yet at the same time, the type of social system in which they are located imposes constraints upon their action and produces effects of which actors are not fully aware. As a consequence of all this, humans constantly seek knowledge about their social environment and act upon it. The better their understanding, the better they are able to reconstruct the social world. This means that by its very nature as an attempt to understand rigorously social life, sociology has a central part to play in the way in which actors come to control their own future. Because of this, sociology cannot avoid being concerned with *both* a quest for true knowledge *and* a struggle to reconstruct society. Sociology can show how the human potential for creativity and self-determination is held back by social systems which embody structures of domination and inequality; this knowledge is inseparable from the struggle to liberate human potential through the reconstruction of society.

REFERENCES TO CHAPTER 12

Durkheim, E. (1974) *Sociology and Philosophy*, New York, Free Press.
Garfinkel, H. (1967) *Studies in Ethnomethodology*, Englewood Cliffs, N.J., Prentice-Hall.
Giddens, A. (1976) *New Rules of Sociological Method*, London, Hutchinson.
Giddens, A. (1977) *Studies in Social and Political Theory*, London, Hutchinson.
Giddens, A. (1979) *Central Problems in Social Theory*, London, Macmillan.
Gouldner, A. (1975) 'Anti-Minotaur', in A. Gouldner, *For Sociology*, Harmondsworth, Penguin.
Lockwood, D. (1964) 'Social Integration and System Integration', in G. K. Zollschan and W. Hirsch (eds), *Explorations in Social Change*, London, Routledge & Kegan Paul.
Lukes, S. (1973) *Emile Durkheim*, London, Allen Lane.
Mead, G. H. (1934) *Mind, Self and Society*, University of Chicago Press.

Merton, R. K. (1949) *Social Theory and Social Structure*, New York, Free Press.

Mills, C. W. (1970) *The Sociological Imagination*, Harmondsworth, Penguin.

Nisbet, R. (1967) *The Sociological Tradition*, London, Heinemann.

Turner, R. (1974) *Ethnomethodology*, Harmondsworth, Penguin.

Weber, M. (1978) *Economy and Society*, University of California Press.

Author Index

766   *Author Index*

Subject Index

crime – *continued*
  victim surveys and   587
  cultural deprivation   433–41
  curriculum   428–31
    'hidden'   12, 428
    and transmission of core values
      384–6, 431

  'dark side' of family life
    309–13
  delinquency   574–83
  denominations   531–3
  deviance   562–623
    amplification   599
    anomie and   576–7
    definition of   562–5
    and labelling process
      588–602
  divorce and marriage in Britain
    299–301
  domestic labour   347–52
  dominant values   28–31, 182,
    198, 200, 229ff
  dual labour markets   343–5

  earnings differences between men
    and women   327–32
  economism   238–9
  education, expansion of   381–2
  Education Act of 1870   381
  Education Act of 1944   381,
    395
  educational achievement
    396–441
    explanations of   402–31
    and language   433–41
    by sex   400–1
    by social class   396–9
  elite
    integration   211–15
    recruitment   208–11
    theory   182–5, 206–7
  employment, gender divisions in
    333–47
  epistemology   629–30
  Equal Pay Act of 1970   323,
    329–31
  equality of opportunity   382,

390–402
ethnomethodological perspectives
  on crime   602–4
  on suicide   617–22
ethnomethodology   652–3,
  741–2
exploitation   54, 57–8

'facts', problems of definition of
  626–8
family, definitions of   255–9
family life, 'dark side' of   309–13
feudalism   50–2, 174–5, 178
football hooliganism   142–3
'fringe' sciences   523, 540
functionalism   21–3, 707–9
functionalist perspectives
  on professions   482
  on religion   525
  on schooling   382, 383–6,
    389–90, 431
  on stratification   126–31

gender and sex, distinction
  between   321–2
gender divisions and child care
  337–40
  in employment   333–47
  and equality   323–7
generation gap, the   135ff

Hawthorne experiments, the
  453–4, 475
'hidden' curriculum   12, 428
historical developments in
  sociology   32–6
housework   347–52
human-relations theory   453–5

ideal types   731
ideological hegemony   245–8
illness and death, distribution of
  88–91
income, distribution of   76–84
independent schools   396, 411,
  419–20
industrial conflict   486–95